THE NATURE AND CHARACTER OF GOD

W.A. PRATNEY

BETHANY HOUSE PUBLISHERS
MINNEAPOLIS, MINNESOTA 55438
A Division of Bethany Fellowship, Inc.

Published by Bethany House Publishers
A Division of Bethany Fellowship, Inc.
6820 Auto Club Road, Minneapolis, Minnesota 55438

Printed in the United States of America

Library of Congress Cataloging-in-Publication Data

Pratney, W. A. 1944–
    The nature and character of God.

    1. God. I. Title.
BT102.P67   1988   231   88–19451
ISBN 1-55661-041-6

THE NATURE AND CHARACTER OF GOD

di·vin·i·ty (n.)

The science of divine things; the science that deals with God, His laws and moral government, and the way of salvation: theology.

—Webster's Third International Dictionary

The science of divine things; the science which unfolds the character of God, His laws and moral government, the duties of man and the way of salvation: Theology as the study of divinity: A system of divinity.

—Noah Webster's 1828 Dictionary, First Edition

*"Write the vision and make it plain
. . . that he may run that readeth it."*

(Habakkuk 2:2)

WILLIAM (WINKIE) PRATNEY is a speaker and author whose effective communication skills keep him traveling extensively with his wife throughout the world. He addresses seminars, conferences and campus audiences on the truths of Scripture and the claims of Christ. He has published three books with Bethany House Publishers: *Youth Aflame*, *Doorways to Discipleship*, and *Handbook for Followers of Jesus*.

CONTENTS

TO THE GENTLE READER
—A COMPILER'S APOLOGY

A BIBLICAL theology is hopefully one in which the BIBLE is patently taken as the single reference point of discussion. All attempts at logical harmony and reconciliation of paradoxical statements are rigorously excluded unless conforming to that criterion. It can allow lexical, hermeneutic and exegetical observations as long as they are not too speculative.

A biblical theology has the merit of being biblical. It ought not to lead to much disagreement or debate, since it supposedly supports no doctrinal bias. It does, of course, omit the interesting records of Church history, the contributions of Christians to the overall testimony of God.

However, since it is assembled by finite beings, it may still be selective in focus, biased, and, not surprisingly, even false. (Satan appealed selectively to the Bible in tempting Jesus.) The logical question then is: Who needs any "biblical" theologies? A Bible, with perhaps a stack of concordances and lexicons, should be perfectly adequate Christian equipment. Yet, the process of teaching always creates the need for some sort of outline; and the best of these are worth calling "biblical."

Then we have the SYSTEMATIC theology—an attempt to set in order those things most surely believed in some form that relates one set of facts to others, utilizing logic, philosophy, Church history, and Scripture to hopefully present a digest of truth pertinent to the views it emphasizes.

A systematic theology allows the writer to attempt originality . . . toward developing an unique emphasis using logic and a set of proof texts. But this leads to a greater polarization of sects with differing views, proof texts, and dogmas. Reformers don't like Mystics who don't seem to stick solely to the Bible. Mystics don't like Fundamentalists who fail to stress the work of the Holy Spirit, using the Bible to defend their loss. Roman Catholics wonder why others do not give as much weight as they do to Church history and are suspect by both Reformers (who *know* Catholics are not biblical) and Mystics (who *know* they are not evangelical).

Of what use then is a "systematic" theology? Generally speaking, a systematic theology is something you can:

- Argue with, hopefully proving what you believe is what God and the Bible say.
- Think with—a filing cabinet for belief, a criteria for testing truth, a filter for all new light.
- Reference from: a topical concordance to things we may think especially important and like to speak about.

Many famous people have written systematic theologies: Augustine, Aquinas, Calvin. Theologians have to have them. Even cults produce them, but call them things like *Make Sure of All Things*, *The Doctrine and Covenants*, or *Science and Health With a Key to the Scriptures*.

Limits of a Systematic Theology

Any theology—mine, yours, your favorite Christian writer's—will be:

- Opinionated. Humans cannot help selectively choosing Scripture to defend a particular view.
- Constrictive. We each tend to lock our minds down to a particular way of looking at all divine truth. Once we've decided, it's hard to change our minds.
- Finite. What is beneficial for one generation may be the weakness of another. What you leave out may hurt as much as what you put in. We all want to see the Church believe truth about God. Unfortunately, when we pick out one thing as important, we minimize others by default. Herein lies the intrinsic weakness of human logic and words.
- Theoretical. A theology does not usually stress practical obedience or character change. But God seems more interested in having us living righteously than reading correct theology. It is easier to talk about Him than obey Him. It is far easier to speculate than surrender. It is simpler to write profoundly about God than live deeply for Him.

So what kind of theology is this?
Well, it:

- Gives plenty of scriptures to use as proof texts for people who do not agree with you.
- May help you think through what you believe, why you believe it, and who else has believed it in the past.
- Focuses on some things that are hopefully important, because it seems others have always thought such things worth thinking about. You can see who some of them were and what they said about these topics.

These are the collected compilations of a Fundamental, Catholic-Evangelical-Mystic who likes Church history, loves the Bible and seeks to practically honor the present work of the Holy Spirit. It will no doubt amuse or annoy professional theologians; but it is not designed for people who write effortlessly in Greek, Aramaic, Hebrew, German, Latin and ancient Egyptian, people who like to fill their writings with words like *dogmatic*, *kerygma*, and *pseudopigraphic*. It hardly has pretensions to profundity other than the intrinsic nature of its subject. I could call it a "devotional apologetic." I offer it as an eclectic theology: an opinionated, constrictive, finite mind-set, complete with attendant omissions, weaknesses, theories, over-emphases, and faulty logic—like all other works of man.

But for the record, this is a theology in which the author tried to be:

- constructive in criticism,
- reasonably fair in defending his particular point of view,
- helpful in putting before young Christians some big issues in little words, and
- more practical than others in applying these grand concepts, often locked away on reference shelves, to the business of ordinary living.

Some themes seem—to me at least—to logically fit with great beauty into all that the universe, history, and revelation testify of the truth. At other times, as Francis Schaeffer said, there is nothing more one can do than to "take off the hat and worship." Critics may point out, as I do also, the many weaknesses of this present volume. There must always be some unavoidable selectivity and simplification among the many great themes of divinity. "Of making many books there is no end"—some such themes have been treated in other works, reserved for later outlines, and others simply left to other writers or thinkers. I must draw the line somewhere, however fallible the selective criteria eventually proves to be.

My gracious Lord, forgive the faults, overlook in mercy the omissions, and bless that which in some small measure gives you the honor, the glory, and absolute worthiness due your name.

W. A. Pratney
(Phil. 1:21)

THE GREATEST STUDY IN THE UNIVERSE

di·vin·i·ty (n.)—The science of divine things; the science that deals with God, His laws and moral government, and the way of salvation: theology. —*Webster's Third International Dictionary.*

di·vin·i·ty (n.)—The science of divine things; the science which unfolds the character of God, His laws and moral government, the duties of man and the way of salvation: Theology as the study of divinity: A system of divinity. —*Noah Webster's 1828 Dictionary, First Edition.*

"Write the vision and make it plain . . . that he may run that readeth it."
(Habakkuk 2:2)

George D. Watson

"It is a beautiful task to study about God. The human mind can never be employed on any subject so full of rich reward as when trying to find out the knowledge of God. To search after the character and perfection of God is the highest science, the deepest philosophy, the loftiest poetry, the sublimest history, the truest theology and the most thrilling biography."[1]

C. S. Lewis

"Everyone has warned me not to tell you what I am going to tell you. . . . They all say 'The ordinary reader does not want Theology; give him plain, practical religion.' I have rejected their advice. I do not think the ordinary reader is such a fool. Theology means 'the science of God' and I think any man who wants to think about God at all would like to have the clearest and most accurate ideas about Him which are available.

---

[1] George D. Watson, *Our Own God* (Schmul Reprints).

13

You are not children; why should you be treated like children?"[2]

Robert Drummond

"I for one should be very much surprised if when the truth about God is reached we should not find something which is very perplexing to human minds and something which betrays the poverty of human speech. I expect the truth about the infinite God will always tax the fullest resources of finite minds and tongues and still leave men wondering, pondering and adoring."[3]

John Watson

"Tell me what your conception of God is and I will work out your doctrine of man, of forgiveness, of life, of punishment. Given the axioms, geometry is only a question of process. Given your God, your whole theology can be constructed within a measurable time. The chief service of a prophet is not to rebuke sin, nor instruct in virtue; it is to give the world a radiant idea of God. . . . If a prophet deal after a satisfying fashion with the idea of God he will be permanent. If a prophet complete and crown the idea of God he will be final. Many may expound him; none can transcend him."[4]

Gregory of Nazianzus

"Rise from thy low condition by thy conversation, by purity of heart unite thyself with the pure. Wilt thou become a theologian and worthy of the Godhead? Then keep the commandments of God, and walk according to His precepts, for the act is the first step to knowledge."

Encyclopaedia Britannica

"To ascend by a chain of reasoning from things visible to things invisible, from palpable to impalpable, from terrestrial to celestial, from the creature even up to the Creator is the business of theology; it is not surprising therefore, that the union of many doctrines is necessary completely to form such a science. To understand, and properly to interpret the Scriptures or revelation demands not less sagacity than assiduity."[5]

William Law

"Read whatever chapter of Scripture you will and be ever so delighted

[2]C.S. Lewis, *Mere Christianity* (Huntington, N.Y.: J.M. Fontana Publishing, 1955), pp. 135–138.
[3]Robert Drummond, *Faith's Perplexities* (New York: American Tract Society), pp. 283–285.
[4]John Watson, *Mind of The Master* (New York: Dodd, Mead, and Company, 1896).
[5]*Encyclopaedia Brittannica*, "Religion, or Theology" (First Ed., 1771), Vol. III, p. 533.

with it—yet it will leave you as poor, as empty and unchanged as it found you unless it has turned you wholly and solely to the Spirit of God, and brought you into full union with and dependence upon Him. . . . Nothing less than this union with God by the power of His Holy Spirit is intended by the Law, the Prophets, or the Gospel."[6]

George MacDonald

"What a believer the man born blind must have become! Nothing should be too grand and good for him to believe thereafter—not even the doctrine hardest to common-place humanity, though the most natural and reasonable to those who have beheld it—that the God of the light is a faithful, loving, upright, honest and self-denying being, utterly devoted to the uttermost good of those whom He has made."[7]

Gerhard Tersteegen

O God, Thou art far other
Than men have dreamed and taught
Unspoken in all language,

Unpictured in all thought.
Thou God art God—he only learns
What that great Name must be
Whose raptured heart within him burns
Because he walks with Thee.

The Spirit of Reformation

Toward a Gospel Treatment of Other Christian Views.

John Wesley

"For God's sake, if it be possible to avoid it, let us not provoke one another to wrath. Let us not kindle in each other this fire of Hell; much less blow it up into a flame. If we could discern truth by that dreadful light, would it not be loss rather than gain? For, how far is love, even with many wrong opinions to be preferred before truth itself without love! We may die without the knowledge of many truths, and yet be carried into Abraham's bosom. But if we die without love, what will knowledge prevail? Just as much as it avails the devil and his angels! The God of love forbid we should ever make the trial!"[8]

---

[6]William Law, *The Power of The Spirit* (1761), p. 17.
[7]George MacDonald, *The Miracles of Our Lord*, ed. Rolland Hein (Wheaton, Ill.: Harold Shaw Publishers, 1980).
[8]John Wesley, *The Works of John Wesley* (Grand Rapids: Baker Books), Preface.

Charles Finney

"I hold myself sacredly bound not to defend these positions at all events; but on the contrary, to subject every one of them to the most thorough discussion; to hold and treat them as I would the opinions of anyone else; that is, if upon further discussion and investigation I see no cause to change, I hold them fast; but if I can see a flaw in any one of them, I shall amend or wholly reject it, as further light demands. . . .

"True Christian consistency does not consist in stereotyping our opinions and views and in refusing to make any improvement lest we be guilty of change; but it consists in holding our minds open to receive the rays of truth from every quarter, and in changing our views and language and practice as often and as fast as we can. . . ."[9]

Robert McAfee Brown

"Very often the man who first appears as a heretic turns out to be the one who was recalling Christendom to a long-neglected truth. He may have shouted a little too loudly as the only way of getting a hearing, but had he not shouted, had he not rocked the boat, his fellow-Christians might not have become aware that they were heading for dangerous shoals. Protestantism has an obligation to 'suffer fools gladly' lest it stifle the message of one who is 'a fool for Christ.'"[10]

John Watson

"No church since the early centuries has had the courage to formulate an ethical creed for even those bodies of Christians which have no written theological creeds, yet have implicit affirmations or denials of doctrines as their basis. Imagine a body of Christians who should take their stand on the Sermon of Jesus and conceive their creed on His lines. Imagine how it would read: 'I believe in the Fatherhood of God; I believe in the words of Jesus; I believe in the clean heart; I believe in the service of love; I believe in the unworldly life; I believe in the Beatitudes; I promise to trust God and follow Christ, to forgive my enemies and seek after the righteousness of God.' . . . Liberty of thought is allowed; liberty of sinning is alone denied. Who would refuse to sign this creed?

"Does one say this is too ideal, too impractical, too quixotic? That no church could stand and work on such a basis? For three too short years the Church of Christ had none else, and it was by holy living and not by any metaphysical subtleties the Primitive Church lived, and suffered, and conquered."[11]

---

[9]Charles G. Finney, *Systematic Theology* (Minneapolis, Minn.: Bethany House Publishers, 1976), Preface.
[10]Robert McAfee Brown, *The Spirit of Protestantism* (London: Oxford University Press, 1965), p. 8.
[11]Watson, op. cit.

John Wesley

"Are you persuaded you see more clearly than me? . . . Then treat me as you would desire to be treated yourself upon a change of circumstances. Point me out a better way than I have yet known. Show me it is so by plain proof of Scripture. And if I linger in the path I have been accustomed to tread and am therefore unwilling to leave it, labor with me a little; take me by the hand and lead me as I am able to bear."[12]

---

[12]John Wesley, op. cit. Preface.

LEXICAL STUDIES: SIGNIFICANCE AND LIMITS[1]

Lexical (or word) studies of the Bible have one great value; they help us see *how* the Holy Spirit used Greek and Hebrew words to express His mind to us. Translations are good; but it is always best, if possible, to go back to the original languages.

The best place to begin is to look at the way people used Hebrew and Greek words in Bible times. Books that help you see *how* Bible writers did this are Greek and Hebrew lexicons and dictionaries; books that show you *where* those words were used are Bible concordances. This book gives you some starting word studies in each area from both concordances and lexicons to show you how some Bible scholars understand the key words of Scripture. You should use these as starting points for your own explorations, taking the time to look up each word the way the Bible uses it in different places.

Words are like people; though each one is uniquely different enough to be distinctly recorded, each one keeps on subtly changing as long as it lives. Languages, like people, stop growing only when they die. Lexical scholars, therefore, are more like psychiatrists than morticians. Like psychiatrists, whose diagnoses and treatments differ somewhat from doctor to doctor, lexical scholars vary in what they believe about word meanings.

Word study, despite all due care and scholarship, is still a touchy science. Even words from old languages (not used in the same, constantly shifting way as today) still express much more than a single idea. Words can overlap with others in meaning, change significance from generation to generation, take on different—or even sometimes, opposite—meaning to the way the words were first used! Because of this, it is not enough to rely just on analysis of key words to define theological concepts. Each

---

[1]All references to Strong's numbers in the sections on lexical studies are taken from the *Strong's Exhaustive Concordance of the Bible*. Strong's numbers, as a standard categorization of the Hebrew and Greek words used in the *Textus Receptus*, are tools for cross-referencing material in other works using those numbers.

study word must then be looked at in context, judged for meaning in the sentences themselves.

This is the proper way to read anything (even *Goldilocks and the Three Bears*) and so much more the Bible.

PART ONE

PROPOSITION ONE:
GOD IS UNCREATED

COROLLARY ONE: GOD IS INFINITE
COROLLARY TWO: GOD IS SPIRITUAL
COROLLARY THREE: GOD IS GLORIOUS

"The profoundest thinkers, headed by Aristotle and Samuel Clarke all affirm there cannot be an infinite series of causes. The other is to admit an uncaused cause. In this there is no absurdity whatever. . . . Such a cause must be a free, self-originating spirit. Beyond that we cannot go and to that we are compelled by reason and logic to go, and from that we cannot escape. In all this there may be much of incomprehensibility of inexplicable mystery; but no absurdity, no self-contradiction."

—*L. D. McCabe*

"The characteristic attitude of the religious man in the presence of deity is an attitude of worship and it is psychologically impossible to worship that which is completely understood. The divine must have something about it of indefinable quality to hold the allegiance of men for as the French so neatly put it 'a God defined is a finite god'. . . . Religion must insist we do not know the whole of God; it must at the same time insist that what we do know of God is true."

—*Bertrand Brasnett*

CHAPTER ONE

PROPOSITION ONE:
GOD IS UNCREATED

Scriptures

"In the beginning God . . ." (Gen. 1:1)

"And Abraham planted a grove in Beersheba, and called there on the name of the Lord, the everlasting God." (Gen. 21:33)

"Before the mountains were brought forth, or ever thou hadst formed the earth and the world, even from everlasting to everlasting, thou art God." (Ps. 90:2)

"Hast thou not known? hast thou not heard, that the everlasting God, the Lord, the Creator of the ends of the earth, fainteth not?" (Isa. 40:28)

"Ye are my witnesses, saith the Lord . . . that ye may know and believe me, and understand that I am he: before me there was no God formed [nothing formed of God], neither shall there be after me." (Isa. 43:10)

"Hearken unto me, O Jacob and Israel, my called; I am he; I am the first, I also am the last." (Isa. 48:12)

"I have not spoken in secret from the beginning; from the time that it was, there am I." (Isa. 48:16)

"He is before all things, and by him all things consist [hold together]." (Col. 1:17)

"Holy, holy, Lord God Almighty, which was, and is, and is to come." (Rev. 4:8)

God Is Called Eternal

"The eternal God is thy refuge, and underneath are the everlasting arms." (Deut. 33:27)

"Now unto the King eternal, immortal, invisible, the only wise God, be honour and glory for ever and ever. Amen." (1 Tim. 1:17)

"That which was from the beginning, which we have heard, which we have seen with our eyes, which we have looked upon, and our hands have handled, of the Word of life; (for the life was manifested, and we have seen it, and bear witness and shew unto you that eternal life, which was with the Father and was manifested unto us)." (1 John 1:1–2)

"And this is the record, that God hath given to us eternal life, and this life is in his Son. He that hath the Son hath life; and he that hath not the Son of God hath not life." (1 John 5:11–12)

"And we know that the Son of God is come, and hath given us an understanding, that we may know him that is true, and we are in him that is true, even in his Son, Jesus Christ. This is the true God, and eternal life." (1 John 5:20)

God Is Called Everlasting

"And Abraham planted a grove in Beersheba, and called there on the name of the Lord, the everlasting God." (Gen. 21:33)

"Blessed be the Lord God of Israel from everlasting, and to everlasting. Amen, and amen." (Ps. 41:13)

"And his name shall be called Wonderful, Counsellor, The mighty God, The everlasting Father, The Prince of Peace." (Isa. 9:6)

"The Lord hath appeared of old unto me, saying, Yea, I have loved thee with an everlasting love: therefore with lovingkindness have I drawn thee." (Jer. 31:3)

"But thou, Bethlehem . . . out of thee shall he come forth unto me that is to be ruler in Israel; whose goings forth have been from of old, from everlasting." (Mic. 5:2)

". . . according to the revelation of the mystery, which was kept secret since the world began, but now is made manifest, and by the scriptures of the prophets, according to the commandment of the everlasting God, made known to all nations for the obedience of faith." (Rom. 16:25b–26)

Bible Word Study

"Uncreated" is not a biblical word, but a technical, theological one. The problem we have in trying to speak simply about this truth is that only God has this quality; no one or nothing else in the universe is uncreated. Therefore, we have nothing in our own realm of experience from which we can draw analogies to help us understand this term.

The word "uncreated" is a summary of some scriptural declarations about the *eternal* and *everlasting* God. What can it mean that God has no beginning or end? Our greatest efforts over the centuries to comprehend this have been at best educated guesses.

Eternal (Hebrew)

Hebrew has more words for *eternal* or *eternity* than either Greek or Arabic. Therefore, it must have been a significant subject to the first people of God.

quedmah (*kayd-maw*)—The front, of a place (eastward) or time. Translated in the KJV as "ancient," "eternal."[1]

olam (*o-lawm*)—Concealed, i.e., the vanishing point; generally time out of mind (past or future), i.e., eternity; always. Translated in the KJV as "ancient" (time), "any more," "continuance," "eternal," "everlasting," "perpetual, "time without end."[2]

"*Olam*, which means 'to hide,' strictly designates the secret time of the past, 'time out of mind' or time immemorial. (Job 22:15; Ps. 25:6; Jer. 6:16; 18:15; Amos 9:11) Prospectively it denotes an infinite time to come, forever—i.e., relatively, as an individual life (Ex. 21:6; Deut. 15:17; 1 Sam. 27:12) of a race (1 Sam. 2:30; 13:13; 2 Sam. 7:16) of the present constitution of the universe (Ps. 78:69; 104:5; Eccl. 1:4) or absolutely (Gen. 17:7, 8; Ex. 12:14; Jer. 51:39). It is also used poetically of a 'good long period' (Isa. 30:8)."[3]

Eternal (Greek)

aion (*ahee-ohn*)—An age; by extension, perpetuity (also past); by implication, the world; specifically (Jewish) a Messianic period (present or future). Translated in the KJV as "age," "course," "eternal," "forever," "evermore," "beginning of the world," "world without end."[4] Used 128 times in the NT.

"From *ao*, *anui*, [to] blow, breathe. The life which hastes away in the breathing of our breath, life as transitory; then, the course of life, time of life, life in its temporal form; then, the space of human life, an age. . . . *Aion* always includes a reference to life, filling time or a space of time. Accordingly—the unbounded time, past and future, in which the history or life of the world is accomplished; and hence, the world as filling the unmeasurable contents of immeasurable time."[5]

aionios (*ahee-o-nee-os*)—Perpetual; also used of past time, or past and future as well. Translated in the KJV as "eternal," "forever," "everlasting," "world" (began).[6]

"Very long time, eternity— a. *of time gone by*, the past, earliest times,

---

[1]*Strong's* 6924—see footnote in Lexical Studies: Significance and Limits.
[2]*Strong's* 5769.
[3]*The People's Bible Encyclopedia*, Charles Randall Barnes, ed. (London: Charles H. Kelley, 1900), p. 334.
[4]*Strong's* 165.
[5]Ethelbert W. Bullinger, *A Critical Lexicon and Concordance to the English and Greek New Testament* (Grand Rapids: Zondervan Publishing House, 1975), p. 36.
[6]*Strong's* 166.

then eternity. . . . b. *of time to come* which, if it has no end, is also known as eternity . . . eternally, in perpetuity."[7]

"Belonging to the *aion*, to time in its movement; constant, abiding, eternal."[8]

Aion corresponds remarkably with the Hebrew *olam* in nearly all of its meanings. Its adjective form has for its general import "enduring," "lasting," with the following uses in the NT: forever (John 6:51, 58; 14:16; Heb. 5:6; 6:20); unto the ages, i.e., as long as the time shall be (Rom. 1:25; 9:5; 11:36); from the ages, i.e., from eternity (Eph. 3:9; Col. 1:26); before time was, i.e., before the foundation of the world (1 Cor. 2:7). In poetical and popular usages, "from the ages" means "from of old" (Luke 1:70; Acts 3:21) from the most ancient times. Elsewhere of the future it is used in an unlimited sense as "endless" (Luke 16:9; 2 Cor. 4:18; Heb. 9:12; 13:20), especially of the happy future of the righteous as "life everlasting" (Matt. 19:16, 29; 25:46) and often of the miserable fate of the wicked (Mark 3:29; Matt. 18:8).[9]

aidios (*ah-id-ee-os*)—Ever-enduring (forward and backward, or forward only. Translated in the KJV as "eternal," "everlasting."[10]

"Always existing, perpetual. (adj. from *aei*, always), occurs only in Jude 6."[11]

"Everlasting, eternal . . . to be without beginning or end."[12]

Everlasting (Hebrew)

'**ad** (*ad*)—Properly a (peremptory) terminus, i.e., by implication duration, in the sense of advance or perpetuity. Translated in the KJV as "eternity," "everlasting," "evermore," "old," "perpetually," "world without end."[13]

ad (*ad*)—Properly the same as '*ad* (used as a preposition, adjective, or conjunction, especially with a preposition). It means, "as far" (or long, or much) "as," whether of space (even unto) or time (during, while) or degree (equally with).[14]

"The word 'everlasting' which the prophet applies to God (Isa. 40:28) does not imply any devaluation of time or history, as in the philosophies and mysticisms of Greece and India. It means a long duration of time whether extending remotely into the past (antiquity) or indefinitely into

[7]Walter Bauer, *A Greek-English Lexicon of the New Testament*, 2nd ed., William F. Arndt and F. Wilbur Gingrich, trans., F. Wilbur Gingrich and Frederick W. Danker, eds. (Chicago: University of Chicago Press, 1979), p. 27.

[8]Bullinger, op. cit. p. 256.

[9]*The People's Bible Encyclopedia*, op. cit. p. 334.

[10]*Strong's* 126.

[11]Bullinger, op. cit. p. 256.

[12]*Theological Dictionary of the New Testament*, Gerhard Kittel, ed., Geoffrey W. Bromiley, trans. (Grand Rapids: Wm. B. Eerdmans Publishing Company, 1964), vol. 1, p. 168.

[13]*Strong's* 5703.

[14]*Strong's* 5704.

the future (futurity) and thus suggests everlasting time, time whose boundaries are hidden from man's view. . . .

"The prophet is not concerned with metaphysical speculations but with historical meaning . . . sense of eternity is occasioned by the realization that Yahweh, unlike the idols, is not bounded by the limitations of man's finite life or by the changing cycles of nature. He is the everlasting God who acts within history to accomplish His purpose and therefore men may rely on Him in faith, confident that His power does not fail."[15]

Questions and Answers

Q: *Who made God?*
A: No one. He had no origin, no beginning. There never was a time when He did not exist. This is impossible to illustrate because He is unlike anything and anyone else in the universe. He made it all. He made us all.

Q: *Where did God come from?*
A: He fills all the universe and everything beyond it, so He didn't come "from" anywhere! He was always here before the worlds were made, so there is no place where He never was in existence.

Q: *What is Ultimate Reality?*
A: God's own uncreated being. Beyond matter and energy, beyond all the creation we see, more basic than anything else in the cosmos is what has always been and always will be—God's own unmade substance.

Q: *What is the difference between God and man?*
A: He is *uncreated*, we are *created*. He is metaphysically unlike us in His basic essence or being; His "stuff" is absolutely and wholly different from ours—or anything else!

Q: *Why can't man become God?*
A: Because it is impossible for the created to become *un*created. We had a point of beginning in created time; we are finite. God did not begin in time and is infinite.

Q: *I didn't choose to be born. How can an uncreated God understand how I feel when I had no say over what package of humanity I was given?*
A: Like you, God had no "choice" in what He is either. He has always had His being, because there was never a time when He began. He is changeless and, unlike you, unchangeable.

---

[15]B.W. Anderson, *Interpreter's Dictionary of the Bible*, George A. Buttrick, ed. (Nashville: Abingdon Press, 1962), vol. 2, pp. 412, 416.

Analysis and Discussion

The concept of *eternity* is simultaneously one of the most puzzling and one of the most essential concepts in theology. What we mean when we say "God is eternal" has been explored historically and philosophically from two key perspectives:

"The notion of eternity, like infinity, has two meanings. . . . We grasp one meaning of eternity by saying there is no beginning or end to time's process. The other sense of eternity we conceive by denying time itself, and with it, change or mutability."[1]

Reduced to essentials, eternity may mean *endless time* and/or *timelessness*. While we cannot imagine what endless time would be like, the idea is not inconceivable; it would be simply a form of time (like that which we experience as creatures of time) but without beginning or end. Since imagination uses definite objects, we can neither imagine nor experience a span of time without end.

The other key concept, the notion of the eternal as timeless and immutable, interprets it as having no sequence of events. From the perspective of eternity, all events and reality coexist; eternity is an "Eternal Now."

Both these ideas have been held in some form by major Christian and non-Christian thinkers in the past. Both have their strengths and weaknesses. Traditionally, many Christian theologians have followed Augustine's lead in his interpretation of God's eternality as an Eternal Now. It will also be seen—at least from our simple list of the Hebrew and Greek words used in Scripture—that a case can be made for exploring the concept of eternity as endless time. (That God as active Sovereign recognizes true time distinction in relation to His creation is expanded in further detail in Chapter 7.) In either case, we are dealing with an absolute of wonder in which even our best thought and study will, at best, give us a finite idea of this awesome reality. However, the view we do adopt as our own will color and form much of our later thinking about God's nature and character, and thus largely determine our personal theology. In our limited views and assumptions, there will be some real dangers and weaknesses that must, if they can, be avoided.

If, for instance, eternity is *endless time*, and God truly acts in sequence, must He have had a beginning? If He can change His mind, could He change His character? If God is subject to time, will He grow older and wiser? Does this make Him finite and fallible?

On the other hand, if eternity is an *Eternal Now*, is the universe itself also eternal? Are we ourselves, when viewed from a true perspective, eternally existent? If all things in time are simply "now" to God, does anything ever really change? Is there only one possible future fixed in His

---

[1]*Great Ideas*, vol. 1, p. 437.

mind? And how does human responsibility fit into this picture? All these and other important difficulties must be considered when we study this aspect of God's nature.

Eternity As Timelessness

We shall first look at the more traditional view of eternity as timelessness, as Augustine introduced it and Aquinas and the Reformers promoted it. This is the classical view, one with much support through history. In questions about God's stability and faithfulness, it affirms that eternity means absolute unchangeableness of action and character as well as nature. It brings some sense of security to the future by absolutely rejecting any alternatives to that future. It gives us as worshipers a view of the Godhead that encourages abandonment to His will whatever the circumstances. Its intent is to uphold the absolute lordship of Christ over human history, even the often evil and contrary actions of individuals. These are its more obvious strengths. Here are observations of thinkers from the past who have held this view:

Augustine of Hippo

"Nor did you by time precede time; else should you not precede all times. But you precede all things past, by the sublimity of an ever-present eternity; and surpass all future because they are future and when they come they shall be past; 'But Thou art the same and Thy years fail not. . . .'

"Thy years are one day; and Thy day is not daily but Today, seeing Thy today gives not place unto tomorrow for neither doth it replace yesterday. Thy today is Eternity; therefore didst Thou beget the coeternal, to whom Thou saidst 'This day have I begotten thee.' Thou hast made all things; and before all times Thou art; neither in any time was time not."[2]

Thomas Aquinas

Augustine's idea is maintained by Aquinas as an early Roman Catholic view: "The now that stands still is said to make eternity according to our apprehension. For just as the apprehension of time is caused in us by the fact that we apprehend the flow of the now, so the apprehension of eternity is caused in us by our apprehending the now standing still."[3]

Charles Hodge

"We affirm that . . . as to the mode of His existence, His thoughts, emotions, purposes and acts are without succession, one and inseparable, the same forever; third, that He is immutable; we deny . . . second that His states or modes of being occur in succession . . . that His essence,

---

[2]St. Augustine, "Confessions," *Great Books of the Western World*, Robert M. Hutchins and Mortimer Adler, eds. (Chicago: Encyclopedia Britannica, 1952), XI, 16.
[3]Thomas Aquinas, "Summa Theologica," *Great Books of the Western World*, Robert M. Hutchins and Mortimer Adler, eds. (Chicago: Encyclopedia Britannica, 1952), vol. 1, Question X, Art. 2, p. 42.

attributes or purposes will ever change.

"Acts of God are never past, present or future as respects God Himself, but only in respect to the objects and effects of His acts in the creature. The efficient purpose comprehending the precise object, time and circumstance was present to Him always and changelessly, the event, however, taking place in the creature occurs in time and is thus past, present and future to our observation."[4]

John Wesley

Wesley, though not a Calvinist, took the same view: "All time, or rather all eternity (for time is only that small fragment of eternity which is allotted to the children of men) being present to him at once, he does not know one thing before another, or one thing after another; but sees all things in one point of view from everlasting to everlasting. As all time with everything that exists therein is present with him at once, so he sees at once, whatever was, is or will be to the end of time.

"The sum of all is this: The almighty, all-wise God sees and knows from everlasting to everlasting all that is, that was, and that is to come, through one Eternal Now. With Him nothing is past or future, but all things equally present."[5]

Charles Finney

Finney, often criticized for his so-called "New Connection" theology, did not see a way out of the implications of the Eternal Now and held to it. Nevertheless, he apparently did so with some wrestlings of heart and mind that he never satisfactorily resolved:

"Times past and future are relative, and respect only finite existences, or such existences as began to be. They cannot possibly respect a being who never began to be and who grows no older. He can no more pass on through duration than through space. Neither space nor duration can have any meaning with him, except as it respects finite existence. All space is to him here, a single point where He exists. All eternity is to him now, or that point which is filled up by His present experience. . . . Nor when He speaks of things as past or future ought we to understand Him as speaking thus in respect to himself. In respect to all finite existences there is in fact locality, time and place, past and future. But to affirm these things as true of God is to suppose Him finite instead of infinite.

"Eternity is to God as present time is to us. . . . By present time we mean that point indicated by present consciousness . . . our mental states or exercises are single and successive. By past, present and future we refer to the order in which they or the occasions of them occur. Time to us is the progression of existence and experience. Present time is that which is filled up by our present experience and consciousness. Successive exercises are successive experience. Successive experience is in-

---

[4]Charles Hodge, *Systematic Theology* (Grand Rapids: Eerdmans, 1960), pp. 142–144.
[5]John Wesley, "On Predestination," *The Works of John Wesley* (Grand Rapids: Baker Books), Vol. VI, pp. 226–230.

creasing knowledge. Succession therefore belongs to a finite being. But God is not a finite being. He cannot be omniscient and yet obtain knowledge from experience. Succession cannot therefore be predicated of Him, either in relation to His existence or mental states. . . . He can have no new thoughts as there is no possible source from which to derive them. He can have no new affections or emotions as He can have no new ideas or knowledge. Therefore His present consciousness is His eternal consciousness and eternity to Him is what present time is to us.

"Eternity to us means all past, present and future duration. But to God it only means *now*. Duration and space as they respect His existence mean infinitely different things from what they do when they respect our existence. God's existence and His acts as they respect finite existence have relation to time and place. But as they respect His own existence, everything is here and now. . . . The Bible seems to favor this view of the subject, although it would guard against pressing our minds with such a metaphysical nicety. Thus God calls himself "I AM. . . ." To Him 'a thousand years are as one day. . . .' By a thousand years we are to understand all time, of which it is said, that it is as one day, or as present time to God."[6]

C. S. Lewis

"Almost certainly God is not in Time. His life does not consist in moments following one another. . . . If a million people are praying to Him tonight at ten-thirty, He need not listen to them all in that one little snippet which we call ten-thirty. Ten-thirty—and every other moment from the beginning of the world—is always the present for Him. If you like to put it that way, He has all eternity in which to listen to the split second of prayer put up by a pilot as his plane crashes in flames. . . .

"God is not hurried along in the time-stream of this universe any more than an author is hurried along in the imaginary time of his own novel. . . . God, I believe, does not live in a time-stream at all."[7]

Dorothy Sayers

"The Church has always carefully distinguished time from eternity as carefully as she has distinguished the Logos from the Father. . . . God, unlike even the greatest of created beings, is not subject to time."[8]

Arthur C. Custance

In his study "Time Contrasted With Eternity In Scripture," Custance offers an interesting implication of the Eternal Now picture of eternity: "When any Christian dies he passes from this realm of time and space into another realm of pure spirit, that is to say out of time as we experience

---

[6]Charles G. Finney, *Lectures on Theology* (Minneapolis, Minn.: Bethany House Publishers, 1968), pp. 68–71.
[7]C.S. Lewis, *Mere Christianity* (Huntington, N.Y.: J.M. Fontana Publishing, 1955), pp. 142–143.
[8]Dorothy Sayers, *A Matter of Eternity* (Grand Rapids: Eerdmans, 1973), p. 40.

it into a state of pure timelessness, the ever-present of God. As he makes this passage, every event in God's scheduled program for the future . . . must crowd instantly upon him. He does not 'wait' for the Lord's return; it is immediate. But the Lord's return is an event which in the framework of historical time cannot take place until the church is complete and the end of the age is come. It must happen for him, therefore, that these events are completed instantaneously, though the living who survive him await those events in the future.

"Yet for him, those who survive him must in his consciousness also have completed their journey home and therefore he will not even experience any departing from them, but they with him will rise to meet the Lord on His way to His second triumph with all the saints. Within the framework of time this general resurrection is future, but to the 'dying' Christian, it is a present event. This is the meaning of the Lord's words, 'The hour is coming—and now is' (John 5:25). There is no difference between 'is coming' and 'now is.' "[9]

The Eastern Concept of Eternity

As can be seen the Eternal Now offers some solutions to puzzling aspects of Scripture. But it is not without problems. Does God's stability and faithfulness, His absolute unchangeableness of nature and character, apply to His plainly stated alternative plans in Scripture? Is our future truly a function of morality if it is secured by absolutely eliminating any alternatives? Does this picture of God essentially differ from the Islam *kismet* or the Hindu *karma*? Can we uphold the absolute lordship of Christ over human history without abandoning individual personal responsibility? Two key criticisms of this view involve its similarity to Eastern ideas of fatality (the loss of human responsibility) and the apparent conflict between God's foreknowledge of man's future and His goodness.

One criticism of the Eternal Now premise is that it is identical to the heart of most Eastern (Indian and Greek) thought. From this same premise the philosophically religious East has built its doctrines of *all life is one with God* (making salvation equal to self-realization), *karma* (whatever people have is what they deserve), and *reincarnation* (death is a temporary recycling of the soul until it merges finally with the Absolute). Unless these ideas can be carefully distinguished from Christianity by a theology adopting the Eternal Now idea, the way remains open to this same resignation and fatalism that has already spiritually and physically hurt those countries and peoples attempting to live by its precepts.

Zen Buddhism

"Now is timeless. That's where you are, in the center of that dimensionless point of the timeless Now. You believe the material world, including your empirical self, endures beyond your thoughts and therefore

---

[9]Arthur C Custance, *The Doorway Papers* (Grand Rapids: Zondervan Publishing House, 1977), p. 42.

you derive your concept of linear time from that belief. The only reality is the 'now' of conscious experience. When one thought disappears to be replaced by another, No-Thing disappears, so there *is* no past. Thoughts yet to appear are likewise No-Thing, so there is no future. The only existence of past, present or future things is the timeless, non-dimensional Now-point of knowing. Western time is measured by motion through space. In Zen understanding, there is neither space or motion; therefore Time is No-Thing."[10]

Buddhism

"The Buddhist teaching on God in the sense of an ultimate reality is neither agnostic as is sometimes claimed, nor vague, but clear and logical. Whatever reality may be it is beyond the finite intellect. . . . If there is a Causeless Cause . . . it must be clearly infinite, unlimited, unconditioned and without attributes. . . . It follows that we can neither define, describe nor usefully discuss the nature of *that* which is beyond the comprehension of our finite consciousness. It may be indicated by negatives and described indirectly by analogy and symbols, but otherwise it must ever remain in its truest sense unknown and unexpressed, as being to us in our present sense unknowable. . . . 'Through the destruction of all that is individual in us we enter into communion with the whole universe and become an integral part of the great purpose.' Perfection is then the sense of oneness with all that is, has ever been and can ever be."[11]

"The essence of the method [of meditation for final enlightenment] lies in the concentration of thought upon a single point, carried so far that the duality of subject and object is resolved into a perfect unity 'when,' in the words of Schilling, 'the perceiving self merges into the self-perceived.' At that moment we annihilate time and the duration of time; we are no longer in time but time, or rather eternity itself is in us."[12]

Neo-Platonism

"We know it [eternity] as a Life changelessly motionless, and ever holding the Universal Content (time, space and phenomena) in actual presence; not this now and now that other, but always all; not existing in one mode and now in another, but a consummation without part or interval. All its content is in immediate concentration at one point; nothing in it ever knows development, all remains identical within itself, knowing nothing of change, *forever in a now*, since nothing of it has passed away or will come into being but what it is now, that it is ever. Eternity, therefore . . . exists as the announcement of the Identity of the Divine, of that state of being thus, and not otherwise—which characterizes what has no future, but is eternal.

"Thus a close enough definition of Eternity would be that it is a life limitless in the full sense of being all the life there is, and a life which

---

[10]Tucker N. Calloway, *The Logic of Zen: Zen-Way; Jesus-Way*, pp. 62–63.
[11]Christmas Humphreys, *Buddhism* (Penguin Books, 1967), pp. 79–80, 128.
[12]Ananda K. Coomaraswamy, *The Dance Of Shiva*, p. 59.

knowing nothing of past or future to shatter its completeness, possesses itself intact forever."[13]

Hinduism

"What does the Vedanta teach us? . . . All the past and all the future are here in the present. No man ever saw the past. When you think you are knowing the past you only imagine the past in the present moment. To see the future you would have to bring it down to the present, which is the only reality—the rest is imagination. This present is all there is. There is only the One. All is here right now. One moment in infinite time is quite as complete and all-inclusive as every other moment. All that is and was and will be is here in the present.

"We shall understand this by and by, and then see it: all the heavens—everything are here *now* and they really are nothing but appearances of the Divine Presence. . . . People think that this world is bad and imagine that heaven is somewhere else. This world is not bad. It is God himself if you know it. It is a hard thing even to understand, harder than to believe. The murderer who is going to be hanged tomorrow is all God, perfect God. It is very hard to understand surely; but it can be understood. Therefore Vedanta formulates not universal brotherhood, but universal oneness. I am the same as any other man, as any animal—good, bad, anything. It is one body, one mind, one soul throughout. Spirit never dies. There is no death anywhere not even for the body. . . . How can the body die? One leaf may fall—does the tree die? The universe is my body. See how it continues. All minds are mine. With all feet I walk. Through all mouths I speak. In everybody I reside."[14]

This connection between eternity as timelessness and man's "true self" being "eternal and identical with God" is obvious in this poem by Vivekananda:

> He who is in you and outside of you
> Who works through all hands
> Who walks on all feet
> Him worship and break all other idols
> *In whom is neither past life*
> *Nor future birth nor death*
> *In whom we have always been*
> *And always shall be one. . . .*[15]

When time, like eternity, is conceived as non-linear, it has led to a picture of history that is not static, but instead circular. This is the root of much of the East's teaching on karma, reincarnation, etc.

"Diverse interpretations of the nature and significance of the individual

---

[13]Plotinus, "Time and Eternity," *Third Ennead*, Tractate VII, *Great Books of the Western World*, Robert M. Hutchins and Mortimer Adler, eds. (Chicago: Encyclopedia Britannica, 1952).
[14]Swami Vivekananda, *The Works of Swami Vivekananda*, vol. 7, pp. 128–129.
[15]Ibid. vol. 7, p. 169.

human being's experience and observation of time . . . have led to equally sharp differences in views of human history and of ultimate reality. . . . Thinkers have been divided between the holders of the cyclical view and holders of the one-way view of time. . . . Variations in the two basic views of time and in the corresponding codes of conduct have been among the salient characteristics distinguishing the principal civilizations, philosophies and higher religions that have appeared in history to date. . . . The cyclic view of history, both cosmic and human has been prevalent among the Hindus, the pre-Christian Greeks, the Chinese, and the pre-Columbian peoples of Central America; it has reappeared in the modern West, although this civilization was originally Christian—that is was nurtured in a religion that sees time as a one-way flow and not a cyclical one."[16]

Divine Foreknowledge and Human Responsibility

If there *is* no past, present, or future with God, then is there *only* one future for each person? Do we merely act out our future without any true options or alternatives as far as God is concerned? If we do, and if that future was already fixed before our physical creation, who is ultimately responsible for our choices? How can there be a place for real human choice or the resulting responsibility in the predetermined future implied by the doctrine of a timelessness eternity? And how then does God view our choices, our future possibilities, our prayers? Does His knowing our future allow either of us to ever change it?

You can see then that whatever we think "eternal" means deeply governs our view of man's salvation, God's treatment of history, and the concept of prophecy. Does a fixed and unchangeable future annul human responsibility?

Augustine

Augustine, who gave a lot of thought to the implications of his idea of the Eternal Now, discussed problems with the concept in his collected works: "Your problem is this. You wonder how . . . these two propositions are not contradictory, and incompatible, namely that God has foreknowledge of all future events and that we sin voluntarily and not by necessity. For if, you say, God foreknows that a man will sin, he must necessarily sin. But if there is necessity, there is no voluntary choice of sinning but rather fixed and unavoidable necessity."[17]

Augustine's answer forms the classic reply of the "eternity-equals-timelessness" view; it is again an *inexplicable paradox* or mystery: "Cicero chooses to reject the foreknowledge of future things and shuts up the religious mind to this alternative. . . . Either that something is in our power or that there is foreknowledge, both of which cannot be true; but if the one is affirmed, the other is denied. . . . But the religious mind chooses both, confesses both and maintains both . . . we assert both that God

---

[16]*Encyclopaedia Britannica*, 15th ed. (1975), vol. 18, p. 411.
[17]St. Augustine, *Freedom of the Will*, Book III, ch. 3, sec. 6.

knows all things before they come to pass and that we do by our free will whatsoever we know and feel to be done by us only because we will it."

He then admits that although everything must be caused by God, including all human choices, he does not want to call this *Fate*. Perhaps God, knowing our choices, somehow keeps us responsible while He still ultimately directs them: "An order of causes in which the highest efficiency is attributed to the will of God, we neither deny nor do we designate by the name of fate. . . . Our wills themselves are included in that order of causes which is certain to God and is embraced by His foreknowledge, for human wills are also causes of human actions; and He who foreknew all the causes of things would certainly among those causes not be ignorant of our wills.

"For one who is not prescient of all things is not God. Wherefore our wills also have just so much power as God willed and foreknew they should have; and, therefore, whatever power they have, they have it within most certain limits; and whatever they are to do they are most assuredly to do, for He whose foreknowledge is infallible foreknew that they would have the power to do it and would do it. Wherefore if I should choose to apply the name of Fate to anything at all, I should rather say that Fate belongs to the weaker of two parties and Will to the stronger, who has the other in his power, than allow that the freedom of our will be excluded by that order of causes which by an unusual application of that word . . . the Stoics call Fate."[18]

John Calvin

Calvin, one of the most influential theologians of church history, developed his later doctrinal ideas logically enough on this same premise. He wrote: "When we attribute foreknowledge to God, we mean that all things have been and perpetually remain before His eyes, so that to His knowledge, nothing is future or past, but all things are present; and present in such a manner that He does not merely conceive of them from ideas formed in His mind, as things remembered by us appear to our minds, but He holds and sees them as if actually placed before Him."[19]

From this he logically progressed beyond Augustine to the following conclusions: "Every action and motion of every creature is so governed by the hidden counsel of God that nothing can come to pass but what is ordained by Him. . . . The wills of men are so governed by the will of God that they are carried on straight to the mark which He has foreordained."[20]

Calvin reached a conclusion similar to Plotinus and other Eastern writers: "I will not scruple to own that the will of God lays a *necessity* on all things and that every thing He wills necessarily comes to pass. . . . God not only foresaw that Adam would fall, but also *ordained* that he

---

[18]St. Augustine *The City of God* (Washington, D.C.: Catholic University Press, 1950), Book V, ch. 9—cf. Plotinus in *The City of God,* Book XI, ch. 21).
[19]John Calvin, *The Institutes of the Christian Religion* (Westminster Press), Book III, ch. 21.
[20]Ibid. Book I, ch. 16, sects. 3, 8.

should. . . . he sinned because God so ordained, because the Lord saw good."[21]

Calvin does not avoid the necessary link between God's actions and knowledge; he does not fall into the trap of thinking that just because God foreknows does not mean He foreordains. To Calvin, it was actually the reverse; God's foreknowledge was not in question, because God's knowledge came from His eternal decrees. God knew it because God himself did it. He did not like this conclusion, but fearlessly held to his convictions:

"All men are not created for the same end; but some are foreordained to eternal life; others to eternal damnation. So according as every man was created for the one end or the other, we say he was elected or predestinated to life, or reprobated that is, predestinated to destruction."[22]

"God, of His own good pleasure ordains that many should be born, who are from the womb devoted to inevitable damnation. If any man pretend that God's foreknowledge lays them under no necessity of being damned, but rather that He decreed their damnation because He foreknew their wickedness, I grant that God's foreknowledge alone lays no necessity on the creature; but eternal life and death depend on the *will* rather than the foreknowledge of God. If God only foreknew all things that relate to all men, and did not decree and ordain them also, then it might be inquired whether or not His foreknowledge necessitates the thing foreknown. But seeing He therefore foreknows all things that will come to pass, because He has decreed they shall come to pass, it is vain to contend about foreknowledge, since it is plain all things come to pass by God's positive decree."[23]

C. S. Lewis

"Another difficulty we get if we believe God to be in time is this. Everyone who believes in God at all believes that He knows what you and I are going to do tomorrow. But if He knows I am going to do so-and-so, how can I be free to do otherwise? Well, here again the difficulty comes from thinking that God is progressing along a time-line like us. . . . But suppose God is outside and above the time-line. In that case what we call 'tomorrow' is visible to Him in just the same way as what we call 'today.' All things are 'now' for Him. He does not remember you doing things yesterday; He simply sees you doing them, because though you have lost yesterday He has not. He does not 'foresee' you doing things tomorrow; He simply sees you doing them, because although tomorrow is not yet there for you, it is for Him. You never supposed that your actions at this moment were any less free because God knows what you are doing. . . . In a sense He does not know your action till you have done it; but then the moment at which you have done it is already 'now' to Him."[24]

[21]Ibid., Book III, ch. 24, sec. 8.
[22]Ibid., Book III, ch. 21, sec. 1.
[23]Ibid., Book III, ch. 23, sec. 6.
[24]Lewis, op. cit. pp. 144–145.

Here Lewis does not define what "in a sense" means, and he does not deal with the problem of God's *will* being the ultimate origination of the *person* who makes the choices. As Calvin saw clearly enough, if God does *not* act in sequence, then all future events *are already fixed and necessary* by the will of God. It is not quite true to say that though God made a person and knows what He will do, He is not responsible for that creation's choices or (as Augustine first pointed out) that you "never supposed that your actions at this moment were any less free because God knows what you are doing."

Human Choices and Time

Thus with this view, the Creator knows absolutely what the creature is going to do before he does it. He creates the person knowing they will do what they will do. As the rationalist and skeptic Bertrand Russell complained: "The world, we are told, was created by a God who is both good and omnipotent. Before He made it, He foresaw all the pain and misery it would contain. Therefore He is responsible for it. It is useless to argue that the pain in the world is due to sin. If I, as a father, begat a child, knowing he was going to be a homicidal maniac, I would clearly be responsible of the crimes for which he was found guilty."[25]

Here then is the other key problem with the Eternal Now: try as you may, it is difficult to avoid the conclusion of Calvin and Plotinus that if it is true, human choices have no real significance. Life, as the East maintains, is but a play, that indeed (apart from the apparent illusion of responsible and history-affecting personal response and decision) a kind of benevolent fatalism rules the universe. If God lives in an absolute Eternal Now, then as far as He is concerned the ultimate reality is that "whatever will be, will be"—by the will of God. Most attempts at compromise either leave the question unanswered or leave the inquirer with John Wesley's puzzled reply, "I frankly confess I know not."

What We Do Know

We have examined the theory of the so called "Eternal Now" in detail to draw some conclusions as to the nature of eternity. We cannot, because of the limits of this volume, examine in detail the second aspect of this question involving the doctrines of foreknowledge, predestination, election, and God's decreed purposes in history. All of these belong properly to the study of God's interaction with His creation and demand thorough treatment. But in considering the key aspects of the two divergent views of God's action in time, we can say that at least these things must be true:

- God's being is, and must be, without beginning or end. If His essential nature and substance are sequential, then He is finite.
- Eternity cannot be created time extended infinitely because God's actions in time are superior in kind to all our experiences of it.

---

[25]Bertrand Russell, *Why I Am Not a Christian* (New York: Simon and Schuster, 1957).

- Time somehow has reality only in association with the created order. Time only has meaning when eternity interacts with creation.
- Time must have its ultimate origin in God, but He himself cannot be a subject of it—at least not in the same sense the universe is subject to time.

The following are conjectures, and not necessarily true:

- God cannot act in sequence without accessing new knowledge or experience, thus being "finite." (See Appendix 2.)
- Eternity precludes any kind of sequence. (Scripture indicates otherwise.)
- All God's acts, experiences, and thoughts are simultaneously existent. He cannot have a new thought, feeling, or make a new decision.—The tenor of the Bible seems to contradict this. (It is certainly not wise to say that a sovereign God cannot do something that is neither wrong nor intrinsically impossible.)
- All the future actions of moral beings are fixed and preordained by the will of God. (If true, it is neither intuitive nor nice; it certainly negates the concept of free choice.)

From all this, if we think hard, we can summarize the three possible views of what eternity is. Comparing time to a film production, we end up with the following choices:

- *There is no real movie.* There is no sequence of events. We have a relativistic 4-D model of our world in which time is but a fourth dimension of space, with all history and reality a single act of creation—an Eternal Now with the appearance of providential government but what is really the illusion of freedom. This has been a popular theory, fitting well with the modern concept of relativity.
- *The whole film is already made and produced.* We can cry over the sad parts, laugh at the funny scenes, but we can only share in the experience; nothing we do can change what we see. God has created the earth in time, but linked the future of that creation to His all-knowing mind; the future is thus fixed and unchangeable. This differs only from the first view in that it allows time as a distinct and real element in an otherwise deterministic process.
- *We live on the set of a movie in production.* The Director knows much of what will happen in the film, but details regarding scenes and minor events are at the option of actors. This is a model of the world in which time is real and the future has options within certain divinely declared limits. This is perhaps our street-level doctrine, the practical view of most Christians, the model we use for thought and action in ordinary life.

Which one is the real picture? Is one exclusively true; or is one more true, tied to the others in a paradox of reality? We do not know what eternity means and probably never will! No finite mind can in modesty come to a comprehensive conclusion on the mystery; but it will capture our best thought and discussion "until time shall be no more," and for "times eternal" we will continue to be filled with wonder over the one who fills all eternity.

Historical Discussion

The profoundest thinkers, headed by Aristotle and Samuel Clarke all affirm there cannot be an infinite series of causes. The other is to admit an uncaused cause. In this there is no absurdity whatever.... Such a cause must be a free, self-originating spirit. Beyond that we cannot go and to that we are compelled by reason and logic to go, and from that we cannot escape. In all this there may be much of incomprehensibility of inexplicable mystery; but no absurdity, no self-contradiction.[1]

—L. D. McCabe

What do we mean when we say something is "timeless"? The idea of a timeless eternity has been critically examined recently by many evangelicals. Some charge that this idea entered theology via neo-Platonism through Augustine to Aquinas. Though at first it was rejected by men like Duns Scotus and William of Ockham, it returned to Catholic theology from the sixteenth century onward. Now it remains the bastion of Reform and related Christian thinkers who seek to uphold it as a key doctrine.

When we say something is "timeless," we mean one or more of the following things:

- That thing has no time *location*; we cannot place it in a time slot; we cannot say anything that makes sense about it using a time word such as "before" or "after."
- That thing has no time *extension*; it has no duration, preceding or ongoing-ness at all; it cannot act for "so long" or be alive "during" any event.
- It has no time *significance*; no time words used of it are either true or meaningful.

Perhaps all these mean that God just does not live in space and time as we do. Two key philosophical objections to God's eternity being timeless are:

- A timeless God cannot be the biblical Creator-God.
- A timeless person is an incoherent notion.

A Creating, Loving God

The first objection, according to Farnell, could be restated something like this: if God created anything, it did not exist before He made it. If it

---

[1]L. D. McCabe, *The Foreknowledge of God and Cognate Themes.*

did exist before He made it, it is eternal as He is and the universe is likewise one with God. If it existed only "after" He made it, the actions of God have a time location (i.e., His eternity is not timeless). "No ancient or recent writer," notes Farnell, "has succeeded in showing how the act of creation is compatible with the idea of timelessness."[2]

Can God timelessly create *in* time? Aquinas argued He could "eternally will" a creation to be made *in* time.[3]

Though true, how does this make the act of creation timeless? We can say that an effect in time need not make its cause temporal, but no one knows what that means.

But can we really discuss whether or not God existed "before" or "after" anything? Do "before" and "after" mean anything when we speak about eternity? We could refuse to use time words when we talk about God; we could insist they have no meaning and simply prevent any further discussion on the nature of eternity. Such a demand also, of course, might be applied to any other words involving God's nature and stops any other kind of discussion about Him (which might sometimes be wiser, but certainly not as much fun).

There are those who say that God in a timeless eternity could not be the personal, caring, involved God of the Bible. Persons *do* things, and do them in sequence or in some sort of time. God plainly states that He remembers, responds to, and remakes lives; He is active in human history, more like the movie-maker than the audience watching the completed movie.

Some insist that all these apparently personal and successive actions mentioned in Scripture are mere analogies, anthropomorphisms, and anthropopathisms; that although the plain language of Scripture seems to state that He *does* do these things, we have to think about God like this because we don't know how He really acts. If so, the simple biblical account could all be, in fact, only an imaginary adaptation to our way of understanding. The objection that the doctrine of eternal timelessness is itself such an adaption, only one even harder to imagine, could also be raised.

Some have suggested that we think of God in two ways: that He does not change His *essential* knowledge, but only His *relational* knowledge about us. On one level, God knows timelessly, without temporal interaction; on another, He knows us through interaction within time. In eternity God sees nothing really change; in time He sees things as they really are—something like parallel lines which meet in infinity. We might also suggest that a pagan might understand this simply as two gods with different knowledge.

Incoherence

The second objection raised to a timeless eternity is that the notion of a timeless being is incoherent. By incoherent we do not mean myste-

---

[2]*Stephen Charnock, The Existence and Attributes of God* (Grand Rapids: Baker Book House, 1979), p. 256.
[3]Thomas Aquinas, "Summa Theologica" *Great Books of the Western World*, Robert M. Hutchins and Mortimer Adler, eds. (Chicago: Encyclopedia Britannica, 1952), Summa Contra Gentiles II. 35, 36.

rious, but nonsensical. We do not mean we cannot understand the idea because it is too wonderful; we mean it cannot be understood because it is too silly. Bible facts about God should give us an interlocking vision of Him; a vision in which each revealed truth really fits with everything else we learn of Him and His universe.

Aquinas, Augustine, and Anselm claimed that all times with God are "simultaneously present." If that means that God knows exactly what is going on at any point in time, that makes sense; the idea matches what the Bible says of Him. But if it means that Jesus was (is) born in A.D. 1 as well as in 1990, it is nonsense. Perhaps it means that *to us* Jesus was born about nineteen centuries ago; but to God He *was*, *is*, or *can be* born at any time. The truth is time is a reality to us, but there is no compelling reason to insist any kind of time is real in God. We can say that, but we cannot prove it.

A More Complete Picture of Truth

Perhaps eternity is a special kind of duration, where God exists without any sort of succession while our time has succession. But what kind of "duration" has no succession? How can a being outside of time observe a creature *in* time without being temporally involved? A being who lives in a "Super-time" might be understood to do this coherently and without paradox. How can a being create a world in time as an effect of a cause outside time?

Is there any reason to prove that God is timeless? Some thinkers offer another dual perspective: perhaps God's acts are "timeless" to Him but temporal to us. We can speak truth about God from our perspective using time words; we do not need to possess any of God's attributes in order to know of them. But the question is not whether or not we should ascribe time to God to explain things about Him, but does His own revelation of himself match what we know of Him in this area.

Dr. Carl Henry avers that while "evangelical theism affirms that God's knowledge is timelessly eternal," this notion is not to be confused with similar ideas from Greek and non-biblical sources. Unlike Boethius, there must be some distinction in God's mind between events occurring yesterday, today, and tomorrow; time does not have to be unreal to God, nor meaningless to Him. Divine personality, he insists, can transcend time because it involves a "more complex and profound selfhood" than man, and that we only bear His image in some aspects. To involve God in history "compromises divine transcendence and portrays Him as being progressively enriched in experience."[4]

"The fact is," writes Henry, "a change in the object of knowledge does not require a change in the knower, nor does it require a change of knowledge. God's knowledge, as Aquinas emphasizes, is 'altogether invariable.' "[5]

---

[4]Carl Henry, *God, Revelation, and Authority* (Waco: Word Publishers), Vol. V, p. 272.
[5]Ibid. p.274.

Henry continues, "The biblical view, it seems to me, implies that God is not in time; that there is no succession of ideas in the divine mind; that time is a divine creation concomitant with the origin of the universe; that God internally knows all things, including all space-time contingencies; that this knowledge includes knowledge of the temporal succession prevalent in the created universe. . . . God includes time not as a constituent aspect of His being or knowing, but as a conceptual aspect of His knowledge of created realities. God's time-transcending knowledge in himself does not cancel out distinctive space-time relationships to His created universe. God is not limited to simply one track of relationships to the temporal order; he knows all historical factualities and contingencies through His eternal decree and He knows them in personal presence in the historical order."[6]

The Uncreated Acting in Time

The idea here is that even in simultaneous knowledge, there remains an *awareness* of sequence; that the divine mind can distinguish between events that are "forever true" or merely "contingent in time." "God's nature need not itself be time-structured in order for Him to know simultaneously all events and also to know them in the way His creatures know them. . . . God's omniscience involves both simultaneous knowledge of all that is past or future and an awareness of the succession of events in the created, temporal order. There is nothing contradictory in saying that God knows all things simultaneously and that within this comprehensive knowledge he distinguishes between what is forever true and factual and what is temporally contingent. He eternally knew that I would write these sentences yesterday and give them a final editing this morning."[7]

Although God's knowledge is not knowledge *in* succession, He has knowledge *of* succession. Augustine argued God is not necessarily spatial just because he knows space. God knows all things at once. . . . He not only knows events as they become actual in time and space, but he also knows them as certain from eternity." Dr. Henry thinks that temporalizing eternity is a compromise: "A deity whose knowledge is time-bound cannot give unqualified assurance about the future or for that matter about the present."[8] This is true unless He can exercise His sovereign power to ensure those assurances.

Attributing fresh experience to God has its dangers. Dr. Henry says it can threaten our sense of divine stability and security: "The more one stresses the possibility of divine surprise by novelty as significant evidence that God is both personal and living, the less predictable will be the final outcome of history, and for that matter the manifest purpose of God in the course of human history itself."[9] This is also true, unless God in His

---

[6]Ibid. p. 276.
[7]Ibid. p. 276.
[8]Ibid. p. 258.
[9]Ibid. p. 278.

greatness and power is even able to accomodate the created contingent into His declared certainties.

Past, Present, and Future as One

Boethius of the 6th century (480–520 A.D.) (On The Consolation Of Philosophy: 5.6) best advanced the recently re-stated argument of men like John Saunders: "Our freedom is no more infringed by God's previously believing that we *will* act in a certain manner than it is by His later believing that we *did* act in a certain manner; we will never perform an act that conflicts with His beliefs no matter what the dates of those beliefs."[10]

It was a neat solution to the problem of divine foreknowledge; if all times are present to God, God as easily sees our future acts as others see our present ones. If having a person knowing how I will decide in a matter does not influence my free choice, why should it be any different with God, with whom future is the same as the present? One difficulty persists however: no human observer created me with the capability of the free choices I presently make. If God sees all time at once, He has seen all my acts before I was made and must have ultimately decreed them.

The Reformers, Henry writes, believed events were fixed because they were determined by God's will; but this does not mean God is wrong in willing sin. Henry notes, "To say God wills sin and redemption as factors in the universe He purposes to create is not at all to say that God sins or that He has a light view of sin. . . . The purpose of God in creation is fully grounded in His wisdom, love, and goodness."

Yet how can an infinitely wise being intelligently author His own unhappiness? "The alternative view," he notes, "is that the creature incurs sin by his own voluntary misdeeds totally outside the purposes of God for His creation." But this is disallowed because it leaves too much to the creation. "This view involves a conception of the universe so open-ended that it nullifies the relevance and significance of God's purposes in the eschatological future as well. God does not force man to sin since sin is deliberate action contrary to the precepts of God. Through man's responsible decision and choice, sin enters a universe in which sin and redemption are integral elements in God's purpose." To put it another way: the creation sins wholly within the purposes of the Creator.

The traditional Reform answer to preserving certainty is not in timeless eternity, but *decree*: the future is finally founded in God's choice, not in His knowledge. Henry writes, while "the mind of God accounts for the intrinsic possibilities of all things . . . [the] power of God accounts for their extrinsic possibilities." Things exist because He ultimately actualizes them. "The argument that God foreknows what He does not purpose and which shifts the grounds of divine foreknowledge to something other than God's purpose raises many difficulties. . . . There can be no other ground of divine foreknowledge of non-existent processes, events, and creatures if they were not divinely purposed. God's purposes are eternal and effec-

---

[10]Saunders, *Of God and Freedom*.

tuate all futurities. The effort to limit divine foreknowledge only to events that do not involve creaturely decision and action, that is, to God's own acts in distinction from so-called 'contingent' events, is conjectural and without biblical basis. In Scripture, divine omniscience embraces even that which is contingent from a human perspective (1 Sam. 23:9ff.; Matt. 11:22ff.). Scripture contravenes the claim that divine non-determination is necessary for human freedom and responsibility, for God's foreordination includes even such events as fallen man's rejection and crucifixion of Jesus Christ, events for which man is held responsible (Acts 2:23)."[11]

Another view is that God's purpose for Christ's death was crucifixion not stoning, and that it is the form of His death, not man's sin itself that was purposed.

The Roots of Our Doctrine

The three main motives for the development of the doctrine of a "timeless" eternity were:

- To reconcile human freedom and divine foreknowledge.
- To retain consistency with other doctrines of God.
- To exalt God's transcendence.

But God is, as Richard Swinburne puts it, "both forwardly and backwardly eternal. . . . A perfectly free person could not be immutable in the strong sense, that is, unable to change. For an agent is perfectly free at a certain time if his action results from his own choice at that time, and if his choice is not itself brought about by anything else. Yet a person immutable in the strong sense would be unable to perform any action at a certain time other than what he had previously intended to do. His own course of actions being fixed by His past choices he would not be perfectly free. . . .

"Why should many theists have wished to suppose that God is immutable in the strong sense? The belief that God is immutable in this sense does not seem to me to be so much in evidence in Christian tradition until the third or fourth century A.D. It came, I suspect from neo-Platonism. For a Platonist, things which change are inferior to things which do not change. . . . It is not, I have suggested, one implicit in the Old or New Testament. Nor, I would think is it one to which very many modern theists are committed unless they have absorbed Thomism fairly thoroughly. . . ."

The theists "only hope" for attempting the inner coherence of a claim that God is timeless would be to "maintain that many words are being used in a highly analogical sense. . . . Although a theist would be justified on occasion in using words in an analogical sense, too many appeals [to analogy] would make sentences in which the words were used empty of the content."[12]

---

[11]Henry, op. cit. p. 284.
[12]Richard Swinburne, *The Coherence of Theism* (London: Oxford Press, 1977), pp. 211, 214–215, 222–223.

CHAPTER TWO

COROLLARY ONE:
GOD IS INFINITE

Scriptures

God Is Infinite in Presence (Omnipresent)

"Can any hide himself in secret places that I shall not see him? saith the LORD. Do not I fill heaven and earth? saith the LORD." (Jer. 23:24)

"But will God indeed dwell on the earth? behold, the heaven and heaven of heavens cannot contain thee." (1 Kings 8:27)

"But who is able to build him an house, seeing the heaven and heaven of heavens cannot contain him?" (2 Chron. 2:6)

"Whither shall I go from thy spirit? or whither shall I flee from thy presence? If I ascend up into heaven, thou art there: if I make my bed in hell, behold, thou art there. If I take the wings of the morning, and dwell in the uttermost parts of the sea; even there shall thy hand lead me, and thy right hand shall hold me." (Ps. 139:7–10)

"The eyes of the LORD are in every place, beholding the evil and the good." (Prov. 15:3)

"For where two or three are gathered together in my name, there am I in the midst of them." (Matt. 18:20)

"God that made the world and all things therein, seeing that he is LORD of heaven and earth, dwelleth not in temples made with hands . . . that they should seek the LORD, if haply they might feel after him, and find him, though *he be not far from every one of us: for in him we live, and move, and have our being.*" (Acts 17:24, 27–28a)

"One God and Father of all, who is above all, and *through all, and in you all.*" (Eph. 4:6)

God Is Infinite in Knowledge (Omniscient)

"Great is our Lord, and of great power; his understanding is infinite." (Ps. 147:5)

"Then hear thou in heaven thy dwelling place, and forgive, and do, and give to every man according to his ways, whose heart thou knowest; (for thou, even thou only, knowest the hearts of all the children of men). . . ." (1 Kings 8:39)

"And thou, Solomon my son, know thou the God of thy father, and serve him with a perfect heart and with a willing mind: for the LORD searcheth all hearts, and understandeth all the imaginations of the thoughts: if thou seek him, he will be found of thee; but if thou forsake him, he will cast thee off for ever." (1 Chron. 28:9)

"Dost thou know the balancings of the clouds, the wondrous works of him which is perfect in knowledge?" (Job 37:16)

"Then Job answered the LORD, and said, I know that thou canst do every thing, and that no thought can be withholden from thee. . . ." (Job 42:1–2)

"Yet they say, The LORD shall not see, neither shall the God of Jacob regard it. Understand . . . He that planted the ear, shall he not hear? He that formed the eye, shall he not see? He that chastiseth the heathen, shall not he correct? he that teacheth man knowledge, *shall not he know?*" (Ps. 94:7–10)

"For God shall bring every work into judgment, with every secret thing, whether it be good, or whether it be evil." (Eccles. 12:14)

"Woe unto them that seek deep to hide their counsel from the LORD, and their works are in the dark, and they say, Who seeth us? and who knoweth us . . . for shall the work say of him that made it, He made me not? or shall the thing framed say of him that framed it, He had no understanding? (Isa. 29:15–16)

"For mine eyes are upon *all* their ways: they are not hid from my face, neither is their iniquity hid from mine eyes." (Jer. 16:17)

"Great in counsel, and mighty in work: for thine eyes are open upon all the ways of the sons of men: to give every one according to his ways, and according to the fruit of his doings." (Jer. 32:19)

"Thus saith the LORD; Thus have ye said, O house of Israel: for I know the things that come into your mind, *every one* of them." (Ezek. 11:5b)

"He revealeth the deep and secret things: he knoweth what is in the darkness, and the light dwelleth with him." (Dan. 2:22)

"And Jesus *knowing their thoughts* said, Wherefore think ye evil in your hearts?" (Matt. 9:4)

"And Jesus knew their thoughts . . ." (Matt. 12:25)

"But he knew their thoughts . . ." (Luke 6:8)

"But Jesus did not commit himself unto them, because he knew all men, and needed not that any should testify of man: for he knew what was in man." (John 2:24–25)

"Come, see a man, which told me all things that ever I did: is not this the Christ?" (John 4:29)

"But there are some of you that believe not. For Jesus knew from the beginning who they were that believed not, and who should betray him." (John 6:64)

"Now we are sure that thou knowest all things, and needest not that any man should ask thee: by this we believe that thou camest forth from God." (John 16:30)

"Lord, thou knowest all things . . ." [Peter to Jesus] (John 21:17)

"For if our heart condemn us, God is greater than our heart, and knoweth all things." (1 John 3:20)

God Is Infinite in Power (Omnipotent)

"Behold, I am the Lord, the God of all flesh: is there any thing too hard for me?" (Jer. 32:27)

"I know that thou canst do every thing, and that no thought can be withholden from thee." (Job 42:2)

"He ruleth by his power for ever; his eyes behold the nations: let not the rebellious exalt themselves. Selah." (Ps. 66:7; Nah. 1:3)

"For who in the heaven can be compared unto the LORD? who among the sons of the mighty can be likened unto the LORD? God is greatly to be feared in the assembly of the saints, and to be had in reverence of all them that are about him. O LORD God of hosts, who is a strong LORD like unto thee? or to thy faithfulness round about thee?" (Ps. 89:6–8)

"Forasmuch as there is none like unto thee, O LORD; thou art great, and thy name is great in might. Who would not fear thee, O King of nations? . . . Among all the wise men of the nations, and in all their kingdoms, there is none like unto thee. . . . But the LORD is the true God, he is the living God, and an everlasting king: at his wrath the earth shall tremble, and all the nations shall not be able to abide his indignation. . . . He hath made the earth by his power, he hath established the world by his wisdom, and hath stretched out the heavens by his discretion." (Jer. 10:6–7, 10, 12)

"And Jesus came and spake unto them, saying, *All power* is given unto me in heaven and in earth. Go ye therefore, and teach all nations, baptizing them in the name of the Father, and of the Son, and of the Holy Ghost." (Matt. 28:18–19; cf. Luke 9:43; 10:19; John 17:2)

"And the stars of heaven fell unto the earth, even as a fig tree casteth her untimely figs, when she is shaken of a mighty wind. And the heaven departed as a scroll when it is rolled together; and every mountain and island were moved out of their places. And the kings of the earth, and the great men, and the rich men, and the chief captains, and the mighty men, and every bondman, and every free man, hid themselves in the dens and in the rocks of the mountains; and said to the mountains and rocks, Fall on us, and hide us from the face of him that sitteth on the throne, and from the wrath of the Lamb: for the great day of his wrath is come; and who shall be able to stand?" (Rev. 6:13–17; cf. 1 Chron. 29:11–12; 2 Chron. 20:6).

God Is Called Mighty

"A great God, a mighty, and a terrible." (Deut. 10:17)

"Our God, the great, the mighty, and the terrible." (Neh. 9:32)

"The Lord mighty in battle." (Ps. 24:8)

". . . remnant of Jacob, unto the mighty God." (Isa. 10:21)

"The Great, the Mighty God, the LORD of hosts is His name . . ." (Jer. 32:18)

"The Lord thy God in the midst of thee is mighty; he will save, he will rejoice over thee with joy." (Zeph. 3:17)

"To the only wise God our Saviour, be glory and majesty, *dominion and power*, both now and ever. Amen." (Jude 25)

God Is Called Almighty

"And will be a Father unto you, and ye shall be my sons and daughters, saith the Lord *Almighty*." (2 Cor. 6:18)

"I am Alpha and Omega, the beginning and the ending, saith the Lord, which is, and which was, and which is to come, the *Almighty*." (Rev. 1:8)

"And the four beasts had each of them six wings about him; and they were full of eyes within: and they rest not day and night, saying, Holy, holy, holy, Lord God *Almighty*, which was, and is, and is to come." (Rev. 4:8)

"Saying, We give thee thanks, O Lord God *Almighty*, which art, and wast, and art to come; because thou hast taken to thee thy great power, and hast reigned." (Rev. 11:17)

"And I heard as it were the voice of a great multitude, and as the voice of many waters, and as the voice of mighty thunderings, saying, Alleluia: for the Lord God omnipotent [*pantokrator*] reigneth." (Rev. 19:6)

Bible Word Study

Infinite (Hebrew)

micpar *(mis-pawr)*—Large, innumerable.[1]

This word translated "infinite" in Ps. 147:5 is "often employed to point out God's greatness: his wonders are without number (Job 5:9; 9:10), as is His host (Job 25:3); he alone knows the number and names of the stars (Ps. 147:4; Isa. 40:26); In the ultimate sense, his eternality (Job 36:26) and understanding (Ps. 147:5) are beyond man's power to fathom"[2]

el *(ale)*—Strength; as adjective means "mighty," especially of the Almighty (but used of any deity). The KJV translates this word as "God," "mighty one," "power," "strong."[3]

"*El* is used in terms showing God's greatness or superiority over all other gods": *ha el haggadol* "the great El" (Jer. 32:18; Ps. 77:13; 95:3); *ha el oseh pele* "El doing wonders" (Ps. 77:14); *el elim* "El of els" ("God of gods," Dan. 11:36); *el elohe haruhot le kol-basar* "El, the God of the spirits of all flesh" (Num. 16:22; 27:16).[4]

(See: Names of God *El* and derivative names of God, Appendix A.)

abiyr *(aw-beer)*—Mighty (spoken of God), mighty one.[5] From a primary root meaning to soar or to fly. It occurs only in poetic passages such as Ps. 132:2, 5.

chazaq *(khaw-zak)*—Strong. Used in a bad sense, it means hard, bold, violent, mighty.[6]

"This adjective means 'strong' in the sense of 'powerful' (including the power to resist). Of its fifty-seven occurrences, twenty-three refer to a 'strong hand.' . . . Although the word often refers to God's powerful hand, it is not used as a substitute for deity."[7]

gibbor *(ghib-bore)*—Powerful; by implication warrior, tyrant.[8]

This word is used 156 times. It means a hero, or champion among the armed forces. "It is not surprising that . . . God was often depicted as a warrior. God is the true prototype of the mighty man, and if an earthly

---

[1]*Strong's* 4557.
[2]*Theological Wordbook of the Old Testament*, Laird R. Harris, ed. (Chicago: Moody Press, 1980), vol. 2, p. 633.
[3]*Strong's* 410.
[4]*Theological Wordbook of the Old Testament*, op. cit. vol. 1, p. 42.
[5]*Strong's* 46.
[6]*Strong's* 2389.
[7]*Theological Wordbook of the Old Testament*, op. cit. vol. 1, p. 277.
[8]*Strong's* 1368.

warrior's deeds are recounted, how much more should God's be. Thus the psalmists recount God's mighty acts (106:8; 145:4, 11, 12) and . . . those attributes which a warrior-king might be expected to possess . . . are all attributed *par excellence* to God (Job 12:13; Prov. 8:14). Isaiah 9:6 (cf. 10:21) indicates . . . that justice and righteousness will accompany [the coming King's] might."[9]

The divine name Yahweh is the most intimately associated with *gebuwrah* "might" (Jer. 10:6). The name of Yahweh is connected with His *gebuwrah* with which He created heaven and earth, and which at the same time is connected with His righteousness and His uprightness (Ps. 89:12–15). By His name God saves, and by His might He vindicates (Ps. 54:3–7). God's name and His *gebuwrah* stand in synonymous parallelism here. God himself says, "I will cause them to know mine hand and my might [*gebuwrah*] and they shall know that my name is The Lord" (Jer. 16:21). God shows His might in His saving acts; these are also done in His name (Ps. 20:7f.). God's name is identical with His *gebuwrah* "might."[10]

"It should be no surprise therefore that in the Rabbinic age when the name of Yahweh was no longer uttered, the word *gebuwrah* was used along with other words as a substitute for the proper name of God. In this way the name and the person of God who has all great attributes, who is Lord and sovereign over all men, and by whom everything is created and whose sovereignty has always been and will always be exercised are best expressed. The best-known example of the use of *gebuwrah* (dynamis) as a designation for God is found in the NT. Jesus uses the expression in His trial before Caiaphas (Matt. 26:64). . . . Undoubtedly none of the other substitute names (and there are many) are able to make the fact of Jesus' authority as clear as this. Thus Jesus' 'blasphemy' did not consist in uttering the name of God but in identifying God with His own power."[11]

"Since God was able to create the world by His *gebuwrah* . . . and since His *gebuwrah* is synonymous with His name Yahweh, the Rabbis later reached the conclusion that God created it by or with His name."[12]

The word "mighty" and its cognates are used *instead of* Yahweh, and are synonymous with His authority, power, and salvation. The one who is called "The Mighty God" is *identical* with Jehovah.

shadad *(shaw-dad)*—A primitive root, which means properly to be burly (i.e., powerful [figuratively], or impregnable when used passively).[13]

shaddai *(shid-dahee)*—It is from *shadad* and means "Almighty."[14]

As a divine title it is used 48 times in the OT. The Septuagint translates

[9]*Theological Wordbook of the Old Testament*, op. cit. vol. 1, pp. 148–149.
[10]*Theological Dictionary of the Old Testament*, G. Johannes Botterweck and Helmer Ringgren, eds. (Grand Rapids: Eerdmans, 1974), vol. 2, p. 370.
[11]Ibid. pp. 370–371.
[12]Ibid. p. 371.
[13]*Strong's* 7703.
[14]*Strong's* 7706.

it *pantokrator* (all-powerful); and the Vulgate translates it *omnipotens*, from which we get our word "omnipotent."

Infinite (Greek)

pantokrator *(pan-tok-rat-ore)*—Almighty.[15] From *pas*, meaning "all"[16] and *kratos*, meaning "might," "power," "strength," or "dominion."[17] (See Eph. 1:19; 6:10; Col. 1:11; 1 Pet. 4:11; 5:11; Rev. 1:6 and 5:13.) The all-ruling (i.e., God as absolute and universal sovereign). Omnipotent.

Pantokrator is used 10 times in the NT, nine of those ten times in the book of Revelation (1:8; 4:8; 11:17; 15:3; 16:7, 14; 19:6, 15; 21:22; and 2 Cor. 6:18).

The Greek term for almighty is derived from the word *kratos*, which denotes the "presence and significance of force or strength rather than its exercise." It first carried the idea of invested or inherent power, or the power the gods gave to rulers. Applied politically it "almost always denotes the legal and valid superior power which confers supremacy and legally, politically and physically turns the scale."[18] It is used in the Septuagint some 50 times.

In no place in the NT is it said that man has or can gain *kratos*, or power. In one verse *kratos* is linked to the Devil; he has control or the power of death—a demonic force that is subject to him and in his service, and the last enemy of Christ (Heb. 2:14). In all other places *kratos* always refers to God or the Lord, and the supremacy of divine strength.[19]

Pantokrator, or Almighty, the "ruler of all things" was not only common as one of God's names, but was used by the early fathers to express the universal claims of Christianity. The references in Rev. 16:14 and 19:15 are not so much to His activity in creation, but His supremacy over all things, a static not dynamic description.[20]

We can see from these Old and New Testament titles that God is described as one with legal, sovereign authority and the utmost ability and enablement to carry out that right. He is not only the supreme ruler of the universe; He is its legal, rightful and actual Sovereign, endued with full power and moral authority to administer that rulership. God is not only infinite in authority; He is infinite in ability. He is the universe's rightful ruler because He is the one best qualified.

---

[15]*Strong's* 3841.
[16]*Strong's* 3956.
[17]*Strong's* 2904.
[18]*Theological Dictionary of the New Testament*, Gerhard Kittel, ed., Geoffrey W. Bromiley, trans. (Grand Rapids: Wm. B. Eerdmans Publishing Company, 1964), vol. 3, p. 905.
[19]Ibid. p. 907.
[20]Ibid. pp. 914–915.

Questions and Answers

Q: *Where is God?*
A: He is in all places at once; His uncreated being literally transcends, fills, and upholds the whole universe. There is no place where we can go that does not contain His presence; He is immanent. "For in Him we live, and move, and have our being." (Acts 17:28).

Q: *Does God have any limits?*
A: He cannot do anything that is unwise, unholy, or intrinsically impossible. So God cannot lie (Heb. 6:18), be unfaithful (2 Tim. 2:13), be tempted to sin (James 1:13), or do anything else that is foolish, unrighteous, or practically contradictory.

Q: *If God can do everything, can He make a rock so big that He can't lift it? (Or any similar question.)*
A: The premise of this dilemma is false and unscriptural—it is a postulate of nonsense. The Bible defines God's infinite power sanely and clearly; "infinite" does not mean "God can do anything." God will always be true to himself. He can do all that is physically, legally, and morally possible. The proper answer to this kind of question is: Your question is as meaningless as "What makes a bee go blue?" As C. S. Lewis said, "Omnipotence means power to do all that is intrinsically possible, not to do the intrinsically impossible. You may attribute miracles to Him, but not nonsense."[1]

Q: *Why can't God be tempted?*
A: Only an infinite person can see all the results of any choice and weigh their values against all other alternatives. God could no more be tempted to sin (knowing its hurtful, destructive outcome) than you could happily, sanely, and enthusiastically eat a plate of live worms.

Q: *The Bible says "God cannot lie." If he is omnipotent, why can't He lie?*
A: The fact that an omnipotent God cannot do some things does not disprove His existence; it merely shows that some activities are incompatible with omnipotence. Omnipotence does not mean the ability to do what is impossible; it entails only the ability to do what is actually possible. If the ability not to do evil, not to go into nonexistence, or not to do the physically contradictory are limitations, then God is severely limited (2 Tim. 2:13; Tit. 1:2; Num. 23:19; Ps. 78:41).

But this is a misuse of the word "limited." The only limits God has are the unlimited possibilities of His own nature and will. God cannot make a stone heavier than He can handle; that is impossible. If He can create it, then He can control it. He alone holds it in existence and He alone can snuff it out of existence.[2]

---

[1]C.S. Lewis, *The Problem of Pain* (New York: MacMillan, 1978), p. 16.
[2]Norman Geisler, *Christian Apologetics* (Grand Rapids: Baker, 1976), p. 248.

Q: *Why can't people discover God by reason alone?*

A: No finite being can "search out" or comprehend exhaustively, the Infinite. By using reason alone, it would take forever to understand enough of God's nature and character to see Him in His true majesty. Thus He must show himself to us (revelation) or we will never know Him (Job 11:7; Isa. 40:28).

Q: *Will we know everything in heaven?*

A: No. We will never stop learning in heaven or eternity, for God is infinite in His knowledge and perfections, and we will always be finite. Our fellowship will be absolutely intimate (1 Cor. 13:12), but the saved will have limitless things to learn, to grow in, and to do. Heaven will be anything but boring or stale!

Q: *If God is everywhere and in everyone, why aren't sinners Christians?*

A: God's infinite being only upholds all reality (including the life and physical being of sinners). Salvation, however, is not metaphysical in the Bible. A sinner is separated morally from God, not by distance, but by an estranged relationship (Isa. 59:1–2).

Q: *Why doesn't God just destroy the Devil?*

A: Perhaps any God-created personality cannot just cease to exist. Maybe creations cannot themselves be wisely "uncreated" by their Creator. But the Devil is no big threat to God's purposes; he is not even remotely comparable in power. He has been given a limited time before his final judgment to try to prove his case, just as all other moral beings who have chosen to live in rebellion against heaven (Rev. 12:12).

Q: *Why doesn't God stop war?*

A: Depending on the sincerity of the question, I could say:

(1) For the same reason He doesn't stop you when you are at war with Him. Why doesn't He stop you from sinning? Answer that and you'll answer your own question.

(2) God is going to stop the war—*all* wars. But, as C. S. Lewis declared, "When the author walks on stage, the play is over." When God comes back (and we expect Him to) it will be the end of the world.

(3) God could stop the war—He could stop *all* wars, and He could do it in the next sixty seconds! He could do it by simply wiping out every selfish person on the face of the earth. But here is a question for you: How many people would be left when He was finished?

(4) God has only two choices with warring nations: let them go on hurting themselves and Him too, or step in personally to stop the fight. If He stepped in and they turned to fight Him, the fight would be over; it would be the end of the world.

Analysis and Discussion

We say that God is infinite, the one without limit. Other sections of this book show that He is not bounded like His creation by constraints of space and time, but here we want to discuss the unlimitedness of His personality.

He is infinite in not only His natural attributes, but also in His moral attributes. He is the utter fullness of love, wisdom, and goodness. In His presence is "fullness of joy" and at His right hand are "pleasures for evermore" (Ps. 16). God is "overflowing," He is what saints of the past used to call "plenipotent," the utter and original fullness of creativity, excitement and power.

This greatness has consequences: He carries in His heart a divine pressure of love which broke His heart at Calvary. This love led Him not only to share himself through the creation, but to also share himself through the incarnation and all that followed: the cross, His resurrection, and the pouring out of the Holy Spirit. He wants to share himself with us.

"That God loves us and wants to share himself with us is wonderful indeed. But there is no sense of *option* in this; this infinite God is all we will ever need. But more than that, we *must* be ruled, directed, and cared for by Him or die.

He is not only limitless in knowledge and presence, but also in power; but what is the heart of God's claim as God over our lives? To put it simply: *why* does God have the right to be God? Is His claim to our devotion based on His ability to *make* us obey Him or on something else? God is Almighty; but is might the ultimate basis of right? To answer this, we must look at a crucial question: the question of authority.

"Lex Rex"

Is the King (Latin: *rex*) the law, or the Law (Latin: *lex*) king? When you ask the basic question: who or what is the foundation of right and wrong in the universe, do you come down to a principle of power or a powerful person? As Francis Schaeffer pointed out in *A Christian Manifesto*, Samuel Rutherford, among others, upheld God's law as the supreme authority for mankind, as opposed to human law constructed merely from finite and limited opinion. He said that society is always faced with a choice in this area of either *Rex Lex*—the King is law, or *Lex Rex*—the Law [of God] is King. Under Rex Lex, might is right; with Lex Rex, right is might. Rex Lex demands freedom and the rights to power; Lex Rex provides power to do right and be free. We either choose to be governed by ultimate law, God's law, or we choose to be governed by the one with the biggest stick, the largest bankroll, or greatest media influence.

Over 200 years ago, the great statesman Edmund Burke saw the problem clearly. We were made to be governed, and we will either submit to

God's rule and govern ourselves or be governed instead by those who have learned the manipulation of desire. Burke wrote: "Men qualify for freedom in exact proportion to their disposition to put moral chains on their own appetites. Society cannot exist unless a controlling power is put somewhere on will and appetite, and the less of it there is within, the more there must be without. It is ordained in the eternal constitution of things that men of intemperate minds cannot be free. Their passions forge their fetters.

"Ancient Greece fell because it represented liberty without authority, beauty without morality and intellectuality without God."

Ramsay wrote, "The Greeks always and everywhere in the world tended to exaggerate the rights of the individual . . . wherever the Greek element is strong, the law is weak and the government is more guided by caprice than by principle. That has been the fact throughout all history; the Greeks are more prosperous under almost any other government than they are under their own. This Greek spirit was diametrically opposed to the Roman law-making and law-abiding spirit."[1]

The Apostle Paul, who preached in Greece under Roman rule, put it like this: "You are the *slaves* of the power you have chosen to obey. All men have a choice of two masters: sin leading to death or obedience to God, bringing a life of right. Thank God you, who were once enslaved to sin, have followed from the heart the challenge given you. Having been delivered from the mastery of sin, you have now willingly become the slaves of Christ and His righteousness. . . . Now being free from sin and being enslaved to God, your lives have begun to show holiness and you are on the path of life that never ends" (Rom. 6:16–22, author's paraphrase).

In his excellent study *The Principle of Authority*, Peter Taylor Forsythe says that the question of our authority is a "religious question first and last. We have no absolute authority over us except in our faith; and without it, all relative authority becomes more and more relative and less and less authoritative."

What do we usually mean by authority? It is *another's certainty taken as the sufficient and final reason for some certainty of ours in thought or action.*

Authority has no meaning at all unless it is external; no moral individual can be an authority to himself. Nor can humanity collectively be its own authority without self-idolatry. If we are to retain authority, it must be as something which does not *depend* but *descend* on us, either to lead or to lift. Dorothy Sayers put it this way: "There is a universal moral law as distinct from a moral code which consists of certain statements of fact about the nature of man, and by behaving in conformity with which man enjoys his true freedom. (It may be described briefly as a force working in history that tends to keep human beings human.) . . . This is what the Christian Church calls 'the natural law.' The more closely the moral code agrees with the natural law, the more it makes for freedom in human

---

[1]Sir William Mitchell Ramsay, *The Cities of St. Paul*, pp. 198–199.

behavior; the more widely it departs from the natural law, the more it tends to enslave mankind and produce the catastrophes called 'judgments of God.' "[2]

The All, the Most, and the Few:

Peter Forsythe notes that most people take authority from the all, most, or *few*:

"The sphere of authority is not in religion alone. In all the affairs of life it has its action. Most people live under what they hold to as the authority of *all*. They do, or seek to do, what everybody else does. They are most secure in those things which are the universal fashion in the primal unities, customs or instincts of society, in immemorial convention.

"Some again are satisfied with the authority of *most*. They live as the politicians do—by majorities. They court and follow the multitude. Their ideal is the popular. Their standard is the majority. What they dread most is . . . to make themselves singular or unpleasant to their side or party. They habitually obey its demands (and they have the flair for them) but they make none. They are never laden prophets to rebuke their own, they are only racy tribunes to champion them.

"Others again follow the authority of the *few*. It may be a minority of experts, as in the case of science. Very many people accept without further question what their favorite paper tells them is the opinion of the scientific leaders, even about things where a mere scientific training does more to disqualify than equip. And here we are growing 'warm' as the children say. We seek more worthy shelter under another form of minority—that for instance of the Church as God's elect and militant minority on Earth, or that of the apostles, fathers and bishops, as men specially commissioned and fitted for a special truth or task. As we have those whose authoritative minority is an 'elite' of culture, so we have those for whom it is an elect of grace.

"Of course, empirically, educationally, we do depend on external authority in the first part of our discipline. As children and youths (of whatever age), we must. It is a necessary stage of growth. It is a mark of our minority. We depend on statements about religion made by other people who are in some historic position of religious authority over us—parents, teachers, churches or apostles. That is to say, our most direct contact at this stage is not with the object of religion but with people produced by that object. The authority for our faith is not yet the object of that faith; it is certain people who themselves have come to own, serve and worship that object. It follows that when we come by these stages to religious maturity our only authority must be faith's object itself, in some direct self-revelation of it. Our authority is what takes the initiative with our faith. Only so is the authority really religious, only as creative. Our only final religious authority is the creative object of our religion to whom we owe ourselves.

[2]Dorothy Sayers, *The Mind of the Maker* (Westport, Conn.: Greenwood Press, 1941), p. 9.

"Narrowing the issue and growing 'warmer' still, most Christian people would take Christ's certainty as a perfectly sufficient ground for any certainty of theirs. His word and teaching is for them the supreme authority in the world. And . . . Christ is indeed the supreme authority; but it is Christ in His gospel more even than in His precept; Christ as present, powerful and absolute Redeemer rather than as past and precious Teacher; Christ as breaking our moral ban by His new creation of eternal life, giving us to our forfeit selves by restoring us from perdition to God's communion and leaving us with no rights but those so given to rebuild faith, creed and action from a new unitary center and a monopolist throne. It is Christ as King in His cross."[3]

Why Does God Have the Right to Rule?

So far, so good; we are reduced ultimately then to God's authority. But we ask an even more basic question: *why* is God's authority legitimate? We say, "Lex Rex"—God's Law is King. We Christians must not acknowledge any other authority as absolute. And why? Because no king, no prophet or priest can make up law. No ruler has the power to invent right or wrong; at best he may qualify to apply, explain, and enforce it. Who then has true authority for action on the scale of all life? Who can say what must be done privately and publicly for now, for the future, for "history as one colossal act"?

The Christian says, "God. Look to Him, for the ultimate example of genuine love, the antithesis of all selfishness and wrong. Look to His lordship and His law; only Christ can free you from selfishness." And yet the world is filled with people who imagine that God is selfish. Satan has always accused Him as such to man (Gen. 3:1–5). You can see they have a point if we are secretly saying that Rex Lex isn't right—unless the *Rex* is God. They may think like one young man who complained, "If God wants us to be unselfish, why does He command us to put Him first? Isn't *that* selfish?"

Did God Make Up Morality?

Now, is God's law arbitrary? Does He just make up right and wrong at His own whim, out of His own will? We say "Lex Rex"—the *law* is king, not "Rex Lex"—the *king* is law, and it seems fair and right that all earthly authority should bow to such law. Are we saying that the law is king *until* it comes to God, then Rex Lex—the King is law—takes effect? Is all law, even divine law, ultimately an invention? Shouldn't law, especially ultimate Law, be fixed, unalterable, unchangeable by anyone?

Again, Dorothy Sayers declares, "Christianity has compelled the mind of man not because it is the most cheering view of man's existence, but because it is truest to the facts. . . . A creed put forward by authority

---

[3]Peter Taylor Forsythe, *The Principle of Authority* (London: Hodder and Stoughton, 1912), pp. 12–15, 21–24, 82–84, 354–56.

deserves respect in the measure that we respect the authority's claim to be a judge of truth. If the creed and authority alike are conceived as being arbitrary, capricious and irrational, we shall continue in a state of terror and bewilderment since we shall never know from one minute to the next what we are supposed to be doing or why or what we have to expect. But a creed that can be shown to have its basis in fact inclines us to trust the judgment of the authority; if this is the case, and it turns out to be correct, we may be disposed to think that it is on the whole correct about everything. The necessary condition for assessing the value of creeds is that we should fully understand that they claim to be not idealistic fancies, not arbitrary codes, not abstractions irrelevant to human life and thought but *statements of fact about the universe as we know it.*"[4]

If God Invented Good, Can He Change It?

This leads to still another set of questions: How can God honestly call himself "good" if He just *makes up* what "good" is? By what standard can we, or anyone for that matter, measure His conduct, if everything He does is by definition right *because He does it?* Could He not, by this definition, one day do all that Satan and sinners do, and still be (by definition) "right" and "holy"? Could He just as easily change the nature of vice and virtue and in the future call right, wrong, and wrong, right? And worse—wouldn't He have every *right* to do so?

God Is Not Selfish at All

When we read the Bible carefully we find a wonderful truth: *God is not selfish* nor has He ever been. He is, of course, faithful and changeless. We need never worry that God will one day have an ultimate character change, or that He might become bad. The Bible is clear that He is not only good, but absolutely and unchangeably loving, just and good. In Scripture He reveals to us His care and concern for as well as His goodness to people who were not only running away from Him, but who were actually His enemies.

But in the truth of that unchangeable faithfulness, there are verses like this: "But if we walk in the light, *as he is in the light*, we have fellowship one with another . . ." (1 John 1:7a). We know roughly what it means to "walk in the light"—to act rightly out of faith and love, to respond to His grace and beauty and keep His laws. But what can it mean for God to walk in the light?

In this Bible description of God's character we can see an amazing thing: *God himself has a law to keep*; God himself has a standard to which He conforms His life. All of the Bible descriptions of His moral nature imply some standard of value to which He has always and will always conform. He has given us nothing He is not first willing to do himself; when He commands us to be holy, it is because *He himself* is holy (Lev. 20:7).

---

[4]Sayers, op. cit. pp. 16–17.

There Is No Law Behind God

What law could possibly apply to the uncreated God who is before all things, and by whom all things hold together? There cannot be a "God" behind God, a law greater than God, or a standard other than God. Accepting this would be to deny the Bible. But there is a Law nevertheless, a law that is *distinct* from God's character, as *eternal* as He is and yet not separate from Him! It is the basis of all right, the standard of value to which all beings in the universe must conform.

Even the Judge of the universe must himself conform to that Law. It is that which gives stability to His decisions, form to His judgment and pronouncements, and absolute virtue to His actions. This standard is the greatest value in the universe and beyond it. It has all the qualities that we hold so dear in human treasure—beauty, light, permanence, uniqueness, rarity, power. It is eternal, changeless—indeed it is the most fundamental reality of all. It is the ultimate *lex*, nothing less than *God's own uncreated being*. It is distinct, though not separate, from His character and personality, the one thing God himself did not make up, create, or have any say over having. And God's *being* is the most valuable thing in the universe.

As we shall see in later discussion, we were made to choose the valuable. God made us like that, because *He* is like that, and we are made in His image. He has always done what we must always do; respond to that which is the most lovely, the most important, the most worthwhile; this is the law of love. God himself unselfishly chooses the highest good of His own being; not just because it is His, but because it is the most valuable. He must. He is obligated to do so. To choose anything less would not only be unwise but wrong. And so must we. We must do what He has always done; put Him first, honor with our lives the revealed ultimate loveliness in the universe, and give Him the glory for what He is.

When God commands, "Thou shalt love (unselfishly choose the highest good of) the Lord thy God . . . and thy neighbor as thyself" (Luke 10:25–28; Matt. 22:34–40; Mark 12:28–34; John 14:21), He is saying simply this: "I am valuable for My own sake. You do what I must always do; put first what belongs first." He deserves first place.

The Final Right to Rule

The one who has the right to rule the affairs of men is the one best qualified to rule. And who is better qualified than God? He made us. He has the wisdom, the understanding, and the love. He has the power to direct and control, the justice to be perfectly fair, and the mercy to be kind. He has the first right to be loved, the only right to be worshiped, and the right to be obeyed. His is the right to be King. Men have marched for their own rights, but who is marching for the rights of God?

God is the most lovely being in the universe. God's being is the source of all life, the power that upholds all of creation. Since everyone's happiness depends on it, God has a responsibility to honor it. God *must* choose His own highest good as the only wisest possible act. He is obliged to rule himself and His creation by informing them of this for their highest good.

Just as we are responsible to love and take care of our own beings, and are able to love and care for our neighbors because we do this, God himself loves and takes care of His own being, and is responsible for His own highest good.

Why should we love God? Because He is the Altogether Lovely. Why should all men and women choose to put God first? Because He is the most valuable person in the universe.

He is not selfish; He has eternally and unvaryingly chosen what He sees and knows, in infinite wisdom, to be the most valuable object in the universe: the incomparable value of His own created being, the foundation of all reality. He is not just important because He *says* so; He actually *is* the most important one there is! When the Bible calls Him "good," it means something. God is good because He has always done what is best and unalterably always will. His law is founded in His being, not His will; it is, therefore, not arbitrary or changeable. His being is distinct from His will, and its infinite value perpetually obligates His will; therefore God himself has a law to keep. Love is not just something He invented. It is the way of supreme intelligence, the way God chooses to live and the way He asks all to live likewise. (See Appendix B for further discussion of God's right to rule.)

An Important Message for Mankind

What is needed for men to give up their sins? *A revelation of the loveliness of the biblical God.* What will induce a man to forsake all and trust Him? A glimpse of His glory. As the song says:

> Turn your eyes upon Jesus
> Look full in His wonderful face
> And the things of earth will grow strangely dim
> In the light of His glory and grace.[5]

We must learn that the motive for change cannot be bribe or threat, but *trust* and *love*; and trust and love can only come from an intelligent devotion to the nature and character of the Bible God. What sinful mankind needs is a vision of Christ; what the Church needs is a God-centered, God-honoring message. The chief content of our preaching must begin, center, and end with *God himself*. It is the "goodness of" God that leads men to repentance (Rom. 2:4). It is not just the "Gospel" we preach, but the Gospel of the kingdom of God that all men must hear before His return. Is this, today, what we are really proclaiming to mankind? (Ex. 33:18–19; 2 Chron. 6:41; Ps. 27:13; 31:19; 33:5; 65:11; 145:7; Jer. 31:12; Luke 2:14.)

---

[5]Helen H. Lemmel.

The Universal Moral Law

This love-law, is eternal; it predates, includes, and supersedes all other laws ever given to man. It was the Law in the Garden of Eden, the law Abraham knew, the law behind the law given to Moses, the law on which hangs "all the law and the prophets." This is the one fundamental without which we cannot enter the kingdom. It applies to all beings in earth and heaven and is unlimited in its scope and eternal in its application. It can never be abrogated, improved on, or reduced. It is the touchstone by which we can measure all religious experience, all claims of spirituality. Do we love God first? Do we exalt Him and His infinite value first in all our daily acts and thoughts? Is He the star of the show? If not, all our claims of righteousness and all our religious service are but dust and ashes. This is the mark that designates the genuine follower of Jesus: he practically puts Christ first. The Lord Jesus means more to him than anything else in the universe. He loves those he can touch the way he cares for his own life. For this, and only this, marks a Christian.

Peter Taylor Forsythe notes: "The question is not, therefore, 'How has God appeared,' but 'What has God done?' God did not come to be seen but obeyed. The Christian answer is in the cross of Christ. The nerve of Christianity is expressed in such a great and sweeping word as 'ye are not your own; ye are brought with a price.' It means Christ's absolute property in us by a new creation. The sinlessness of Jesus, His ideal perfection is not enough. It really means the active holiness of Jesus, not merely as keeping himself unspotted from the world, cherishing a pure experience or going about doing good, but gathered into a universal, victorious and creative head in the cross. The whole range of right and demand opened by the holiness of God and its judgment must be surveyed. It is there that the crucial issue of the cross lies. It is in this nature and action of the cross that the solution lies for the question of authority for Christianity, for history, for ever. . . .

"Faith is in its nature an obedience; it is not primarily a sympathy. It is sympathetic obedience, truly, but obedience always. Eternal life is absolute obedience, an attitude to one who has a right over us high above all His response to us, one to be trusted and obeyed even amid any dereliction by Him and refusal of His response. He is our God, not because He loved and pitied but because in His love and pity He redeemed us. God is for us and our release only that we may be for Him and His service. He is for us to help, save and bless, only that we may be for Him, to worship Him in the communion of the Spirit and serve Him in the majesty of His purpose forever. *First we glorify Him, then we enjoy Him forever.*

"The whole nature of authority is changed as soon as it ceases to be statutory and becomes thus personal and religious. It is no longer then what it is to most people—a limit—it becomes a *source of power.* It is not, in the first instance regulative and depressive; it is expansive, it is creative. . . . It makes the soul to be more than in its egotism it could ever be. . . . By the true obedience we *are* more. It is the great culture, the great enrichment. Our great authority is what gives us most power to go forward; it is not what ties us up most to a formal past. It is of grace and not of law. It cannot be a doctrine, nor a book, nor an institution; it must, for a person, be a Person."[6]

Collective Witness of Authority

Historically, religious people have looked to three main sources for authority: (1) the direct inner witness of the *Holy Spirit* to the living Christ, making the claims of the Lord Jesus real to the individual believer; (2) the objective, propositional revelation of the *Holy Scriptures* as inspired, inerrant, and comprehensive for all matters of faith and life; and (3) the combined testimony of the *Church* down through the centuries bearing common witness to the reality and power of the Gospel of the grace of God.

Hence we have the *Mystic* stream of the Church focusing on the inner experience and witness; the *Reformed* and *Conservative* stream focusing on the Scriptures as the fundamental source of truth, faith, and authority; and the *Catholic* historical stream honoring the collective cross-section of testimony of true believers through time. So what is right? What can preserve us from fantasy and fanaticism, legalism and bibliolatry, formalism and entrenched traditional error?

E. Stanley Jones observed: "Where then do we find the place of authority? In which one of these three—the Infallible Church, the Infallible Bible, the Infallible Christian experience—does it lie? It lies in *all three*. Each contributes. That place of final certainty and authority is at the junction where the Jesus of history becomes the Christ of experience and where the resultant individual experience is corroborated and corrected by the collective experience. The place of authority then is Christ revealed in the past, experienced in the present and corroborated by collective Christian experience. . . . The Historical speaks and says, 'Come unto Me and I will give you rest.' The Experimental cries, 'I've tried it and experienced it—it's true,' and the Collective witnesses say, 'Through all times and climes we have verified it—it is so.' There is no higher certainty possible."[7]

When Famous Christians Sin

Every so often we hear a sad story of some well-known Christian who gets into some kind of financial, moral, or legal trouble and winds up publicly embarrassing the Church and the cause of Christ. What makes it especially sad is that they may have been in a place of power or authority, and their failure seems all the more shocking. Yet we must remember that the basis of all Christian authority is only borrowed, that no man or woman has that authority in themselves, and that we retain the right to that au-

---

[6]Forsythe, op. cit.
[7]E. Stanley Jones, *Christ at the Round Table* (Philadelphia: Century Bookbindery, 1981).

thority only as we properly represent Christ and His Word and His Church. It is in this derived authority that Christian authority is best expressed.

As Forsythe again comments: "The best documents are human sacraments. Holy men are the best argument of the Gospel, short of the Gospel itself, short, i.e., of Christ's real presence with us in the Holy Ghost as our active Savior. And when men have done their proper work, when they have introduced us personally to God and left us together, it is not fatal if we find flaws in their logic, character or faith."[8]

Isn't Christian Experience Only Psychological?

Sometimes in an evangelistic crusade, commitments to Christ are called "emotionalism" or "mass hypnotism." The public failure of a noted Christian leader is claimed to mean the whole Christian experience is only psychological. The proper reply might be, "Your statement is only psychological!"

Psychology claims to deal with the human personality. Such a man-made discipline must supply its own validity qualifications. At best, psychology only claims to be a science; and science, says Forsythe, "cannot go beyond method. It has no machinery with which to reach or test reality, and therefore it has no jurisdiction in the ultimates of religion. When it is a question of the reality of an object and its value, we are treating it in another dimension from that of science; for science but coordinates our impressions and cannot gauge their ultimate weight or worth. *The Judge of all the earth is not an object of knowledge, but of obedience and worship. He is to be met neither with an intuition nor an assent but with a decision, a resolve....*"[9]

A. W. Tozer said it in a similar vein: "Hearts that are fit to break with love for the Godhead are those who have been in the presence and have looked with open eye upon the majesty of deity. Men of the breaking hearts had a quality about them not known to or understood by common men. They habitually spoke with spiritual authority. They had been in the presence of God and they reported what they saw there. They were prophets, not scribes, for the scribe tells us what he has read and the prophet tells us what he has seen."[10]

---

[8]Forsythe, op. cit. p. 356.
[9]Ibid. p. 356
[10]A.W. Tozer, *The Pursuit of God* (Camp Hill, Penn.: Christian Publications Inc., 1982), pp. 42–43

Historical Discussion

"A comprehended God is no God at all."

Gerhard Tersteegen

Infinity Is Inexpressible

St. Maximus the Confessor

"When the mind reflects on the absolute infinity of God, on this unfathomable and greatly desirable deep, it is first filled with wonder; and then it is struck with amazement how God has brought into being from nothing all that is. But as there is no end to His greatness, so too is His wisdom unsearchable (Ps. 144:3). For how will he not be filled with wonder, who contemplates this unapproachable and awe-inspiring cause of goodness?"[1]

Thomas Brooks

"We are as well able to comprehend the sea in a cockle-shell as we are able to comprehend God. God is above all name, all notion and all comprehension. . . . you shall as soon tell the stars of heaven, number the sand of the sea, stop the sun in its course, raise the dead and make a world as be able to comprehend the infiniteness of God's essence: 'His greatness is unsearchable' (Ps. 145:3). The most perfect knowledge we can have of God is that we cannot perfectly know Him because we do know Him to be infinitely and incomprehensibly perfect: 'Oh the depth both of the wisdom and knowledge of God! How unsearchable are His judgments and His ways past finding out' (Rom. 11:33). . . . There is infinitely more in God than the tongues of men or angels can express."[2]

William Pope

"It is not that He fills immensity with His presence; He is the only immensity, all things created being measurable and limited. The universe cannot contain Him; not because His essence stretches beyond the confines of created things, but because His eternal Spirit transcends and is inconsistent with all notions of space. Space is born out of His immensity, as time out of His eternity; but none can declare the generation of either. . . . 'In Him we live and move and have our being' (Acts 17:28); as our time is enfolded by the divine eternity, so our place is in the bosom of the divine immensity."[3]

---

[1]St. Maximus the Confessor, *Writings From the Heart: The Philokalia.*
[2]Thomas Brooks, "An Ark for All God's Noahs," *The Complete Works of Thomas Brooks*, Alexander Groshart, ed. (AMS Press, 1866), pp. 28–29.
[3]William Pope, *Compendium of Christian Theology* (1881), vol. 1, pp. 295–296.

Anselm of Canterbury

"God is that, the greater than which cannot be conceived."[4]

Augustine

"What art Thou then, my God?. . . Most highest, most good, most potent, most omnipotent; most merciful, yet most just; most hidden, yet most present; most beautiful, yet most strong; stable, yet incomprehensible; unchangeable, yet all-changing; never new, never old . . . ever working, ever at rest; still gathering, yet nothing lacking; supporting, filling and over-spreading; creating, nourishing and maturing; seeking, yet having all things. Thou lovest without passion; art jealous without anxiety; repentest, yet grievest not; art angry, yet serene; changest Thy works, Thy purpose unchanged; receivest again what Thou findest, yet didst never lose; never in need, yet rejoicing in gains. . . . And what have I now said, my God, my life, my holy joy? Or what saith any man when he speaks of Thee?"[5]

John Fletcher

"The Royal Academy of Paris offered a prize to the man who should write the best copy of verses upon the divine nature. Many wrote largely on the awful subject; but Professor Crousaz sent only two lines: 'Cease to expect from man a proper description of the Supreme Being; None can speak properly of Him but himself.' And the judicious Academicians agreed to crown this short performance, because it gave the most exalted idea of Him, whose dazzling glory calls for our silent adoration and forbids the curious disquisitions of our philosophical pride. . . . As we cannot grasp the Universe with our hands, so we cannot comprehend the Maker of the Universe with our thoughts."[6]

Infinity Involves No Contradiction

Bertrand Brasnett

"It is probably true to say that the more a man knows, the fewer things seem possible. To the quite small child, fairy tales present no scientific difficulty, for the laws of nature can be set aside at will. . . . Secondly (in the abstract concept of number) to the human mind, infinity is theoretically possible; no human mind can ever answer 'two squared to infinity' but a human mind can set the problem; are we to suppose that the problem is unanswerable or are we to say God alone knows the answer? . . . If to attempt to sum an infinite series is a contradiction in terms, God is aware of the contradiction and cannot be pictured as embarking on an

[4]Anselm, *Proslogium: Faith Seeking Understanding*.
[5]St. Augustine, "Confessions," *Great Books of the Western World*, Robert M. Hutchins and Mortimer Adler, eds. (Chicago: Encyclopaedia Britannica, 1952), Vol. I, Chap. IV, p. 2.
[6]John Fletcher, *The Works of John Fletcher* (Schmul Reprints, 1974), vol. 2, pp. 402–403.

attempt which from the nature of the case must be abortive. . . . Number is after all an abstraction. . . . Something similar may be said in relation to space and time. . . . Space and time may be genuinely infinite to us and yet to the wider vision of God, finite.

"That which is finite does not demand an infinite creator; it is possible for the finite to be created by the infinite, but the mere existence of the finite does not by itself establish the existence of the infinite. An effect postulates a cause adequate to the effect, but a limited effect does not by itself establish an unlimited cause."[7]

The Infinite Must Communicate With the Finite

Thomas F. Torrance

"Our relations with God are only possible because there are things about God which we understand. We can have no conscious relations with any person or thing that is to us utterly and absolutely unintelligible. But on the other hand, in relationships with friends it is necessary that there should be in them and us a certain depth of personality. There is no satisfaction in friendship with a shallow person because he is so quickly understood. There is no richness of character, no hidden depths of personality which we can delightedly explore and never wholly exhaust. Similarly with God; it is an essential demand of the religious conscious-ness that God should be profound beyond our understanding, and deep beyond the plummet line of our human spirits. It is essential that we understand much about God, for otherwise we would never turn to Him; it is equally essential that there should be much about God that we do not and cannot understand, for otherwise He would be inadequate to our religious needs. The charm of a wide prospect does not consist in the ability to see all things both far and near with equal clarity; its joy is the opportunity it affords of clearness of vision, close at hand coupled with a wide vista fading by imperceptible gradations into the far horizon. So it is when man stands, or kneels to look upon God."[8]

Finite Truth About the Infinite

Thomas F. Torrance

"God is present to us and gives himself to our knowing only in such a way that He remains the Lord who has ascendancy over us, who distin-guishes himself from us and makes himself known in His divine otherness even when He draws us into communion with himself. He is present to us in such a way that He never resigns knowledge of himself to our mastery. . . . Hence we can never give an account of our knowledge of God in such a way as to reduce His holiness, His transcendence, His

---

[7]Bertrand Brasnett, *The Infinity of God* (London: Longmans, Green, and Co., 1933), p. 43.
[8]Thomas F. Torrance, *Theological Science* (New York: Oxford University Press, 1969), pp. 73–74.

unapproachable majesty to a vanishing point, but only in such a way that we are thrown ultimately upon His mercy, upon His transcendent freedom to lower himself to us and to lift us up to Him beyond anything we can think or conceive out of ourselves. To know God in His holiness means our human subjectivity is opened out and up toward that which infinitely transcends it."[9]

Bertrand Brasnett

"The characteristic attitude of the religious man in the presence of deity is an attitude of worship and it is psychologically impossible to worship that which is completely understood. The divine must have something about it of indefinable quality to hold the allegiance of men for as the French so neatly put it 'a God defined is a finite god'. . . . Religion must insist we do not know the whole of God; it must at the same time insist that what we do know of God is true. . . . God is a unity, utterly devoid of inconsistency or lack of stability, and therefore what is known of deity is an adequate guide to that which is hidden. Yet logic after all is powerless before experience and we are unable to preclude the possibility of fresh surprises emerging from the unknown realms of deity for man's confounding. In one sense indeed it has always been part of the Christian tradition to insist on the possibility of fresh revelation and the outpouring of new treasures by a God the riches of whose being are inexhaustible . . . It is the privilege of the pure in heart to see God; it is the penalty of the less pure that they are granted a less full vision . . . Both for weal and woe, both as Savior and as Judge, we do not yet know the full potentialities of God. . . . We may not know the whole of God, but such of God as we do not know will not refute or overthrow such knowledge of Him we already have."[10]

Francis Schaeffer

"When God reveals His attributes to man they are true not only to man but to God. God is not just telling a story. God is really telling us what is true to himself. What He tells us is not exhaustive, because we are finite, and we know nothing in an exhaustive way. We cannot even explain to each other exhaustively because we are finite. But He tells us truly, even the great truth about himself. He is not just playing games with us."[11]

Authority Is Not Arbitrary

Stephen Clark

"Modern man cannot easily understand the scriptural portrayal of the husband's role in the family, unless they understand the difference between the biblical and contemporary view of authority. Contemporary peo-

---

[9]Ibid. p. 53.

[10]Brasnett, op. cit. pp. 73–74.

[11]Francis Schaeffer, *He Is There and He Is Not Silent* (London: Hodder and Stoughton, 1972), p. 80.

ple often react against the ideas of rule, government and exercise of authority. . . . they react against the exercise of directive authority in the lives of others because they see the direction mainly as the imposition of one person's will and way on others. Indeed, since people in modern society often do not have any objective standard of right and wrong or good and bad, they cannot imagine directive authority being anything but arbitrary. . . .

"The scriptural writers were familiar with the exercise of arbitrary authority in which one person imposed his decisions and preferences on another. However, they normally did not consider this exercise of authority inevitable. They could have a real alternative because they believed in an objective right and wrong and an objective good and bad—a standard of right living revealed by the Lord. In their view the Lord revealed a pattern of human life that reflects His own character. Therefore, a ruler or a head can know what is right and good. He can know if the life of his household, community or kingdom is healthy because he possesses a standard that both he and his subordinates acknowledge as objective. In fact . . . a ruler must first submit to the Lord's standard and become a righteous man in order to become a just ruler over others (Deut. 17:18–20). His rule then becomes an extension of the Lord's rule."[12]

George MacDonald

"Oh the folly of any mind that would explain God before obeying Him! That would map out the character of God instead of crying 'Lord what would you have me to do?' "[13]

Robert Herbert Story, D.D.

"It is still as in the days of Him who spake as never man spake. Those who are brought into contact with new thought, new teaching, with what professes at least to be clearer light and wider truth than men before possessed, rather than look at the thing itself will demand—'Whence comes it? What authority has it? Who gave it its authority?' They will not search into its character to see whether that does or does not bear the mark of the Spirit of Christ, but merely seek to know whether any opinion has been pronounced in its favor—what system it agrees with, what usage is on its side. But that is not the point to settle. Anyone who believes in Christ's work as a living work, who believes that He still teaches His people and leads them by His Spirit into clearer and clearer light is ready from the very fact of his belief to receive illumination whencesoever it may come; and is ready also . . . to apply to it the test; not 'What authority has it?' but 'What character has it?' not 'What external claim has it to be received with respect?' but 'What inner claim speaking from it tells me that it is of Christ, convinces me that it comes from Him?' The external authority is but the stamp upon the coin. The stamp may be a forgery.

[12]Stephen B. Clark, *Man And Woman in Christ* (Ann Arbor, Mich.: Servant Publications, 1980), pp. 55–56.
[13]George MacDonald, *Anthology*, C.S. Lewis, ed. (New York: Macmillan, 1986), p. 86.

The internal evidence is the fine gold of which the true coin is made, and which, stamped or unstamped, is of the same intrinsic and unalterable value."

Authority of Scripture

James Hervey

"God, in tender indulgence to our different dispositions, has strewed the Bible with flowers, dignified it with wonders, and enriched it with delights."

Rev. T. M. Eddy, D.D.

"Eusebius said it was alike rashness and presumption to venture to prove that the divine Scriptures have erred. . . . Cranmer speaks of the Scripture as 'the sure rock of God's infallible written Word.' Bullinger terms it 'the very true Word of God, absolutely perfect'; Jewell, 'the very sure and infallible rule'; Archbishop Parker, 'the fountains of divine knowledge'; Hooker, 'heavenly truth uttered by immediate divine inspiration'; Bishop Hall, 'a perfect Word, so exquisite a rule of knowledge and obedience, as cannot admit of any defect or supplement.' Bishop Jeremy Taylor says, 'It is the immediate and sole ministry of entire salvation and the whole depository of the divine will.' Chillingworth says, 'The Scriptures being all true, I am secured by believing nothing else, that I should believe no falsehood' And Stillingfleet speaks of 'the infallible records of the Word of God.'

"In short, from the days of Christ and His apostles down to the present day, a belief in the infallible authority of the Bible has been the belief of the Church of Christ. I know there are difficulties . . . but each year research diminishes these, and I am persuaded that further research will altogether remove them. The Bible not only contains, but *is* the Word of God. It is a living Book, instinct with a living Spirit, and in it we hold converse with the living God. When we study it prayerfully, a sense of His presence, a consciousness of His glory pervades our souls, our love to Him is inflamed, we enter into the very heart of God."

Augustine

"The Scripture so speaks that with the height of it, it laughs proud and lofty-spirited men to scorn; with the depth of it, it terrifies those who with attention look into it; with the truth of it, it feeds men of the greatest knowledge and understanding; and with the sweetness of it, it nourishes babes and sucklings."

William Chillingworth

"I profess plainly that I cannot find any rest for the sole of my foot but this rock only. In a word, there is no sufficient certainty but of Scripture only for any considering man to build on. This therefore, and this only I have reason to believe; this I will profess; according to this will I live; and for this, if there be occasion I will not only willingly but very gladly lose my life.

"Propose me anything out of this Book and enquire whether I believe it or no, and seem it ever so incomprehensible to human reason, I will subscribe to it with hand and heart, as knowing no demonstration can be stronger than this—God hath said so, therefore it is true.

"In other things I will take no man's liberty of judgment from him, neither shall any man take mine from me. I will think no man the worse man nor the worse Christian, I will love no man the less for differing in opinion from me; and what measure I mete to others I expect from them again. I am fully assured that GOD does not, and therefore man ought not to require any more of any man than this—to believe the Scripture to be God's Word, and find the true sense of it, and live accordingly."

Authority and Paradox

E. Stanley Jones

"It is inevitable that we have the radical and conservative in religion also. It would be a tragedy if we did not have them both. If we were all radicals, we would blow up! If we were all conservatives, we would dry up! But between the pull of the two we make very definite progress in a middle direction.

"Everywhere we find both the conservative and radical appealing to Jesus as approving their standpoint. As I hear Him challenging almost every single religious conception and institution of that day . . . I am convinced He is a radical. But when I see Him gather up every truth out of the past, conserving it and completing it and saying 'I came not to destroy but to fulfill' I know He is a conservative. He is both. He says 'The Kingdom of Heaven is like unto a man . . . that brings forth out of his treasures things new and old.' The wise scribe of the Kingdom is to be both radical and conservative—he brings forth 'things new and old.' But note the order; the new is first. At Pentecost the young men seeing visions came before the old men dreaming dreams. The Gospel does lean toward the radical for it involves change. It is the 'ought-to-be' standing over against the 'is.' "[14]

A. W. Tozer

"Truth is like a bird; it cannot fly on one wing. . . . I believe it was G. Campbell Morgan who said that the whole truth does not lie in 'It is written' but in 'It is written' and 'Again it is written.' The second text must be placed over against the first to balance it and give it symmetry just as the right wing must work with the left to balance the bird and enable it to fly. . . . For it is not denial only that makes a truth void; failure to emphasize it will in the long run be equally damaging."[15]

---

[14]E. Stanley Jones, *The Christ of Every Road* (Nashville, Tenn.: Abingdon, 1930), pp. 126, 128–129.

[15]A.W. Tozer, "Truth Has Two Wings," *That Incredible Christian* (Camp Hill, Penn.: Christian Publications, Inc., 1964).

Rev. C. J. Vaughan

"Theology, gendered of controversy, is cautious and balancing; revelation, flashing from heaven, is bold and free. Human hands have soiled, feet have trampled, the bright, the precious deposit of the faith once delivered. Heresy has corrupted, schism has torn the simplicity which is in Christ. Then the Church must mend and patch, must restore and reconcile, must define and systematize; and the result is theology—a thing of creeds and formulas, of accuracies and harmonies, necessitated by the existence of error and accepted as a safeguard by all but the presumptuous.

"Still this theology was not the first utterance, but the second; not the voice, but the letter; not the lively, living, life-giving Word, but the drier, duller, less sparkling form, in which as a protecting casket the original jewel of revelation is packed and folded. The very Word itself, conscious of truth, majestic in its divinity, speaks here, speaks there, as God prompts it, as man needs it. It stays not to guard against right-hand mistake or left-hand abuse; it flings forth its broad, free saying and waits not to fence itself against each possible misconstruction. Sometimes, to the careless ear it seems ambiguous or double-tongued—seems even to contradict itself—seems even to say here what it denies there, or to unsay in this place what it emphasized in that.

"The explanation of all this is that truth has ever at least *two aspects*. To see but one of these is error; to allow for both is a condition of sound doctrine. Yet to state both sides in one breath is seldom possible; to stay to reconcile is to miss the force of both; let each have its rush, its swing, its stroke—the 'via media,' theologically safe, is practically feeble. God speaks the free word on this side and the free word on that; the result is conviction, is wisdom, is strength."[16]

Clement of Rome

"Brothers, the God of the universe has need of nothing."

---

[16]Rev. C.J. Vaughan, "Suggestive Thoughts," *Half-Hours in the Temple Church*, pp. 27–28.

CHAPTER THREE

Corollary Two:
God Is Spiritual Not Material

Scriptures

"Thou shalt not make unto thee any graven image, or any likeness of any thing that is in heaven above, or that is in the earth beneath, or that is in the water under the earth. Thou shalt not bow down thyself to them, nor serve them: for I the LORD thy God am a jealous God. . . ." (Ex. 20:4)

"And he [Moses] said, I beseech thee, shew me thy glory. And he said, I will make all my goodness pass before thee, and I will proclaim the name of the Lord before thee . . . thou canst not see my face: for there shall no man see me and live." (Ex. 33:18–20)

"But will God indeed dwell on the earth? behold, the heaven and heaven of heavens cannot contain thee; how much less this house that I have builded?" (1 Kings 8:27)

"Of old thou hast laid the foundation of the earth: and the heavens are the work of thy hands. They shall perish, but *thou shalt endure*: yea, all of them shall wax old like a garment; as a vesture shalt thou change them, and they shall be changed: but *thou art the same*, and thy years shall have no end." (Ps. 102:25–27)

"Wherefore should the heathen say, Where is now their God? But *our God is in the heavens*: he hath done whatsoever he hath pleased. Their idols are silver and gold, the work of men's hands. They have mouths, but they speak not: eyes have they, but they see not. . . . They that make them are like unto them; so is every one that trusteth in them." (Ps. 115:2–5, 8)

"Whither shall I go from thy spirit? or whither shall I flee from thy presence? If I ascend up into heaven, thou art there: if I make my bed in hell, behold, thou art there. If I take the wings of the morning, and dwell in the uttermost parts of the sea; even there shall thy hand lead me, and thy right hand shall hold me." (Ps. 139:7–10)

"Thus saith the LORD, The heaven is my throne, and the earth is my footstool: where is the house that ye build unto me? and where is the place of my rest? For all those things hath mine hand made . . ." (Isa. 66:1–2a)

"After this manner therefore pray ye: Our Father *which art in heaven*, Hallowed be thy name. Thy kingdom come, Thy will be done in earth, as it is in heaven." (Matt. 6:9–10)

"Teaching them to observe all things whatsoever I have commanded you: and, lo, *I am with you alway*, even unto the end of the world." (Matt. 28:20)

"But the hour cometh, and now is, when the true worshippers shall worship the Father in spirit and in truth: for the Father seeketh such to worship Him. God is a Spirit: and they that worship him must worship him in spirit and in truth." (John 4:23–24)

"God that made the world and all things therein, seeing that he is Lord of heaven and earth, dwelleth not in temples made with hands . . . that they should seek the Lord, if haply they might feel after him, and find him, *though he be not far from every one of us*: for in him we live, and move, and have our being." (Acts 17:24, 27–28a)

"And changed the glory of the uncorruptible God into an image made like to corruptible man, and to birds, and fourfooted beasts, and creeeping things . . . who changed the truth of God into a lie, and worshipped and served the creature more than the Creator." (Rom. 1:23, 25)

"One God and Father of all, who is above all, and *through all*, and *in you all*." (Eph. 4:6)

"And immediately I was in the spirit: and, behold, a throne was set in heaven, and one sat on the throne. And he that sat was to look upon like a jasper and a sardine stone: and there was a rainbow round about the throne, in sight like unto an emerald. . . . And out of the throne proceeded lightnings and thunderings and voices: and there were seven lamps of fire burning before the throne, which are the seven Spirits of God." (Rev. 4:2–3, 5)

"And I beheld, and I heard the voice of many angels round about the throne and the beasts and the elders: and the number of them was ten thousand times ten thousand, and thousands of thousands; saying with a loud voice, Worthy is the Lamb that was slain to receive power, and riches, and wisdom, and strength, and honour, and glory and blessing. And every creature which is in heaven, and on the earth, and under the earth, and such as are in the sea, and all that are in them, heard I saying, Blessing, and honour, and glory, and power, be unto him that sitteth upon the throne, and unto the Lamb for ever and ever." (Rev. 5:11–13)

"And I saw a great white throne, and him that sat on it, from whose face the earth and the heaven fled away; and there was found no place for them." (Rev. 20:11)

God's Spirit Can Be Manifested Audibly or in Visible Form

"Now Moses kept the flock . . . And the angel of the Lord appeared unto him in a *flame of fire* out of the midst of a bush: and he looked, and, behold, the bush burned with fire, and the bush was not consumed. . . . And when the Lord saw that he turned aside to see, God called unto him out of the midst of the bush, and said, Moses, Moses. And he said, Here am I." (Ex. 3:1–2, 4)

"And the child Samuel ministered unto the LORD before Eli. And the word of the LORD was precious in those days; there was no open vision. And it came to pass . . . ere the lamp of God went out in the temple of the LORD, where the ark of God was, and Samuel was laid down to sleep; that the LORD called Samuel: and he answered, Here am I. . . . And the LORD came, and stood, and called as at other times, Samuel, Samuel. Then Samuel answered, Speak; for thy servant heareth." (1 Sam. 3:1, 3–4, 10)

"And let it be, when thou hearest the sound of a going [marching] in the tops of the mulberry trees, that then thou shalt bestir thyself: for then shall the LORD go out before thee, to smite the host of the Philistines." (2 Sam. 5:24–25; cf. 1 Chron. 14:15)

"Belshazzar the king made a great feast . . . they drank wine, and praised the gods of gold, and of silver, of brass, of iron, of wood, and of stone. In the same hour came forth *fingers of a man's hand*, and wrote over against the candlestick upon the plaster of the wall of the king's palace: and the king saw the part of the hand that wrote. Then the king's countenance was changed, and his thoughts troubled him, so that the joints of his loins were loosed, and his knees smote one against another." (Dan. 5:1, 4–6)

"And John bare record, saying, I saw the Spirit descending from heaven like a dove, and it abode upon him." (John 1:32)

"Father, glorify thy name. Then came there a *voice* from heaven, saying, I have both glorified it, and will glorify it again. The people therefore, that stood by, and heard it, said that it thundered: others said, An angel spake to him." (John 12:28–29)

"And suddenly there came a sound from heaven as of a rushing mighty *wind*, and it filled all the house where they were sitting. And there appeared unto them cloven tongues like as of *fire*, and it sat upon each of them. And they were all filled with the Holy Ghost, and began to speak with other tongues as the Spirit gave them utterance." (Acts 2:2–4)

"And as he [Saul] journeyed, he came near Damascus: and suddenly there shined round about him a light from heaven: and he fell to the earth, and heard a voice saying unto him, Saul, Saul, why persecutest thou me? And he said, Who art thou, Lord? And the Lord said, I am Jesus whom thou persecutest: it is hard for thee to kick against the pricks." (Acts 9:3–5)

"And of the angels he saith, Who maketh his angels spirits, and his ministers a *flame of fire*." (Heb. 1:7)

This Manifestation Can Be Human in Form

"And the LORD appeared unto him in the plains of Mamre: and he sat in the tent door in the heat of the day; and he lifted up his eyes and looked, and, lo, *three men* stood by him: and when he saw them, he ran to meet them from the tent door, and bowed himself toward the ground. . . . And they said unto him, Where is Sarah thy wife? And he said, Behold, in the tent. And he said, I will certainly return unto thee according to the time of life; and, lo, Sarah thy wife shall have a son. And Sarah heard it in the tent door, which was behind him. And the LORD said unto Abraham, Wherefore did Sarah laugh, saying, Shall I of a surety bear a child, which am old? Is any thing too hard for the LORD? At the time apppointed I will return unto thee, according to the time of life, and Sarah shall have a son. And the men rose up from thence, and looked toward Sodom: and Abraham went with them to bring them on the way." (Gen. 18:1–2, 9–10, 13–14, 16)

In this preceding passage, one of the three men to visit Abraham was Jehovah. We know this because in chapter 19 only *two* men arrive at Sodom; the one who remains to talk with Abraham is the LORD (Gen. 18:17–20), who stood before Abraham in the form of a man (Gen. 18:22, 33; cf. 19:27).

"And Jacob was left alone; and there wrestled a man with him until the breaking of the day. . . . And he said unto him, What is thy name? And he said, Jacob. And he said, Thy name shall be called no more Jacob, but Israel: for as a prince hast thou power with God and with men, and hast prevailed. And Jacob asked him, and said, Tell me, I pray thee, thy name. And he said, Wherefore is it that thou dost ask after my name? And he blessed him there. And Jacob called the name of the place Peniel: for I have seen God face to face, and my life is preserved." (Gen. 32:24, 27–30)

"Then went up Moses, and Aaron, Nadab, and Abihu, and seventy of the elders of Israel: and *they saw* the God of Israel: and there was under his feet as it were a paved work of sapphire stone, and as it were the body of heaven in his clearness." (Ex. 24:9–10)

"And it came to pass, when Joshua was by Jericho, that he lifted up his eyes and looked, and, behold, there stood a man over against him with his sword drawn in his hand: and Joshua went unto him, and said unto him, Art thou for us, or for our adversaries? And he said, Nay; but as captain [prince] of the host of the LORD am I now come. And Joshua fell on his face to the earth, and did worship, and said unto him, What saith my Lord unto his servant? And the captain of the LORD'S host said unto Joshua, Loose thy shoe from off thy foot; for the place whereon thou standest is holy. And Joshua did so." (Josh. 5:13–15)

"In the year that king Uzziah died *I saw* also the Lord sitting upon a throne, high and lifted up, and his train filled the temple. . . . And one [seraphim] cried unto another, and said, Holy, holy, holy, is the LORD of hosts: the whole earth is full of his glory. And the posts of the door moved at the voice of him that cried, and the house was filled with smoke." (Isa. 6:1, 3–4)

The Angel of the LORD Is One Such Manifestation

"And the angel of the Lord found her by a fountain of water in the wilderness . . . and the angel of the LORD said unto her, Return to thy mistress, and submit thyself under her hands. And the angel of the LORD said unto her, *I* will multiply thy seed exceedingly, that it shall not be numbered for multitude. And she called the name of the LORD *that spake unto her*, Thou God seest me: for she said, Have I also here looked after him that seeth me?" (Gen. 16:7, 9–10, 13)

"And God heard the voice of the lad; and the angel of God called to Hagar out of heaven, and said unto her, What aileth thee, Hagar? fear not; for God hath heard the voice of the lad where he is. Arise, lift up the lad . . . for *I will make* him a great nation." (Gen. 21:17–18)

"And the angel of the LORD called unto him out of heaven, and said, Abraham, Abraham: and he said, Here am I. And he said, Lay not thine hand upon the lad, neither do thou any thing unto him: for now I know that thou fearest God, seeing thou hast not withheld thy son, thine only son *from me*." (Gen. 22:11–12)

"And the angel of the LORD appeared unto the woman . . . then the woman came and told her husband, saying, A man of God came unto me, and his countence was like the countenance of an angel of God, very terrible . . . and Manoah said unto the angel of the Lord, What is thy name, that when thy sayings come to pass we may do thee honour? And the angel of the LORD said unto him, Why askest thou thus after my name, seeing it is secret [wonderful]?" (Judg. 13:3, 6, 17, 18–19; cf. Isa. 9:6)

This "Angel of the Lord" (used 70 times in the Bible) is thus a "Theophanes," or more properly—an Old Testament manifestation of God, an appearance of the Word, or God the Son before His permanent incarnation as Jesus. Whenever man sees God in human form, he sees a manifestation of Christ, who (himself the uncreated God) is the "express image" (the exact likeness) of the invisible spiritual essence of God. The expression *The* angel of the Lord "does not appear after the birth of Christ. The expression occurs in the KJV, but is always a mistranslation, as the RV shows." The proper translation is "*An* angel of the Lord." (See Matt. 1:20; 28:2; Luke 2:9; Acts 8:26; 12:7, 23 in the RV.)[1]

---

[1] R.A. Torrey, *What The Bible Teaches*, (Fleming H. Revell Company), pp. 16–17.

Bible Word Study

Spirit (Hebrew)

ruah Wind, breath, mind.[2]

"This noun occurs 387 times in the Old Testament, usually feminine. . . . The basic idea of *ruah* is 'air in motion' from air which cannot come between a crocodile's scales (Job 41:16) to the blast of a storm (Isa. 25:4). . . . In living beings the *ruah* is their breath, whether of animals (Gen. 7:15; Ps. 104:25), men (Isa. 42:5; Ezek. 37:5) or both (Gen. 7:22–23); whether inhaled (Jer. 2:24), or on the lips (Isa. 11:4; cf. Job 9:18; contrast dead idols, Jer. 10:14; 51:17). God creates it: 'The [*ruah*] spirit[s] of God [from God] is in my nostrils'(Job 27:3).

"The connotations of breath include power (1 Kings 10:5, where the Queen of Sheba 'had no more spirit [*ruah*].' She was 'breathless' [overwhelmed]); courage (Josh. 2:11; 5:1, where the 'spirit' of Israel's enemies failed them); or value (Lam. 4:20, where the Davidic king was the 'breath of our nostrils'—a phrase borrowed from the common Egyptian, 'the breath of their nose').

"False prophets become *ruah* 'wind' because they lack the word (Jer. 5:13), the connotation being emptiness, the futility of 'mere breath' (Job 7:7; Isa. 41:29). As a rush of air, a snort through one's nose, *ruah* depicts emotions of agressiveness (Isa. 25:4) or anger (Judg. 8:3; Prov. 29:11, KJV, RSV). "Ultimately, breath signifies activity and life. One's 'spirit' is consumed when he is sick or faint (Job 17:1), but it comes back as a second wind and he 'revives' (1 Sam. 30:12; cf. Gen. 45:27). In God's hand is the breath of all mankind (Job 12:10; Isa. 42:5). . . .

"The 'breath' of man was bestowed by a special creative act of God (Gen. 2:7; contrast the beasts in 1:24). But it is his inner being that reflects the image of God, formed by the counsel of the Trinity ('us,' 1:26) and sovereign over all other living things (2:20). Biblical Hebrew therefore speaks of things that come into your mind [*ruah*] (Ezek. 11:5; 20:32). Daniel's Aramaic refers likewise to Nebuchadnezzar's mind (spirit, ASV) being hardened (Dan. 5:20). . . .

"On a higher plane, *ruah* may then designate a supernatural, angelic being, a 'spirit from God' (1 Sam. 16:23, NASB).

"The preeminent example of a spiritual personality is God (Isa. 31:3). *Ruah* can exhibit a range of meaning. The 'breath' of God may be a strong wind (Isa. 40:7; 59:19, NASB; cf. Num. 11:31). His 'spirit' may indicate no more than active power or mood. (Isa. 40:13—'Who hath directed the Spirit [intention] of the Lord?' or, 1 Cor. 2:16—'Who hath known the mind

---

[2]*Strong's* 7307.

[intention] of the Lord?'). At most points, however, context approves and the analogy of the New Testament strongly suggests that *ruah YHWH* is the Holy Spirit 'in the fullest Christian sense.' (A. F. Kirkpatrick, *Cambridge Bible, Psalms*, II, p. 293)."[3]

God's *ruah* is the power behind the cherubim (Ezek. 1:12, 20), the power behind unusual strength like Samson's (Judg. 13:25), and special physical power (Judg. 14:6, 19; 15:14). It sets the prophet on his feet (Ezek. 2:2; 3:24), and is the power for prophecies and miracles (Num. 11:17, 25, 29; 1 Sam. 10:6, 10; 19:20, 23; 2 Kings 2:9, 15). It lifts him up (2 Kings 2:16; Ezek. 3:12, 14; 8:3; 11:1, 24; 43:5), snatches him away (Ezek. 3:14), and sets him down in another place (2 Kings 2:16; Ezek. 8:3; 11:1, 24; 43:5; 37:1).[4]

It inspires preaching (Num. 24:2; 2 Sam. 23:2; 1 Kings 22:24; 2 Chron. 24:20; Isa. 61:1; Ezek. 11:5; Joel 2:28; Zech. 7:12), and visions (Ezek. 8:3; 11:24).[5]

"God's *ruah* power (Ezek. 37:9–10) created both the cosmos (Gen. 1:2) and all physical life (Job 33:4; Ps. 33:6). It gives mental and creative abilities (Deut. 34:9) like insight, artistic sense and skill (Ex. 31:3; 35:31), and enlightenment and wisdom (Dan. 5:14).[6]

"The prophet and the leader owe their divine charisma to *ruah* (Neh. 9:30; Isa. 48:16; Mic. 3:8) which also equips a ruler with wisdom, understanding, true kingly action, constancy, and godliness (Isa. 11:2; cf. Isa. 42:1).[7]

Spirit (Greek)

pneuma (*pnyoo-mah*)—A current of air (i.e., breath, blast or breeze). By analogy or figuratively, it means a spirit (i.e., human), the rational soul; by implication it means vital principle, mental disposition, etc., or superhuman spirit—an angel, demon, or (divine) God, Christ's Spirit, the Holy Spirit; ghost, life, mind.[8] Used 385 times in the NT.

"The verbal noun *pneuma* means the elemental natural and vital force which, matter and process in one, acts as a stream of air in the blowing of the wind and the inhaling and exhaling of breath, and hence—tranf. as the breath of the spirit which, in a way that may be detected both outwardly and inwardly, fills with inspiration and grips with enthusiasm."[9]

Early secular Greek uses of *pneuma* convey the idea of something out of man's control, an elemental dynamic, which imparts inspiration, fills with life and snatches away in enthusiasm. It is the breath of true poetry,

[3]J. Barton Payne, *Theological Wordbook of the Old Testament*, Laird R. Harris, ed. (Chicago: Moody Press, 1980), vol. 2, pp. 836–837.
[4]*Theological Dictionary of the New Testament*, Gerhard Kittel, ed., Geoffrey W. Bromiley, trans. (Grand Rapids: Wm. B. Eerdmans Publishing Company, 1964), vol. 6, p. 362.
[5]Ibid. pp. 362–363.
[6]Ibid. p. 363.
[7]Ibid. p. 363.
[8]*Strong's* 4151.
[9]*Theological Dictionary of the New Testament*, op. cit. vol. 6, pp. 334–335.

the ecstatic and rapturous passion of the inspired prophet, complete sometimes even with physical effects like the real wind: streaming hair, panting breath, violent filling, or being snatched away.

The scene on the day of Pentecost was much the same. "As something 'other' . . . which comes from without, *pneuma* fills the interior of the house [of the disciples] . . . either with a sound as of thunder or with a costly divine aroma; it fills everything around, both men and beasts . . . but especially the inner being of [the oracle]." Like a bride-groom spirit it "powerfully takes possession of the whole man and carries him off like a stormy wind. . . . It makes of him a winged and light being . . . catches him up out of the usual orders of life into the extraordinary . . . chasing the understanding out of his head and taking its place." It liberates, discloses and reveals "what was hidden, unknown, at most only suspected, and thus establishes a relation to the truth of things."[10]

aoratos (*ah-or-at-os*)—Something gazed at; by implication it means capable of being seen. The KJV translates it as "visible."[11]

horao (*hor-ah-o*)—Properly means to stare at; to discern clearly (physically or mentally). By extension it means to attend to. The KJV translates it "behold," "perceive," "see," "take heed."[12]

Questions and Answers

Q: *What is Spirit?*

A: A spirit is bodiless, invisible reality. R. A. Torrey says, "To say God is Spirit is to say God is incorporeal and invisible." (Luke 24:39; Deut. 4:15–18)[1]

Q: *What does the Bible mean when it says, "God created man in His own image" (Gen. 1:27)?*

A: "The words 'image' and 'likeness' evidently do not refer to visible or bodily likeness, but to intellectual and moral likeness—likeness in 'knowledge,' 'righteousness,' and 'holiness of truth.' "[2]

"And have put on the new man, which is renewed in knowledge after the image of him that created him" (Col. 3:10). "And be renewed in the spirit of your mind; and that ye put on the new man, which after God is created in righteousness and true holiness" (Eph. 4:23–24). "Who is the image of the invisible God, the firstborn of every creature" (Col. 1:15).

---

[10]Ibid. pp. 346–347.
[11]*Strong's* 3707.
[12]*Strong's* 3708.
[1]R.A. Torrey, *What the Bible Teaches* (Tappan, N.J.: Fleming H. Revell Company), p. 13.
[2]Ibid. p. 13.

Q: *If "no man can see God's face and live," how could Moses, Isaiah, or even Jesus' disciples see God?*

A: As our face is the ultimate focused expression of our own nature, character, and personality, God's gentle warning to his zealous but ingenuous friend was to simply remind him just who he was speaking with. The expression "to see My face" refers to the unmediated essence of God's glory, the fundamentally awesome and focused power of His substance, nature, and character. God never speaks to mortals without mediation: in the Old Testament through His angel (Exod. 3:2–6), the flame of fire, or the cloud of glory in the wilderness and in the New Testament through His Son (2 Cor. 4:6). Gleason Archer says, "The Bible draws a clear distinction between gazing on God in His unveiled glory and beholding a representation or reflection of God (like a TV broadcast) in a personal interview or encounter with Him."[3] The expression speaking "face to face as a man talks with his friend" (Exod. 33:11) carries the image of frankness and intimacy and does not refer to any unveiled revelation of God (cf. 1 Tim. 6:16). God hid Moses in a cleft of a rock and revealed His "afterglow" to honor Moses' request (Exod. 33:23; 34:6–7).

Q: *If God is spirit, and Jesus is God, did Jesus give up being God when He became a man?*

A: No, because an uncreated being cannot ever surrender its unmade nature. You cannot unmake an unmade! Jesus gave up His rights and privileges as God when He became a man (Phil. 2:6–8) but always retained His essential nature.

Q: *Does God have a body?*

A: No, but He can manifest himself in one locality if He chooses. We call this a *theophany* (an appearance of God) or even more specifically a *logophany* (an appearance of the Eternal Word, the Son, or second person of the Godhead in human form, often called "the angel of the Lord"). That Word became flesh (John 1:14); God incarnated himself as a real human being with a flesh-and-blood body (Heb. 2:16) so that in a true sense God, in the person of the Son, has a literal body.

Q: *But doesn't God need some kind of physical or material form in order to exist at all?*

A: If God were material being like that, no other matter could exist; He would exclude or else incorporate all other material existences. But neither physical or human form are necessary to retain or communicate intelligence and personality. Electron patterns communicate daily via radio, TV, video and audio tape, or telephone. Computers demonstrate the possibilities of "intelligence" which would not require human form. It is a much more obvious possibility to modern man that intelligence, order and personality can exist and communicate without human shape or form, or even "solid" existence apart from

---

[3]Gleason Archer, *Encyclopedia of Bible Difficulties* (Grand Rapids: Zondervan Publishing House, 1982), pp. 124–125.

the actual interface to the person.

Q: *But doesn't the Bible say God made man "in His image and after His likeness?" (Gen. 1:26; Heb.1:3).*

A: In what way can a creation be *made* like his uncreated Creator? Certainly not in substance or essence; you cannot *make* an unmade. By "image and likeness" we understand mankind to be creative like the Creator, a unique and distinct race from the rest of the creation (Gen. 1:26) modeled after God's own attributes of personality and with potential to have the same character likeness as our Heavenly Father.

Q: *What does the Bible mean when it says God sits (Isa. 6:1) and stands (Isa. 3:13), and why does it speak about God's hand (Job 40:4), eye (Ps. 32:8), and other parts of His body as if He were human?*

A: When the Bible attributes physical features to God (anthropomorphism), it refers to His actions by means of their human or physical counterparts, which we understand. Likewise when Scripture says we are to be kept under the "shadow of His wings" (Ps. 57:1), we are certainly not to understand that God is a giant eagle or a chicken!

Q: *People can draw near to God (Ps. 73:28) or depart from Him (Jer. 17:13). How can that be if He is not corporeal?*

A: The omnipresent God who upholds the entire creation by His Word of command cannot be physically approached or abandoned. All such words are words of *relationship*. "The Lord's hand is not shortened, that it cannot save," but "your iniquities" (Isa. 59:1–2) can certainly separate you from His fellowship.

Q: *If God really is in all things, He would dwell in Satan and the demons, but the Bible teaches there is no fellowship between light and darkness (2 Cor. 6:14). Is the Devil somehow filled with the Holy Spirit? If not, then how can God then be infinite?*

A: Again, good and evil are not qualities of substance or essence, but character. God does uphold the reality of the entire created universe, and is the absolute author of its original existence. However, sin itself is a moral (not physical) creation of rebellious moral beings, and each moral member of the creation will be held responsible for his own actions. Moral character (unlike metaphysical substance), related to God's own creative personality, goes on forever in redeemed or unredeemed alike; heaven and hell are eternal realities because of God's omnipresence.

Q: *The Bible ascribes height, depth, and breadth to God (Job 11:8–9). Doesn't this mean that He has form or shape of some sort?*

A: In all these descriptions God transcends known dimensions. Our own dimensions of space may be created—and thus finite—analogues of His own infinite extension. Our three-dimensional space may be a lesser and perceivable correspondence to His omnipresence. Some have thought the terms of size are instead used as illustrations of God's power, wisdom, and love; depth meaning unfathomable wisdom; length, the extension of His reality and pervasion of His power;

breadth, His comprehensive protection and care for creation, and height, His infinite rule and power over all things.

Q: *How can God be* in *all things as well as* above *all things as in Ps. 113:4?*

A: Not hard for an omnipresent being. He is there in the same way that Christ, who already dwells in our hearts by faith by the Holy Spirit, can yet baptize and flood our lives with power from on high. Again, these are questions about manifestation, revelation, and communication with the God who is there.

Analysis and Discussion

What do you think of when you see the word *spiritual?* People think two things. Morally, they think of something to do with being religious or holy; metaphysically, of something not quite real, not quite solid, and not quite all there.

As people of flesh and blood, we naturally assume that something *spiritual* such as a ghost (though we may see it and it may even do things to frighten us) is somehow not as real as we "solid" people are.

"We are born of material parents into a material world," says A. W. Tozer, "we are wrapped in material clothes, fed on material milk and lie on a material bed and sleep and walk and live and talk and grow up in a world of matter. Matter presses upon us so obtrusively and takes over our thinking so completely that we cannot speak of spirit without using materialistic terms. God made man out of the dust of the ground and man has been dust ever since, and we can't quite shake it off."[1]

Yet, as our studies in physics have shown us, we know that matter itself is not really solid. Remove the empty space from a man and what is left as "matter" would be fly-speck size. What we think of as solidness is only energy bundles held together by subatomic forces, entire universes of swarming electromagnetic and nuclear fields. All we see is unsubstantial at heart; coalesced force bound by yet deeper invisible cords. The nature of reality remains the subject of scientific and even mystic speculation. People who attempt to describe it find even illustration difficult and are forced instead either to mathematical representations, poetic analogies, or notational models in their thought processes.

The Visible Is Merely Symbolic

What we perceive is essentially a *representation* of reality. Sir James Jeans said years ago that the more we study the universe, the less and less it looks like a great machine and the more and more it begins to look like a great idea.

---

[1]A.W. Tozer, *How To Be Filled With the Holy Spirit* (Camp Hill, Penn.: Christian Publications, Inc.), p. 3.

Owen Barfield declares: "Atoms, protons, and electrons of modern physics are now more generally regarded not as particles but as notational models or symbols of an unknown supersensible or subsensible base. . . . Whatever may be thought about the 'unrepresented' background of our perceptions, the familiar world which we see and know around us—the blue sky with white clouds in it, the noise of a waterfall or a bus, the shapes of flowers and their scent . . . is a system of collective representations. The time comes when one must either accept this as the truth about the world or reject the theories of physics as an elaborate delusion. We cannot have it both ways. . . . Descriptions may still . . . be valuable, not as actual descriptions, but as notational models. What is important is to remember that that is *all* they are. . . . Their nature is that of artificial imagery. And when the nature and limitations of artificial images are forgotten they become idols."[2]

Roots of Reality

This is not to say that the material is unreal or illusory; the Bible does not treat created matter as unworthy or dishonorable. As the loved creation of God, it is both real and valuable. Even in the spiritual world a thing may be false and still be "real."

"In fact," said C. S. Lewis, "we should never ask the question, 'Is it real?' for everything is real. The proper question is 'A real what?' e.g., a real snake or real delirium tremens? The objects around me and my idea of 'me' will deceive if taken at their face value. But they are momentous if taken as the end-products of divine activities.

"Or put it this way. I have called my material surroundings a stage set. A stage set is not a dream nor a nonentity. But if you attack a stage house with a chisel you will not get chips of brick or stone; you'll only get a hole in a piece of canvas and beyond that, windy darkness. Similarly if you start investigating the nature of matter you will not find anything like what imagination has always supposed matter to be. You will get mathematics. From that unimaginable physical reality my senses select a few stimuli. These they translate or symbolize into sensations which have no likeness at all to the reality of matter."[3]

Creation by a Spoken Word

If we accept our own universe as a creation God originally spoke into existence (and now upholds by that same word of command), we can think of all space-time-matter reality as a spectrum of vibration; from that which we can see and touch and hear in our own very tiny portion of perception, to that above and below our ability to perceive, the infra- and super-structures of created reality. For instance, we can hear sounds as

---

[2]Owen Barfield, *Saving the Appearances: A Study in Idolatry* (Harcourt Brace Janovich, 1965), pp. 17–18, 39.

[3]C.S. Lewis, *Letters to Malcolm* (Huntington N.Y.: John M. Fontana Publishers, 1975), p. 82.

low as 20 cycles or vibrations per second (a very low note) and up to 18,000–20,000 cycles per second. Lower than 20 cps, a sound may be perhaps felt as a deep throbbing or sense of uneasiness, without ever being heard; higher than this, it may be perceived, if at all, only as a tension, a sense of keen disorientation. Dogs, with a wider scale of sound perception, can hear a whistle inaudible to a man. Bats regularly use such sounds (ultrasonics) to navigate in darkness. We now utilize ultrasonics in cleaning devices for watches and jewelry, special dental drills and for special kinds of welding and soldering.

Push frequency still higher, and the "sound" waves move right out of the audible range, becoming radio waves that can be picked up and translated into audio waves by a radio receiver. Even higher frequencies we classify as the microwave and radar spectrums; higher still they become the narrow band of visible light, where we can again pick them up with different sensors of our eyes, from the deep reds to the high violets. A little too low in frequency for our eyes, and they disappear from sight but can be felt as infra-red rays which heat; too high and they again vanish from the visible, becoming ultraviolet light or even higher frequency. Above these in turn are X-rays, gamma rays, and cosmic rays. Each frequency and wavelength has different properties; ultraviolet in sunlight, for instance, is blocked by glass, but passes through quartz; ultraviolet rays in sunshine tan or burn your skin. The infra-red in sunlight, however, passes right through glass, which is why you can hot sunbathe behind glass without tanning!

Energies in Harmony

What you "feel" when you touch something is not a collision of solids but of energies in tune, in harmony with one another. If it were possible to somehow alter the basic nature of the frequencies of matter, to somehow throw matter "out of phase" with matter as we know it, *another world could co-exist with this one,* each equally "real," with its own flowers, trees, and people. This world might simultaneously exist in the same physical space and the same continuum of time as our own world, yet it would be as "solid" and as "real" as ours is to us; yet each world could freely pass through the other without either being aware of the other world's existence! Someone "shifted" in frequency from our world to the alternate one would be largely unaffected by the properties of this one— properties of radiation, gravity, and tactile response would all be out of phase and pass through as cleanly as light passes through glass. He could walk through a wall, on top of the sea, or even be thrown into a furnace and walk out unharmed without even the smell of smoke on his clothes.

And the Bible tells us such a world *does* exist. Rarely now do we sense it, see it, or cross paths with it; but that world is real, and as "solid"—if not indeed far more so—as the one we think of as so fundamental.

A. W. Tozer declared, "A spiritual kingdom lies all about us, enclosing us, embracing us, altogether within reach of our inner selves, waiting for us to recognize it. God himself is here waiting our response to His presence. This eternal world will come alive to us the moment we begin to reckon upon its reality."[4]

When we try to explain the nature of this spiritual world, words fail. It is difficult enough trying to describe the nature of the created spiritual world; but when we try to illustrate God's own nature of *uncreated* Spirit we are again speaking of something marvelous and incomprehensible. As Stephen Charnock notes: "God is Spirit; that is, He hath nothing corporeal, no mixture of matter, not a visible substance, a bodily form. He is a Spirit, not a bare spiritual substance, but an understanding, willing Spirit, holy, wise good and just. . . . When we say God is a Spirit, it is to be understood by way of negation. There are two ways of knowing or describing God: by way of *affirmation*, affirming that of Him by way of eminence, that which is excellent in the creature, as when we say God is wise, good; the other by *negation* when we remove from God in our conceptions what is tainted with imperfection in the creature. . . . His way of negation is more easy; we better understand what God is not, than what He is; and most of our knowledge of God is by this way; as when we say God is infinite, immense, immutable, they are negatives. . . . We call Him so, because in regard of our weakness we have not any other term of excellency to express or conceive of Him by; we transfer it to God in honor. . . . His nature is so great that He cannot be declared by human speech, perceived by human sense or conceived by human understanding."[5]

Ultimate Reality: Uncreated Spirit

All we can really say is that final reality is in the highest and deepest way the substance of God himself; and that this *uncreated spirit* which is God's essence, totally transcends our idea of what is real or solid; it is another ultimate mode of being.

Finney expressed the dilemma like this: "By the spirituality of God, we understand that His existence or substance is immaterial—a substance or existence possessing properties essentially different from those of matter. . . . If God were material, no other material could exist. As He is omnipresent, He would of course, if He were material, exclude all other material existences."[6]

God is the Source of Reality

God's ultimate uncreated reality is the very opposite of tenuousness or shadow, as C. S. Lewis urged: "God is basic fact or actuality, the source of all other facthood. At all costs therefore, He must not be thought of as a featureless generality. . . . He is the most concrete thing there is, the

---

[4]A.W. Tozer, *The Pursuit of God* (Camp Hill, Penn.: Christian Publications, Inc., 1982), p. 52.

[5]Stephen Charnock, *The Existence and Attributes of God* (Grand Rapids: Baker Book House, 1979), vol. 1, pp. 178, 182.

[6]C.G. Finney, *Skeletons of a Course of Theological Lectures* (London: Milner and Company), p. 86.

most individual, organized and minutely articulated. He is unspeakable, not by being indefinite but by being too definite for the unavoidable vagueness of language. The words 'incorporeal' and 'impersonal' are misleading because they suggest He lacks some reality which we possess. It would be safer to call Him trans-corporeal, trans-personal. Body and personality as we know them are the real negatives—they are what is left of positive being when it is sufficiently diluted to appear in temporal or finite forms. Even our sexuality should be regarded as the transposition into a minor key of that creative joy which in Him is unceasing and irresistible. . . . Divine Sonship is, so to speak, the solid of which biological sonship is merely a diagrammatic representation on the flat.

"The ultimate spiritual reality is not vaguer, more inert, more transparent than the images, but more positive, more dynamic, more opaque. . . . If we must have a picture to symbolize Spirit, we should represent it as something 'heavier' than matter.

"The stillness in which the mystics approach Him is intent and alert—at the opposite pole from sleep or reverie. They are becoming like Him. Silences in the physical world occur in empty places; but the Ultimate peace is silent through the very density of life. Saying is swallowed up in being. . . . You might if you wished call it movement at an infinite speed, which is the same thing as rest, but reached by a different—perhaps less misleading—way of approach."[7]

Four-Dimensional Reality

Although this uncreated spiritual being of God is ultimate reality, we can say there are at least two other lower levels of being in the created realm: created spirit and created matter. Reality intensifies and substantially densifies as we move from realm to realm, closer to uncreated God himself. It follows that our world, spoken into existence and upheld by His Word alone is subject to rule and control by that which is intrinsically greater; the spiritual ultimately transcends and has power over the material.

Is this transcendence intrinsic and inherent in the nature of these distinctions of reality? Dr. Paul Yonggi Cho, pastor of the world's largest church in Seoul, Korea, believes this explains the claims and demonstrations of the occult miraculous in Buddhism, Yoga, Sokagakki, and other Oriental religions. How can even the demonic world have a measure of control over matter?

The analogy given Dr. Cho in prayer was spatial: lesser space is both incorporated and transcended by the next highest level of extension. As a line (one dimension) transcends a point, and a plane (two dimensions) in turn transcends the line, so a solid (three dimensions) transcends the plane. Each higher realm dominates (has power) over the lower.

What transcends our own space-time world? The spiritual world which he calls *the fourth dimension*: "Every human being is a spiritual being as

---

[7]C.S. Lewis., *Miracles* (New York: MacMillan, 1978), p. 291.

well as a physical being. They have the fourth dimension as well as the third dimension in their hearts. . . . When God created us, He created in us the fourth dimension, the spiritual world.

"Access to that world with a measure of power and influence over the space-time-matter realm comes via the spiritual perceptions of man, in areas of the human spirit like the imagination through the door of visions and dreams." So men, "by exploring their spiritual sphere of the fourth dimension through the development of concentrated visions and dreams in their imaginations can brood over and incubate the third dimension, influencing and changing it."[8]

Imagination: A Link to the Spiritual World

There are nine different words in the Bible used for the right or wrong use of imagination; it is a deeply significant facet of man's being. The misuse of human imagination results in the most serious divine judgment; the scattering of nations and confusion of language, the divine abandonment of a culture, even the destruction of the world (Gen. 6:5; 11:6; Rom. 1:21). It is listed as one of the seven abominations that God hates (Prov. 6:18).

Cho points out that because the faculty of vision and imagination is spiritual, it is through this avenue that true creativity functions. The Holy Spirit, unlimited by our physically imposed limits of space and time can cooperate with us—to create by ". . . helping young men to see visions and old men to dream dreams. Through envisioning and dreaming dreams we can kick away the wall of our limitations and can stretch out to the universe. That is the reason that God's Word says, 'Where there is no vision the people perish' (Prov. 29:18). If you have no vision, you are not being creative; and if you stop being creative, then you are going to perish." Cho calls visions and dreams "the language of the fourth dimension," and says "the Holy Spirit communicates through them."[9]

Misuse of Vision and Imagination

Cho believes the misuse of imagination, trained and channeled to false, deceptive, or destructive ends is the chief source from which the occult world functions: "Occult or mentalist believers explore and develop their human fourth dimension—their spiritual sphere—by incubating over their bodies with clear-cut visions and mental pictures. . . . By natural order the fourth dimension has power over the third dimension, and the human spirit, within limitations, has power to give order and creation. God gave power to human beings to control the material world and to have dominion over material things, a responsibility they can carry out through the fourth dimension. Unbelievers, by exploring and developing their inner spiritual beings in such a way can carry out dominion upon

[8]Dr. Paul Yonggi Cho, *The Fourth Dimension* (Plainfield, N.J.: Logos Int.), p. 40.
[9]Ibid. p. 42.

their third dimension which includes their physical sicknesses and diseases."

Non-Christians can exercise occult powers just as Pharaoh's magicians in Egypt did, because their human spirit "joins up with the evil fourth dimension" ruled by Satan and they "carry out dominion over their bodies and circumstances." But the Christian has available in Christ an even greater source of power. In this he can become "fantastically creative and exercise great control and power over the third dimension" over circumstances, by his dependence on "the fourth dimension of the Holy Father— the Creator of the universe." It is important to note that the power of uncreated Creator-God is not just another higher level of magic or the manipulation of appearances of reality; it is of a *totally different order entirely*—absolute, ultimate, creative and life-giving, recognized even by Pharaoh's magicians as completely out of their realm, the very "finger of God" (Ex. 8:19).

Cho warns about the danger of exalting the power of the subconscious, the human spirit, as *deception*: "The Bible calls the subconscious the inner man, the man hidden in your heart. . . . The subconscious has certain influence, but it is quite limited and cannot create like our Almighty God can. . . . To put that spirit in the place of Jesus Christ . . . is indeed a great deception and a great danger."[10] Because this realm can be the playground of the occult, we must give our spiritual vision wholly to God: "Do not be deceived by talk of mind expansion, yoga, transcendental meditation, or Sokagakkai. They are only developing the human fourth dimension, and in these cases are not in the good, but rather the evil fourth dimension. Let us rise up and do more than an Egyptian magician. There are plenty of magicians in the Egypts of this world but let us use all our visions and dreams for our Holy God. Let us become Moses and go out and perform the most wonderful of miracles."

The Spiritual Structure of Scripture

God says His Word is "living and powerful" (Heb. 4:12); far more than a book because it, like the creation itself, is the Word of God (Psa. 138:2; 119:89). Cho points out that the Bible also is fourth-dimensional; there "we can read of God and the life He has for us and can learn the language of the Holy Spirit. By reading Scripture you can enlarge your visions and your dreams. . . . Let the Holy Spirit come and quicken the scriptures you read, and implant visions in the young and dreams in the old."

Captured spiritual vision is dangerous because in the fourth dimension, "either good or evil is created. . . . If seeing is not important, why did the angel of God give such a grievous judgment to the wife of Lot (Gen. 19:17)? It is a simple command—do not look behind you. . . . You might say that the judgment was too harsh but when you understand this law of the spirit, it is not, for when she looked back she did not only see with her physical eyes; when she looked, that sight came to her inner self,

---

[10]Ibid. p. 42.

and gripped hold of her imagination. Lust for her former life began to take hold of her, and God carried out His just judgment on her."[11]

The Role of Vision in Intercession

Despite the overwhelming nature of some of life's crises, a divine perspective can give us a whole new picture of the situation (see 2 Kings 6:15–17). All of us interpret our encounters in life through a mental perspective colored by our own preconceptions; it is important that these preconceptions be constantly corrected by the Word of God, the Spirit of God, and the testimony of His works and His ways in His Church. Begin with a false premise, and with all the right facts and correct logic we can still come to a wrong conclusion for all the right reasons! God wants to correct and lift our spiritual vision, so that we see all life His way. Spiritual vision is also important to prayer and intercession.

C. S. Lewis comments: "Now the moment of prayer is for me—or involves for me as its condition—the awareness—the re-awakened awareness—that this 'real world' and 'real self' are very far from being rock-bottom realities. I cannot, in the flesh leave the stage, either to go behind the scenes or to take my seat in the pit; but I can remember that these regions exist. And I also remember that my apparent self—this clown or hero or superman under his greasepaint—is a real person with an off-stage life. The dramatic person could not tread the stage unless he concealed a real person; unless the real and the unknown 'I' existed, I would not even make mistakes about the imagined me. And in prayer this real 'I' struggles to speak, for once, from His real being and address, for once, not the other actors but—what shall I call Him?—The Author, for He invented us all? The Producer, for He controls all? Or The Audience, for He watches and will judge the performance?"[12]

Cho encourages the homebound: "If you lack the mobility and opportunity of a missionary, then at least you can sit in your chair and dream. That is powerful. Let the Holy Spirit come and teach you the language of the Holy Spirit, the language of visions and dreams. Then keep those visions, keep those dreams and let the Holy Spirit flow through that language and create.

"Through dominion in the forth dimension—the realm of faith—you can give order to your circumstances and situations, give beauty to the ugly and chaotic and healing to the hurt and suffering."[13]

Matter as Extended Mind

We see in creation a phenomena Hans Jenny named *cymatics*, his idea that environmental pressures create wave patterns and matter responds to these patterns in a form dependent on the frequency.[14] Nature

[11]Ibid. pp. 45–46.
[12]Lewis, *Letters to Malcolm*, op. cit. p. 83.
[13]Cho, op. cit. pp. 65–66.
[14]Hans Jenny, *Cymatics Basel* (Basileus Press, 1966).

does show many recurring patterns as God's ergonomic design of the universe; the helical spiral of a thermal updraft is a mirror of the DNA molecule and the path of a creeper around a tree. We say *function follows form*; we could also say *form follows frequency*. It might be more accurate to say that God speaks things into existence which are shaped by the distinctions of His original naming; and while we speak words, God speaks pattern, reality, and life.

In fact, *matter is shaped by mind*, as A. C. Custance observes: "If . . . matter is taken as a form of congealed consciousness, a direct creation out of the mind of God, then mind is not an epiphenomenon of matter, but matter is an epiphenomenon of mind. The brain as a physical organ is not the originator of consciousness, will or volition as commonly held, but merely a specialized housing of consciousness in a concentrated form, an important locus of involvement but by no means the only seat of it. Every cell in the body should be expected to have or to be a locus of consciousness, for every cell would in fact be an expression of it. . . ." (Mindedness extends right down to cellular level, and the brain is more a processor and container of mind.)

"What I am arguing is that the basic reality is spiritual (of which mindedness is only one mode) and that matter is a kind of secondary congealing of it, in which the true identity of mindedness is by no means lost, but only apportioned appropriately depending on its organization. Inanimate matter would still then be mindedness objectified, but objectified in such a way that our research tools are not designed to elucidate. When plant life was created, mindedness could be displayed more completely. . . . when animal life was created, mindedness was provided with an even more liberating mode of expression. When man was created, liberation went one step further, appearing not merely as consciousness, but as self-consciousness. At the time of the Incarnation we meet with the epitome of pure Spirit objectified within the material order. . . . There is a very real sense in which it is the *material* order that is mystical, and not the spiritual order as we so commonly view it. *The real mystery is how the spiritual can be materialized.* . . . What the Scripture sees as real mystery, the 'great mystery' (1 Tim. 3:16), is how pure spirit can be materialized, as happened when God was manifested in the flesh. And this is really the secret also of what happened when God created the universe in the first place."[15]

Spiritual Substance Is Still Reality

Harry Rimmer comments on the *form* of Christ from Phil. 2:5–11: "In the Greek text, the word is *morphe* and is the basis for our scientific term morphology. This science deals with the gross bodily structure of the living creature and is in contrast to histology, the microscopic structure of the cell. . . . Before Christ came to earth He existed in the *morphe* or bodily

---

[15]Arthur C. Custance, *The Doorway Papers* (Grand Rapids: Zondervan Publishing House, 1977), Vol. III, pp. 326–327.

substance of God. . . . The Holy Spirit caused Paul the Apostle to say, 'Jesus existed in the *morphe* of God. . . .'

"We cannot conceive of intelligence apart from personality, nor can we grasp the fact of personality apart from some sort of bodily substance. Our difficulty here is rooted in the fact that we are prone to conceive of all substance as physical matter. We fail to grasp the fact that spiritual substance may be as real as physical matter. . . . In the resurrection, the believer in Christ receives a body that is literal and real but which is not made of physical substance. After the resurrection our Savior manifested a body composed of translated flesh and bones capable of passing through walls and locked doors into a sealed room. This body was not restricted by the influence of gravity. When it desired to, it could exercise sovereignty over different, common earthly factors. We are so tremendously ignorant about all things beyond the world of the senses that we are only capable of a stumbling approach to a subject which bewilders our darkened human mentality."[16]

God Is Not a Man

Because God *is* that Ultimate Reality, we must measure everything against the criterion of His self-revelation and work, from what He says outward, not attempting to make Him fit our own personal images and imaginations.

James Packer comments: "How often do we hear this sort of thing: 'I like to think of God as the great Architect (or Mathematician; or Artist). I don't like to think of God as a Judge; I like to think of Him as a Father.' We know from experience how often remarks of this kind serve as a prelude to a denial of something that the Bible tells us about God. It needs to be said with the greatest possible emphasis that those who hold themselves free to think of God as they like are breaking the second commandment. At best they can only think of God in the image of man—as an ideal man perhaps, or a superman. But God is not any sort of man."[17]

The Bible does not command belief in *a* god; it commands belief in *the* God. The first of the Ten Commandments prohibits *idolatry*, not atheism. The great danger of a civilization is not that they will not believe in God, but that they will give themselves over to fantasies, wicked imaginations, and demons.

Packer goes on to write, "Those who make images and use them in worship, and thus inevitably take their theology from them, will in fact tend to neglect God's revealed will at every point. The mind that takes up with images is a mind that has not yet learned to love and attend to God's Word. Those who look to man-made images—material or mental—to lead them to God, are not likely to take any part of His revelation as seriously as they should."[18]

---

[16]Harry Rimmer, *The Magnificence of Jesus* (1943), pp. 100–101.
[17]J.I. Packer, *Knowing God* (Downers Grove, Ill.: Inter-Varsity Press, 1973), p. 48.
[18]Ibid. p. 49.

Obedience Opens the Spiritual Eye

Disobedience dims spiritual vision; ultimately, *truth can only be known by revelation*. We are dependent on God speaking to us; He as infinite must reveal himself to us as finite. God has conditioned this to obedience.

As F. W. Robertson says: "The universe is governed by laws. . . . By submission to them you make them your own. The condition annexed to a sense of God's presence—in other words, that without which a sense of God's presence cannot be—is *obedience* to the laws of love. 'If we love one another God dwells in us and His love is perfected in us.' The condition of spiritual wisdom and certainty in truth is obedience to the will of God, and surrender of our private will. 'If any man will do His will He shall know.' . . . See the beauty of the divine arrangement. If the certainty of truth depended upon the proof of miracles, prophecy or the discovery of science, then the truth would be in the reach chiefly of those who can weigh evidence, investigate history and languages and study by experiment; whereas it is 'The meek will He guide in judgment and the meek will He teach His way. Thus saith the High and Holy One that inhabits eternity whose name is Holy; I dwell in the high and holy place with him also that is of a contrite and humble spirit.' The humblest and weakest may know more of God, or moral evil and of good, by a single act of charity or a prayer of self-surrender than all the sages can teach or all the theologians can dogmatize on.

"Annexed to this condition is *earnestness*. If any man *will do* his will. Now that word *will* is not the will of future tense, but will meaning volition—if any man wills, resolves, has a mind to do the will of God. So then it is not a chance, fitful obedience that leads to truth; nor an obedience paid while happiness lasts and no longer—but an obedience rendered entire and in earnest."[19]

Historical Discussion

Always the Church has been tempted to think of God by the use of images and forms and always when she has done so she has fallen into externalism and spiritual decay. Some of the greatest books apart from inspired Scripture have been written to call the church back to a purer view of God. . . . I think it may be said with a fair degree of accuracy that all the great devotional theologians of the centuries taught the futility of trying to visualize the Godhead. Molinos warned against every effort of the intellect to image God forth. "She ought to go forward with her love," he says of the Christian soul, "leaving all her understanding behind. Let her love God as He is and not as her understanding says He is, and pictures Him."

---

[19]F.W. Robertson, *Sermons on Religion and Life* (London: J.M. Dent and Co., 1906), pp. 95–104.

The teaching of the New Testament is that God and spiritual things can only be known by a direct work of God within the soul.[1]

—A.W. Tozer

Spiritual Truth Comes by Revelation

Bonaventure

"Nothing can be understood unless God himself by His eternal Truth immediately enlightens him who understands. . . . God is to be called our Teacher, because our intellect attains to Him as to the light of our minds and the principle by which we know every truth."[2]

Joseph Parker

"Any suggestion will do when men want to get rid of the supernatural. . . . Anything that will rid us of lines beyond our own personal experience and give us a sense of comfortable smugness within four visible points will be received with gratitude by the natural heart. We like insulation. We are pleased with a clock that we can see, every tick of which we can hear and every indication of which we can read. But the clock is not the time. Time is invisible, impalpable, in many ways incalculable; quite a ghost, a very solemn thing, always talking and yet talking in a way that is not always clearly apprehended or understood. People like to be comfortable and nobody can be comfortable with the supernatural who is not in harmony with it. If a certain miracle has not been wrought in the soul the supernatural becomes a kind of ghost, a spectral presence, an uncanny possibility in the life, and had better be got rid of; and when the mind wants such riddance, any suggestion that will aid it in that direction is received with effusive thankfulness."[3]

Anselm

"I am not trying Lord, to penetrate Your sublimity, for my understanding is not up to that. But I long in some measure to understand Your truth which my heart believes and loves. For I am not seeking to understand in order to believe, but I believe in order that I may understand. For this too I believe; that unless I believe, I shall not understand."[4]

Adolph Saphir

Speaking of the life of faith, Saphir says: "The things hoped for and the things not seen which are now made manifest in full perfection by the Gospel of Christ can only be realized by faith, even as it was by faith that all the godly, since the beginning of the world, lived and suffered,

[1]A.W. Tozer, *That Incredible Christian* (Camp Hill, Penn.: Christian Publications Inc., 1964), pp. 90–91.
[2]Bonaventure, *Disputed Questions Concerning Christ's Knowledge.*
[3]Joseph Parker, *Preaching Through the Bible* (Grand Rapids: Baker Books, 1978), vol. 3, p. 315.
[4]Anselm, *Proslogian: Faith Seeking Understanding.*

obeyed and conquered. . . . What was their greatness but that they were men of God? And what made them men of God but that they believed God and waited for the fulfillment of His promise? Faith was the characteristic attitude of all the saints. It is the attitude of heart without which there is no communion with God and without which we cannot please Him.

"The apostle gives the most comprehensive definition of faith, describing the radical and essential disposition of heart Godward in whatever dispensation men lived. . . . It consists at all times in a firm confidence of unseen and future realities.

"There are things hoped for in future, in eternity; there are things not seen, both past and present. The latter expression is more comprehensive than the former. The second advent, our resurrection and glory are future things hoped for; God as the Creator and Upholder of all things, and all spiritual truths and heavenly realities, belong to the unseen, of which faith alone can have assurance. The heart of man, gravitating since the fall toward the things seen and which are present, is never satisfied with the visible and temporary, cannot rest except in the spiritual and eternal. God in His great mercy has revealed to us the things of God; eternal and spiritual realities have been manifested by God's Spirit. There is a divine revelation; the things which man's reason cannot discern or his imagination and intuition discover have been unveiled."[5]

Faith Is the Organ of Sight

Adolph Saphir

"How is this revelation received? What is the eye that sees, the organ that beholds and appropriates this gift? *Faith* is the eye that beholds the King in His beauty, and that sees the land afar off. Not man's intellect, not man's imagination, not man's conscience; all these become indeed most deeply, radically and thoroughly servants of faith; but that which discerns and beholds spiritual realities and appropriates them, that which beholds future blessings, and so grasps and cherishes them as to prefer them to things visible and to make them the object and joy of life is what Scripture calls faith.

"To assent to the Word of God is therefore to enter into a perfectly new life, a perfectly new mode and power of existence. Nothing but God's Word could have ever called forth that which we call faith, and God's Word, Spirit-given as it is, only when vitalized by the Holy Ghost. Where then is the *seat* of faith? Not in the intellect, which sees the logical connection or the historic evidence; not in the imagination, which recognizes the beauty and organic symmetry and reproduces the picture; not in the conscience, which testifies to the righteousness and truth of the revelation; but in a something which lies deeper than these, in which all these center, and to which all these return. With the *heart*, as Scripture teaches, man believeth. There, where are the issues of life, emotional, intellectual,

---

[5]Adolph Saphir, *The Life of Faith* (N.Y.: Gospel Publishing House).

moral, spiritual in that secret place to which God alone has access, God's Word as a seed begets faith; God's Word, as light, kindles light and the man becomes a believer. . . . Without desiring the things future, without turning in sorrow and self-condemnation to the unseen God—revealed without the heart clinging in trustfulness to God the Savior—there is no faith. God speaks to the heart of Jerusalem, and faith is the heart hearing and responding."[6]

Bonaventure

"But if you wish to know how these things come about, [it is] as grace not instruction, desire not understanding, the groaning of prayer not diligent reading, the Spouse (Christ) not the teacher, God not man, darkness not clarity, not light but the fire which totally inflames and carries us into God by ecstatic unctions and burning affections."[7]

Gregory Palmas (1330)

"The mark made on the mind by the Divine and mysterious signs of the Spirit is very different from apophatic [negative] theology. . . . Theology is as far from the vision of God in light, and as distinct from intimate conversation with God as knowledge is different from possession."[8]

Spiritual Reality Counteracts Deception

Watchman Nee

"Of all the works of the Holy Spirit, two are of prime importance; namely the *revelation* of the Spirit and the *discipline* of the Spirit. The first enables us to know and see spiritual reality, while the second guides us into the experience of spiritual reality through environmental arrangements. Revelation is the foundation of all spiritual progress. Without the revelation of the Holy Spirit, no matter how good one's knowledge and how excellent one's outward conduct, that Christian remains superficial before God . . . We may say that the revelation of the Holy Spirit is the foundation while the discipline of the Holy Spirit is the construction.

"We ought to realize that all spiritual life and teaching has its reality before God. *If one has not touched that reality*—and no matter how well he may preach the doctrine—he produces nothing of spiritual value. . . . A wonderful thing happens after you touch reality. Whenever you encounter someone who has not touched, or entered into reality, you immediately sense it. . . . Before God there is something which the Bible calls 'true.' . . . In relating to this trueness—this reality—one is delivered from doctrine, letter, human thoughts and human ways. Be it baptism or breaking of bread or the church, there is a reality. Nothing is mere form, procedure or doctrine. . . .

"We must learn to live before God according to what we verily are. We

---

[6]Ibid. pp. 10–15.
[7]Bonaventure, *The Soul's Journey Into God.*
[8]Gregory Palmas, *Triads.*

should ask Him to cause us to contact that which is spiritually real. Sometimes we are close to being false simply because we know too much. . . . The power of discerning comes out of what one has already seen. If we have touched spiritual reality in a certain matter, no one can ever deceive us in that particular matter. A truly saved believer has at least touched the spiritual reality of salvation."[9]

God's Word Brings Reality to Man

Watchman Nee

"[Faith] is nothing else but receiving the Word of God. We know what it is to receive the word of a man, to believe statements though strange and surpassing our experience, because we regard the character of him who makes them with respect and confidence. Faith in God's Word is receiving God's testimony. But then remember, as God is greater than man, as God's Word is heaven-high above any human word, so the reception of this Word, the believing of this Word, is necessarily something quite different from the reception of any human word or testimony. As is the voice, so is the echo; as is the seal, so is the impression; as is the word, so is the faith. The divine Word produces in the heart of man faith, which is divine in its nature and power. When God speaks, when God discloses to the soul the world of spiritual realities and of future blessings, this very Word of His creates within the soul a new world of fear, shame, contrition, desire, reverence, longing, hope, trust which no other word could call forth, perfectly unique in its character as God's Word is unique in its character."[10]

Unseen Substance and Reality

Adolph Saphir

"Things unseen are not doubtful to faith; but faith is the evidence, the clear and sure beholding of the things of God, shown or demonstrated by the Holy Ghost. Things future are not vague and shadowy, for faith gives them substance, so that they influence, gladden and uphold us in our earthly life. Not as the world giveth gives God unto us. Our faith is not a pale and uncertain light; it is not inferior to the knowledge of reason, or memory, or the senses; it is light, conviction, substance. We have the things we believe and which God has freely given us."[11]

Christ Reveals Himself to Us

John Fletcher

"I am presuming that it is now obvious to you, as it is to myself, that

---

[9]Watchman Nee, *Spiritual Reality* (Richmond, Va.: Christian Fellowship Publishers, 1970), pp. 39–40, 13, 29.
[10]Ibid.
[11]Saphir, op. cit. p. 34.

spiritual senses not only exist, but also are the means of communication used by the Lord when He chooses to reveal Himself to us.

"I can more easily tell you what this revelation is *not* than what it is. The tongues of men and angels need proper words to express the sweetness and glory with which the Son of God visits the soul that cannot rest without Him. This blessing is not to be described but enjoyed. It can be written not with ink, but only with the Spirit of the Living God, not on paper but in the fleshly tables of the heart.

"The revelation of Christ by which an unconverted man becomes a holy and happy possessor of the faith is a supernatural, spiritual, experimental manifestation of the spirit, power and love (and sometimes of the Person) of God, manifest in the flesh, whereby He is known and enjoyed in a manner which is altogether new. . . .

"This manifestation is given sooner or later in a higher or lower degree . . . to every sincere seeker, through one or more spiritual senses opened in his soul; it may be gradual or an instantaneous way that manifestation comes, according to God's good pleasure. As soon as the veil of unbelief covering the human heart is rent by the power of the Holy Spirit; as soon as the soul has struggled into a living belief in the Word of God; as soon as the door of faith is opened—the Lord Jesus Christ comes in and reveals Himself as being full of grace and truth. Only then is the tabernacle of God with man; His Kingdom come with power; righteousness, peace and joy in the Holy Spirit are spread through the newborn soul; eternal life has begun; heaven has come upon earth; the conscious heir of glory cries 'Abba Father'; and from blessed experience he witnesses that he has come to Mount Zion, the heavenly Jerusalem.

"If you desire to know the Lord in a more intimate way, you will need to use what means are available to you. The Agent or Author of every divine manifestation is the eternal God, one in three and three in one. The Father reveals His Son, the Lord Jesus Christ shows himself and the Holy Spirit freely testifies of Him. Nevertheless, the Scriptures—in general—attribute the wonder of Divine manifestations to the blessed Spirit. No man can experimentally say 'Jesus is Lord' but by the Holy Ghost. It is His peculiar office to convince the world of righteousness, by enabling us to know the Lord our Righteousness in a saving way. 'He shall glorify Me,' said Christ, 'for He shall take of Mine and show it unto you . . .' "[12]

True God or Idolatry

Joy Davidman

"The man who says, 'One God,' and does not care is an atheist at heart. The man who speaks of God and will not recognize the presence of God burning in his mind as Moses recognized him in the burning bush—that man is an atheist, though he speak with the tongues of men and of angels, and appear in his pew every Sunday, and make large contributions to the church. . . .

[12]John (of Madeley) Fletcher, *Christ Manifested* (1800), pp. 30–31, 52–53.

"For the beast gods have come creeping back. If we will not have the One, we must in the end accept the many after all. A man with nothing to worship is a man in a vacuum, and the false gods will rush in. . . . The false gods of today are things of the spirit, and as hard to pluck forth as it is hard for a man to pluck out his right eye. The beast in the heart is always the self."[13]

Christ Alone Overcomes the Tug of the Seen

Adolph Saphir

"What is this belief worth—this rational intellectual belief that God is Creator—a belief independent of Scripture and independent of the God of salvation revealed in Christ Jesus? Soon—thus the history of human thought shows us—this belief vanishes either before the lofty and alluring specula- tions of pantheism or the powerful and fascinating science of materialism.

"We find it difficult to look from earth, from things visible, from second causes to heaven, to spiritual and eternal realities, to the Lord, from whom comes every good and perfect gift. And as civilization advances, as men who have not the love of God in their hearts become more fully acquainted with the laws of nature, the tendency to materialism becomes stronger; and resting satisfied with the phenomenal and secondary causes and powers, men fail to rise above the inanimate and visible to the fatherly heart in heaven, whose omnipotent love and wisdom day by day, hour by hour, cherishes, rules and sustains all things."[14]

Virginia Stem Owens

"At present the scientific community is preparing to line up on entirely different issues. On the one hand are those who see matter as fundamen- tally dead and dumb inhabiting an equally dead void of space. Often they are the very ones intent on the possibilities of finding extraterrestrial life somewhere, out there, in space. The matter they see right here on earth of which they themselves are made they assume follows basic mechanical laws, completely passive under scientific investigation with no 'mind of its own.' Any mysterious goings-on observed in it they dismiss as mysti- cism and folderol.

"On the other hand are those scientists who have reason to suspect that matter itself is at some level sentient, informed with knowledge. In other worlds we are living in an at least potentially conscious cosmos. Those in this second group find themselves unprovided with ways of thinking about the cosmos except as they discover them in Eastern religions. . . .

"Only a full embrace of the Incarnation can open our eyes to its in- terpenetration of all being, its redemption of the whole cosmos which is the biblical claim. To see ourselves as separate and distinct from the physical world is our terrible inheritance from the Manichees. Such a heresy leads to the enormous excesses of our current technology."[15]

---

[13]Joy Davidman, *Smoke on the Mountain* (Philadelphia: Westminister Press), p. 23.
[14]Saphir, op. cit. p. 44.
[15]Virginia Stem Owens, *And the Trees Clap Their Hands* (Grand Rapids: Eerdmans, 1983), pp. ix-xi.

A Christian View of Matter

Thomas Merton

"Detachment from things does not mean setting up a contradiction between 'things' and 'God' as if God were another thing and as if His creatures were His rivals. We do not detach ourselves from things in order to attach ourselves to God, but rather that we become detached *from ourselves* in order to see and use all things in and for God. . . . There is no evil in anything created by God, nor can anything of His become an obstacle to our union with Him. The obstacle is our '*self*,' that is to say in the tenacious need to maintain our separate, external, egoistic will. It is when we refer all things to this outward and false 'self' that we alienate ourselves from reality and from God. It is then the false 'self' that is our God, and we love everything for the sake of this self. We use all things so to speak, for the worship of this idol which is our imaginary self. In so doing we pervert and corrupt things, or rather we turn our relationship to them into a corrupt and sinful relationship. . . . Those who try to escape from this situation by treating the good things of God as if they were evils are only confirming themselves in a terrible illusion. . . .

"It is not true that the saints and the great contemplatives never loved created things and had no understanding or appreciation of the world, with its sights and sounds and people living in it. They loved *everything* and *everyone*. . . . It was because those saints were absorbed in God that they were truly capable of seeing and appreciating created things and it was because they loved Him *alone* that they *alone* loved everybody."[16]

Virginia Stem Owens

"The task begins with answering one of those annoying questions science thought it had left behind: *how important is matter?* The Manichean contempt for matter that early infected the Church still plagues it today and indeed undermines all human endeavor. We continue to imagine we can exist as disembodied intelligences. The resurrection of the body has only the dimmest possible meaning for us. Such contempt for creation lays the groundwork for an unwitting alliance between religious spiritualizers (whether of the demythologizing or supposedly literalist school) and a science that would have us believe matter itself is dead and thus would strip everything 'merely' material of significance. Even, ultimately, ourselves.

"I declare that the prophet's figures of trees clapping their hands is a living reality and that Paul's image of living Christ's life is simultaneously symbol and fact. This is the reality of matter we have not dared to dream."[17]

A. E. Wilder-Smith

"The history of scientific progress in the past thirty years or so has demonstrated that purely mechanistic explanations of reality are usually

---

[16]Thomas Merton, "Everything That Is, Is Holy," *Seeds of Contemplation* (Greenwood, 1949), pp. 17–18.
[17]Owens, op. cit. pp. xii.

unsatisfactory in that they represent only a part or one side of the truth. . . . the answer to the problem of consciousness does not lie in the assumption that matter can mechanistically produce or even bear the phenomenon of thought or consciousness. In fact the evidence for the exact reverse is quite strong; matter itself was produced and is maintained by thought. [Or better] . . . thought is not the result of matter but matter is more probably the result of thought. . . . Matter is rather an end product, manifestation and function of mind. . . . Progressive thought is leading scientists to conceive of matter as being molded in a kind of thought matrix which upholds matter after having produced it, as the expression of mind and consciousness."[18]

Sir James Jeans

"Energy, the fundamental entity of the universe, had again to be treated as a mathematical abstraction—the constant of integration of a differential equation. The same concept implies of course that the final truth of a phenomenon resides in the mathematical description of it. . . . The making of models or pictures to explain mathematical formulae and the phenomenon they describe is not a step toward, but a step away from reality; it is like making graven images of a spirit."[19]

Alexander Whyte

"Our more thoughtful men of science in some of their profoundest speculations, try to penetrate to the true 'constitution' of the physical universe. . . . But to us . . . God is the ultimate analysis and the innermost essence, and the deepest root and the all-sustaining cause of all existence. The whole universality and immensity of things, created and uncreated is all one and the same mystery of Godliness. All created things—the most firm and stable—would instantly stagger and reel back and dissolve into their original nothingness and annihilation if Almighty God withheld His all-upholding hand from them for one moment. The pillars of the earth are His and it is He Who established the world on its foundations. From a grain of sand on the seashore up to all the endless systems of suns and stars in the heavens; from those creatures of God that are too small for the eye to see up to the choirs of Cherubim and Seraphim before the throne—to our ears they all unite and rejoice to sing—'In Him we live and move and have our being, for of Him and through Him and to Him are all things.' "[20]

Matter: Not a Manifestation of God

Owen Barfield

"Turn from an Attic chorus or a Platonic dialogue to say the 104th

---

[18]A.E. Wilder-Smith, *The Creation of Life: A Cybernetic Aproach to Evolution* (Wheaton, Ill.: Harold Shaw Publishers, 1970) p. 176.
[19]Sir James Jeans, *The Mysterious Universe*, pp. 150–151.
[20]Alexander Whyte, *With Mercy and Judgement* (London: Hodder and Stoughton), pp. 6–7.

Psalm and you are in a different climate of soul altogether. More than that—you are among different *representations*. . . . Here is not only no hint of mythology, but no real suggestion of manifestation. Everything proclaims the glory of God, but nothing represents Him. Nothing could be more beautiful and nothing could be less Platonic. . . . The Jew could rejoice in the appearances; but he was not curious about them. He was not interested in them. He was, above all, detached from them. . . . this detachment from knowledge arose in the case of the Jews, not so much from any want of mental alertness as from a positive objection to participation as such. . . . Participation and the experience of phenomena as representations go hand in hand; and the experience of representation as such is closely linked with the making of images.

"The children of Israel became a nation and began their history in the moment when Moses, in the very heart of the ancient Egyptian civilization, delivered to the them those Ten Commandments which include the unheard of injunction: 'Thou shalt not make unto thee any graven image or any likeness of anything that is in heaven above, or that is in earth beneath, or that is in the water under the earth.' That is perhaps the *unlikeliest* thing that ever happened. As far as we know, in every other nation at that time there prevailed unquestioned the participating consciousness which apprehends the phenomena as representations and naturally expresses itself in making images. . . . Everywhere throughout the world original participation was in full swing. For the Jews, from that moment on, original participation, and anything smacking of it became a deadly sin.[21]

George MacDonald

"*Things* are given to us—this body, first of things—that through them we may be trained both to independence and true possession of them. We must possess them; they must not possess us. Their use is to *mediate*—as shapes and manifestations in lower kind of the things that are unseen, the things that belong, not to the world of speech, but the world of silence, not to the world of showing, but the world of being, the world that cannot be shaken and must remain. These things unseen take form in the things of time and space—not that they may exist, for they exist in and from the eternal Godhead, but that their being may be known to those in training for the eternal; these things unseen the sons and daughters of God must possess. But instead of reaching out after them, they grasp at their forms, regard the things seen as the things to be possessed, fall in love with the bodies instead of the souls of them."[22]

Touched by Another World

A. W. Tozer

"One power of spirit, of any spirit (for I am talking about spirit now,

[21]Owen Barfield, *Saving the Appearances: A Study in Idolatry* (Harcourt Brace Janovich, 1965), pp. 107–109.
[22]George MacDonald, "Unspoken Sermons: The Hardness Of The Way," *Anthology*, C.S. Lewis, ed. (New York: Macmillan, 1986), p. 44.

not about the Holy Spirit) is its *ability to penetrate*. . . . Spirit can penetrate everything. Your body is made of matter, yet your spirit has penetrated your body completely. Spirit can penetrate spirit. It can penetrate personality—Oh if God's people could only learn that spirit can penetrate personality, that your personality is not an impenetrable substance but can be penetrated. A mind can be penetrated by thought, the air can be penetrated by light and material things and mental things and even spiritual things can be penetrated by spirit."[23]

Samuel Rutherford

"Jesus Christ came into my prison cell last night, and every stone flashed like a ruby."[24]

Sadhu Sundar Singh

"Sometimes without any tangible cause, one feels a sense of joy or pain which is a 'touch' from the spiritual world; that is from heaven or hell. These 'touches' are continually casting their shadows upon the hearts of men. Gradually this contact with one sphere or the other of the spiritual world becomes permanent. According to our good or our bad deeds and habits we come under the influence of one or the other and this tendency decides our destiny. So even in this world, the foundations of heaven and hell are being laid. When the soul leaves the body at death it enters that state for which it was prepared here on earth."[25]

Wilfrid Hannum

Two worlds are ours; tis only sin
Forbids us to descry
The mystic heaven and earth within
Plain as the sea and sky.
Thou who hast given me eyes to see
And love this sight so fair
Give me a heart to find out Thee
And read Thee everywhere[26]

---

[23]A.W. Tozer, *How to Be Filled With the Spirit* (Camp Hill, Penn.: Christian Publications), p. 4.
[24]Samuel Rutherford, *Letters*, ed. Frank Gaebelein. (Chicago: Moody Press, 1951).
[25]Sadhu Sundar Singh, *The Gospel of Sadhu Sundar Singh* (Allen Unwin), p. 193.
[26]Wilfred Hannum, *In the Things of My Father*, p. 117.

CHAPTER FOUR

COROLLARY THREE:
GOD IS GLORIOUS;
HE IS OF ULTIMATE VALUE

Scriptures

"And they saw the God of Israel: and there was under his feet as it were a paved work of a sapphire stone, and as it were the body of heaven in his clearness. And the sight of the glory of the Lord was like devouring fire on the top of the mount in the eyes of the children of Israel." (Ex. 24:10, 17)

"And he [Moses] said, I beseech thee, shew me thy glory. And he said, I will make all my goodness pass before thee, and I will proclaim the name of the Lord before thee. . . . And it shall come to pass, while my glory passeth by, that I will put thee in a clift of the rock, and will cover thee with my hand while I pass by . . . thou shalt see my back parts [afterglow]: but my face shall not be seen." (Ex. 33:18, 19, 22–23)

"Then a cloud covered the tent of the congregation, and the glory of the Lord filled the tabernacle. And Moses was not able to enter into the tent of the congregation, because the cloud abode thereon, and the glory of the Lord filled the tabernacle." (Ex. 40:34)

"For the Lord your God is God of gods, and Lord of lords, a great God, a mighty, and a terrible . . . (Deut. 10:17)

"That thou mayest fear this glorious and fearful name, the Lord thy God." (Deut. 28:58)

"He shined forth from mount Paran, and he came with ten thousands of saints. . . . There is none like unto the God of Jeshurun, who rideth upon the heaven in thy help, and in his excellency on the sky." (Deut. 33:2, 26)

"Shall not his excellency make you afraid? and his dread fall upon you?" (Job 13:11)

"God thundereth marvellously with his voice; great things doeth he, which we cannot comprehend . . . with God is terrible majesty." (Job 37:5, 22)

"The heavens declare the glory of God; and the firmament sheweth his handiwork." (Ps. 19:1)

"Who is this King of glory? The Lord strong and mighty, the Lord mighty in battle. Lift up your heads, O ye gates; even lift them up, ye everlasting doors; and the King of glory shall come in." (Ps. 24:8)

"Be still, and know that I am God: I will be exalted among the heathen, I will be exalted in the earth." (Ps. 46:10)

"Be thou exalted, O God, above the heavens; let thy glory be above all the earth." (Ps. 57:5)

"His name shall endure forever: his name shall be continued . . . and men shall be blessed in him: all nations shall call him blessed." (Ps. 72:17)

"Blessed be the Lord God, the God of Israel, who only doeth wondrous things. And blessed be his glorious name for ever: and let the whole earth be filled with His glory . . ." (Ps. 72:18–19)

"Let thy work appear unto thy servants, and thy glory unto their children. And let the beauty of the Lord our God be upon us: and establish thou the work of our hands upon us . . ." (Ps. 90:16–17)

"For the Lord is great, and greatly to be praised. . . . Honour and majesty are before him: strength and beauty are in his sanctuary." (Ps. 96:4, 6)

"O worship the Lord in the beauty of holiness: fear before him, all the earth." (Ps. 96:9)

"Enter into the rock, and hide thee in the dust, for fear of the Lord, and for the glory of his majesty." (Isa. 2:10)

"I saw also the Lord sitting upon a throne, high and lifted up, and his train filled the temple. . . . And one [seraphim] cried unto another, and said, Holy, holy, holy, is the Lord of hosts: the whole earth is full of his glory." (Isa. 6:1, 3)

"In that day shall the Lord of hosts be for a crown of glory, and for a diadem of beauty, unto the residue of his people." (Isa. 28:5)

"I am the Lord: that is my name; and my glory will I not give to another, neither my praise . . ." (Isa. 42:8)

"The Lord hath made bare his holy arm in the eyes of all the nations; and all the ends of the earth shall see the salvation of our God." (Isa. 52:10)

"But the Lord shall be unto thee an everlasting light, and thy God thy glory . . . the Lord shall be thine everlasting light." (Isa. 60:19–20)

"Then there came a voice from above the expanse over their heads as they stood with lowered wings. . . . High above on the throne was a figure like that of a man. I saw that from what appeared to be his waist up he looked like glowing metal, as if full of fire . . . brilliant light surrounded him. Like the appearance of a rainbow in the clouds on a rainy day, so was the radiance around him. . . . This was the appearance of the likeness of the glory of the Lord. When I saw it I fell facedown, and I heard the voice of one speaking." (Ezek. 1:25–28, NIV)

"His glory covered the heavens and his praise filled the earth. His splendor was like the sunrise; rays flashed from his hand, where his power was hidden." (Hab. 3:3–4, NIV)

"And suddenly there was with the angel a multitude of the heavenly host praising God, and saying, Glory to God in the highest, and on earth peace, good will toward men." (Luke 2:13–14)

. . . because that, when they knew God, they glorified him not as God, neither were thankful . . ." (Rom. 1:21)

"Who only hath immortality, dwelling in the light which no man can approach unto; whom no man hath seen, nor can see: to whom be honour and power everlasting." (1 Tim. 6:16)

"The temple was filled with smoke from the glory of God, and from his power." (Rev. 15:8)

His Value Is the Basis of Worship

"Stand up and bless the Lord your God for ever and ever: and blessed be thy glorious name, which is exalted above all blessing and praise." (Neh. 9:5)

"Give unto the Lord the glory due unto his name; worship the Lord in the beauty of holiness." (Ps. 29:2)

"Declare his glory among the heathen, his wonders among all people. For the Lord is great, and greatly to be praised: he is to be feared above all gods. . . . Honour and majesty are before him: strength and beauty are in his sanctuary. Give unto the Lord, O ye kindreds of the people, give unto the Lord glory and strength." (Ps. 96:3–4, 6–7; cf. 1 Chron. 16:24–25, 27–28)

"Give unto the Lord the glory due unto his name: bring an offering, and come into his courts . . ." (Ps. 96:8)

"Arise, shine; for thy light is come, and the glory of the Lord is risen upon thee. For, behold, the darkness shall cover the earth, and gross darkness the people: but the Lord shall arise upon thee, and his glory shall be seen upon thee. . . . They shall shew forth the praises of the Lord." (Isa. 60:1–2, 6)

"The kingdom of heaven is like unto treasure hid in a field; the which when a man hath found, he hideth, and for joy thereof goeth and selleth all that he hath, and buyeth that field. Again, the kingdom of heaven is like unto a merchant man, seeking goodly pearls: who, when he had found one pearl of great price, went and sold all that he had, and bought it." (Matt. 13:44–46)

"What is written in the law? how readest thou? And he answering said, Thou shalt love the Lord thy God with all thy heart, and with all thy soul, and with all thy strength, and with all thy mind; and thy neighbour as thyself. And he said unto him, Thou hast answered right: this do, and thou shalt live." (Luke 10:26–28)

"Of him, and through him, and to him, are all things: to whom be glory for ever." (Rom. 11:36)

"Unto him be glory in the church by Christ Jesus throughout all ages, world without end." (Eph. 3:21)

"Thou art worthy, O Lord, to receive glory and honour and power: for thou hast created all things, and for thy pleasure they are and were created." (Rev. 4:11)

His Value Is the Basis for All Living and Ministry

"Great is the Lord, and greatly to be praised. . . . I will speak of the glorious honour of thy majesty, and of thy wondrous works. . . . All thy works shall praise thee, O Lord; and thy saints shall bless thee. They shall speak of the glory of thy kingdom, and talk of thy power; to make known to the sons of men his mighty acts, and the glorious majesty of his kingdom." (Ps. 145:3, 5, 10–12)

"Every one that is called by my name: for I have created him for my glory, I have formed him; yea, I have made him. . . . This people have I formed for myself; they shall shew forth my praise." (Isa. 43:7, 21)

"The branch of my planting, the work of my hands, that I may be glorified." (Isa. 60:21)

"To the praise of the glory of his grace, wherein he hath made us accepted in the beloved . . . that we should be to the praise of his glory, who first trusted in Christ . . . the redemption of the purchased possession, unto the praise of his glory." (Eph. 1:6, 12, 14)

"For ye are bought with a price: therefore glorify God in your body, and in your spirit, which are God's." (1 Cor. 6:20)

"Whether therefore ye eat, or drink, or whatsoever ye do, do all to the glory of God." (1 Cor. 10:31)

"All the promises of God in him are yea, and in him Amen, unto the glory of God by us." (2 Cor. 1:20)

"That every tongue should confess that Jesus Christ is Lord, to the glory of God the Father." (Phil. 2:11)

"My God shall supply all your need according to his riches in glory by Christ Jesus." (Phil. 4:19)

He Is the True Future Focus of the Universe

"I saw in the night visions, and, behold, one like the Son of man came with the clouds of heaven, and came to the Ancient of days. . . . And there was given him dominion, and glory, and a kingdom, that all people, nations, and languages, should serve him: his dominion is an everlasting dominion, which shall not pass away, and his kingdom that which shall not be destroyed." (Dan. 7:13–14)

"And then shall appear the sign of the Son of man in heaven. . . . And they shall see the Son of man coming in the clouds of heaven with power and great glory." (Matt. 24:30)

"And the city had no need of the sun, neither of the moon, to shine in it: for the glory of God did lighten it, and the Lamb is the light thereof. And the nations of them which are saved shall walk in the light of it: and the kings of the earth do bring their glory and honour into it. And the gates of it shall not be shut at all by day: for there shall be no night there. And they shall bring the glory and honour of the nations into it." (Rev. 21:23–26)

Bible Word Study

Glory (Hebrew)

There are some general words in Hebrew used for honor and power:

hadar *(had-ar)*—A Chaldean word that means magnificence. The KJV translates it as "honour," or "majesty."[1]

hadar *(haw-dawr)*—Magnificence (i.e., ornament or splendour). Translated in the KJV as "beauty," "comeliness," "excellency," "glorious," "honour," "majesty."[2]

tiph'ereth *(tif-eh-reth)*—Ornament (abstract or concrete, literal or figuratively). Translated in the KJV as "beauty," "bravery," "comely," "fair," "honour," "majesty."[3]

But a special family of words is used especially of God:

---

[1] *Strong's* 1923.
[2] *Strong's* 1926.
[3] *Strong's* 8597.

kabed *(kaw-bade)*—To be heavy . . . in the good sense it means "numerous," "rich," "honorable."[4]

kabod *(kaw-bode)*—properly means "weight," but only figuratively in a good sense. Also "splendour" or "copiousness." Translated in the KJV as "glory," and "honour."[5]

The root, *kabed*, with its derivatives occurs 376 times in the Hebrew Bible. John Oswalt comments: "Over against the transience of human and earthly glory stands the unchanging beauty of the manifest God (Ps. 145:5). In this sense, the noun *kabod* takes on its most unusual and distinctive meaning. Forty-five times this form of the root relates to a *visible manifestation* of God and whenever the 'glory of God' is mentioned this usage must be taken account of. Its force is so compelling that it remolds the meaning of *doxa* from an opinion of men in the Greek classics to something absolutely objective in the LXX and NT."[6]

"*Kabod* was always used in a secular sense for 'honour.' Yet honour was not thought of as a purely ideal quality, but in accordance with the basic meaning, as something 'weighty' in man which gives him 'importance.' Thus *kabod* could be used for wealth, or for the position of honour conferred by material substance. . . . Even primarily *kabod* can denote what is weighty in the figurative sense, i.e., what is impressive to men, so that *kabod* approximates to an anthropological term. . . .

"If in relation to man *kabod* denotes that which makes him impressive and demands recognition . . . in relation to God it implies that which makes God impressive to man, the force of His self-manifestation. As everywhere attested in the OT, God is intrinsically invisible. Nevertheless, when He reveals Himself, or declares Himself . . . one may rightly speak of . . . a manifestation which makes on man a highly significant impression."[7]

Again Oswalt says: "The bulk of occurrences where God's glory is a visible manifestation have to do with the tabernacle (Ex. 16:10; 40:34; etc.) and with the temple in Ezekiel's vision of the exile and restoration (Ezek. 9:3). These manifestations are directly related to God's self-disclosure and his intent to dwell among men. As such they are commonly associated with his holiness. God wishes to dwell with men, to have his reality and his splendor known to them. But this is only possible when they take account of the stunning quality of his holiness and set out in faith and obedience to let that character be manifested in them (Num. 14:10; Isa. 6:3; Ezra. 10:11)."[8]

Kittel further explores the imagery of a thunderstorm used in such

[4]*Strong's* 3513.
[5]*Strong's* 3519.
[6]*Theological Wordbook of the Old Testament*, Laird R. Harris, ed. (Chicago: Moody Press, 1980), vol. 1, p. 427.
[7]*Theological Dictionary of the New Testament*, Gerhard Kittel, ed., Geoffrey W. Bromiley, trans. (Grand Rapids: Wm. B. Eerdmans Publishing Company, 1964), vol. 2, pp. 238–239.
[8]*Theological Wordbook of the Old Testament*, op. cit. vol. 1, p. 427.

scriptures as Psalms 97 and 29. There are clouds, lightnings, thunder, fire, and the hills melt "like wax." He says, "It is striking that the basic thought of weight is no longer present where there is reference to [this 'glory']. Hence it is not impossible that *kabod* was used to define that which is intrinsically impressive in the being of God."[9]

Glory (Greek)

doxa *(dox-ah)*—Glory (as very apparent). Has a wide application (literally, figuratively, objectively, or subjectively). Translated in the KJV as "radiance," "dignity," "honour," "praise," "worship."[10] Used 168 times in the New Testament.

Doxa is a Greek word radically changed by biblical usage. It originally meant an opinion, conjecture or an estimate ranging from the "person or thing that I am prepared to defend" to the "evaluation placed on me by others." The noun in secular Greek accordingly meant "expectation, view, opinion, conjecture, repute, praise, fame."[11]

While it is used in the Septuagint for the idea of pomp, power and earthly majesty (Isa. 17:4; 35:2; Hag. 2:3), above all *doxa* is used of God's power and glory (Ps. 24:7ff.; 29:3; Isa. 42:8). The essential key idea is appearance or "manifestation of a person, with special stress on the impression this creates on others."[12]

"The subjective sense [in non-biblical Greek] can be applied in many ways. It may imply 'expectation' . . . but it may well equally imply the 'opinion' or 'view which I represent.' . . . In this sense the term becomes a philosophical catchword for a 'philisophical opinion,' whether sound or unsound, true or false. . . . Counterparts are insight and knowledge. . . . It stands midway between knowledge and certainty. . . . From this sense of philosophical opinion it comes to be used for a 'philosophical tenet.'"[13]

"Even a cursory survey of the NT reveals a totally different picture. The old meaning 'opinion' has disappeared completely. There is not a single example in either the NT or the post-apostolic fathers. . . . There has been added the meaning 'radiance,' 'glory' which is not found in secular Greek. . . . *Doxa* can also mean 'reflection' in the sense of 'image' *eikon*: man is the *doxa theo* and woman the *doxa anthropos* (1 Cor. 11:7)."[14]

The word is used in the NT, however, "in a sense for which there is no Greek analogy whatever and of which there is only an isolated example in Philo. That is to say, it denotes 'divine and heavenly radiance,' the 'loftiness and majesty' of God, and even 'the being of God' and His world." This new significance came from the concepts and influence of the Old Testament *kabod*.[15]

---

[9]*Theological Dictionary of the New Testament*, op. cit. vol. 2, p. 239.

[10]*Strong's* 1391.

[11]Sverre Aalen, *The New International Dictionary of New Testament Theology*, Colin Brown, ed. (Grand Rapids: Zondervan Publishing House, 1971), vol. 2, p. 44.

[12]Ibid. p. 45.

[13]*Theological Dictionary of the New Testament*, vol. 2, p. 234.

[14]Ibid. p. 237.

[15]Ibid. p. 237.

Unlike the Hebrew concept of glory (which focuses not so much on God in His essential *nature* but on the luminous *manifestation* of His Person, His glorious revelation of himself) *doxa* also means the *divine reality*, or manner of existence.

Through salvation, man is able to share in this reality (John 17:22; Rom. 8:30; 2 Cor. 3:18) or will do so (Rom. 8:17–18, 21; 1 Cor. 2:7; Phil. 3:21; 1 Thess. 2:12; Heb. 2:10; 1 Pet. 5:1, 4, 10). The Christian hope is the "hope of glory" (Col. 1:27; cf. Eph. 1:18; 2 Thess. 2:14; 2 Tim. 2:10).[16]

Doxa is used "of the nature and acts of God in self-manifestation, i.e., what He essentially is and does, as exhibited in whatever way He reveals Himself in these respects, and particularly in the person of Christ, in whom essentially His glory has ever shone forth and ever will do."[17]

E. W. Bullinger comments that in secular Greek it "denotes the recognition which anyone finds, or which belongs to him, renown (differing from honour as recognition does from estimation). Then from the meaning *seeming* comes appearance, form, aspect, viz., that appearance of a person or thing which attracts attention or commands recognition, looks like something, equivalent therefore to splendour, brilliance, glory.

"In this sense *doxa* denotes, the appearance of glory attracting the gaze, manifestation of glory (not the person or thing itself whose glorious appearance attracts attention, but the appearance which attracts attention), splendour, glory, brightness.

"The *doxa* of God is, as explained by Philo, the unfolded fulness of the Divine *dunamis* (manifested powers); and coincides with His self-revelation (Ex. 33:18–19). . . . Hence as it comprises all that God is for us for our good, the fulness of all that is good in Him, so is it the form in which He reveals himself in the economy of salvation, and becomes the means (2 Pet. 1:3), and the goal of the Christian vocation and hope (1 Thess. 2:12; 1 Pet. 5:10), for its disclosure belongs to the future and the close of the history of redemption."[18]

It appears in the Old Covenant (2 Cor. 3:7–11), in believers (John 17:22; 2 Cor. 3:18; Eph. 1:18; 3:16; Col. 1:11), and "above all in Christ and his work of salvation (Matt. 17:2–5; Mark 9:2–7; Luke 9:29–35; John 1:14; 2:11; 2 Cor. 4:4, 6). . . . Just as in the OT, glory is partly linked with God's action (Rom. 6:4) and is partly an attribute of His being . . . it suggests something which radiates from the one who has it, leaving an impression behind."[19]

doxazo (*dox-ad-zo*)—To render or esteem glorious (in a wide application). Used 62 times in the KJV as "make glorious," "glorify," "full of glory," "honour," "magnify."[20]

"To think, be of opinion, hold any one for anything; in later Greek

[16]Aalen, op. cit. pp. 45–46.
[17]W.E. Vine, *The Expanded Vine's Expository Dictionary of New Testament Words*, John R. Kohlenberger III, ed. (Minneapolis, Minn.: Bethany House Publishers, 1984), p. 483.
[18]Ethelbert W. Bullinger, *A Critical Lexicon and Concordance to the English and Greek New Testament* (Grand Rapids: Zondervan Publishing House, 1975), p. 323.
[19]Aalen, op. cit. pp. 44, 46–47.
[20]*Strong's* 1392.

writers, to recognize, honour, praise; in the LXX, to invest with dignity, make any one important, to cause him honour by putting him into an honourable position. Hence the NT meanings are, (1) to recognize, honour, praise; (2) to bring to honour, make glorious, glorify, but strictly to give any one importance. (When predicated of Christ it means that His innate glory is made manifest and brought to light.)"[21]

Questions and Answers

Q: *What is the glory of God?*
A: His glory is who He is, what He does and how He shows himself. It is His intrinsic uncreated divine nature, His matchless character and His awesome revelation in holiness and power to His creation. As Bengel says, "His glory is Divinity manifest."

Q: *How can a mere creature give glory to God?*
A: Man and the creation were originally intended to be living demonstrations of God's greatness and goodness (Ps. 96:8; 66:2). When the creation returns to its original purpose, it honors God in the same way that an artist is honored by his classic creation or in the way an outstanding child honors a wise and loving parent.

Q: *Why will God not share His glory with man* (Isa. 42:8)?
A: God's glory is the value of what He is—and He is of ultimate worth and supreme importance. This, of course, is not true of any of the rest of His creation, and to "take glory" that belongs by intrinsic right to God alone is essentially to play God. (Jer. 9:23–25; Rom. 1:23).

Q: *What does it mean for me to be a "partaker of His glory" (1 Pet. 5:1) if God doesn't share His glory with anyone?*
A: Although God cannot share the claim to His intrinsic worth with any creature, He longs to share the joy of what He is with others. To be invited into the presence of a king is to be honored by that king; to be invited into the presence of the King of all kings is to be honored indeed. To have the privilege of the companionship of God is to be a partaker of His glory.

Q: *What does it mean to "fall short of the glory of God" (Rom. 3:23)?*
A: Falling short is to miss most of what God designed us to be: a people and a creation that bring Him the honor He deserves by our lives and relationships with Him and with each other. Man as a rebel ruins his God-given glory.

Q: *God's wanting everyone to love Him and put Him first hardly sounds like the essence of unselfishness. Isn't that purely egocentric?*
A: God wants everyone to live according to ultimate intelligence and truth. The truth is this: God wholly *deserves* to be first in all things.

---

[21]Bullinger, op. cit. p. 322.

To live in accord with this reality is not only the ultimate good, but absolute wisdom. Put simply: if we don't put God first, we are not only selfish, but stupid.

Q: *Does God need praise from people?*

A: No, God has no intrinsic or extrinsic needs; He is happy in himself and knows fully who He is. Nevertheless, receiving praise from His creation is not only what He deserves, but it is beneficial to His creature; for in properly honoring God by our thoughts, our lives, and our words, we likewise recognize and take our proper place in His universe and add to the total happiness in it.

Q: *Why does the Bible describe glory as if it were light?*

A: Light in Scripture is not only that which reveals, illumines, and banishes darkness; it also symbolizes that which is most wise, true, and pure. Light is radiant, not absorbent; energy, not matter; tangible, though itself formless. As God must show himself in some way to mankind, light-glory becomes His most common appearance (Ex. 24:16–18; 29:43; 40:34ff.; 1 Kings 8:10ff.; 2 Chron. 7:1ff.; Ezek. 1:28; 3:12ff.; Acts 9:3).

Q: *How do we give glory to God?*

A: We treat Him the way He deserves to be treated; speak to (and of) Him with the full honor He deserves; and live our lives under His wise and wonderful watching eyes. Christians are to receive each other "for the glory of God" (Rom. 15:7) and to speak and minister "that God in all things may be glorified through Jesus Christ" (1 Pet. 4:11). Our bodies must be kept pure for His glory (1 Cor. 6:20; Phil. 1:20); "whether we eat or drink or whatsoever we do" we are to "do all to the glory of God" (1 Cor. 10:31).

Q: *How did Jesus glorify His Father?*

A: He did what no man ever did: in suffering or joy, conflict or conquest, victory or agony, He brought honor to His Father in all that He ever said and did. He shared His Father's glory before He came to earth (John 17:5, 24). He was the fulfillment of prophecy in His birth—"the glory of the Lord shall be revealed; and all flesh shall see it together" (Isa. 40:5; see also Isa. 4:5; 11:10; 24:23) and "the Word was made flesh and dwelt among us; and we beheld His glory . . ." (John 1:14).

His own personal glory of a perfect, pure and courageous life directed total honor to the Father—"I have glorified thee on the earth: I have finished the work which thou gavest me to do" (John 17:4). Even in His betrayal, suffering, and death He showed the greatness and the grandeur of God (John 12:23; Luke 9:31; John 7:39; 12:16; 13:31ff.; 17:1, 4). He went to the cross as a King to his coronation; and with death itself the astonished victim, at the resurrection He took up again the glory He had laid aside in His incarnation. Raised from the dead by His Father's glory (Rom. 6:4), restored to glory (1 Pet. 1:21), received in glory (1 Tim. 3:16), He now reigns forever in glory at His Father's right hand (Acts 7:55ff.; 2:33; 3:13; 3:21; 1 Cor. 15:27; Eph. 1:20; Phil 2:9ff.; Heb. 1:3ff.).[1]

Q: *What is this "glorious body" like Christ's* (Phil. 3:21)?
A: Redeemed mankind will not only have characters like their King (1 John 3:2); we will have transfigured bodies to match (1 Cor. 15:42ff.). We will once again in Him be "crowned with glory and honor" (Ps. 8:5ff.) and shine like stars in the heavens (Dan. 12:3), sharing in the riches of Christ our King (Eph. 1:18; Rom. 9:23).

Analysis and Discussion

The *glory* of God—what a wonderful and mysterious word! It is not shared with man, yet we are promised that one day we shall partake of it. It is a glory that both shone around shepherds to announce Christ's birth and terrified soldiers to declare His resurrection. It was hidden with Him before the world was, signifies God's present presence and power, and surrounds our understanding of His second coming. Moses cried out to see it, but no man can behold it and live. The glory of God . . . what does it mean?

As we can see from Bible study words like *kabod* and *doxa*, this awesome characteristic of God seems to be at least a summary of two great descriptive truths about Him: what He *is* (His metaphysical nature), and what He *does* (His moral nature). God's glory speaks of what He is like in both His infinitely wonderful being and also in His absolute moral perfection.

G. D. Watson writes, "We must remember that God has two kinds of glory; first the glory that is *inherent* inside the Divine nature, and then the glory that is *external* to God in His creation of worlds and creatures. The glory in the divine nature consists in His natural perfection, in His eternity, His sanctity, the communion of the three divine Persons and the infinite joy which He has in himself. The external glory of God consists in the magnitude, the variety and the splendor of the created worlds, and the various ranks of angels, men and lower orders of sentient creatures. Added to this is the glory which He obtains by redeeming fallen men, by the systems of grace, providence, of rewards and punishments, of the application of His mercy, justice to His creatures and the praises, love and the worship that are rendered back to Him from His creatures."[1]

Metaphysical Nature

God's *being* is the *substance* of this glory. Remember the "Shekinah Glory" in the pillar of cloud and the Holy of Holies? "The glory of the

---

[1]M.R. Gordon, *The Zondervan Pictorial Encyclopedia of the Bible*, Merrill Tenney, ed. (Grand Rapids: Zondervan Pub. House, 1976), vol. 2, p. 734.
[1]G.D. Watson, *Our Own God* (Schmul Reprints).

Lord" that "appeared in the cloud" (Ex. 16:10) was some visible manifestation of the being of God—a brightness or a splendor. Moses, one of the greatest lovers of God in the Old Testament and a real adventurer into His presence, prayed: "Now therefore, I pray thee, if I have found grace in thy sight, show me now thy way, that I may know Thee, that I might find grace in Thy sight . . . I beseech Thee, show me Thy glory" (Ex. 33:13–23; 34:5–8).

That brief contact made Moses himself an object of awe and wonder to Israel (Ex. 34:29–30). The same tangible manifestation happened to the shepherds in Bethlehem: "And, lo, the angel of the Lord came upon them, and the glory of the Lord shone round about them: and they were sore afraid" (Luke 2:9). Saul, struck by this same divine radiance, became the Apostle Paul and later recorded: "I could not see for the glory of that light . . ." (Acts 22:11).

God's glory can be a tangible, physically manifested demonstration of light and terrible power, a place where He reveals himself in a *divine "radiation zone"* that can literally affect and transform created objects of matter and energy. Isaiah saw the seraphim crying, " 'Holy, Holy, Holy is the Lord of hosts: the whole earth is full of His glory.' And the posts of the door moved at the voice of him that cried, and the house was filled with smoke" (Isa. 6:3–4).

Only in this limited metaphysical way can we and the rest of creation really "partake of His glory." Other similar scriptures refer to God's manifested presence giving great value to the Church, or to our transformed future physical beings, or that this glory will be finally visible within the whole re-creation. Paul says the Lord Jesus will "change our vile body, that it may be fashioned like unto his glorious body, according to the working whereby he is able even to subdue all things unto himself" (Phil. 3:21).

We are told that eventually the creation will be "delivered from the bondage of corruption into the glorious liberty of the children of God" (Rom. 8:21). This may refer to its present enslavement to entropy and decay, which will be ultimately broken by the power of Christ. John on Patmos records in Rev. 21:10–12: "And showed me that great city, the holy Jerusalem, descending out of heaven from God, having the glory of God: and her light was like unto a stone most precious, even like a jasper stone, clear as crystal. (Jasper is a translucent stone of various colors, especially that of fire.)

Moral Character

The second aspect of God's glory is His *worth* as an infinitely lovely, pure, and holy person, one who made man in a finite, miniature image to himself. If there is a fundamental reason why He will not share His glory with another, it would be this: all ultimate power, honor, worth, and value belong to God (Ps. 62:11; Isa. 42:8; Ezek. 31:18). Yet Scripture suggests that we shall also participate or share in this honor paid to God in some real way, not by our own personal merit or worthiness of course, but by being linked forever by grace and love with the honor due to Christ as Head of the Church.

Paul prayed that the "Father of glory" would give the church at Ephesus "the spirit of wisdom and revelation in the knowledge of him," that the eyes of their understanding being enlightened, they might know what was the "hope of his calling," and that they would understand what were "the riches of the glory of his inheritance in the saints" (Eph. 1:17–18).

God's revealed glory, the progressive revelation to believers of His radiantly pure and lovely character, is the secret of all Christian sanctification and growth: "But we all, with open face beholding as in a glass the glory of the Lord, are changed into the same image from glory to glory, even as by the Spirit of the Lord" (2 Cor. 3:18). This means moral growth and change, not alteration into God's substance.

"In a word," said George MacDonald, "there is no way of thought or action which we count admirable in man in which God is not altogether adorable. There is no loveliness, nothing that makes man dear to his fellowman that is not in God, only it is infinitely better in God."[2]

Again, we are partakers, but not originators of this glory, "For God . . . hath shined in our hearts, to give the light of the knowledge of the glory of God in the face of Jesus Christ. But we have this treasure in earthen vessels, that the excellency of the power may be of God, and not of us" (2 Cor. 4:6–7).

What is the *essence* of the tragedy of sin and rebellion? Why is sin so bad and human disobedience so disappointing to God? Because He had in His heart so much to share with us; He carried a "pressure of love" when He came unto His own, and His own did not receive Him (John 1:9–11). Man's awful failure is that we have all, without exception, become active participants in a world that has broken off friendship with this ultimately lovely Person: "All have sinned, and come short [fallen, failed] of the glory of God" (Rom. 3:23). All are "without excuse" because "when they knew God," they did not give Him the glory as God, "neither were thankful . . . changed the glory of the uncorruptible God into an image made like to corruptible man" (Rom. 1:20–23).

And yet there is an even more basic and wonderful truth conveyed by the biblical image of glory. It has to do with the reason why we think anything ought to be sought after or paid devotion; what we think of when we say "worthwhile." It has to do with the whole idea of *value*, of prizing and giving our lives to one end rather than another. It has to do with the basis of worth.

The Idea of Worth

Why do you choose what you do? What is there about a person or a thing that makes us prefer it above another? When we say "It was *worth* it!" on what basis do we make our decision? Whether we have ever se-

---

[2]George MacDonald, *Creation in Christ*, Rolland Hein, ed. (Wheaton, Ill.: Harold Shaw Publishers, 1976).

riously thought about it or not, and whatever we assume it is, we use our idea of worth as the basis for every decision, small or great, that we ever make in life. In earthly society we attach value to people and things that show properties such as:

- *Beauty*—We value a sense of fitness, perfection, loveliness, worthwhileness, attractiveness, and form.
- *Permanence*—We all like things to last. Precious metals and gems communicate this.
- *Luminosity*—We are fascinated with the interplay of light and color.
- *Uniqueness*—We seek the one-of-a-kind because an original is worth more.
- *Rarity*—Our society attaches value to something scarce or uncommon, and its worth usually increases like the world's rarest—and most valuable—stamp, the *Penny Magenta*, is the only surviving copy of that stamp known to exist.
- *Power*—Man covets anything that provides a source of energy or power in a world with constant energy needs.

These are at least some of the things we look for in what we call *treasures* on earth. But this is a serious, all-consuming question to pose to everyone: *Why should we seek what we seek?* People have given their lives for things that represent in their minds and hearts the fulfillment of just one of these attributes of worth. Right or wrong, individuals have sacrificed or struggled, armies have marched, nations have competed or gone to war, people have risked death and dishonor to obtain or defend a person or property. Those who have done this voluntarily would have only one answer when asked why they did it: they were convinced it was "worth it."

Try to imagine the impossible: think of all the lovely things you have ever seen, all the most wonderful times and places and people you have ever known; and imagine you could contain *all* of that beauty and loveliness, concentrate and distill all those experiences of awe and wonder and happiness in your life into one moment. It would be so painfully lovely, so breath-takingly beautiful that you could not bear for it to go on any more or you would die, nor could you bear having it cease for the same reason. What would you give to be part, even for a moment, of something so utterly wonderful as that, so intensely joyful?

Take any of the treasures we value highly, take them all to their ultimate essence. We have not yet begun to approach the truth; power beyond conception, radiance of inconceivable splendor and brightness, stability beyond imagination, a one-of-a-kind and absolutely uncommon Reality.

Paul knew it. He declared, "But we speak the wisdom of God in a mystery, even the hidden wisdom, which God ordained before the world unto our glory: which none of the princes of this world knew: for had they known it, they would not have crucified the Lord of glory. But as it is written, eye hath not seen, nor ear heard, neither have entered into the heart of man, the things which God hath prepared for them that love him" (1 Cor. 2:7–9).

C. S. Lewis noted: "We usually notice . . . just as the moment of vision dies away, as the music ends or the landscape loses its celestial light. For just a few moments we had the illusion of belonging to that world. Now we wake to find that there is no such thing. We have been mere spectators. Beauty has smiled, but not to welcome us; her face was turned in our direction, but not to see us. We have not been accepted, welcomed, or taken into the dance. . . .

"It is not the physical objects . . . but that indescribable something of which they become for a moment, the messengers . . . We want something else, we can hardly put in words; to be united with the beauty we see, to pass into it, to receive it into ourselves, to bathe in it, to become part of it . . . someday, God willing, we shall get in.

"The faint, far-off results of those energies which God's creative rapture implanted in matter when He made the worlds are what we now call physical pleasures; and even thus filtered, they are too much for our present management. What would it be like to taste at the fountain-head of that stream of which even these lower reaches proves so intoxicating? Yet that, I believe, is what lies before us."[3]

The mystics, the God-lovers, those people raptured by His presence, all wrote like this. Some may say they seemed too subjective, too pietistic, too other-worldly, too "heavenly-minded to be of any earthly good." But it is debateable whether we can ever get too heavenly-minded. Men and women who truly live in the heavenlies are building for a kingdom that never passes away. Perhaps their language is not too extravagant but, rather, our vision is too small.

Historical Discussion

Two men please God; he who loves Him with all his heart because He knows Him; he who seeks Him with all his heart because he knows Him not.

Power is honored by submission; merit, by respect; and beauty, by admiration. In God the three are to be honored by worship.[1]

Ivan Panin

God Himself Our Goal

F. B. Meyer

"The life of fellowship with God cannot be built up in a day. It begins with the habitual reference of all to Him, hour by hour as Moses did. . . . But it moves on to more and longer periods of communion. . . . Ah, what patterns are seen in the Mount! What cries are uttered there! What injunctions are received there! Alas for us that we remove so far away from

[3]C.S. Lewis, *The Weight of Glory* (Grand Rapids: Eerdmans, 1973), pp. 8–13.
[1]Ivan Panin, *The Writings of Ivan Panin*, pp. 27, 29.

it, or at best are admitted to stand only with the elders and see paved work of sapphire beneath God's feet. Oh for the closer access, the nearer view, the more intimate face to face intercourse, such as is open still to the friends of God!"[2]

A. W. Tozer

"In this hour of all-but-universal darkness one cheering gleam appears; within the fold of conservative Christianity there are to be found increasing numbers of persons whose religious lives are marked by a growing hunger after God himself. They are eager for spiritual realities and will not be put off with words, nor will they be content with correct 'interpretations' of truth. They are athirst for God, and they will not be satisfied till they have drunk deep at the Fountain of living water."[3]

Alexander MacClaren

"And is not the very essence and innermost secret of the religious life this: that the heart turns away from earthly things and deliberately accepts God as its supreme good and only portion? . . . There must be first of all a fixed, deliberate, intelligent conviction lying at the foundation of my life that God is best and that He and He only is my true delight and desire. . . . And remember that nothing less than this is Christianity; the conviction that the world is second and not first; that God is best, love is best, truth is best, knowledge of Him is best; likeness to Him is best; and the willingness to surrender it all if it comes in contest with His supreme sweetness. He that turns his back upon the earth by reason of the drawing power of the glory that excelleth, is a Christian. The Christianity that only trusts to Christ for deliverance from the punishment of sin and so makes faith a kind of fire insurance is a very poor affair. We need the lesson pealed in our ears as much as any generation has ever done: 'Ye cannot serve God and mammon.' A man's real working religion consists in his loving God most and counting His love the sweetest of all things."[4]

Vance Havner

"There ought to be in every child of God a sense of surprise, a glad expectancy. This is his Father's world and anything can happen. We live on a miracle level and faith is not believing that God *can*, but that He *will* do wonderful things. . . . We get used to being Christians; we take it for granted, and we lose the wonder. . . . Once we stood amazed in the presence of Jesus the Nazarene; now we want to sit amused. Once we were edified; now we must be entertained. It is all work and no wonder."[5]

---

[2]F.B. Meyer, *Friendship With God: Moses* (London: Morgan and Scott), p. 121.

[3]A.W. Tozer, *The Pursuit of God* (Camp Hill, Penn.: Christian Publications Inc., 1982), p. 7.

[4]Alexander MacClaren, "Man's True Treasure in God," *A Year's Ministry* (1903), pp. 205, 211.

[5]Vance Havner, *Have You Lost the Wonder?* (Old Tappan, N.J.: Fleming H. Revell Co., 1969), p. 93.

Christ Himself Is Wonderful

Charles Finney

" 'His Name shall be called *Wonderful*.' No inward or audible exclamation is more common to me of late years . . . When contemplating the nature, character, the offices, the relations, the salvation of Christ, I find myself often mentally and frequently [verbally] exclaiming *wonderful*! My soul is filled with wonder, love and praise as I am led by the Holy Spirit to apprehend Christ . . . I am more and more 'astonished at the doctrine of the Lord' and at the Lord himself from year to year. I have come to the conclusion that there is no end to this, either in time or eternity. He will, no doubt, to all eternity continue to make discoveries of himself to His intelligent creatures, that shall cause them to exclaim 'wonderful!' . . . Look steadfastly at Him, as He is revealed through the Gospel by the Holy Spirit, at any time and place, in any of His works and ways, and the soul will instantly exclaim, *wonderful!*"[6]

The Ultimate Study

Father John Sergieff

"Thou hast opened to me all the riches of faith and of nature and of the human mind. I have studied the laws that regulate the mind of man in its pursuit of truth and the growth and the beauty of the languages of men. I have penetrated with some depth into the mysteries of nature, into her laws . . . I know something of the wonderful history of our own earth. I have acquainted myself with different peoples; with its celebrated men and with their great achievements. I have spent no little time and strength in the study of myself also, and of Thee, and of the way I must take to know Thee and to come to Thee. And I hope still to learn much more of all that in the years to come. But, with all that, neither my mind nor my heart is satisfied; no, nor ever will be. My mind still hungers, my heart still hungers and thirsts and cries: 'Give, give'. . . . I shall be satisfied only when I awake with Thy likeness and when the Lamb leads me to living fountains of water. For He says to me and I believe Him: 'The water that I shall give you, shall be in you a well of water springing up into everlasting life.' "[7]

God Alone Satisfies

Santa Teresa

"The soul has her own ways of understanding, and of finding in herself by certain signs and great conjectures whether she really loves His Divine Majesty or not. Her love is full of high impulses, and longings to see and

---

[6]Charles G. Finney, *Sanctification*, W.E. Allen, ed. (Fort Washington, Penn.: Christian Literature Crusade, 1963), p. 88.
[7]Alexander Whyte, *Father John of the Greek Church: An Appreciation* (Olipant, Arduson, and Ferrur, 1898).

be with and to be like God. All else tires and wearies out the soul. The best of created things disappoint and torment. . . . God alone satisfies the soul, till it is impossible to dissemble or mistake such love. When once I came to see the great beauty of our Lord, it turned all other comeliness to corruption in me. My heart could rest on nothing and on no one but himself. When anything else would enter my heart, I had only to turn my eyes for a moment in upon that Supreme Beauty that was graven within me. . . . What a difference there is between the love of the Creator and the love of the creature! May His Divine Majesty . . . let us see and taste and understand something of this before He takes us out of this prison-house life. It will be a magnificent comfort in the hour of death to know we are on our way to be judged by Him whom we have loved above all things. We are not going to a strange country; it is His country; it is He whom we love and who loves us."[8]

A. W. Tozer

"In the midst of this great chill there are some, I rejoice to acknowledge, who will not be content with shallow logic. They will admit the force of the argument, and then turn away with tears to hunt some lonely place and pray 'O God, show me Thy glory.' They want to taste, to touch with their hearts, to see with their inner eyes the wonder that is God."[9]

Love Without End

George Fox

Fox, founder of the Quakers, was a man of vision beyond his time. After his conversion, he set his heart to seek the glory of God and noted in his diary: "I could have wept night and day with tears of joy to the Lord in humility and brokenness of heart. I saw into that which was without end, and things which cannot be uttered, and of the greatness and infiniteness of the love of God which cannot be expressed by words. For I had been brought through the very ocean of darkness and death, and through and over the power of Satan by the eternal glorious power of Christ; even through that darkness was I brought which covered up all the world, and which chained down all and shut up all in death."[10]

David Brainerd

Brainerd, like Fox, was also a young man consumed by love for Christ. In his journal he wrote that the Lord "should be God over all for ever and ever. My soul was so captivated and delighted with the excellency, loveliness, greatness and other perfections of God, that I was even swallowed up in Him. At least to that degree that I had no thought (as I remember)

[8]Whyte, Alexander, *Santa Teresa: An Appreciation* (Olipant, Arduson, and Ferrur, 1898), pp. 51–52.
[9]A.W. Tozer, *The Pursuit of God* (Camp Hill, Penn.: Christian Publications Inc., 1982), p. 17.
[10]George Fox, *The Journal of George Fox*, p. 12.

at first, about my own salvation, and scarce reflected there was such a creature as I. Thus God, I trust, brought me to a hearty disposition to exalt Him and set Him on the throne, and principally and ultimately to aim at His honor and glory, as King of the Universe.

"One convert of the revival was captured by the same glory that had so overwhelmed Brainerd: "While he was musing in this manner, he saw, he said 'with his heart' (a common phrase among them) something that was unspeakably good and lovely, and what he had never seen before; and this stole away his heart, whether he would or no, he did not, he said, know what it was he saw. He did not say 'This is Jesus Christ'; but it was such glory and beauty as he had never seen before. He did not now give away his heart as he had formerly intended and attempted to do, but it went away of itself after that glory he then discovered."[11]

Source of True Genius

A. W. Tozer

"Every one of us has had experiences which we have not been able to explain: a sudden sense of loneliness, or a feeling of wonder or awe in the face of universal vastness. Or we have had a fleeting visitation of light from some other sun, giving us in a quick flash an assurance that we are from another world, that our origins are divine. . . . Explain such things as we will, I think we have not been fair to the facts until we allow at least the possibility that such experiences may arise from the presence of God in the world and His persistent effort to communicate with mankind. . . . It is my own belief (and here I shall not feel bad if no one follows me) that every good and beautiful thing which man has produced in the world has been the result of his faulty and sin-blocked response to the creative Voice sounding over the earth. The moral philosophers who dreamed their high dreams of virtue; the religious thinkers who speculated about God and immortality, the poets and artists who created out of common stuff pure and lasting beauty . . . it is not enough to say simply, 'It was genius.' What then is genius? Could it be that a genius is haunted by the Speaking Voice, laboring and striving like one possessed to achieve ends which he only vaguely understands?"[12]

The Passion and Purity of Glory

John Henry Jowett

"If the Church would be pure, the Church must be passionate. Why, the very heart of the word 'pure' is suggestive of fire. It is significant of an end which has been reached through the ministry of flame. You cannot have purity without burning; you cannot have holiness without the baptism of fire. Our fathers steeped their souls in meditation. They appointed

---

[11]David Brainerd, *Journal of David Brainerd*, Jonathan Edwards, ed. (Chicago: Moody Press), pp. 30–32, 188.
[12]Tozer, op. cit. pp. 78–79.

long seasons for the contemplation of God in Christ. And as they mused the fire burned. Passion was born of thought. What passion? The passion which Faber so beautifully describes as the desire which purifies man and glorifies God:

> Nought honors God like the thirst of desire,
> Nor possesses the heart so completely with Him
> For it burns the world out with the swift ease of fire
> And fills the life with good works till it runs o'er the brim.

"The Church must give herself time to kindle and pray. We must give ourselves time for visions if we would worthily accomplish our tasks. Let us muse upon the King in His beauty, let us commune more with His loveliness, let us dwell more in the secret place, and the unspeakable glory of His countenance shall create within us that enthusiastic passion which shall be to us our baptism of fire, a fire in which everything unchristian shall be utterly consumed away."[13]

Living for the Glory of God

Chrysostom

"Let all things which you undertake and accomplish have this root and foundation; namely thus tend to the glory of God and let no action of yours fail to have this foundation. . . . In this brief text he has gathered together our whole life . . . enclosed our existence in a single word: *all*. He desires that we never perform any act of virtue with an eye to human glory.

" 'Let your light so shine before men that they may see your good works and glorify your Father which is in heaven.' Nothing brings such glory to our master as does the best conduct. . . . Let us do everything we do in such a way as to move each one who sees us to glorify God. . . . If you ever wish to associate with someone, make sure that you do not give your attention to those who enjoy health and wealth and fame as the world sees it but take care of those in affliction, those in critical circumstances, those in prison, those who are utterly deserted and enjoy no consolation. Put a high value in associating with these; for from them you shall receive much profit. You will be a better lover of the true wisdom and you will 'do all for the glory of God.' God himself has said 'I am the father of orphans and protector of widows.' And again 'Judge for the fatherless, defend the widow. Then come and let us talk, saith the Lord.' "[14]

Charles G. Finney

"Nothing is innocent unless it proceeds from supreme love to God and equal love to man, unless the supreme and ultimate motive be to

---

[13]John Henry Jowett, "The Baptism of Fire," *The Best of John Henry Jowett*, Gerald Kennedy, ed. (London: Epworth Press, 1951), pp. 65, 68.

[14]Chrysostom, "Sixth Instruction," *Twenty Centuries of Great Preaching*, Clyde E. Fant Jr. and William M. Dinson Jr., eds. (Waco, Texas: Word Books, 1971), vol. 1, pp. 65–66.

please and honor God. In other words to be innocent, any amusement must be engaged in because it is believed to be at the same time the most pleasing to God, and is intended to be a service rendered to Him as that which upon the whole will honor Him more than anything else that we can engage in for the time being.

"Let no one say this prohibits all rest, recreation and amusement whatever. It does not. It freely admits all rest, recreation and amusement that is regarded by the person who resorts to it as a condition and means of securing health and vigor of body and mind with which to promote the cause of God. This . . . only insists as the Bible does that 'whether we eat or drink,' rest, recreate, or amuse ourselves, all must be done as a service rendered to God. God must be our end. To please Him must be our aim in everything or we sin."[15]

D. L. Moody

"When the cloud came and received Moses and Elijah out of sight and they were taken back into the other world, what would have been the results if Jesus Christ had gone too? . . . But Moses disappeared and Elijah disappeared and Christ only was left, for Christ is all. The law and the prophets were fulfilled in Him. My dear friends, the longer I live the more I am convinced that what the world wants is Jesus Christ. If we preach Him more, live Him more and love Him more and let Him be constantly held up to this lost world we shall accomplish something. All our work that is separate from Christ will be just wood, hay, stubble and chaff; it will be burned up when God comes to test our works. . . . If you want power with God, just get as far from the world as you can. It seems to me that if we get one look at Christ and His love and beauty, the world and its pleasures will look very small to us. . . . Get near to Christ and you will never want to go back to the world."[16]

Isaac Watts

> When I survey the wondrous cross
> On which the Prince of Glory died,
> My richest gain I count but loss,
> And pour contempt on all my pride.

Jesus Christ Is All in All

Samuel Rutherford

"Come in, come in to Christ and see what you want and find it in Him. He is the short cut (as we used to say) and the nearest way to an outgate of all your burden. . . . I dare say that angels' pens, angels' tongues, nay, as many worlds of angels as there are drops of water in all the seas and fountains and rivers of the earth cannot paint Him out to you. I think His

---

[15]Charles G. Finney, "Innocent Amusements," *Lectures To Professing Christians* (New York: Garland Publishing Inc.), 1985.

[16]Dwight L. Moody, "The Transfiguration," *Sermons of D.L. Moody* (1900), pp. 80–81.

sweetness since I was a prisoner has swelled upon me to the greatness of two heavens. Oh for a soul as wide as the utmost circle of the highest heaven that containeth all to contain His love! . . . His bare shadow were enough for me. A sight of Him would be the earnest of heaven to me. . . . Christ, Christ, nothing but Christ can cool our love's burning languor. Oh thirsty love! Wilt thou set Christ the well of life to thy head and drink thy fill!

"The very dust that falleth from Christ's feet, His old ragged clothes, His knotty and black cross are sweeter to me than kings' golden crowns and their time-eaten pleasures. I should be a liar and a false witness if I would not give my Lord Jesus a fair testimonial with my whole soul. My world, I know will not heighten Him; He needed not such props under His feet to raise His glory high. But oh that I could raise Him the height of heaven and the breadth and length ten heavens in the estimation of all his young lovers! For we have all shapen Christ but too narrow and too short and formed conceptions of His love in our conceit very unworthy of it."

"Oh that men were taken and catched with His beauty and fairness! They would give over playing with idols in which there is not half room for the love of one soul to expiate itself. . . . We seek to thaw our frozen hearts at the cold smoke of the short-timed creature and our souls gather neither heat nor life, nor light; for these cannot give what they have not in themselves. Oh that we could thrust in through these thorns and this throng of bastard lovers and be ravished and sick of love for Christ! We should find some footing and some room, and sweet ease for our tottering and witless souls in our Lord. I wish it were in my power . . . to cry down all love but the love of Christ, and to cry down all gods but Christ, and all soul-suitors and love-beggars but Christ."[17]

John Watson

"The passion for Jesus has no analogy in comparative religion; it has no parallel in human experience. It is a flame of unique purity and intensity. . . . At the sight of His face seven devils went out of Mary Magdalene; for the blessing of His visit a chief publican gave half his goods to the poor. When a man of the highest order met Jesus he was lifted into the heavenly places and become a man whose eyes saw with the vision of Christ, whose pulse beat with the heart of Christ. . . . We ought to discern the real strength of Christianity and revive the ancient passion for Jesus. It is the distinction of our religion; it is the guarantee of its triumph. Faith may languish; creeds may be changed; churches may be dissolved; society may be shattered. . . . [Jesus] can never be superseded, He can never be exceeded. Religions will come and go, the passing shapes of an eternal instinct, but Jesus will remain the standard of the conscience and the

---

[17]Samuel Rutherford, *Letters*, Frank Gaebelein, ed. (Chicago: Moody Press, 1951), pp. 51, 101–102.

satisfaction of the heart, whom all men seek, in whom all men will yet meet."[18]

Helen Howarth Lemmel

> Turn your eyes upon Jesus;
> Look full in His wonderful Face;
> And the things of earth will grow strangely dim
> In the light of His glory and grace.

---

[18]John Watson, *Mind of the Master* (New York: Dodd, Mead and Company, 1896), pp. 191, 198.

PART TWO

PROPOSITION TWO:
GOD IS CREATOR

COROLLARY ONE: GOD IS A LOVING PERSON
COROLLARY TWO: GOD IS ACTIVE IN HISTORY
COROLLARY THREE: GOD IS AWESOMELY HOLY

I give myself over to my rapture. I tremble; my blood leaps. God has waited six thousand years for a looker-on to His work. His wisdom is infinite; that of which we are ignorant is contained in Him as well as the little we know.

—*Johannes Kepler*

CHAPTER FIVE

PROPOSITION TWO:
GOD IS CREATOR

Scriptures

"In the beginning God created the heaven and the earth. . . .
"And God said, Let there be light: and there was light. . . .
"And God made the firmament, and divided the waters. . . .
"And God said, Let the earth bring forth grass. . . .
"And God made two great lights. . . .
"And God said, Let the waters bring forth abundantly. . . .
"And God created great whales, and every living creature that moveth. . . .
"And God said, Let the earth bring forth. . . .
"So God created man in his own image, in the image of God created he him; male and female created he them." (Gen. 1)

"Thou, even thou, art LORD alone; thou hast made heaven, the heaven of heavens, with all their host, the earth, and all things that are therein, the seas, and all that is therein, and thou preservest them all; and the host of heaven worshippeth thee. Thou art the LORD . . ." (Neh. 9:6–7a)

"The heavens declare the glory of God; and the firmament sheweth his handywork. Day unto day uttereth speech, and night unto night sheweth knowledge." (Ps. 19:1–2)

"I will praise thee; for I am fearfully and wonderfully made: marvellous are thy works; and that my soul knoweth right well." (Ps. 139:14–15)

"The LORD is good to all: and his tender mercies are over all his works. All thy works shall praise thee, O Lord; and thy saints shall bless thee." (Ps. 145:9–10)

"The LORD hath made all things for himself . . ." (Prov. 16:4)

"Remember now thy Creator in the days of thy youth." (Eccles. 12:1)

"Lift up your eyes on high, and behold who hath created these things, that bringeth out their host by number: he calleth them all by names." (Isa. 40:26)

"Hast thou not known? hast thou not heard, that the everlasting God, the LORD, the Creator of the ends of the earth, fainteth not, neither is weary? there is no searching of his understanding . . ." (Isa. 40:28)

"That they may see, and know, and consider, and understand together, that the hand of the LORD hath done this, and the Holy One of Israel hath created it." (Isa. 41:20)

"Thus saith God the LORD, he that created the heavens, and stretched them out; he that spread forth the earth, and that which cometh out of it; he that giveth breath unto the people upon it, and spirit to them that walk therein . . ." (Isa. 42:5)

"I am the LORD that maketh all things; that stretcheth forth the heavens alone; that spreadeth abroad the earth by myself." (Isa. 44:24)

"I have made the earth, and created man upon it; I, even my hands, have stretched out the heavens, and all their host have I commanded." (Isa. 45:12)

"For, behold, I create new heavens and a new earth. . . . Be ye glad and rejoice for ever in that which I create: for, behold, I create Jerusalem a rejoicing, and her people a joy." (Isa. 65:17–18)

"Have we not all one father? hath not one God created us?" (Mal. 2:10)

"All things were made by him; and without him was not any thing made that was made." (John 1:3)

"He was in the world, and the world was made by him, and the world knew him not." (John 1:10)

"God that made the world and all things therein . . ." (Acts 17:24a)

"For the invisible things of him from the creation of the world are clearly seen, being understood by the things that are made, even his eternal power and Godhead." (Rom. 1:20)

"Who changed the truth of God into a lie, and worshipped and served the creature more than the Creator." (Rom. 1:25)

"For of him, and through him, and to him, are all things: to whom be glory for ever. Amen." (Rom. 11:36)

"For by him were all things created, that are in heaven, and that are in earth, visible and invisible . . . all things were created by him and for him; and he is before all things, and by him all things consist [hold together]." (Col. 1:16–17)

"God . . . hath in these last days spoken unto us by his Son, whom he hath appointed heir of all things, by whom also he made the worlds . . ." (Heb. 1:1–2)

"Thou art worthy, O Lord, to receive glory and honour and power: for thou hast created all things, and for thy pleasure they are and were created." (Rev. 4:11)

Bible Word Study

Create (Hebrew)

bara (*baw-raw*)—To create, select. Translated in the KJV as "creator," "choose," "do," "dispatch," "make."[1]

Baraar is translated "choose" in Ezek. 21:19; and "make" in Num. 16:30, 38, 46; 17:5. (KJV)

It's translated "create" in Ps. 51:10; Isa. 4:5; 45:7; 65:17, 18. And "created" in Gen. 1:1, 21, 27; 2:3, 4; 5:1–2; 6:7; Deut. 4:32; Ps. 89:12; 102:18; 104:30; 148:5; Isa. 40:26; 41:20; 42:5; 43:1, 7; 45:8, 12, 18; 48:7; 54:16; Jer. 31:22; Ezek. 21:30; 28:13, 15; Mal. 2:10.

Create (Greek)

ktizo (*ktid-zo*)—To fabricate, i.e., found (form originally). Translated in the KJV as "create," "Creator," "make."[2]

"*Ktizo*, create, produce and its derivatives are found 38 times in the NT. Of these there are 14 instances of the verb and 19 of the noun. . . . The occurrences of this group of words do not, however, exhaust the terminology of creation. The following are also found, though less frequently: *poieo*, to make; *plasso*, to form; and less frequently still, *kataskeuazo*, prepare (Heb. 3:4); *themelioo*, found; and *demiourgos*, craftsman, shaper. Other terms like *ta panta*, all; *arche*, beginning (used absolutely in John 1:1), and lists of the separate areas of creation (heaven, earth, sea, etc.) and their inhabitants likewise refer to the doctrine of creation. . . .

"The Creator alone is worthy of worship and veneration. The creature is limited by the fact that it is created. The limitation of creaturehood cannot be overcome from man's side. Where worship is nevertheless offered to creatures, God gives up those who have thus transgressed to their own evil ways (Rom. 1:25)."[3]

"Used among Greeks to mean the founding of a place, a city or colony. Signifies, in Scripture, to create, always of the act of God whether (a) in the *natural creation* (Mark 13:19; Rom. 1:25 . . . Eph. 3:9; Col. 1:16; 1 Tim.

---

[1]*Strong's* 1254.

[2]*Strong's* 2936.

[3]Hans-Helmut Esser, *The New International Dictionary of New Testament Theology*, Colin Brown, ed. (Grand Rapids: Zondervan Publishing House, 1971), vol. 1, pp. 383–385.

4:3; Rev. 4:11; 10:6), or (b) *spiritual creation* (Eph. 2:10; 4:24; Col. 3:10)."[4]

"To bring under tillage and settlement (e.g., land), to people a country, build houses and cities in it, hence, to found, set up, establish, produce, bring into being."[5]

Creation (Greek)

Ktisis (*ktis-is*)—Original formation (properly the act; by implication, the thing, literally or figuratively). Translated in the KJV as "building," "creation," "creature," "ordinance."[6]

"A founding, settling, foundation; a making or creation, then, that which was created, creation (denoting the action as incomplete and in progress). Mark 10:6; 13:9; Rom. 1:20; Rom. 8:22; 2 Pet. 3:4; Rev. 3:14."[7]

"The act of creating, or the creative act in process . . . Rom. 1:20 and Gal. 6:15."[8]

"The act of creation. . . . The Son of God was . . . counselor to the Father in His creative work. That which is created as a result of that creative act."[9]

Creature—"Product of a creative act. Mark 16:15 (RV); Rom. 1:25; 8:19. . . . Mark 16:15 and Col. 1:23 [have] special reference to mankind in general." Concerning Gal. 6:15; and 2 Cor. 5:17, "in the former . . . 'the reference is to the creative act of God, whereby a man is introduced into the blessing of salvation. . . . In 2 Cor. 5:17 the reference is to what the believer is in Christ; in consequence of the creative act he has become a new creature.' . . . *Ktisis* is used once of human actions, 1 Pet. 2:13, 'ordinance.'

"In all non-Christian Greek literature these words are never used by Greeks to convey the idea of a creator or of a creative act by any of their gods. The words are confined by them to the acts of human beings."[10]

Ktizo is translated "created" in these verses: 1 Cor. 11:9; Eph. 2:10; 3:9; 4:24; Col. 1:16; 3:10; 1 Tim. 4:3; Rev. 4:11; 10:6.

Non-Christian Ideas

"In this connection we should also mention the many and varied attempts to understand creation as a miracle, as a personal act of power, whether it be creation by word or creation by certain psychic states of the

---

[4]W.E. Vine, *The Expanded Vine's Expository Dictionary of New Testament Words*, John R. Kohlenberger III, ed. (Minneapolis, Minn.: Bethany House Publishers, 1984), pp. 246–247.

[5]Ethelbert W. Bullinger, *A Critical Lexicon and Concordance to the English and Greek New Testament* (Grand Rapids: Zondervan Publishing House, 1975), p. 194.

[6]*Strong's* 2937.

[7]Bullinger, op. cit. p. 194.

[8]Vine, op. cit. p. 247.

[9]Walter Bauer, *A Greek-English Lexicon of the New Testament*, 2nd ed., William F. Arndt and F. Wilbur Gingrich, trans., F. Wilbur Gingrich and Frederick W. Danker, eds. (Chicago: University of Chicago Press, 1979), p. 455.

[10]Vine, op. cit. p. 247.

creator, e.g., ecstacy. The point here is to emphasize that creation is an act which is beyond human conception. But if it is a magical act, the decisive force does not lie in the meaning of the word spoken, but in the magical power of the word itself which may at a pinch be divorced from the meaning.

"To understand creation as magic is to see at work in it a mysterious power which may be separated from the creator. It is not to see the creator as a person. These notions are all moving in the direction of a personal act of will, but they cannot reach this because creation alone is not enough to give a personal view of God. Hence these divine figures cannot be grasped as truly personal. The decisive personal element, action in history, is not stated of them. This is true in the Greek world. Philosopical reflection makes of Zeus an abstract quantity. . . ."[11]

"In Jer. 27:5 . . . there appears the first clear and comprehensive statement concerning creation. . . . The absolute power of God over history is now for the first time traced back to His being as Creator. The connection between power in history and power as Creator is a very close one in the OT, for the shaping of history is also a creation, and the same words are used of it as are applied to the creating and fashioning of the world and man . . . Isa. 22:11; 29:16f.; Jer: 18:11; Hab. 1:15. . . ."[12]

"In the beginning God is, but the creature comes into being. The beginning is thus the beginning of the creature, before which it does not exist. It is in keeping with the practical nature of the OT that it does not formulate creation out of nothing as a dogmatic principle but always, so far as we can see, makes about God only statements which do not subject Him to, or bring Him under the influence of any pre-existent conditions."[13]

"The more clearly the concept of creation is worked out, the broader is the circle of ideas which are linked with it or based on it. Creation displays not only the omnipotence but also the wisdom and omniscience of God, Jer. 10:12—51:15; Ps. 104:24; Job 28:24–26; Prov. 3:19; 8:27. . . .

"The creative act of God is also the basis of His power in history, Jer. 27:5, of the duty of trust in Him, of His claim to trust and gratitude, Isa. 17:7; 22:11; 40:26ff.; 43:1; 44:2; Hos. 8:14; Deut. 32:6, 15; Ps. 103:22 and of the duty of obedience, Ps. 119:73. . . .

"The fact that He has created heaven and earth distinguishes the God of Israel from idols, Jer. 10:12–16 (cf. 14:22); 51:15–19; Ps. 96:5, 115:3f.; Jon. 1:9. This does not mean that God's being as Creator is added as a necessary qualification to a general concept of God. It means that witness is borne to the fact that Yahweh, the God of Israel, is the Creator, and none else. The uniqueness of God is indissolubly linked to the fact that He is the Creator, e.g., Isa. 44:24."[14]

---

[11]*Theological Dictionary of the New Testament*, Gerhard Kittel, ed., Geoffrey W. Bromiley, trans. (Grand Rapids: Wm. B. Eerdmans Publishing Company, 1964), vol. 3, p. 1004.
[12]Ibid. vol. 3, p. 1006.
[13]Ibid. vol. 3, p. 1012.
[14]Ibid. vol. 3, pp. 1012–1013.

Questions and Answers

Q: *How could God make something out of nothing?*
A: Strictly speaking, He didn't. His creation came from the resources of His own infinite being, that which was always here. When we say He makes things "out of nothing" (*ex nihilo*), we mean that He does not need any resource external to himself, does not lose part of himself in creating, and that His creation is distinct from himself rather than an extension of His being.

Q: *How could a universe as vast and complex as this be created in so short a time?*
A: Henry Ford took around 30 years to make a car that can now be made in less than 18 hours. Creation "time" is a function of available energy and wisdom. God, with infinite wisdom and power, has no problem doing extremely complex things in short time intervals.

Q: *If God made everything, did He create sin?*
A: No. Sin is represented everywhere in Scripture as an alien intrusion on the divine happiness. A wise God could not intelligently author His own unhappiness. God created moral beings—each a tiny "creator" who had the power to make choices for right or for wrong. Our own creative choices, like the Devil's rebellion against God's expressed will, create sin.

Q: *Doesn't the Bible teach that God creates good and evil?*
A: No. The Bible words are "I make *peace*, and create evil" (Isa. 45:7). Although sin is evil, evil is not always sin. Punishment or judgment are called "evil" (Deut. 29:21; 30:15); some bad or painful event, that is not necessarily morally wrong (Ps. 34:21; Gen. 37:20, 33) or the righteous wrath of God (Jer. 44:11). When bad men create wrong choices, these sins are evil; but when God brings on them an evil for these choices, He is not wrong, just as any loving and just father would not be wrong in punishing a bad child, or as a fair judge would be in sentencing a criminal. The passage in Isaiah refers to an evil whose opposite is not *good* but *peace*, and it obviously refers to God's blessing or judgment on a nation.

Q: *Did God make the Devil? If so, why did He do it?*
A: No. God did not make the Devil. He made Lucifer, a beautiful archangel who chose to set his created will against God, and by his sinful choice made himself the Devil, bringing great hurt and sadness to heaven and earth.

Q: *If there is a God, why do the innocent suffer?*
A: But a universe of evil like ours is inconsistent with the existence of a Creator of infinite goodness, knowledge, or power. Either God did not foresee these evils (in which case He is not omniscient); or foreseeing it, He had no power to prevent evil (in which case He is not omnipo-

tent); or foreseeing it and being able to prevent it, He did not have the goodness to do so.

This assumes that a better universe would be naturally possible, that under a government administered morally in the wisest and best manner, moral beings could be wholly restrained from sin; but who ever said so? Infinite goodness, knowledge, and power imply only that a universe created would be the best universe *naturally* possible. Moral and physical evils do exist, but why should their existence be less preferable in a universe in which they were not allowed to exist? And why should we assume that things which we cannot adequately explain or understand set aside a world of evidence telling us that God designed and governs what we do know?

Q: *If God is unchangeable, how could He create the world?*

A: God is unchanging or immutable in His nature and character. But, Finney says, "Creation implies no change in either of these but only the exercise of His natural and moral attributes; character consists in design or intention and God always intended to design or create the universe; therefore creation implies no formation or change of character with Him."[1]

Objections to Creation

Q: *Isn't evolution a proven fact? The world is full of examples of creatures that have changed or are changing in some way.*

A: Creationists believe in that kind of evolution—if all we mean by "evolution" is certain kinds of change. Creationists do not reject *micro*- but *macro*-evolution, not small changes in species that allow them to adapt to their changing environments and needs, but the idea of major changes from one kind of creation to another by indiscriminate chance.

Q: *Don't creationists misuse the word "theory" to convey the false impression that evolutionists are covering up some faulty core in their idea?*

A: It is fair to point out well established rules for doing science, and according to these rules evolution doesn't even qualify as a scientific *theory*, much less as proven *fact*. A theory is scientific if it fits known facts compiled, studied, and verified by trained observation. These facts are generalized as a scientific hypothesis and used as a rough working model to test an idea through further observation. If the hypothesis fits the facts, it is a *theory*; its accuracy as a law depends on experimental repeatability, predictability, and proper control. And since no one has *ever* observed life evolving—then or now—and we cannot repeat it or verify it, macro-evolution is, at best, a premise based on naturalistic philosophy.

Q: *Isn't it true that creationists misuse popular scientific philosophy to*

---

[1]Charles G. Finney, *Lectures on Theology* (Minneapolis, Minn.: Bethany House Publishers, 1968), p. 29.

argue that they are behaving scientifically in attacking evolution?

A: While true scientific method cannot be used to resolve this controversy, we can still prove or disprove the ideas in question another way;
by weighing evidence as in a law court, to determine which position
best fits the facts of the world around us. Creationism is a theory
specific enough that not every imaginable fact or evidence, hypothetical or real, can be used to support it; it is properly falsifiable and
could hypothetically be proved wrong. In this it is perfectly proper to
criticize another (and the only other) competing idea in the light of
direct scientific evidence such as the fossil record, laws of probability,
thermodynamics, and the laws of genetics.

Q: *Don't creationists use selective quotations, putting them together in
such a way to make an argument that the writer quoted had no intention of making?*

A: Creationist authors usually do two things: they quote only from evo-
lutionist sources and they document everything so you can check the
quotes out in context for yourself. Honest researchers, creationist or
not, admit facts even if they cannot follow them through to their own
conclusions. It is certainly legitimate for creationists to show how
these problems can be explained in terms of a creationist position.

Q: *But surely creationism isn't "science" as it is universally defined today,
is it?*

A: That is not the fault of science. Science has not always been the ally
of materialism. Many of the sciences, locked into a hundred years of
Industrial Revolution mindset and world view as well as succumbing
to the influence of that era's mechanistic physics, are now under intense scrutiny and challenge. Significantly, the cutting edge of much
new research today points directly toward the existence of spiritual,
or metaphysical, reality.

Q: *But how can creationists claim they have a scientific theory when they
have merely torn into an opposing scientific theory?*

A: Conversely, assuming creation a "religious doctrine based on blind
faith" does not make evolution an empirical scientific and emotionally
neutral theory. Creation and macro-evolution are the only two basic
possibilities; if one is true, then the other is false. Although neither
evolutionism or creationism can be observed or repeated, creation has
certainly not been proven false. We believe it not just because macro-
evolution is deemed insupportable, but because creation (even beyond the declaration of God's record) from the weight of all the best
evidence appears to be true.

Creation can be argued evidentially without reference to the Bible.
If evolution can't best fit the facts, why not go for the theory that does?
Christian researchers don't "bring in God" just to explain what cannot
currently be explained. He is not invoked to "fill gaps" for faulty theories, perhaps to be squeezed out by the next scientific advance. We
honor Him as Creator God, evident in His universe not because other
explanations fail, but because studies point to His mind, His purpose,

or His planning. Can we allow "gaps" in our knowledge of origins? To acknowledge God as Creator is to honor Him where science reaches its limits and can never expound.

Q: *What if there is intellect and personality behind man's creation? You don't have to believe in divine creation. Some people have concluded that we were put here by super-beings from space.*

A: Do we need to talk about how *they* came into existence? Perhaps "long, long ago, in a galaxy far, far away . . ." No matter how far back we move the problem and how long ago we set the beginning, the problem of origins will not go away.

Q: *If creation is true, why are so many things explained by evolution? Why does evolution seem to have explanations that appear to fit the facts?*

A: Much depends on our *premises*—the ideas you start with, your pre-suppositions. It is not often the facts themselves that cause arguments; conflicts come because two people start with very different bases by which they interpret what they see. For instance, a fish and a submarine are alike in some ways, they both have tails, move underwater, and so on. The facts declare they are similar in many ways.

Now assume the premise *similarity equals common ancestry*. With all the right facts, we could decide that the fish is a highly-advanced, miniaturized great-nephew of the submarine. This is no doubt offensive to both fish and human common sense, but "facts are facts!"

Change your premise to *similarity equals common design*, and with the same set of facts you see something very different: both fish and submarines were designed to work underwater, one by man, one by man's Creator.

With the right facts but a wrong premise you can come up with the wrong answer for all the right reasons.

Analysis and Discussion

Here is the second of the three great mysteries of God: He is Creator! Just as we cannot explain His uncreatedness, we cannot explain His creativity; but *un*like His uncreatedness, we do have an illustration of this wonderful attribute. The fact that God is the creator means that personality, responsibility, and morality are all founded in ultimate reality; they are not an imaginary projection of human consciousness that would be itself the random and accidental product of time, matter-energy, and chance in the universe. Although we can never fully approach God nor even begin to communicate with Him as the infinite being He is, there is a basis for true fellowship—He, as Creator, made us in His image and we have been made like Him as persons.

Out of Nothing

How did God begin everything? God created the world by His Word according to Genesis 1. Passages like Ps. 33:9; 148:5; and Isa. 45:12 emphasize the Creator's transcendent majesty. These are amplified in NT verses like John 1:1–3; Heb. 11:3 and 2 Pet. 3:5–6.

R. K. Harrison declares, "Creation *ex nihilo* rules out the idea that matter is eternal, and also rejects any kind of *dualism* in the universe in which another entity, power or existence stands over against God and outside His control. . . . Furthermore, the concept of creation from nothing affirms that God is separate from His creation and denies that the latter is a phenomenal manifestation of the Absolute as *pantheism* maintains."[1]

Francis Schaeffer notes regarding the idea of an impersonal beginning to the universe, that "everything began with an impersonal something," is not only the consensus of almost all Eastern thinking, but now also a strong component of the Western world view. "It is the view of scientism . . . and embodied in the notion of the uniformity of natural causes in a closed system. It is also the concept of much modern theology if one presses it back far enough." But it raises "two overwhelming problems which neither the East nor modern man has come anywhere near solving.

"First, there is no real explanation for the fact that the external world is not only real but has specific *form*. . . . One can go from particulars to a greater unity, from the lesser laws to more and more general laws or super-laws." Second, and more important, "there is no explanation of *personality*. In a very real sense, the question of questions for all generations—but overwhelmingly so for modern man—is: 'Who am I?' . . . In short, an impersonal beginning explains neither the form of the universe nor the personality of man."[2]

The Foundation of Science

Perhaps the biggest opposition today to the doctrine of creation comes from the discipline that strangely enough is ultimately its child—the world of science! Robert Blaikie pointed out that science owes its origin to five influences: (1) Greek geometry (while replacing the Greek approach to knowledge by deduction from principle with observation and experiment), (2) the collected contributions of classical astronomy, (3) Arabian arithmetic and algebra, (4) a combined approach to truth linking both rational thought and empirical fact, and—finally and most importantly—(5) a belief in the "regularity of nature, the rationality of God and the certainty that the universe was really there." We will see that "God as World Creator is our fundamental starting-point for all true science. Acknowledging what He *is* (ontology) also profoundly affects the area of *how* we can know (epistemology) the foundation of all true knowledge."[3]

What are the implications of God as Creator in the realm of science? If this concept laid the foundation of true science, why is theology so

---

[1]"Creation," *The Zondervan Pictorial Encyclopedia of the Bible*, Merrill Tenney, ed. (Grand Rapids: Zondervan Pub. House, 1976), vol. 1, p. 1023.

[2]Francis A. Schaeffer, *Genesis in Space and Time* (Downers Grove, Ill.: InterVarsity Press, 1972), p. 25.

[3]Dr. Robert J. Blaikie, *Secular Christianity and the God Who Acts* (London: Hodder and Stoughton, 1970).

often divorced from science today? Thomas F. Torrance in his *The Ground and Grammar of Theology*[4] argues convincingly that there should never have been such a dichotomy, and that the seeds of this mutual distrust were sown by the reintroduction of Eastern, dualist ideas into the theology after the era of the early Church.

You cannot think scientifically and productively about God, Torrance says, without also holding some kind of basic belief in sensible, practical, and testable connections to the world of space and time. Thus the more deeply committed and careful both the scientist and theologian are to their respective work, the better they should be able to talk to each other, "if only because both have to develop fundamental attitudes to the world."

Torrance begins with the classical theology of the early Church, (including Nicene theology and all that followed in the next two centuries, especially in Greek theology) as the "foundations of the theology upon which all Christendom rests and to which all our creeds go back."

The Pagan World View

Early Christian theology battled to break through a pagan view of the world, which not only saw cosmology (the study of the universe) and theology (the study of God) as the same thing, but often identified God with the world. Stoic thinkers thought God was the soul of the world, animating it and giving it motion much as the human soul does to the body. Aristotle viewed God as finite, the "Unmoved Mover of the finite universe." So it was natural for him to include theology under the rubric of "cosmology."

This led to a mighty confrontation in the early centuries between the Judeo-Christian understanding of God as the transcendent Lord of the universe and the fatalistic Graeco-Roman philosophy and religion. It was the "revelation of the one God as Creator of the earth and heaven and of all things visible and invisible" versus the dualistic structures of the ancient world with its two branches of the "real, eternal and changeless and the unreal, apparent and evanescent."

Old Testament Foundation and New Testament Reality

Torrance maintains that the OT concept of the "living God who interacts through His word and Spirit providentially and savingly with the world He has made" was foundational to Christianity. Not only was He real and good to His creatures, but the world He made was real and good also. Even this brought a "head-on clash at essential points within basic structures of thought." The fight centered around the "contrast between God as the mighty living and active source of all that is good and real and orderly" and the pagan picture of a God "statically and timelessly changeless—bound up with the eternal forms that constitute the nature of ulti-

---

[4]Thomas F. Torrance, *The Ground and Grammar of Theology* (Edinburgh, Scotland: University Press, 1980), pp. 45–46, 54–56, 59–61.

mate reality." God was the mere "inertial source of all the immanent processes in the universe, regularly identified in literature with fate or necessity, and therefore also with the evil as well as the good that overtakes the world and all the inexorable processes within it."

When Christianity blossomed and spread, the clash heightened. It not only taught the "overwhelming love of God, of creation out of nothing," but also the incarnation and resurrection. God himself had interacted personally with the world, becoming a man in Jesus Christ! These facts demanded a "radical reconstruction of the foundations of ancient philosophy, science, and culture" for this "Christian Gospel to take root in a civilized world and to transform its society until it was brought within the Kingdom of Christ."

Did Christians try to adapt their message to make it understandable and relevant to the modern world? No. "Whole generations of preachers, scholars, and theologians have been asking how they can communicate the Gospel. . . . In answer they have been trying to fit the Christian message to the paradigms of the community—otherwise they argue, 'people today would not understand what Christianity is about.' Thus, while science advances through changing our thought, the preaching and teaching of the Church has become more and more obsolescent. Is that not why in the last few decades, the more we have tried to make the Gospel relevant, the more it has become irrelevant to our contemporaries while theology has fallen into the deep fissures that have opened up in our split culture?"

This "staggering conquest of the ancient world by the Galilean . . . took place precisely as early Christian theology—instead of trying merely to operate within the paradigms of the ancient pagan world—undertook the enormous task of recreating the very foundations of human philosophy, science, and culture, so that the Gospel could take deep root and develop within human society in such a way as to evangelize and convert it, and would thus fulfill its cultural role in clarifying and unifying all human knowledge and life under the creative impact of God's self-revelation in Christ and the ordering power of His love."

"Dogmatic" Theology

During this time, Torrance notes, proper theology (dogmatics) developed. In the ancient world the so-called *nee Academy* followed the schools of Plato and Aristotle, whose philosophers (soon to be called *skeptics*) concentrated on "asking questions, and questions, and questions—but were not prepared to entertain positive answers—the kind of questions that people so often ask in the ecumenical movement—that is, the kind of questions that do not yield the kind of answers that commit you to decision and change. (We still dub these 'academic' questions). . . ." The "dogmatics," however, "claimed they were concerned not with abstract and useless questions, but with the kind of answers forced on them by the nature of things, which they could not refrain from accepting and acting upon. Thus the dogmatic person turns out to be, not a philosopher, but a scientist who thinks only as he is compelled to think by the objective and intrinsic structures of nature."

Faithful to What Is There

Christian theologians took up the cause and developed dogmatics, changing it and its foundations by relating the intrinsic structures of nature to God's creation out of nothing. Cyril of Alexandria called this *dogmatike episteme* ("dogmatic science"). He applied the term to Christian theology as we find it in the great councils of the Church.

This was not some kind of theological freethinking, but the kind of theology that is forced upon us by the interaction of God with the universe He has made and by His intelligible self-revelation within that interaction. As we allow our minds to fall under the power of what we hear and find in this discussion of God, we find ourselves committed to saying fundamental things about Him, the Spirit, and the Church. Thus there arose *dogmatic science* or theology, which developed basic ideas that changed the whole course of science.

Torrance explains that the word "dogmatic" now tends to be used in an opposite sense: to state "definite ideas and propositions apart from any controlling evidential grounds and merely under the constraint of external authorities and preconceptions—traditional, ecclesiastical, political, or even scientistic." These ideas are not those forced on us by the objective structures of reality. " 'Laws of nature' are dogmas . . . imposed on the scientific mind by the immanent rationality of the universe, just as crystalline formations impose upon our thinking the geometric patterns imbedded in them."

Three Key Ideas

Torrance notes that "in its reconstruction of the foundations of ancient philosophy, science, and culture, Christian theology of this rigorous spirit in the early Church developed three masterful ideas . . . that had a powerful effect on all subsequent thought in natural science as well as in theological science." These ideas of the rational unity of the universe, contingent rationality, and contingent freedom "arose out of careful thinking together of the doctrines of the incarnation of the eternal Logos and of the creation of the world out of nothing."

The Rational Unity of the Universe Under Its Creator

Accepting this meant rejecting all the "polytheism, dualism, pluralism, and polymorphism of ancient religions, philosophies, and science, and produced the concept of one harmonious system of things characterized by one pervasive, if multi-variable, unity in the universe." In his *Contra Gentes*, St. Athanasius uses musical terms again and again to "describe the kind of symphonic texture that was the order of the universe under one God the Creator. This masterful idea of a *unified rationality* sweeps away the Aristotelian, the Neoplatonic, and certainly the Ptolemaic duality between celestial and terrestrial worlds, celestial and terrestrial mechanics and all the dualism and pluralism that goes with it, for this universe as it comes from the creative Word of God has one pervading *taxis*, or order, everywhere; so that wherever you go in the universe it is accessible to rational inquiry." This, says Torrance is "a correlate of the doctrine of one God who created the universe out of nothing" and on this idea of the rationality or intelligibility of the universe the confidence of all scientific inquiry has rested ever since.

Contingent Rationality or The Intelligibility of the Universe

Another immense step forward, considered even more difficult, according to Torrance, was "the idea that the rationality of the universe was contingent (i.e., neither necessary nor eternal); that there is an order in the universe created—along with the universe—out of nothing, was quite impossible for Greeks and Orientals alike." Christians teaching the doctrine of creation out of nothing were accused of "impiety." To their scandalized Platonist, Aristotelian, or Stoic world view listeners, teaching that questioned the "rationality of the eternal forms and denied the necessary connection between the rationality immanent in things and its source," and was a form of atheism. To them it "undermined the stability of the natural principles, . . . without which there would be nothing to stand between cosmos and chaos."

This had even more radical implications. "In creating the universe out of nothing," Torrance declares, "God created time and space out of nothing as well. . . . On one hand this doctrine of creation changed the basic understanding of space and time—destroyed the container concept applied to their understanding in different ways by Platonic, Aristotelian, and Stoic philosophy and replaced it with a *relational* concept. This represents one of the greatest changes imaginable and is indeed a change with which we have only managed to catch up in our own day with relativity theory. The relational notions of space and time developed by theology were then translated into physics by John Philpanonos of Alexandria, whose work later had some influence in the West through Al Ghazali and Grosseteste. . . .

"On the other hand, since space and time are the bearers of rational order in the universe, the creation of space and time out of nothing meant that the rational order of the universe is created out of nothing. That was a staggering concept for the Greeks, but there was more—*man* and the *human mind* were likewise! All Greek thought and religion were informed by the Orphic idea that mind or intelligence is the 'spark of the Divine'— so the light of reason could no more be considered to be created out of nothing than could God." Christians however, thought this Greek idea divinized creation, "damaging the true status of the creature . . . detracting from the glory and majesty and truth of God himself." Christians rejected dualism, and made a "distinction between created and uncreated light, or created and uncreated rationality—the former deriving from the latter, but not as an extension or emanation of it—which had the effect of maintaining the creaturely integrity of the creature and the human integrity of man."

God made in man an intelligent counterpart to the rational order immanent in His creation. "By positing the human intelligence along with space and time in His creation of the universe out of nothing, God conferred upon it a rationality of its own, independent of, yet contingent upon His own uncreated and transcendent rationality. This does not mean that the rationality of the universe is a sharing in God, or that the created light of the human mind is an 'ontologistic' participation in the mind of God— as for example the Neoplatonists seemed to think. On the contrary, while as created light it derives from the uncreated light of God, it is independent of it, yet by no means self-sufficient—as God's light is. By very nature created and contingent, it points away from itself to the Uncreated Light and in a creaturely way reflects it. This doctrine of contingent intelligibility, inherent in the creation, means that if you are to understand any natural process in the universe, you cannot do so by any *a priori* thought or any kind of theological reasoning from what we know of God but only by going to the natural process itself and probing into its natural or intrinsic order.

"The doctrine of contingent intelligibility or rationality is the foundation of all empirical and theoretical science while the essential connection between 'contingence' and 'intelligibility' means that in all our science we have to operate with an indissoluble connection between empirical and theoretical factors, both in what we seek to know and in our knowing of it. Today general relativity and the singularity of the universe so astonishingly disclosed by modern cosmology provides massive support for this masterful idea as never before in the history of science. This idea, which is quite impossible for the pagan mind, is a direct product of Christian theology."

Contingent Freedom or Freedom of the Universe

"Behind this lies a powerful conception of the freedom of God, which stems from the deep background of the Church in Judaic thought. As Creator of the whole cosmos out of nothing, God is the transcendent Lord over all space and time. He is not indebted to the universe in any way or bound to it by some sort of dualist synthesis such as monistic philosophy or pantheistic religion evidently entailed. The universe is indebted to God and utterly dependent on Him both in its origin and its continuity. He does not need the universe to be God. He is majestically and almightily free over all created existence, and in that sense He was often spoken of as 'superessential' or 'beyond being' (i.e., beyond created being). Yet God's freedom is not arbitrary freedom, for almighty though He is, He is in His own transcendent being intrinsically and supremely rational, and as such He is the transcendent source of all truth, rationality, and order in the universe."

Freedom From the Cycles of "Fate"

The universe to a pagan mind was like an inexorable wheel, self-sufficient and closed, his world locked up to fate, deterministic; but a universe contingent upon God and His freedom is no slave to some alien power or destiny. The doctrine of the freedom of the universe grounded in the freedom of God came like a proclamation of emancipation. According to Torrance early Christian thinkers like Clement, Athanasius of Alexandria, and Athenagoras of Athens "tried to lift the concept of 'pronia' or divine providence on an altogether higher level . . . destroying the fatalistic outlook upon things derived from the deadening idea of a universe shackled to unending recurrence and harnessed to an altogether necessitarian and blind destiny. This has nowhere been more fully and effectively shown than by Stanley L. Jaki in two recent works, *Science and Creation* and the *Road of Science and the Ways of God*. The doctrine of creation out of nothing and the continual preservation of creation from lapsing back into nothing, shattered the notion of *eternal cyclical processes*, with its built-in futility, for it revealed the universe had an absolute beginning and thus replaced the idea of time ever turning back on itself with a *linear* view of time moving irreversibly toward its consummation or end in the purpose of the Creator. But it also grounded the ongoing order of the universe in the steadfast love and faithfulness of God, which gave it a stability as well as freedom in its contingency, for it meant that its natural ability, its openness to change was undergirded by God himself.

"The contingent freedom of the universe then is not something bound up with randomness of chance, for it is no more arbitrary than the freedom of the God of infinite love and truth upon which it rests and by which it is maintained. It is a freedom that derives from the unlimited freedom of God, but it is a contingent freedom and is therefore a limited freedom. An unlimited, contingent freedom would be an inherent contradiction— that would spell arbitrariness. Limited though contingent freedom is, it is limited by the very freedom of God on which it is grounded. It is nonetheless a genuine freedom, the kind of freedom proper to a finite and contingent universe. On the other hand because it is contingent upon the unlimited freedom of God, it is a freedom that embraces inexhaustible possibilities.

"That is why as we explore the universe in our scientific activities, it keeps surprising us, disclosing to us patterns and structures in an indefinite range of intelligibility which we could never anticipate on our own— such is the excitement of scientific enterprise. Indeed it is the hallmark of a true scientific theory in its bearing on reality that it indicates far more than it can express, so that the more we probe through it into the intelligibilities of the universe the more exciting are the aspects and forms of reality that become disclosed to us. The universe constantly takes us by surprise in this way because it is correlated to the infinite inexhaustible freedom and rationality of God its Creator."

John Philoponos

Torrance goes on to declare, "In terms of these masterful ideas, that Christian theology of the fourth through sixth centuries worked its outlook on the universe, reconstructing the cultural foundations in philosophy and science on which the pagan picture of God and the cosmos rested. . . . John Philoponos . . . was the first Christian physicist; who, following the theological work of Anathansius and Cyril in Alexandria, developed a physics of light—and in that connection a new concept of motion—as well as relational notions of space and time which are an astonishing anticipation of our own scientific notions today. The profound interconnection revealed there between theology and science in respect to these basic ideas was, as it were a prophecy of what was to follow in the subsequent history of thought but at no time has that interconnection been more evident than it is today."

But "John's views were rejected as 'monophysite' (someone who denies that there are 'two natures'—a divine and human in Christ, where *nature* is interpreted in an Aristotelian way) and heretical. John, however, did not think that way—in line with scientific and theological tradition to which he belonged 'nature' meant 'reality' so that for him to think of Christ as 'one nature' meant that he was 'one reality' and not a schizoid being. John was no monophysite in the heretical sense, but the accusation of heresy had the effect of denigrating also his anti-dualistic thought in science and philosophy. This represents, in my view, one of the greatest tragedies in the history of science as well as of theology, for it really means that the Church was ultimately unwilling to work out, in the rigorous way required, the distinctively Christian ideas of the relation between God and the world."

The Influence of Neoplatonism

These masterful ideas then tragically became "submerged in a massive upsurge of dualist modes of thought and the container notions of space in the East and West in Byzantine and Latin Christian cultures. To a large extent this was due to the powerful influence of Neoplatonic philosophy with its reinterpretation of Plato and Aristotle (especially Aristotle's logic) and the survival of the dualistic Stoic notions of law in the development of canon law. All the way from the fifth through the seventh century, when the great theological and scientific reconstruction was going on, the old dualism operated below the surface, corroding the new ideas (not the least ruined were those of John Philoponos) and then broke out into the open and were given paradigmatic status in the West through the subtle but admittedly beautiful blending of Christian theology with Neoplatonic theology and Ptolemaic cosmology by the great St. Augustine.

Augustinian Impact on Science

Torrance continues, "Thus the great advances in Alexandrian science and the extensive interconnection between science and theology worked out there were largely lost, if only because in the Augustinian dualist outlook this world of space and time has no ultimate place in the Christian hope but belongs to the world that passes away—that is the world out of which we must be saved."

In his *Theological Science*, Torrance also points out that medieval theology held a deeply entrenched patristic notion of God (similar to Aristotle's "Unmoved Mover"). They understood Him as impassive and changeless, to the point that all creation existed only as objects of His eternal knowing and willing; human existence was directly grounded in God's eternity. It was difficult to explain how something created was never non-existent, though men like St. Thomas tried. However, their attempts to "interpret nature in the light of final and primary causes" left "little room for the element of real contingency in nature," the basis of modern experimental science. It took the Reformation for men to "learn to think differently of the nature of God and His relation to the creation as utterly distinct from Him while yet dependent on His will for its being and ultimate order, and therefore learned to think differently of the order of nature and of the creaturely nature of its order."

Modern science could replace the more or less static science of the ancient and medieval world only when nature was liberated from medieval rationalism and disenchanted of its secret "divinity" and man admitted that one could only know natural order by observing and interpreting the creaturely processes themselves.[5]

In *The Ground and Grammar of Theology*, Torrance expanded, "The doctrine of the one God—with its correlate in the unitary rationality of the universe—remained and indeed received considerable attention and development in Latin medieval thought which played its due part in the emergence of modern science. But the medieval Ptolemaic cosmology, "with its hard separation between celestial and terrestrial motion—had to be radically questioned before modern astronomy and science could arise based on a unitary physics spanning the heavenly bodies and the earth."

Man in God's Image

We often forget that God made the creation creative when He created. Even in the beginning, God called the waters and the earth to "bring forth," allowing His own creativity to spill forth via His creation. As Terry Fretheim brings out, "The creative activity is often depicted only in terms of a sovereign unilateral Divine act; it is a command performance. . . . As a result, creatureliness tends to be viewed solely in terms of dependence and humility, even impotence. But . . . the common use of *'asah* ('make') with its many uses in the human sphere, makes it clear that God's creative work is not without analogy. Moreover Genesis 1 speaks of creation as both mediate and immediate, indirect and direct. . . . Although the emphasis throughout is on the Divine initiative, the creative capacities of the created are clearly attested."[6]

One final observation comes out of the doctrine of God as Creator—

---

[5]Thomas F. Torrance, *Theological Science* (New York: Oxford University Press, 1969), pp. 59–60.
[6]Terence Fretheim, *The Suffering of God* (Fortress, 1984), p. 73.

in making man "in His image," man himself has been given the ability to be like God in at least one way: the ability to create. Of course, unlike God, our creativity is not expressed matter and energy; these are gifts already given by the Uncreated. But we do have the ability to originate in the realm of the personal and the moral; we have the ability to be His finite "created creators."

The closest parallel to God that exists in man is our ability to *make*, to be a *maker* in miniature. It is entirely possible that the ability of free will or choice is the one facet of God's own personality that makes us most like Him. (It certainly underlies all the biblical judgments of our character and appeals to our responsibility.) We never come nearer to an act like God than when we originate a choice based on what is given to us as the highest good. Our choices actually call into existence moral paths and realities that never before existed in the universe. Thus a man is significant, valuable, and utterly special regardless of whether he ever returns to God or not.

As Francis Schaeffer noted, "Prior to the material universe (whether we think of it as matter or energy), prior to the creation of all else, there is love and communication. This means love and communication are intrinsic. And hence, when modern man screams for love and communication, . . . Christians have an answer: there is value to love and value to communication because it is rooted into what intrinsically always has been."[7]

Here then is an absolute basis for all analysis of personality as well as questions of axiology—of morals, values, judgments and ethics. Because God is a Creator, a person able to originate that which has never before been, so man, made in His image, is also able to originate choices for which he must be held responsible. This leaves us with one awesome conclusion: *everything we do is important*. Choices are creations that can never be recalled; sin and righteousness are real; and heaven and hell are real. Man is not a nothing, whether he is a sinner or a saint; man is himself an originator, a creator and the choices he makes will affect both the universe and the future.

Historical Discussion

The Great Creator

Robert Blaikie

" 'In the beginning God created the heavens and the earth.' This very first affirmation in the Bible presupposes the living Creator-God, God before and beyond all things, God in action as Creator of all else that is. It is this which is the basic and constant presupposition of the whole Bible, Old Testament and New. There is no attempt in the Bible to prove or

---

[7]Schaeffer, op. cit. pp. 20–21.

defend this presupposition. It is simply assumed, as what is basically 'given' to be accepted 'by faith alone.' God is the creative primary Agent: living, personal and able to act in fulfillment of His purposes."[1]

Issac Newton

"It became Him Who created them to set them in order. And if He did so it is unphilosophical to seek for any other origin of the world, or to pretend it may arise out of a chaos by the mere laws of Nature; though being once formed it may continue by those laws for many ages. . . . If natural philosophy in all its parts . . . shall at length be perfected, the bounds of moral philosophy will be also enlarged. For so far as we can know by natural philosophy what is the First Cause, what power He has over us and what benefits we receive from Him, so far as our duty towards Him as well as that towards one another will appear to us by the light of nature. And no doubt if the worship of false gods had not blinded the heathen, their natural philosophy would have gone further than to the four cardinal virtues; and instead of teaching the transmigration of souls, to worship the sun and the moon, and dead heroes, they would have taught us to worship our true Author and Benefactor as did their ancestors under the government of Noah and his sons before they corrupted themselves."[2]

The Foundation of Knowledge

Robert Blaikie

"The basic presupposition of biblical theology therefore is ontological, affirming the existence of God who acts. The immediate epistemological consequence of this must be the recognition of 'revelation' as a source of knowledge alongside the knowledge yielded by science. Revelation comes to man through the acts of God together with a 'word'—a conceptual interpretation of these particular acts as God's acts."[3]

Henry Drummond

"No one who knows the content of Christianity or feels the universal need of a Religion can stand idly by while the intellect of his age is slowly divorcing itself from it. What is required therefore to draw Science and Religion together again—for they began the centuries hand in hand—is the disclosure of the naturalness of the supernatural. Then and not till then will men see how true it is that to be loyal to all of Nature they must be loyal to that part defined as spiritual. As the contribution of Science to Religion is the vindication of the naturalness of the supernatural, so the gift of religion to Science is the demonstration of the supernaturalness of the Natural. Thus, as the supernatural becomes slowly natural will also

---

[1]Dr. Robert J. Blaikie, *Secular Christianity and the God Who Acts* (London: Hodder and Stoughton, 1970), p. 48.
[2]Isaac Newton, "Optics," *Great Books of the Western World*, Robert M. Hutchins and Mortimer Adler, eds. (Chicago: Encyclopedia Britannica, 1952), vol. 3, pp. 542–544.
[3]Blaikie, op. cit. p. 48.

the natural become slowly supernatural, until in the impersonal authority of Law men everywhere recognize the Authority of God."[4]

The Foundation of Activity and Reality

Robert Blaikie

"For those whose starting-point is biblical rather than secular, the basic presupposition is the reality, power and over-all authority of God as Agent, God who acts. This is the fundamental faith-affirmation of the biblical Christian: God is real and active, and all other reality and activity originates from Him. It is in terms of this fact, for the Christian, that every claim to truth must ultimately be assessed."[5]

Blaise Pascal

"The God of the Christians is not a God who is simply the author of mathematical truths or of the order of the elements; that is the view of the heathens and Epicureans. He is not merely a God who exercises His providence over the lives and fortunes of men, to bestow on those who worship Him a long and happy life. That was the portion of the Jews. But the God of Abraham, the God of Isaac, the God of Jacob, the God of the Christians is a God of love and comfort, a God who fills the soul and heart of those He possesses, a God who makes them conscious of their inward wretchedness and His infinite mercy, who unites himself with their innermost soul, who fills it with humility and joy, with confidence and love, who renders them incapable of any other end but himself.

"All who seek God without Jesus Christ, and who rest in nature, either find no light to satisfy them or come to form for themselves a means of knowing God and serving Him without a mediator. Thereby they fall either into atheism or deism, two things which the Christian religion abhors almost equally."[6]

The Foundation of the Miraculous

C. S. Lewis

"He is the opaque center of all existences, the thing that simply and entirely *is*, the fountain of facthood. And yet, now that He has created, there is a sense in which we must say that He is a particular Thing and even one Thing among others. To say this is not to lessen the immeasurable difference between Him and them. On the contrary, it is to recognize in Him a positive perfection which Pantheism has obscured; the perfection of being creative. He is so brim-full of existence that He can give existence away, can cause things to be, and to be other than himself, can make it untrue to say that He is everything. . . . We know that He invents, acts,

---

[4]Henry Drummond, *Natural Law in the Spiritual World* (London: Hodder and Stoughton, 1884), pp. xxii-xxiii.
[5]Blaikie, op. cit. p. 49.
[6]Blaise Pascal, *Pensees*, Section VIII.

creates. After that there can be no ground for assuming in advance that He does not do miracles."[7]

The Foundation of Art

George MacDonald

> To be on earth a poem of God's making
> To have one's soul a leaf, on which God's pen
> In various words, as of triumphant music,
> That mingles joy and sorrow, setteth forth
> That out of darkness He has brought the light
> To such perchance, the poet's voice is given
> To tell the mighty tale to other worlds.[8]

Francis Schaeffer

"As a younger Christian I never thought it right to use the word *creation* for an artist's work. I reserved it for God's initial work alone. But I have come to realize this was a mistake, because while there is indeed a difference, there is a very important parallel. The artist conceives in his thought-world and then he brings forth into the external world. . . . And it is exactly the same with God. God who existed before had a plan, and He created and caused these things to become objective. Furthermore, just as one can know something very real about the artist from looking at his creation, so we can know something about God by looking at His creation. . . .

"And yet the differences between the artist and God are overwhelming because we, being finite, can only create in the external world out of that which is already there. . . . God is quite different. Because He is infinite, He created originally out of nothing—*ex nihilo*. There was no mass, no energy particles, before He created. We work through the manifestation of our fingers. He, in contrast, created merely . . . by His word. Here is power beyond all that we can imagine in the human, finite realm. He was able to create and shape merely by His spoken word."[9]

Dorothy Sayers

"It is true that everyone is a 'maker' in the simplest meaning of the term. We spend our lives putting matter together in new patterns and so 'creating' forms which were not there before. . . . Though we cannot create matter, we continually by rearrangement create new and unique entities.

"It is the artist who more than other men is able to create something out of nothing. A whole artistic work is immeasurably more than the sum of its parts. . . . The 'creation' is not a product of matter, and is not simply

---

[7]C.S. Lewis, *Miracles* (New York: Macmillan, 1978), pp. 92–93.

[8]George MacDonald, *Diary of an Old Soul* (Minneapolis, Minn.: Augsburg Publishing House, 1965), Introduction.

[9]Francis A. Schaeffer, *Genesis in Space and Time* (Downers Grove, Ill.: InterVarsity Press, 1972), pp. 27–28.

a rearrangement of matter. The amount of matter in the universe is limited, and its possible rearrangements, though the sum of them would amount to astronomical figures, is also limited. But no such limitation of numbers applies to the creation of works of art. . . . The components of the material world are fixed; those of the world of imagination increase by a continuous and irreversible process, without destruction or rearrangement of what went before. This represents the nearest approach we can experience to 'creation out of nothing' and we conceive of the act of absolute creation as being an act analogous to that of the creative artist."[10]

The Difference Between Divine and Human Creativity

Bertrand Brasnett

"It is perhaps worthwhile to remind ourselves that creation, although it is *from* nothing is not *by* nothing. It is no part of the Christian tradition that the universe is self-caused or its own creator. . . . In the Christian view, the universe is dependent for its existence upon God. It is created *by* God but not *out of* God. Were it created out of God, such creation might impart to it something of the infinite quality . . . of Deity. . . .

"In human experience there is nothing that corresponds precisely to creation in the theological sense of the term. Man does not create, he modifies already existing material. It is true we speak of creative work and in one sense such work is calling into existence of that which formerly was not. The great sculptor 'creates' a statue, but the statue was already there hidden in the stone, and if there had been no stone there would have been no statue. . . . But creation as understood theologically is creation *ex nihilo*, creation with no previously existing ground. To creation of this kind there is no parallel in human activity."[11]

The Foundation of Experimentation and Discovery

George Washington Carver

"It is not we little men who do the work; it is our blessed Creator working through us. . . . Other people can have this power if they only believe. The secret lies right here in the Bible, in the promises of God. They are real, but so few people believe them to be real.

"Without God to draw aside the curtains I would be helpless. No books ever go into my laboratory. The thing that I am to do and the way of doing it come to me. I never grope for methods, the method is revealed at the moment I am inspired to create something new. . . . My discoveries come like a divine revelation from God. The idea and the method of working out a new product come all together. . . . Anything will give up its secrets if you love it enough."[12]

---

[10]Dorothy Sayers, *Christian Letters to a Post-Christian World* (Grand Rapids, Mich: Eerdmans, 1969), pp. 104–105.
[11]Bertrand Brasnett, *The Infinity of God* (London: Longmans, Green, and Co., 1933), pp. 43, 44.
[12]Basil Miller, *George Washington Carver*, pp. 80, 104, 161.

C. F. Von Wiezacker

"The concept of strict and generally valid laws of nature could have hardly arisen without the Christian concept of creation. Matter in the Platonic sense which must be 'prevailed upon' by reason will not obey mathematical laws exactly; matter which God created from nothing may well strictly follow the rules which its Creator had laid down for it. In this sense I called modern science a legacy; I might even have said a child of Christianity."[13]

Robert E. D. Clark

"Part of the 'hidden history' of science is the record of Christians who contributed deeply to major research breakthroughs; although there have been many fine thinkers and researchers who were not believers, the idea that a belief in creationism halts human inquiry, that a picture of reality starting off with God 'finishes off any ideas of research' is a modern fiction. The life-sciences once again have many Christian researchers like those in the past, such as Linnaeus, the great Swedish botanist, and his predecessor John Ray, (whose book *The Wisdom of God Manifested in the Works of Creation* blocked evolutionary thought in science for two hundred years). History is filled with the Christian genius of men like Kepler, Galileo, Bacon, the brilliant Isaac Newtons, Pascals and Leibnitzs who, despite the strange silence on this aspect of their lives from the secular researcher, all outspokenly and unashamedly loved God and studied with joy His world."[14]

Francis Bacon

"This I dare affirm in knowledge of Nature, that a little natural philosophy at the first entrance into it, doth dispose the opinion to atheism; but on the other side, much natural philosophy, and wading deep into it, will bring about men's minds to religion."[15]

Henry Drummond

"When I began to follow out these lines I had no idea where they would lead. . . . But in almost every case after stating what appeared to be the truth in words gathered direct from the lips of Nature, I was sooner or later startled by a certain similarity in the general idea to something I had heard before, and this often developed in a moment and when I was least expecting it, into recognition of some familiar article of faith. . . . I did not begin by tabulating the doctrines as I did the laws of nature and then proceed with the attempt to pair them. The majority of them seemed at first too far removed from the natural world even to suggest this. Still less did I begin with doctrines and work downwards to find their relations

---

[13]Colin Chapman, *Christianity on Trial* (Berkhamsted, England: Lion Publishing, 1974), vol. 2, p. 121.
[14]Robert E.D. Clark, "Creator God or Cosmic Magician?," *Symposium on Creation*, Vol. IV, pp. 117–118.
[15]Francis Bacon, *Meditationes Sacrae*, p. x.

in the natural sphere. It was the opposite process entirely. I ran up the Natural Law as far as it would go and the appropriate doctrine seldom ever loomed in sight till I had reached the top. Then it burst into view in a single moment. I can scarcely now say whether in those moments I was more overcome with thankfulness that Nature was so like Revelation or more filled with wonder that Revelation was so like Nature. . . .

"There is a sense of solidity about a Law of Nature which belongs to nothing else in our world. Here, at last, amidst all that is shifting, one thing is sure; one thing outside ourselves, unbiased, unprejudiced, un-influenced by like or dislike, by doubt or fear; one thing that holds on its way to me eternally incorruptible and undefiled. This, more than anything else, makes one eager to see the Reign of Law traced in the spiritual sphere."[16]

Creation and the Next Creation

T. DeWitt Talmage

"It is exciting to see a ship launched. The people gather in a temporary gallery erected for their accommodation. The spectators are breathless, waiting. . . . But my Lord Jesus saw this ship of a world launched, with its furnaces of volcano, and flags of cloud and masts of mountain and walking-beams of thunderbolt, while the morning stars shouted and the orchestra of heaven played 'Great and marvelous are thy works Lord God Almighty!'

"The same Hand that put up this universe will pull it down. . . . The furnaces already on fire in the heart of the earth will burst their bounds and the mountains kindle, and the great forests begin to crackle, and the wild beasts tumble off the crags in an avalanche of terror, and the metals melt flowing in liquid down the gulches and the ocean to steam and bubble and finally to flame, and the round earth from all sides shoot out forked tongues of fire. All the Universe will know who set on fire the one world, and who shattered the others, for Christ, my Lord will stand amidst the roar and crackle and thunder and crash of that final undoing proclaim-ing, 'I AM THE OMEGA!' "[17]

The Heavens Declare

Chrysostom

"We differ from unbelievers in our estimate of things. The unbeliever surveys the heavens and he worships them because he thinks they are a divinity; he looks to earth and makes himself a servant to it and longs for the things of sense. But not so with us. We survey the heavens and admire

---

[16]Drummond, op. cit., pp. xvi-viii, p. 23.

[17]T. De Witt Talmage, "The A and the Z," *Twenty Centuries of Great Preaching*, Clyde E. Fant Jr. and William M. Dinson Jr., eds. (Waco, Texas: Word Books, 1971), vol. 1, p. 272.

Him that made them; for we do not believe them to be a god, but a work of God. I look on the whole creation, and am led by it to the Creator."[18]

Henry Drummond

"We have Truth in Nature as it came from God. And it has to be read with the same unbiased mind, the same open eye, the same faith, and the same reverence as all other Revelation."[19]

He Is Not Silent

Samuel Shoemaker

"Whatever happens in prayer depends on what kind of god God is. If He created the universe and gave everything a primeval push and then retired beyond where we can get in contact with Him prayer is a vain effort. But if He be 'God and Father of our Lord Jesus Christ' He is not like that. He is concerned for the creation He made and concerned with the people in it who are meant to be His children. Most people in our day believe in some kind of God. There are very few atheists. Someone said an atheist is just a theologian with the jitters. But there are many who think God is so great and so impersonal that He cannot possibly mean anything personal to us and we cannot even say He is a 'personal God.'

"Let me try to answer that not from my own wisdom but from that of a man who graduated from Princeton with the highest honors in all of its history—signe cum laude—the late Dr. Henry Norris Russell of the Department of Astronomy. One evening he had been giving us some head-splitting figures on the size of the universe. Talking with him afterwards I said 'Dr. Russell, how is it possible for an infinite God to have time for us?' He replied (and I recall his exact words), 'The trouble is that your infinite God is not infinite enough. If He is really infinite He can dispatch the affairs of this universe in the twinkling of an eye, and then have all the time in the world for you.' "[20]

C. S. Lewis

"Men are reluctant to pass over from the notion of an abstract and negative deity to the living God. I do not wonder. . . . The Pantheist's God does nothing, demands nothing. He is there if you wish for Him, like a book on a shelf. He will not pursue you. There is no danger that at any time heaven and earth should flee away at His glance. But Christ the Creator King is *there*. And His intervening presence is a terribly startling thing to discover—You have had a shock like that before . . . when the line pulls at your hand, when something breathes beside you in the darkness. So here; the shock comes at the precise moment when the thrill of

---

[18]Chrysostom, *Twenty Centuries of Great Preaching*, Clyde E. Fant Jr. and William M. Dinson Jr., eds. (Waco, Texas: Word Books, 1971), vol. 1, p. 73.
[19]Drummond, op. cit. p. 11.
[20]Samuel M. Shoemaker, *Twenty Centuries of Great Preaching*, Clyde E. Fant Jr. and William M. Dinson Jr., eds. (Waco, Texas: Word Books, 1971), vol. 1, p. 102.

life is communicated to us along the clues we have been following. It is always shocking to meet life where we thought we were alone. 'Look out!' we cry 'It's alive!' . . . An impersonal God—well and good. A subjective God of beauty, truth and goodness, inside our own heads—better still. A formless, life-force surging through all of us, a vast power which we can tap—best of all. But God himself, alive, pulling at the other end of the cord, perhaps approaching us at an infinite speed, the hunter, King, husband—that is quite another matter.

"There comes a moment when the children who have been playing at burglars hush suddenly; was that a *real* footstep in the hall? There comes a moment when people who have been dabbling in religion ('Man's search for God!') suddenly draw back. Supposing we really found Him? We never meant it to come to that! Worse still, supposing He had found us? So it is a sort of Rubicon. One goes across; or not. But if one does, there is no manner of security against miracles. One may be in for *anything*."[21]

Participating in Creation

Harry Emerson Fosdick

"Surely this principle runs through all of life. Life is not what you find; it is what you create. Many people wander into the world and pick up everything they can get their hands upon looking for life. They never get it. What they get is *existence*. Existence is what you *find*; life is what you *create*. . . . One wonders if this ability to tackle life as Titus tackled Crete, without which America would lose nine-tenths of its glory is going to be distinctive of the new generation. . . . We are surrounding them in our families with luxuries that we never knew, that our fathers never dreamed. They are told on every side that personality is a creature of environment and that the great thing is for everybody to be surrounded by commodious and comfortable circumstances. I do not think that it is going to make them morally wild but I am sure that it is deceiving many of them as to the real secret of living. They are expecting to find life, pick it up, get it out of circumstances and that is a fallacy. You never find life, you create it. Often the best friend a man ever has is not comfort, but the stimulus and challenge of antagonistic environment to awaken the resistance of his slumbering soul. . . .

"When a man does live in this spirit of Jesus, it is more satisfying than anything besides. Consider; the deepest joy in life is creativeness. To find an undeveloped situation, to see its possibilities to brood over it, pray about it, think concerning it, work for it, to get something done there that would not have been done except for your creative soul—that is a satisfaction in comparison with which superficial joys are trivial."[22]

---

[21]Lewis, op. cit. pp. 97–98.
[22]Harry Emerson Fosdick, *Twenty Centuries of Great Preaching*, Clyde E. Fant Jr. and William M. Dinson Jr., eds. (Waco, Texas: Word Books, 1971), vol. 9, pp. 36, 38.

CHAPTER SIX:

COROLLARY ONE:
GOD IS A LOVING PERSON

Scriptures

God Has a Mind and He Thinks

"I will raise me up a faithful priest, that shall do according to that which is in mine heart and in my mind . . ." (1 Sam. 2:35)

"Jesus increased in wisdom and stature, and in favour with God and man." (Luke 2:52)

"O the depth of the riches both of the wisdom and knowledge of God! how unsearchable are his judgments, and his ways past finding out! For who hath known the mind of the Lord? or who hath been his counsellor?" (Rom. 11:33–34)

"For who hath known the mind of the Lord, that he may instruct him? But we have the mind of Christ." (1 Cor. 2:16)

He Has Thoughts

"For my thoughts are not your thoughts, neither are your ways my ways, saith the LORD. For as the the heavens are higher than the earth, so are my ways higher than your ways, and my thoughts than your thoughts." (Isa. 55:8–9)

"For I know the thoughts that I think toward you, saith the LORD, thoughts of peace, and not of evil, to give you an expected end." (Jer. 29:11)

He Reasons

"If thou sayest, Behold, we knew it not; doth not he that pondereth the heart consider it? and he that keepeth thy soul, doth not he know it? and shall not he render to every man according to his works?" (Prov. 24:12)

"Come now, and let us reason together, saith the LORD: though your sins be as scarlet, they shall be as white as snow." (Isa. 1:18)

He Remembers

"Go and cry in the ears of Jerusalem, saying, Thus saith the LORD; I remember thee, the kindness of thy youth, the love of thine espousals, when thou wentest after me in the wilderness . . ." (Jer. 2:2)

"And they consider not in their hearts that I remember all their wickedness: now their own doings have beset them about; they are before my face." (Hos. 7:2)

God Has Emotions

He Grieves

"And God saw that the wickedness of man was great . . . and it repented the LORD that he had made man on the earth, and it grieved him at his heart." (Gen. 6:5–6)

"His soul was grieved for the misery of Israel." (Judg. 10:16)

"Forty years long was I grieved with this generation, and said, It is a people that do err in their heart, and they have not known my ways." (Ps. 95:10)

"A man of sorrows, and acquainted with grief." (Isa. 53:3)

"Grieve not the Holy Spirit of God." (Eph. 4:30)

"In the days of his flesh, when he had offered up prayers and supplications with strong crying and tears unto him that was able to save him from death, and was heard in that he feared." (Heb. 5:7)

He Can Be Angry

"Kiss the Son, lest he be angry, and ye perish from the way, when his wrath is kindled but a little. Blessed are all they that put their trust in him." (Ps. 2:12)

"God judgeth the righteous, and God is angry with the wicked every day." (Ps. 7:11)

"They provoked him to anger with their high places, and moved him to jealousy with their graven images." (Ps. 78:58)

"Who knoweth the power of thine anger? even according to thy fear, so is thy wrath." (Ps. 90:11)

"Thou wast angry with me, thine anger is turned away, and thou comfortedst me." (Isa. 12:1)

"For my name's sake will I defer mine anger, and for my praise will I refrain for thee, that I cut thee not off." (Isa. 48:9)

"Thus saith the LORD of hosts; I am jealous for Jerusalem and for Zion with a great jealousy. And I am very sore displeased with the heathen that are at ease: for I was but a little displeased, and they helped forward the affliction." (Zech. 1:14–15)

He Shows Mercy

"But he, being full of compassion, forgave their iniquity, and destroyed them not: yea, many a time turned he his anger away, and did not stir up all his wrath." (Ps. 78:38)

"The LORD is gracious, and full of compassion; slow to anger, and of great mercy." (Ps. 145:8)

"Who is a God like unto thee, that pardoneth iniquity, and passeth by the transgression of the remnant of his heritage? he retaineth not his anger for ever, because he delighteth in mercy." (Mic. 7:18–19)

"I beseech you therefore, brethren, by the mercies [oiktirmoi—compassionate feelings] of God, that ye present your bodies a living sacrifice." (Rom. 12:1)

"Blessed be God, even the Father of our Lord Jesus Christ, the Father of mercies [compassionate feelings: ton oiktirmon], and the God of all comfort; who comforteth us in all our tribulation, that we may be able to comfort them which are in any trouble, by the comfort wherewith we ourselves are comforted of God." (2 Cor. 1:3–4)

He Rejoices

"And the Lord thy God will make thee plenteous in every work of thine hand . . . for the Lord will again rejoice over thee for good, as he rejoiced over thy fathers." (Deut. 30:9)

"The glory of the LORD shall endure for ever: the LORD shall rejoice in his works." (Ps. 104:31)

"Yea, I will rejoice over them to do them good, and I will plant them in this land assuredly with my whole heart and with my whole soul." (Jer. 32:41)

"The LORD thy God in the midst of thee is mighty; he will save, he will rejoice over thee with joy; he will rest in his love, he will joy over thee with singing." (Zeph. 3:17)

"In that hour Jesus rejoiced in spirit [agaliao—to jump for joy, exalt, be exceedingly glad], and said, I thank thee, O Father, Lord of heaven and earth, that thou hast hid these things from the wise and prudent, and hast revealed them unto babes: even so, Father; for so it seemed good in thy sight." (Luke 10:21)

"I say unto you, that likewise joy shall be in heaven over one sinner that repenteth, more than over ninety and nine just persons, which need no repentance." (Luke 15:7)

"And I am glad [rejoice] for your sakes that I was not there, to the intent ye may believe . . ." (John 11:15)

He Suffers

"In all their affliction he was afflicted . . . in his love and in his pity he redeemed them." (Isa. 63:9)

"And they that escape of you shall remember me among the nations whither they shall be carried captives, because I am broken with their whorish heart, which hath departed from me." (Ezek. 6:9)

"O Jerusalem, Jerusalem, thou that killest the prophets, and stonest them which are sent unto thee, how often would I have gathered thy children together, even as a hen gathereth her chickens under her wings, and ye would not!" (Matt. 23:37)

"And when he was come near, he beheld the city and wept over it." (Luke 19:41)

"Jesus wept." (John 11:35) (The shortest verse in the Bible.)

"Jesus therefore again groaning in himself cometh to the grave . . ." (John 11:38)

God Has Choice and He Decides

"And God said, Let us make man in our image, after our likeness: and let them have dominion . . ." (Gen. 1:26)

He Wills

"And it repented the LORD that he had made man on the earth. . . . And the LORD said, I will destroy man whom I have created . . ." (Gen. 6:6–7)

"And God said, This is the token of the covenant which I make between me and you and every living creature . . . for perpetual generations." (Gen. 9:12)

"And the LORD said unto Moses, I have seen this people, and, behold, it is a stiff-necked people: now therefore let me alone, that my wrath may wax hot against them, and that I may consume them: and I will make of thee a great nation." (Ex. 32:9–10)

"Turn again, and tell Hezekiah the captain of my people, Thus saith the LORD, the God of David thy father, I have heard thy prayer, I have seen thy tears . . . I will add unto thy days fifteen years." (2 Kings 20:5–6)

"Thus saith the LORD, Ye have forsaken me, and therefore have I also left you in the hand of Shishak. Whereupon the princes of Israel and the king humbled themselves. . . . And when the LORD saw that they humbled themselves, the word of the LORD came to Shemaiah, saying, They have humbled themselves; therefore I will not destroy them, but I will grant them some deliverance." (2 Chron. 12:5–8)

"And there came a leper . . . saying unto him, If thou wilt, thou canst make me clean. And Jesus, moved with compassion, put forth his hand, and touched him, and saith unto him, I will; be thou clean." (Mark 1:40–41)

"What if God, willing to shew his wrath, and to make his power known, endured with much longsuffering the vessels of wrath fitted to destruction. . . ?" (Rom. 9:22)

"But now hath God set the members every one of them in the body, as it hath pleased him [lit. *as he willed*]." (1 Cor. 12:18)

"Having predestinated us unto the adoption of children by Jesus Christ to himself, according to the good pleasure of his will." (Eph. 1:5)

"In whom also we have obtained an inheritance, being predestinated according to the purpose of him who worketh all things after the counsel of his own will." (Eph. 1:11)

"Who will have all men to be saved, and to come unto the knowledge of the truth." (1 Tim. 2:4)

"For that ye ought to say, If the Lord will, we shall live, and do this, or that." (James 4:15)

"For it is better, if the will of God be so [lit. *if wills the will of God*], that ye suffer for well doing, than for evil doing." (1 Pet. 3:17)

He Chooses

"For thou art an holy people unto the LORD thy God: the LORD thy God hath chosen thee to be a special people unto himself. . . . The LORD did not set his love upon you, nor choose you, because ye were more in number than any people . . ." (Deut. 7:6–7)

"For the LORD thy God hath chosen him out of all thy tribes, to stand to minister in the name of the LORD . . ." (Deut. 18:5)

"Then Jesse called Abinidab . . . and he [Samuel] said, Neither hath the LORD chosen this." (1 Sam. 16:8)

"For David my servant's sake, and for Jerusalem's sake which I have chosen." (1 Kings 11:13)

"Many are called, but few are chosen." (Matt. 22:14)

"And except that the Lord had shortened those days, no flesh should be saved: but for the elect's sake, whom he hath chosen . . ." (Mark 13:20)

To whom coming, as unto a living stone, disallowed indeed of men, but chosen of God, and precious . . ." (1 Pet. 2:4)

"But ye are a chosen generation, a royal priesthood, an holy nation, a peculiar people; that ye should shew forth the praises of him who hath called you out of darkness into his marvellous light." (1 Pet. 2:9)

"For he is Lord of lords, and King of kings: and they that are with him are called, and chosen, and faithful." (Rev. 17:14)

Bible Word Study

When considering God as a divine Person, we come face to face with a rewarding, yet overwhelming task. If we are to properly study His thoughts, feelings, and actions as they are outlined in Scripture, we are naturally launched into a study of everything God does and is. But no examination of God's personality can ever be exhaustive.

One thing to realize in studying is that biblical images used to describe God's personality also describe our own human reactions, yet wholly transcend them in every perfection. God is not only loving, He is love— the essential statement of what love is and more than can ever be expressed in the highest forms of human affection. Likewise, when God is "provoked to anger" no words can adequately describe the depths of divine emotion and expression in His unchanging and ultimate hatred of wrong. As Kittel comments:

"By using human terms of reference, these images show that God's work far exceeds human terms of reference. The One whose hand has stretched out the heaven is not a giant man; He is quite other than man; He is God, the First and the Last, who will still abide when heaven and earth, the work of his hands (Ps. 102:25f.), have perished and in face of whom it is nonsensical to fear men (Isa. 51:13). The firmness with which earth is established is a guarantee of the faithfulness of God (Ps. 119:90). Finally, these figurative expressions point to the power and wisdom of God: Jer. 10:12; cf. Prov. 3:19; 8:27; Job 38f.; Ps. 65:6."[1]

There are three great absolute statements about God in the New Testament: "God is *spirit*" (John 4:24); "God is *light*" (1 John 1:5); and "God is *love*" (1 John 4:8). Each reflects a fundamental facet of His nature; His essential being, His wisdom, and His goodness. They might be combined to give us the word describing His essential personality: God is *holy* (1 Pet. 1:16; Rev. 4:8).

Our focus here will be on just one of these great attributes, the one that comprehends all the affection and good will of God's nature: love.

Love (Hebrew)

chashaq (*khaw-shak*)—To cling (i.e., to join, [figuratively]) to love, delight in.[2]

"Emphasizes that which attaches to something or someone; in the case of emotions (to which the biblical usage is limited) it is that love which is already bound to its object. It should be distinguished from *ahab*

---

[1]*Theological Dictionary of the New Testament*, Gerhard Kittel, ed., Geoffrey W. Bromiley, trans. (Grand Rapids: Wm. B. Eerdmans Publishing Company, 1964), vol. 3, p. 1009.
[2]*Strong's* 2836.

'love'; *awa* 'desire, wish'; *hamad* 'desire, take pleasure in.' "[3]

God describes His love for Israel (Deut. 10:15) as this deep inner attachment. "He was bound to them of His own volition (love) and not because of anything good or desirable in them (Deut. 7:7). It is to God's attachment (love) Hezekiah attributes his deliverance (Isa. 38:17). This is the love that will not let go."[4]

ahab *(ah-hab)*—Affection, in a good or bad sense. Translated in the KJV as "love."[5]

The meaning of this word varies in intensity from "God's infinite affection for his people to the carnal appetites of a lazy glutton." God commands men to love Him (Deut. 6:5), and "the Psalms contain testimonies of obedience to that commandment (116:1; 145:20). Conversely God 'loves' men, especially his people Israel (Deut. 4:37; Isa. 43:4; Mal. 1:2)."[6]

checed or hesedh *(kheh-sed)*—Kindness; by implication (toward God) piety, or (subjective) beauty; reproof (rarely). Translated in the KJV as "favor," "good deed," "kindly," "kindness," "merciful," "pity," "reproach."[7] This word is used 245 times in the OT.

Leon Morris calls this term *hesedh*, "a term extraordinarily difficult to translate into English. Our language has no obvious equivalent." E. W. Heaton says the word expresses "one of the most profound ideas in Hebrew religion" and links it to terms like loyalty, devotion, fidelity, and "even the knowledge of God." The King James uses 11 different words to translate it, the favorite being "mercy"; the RSV renders it "steadfast love" 178 times.[8]

Important translation groups would be words meaning "love, kindness, lovingkindness, mercy, loyalty, promise, devotion, favor, and goodness."[9]

Nelson Glueck says it always indicates some kind of relationship, and a deep, lasting affection. "But what does the word tell us about that relationship? What is the attitude it denotes? Very plainly, it is an attitude of goodwill. But it is more than that—it is love strengthened by loyalty. . . . *Hesed* was not merely love dependent solely on the subject, but was, at the same time, loyalty and duty."[10]

Norman Snaith says it means "faithfulness rather than kindness, for we find the word to involve in almost every case a substratum of fixed, determined, almost stubborn steadfastness." C. H. Dodd combines both

---

[3]*Theological Wordbook of the Old Testament,* Laird R. Harris, ed. (Chicago: Moody Press, 1980), vol. 1, p. 332.

[4]Ibid. vol. 1, p. 332.

[5]*Strong's* 158.

[6]*Theological Wordbook of the Old Testament,* op. cit. vol. 1, p. 14.

[7]*Strong's* 2617.

[8]Leon Morris, *Testaments of Love* (Grand Rapids: Wm. B. Eerdmans Publishing Company, 1981), p. 65.

[9]Ibid. p. 66.

[10]Ibid. pp. 67, 69.

concepts, calling it "loyal affection."[11]

"To love God is to have pleasure in Him and strive impulsively after Him. Those who love God . . . seek God for His own sake."[12]

"Love of God for Israel (Deut. 7:13) is not impulse, but will; the love for God and the neighbor demanded of the Israelite (Deut. 6:5; Lev. 19:18) is not intoxication but act. . . . It is a love which makes distinctions, which chooses, which prefers."[13]

Love (Greek)

stergein—One of a number of NT words used for love. It means natural affection or family love, the lack of which is a characteristic of the last days (Rom. 1:31; 2 Tim. 3:3). *Stergein*, comments Kenneth Wuest, is compounded in Rom. 12:10 with the word *philos*, and is translated "kindly affectioned."

"*Stergein* designates the 'quiet and abiding feeling within us, which, resting on an object near to us, recognizes that we are closely bound up with it and takes satisfaction in that recognition.' It is a love that is 'a natural movement of the soul,' 'something almost like gravitation or some other force of blind nature.' It is the love of parents for children and children for parents, of husband for wife and wife for husband, of close relations one for another. It is found in the animal world in the love which the animal has for its offspring. It is a love of obligatoriness, the term being used here not in its moral sense, but in a natural sense. It is a necessity under the circumstances. This kind of love is the binding factor by which any natural or social unit is held together."[14]

philein—Friendship, built on common insight, interest or taste. This word is used 45 times in the NT in its various noun and verb forms. *Philein* is "an unimpassioned love, a friendly love. It is a love that is called out of one's heart as a response to the pleasure one takes in a person or object."[15]

It can be used of the joy a hypocrite experiences praying publicly (Matt. 6:5), or the pleasure many people get out of lying (Rev. 22:15).[16]

Men can be "lovers of their own selves" (2 Tim. 3:2) or have the "love of money," which is the "root of all evil" (1 Tim. 6:10; Luke 16:14; 2 Tim. 3:2). Likewise, the one who "loves" his own life will lose it (John 12:25). The world that "loves its own" (John 15:19) speaks of an inner affinity, a liking for that which is like itself. "*Philein* is a love of liking, and we like that which is like us . . . and for that reason the world hates the Christian."

---

[11]Ibid. p. 70.

[12]*Theological Dictionary of the New Testament*, op. cit. vol. 1, p. 28.

[13]Ibid. vol. 1, p. 38.

[14]Kenneth S. Wuest, *Word Studies in the Greek New Testament* (Grand Rapids: Eerdmans Publishing Company, 1973), vol. 3, p. 110.

[15]Ibid. vol. 3, p. 111.

[16]Ibid. vol. 3, pp. 118–119.

Alternately one can be a "lover of that which is [intrinsically] good" (Titus 1:8).[17]

"Kindness" in Acts 28:2, "love toward man" in Titus 3:4, and "courteously" in Acts 27:3, are all from *philein*, and a Greek word for man. Together, we often translate them as "philanthropy." *Philein* is often used with another word literally meaning "from the same womb." We translate the combination as "brotherly love" (Rom. 12:10; 1 Thess. 4:9; Heb. 13:1) or "love of the brethren" (1 Pet. 1:22; 1 Pet. 3:8; 2 Pet. 1:7).[18]

The verb form of *philein* occurs throughout the NT and is translated "love" or "kiss" (Matt. 6:5; 10:37; 23:6; 26:48; Mark 14:44; Luke 20:46; 22:47; John 5:20; 11:3, 36; 12:25; 15:19; 16:27; 20:2; 21:15–17; 1 Cor. 16:22; Titus 3:15; Rev. 3:19; 22:15).[19]

Wuest says *philein* is based on an inner community, a bond between the person loving and the person or object loved, and a sharing of things in common. The one loving finds a reflection of his nature in the person or object loved. "It is a love of liking, an affection for someone or something that is the outgoing of one's heart in delight to that which affords pleasure."[20]

When Jesus asks Peter twice, "Do you love [*agapan*] me?", He was asking, "Do you love me because I am precious to you, with a sacrificial love that would make you willing to die for me?" Three times Peter replied, "Yes Lord, you know I am fond of [*philein*] you; I have an affection for you because of the pleasure I take in you" (John 21:15–19). Wuest comments: "Jesus asked for a love of complete devotion. Peter offers Him a love of pesonal heart emotion. Jesus asked for a love of surrendering obedience. Peter offers Him a love of personal attachment."[21]

The noun form of *philein* is *philos* and is translated "friend" (Matt. 11:19; Luke 7:6, 34; 11:5, 6, 8; 12:4; 14:10, 12; 15:6, 9, 29; 16:9; 21:16; 23:12; John 3:29; 11:11; 15:13–15; 19:12; Acts 10:24; 19:31; 27:3; James 2:23; 4:4; 3 John 14).[22]

"The Greeks made much of friendship, and this word was used by them to designate mutual attraction. 'Whatever in an object that is adapted to give pleasure, tends to call out this affection.' It is connected with the sense of the agreeable in the object loved. The words which best express this kind of love are 'fondness,' 'affection,' 'liking.' . . . As an outgrowth of its meaning of fondness, it sometimes carries that sentiment over into an outward expression of the same, that of kissing.

"*Philein* is used in John 16:27 where God the Father takes pleasure in and loves those believers who take pleasure in His Son and therefore love Him. It is a love of friendly affection. The Father finds the same kind of love for the Son in the hearts of the saints that is in His own heart for His Son."[23]

---

[17]Ibid. vol. 3, pp. 119, 123.
[18]Ibid. vol. 3, p. 123.
[19]Ibid. vol. 3, p. 122.
[20]Ibid. vol. 3, p. 111.
[21]Ibid. vol. 3, p. 120.
[22]Ibid. vol. 3, p. 122.
[23]Ibid. vol. 3, pp. 111–112, 121.

epithumia—Strong desire, or passion. Is a word sometimes used positively as in Luke 22:15; Matt. 13:17 and Phil. 1:23 ("I have a deep desire to depart and be with Christ") but most often to refer to lust or covetousness (1 John 2:16; Col. 3:5).

All these words are important but will not be dealt with in detail here. Each of these forms of love can be a blessing if used rightly, or a curse if misused. Family affection may lead to unfairness with another family. A friendship may selfishly discriminate. A strong desire to do God's will could equally become a strong desire to do our own. The key word we focus on is *agape*, that special noun rescued from an obscure family of Greek words and given meaning and import as never before by NT Christians.

agape (*ag-ah'-pay*)—Love, i.e., affection or benevolence.[24]

agapeo (*ag-ap-ah'-o*)—perhaps from *agan* (much); to love in a social or moral sense.[25] *Agape* is used 116 times, *agapao* 143, the adjective *agapetos* 61, a total of 320 times, contrasted to *philia* (once), *phileo* 25, and *philos* 29, or 55 times. "Clearly it is agape and its cognates that mattered to the writers of the New Testament."[26]

Agape, says Wuest, was never common in classical literature; it is used in Homer "only ten times, in Euripides but three. Its noun form *agapesis* is rare. The form *agape*, so frequently found in the New Testament, does not occur at all. Its first appearance is in the Greek translation of the Old Testament. It conveyed the ideas of astonishment, wonder, admiration, and approbation when connected with the word *agamai* which meant 'to wonder at or admire.' It was used in classical literature in the same sentence with *philein*, and had its distinctive sense of 'a love of prizing' as contrasted to *philein*, 'a love of liking.' . . . Its relative emptiness, so far as the general knowledge of the person was concerned who spoke Greek as his second language, made it the ideal recepticle into which the new moral and ethical content of Christianity could be poured."[27]

In pre-biblical Greek it meant only "to be satisfied with something . . . 'to receive,' or 'to greet,' or 'to honour,' i.e., in terms of external attitude. It relates more to the inward attitude in its meaning of 'seeking after something,' or 'desiring someone or something.' Particularly characteristic are the instances in which *agapan* takes on the meaning of 'to prefer,' 'to set one good or aim above another,' 'to esteem one person more highly than another.' "[28]

Agape love is a "love which makes distinctions, choosing and keeping to its object . . . a free and decisive act determined by its subject . . . the love of the higher lifting up the lower." It "must often be translated 'to

---

[24]*Strong's* 26.
[25]*Strong's* 25.
[26]Morris, op. cit. p. 125.
[27]Wuest, op. cit. vol. 3, p. 114.
[28]*Theological Dictionary of the New Testament*, op. cit. vol. 1, p. 35.

show love'; it is a giving, active love on the other's behalf."[29]

"*Agapan* is used in its verb, noun, and adjective forms about three hundred and twenty times in the New Testament. It is a love called out of a person's heart by an 'awakened sense of value in an object which causes one to prize it.' It expresses a love of approbation and esteem. Its impulse comes from the idea of prizing. It is a love that recognizes the worthiness of the object loved. Thus, this love consists of the soul's sense of the value and preciousness of its object, and its response to its recognized worth in admiring affection.

"In contrasting *philein* and *agapan*, we might say that the former is a love of pleasure, the latter a love of preciousness; the former a love of delight, the latter a love of esteem; the former a love called out of the heart by the apprehension of pleasurable qualities in the object loved; the latter a love called out of the heart by the apprehension of valuable qualities in the object loved; the former takes pleasure in, the latter ascribes value to; the former is a love of liking, the latter a love of prizing."[30]

"Love can be known only from the actions it prompts. God's love is seen in the gift of His Son. . . . But obviously this is not the love of complacency or affection, that is, it was not drawn out by any excellency in its objects. . . . It was an exercise of the divine will in deliberate choice, made without assignable cause save that which lies in the nature of God himself."[31]

Agapao is used of both human and divine actions; it is basically a choice for the highest good that expresses one's character. That it is basically a choice and neither a metaphysical necessity nor an intrinsic virtuous substance is shown by the fact that it is also used of people making a wrong choice. Someone may take as their highest good that which is not of greatest worth in God's evaluation; someone may prize and esteem as precious that which God condemns. "Love not the world" (1 John 2:15), "Men loved darkness rather than light" (John 3:19), "They loved the praise of men" (John 12:43), and "Demas hath forsaken me, having loved this present world" (2 Tim. 4:10) all use forms of agapao.

Michael Harper says, "Because God is love we do not discover God from our experience of love, but we discover love from our experience of God." Brunner says, "Every attempt to conceive love as a principle . . . becomes distorted either in the rigorist legalistic sense or in the hedonistic sense. Man only knows what the love of God is when he sees the way in which God acts, and he only knows how he himself ought to love by allowing himself to be drawn by faith into this activity of God."[32]

We can put all the ideas of the Bible words for this divine love together and say that *agape is a heartfelt supreme preference for the highest good of God and His universe, according to all their real, relative values.*

---

[29]Ibid. vol 1, p. 37.

[30]Wuest, op. cit. vol. 3, p. 112.

[31]W. E. Vine, *The Expanded Vine's Expository Dictionary of New Testament Words*, John R. Kohlenberger III, ed. (Minneapolis, Minn.: Bethany House Publishers, 1984), p. 693.

[32]Michael Harper, *The Love Affair* (Grand Rapids: Wm. B. Eerdmans Publishing House, 1982), pp. 22–23.

It is an *intelligent* choice, not just a pleasant, passing feeling. It is an *ultimate* choice, a wholehearted commitment involving loyalty, faithfulness, and trustworthiness. It is truly unselfish, opposing wrong.

Ultimately loyal to God, it prizes and prefers Him above all other objects of devotion or affection, because He alone deserves this honor. Consequentially, it deals with all of God's creation truthfully and wisely, always considering with care its highest good. It is the foundation of all true Christianity.

Questions and Answers

Q: *If there is a creator God, why do the innocent suffer?*

A: If there *is* no God, why are they *innocent* and *who cares* if they suffer? Innocence implies moral standards, and the sadness of suffering implies that someone cares about suffering, that it is not natural or ordinary, right or just. Only believers in a personal, omnipotent, and loving God ask this kind of question. If there is no personal God, there are no morals, no innocence, and suffering is a first truth of existence.

As to suffering, God is innocent and *He* suffers. The Lord Jesus, who suffered more than any man for our sake, did not promise to free mankind from suffering, but sin. And because suffering comes from our sin, each reborn person helps take some of the hurt from the heart of the universe.

Q: *If God is a God of love, why does the Bible say He is "angry with the wicked every day" (Ps. 7:11)?*

A: It is perfectly possible to love and be angry at the same time. You have done it yourself if you got mad at yourself when you did something foolish or wrong. The reason you were angry with yourself was that you knew you were capable of better things, but did not do them. God is angry with the wicked every day because He knows what they are capable of and to what depth they have fallen.

Q: *If God is good, how can He be jealous?*

A: Jealousy is the emotion of single-minded devotion. Jealousy is only wrong when it is self-centered, creating envy and hatred for others. But jealousy can also be positive—the single-mindedness of commitment and zeal. Jealousy is the only correct emotional response when a rightful love is threatened by some rival claiming an already pledged affection.

God loves us wholly, utterly and without reserve. We by right belong to Him, and an utterly faithful and committed God of covenant love cannot allow a rival to His rightful ultimate affection (Ex. 20:5; Deut. 5:9; 6:15). His response to all that would lead us to idolatry, wavering commitment, and spiritual seduction is a holy protective anger that flames against that which threatens His beloved (Deut. 4:23–31; 32:16–21; Ps. 78:52–58; Zech. 1:14–16; 8:2–8).

Q: *I hear Christians say that Jesus was perfect, yet He cursed a poor fig tree because it didn't have any figs and killed it (Mark 11:12–14). Doesn't this reveal a bad temper?*

A: No, it shows He was God! This incident happened on the way to the Temple, His Father's house, which had become badly corrupted (Mark 11:15–18). Certain trees in the Bible are consistent symbols: the *vine* represents the political history of the nation and the *olive*, its genuine spiritual history.[1] The *fig* tree is likewise a symbol, representing the religious history of a nation. It is unique in that the *fruit appears before the leaves.* On His way to the temple of the backslidden people of Israel, a place with all the trappings and no fruit, Jesus came across a fig tree with only leaves, *just as if it had fruit,* in violation of its proper function. He used the anomaly as an unforgettable object lesson to the disciples (Mark 11:20–22).

Q: *How can anyone know what God is like? An infinite God, far beyond our mortality, is too strange for finite man to understand.*

A: True, unless God is somehow related to us. We could never know God as the uncreated infinite being He is except for the fact that He is the personal Creator. An atheist asked Francis Schaeffer, "What sense does it make for a man to become an ant and die for the ants in order to save the ants?" Schaeffer answered, "No sense at all, for man is not related to the ant. But God made man in His own image and likeness; we are related to Him by creation in His image."

Q: *But how could anyone find an infinite God?*

A: No one can, unless that infinite God chooses to reveal himself. Zophar said to Job, "Canst thou by searching find out God? canst thou find out the Almighty unto perfection?" (Job 11:7). Truth comes by revelation and is possible because God, even though infinite, is also a person and thus able to communicate with us who are also persons—even though we are finite. In Scripture and in history, God has revealed himself to all who set their hearts on seeking Him. "And ye shall seek me, and find me, when ye shall search for me with all your heart. And I will be found of you, saith the Lord" (Jer. 29:13–14).

Q: *If that is true, why hasn't God disclosed himself to more people than just a few Jews and Christians?*

A: "The wicked, through the pride of his countenance, will not seek after God: God is not in all his thoughts" (Ps. 10:4). "The Lord looked down from heaven upon the children of men, to see if there were any that did understand, and seek God. They are all gone aside, they are all together become filthy: there is none that doeth good, no, not one" (Ps. 14:2–3). Because we run from God, He had to take the initiative to seek us, a rebel and runaway race. Through His Spirit and in His Son, anyone who will respond to Him can meet the same God who made Jews "Israelites indeed" and who is making heathen of all ages and places into Christians.

---

[1]Arthur C. Custance, *Time and Eternity,* pp. 60ff.

Q: *How can God possibly care for all the people in the world?*

A: God is not only a person, but an infinite person. He names every star (Ps. 147:4), attends the funeral of every sparrow (Matt. 10:29), and knows all our names as well as the number of hairs on our heads (Matt. 10:30). His care is real, His concern is genuine, and His ability is unlimited.

Q: *With so much hurt, pain, and horror in the world, what keeps God from going crazy?*

A: His love and His purposes. He who declares the end from the beginning (Isa. 46:10) is the only being great enough to carry the sins and sorrows of a world and live. Although our sin has caused God great suffering, He moves toward His final goal of a redeemed Church in a recreated universe filled with happiness and harmony (Rev. 21:1–7).

Q: *I don't believe God can really suffer. How can you say God is all-powerful, sovereign, and in total control of the universe and in the next breath say He can be affected by problems and evil in His creation?*

A: Because God is all-powerful, He is able to suffer without damage to either His character or purposes. Because He is truly sovereign, He is able to take existing evil in a fallen world and use it for His own purposes (Gen. 50:20). Because He is in total control of the universe, He is capable of managing His grief, knowing that the ultimate eternal outcome will be worth the passing pain. It was for the "joy that was set before him" (Heb. 12:2) that Jesus went to the cross, and both the incarnation and crucifixion demonstrate the reality of God's suffering; not out of His own weakness, but on behalf of ours (1 Pet. 2:21).

Q: *But if God really suffers, isn't He then at the mercy of turmoil and pain? How does that concur with an all-powerful God?*

A: God is not at the mercy of suffering. He has chosen to enter into it, bear it, and yet triumph over it (Luke 24:43–46; Acts 3:18). His alternative is to divorce himself from His creation, leave it a deist universe, and walk out. But long before the incarnation, God chose to fully enter into and wholly identify with all the potential sufferings of a world that, as yet, had never experienced them; He is the "Lamb slain from the foundation of the world" (Rev. 13:8).

Q: *If God cannot sin, what does it mean that God "repented" (1 Chron. 21:15; Amos 7:6; Jon. 3:10)?*

A: The word "repent" used of God is called an "anthropopathism," an image ascribing human feelings or reactions to God, because we know that God cannot change (Num. 23:19; 1 Sam. 15:29; James 1:17). But we can think of God's changelessness in terms of His uncreated being and eternally faithful character, not as some inability to make new decisions. God as Creator not only can make new choices (see Chapter 7) but because He is faithful and righteous He is perfectly able to respond with integrity and justice when men change their choices for or against His purposes and laws.

Q: *Are you saying then that God was wrong before He changed His mind?*

A: No, but that the world was. It seems clear that God was initially happy over His creation, and that the space-time fall of man and the subsequent spread of deep rebellion brought Him real grief. In Gen. 6:6–7 (and 37 other times in the Bible) the special word *"nacham"* is used for "repent." It comes from a root that means "to draw the breath forcibly, to pant, to breathe strongly, to groan," and is difficult to translate into English.

It is usually used of God instead of the other word *"shuwb"* used of man's repentance, his turning from sin. Zodhiates writes, "Essentially *nacham* is a change of heart or disposition, a change of mind, purpose, or conduct. When a man changes his attitude, God makes the corresponding change. God is morally bound not to change His stance if man continues to travel on an evil path. . . . When God did change His mind it was because of the intercession of man and because of man's true repentance (Ex. 32:12, 14; Jer. 31:19–20; Jon. 3:10). God is consistent (Ps. 110:4; James 1:17). Though it may appear that God's purpose has changed, according to God's perspective nothing has changed. Most prophecy is conditional upon the response of man."[2]

Q: *God loved the world (John 3:16), yet He tells us not to love it (1 John 2:15). What does He mean?*

A: God loved the world by dying in it to free it. We, too, must die to the world and its influence in order to demonstrate God's love for it in Christ so that He might redeem it (John 1:7; 9:5; Matt. 5:14; John 17:14–23).

Analysis and Discussion

Almighty God, whose most dear Son went not up to joy but first He suffered pain, and entered not into glory before He was crucified; mercifully grant that we, walking in the way of the cross may find it none other than the way of life and peace through the same Jesus Christ our Lord.[1]
                                                —The Book of Common Prayer

Even a cursory reading of the Bible shows us a striking fact: God really is *personal*. We tend (perhaps even prefer) to think of Him as aloof, apart, the great Unmoved Mover. Philosophically and theologically it is convenient to study Him from a "safe" distance. But the trouble with the real God, the biblical God, is that He will not remain safely distant. The "impartial" study of God is rather like impartial fishing for giant sharks by hanging a line over the side of the boat. Debate the merits of various baits

---

[2]Spiros Zodhiates, *Lexicon to the Old and New Testaments*, p. 1613.
[1]*The Book of Common Prayer* (London: Oxford University Press).

if you wish, but what do you do when you suddenly feel a violent tug on the line and realize in shock that something is really there? As C. S. Lewis would put it: "Look out! It's alive!"

God's personality *is* alive in the Bible; He is constantly represented as one who sees, hears, acts, moves, reacts, and responds to a living, moving creation as its living, moving Creator. Our revelation of the Hebrew God is far different from the impersonal World-Soul, the Hindu *atman*, or the "Force" of *Star Wars*!

J. Oliver Buswell contends Scripture is "radically contrary to some philosophical statements that have crept into the history of theology. A biblical view of God as a *personal* Spirit is contrary to the view of Thomas Aquinas who said that God is the 'fully realized' in 'whom there is no potential.' It is also contrary to the pantheistic God of Spinoza, the transcendent timeless God of Kant and contrary to the pseudo-Calvinism of some of our contemporaries who teach that God is timeless, and those who hold with Jonathan Edwards that God has no freedom of choice. To say that these eminent writers hold views of God which deny His personality seems radical indeed. Some of them of course do believe in a personal God, but inconsistently. My point is that to deny that God performs self-conscious, self-determined specific actions in the process of time and that He is causally related to specific events is to deny something which is essential to the concept of personality."[2]

John Watson writes, "Jewish piety has laid the world under a hopeless debt by imagining the austere holiness of God and has doubled the obligation by adding His tenderness. It was an achievement to carve the white marble; it was greater to make it live and glow. The saints of Israel touched their highest when they infused the idea of Divine spirituality with passion and brought it to pass that the Holy One of Israel is the kindest deity that has ever entered into the heart of man. There was no human emotion they did not assign to God; no relationship they did not use as illustration of His love; no appeal of affection they did not place in his lips; no sorrow of which they did not make Him partaker. When a prophet's inner vision had been cleansed by the last agony of pain he dared describe the Eternal as a fond mother who holds Ephraim by the hands, teaching him to go; who is outraged by his sin, and yet cannot bear that Israel should perish; as a Husband who has offered a rejected love and still pleads; who is stained by a wife's unfaithfulness and pursues an adulteress with entreaties. You cannot lay your hand on the body of prophetical scripture without feeling the beat of the divine heart; one can detect in its most distant member the warmth of the divine love."[3]

What Is a Person?

Apart from the qualities with which we categorize all living things, from the most basic cell on up to the highest of animals, what are the

---

[2]J. Oliver Buswell, *Systematic Theology of the Christian Religion* (Grand Rapids: Zondervan Publishing House), vol. 1, p. 37.

[3]John Watson, *Mind of the Master* (New York: Dodd, Mead, and Company, 1896), pp. 255–256.

unique qualities held by a person? We say morality is essentially the ability to think, feel, freely originate choice, and perhaps most importantly perceive and respond freely to moral light, the knowledge of what is best or right.

Richard Swinburne observes that persons use language not only to communicate and for private thought, but to argue, to raise a consideration to object to another. Unlike animals, which show only evidence of "first-order wants" such as food or drink, people have "second-order wants." They can want *not* to want something, like a fasting man wanting not to want food, or a girl who does not want to hate her sister.

Persons can also "form and state theories about things beyond observation. . . . Above all they can make moral judgments; judgments that this or that action is morally obligatory" as distinct from advantageous or gratifying to the senses. They can decide that a certain pattern of life is supremely worthwhile. "If a thing is characterizable by all of the above predicates," says Swinburne, "then it is a person; and if it is characterizable by none it is not."[4]

Non-Biological Consciousness

This suggests interesting possibilities in the science of Artificial Intelligence (AI), the field of computer science in which man teaches computers to think for themselves about a particular subject area. Might a fourth- or fifth-generation computer system capable of performing independent analysis and judgment be called a real person?

One scientist suggests that developments in AI demonstrate a foundational claim of Scripture: you don't need a body to be a person. A. E. Wilder-Smith says, "It is now known that both intelligence and probably consciousness can theoretically exist independently of biology and of man. Such artificially induced intelligence rides on electronic gear, and it needs no anthropomorphology to explain it. In short, artificial intelligence puts energy, coding, programming, and patterns as we see them in life, matter, speciation, and evolution on a thermodynamic basis without any appeal to biology. . . ."[5]

If we call even early attempts in this field an expression of crude "personality," more complex personality can surely exist without an organic body. Intelligence can reside outside the limits of a biological frame. If jumping energy levels in a complex silicon matrix show what some contend are elements of true personality, then why is it an absurdity to believe in and worship a person who is wholly an immaterial spirit? There is no need to imagine a giant man in order to picture God as a person. Personality can be directly communicated by a phone call, a record, or a video tape; a body does not have to be physically present.

All this, of course, has bearing on God's immaterial nature; but do we

---

[4]Richard Swinburne, *The Coherence of Theism* (London: Oxford Press, 1977), p. 101.
[5]A.E. Wilder-Smith, *The Creation of Life: A Cybernetic Aproach to Evolution* (Wheaton, Ill.: Harold Shaw Publishers, 1970), p. 161.

mean more when we say *God* is a person? We know persons like us feel, think, and do things; the Bible says God also feels, thinks, and acts. We assume our own ability to do these things comes from being made in His image. But when it says He does those things, is it really like us, but on a much greater scale; or like us, but only by an adaptation to our human way of understanding? When the Bible says He is "provoked to anger" or that He "loves with an everlasting love," is there some sort of direct correspondence between the feelings, thoughts, and choices of God and the ones I feel, in at least a tiny and limited way?

Similarity and Difference

Perhaps, some say, these will be merely metaphors, language that applies a name or description to an object to which it is not literally applicable. But as Terence E. Fretheim points out, "Metaphors matter. . . ." A memorable metaphor, says Max Black, has the "power to bring two separate domains into cognitive and emotional relation by using language directly appropriate to the one as a lens for seeing the other."[6] J. Martin of Oxford University, in her Ph.D. dissertation on the use of metaphor in religious language, makes a strong case for the idea that a metaphor does not have a double meaning (literal and metaphorical) but a single meaning that results from the "interanimation of two networks of association" (the tenor and the vehicle).

Proper insight in a metaphor comes when we think about what is the *same* and what is *different* between the idea used for illustration and the idea illustrated; between the known and experienced and the less well known (perhaps only partially or dimly experienced). Virtually all words used about God in the Bible (except "God") *are* metaphors, though some use either the inanimate (God is our Rock, Ps. 31:2–3) or the animate world (God is an eagle, Deut. 32:11), the vast majority are drawn from the human creation in either form or function, personal acts, thoughts and feelings, or roles and activities in the family or society.

An Imperfect Correspondence

Fretheim points out two opposite dangers in using human form and function metaphors about God. The first is the temptation to imagine a continuous and real one-on-one correspondence of the image with the illustrated. "Anthropomorphic metaphors ought not to be conceived in terms of pictures, replicas, scale models, copies or the like." The variety of biblical metaphors (like Husband-Wife, Parent-Child) should prevent us from such literalism, and we should thus be careful not just to select one set, (like, for instance, the legal or judicial metaphors of God as Judge) to build our picture of Him. . . . There is always that in the metaphor which is discontinuous with the reality of God. God outdistances all

---

[6]Max Black, *Models and Metaphors: Studies in Language and Philosophy* (Ithaca, N.Y.: Cornell University Press, 1962).

our images; God cannot be finally captured by any of them."[7]

People who tend to "think of God" in terms of literal correspondence between metaphor and reality also tend to embrace idolatry and heresy. As Dorothy Sayers observed, "When we are dealing with simile or metaphor, it has to be remembered that every image is true and helpful only at its relevant point. . . . 'My love is like a red, red rose'; but it is not advisable to mulch her with manure. The common sense of mankind can usually be trusted to disentangle the relevant from the irrelevant—but not always. The great dispute that was fought out at Nicaea turned upon the relevant point of a metaphor. That the Divine Son was begotten of the Divine Father was common ground; the Arians, a literal-minded set of people, argued that He must therefore be subsequent to Him, like a bodily procreation. The Orthodox, more sensitively aware of the trap concealed in the metaphor, rejected the temptation to enclose God in space-time, holding stubbornly to the paradox of the Son's co-eternity. Indeed, nearly all heresies arise from pressing a metaphor beyond the point where the image ceases to be relevant."[8]

A Real Continuity

The opposite danger, says Fretheim, is to posit "no real or essential relationship between the metaphor and God as God really relates to the world. Hence people speak of "mere" metaphor, consider it to be only illustrative or decorative of thought to be dispensed with as one moves on to more abstract definitions. But . . . while there is no one-to-one correspondence, the metaphor does say some things about God that correspond to the reality which is God, while saying other things as well. . . ." The metaphor does, in fact, describe God and does contain information about God, but it is not *fully* descriptive. "It does not stand over against the literal; though the use of the metaphor is not literal, there is a literalness intended in the relationship to which the metaphor has reference. God *is* actually good or loving; God *is* the supreme exemplification of goodness and love. . . . Metaphors reveal an 'essential continuity with the reality which is God'; to use J. Martin's apt phrase, the metaphors are 'reality depicting.' "[9]

Does God Really Feel?

"Jesus will be in agony even to the end of the world. We must not sleep during that time."

Blaise Pascal

Early Christians did not seem to wonder about this question much. Certainly the disciples who were with Jesus never seemed to worry about it; they saw Him angry, sad, happy, and decisive; they may have wondered

[7]Terence Fretheim, *The Suffering of God* (Fortress, 1984), pp. 7–8.
[8]Dorothy Sayers, *A Matter of Eternity* (Grand Rapids: Eerdmans, 1973), p. 91.
[9]Fretheim, op. cit. p. 7.

why He was sad, but it is doubtful whether they debated as to whether *His* kind of "sad" was anything like *their* kind of sad. They saw God on display in these characteristics of Jesus; after all, His favorite description of himself was "Son of Man."

Where the credal confession says God is "without parts or passions," it ,seems the Westminster fathers were referring to "bodily" parts or passions (i.e., that He is an incorporeal spirit).

As C. S. Lewis points out, such credal statements were written primarily to show how much greater and more wonderful God is than our human limitations: "Great prophets and saints had an intuition of God which was positive and concrete to a high degree. Because just touching the fringes of His being they see He is plenitude of life, energy, and joy. . . . For no other reason, they have to pronounce that He transcends those limitations we call personality, passion, change, materiality, and the like. . . . The purpose for all this unclothing is not that our idea of God should reach nakedness but that it should be reclothed. But unhappily we have no means of doing the re-clothing. When we have removed from our idea of God some puny human characteristic . . . we have no resources from which to supply that blindingly real and concrete attribute of Deity to replace it."[10]

Divine Apathy?

Some say God is not only unlike us in His substance and His sinlessness, but also in His reactions: what they call the "Divine apathy." Yet if God knows exactly how we experience, how can He stand our sin? Brasnett says, "In what sense can God know the feelings of a man engaged in some terrible act of sadistic passion, or the mind of a would-be murderer calmly and gloatingly planning the brutal execution of a man he hates? We find it difficult to believe that even God can know the mental and psychological states of such persons as their possessors themselves experience them. Because God can never will evil, it seems hard to imagine Him really entering into the psychological experience of a man who is planning and willing evil and glorying in so doing. Yet if God does not know the mind and feelings of such a one, He does not possess all knowledge."[11]

"Divine apathy" is a philosophical idea first developed by Greek philosophers and adapted by some of the early Christian theologians. We can easily see why—they wanted to protect the Christian idea of God by preventing any identification of Him with things subject to failure, change, and decay. It is surely unthinkable that the omnipotent God is subject to physical hurt or susceptible to damage. Perhaps it would also be wrong to think of Him as even having emotional feelings of hurt like us. The Greeks thought difference, diversity, movement, and suffering in the divine

---

[10]C.S. Lewis, *Miracles* (New York: MacMillan, 1978), pp. 287–288.
[11]Bertrand Brasnett, *The Infinity of God* (London: Longmans, Green, and Co., 1933), p. 101.

nature inappropriate to deity. After all, if divine substance were capable of suffering, how could it be divine? Man and other transient non-divine beings all suffer as well as die; God must be different. If God shares His eternal life in saving a man and brings him immortality and non-transience, that life ought to give him "impassibility" too; in eternity he shouldn't be able to hurt or feel badly.

Some early Church fathers, drawing from Greek philosophy (which they saw as "natural theology" and adapted as their own foundation), saw apathy as the essence of the divine nature and the purest manifestation of human salvation in fellowship with God. While practically they adored the crucified Christ as God and preached about God's suffering, many felt obliged in defining their theology to follow the philosophers' lead. The "absolute Subject" [God] of Nominalist and Idealist philosophy surely could not suffer; otherwise it would not be absolute.

Yet the simple texts of Scripture seem to show that God *does* experience joy and suffering. How can we explain this? Lewis comments, "If God sometimes speaks as though the Impassible could suffer passion and as if eternal fullness could be in want . . . this can mean only, if it means anything intelligible by us, that the God of mere miracle has made Himself able to hunger and created in Himself that which we can satisfy. If He requires us, the requirement is of His own choosing. If the immutable heart can be grieved by the puppets of His own making, it is Divine omniscience that has so subjected it freely and in a humility that passes understanding. . . . If He who in Himself can lack nothing chooses to need us, it is because we need to be needed."[12]

Theopathy—Divine Feelings

"A healthy child is somehow very much like God. A hurting child, His Son."[13]

Calvin Miller

In his detailed study of the trinity, Jurgen Moltmann is one of a number of theologians who opt for *Theopathy*—the doctrine of God's passion rather than His apathy. He says it seems more consistent to understand the suffering of Christ as the suffering of the passionate God "if we cease to make the axiom of God's apathy our starting point and start instead from the axiom of Gods passion.

"Impassible, immoveable, united and self-sufficient the deity confronts a moved, suffering and divided world that is never sufficient for itself. . . ." But in contrast, God's passion and suffering are the very center of Christian history and tradition. Are these the only alternatives then; a God who is *unable* to suffer or a God who is *at the mercy* of suffering? No, he suggests, "There is a third form of suffering—*active* suffering—the voluntary laying oneself open to another and allowing oneself to be intimately affected by

---

[12]C.S. Lewis, *The Problem of Pain* (New York: MacMillan, 1978), pp. 38–39.
[13]Calvin Miller, *The Singer* (Downers Grove, Ill.: InterVarsity Press, 1975).

him; that is to say, the suffering of passionate love. . . . In Christian theology, the apathetic axiom only really says that God is not subjected to suffering in the same way as transient, created beings. It is not in fact a real axiom at all. It is a statement of comparison. It does not exclude the deduction that in another respect God certainly can and does suffer. If God were incapable of suffering in every respect then He would also be incapable of love. He would at most be capable of loving himself, but not of loving another as himself. . . . But if He is capable of loving something else, then He lays himself open to the suffering which love for another brings Him; and yet by virtue of His love He remains master of the pain that love caused Him to suffer. God does not suffer out of deficiency of being, like created beings. . . . But He suffers from the love which is the superabundance and overflowing of His being."[14]

William Temple writes, "The Son of Man *must* suffer. For the manifestation of love by which it wins its response is always sacrifice. The principle of sacrifice is that we choose to do or to suffer what apart from our love we should not choose to do or suffer. When love is returned, this sacrifice is the most joyful thing in the world, and heaven is the life of joyful sacrifice. But in a selfish world it must be painful and the pain is the source of the triumph."

Likewise Buswell comments: "Unless we wish to reduce the love of God to the frozen wastes of pure speculative abstraction, we should shake off the static ideology which has come into Christian theology from non-biblical sources, and insist on preaching the living God of intimate actual relationships with His people. God's immutability is the absolutely perfect consistency of His character in His actual relationships throughout history with His finite creation."[15]

Some Christians still feel that although this is the simplest picture of God as He reveals himself in Scripture, it nevertheless might make God out to be "too vulnerable." But what picture does the other emphasis give us of Him? While arguably preserving the "otherness" of God, apathy still tends to represent Him in a more "alien," remote light. Nothing in the voluntary passion of God appears to challenge His power, His abilities, or His sovereign rulership over the universe. Yet "right down to the present day, the apathy axiom has left a deeper impress on the basic concept of the doctrine of God than has the history of Christ's passion. Incapacity for suffering apparently counts as being the irrelinquishable attribute of divine perfection and blessedness. But does this not mean that to the present day Christian theology has failed to develop a consistent Christian concept of God? . . ."[16]

Some of the early Church fathers thought so. Origen wrote, "He, the Redeemer, descended to earth out of sympathy for the human race. He took our sufferings upon himself before He endured the cross . . . for if He had not felt these sufferings He would not have come to partake of

---

[14]Jurgen Moltmann, *The Trinity and the Kingdom of God* (SCM, 1981), pp. 21–23.
[15]Buswell, op. cit. vol. 1, p. 56.
[16]Moltmann, op. cit. p. 21.

our human life. What is this passion he suffered for us? It is the passion of love. And the Father himself, God of the Universe, 'slow to anger and plenteous in mercy' (Ps. 103:8), does He not also suffer in a certain way? Or know you not that He, when He condescends to men, suffers human suffering? For the Lord thy God has taken thy ways upon Him 'as a man does bear his son' (Deut. 1:31). . . . Even the Father is not incapable of suffering. When we call on Him He is merciful and feels our pain with us. He suffers a suffering of love, becoming something which, because of the greatness of his nature, He cannot be, and endures human suffering for our sakes."[17]

Charles Hodge draws attention to this when he comments, "Again the Schoolmen and often the philosophical theologians tell us there is no feeling in God. This, they say, would imply passivity or susceptibility of impression from without . . . which if assumed is incompatible with the nature of God. . . ." But such a view is "in real contradiction to the representations of God in the Old and New Testament. . . . Here again we have to choose between a mere philosophical speculation and the clear testimony of the Bible and our own moral and religious nature. Love, of necessity, involves feeling, and if there be no feeling in God there can be no love."[18]

Can God Feel Our Feelings?

Now then, how does God as a person perceive other sinful or finite created consciousnesses? Could God possess these various kinds of flawed or limited knowledge and experience without injuring His own perfectness? "What we particularly need," says Brasnett, "is to see more clearly into the nature of *sympathetic insight*. . . . The actor . . . sinks his personality into the part; he speaks and acts through them . . . he even thinks through them." The actor who can do this with reality and conviction is enriched even when the part played is ignoble; he gains from such a part only an increased breadth of sympathy for the fallen and the frail. Further, God is not only the actor who so could wholly 'understudy us' and play our parts to perfection; He is also the dramatist who wrote the play and created the characters. He knows not only how we in fact play them, but also how we ought to play them if we were the actors we ought to be." God is the "Creative Spirit who made the world and its inhabitants. He knows the purpose of His creation and how far it has fulfilled its destiny. . . . When we are as we ought to be, the ideal and the actual coincide, and God wills with our wills, thinks with our minds, speaks in our words and acts in our acts. But when we fall away from the ideal . . . God still knows our thoughts and words and acts, but He does not identify himself with them. He has knowledge of them but He does not make them His own."[19]

---

[17]Origen. "Homily VI in Ezekiel."
[18]Charles Hodge, *Systematic Theology* (Grand Rapids: Eerdmans, 1960), vol. 1, p. 428.
[19]Brasnett, op. cit. pp. 105–109.

A deity with zeal does not need harm our perception of God. On the contrary, says William Pope, it is the foundation of our very ability to speak meaningfully and worshipfully of Him.

Pope goes on, "If our conscience and sense of responsibility to a Judge, if our desires for communion with a Personal Father have no corresponding realities, where is our religion and where the Gospel on which it rests? We cannot exaggerate the importance of what is at stake here . . . there are many ways in which it pleases the Supreme to reveal Himself; but they all imply that He gives us a true perception of His own nature so far as it goes. This is the prevalent method of the Bible; where God speaks to man as a finite copy of His infinite Self. . . . 'My thoughts are not your thoughts' but only in the sense of being nobler; and 'neither are my ways your ways' but only in the sense of being better. . . . Personality, power, goodness, truth and love are reflections in us of His image; realities in us corresponding to realities in Him. 'He that planted the ear, shall He not hear? He that formed the eye, shall He not see?' We are transcripts from an Eternal Archetype. . . . The Incarnation is the pledge that human nature may have a true knowledge of the Divine."[20]

God's Moral Immanence in Creation

Not only does the doctrine of God's passion shed light on His relationship with man; it also illuminates His interaction with the rest of His creation. A deist view of God puts Him *out* of His creation; a pantheist view puts Him *into* it. For the deist, God has actively *left* the world; for the pantheist, He is actually *part* of it. Many with a deist view of Him seek to uphold His transcendence, but lose something lovely in so doing: His immanence in nature.

Brasnett thinks a re-examination of the way God experiences would return to the Christian that missing element without the pantheist weakness. He writes, "We are disposed to believe that the Divine omniscience has a very wide range in the animal kingdom." God knows all animal activities not only as a "superhuman Keeper of records might know them, but also as we can never know them, from within. God knows what the tiger's spring means to the tiger and also what it means to the fawn; He knows what the sweep of sunlight means to the soaring lark and is consciously present with the deep-sea monsters when they rejoice in the oceans' depths. . . .

"We might even go further, for what is true of the animal kingdom is likewise true in proportionate degree of all material things. With them, as with animals we tend to be deistic, to regard them as somehow started by God and then left to follow their own devices, or to be hammered into some shape or form by the rough clash of competing forces. And yet even pantheism, incomplete and unsatisfactory as it is, could have taught us better and enriched our creed. For pantheism knows that the stone is something more than a stone; it is in one sense part of the living God;

---

[20]William Pope, *Compendium of Christian Theology* (1881), Vol. I, pp. 245, 247.

and the tree that waves in the summer breeze does not wave alone, God waves with it. To us it does not seem that trees can feel or stones know emotion; but if there be in tree or stone some sentience of any kind, we should hold that God knows it and God shares it." [21]

"He Shines in All That's Fair . . ."

Catherine of Siena said, "The reason why God's servants love creatures so much is that they see how much Christ loves them, and it is one of the properties of love to love what is loved by the person we love."

The old song says it beautifully, if we do not confuse its message with mere pantheism, the world is as alive with the presence of God for those who have eyes to see, as it is fully alive to its glorious Creator, who senses all its moods and seasons like one great psalm of praise:

> This is my Father's world,
> He shines in all that's fair,
> In the rustling grass I hear Him pass;
> He speaks to me everywhere.
>
> *Maltbie Babcock*

Blind Helen Keller wrote:

> I run with playful winds that blow the scent
> Of rose and jessamine in eddying whirls.
> At last I come where tall lilies grow,
> Lifting their faces like white saints to God.
> While the lilies pray I kneel upon the ground;
> I have strayed into the holy temple of the Lord.

So too, we have a message to the broken-hearted of the world: *there is someone who really understands, who sees the sparrow fall, and who is never indifferent to our grief and sorrow.*

Calvin Miller writes, "A child who cries at the coffin of his father is only mature when he has lived long enough to cry at the coffin of his son. Never was a boy crucified but that the weeping Father has always found the nail-prints in his own hands."[22]

For this reason, the Gospel has a simple and direct appeal to the human heart: people know a little bit about what God feels like because they are made in His image, and they know how they feel when they are hurt, sad, or happy. C. S. Lewis says, "When Christianity says that God loves man it means that God *loves* man; not that He has some . . . indifferent concern for our welfare, but that in an *awful* and surprising truth, we are the objects of His love. You asked for a 'loving God'; you have one. The great Spirit you so lightly invoked, the 'Lord of terrible aspect' is present; not a senile benevolence that drowsily wishes you to be happy in your own way, not the cold philanthropy of a conscientious magistrate,

---

[21]Brasnett, op. cit. pp. 122–123.
[22]Miller, op. cit. p. 121.

nor the care of a host who feels responsible for the comfort of his guests, but the Consuming Fire himself, the Love that made the worlds, persistent as an artist's love for his work and despotic as a man's love for his dog, provident and venerable as a father's love for a child, jealous, inexorably exacting as love between the sexes. . . .

"The Impassible speaks as if it suffered passion, and that which contains in Itself the cause of its own and all other bliss talks as though it could be in want and yearning (Jer. 31:20; Hos. 11:8). . . . We were made not primarily that we may love God (though we were made for that, too) but that God may love us, that we may become objects in which the Divine love may rest 'well pleased.' "[23]

"When I think upon my God," said the musician Franz Josef Haydn, "my heart is so full of joy that the notes dance and leap from my pen; and since God has given me a cheerful heart, it will be pardoned me that I serve Him with a cheerful spirit."

Historical Discussion

Only a person can truly utter a person. Only from a character can another character be echoed. You might write all over the skies that God was just, but it would not burn there. It would be, at best, only a bit of knowledge; never a Gospel; never something which would gladden men's hearts to know. That comes only when a human life, capable of justice like God's, made just by God, glows with His justice in the eyes of men, a candle of the Lord.

Phillips Brookes

We have already seen that God has real feelings and experiences just as we do. On a much grander and greater scale, we now ask an even more important question: Does He make decisions too, just as His creation does? We know He is "righteous in all His ways" (Ps. 145:17); but is this because He does righteous acts, because He himself in some way is righteous*ness*? We know He is kind because the Bible calls Him kind; but how does God know that He *is* kind? By what standard does God measure His own behavior, and on what basis does He call himself holy?

Why is this important at all? Because the answer to this question is also the answer to a fundamental question: What is the ultimate basis of right and wrong? If we say, as we should, "God is _____," then the next question can be, "Why?" God *is* good. Is God good *just because* He says so or because He gets to make up the rules, or does *He himself* have some moral criteria or measurement for His own character and actions?

Both history and government reveal a constant shift in the tension

---

[23]C.S. Lewis, op. cit. pp. 34–36.

between *form* and *freedom*. We trace the basis for all law, structure, government and obligation to some perceived *form*. Responsibility, independence, decision, and morality all have roots in the idea of *freedom*. If these two principles are fundamental, we ought to find their source in God. All law finds its basis in the uncreated being of God. But from what does freedom originate? If freedom were identical with what God unchangeably is, then it would ultimately be an illusion, because it would be based on something that has no real alternative to change.

But there is another possibility. Perhaps we can make a distinction between what God *is* as a divine being (His uncreated substance and essence) and what God *does* as a divine person (His character and actions as the holy Creator). When we look at God as the ultimate divine person, we are also asking again this important question: Is God really free?

Is God a Moral Being?

Charles Finney said a moral being is someone who has *moral agency*; attributes of *intellect* (including reason, conscience, and self-consciousness), *sensibility* (the faculty of feeling, all sensation, desire, emotion, passion, pain, or pleasure), and *free will* (the power of choosing or refusing to choose in every instance in compliance with moral obligation). What we traditionally call free will is "the power of originating and deciding our own choices and of exercising our own sovereignty, in every instance of choice upon moral questions—of choosing in conformity with duty or otherwise in all cases of moral obligation."[1]

Our own human sensibility (which includes feelings and other sense perceptions) helps supply us with some idea of what is valuable; therefore, even a dumb dog won't kiss a hot stove twice. Redeemed and purified, our senses and understanding contribute to a better idea of our moral obligation to choose the best and helps us sense what alternatives we have.

Loving Ourselves

Because we are "wired" to serve God, we ought to feel good when we choose right. We were made to appreciate the best and avoid the worst. "Self-love," said Finney, "is constitutional. Its gratification is the chronological condition of the development of that moral law. In other words, we affirm that this intrinsic good ought to be universally chosen and sought for its own sake. . . . The sensibility, like the intellect, receives in a purely passive way, as distinct from a voluntary faculty. All its phenomena are under the law of necessity."[2]

Feelings thus help supply the understanding of which choice is of greater or lesser value and which ought to be chosen. But feelings themselves are amoral. We have no direct control or choice as to how we will

---

[1]Charles Finney, *Systematic Theology* (Minneapolis, Minn.: Bethany House Publishers, 1976), pp. 13–15.
[2]Ibid. p. 14.

feel when we expose ourselves or are exposed to different emotional influences.

Two Different Kinds of Law

Finney distinguished between *moral* and *physical* law. Physical law, like gravity or mathematical relationships, describes a way something *always* behaves. Someone slipping off a fourteen-story building has no choice but to fall, and 8×8 cannot optionally be 15. Physical law leaves no choice. It describes rules of action, what is true in the interlocking relationships of space, time, and matter. Find what is true, define it, and you will have physical law. In God's universe, things maintain the fixed relationships to each other that we discover in the sciences.

But God, though He runs the creation by physical law, gave moral beings a different and higher order of law: *moral law*. It does not describe the way creatures *do* behave; it reveals the way people *ought* to behave.We can call it a set of rules for action, describing what is true in the world of relationships and the consequences of trying to live outside this moral design.

Moral law describes what is true about the world of personal relationships and the consequences of trying to live differently from the way we were intended to. Moral law, Finney said, "is a rule of action with sanctions." It is that rule to which "moral agents ought to conform all their voluntary actions, and is enforced by sanctions equal to the value of the precept. It is the rule for the government of free and intelligent action as opposed to necessity and unintelligent action. It is the law of liberty, as opposed to the law of necessity—of motive and free choice as opposed to force of every kind." He goes on to say that if there is no real choice involved, no intelligent action allowed, no possible option, then the rule is physical rather than moral law.[3]

Both reason and emotion function under physical laws. No moral being can change his perceptions and emotions about anything he hears, sees, or reads. But free choice means you know you can always *do* something else. If you cannot, you are not under moral but physical law. If you can't help but do it, you have no true choice.

Relativity, Quantum Theory, and Choice

Today the concept of freedom is under major discussion, not only in the fields of psychology and sociology, but even in the hard sciences like physics. Although relativity theory postulates a future that unalterably exists already in some sense, it does not deny cause and effect relationships. Its quarrel is with the notion of an absolute past, present, and future; not with causation.

Quantum theory postulates that an observer has a key part to play in the nature of events. Human beings seem to be able to influence the

[3]Ibid. p. 1.

physical universe in a way nobody ever thought in Newton's day. For instance, in atomic study it seems that how you decide to measure an event affects the way the electrons actually behave; whether they remain stationary or move seems to be determined by what we decide we want to look at. The human choice seems to govern atomic behavior! The idea of a creative choice, originating in the being of man himself, suggests a causeless cause, something that brings into existence, affects, or changes some other event that is not itself determined.

Because we are most like God in this ability to create choice, the question of freedom and morality is a very important study. God has entrusted us with a very significant gift: we are able to genuinely affect the universe around us. While the laws of nature are statements of how things in God's creation actually behave; the moral laws of God apply to man and tell him how he ought to behave.

Moral Law

This moral law is God's basic rule for free moral agents. It consists of a revealed idea entering our mind via the conscience, a rule of obligation, an *oughtness* as opposed to necessity. There is no moral law when there is no choice. It cannot have elements of force, or be unavoidable.

All this, most people will readily admit, is true enough of man. We are moral agents. We cannot help feeling or thinking what we sense or perceive, but we have true freedom of choice and know the alternatives to our choices.

The important question is: Is *God* a moral being, not only in the sense of being able to discern and differentiate between good and evil, but in the sense of having His own infinite freedom to choose on the basis of His perception and sensibilities? Is He holy because of an ultimate moral obligation, because He too has eternally made some kind of free choice to be loving and kind, a choice not demanded by metaphysical necessity?

In humans, the intentions of the will resolve into choices. When someone wills an end, they know they could will differently; a person is genuinely free to make any end his goal. Of course man's freedom is circumscribed; he is not an absolutely autonomous or self-sufficient being like God himself, who is the only true claimant to that right.

A True Moral Equivalence

When God says, "Ye shall be holy: for I the Lord your God am holy" (Lev. 19:2), what does He mean? We know what it means to be holy—to conform our lives to the truth, to so feed on His life and nature that our own lives will be an expression of reality and love. But why would God tell us to be holy as God is? The simple answer is that when God gave us moral law, He did not just invent it for humans. *He himself* is a subject of that same law. It is not His invention but a *description of reality*, His own unchangeable reality. God's own character is under a law, governed by the value of His intrinsically great being, which He himself cannot change. If God himself is a moral being, His immutable holiness and moral perfection are qualities of His character and not of His substance.

Does God choose between what He perceives as good and evil as the basis for His thoughts and actions? Is morality the same with the infinite God as it is for finite humanity in regard to His ability to freely decide between alternative choices? Let's read a few thoughts from those who have spent some time pondering the idea:

Jonathan Edwards

Jonathan Edwards, along with many other Christian thinkers of his time, believed that while God was truly free to express His will, He nevertheless could choose only that which is best. He argued that God's will was "necessitated" by His wisdom:

"It is no disadvantage or dishonor to a being necessarily to act in the most excellent or happy manner from the necessary perfection of His own nature. This argues no imperfection, inferiority, or dependence, nor any want of dignity, privilege or ascendancy."[4]

He quotes Clarke and Locke to amplify his thought on this matter as follows: "This is a necessity not of nature or fate but of fitness and wisdom; a necessity consistent with the greatest freedom and the most perfect choice. For the only foundation of this necessity is such an unalterable rectitude of will, and perfection of wisdom as makes it impossible for a wise being to act foolishly.

"God is a most perfect free Agent, yet He cannot but do always what is best and wisest in the whole. The reason is evident; because perfect wisdom and goodness are as steady and certain principles of action as necessity itself; and an infinitely wise and good being, endued with the most perfect liberty can no more choose to act in contradiction to wisdom and goodness than a necessary agent can act contrary to the necessity by which it is acted; it being as great an absurdity and impossibility in choice for Infinite Wisdom to choose to act unwisely or Infinite Goodness to choose what is not good as it would be in nature for absolute necessity to fail of producing its necessary effect."[5]

"If we look on those superior beings above us who enjoy perfect happiness, we shall have reason to judge that they are more steadily determined in their choice of good than we; and yet we have no reason to think that they are less happy or free than we are. And if it were fit for such poor finite creatures as we are to pronounce what Infinite Wisdom and Goodness could do, I think we might say that God himself cannot choose what is not good. The freedom of the Almighty hinders not His being determined by what is best."[6]

"This Being, having all things always necessarily in view, must always

---

[4]Jonathan Edwards, *The Works of Jonathan Edwards* (University Press, 1977), Vol. I, p. 70.

[5]Clarke, *Demonstration of Being & Attributes of God*, Ed. 6, pp. 64, 112–113.

[6]John Locke, *An Essay Concerning Human Understanding*, Peter H. Nidditch, ed. (New York: Oxford University Press, 1975), Vol. I, Edit. 7, pp. 215–216.

and eternally will according to His infinite comprehension of things; that is, must will all things that are wisest and best to be done. There is no getting free of this consequence. . . . Infinite knowledge must direct the will without error. Here then is the origin of moral necessity; and that is really of freedom. . . . It is the beauty of this necessity that it is as strong as fate itself with all the advantages of reason and goodness."[7]

Edwards defines God's will as part of His sovereignty (His ability and authority to do whatever pleases Him). His will is "supreme, underived, and independent of anything outside himself . . . determined in everything by His own counsel, having no other rule but His own wisdom." He goes on, "His Wisdom, which determines His will, is supreme, perfect, underived, self-sufficient, and independent. . . . If God's will is steadily and surely determined in every thing by supreme wisdom then it is in every thing necessarily determined to that which is most wise."[8]

Charles Finney

Finney enlarged on these essential attributes of moral law by writing, "*Independence* . . . is an eternal and necessary idea of the Divine reason. It is the eternal self-existent rule of the Divine conduct, the law which the intelligence of God prescribes to himself. Moral law . . . does not and cannot originate in the *will* of God. It eternally existed in the Divine reason. It is the idea of that state of will which is obligatory upon God, upon condition of His natural attributes, or in other words, upon condition of His nature. As a law it is entirely independent of His will just as His own existence is. It is obligatory also upon every moral agent, entirely independent of the will of God. Their nature and relations being given and their intelligence being developed, moral law must be obligatory upon them and it lies not in the option of any being to make it otherwise."

We see from this that:

- Moral law is not for man alone; it is an eternal, self-existent rule. God lives this way based on His intelligence and not on some created imposition of His will.
- Moral law is an idea eternally existing in the divine reason, one that is not derived arbitrarily from His will but rather from His own infinite wisdom: He perceives the reality of His uncreated supreme value.
- Moral law is what God prescribes for himself, or the law He eternally lays down or authoritatively imposes on himself.

Furthermore, it should be obvious, Finney said, that moral law is "*immutable*—Moral law cannot change or be changed. It always requires a course of conduct precisely suited to his nature and relations. . . . It never changes its requirement. 'Thou shalt love' or be perfectly benevolent is its uniform and only demand. This demand never varies and can never vary. It is immutable as God is and for the same reason.

---

[7]Edwards, *Works* op. cit. Vol II, pp. 403–404.
[8]Edwards, *Works* op. cit. Vol I, p. 71.

"Unity—Moral law proposes the same one ultimate end of pursuit to God and to all moral agents. All its requisitions in their spirit are summed up and expressed in one word—*love* or benevolence. Moral law is a pure and simple idea of the reason. It is the idea of perfect, universal, and constant consecration of the whole being to the highest good of being. Just this and nothing more nor less can be moral law."[9]

Is God Really Good?

C. S. Lewis

Battling with deep grief over the loss of his wife, C. S. Lewis faced the ancient question: Is God really good? He responded:

"Not that I am (I think) in much danger of ceasing to believe in God. The real danger is of coming to believe such dreadful things about Him. The conclusion I dread is not 'So there's no God after all' but 'So this is what God's really like. Deceive yourself no longer.' " What if, he reasons, our worst fears are true; that all the characteristics we regard as bad; "unreasonableness, vanity, vindictiveness, injustice, cruelty" are after all part of God's nature and it is only our own depravity that makes them look bad to us?

But, he concludes, "this knot comes undone when you try to pull it tight—And so what? This, for all practical (and speculative) purposes sponges God off the slate. The word 'good' applied to Him becomes meaningless, like 'abracadabra.' We have no motive for obeying Him. Not even fear. It is true we have His threats and promises. But why should we believe them? If cruelty is from His point of view 'good,' telling lies might be 'good' too. Even if they are true, what then? If His ideas of good are so very different from ours, what He calls 'Heaven' might well be what we should call Hell, and vice-versa. Finally, if reality at its very root is so meaningless to us—or putting it the other way around, if we are such total imbeciles—what is the point of trying to think either about God or about anything else?"[10]

Earlier, in his *Reflections on the Psalms*, he observed: "There were in the eighteenth century terrible theologians who held that God did not command certain things because they were right, but certain things are right because God commanded them. To make the position perfectly clear, one of them even said that though God has, as it happens, commanded us to love Him and one another, He might have equally well commanded us to hate Him and one another and hatred would then have been right. It was apparently a mere toss-up which He decided on. Such a view, in effect, makes God an arbitrary tyrant. It would be better and less irreligious to believe in no God and to have no ethics than to have such an ethics and such a theology as this. The Jews, of course, never discuss this in abstract and philosophical terms. But at once, and completely, they assume the right view, knowing better than they know. They know that the

---

[9]Finney, op. cit. pp. 3–4.
[10]C.S. Lewis, *A Grief Observed* (Harper and Row, 1963), p. 28.

Lord (not merely obedience to the Lord) is 'righteous' and commands 'righteousness' because He loves it (Ps. 11:7). He enjoins what is good because He is good. Hence His laws have *emeth* ('truth'), intrinsic validity, rock-bottom reality, being rooted in His own nature and are therefore as solid as that Nature which He has created."[11]

God Is Not Only Good but Faithful

Charles Finney

Finney argues for God's goodness on the basis of His omniscience: "He could not but know all the reasons in favor of benevolence and all the reasons against malevolence. He could not by any possibility be ignorant of the reasons on either side, nor so divert His mind from them as that they should not have their full influence in deciding His character and confirming it forever."[12]

In *Power From on High* he also says: "What is this love of God as a mental exercise? It must be benevolence, or good will. God is a moral agent. The good of universal being is infinitely valuable in itself. God must infinitely appreciate this. He must see and feel the moral propriety of choosing this for its own sake. He has chosen it from eternity. . . . God's infinite choice of the good of universal being is righteousness in Him because it is the choice of the intrinsically and infinitely valuable for its own sake. It is a choice in conformity with the nature and relations He has constituted. It must be a choice in conformity with His infinitely clear conscience or moral sense. Righteousness in God, then, is conformity to the laws of universal love or good will. It must be an ultimate, supreme, immanent, efficient preference or choice of the highest good of universal being, including His own."[13]

George MacDonald

"Let no one persuade you that there is in Him a little darkness because of something He has said which His creature interprets as darkness. The interpretation is the work of the enemy; a handful of tares of darkness sown in the light. Neither let your cowardly conscience receive any word as light because another calls it light while it looks to you dark. Say either the thing is not what it seems, or God never said it or did it. But, of all evils, to misinterpret what God does and then say the thing as interpreted must be right because God does it, is of the devil."[14]

---

[11]C.S. Lewis, *Reflections on the Psalms* (Huntington, N.Y.: John M. Fontana Publishers, 1961), pp. 54–55.

[12]Finney, op. cit. p. 77.

[13]Charles Finney, *Power From on High* (Fort Washington, Pa.: Christian Literature Crusade, 1962), p.76.

[14]George MacDonald, *Creation in Christ*, Rolland Hein, ed. (Wheaton, Ill.: Harold Shaw Publishers, 1976), p. 42.

The Basis of God's Right to Govern

Ultimately then, the moral right to govern is based on *qualification* and the implementation of that right, based on *ability*. God's qualifications oblige Him to govern us and oblige us to yield to His government. Those qualifications are His wisdom, love, power, and the rest of His natural and moral attributes. His ability to govern is a function of these attributes, and the intrinsic value of His own uncreated being gives His character a faithful reference point. Thus, His moral attributes are not from an arbitrary foundation, but are instead founded on that which is absolutely fit and in perfect accord with the nature of things: His own being.

In reference to God's love for himself, Jonathan Edwards said: "The Divine virtue, or the virtue of the Divine mind must consist primarily in love to himself, or in the mutual love and friendship which subsists eternally and necessarily between the several persons in the Godhead or that infinitely strong propensity there is in these Divine persons one to another. There is no need of multiplying words to prove this. . . . virtue in its most essential nature consists in benevolent affection or propensity of heart towards being in general; and so flowing out to particular beings in a greater or lesser degree according to the measure of existence and beauty which they possess. . . . God's goodness and love to created beings is derived from and subordinate to His love to himself.

"By these things it appears that the truly virtuous mind, being as it were under the sovereign dominion of love to God above all things, above all things seeks the glory of God and makes that his supreme, governing, and ultimate end. This consists in the expression of God's perfections in their proper effects—the manifestation of God's glory to created understandings—the communications of the infinite fullness of God to the creature—the creature's highest esteem of God, love to and joy in Him—and in the proper exercises and expressions of these. And so far as a virtuous mind exercises true virtue in benevolence to created beings, it chiefly seeks the good of the creature; consisting in its knowledge or view of God's glory and beauty, its union with God, conformity and love to Him, and joy in him. And that disposition of heart, that consent, union, or propensity of mind to being in general, which appears chiefly in such exercises, is virtue truly so called; or in other words, true grace and real holiness. And no other disposition or affection but this is of the nature of true virtue."[15]

"It may be asserted in general that nothing is of the nature of true virtue in which God is not the first and the last; or . . . have not their first foundation and source in apprehensions of God's supreme dignity and glory and in esteem and love of him and have not respect to God as the supreme end."[16]

In a sense, these are all part of one reality; each consideration a different perspective on the same truth or a different analysis of the same thing. The changeless *intrinsic value of His being* is the basis of His

---

[15]Edwards, *Works* op. cit. p. 127.
[16]Edwards, *Works* op. cit. pp. 122–126.

changeless character, and thus of all law. The *revelation of His character* is the moral basis of our glad surrender to Him and His ability to govern is the *power to implement that law* and that government or to fitly pursue that which He has moral and legal right to do.

The Faithfulness of God

> He cannot fail, for He is God
> He cannot fail, He pledged His Word
> He cannot fail, He'll see you through
> He cannot fail, He'll answer you.
>
> C. E. Mason, Jr.

We may sum up this wonderful attribute of the eternal self-consistency and unwavering goodness of God by the word used more often of His nature than any other word in the Bible: God is *faithful*. God is utterly trustworthy. It is the rock-bottom reality on which everything depends; it is why the Christian life at heart is to be a life of trust.

When the Lord Jesus was asked, "What shall we do, that we might work the works of God?" (John 6:28), the answer given by Him was wholly different from what other religious systems might have offered. The Buddhist would recommend the eight-fold path; the Muslim, fasting, prayer and a trip to Mecca; the modern Christian might say, "Bible study, prayer, tithing, and regular fellowship in the Church." But the answer Jesus gave was: "This is the work of God, that ye *believe on him* whom he [the Father] hath sent" (John 6:29).

R. Kelso Watson wrote:

> Standing on the promises of Christ my King
> Through eternal ages let His praises ring. . . .
> Standing on the promises that cannot fail
> When the howling storms of doubt and fear assail
> By the living Word of God I shall prevail
> Standing on the promises of God.

George Watson said: "To trust the Origin of our existence is the fundamental grace of life. Every virtue, every grace possible to the soul, must be the outcome of that fundamental trust. One of the infallible proofs that Scripture is the Word of God is that its revelation of a life of faith agrees exactly with the constitution of things in relationship to our makeup and environment. The very men that deny the supernatural in religion and deny a life of faith in matters of salvation are themselves living a life of faith in matters of material, social, and financial things.

"Every animal, fish, bird, and human being in this world is constantly living in faith and is taking steps, or moving forward, giving credence either instinctively or rationally to something that lies beyond the five senses, and is reposing on a broad bed of boundless providence, of which each knows neither the beginnings, endings, or a million-fold intricacies.

"The fidelity of God is that adorable perfection in His nature upon which everything in the universe lies down to rest. Our blessed Creator refers to His faithfulness more frequently in His Word than any of His other attributes because it is His faithfulness that His creatures have to deal with more constantly and more universally than any other one attribute of His nature. . . . There is one virtue that stands out forever more conspicuously than friendship, or love, or knowledge, or wisdom, or any other human virtue. God's fidelity is in Him just what trust is in us."[17]

> How firm a foundation, ye saints of the Lord
> Is laid for your faith in His excellent Word!
> What more can He say than to you He hath said
> To you who for refuge to Jesus have fled?
>
> Anne Steele

---

[17]George Watson, "Necessity Of Trusting God," *Our Own God* (Schmul Reprints), pp. 150–151.

CHAPTER SEVEN

COROLLARY TWO:
GOD IS ACTIVE IN HISTORY

Scriptures

"In the beginning God created . . . and the evening and the morning were the first day." (Gen. 1:1, 5)

"And God said, Let there be a firmament. . . . And God made the firmament . . . and it was so. And God called the firmament Heaven. And the evening and the morning were the second day." (Gen. 1:6–8)

"And God blessed them, and God said unto them, Be fruitful, and multiply, and replenish the earth, and subdue it." (Gen. 1:28)

"And God saw every thing that he had made, and, behold, it was very good. And the evening and the morning were the sixth day." (Gen. 1:31)

"And God looked upon the earth, and, behold, it was corrupt; for all flesh had corrupted his way upon the earth. And God said unto Noah, The end of all flesh is come before me; for the earth is filled with violence through them; and, behold, I will destroy them with the earth." (Gen. 6:12–13)

"And the LORD smelled a sweet savour; and the LORD said in his heart, I will not again curse the ground any more for man's sake; for the imagination of man's heart is evil from his youth; neither will I again smite any more every thing living, as I have done." (Gen. 8:21)

"Why, seeing times are not hidden from the Almighty, do they that know him not see his days?" (Job 24:1)

"The LORD shall count, when he writeth up the people, that this man was born there. Selah." (Ps. 87:6)

"I have shewed thee new things from this time; even hidden things, and thou didst not know them. They are created now, and not from the beginning; even before the day when thou heardest them not; lest thou shouldest say, Behold, I knew them." (Isa. 48:6–7)

"I have spread out my hands all the day unto a rebellious people." (Isa. 65:2)

"I go to prepare a place for you. And if I go and prepare a place for you, I will come again, and receive you unto myself; that where I am, there ye may be also." (John 14:2–3)

God Changes His Actions When People Change

"And God saw that the wickedness of man was great in the earth, and that every imagination of the thoughts of his heart was only evil continually. And it repented the LORD that he had made man on the earth, and it grieved him at his heart." (Gen. 6:5–6)

"Let me alone, that my wrath may wax hot against them, and that I may consume them: and I will make of thee a great nation. And Moses besought the LORD his God, and said . . . Turn from thy fierce wrath, and repent of this evil against thy people. And the LORD repented of the evil which he thought to do unto his people." (Ex. 32:10–12, 14)

"If ye forsake the LORD, and serve strange gods, then he will turn and do you hurt, and consume you, after that he hath done you good." (Josh. 24:20)

"David said . . . Let me now fall into the hand of the LORD; for very great are his mercies: but let me not fall into the hand of man. And God sent an angel unto Jersualem to destroy it: and as he was destroying, the Lord beheld, and he repented him of the evil, and said to the angel that destroyed, It is enough, stay now thine hand." (1 Chron. 21:13, 15)

"Nevertheless he regarded their affliction, when he heard their cry: and he remembered for them his covenant, and repented according to the multitude of his mercies." (Ps. 106:44–45)

"The fear of the LORD prolongeth days: but the years of the wicked shall be shortened. . . . Be not over much wicked, neither be thou foolish: why shouldest thou die before thy time?" (Prov. 10:27; Eccles. 7:17)

"If that nation, against whom I have pronounced [judgment], turn from their evil, I will repent of the evil that I thought to do unto them . . . If it do evil in my sight, that it obey not my voice, then I will repent of the good, wherewith I said I would benefit them." (Jer. 18:8, 10)

"Stand . . . and speak . . . diminish not a word: if so be they will hearken, and turn every man from his evil way, that I may repent me of the evil, which I purpose to do unto them because of the evil of their doings." (Jer. 26:2–3)

"If Ye will still abide in this land, then will I build you, and not pull you down, and I will plant you, and not pluck you up: for I repent me of the evil that I have done unto you." (Jer. 42:10–12)

"Mine heart is turned within me, my repentings are kindled together.

I will not execute the fierceness of mine anger, I will not return to destroy Ephraim: for I am God, and not man; the Holy One in the midst of thee: and I will not enter into the city." (Hos. 11:8–9)

"Turn unto the LORD your God: for he is gracious and merciful, slow to anger, and of great kindness, and repenteth him of the evil. Who knoweth if he will return and repent, and leave a blessing behind Him?" (Joel 2:13–14)

"The LORD repented for this: it shall not be, saith the LORD." (Amos 7:3; see also v. 6)

"And God saw their works, that they turned from their evil way; and God repented of the evil, that he had said that he would do unto them; and he did it not." (Jon. 3:10; cf. 3:2, 4; 4:2)

God Tests People and Responds to Their Response

"Then said the LORD unto Moses, Behold, I will rain bread from heaven for you; and the people shall go out and gather a certain rate every day, that I may prove them, whether they will walk in my law or no." (Ex. 16:4)

"And thou shalt remember all the way which the LORD thy God led thee these forty years in the wilderness, to humble thee, and to prove thee, to know what was in thine heart, whether thou wouldest keep his commandments or no." (Deut. 8:2)

"Thou shalt not hearken unto the words of that prophet, or that dreamer of dreams: for the LORD your God proveth you, to know whether ye love the LORD your God with all your heart and with all your soul." (Deut. 13:3)

"Because that this people hath trangressed . . . I also will not henceforth drive out any from before them of the nations which Joshua left when he died: that through them I may prove Israel whether they will keep the way of the Lord to walk therein, as their fathers did keep it, or not." (Judges 2:20–22; cf. Ex. 33:2; 34:24)

"And they were to prove Israel by them, to know whether they would hearken unto the commandments of the LORD." (Judg. 3:4)

"Wherefore the Lord God of Israel saith, I said indeed that thy house, and the house of thy father, should walk before me for ever: but now the LORD saith, Be it far from me; for them that honour me I will honour, and they that despise me shall be lightly esteemed." (1 Sam. 2:30)

"Whereupon the princes of Israel and the king humbled themselves; and they said, The LORD is righteous. And when the LORD saw that they humbled themselves, the word of the LORD came . . . therefore I will not destroy them, but I will grant them some deliverance; and my wrath shall not be poured out upon Jerusalem by the hand of Shishak." (2 Chron. 12:6–7)

"For the eyes of the LORD run to and fro throughout the whole earth, to shew himself strong in the behalf of them whose heart is perfect toward him." (2 Chron. 16:9)

"Oh that my people had hearkened unto me, and Israel had walked in my ways! I should soon have subdued their enemies, and turned my hand against their adversaries." (Ps. 81:13–14)

God's Future Decisions Appear to Be Future to Him

"And God said, Let there be light: and there was light. And God saw the light, that it was good. . . . And the evening and the morning were the first day." (Gen. 1:3–5)

"And God said, Let us make man in our image, after our likeness. . . . So God created man in his own image, in the image of God created he him; male and female created he them." (Gen. 1:26–27)

"For the Lord had said unto Moses, Say unto the children of Israel, Ye are a stiffnecked people: I will come up into the midst of thee in a moment, and consume thee: therefore now put off thy ornaments from thee, that I may know what to do unto thee." (Exod. 33:5)

"And God's anger was kindled because he went: and the angel of the Lord stood in the way for an adversary against him. Now he was riding upon his ass, and his two servants were with him." (Num. 22:22)

"And Samuel said to Saul, Thou hast done foolishly: thou hast not kept the commandment of the Lord thy God, which he commanded thee: for now would the Lord have established thy kingdom upon Israel for ever. But now thy kingdom shall not continue: the Lord hath sought him a man after his own heart, and the Lord hath commanded him to be captain over his people, because thou hast not kept that which the Lord commanded thee." (1 Sam. 13:13–14)

"And said, Remember now, O Lord, I beseech thee, how I have walked before thee in truth and with a perfect heart, and have done that which is good in thy sight. And Hezekiah wept sore. Then came the word of the Lord to Isaiah, saying, Go, and say to Hezekiah, Thus saith the Lord, the God of David thy father, I have heard thy prayer, I have seen thy tears: behold, I will add unto thy days fifteen years." (Isa. 38:3–5)

"Thus saith the Lord unto this people, Thus have they loved to wander, they have not refrained their feet, therefore the Lord doth not accept them; he will now remember their iniquity, and visit their sins." (Jer.14:10)

"And rend your heart, and not your garments, and turn unto the Lord your God: for he is gracious and merciful, slow to anger, and of great kindness, and repenteth him of the evil." (Joel 2:13)

"For thus saith the Lord of hosts; As I thought to punish you, when your fathers provoked me to wrath, saith the Lord of hosts, and I repented not: So again have I thought in these days to do well unto Jerusalem and to the house of Judah: fear ye not." (Zech. 8:14–15)

"David said . . . Let me fall now into the hand of the Lord; for very great are his mercies . . . And God sent an angel unto Jerusalem to destroy it: and as he was destroying, the Lord beheld, and repented him of the evil, and said to the angel that destroyed, It is enough, stay now thine hand." (1 Chron. 21:13, 15)

"Oh that my people had hearkened to me, and Israel had walked in my ways! I should soon have subdued their enemies, and turned my hand against their adversaries." (Ps. 81:13–14)

"Nevertheless he regarded their affliction, when he heard their cry: and he remembered for them his covenant, and repented according to the multitude of his mercies." (Ps. 106:44–45)

"If that nation, against whom I have pronounced, turn from their evil, I will repent of the evil that I thought to do unto them. . . . If it do evil in my sight, that it obey not my voice, then I will repent of the good, wherewith I said I would benefit them." (Jer. 18:8, 10)

"Stand . . . and speak . . . if so be they will hearken, and turn every man from his evil way, that I may repent me of the evil, which I purpose to do unto them because of the evil of their doings." (Jer. 26:2–3)

"If ye will still abide in this land, then will I build you, and not pull you down, and I will plant you, and not pluck you up: for I repent me of the evil I have done unto you." (Jer. 42:10)

"Turn unto the Lord your God: for he is gracious and merciful, slow to anger, and of great kindness, and repenteth him of the evil. Who knoweth if he will return and repent, and leave a blessing behind him?" (Joel 2:13–14)

"Ye also shall sit upon twelve thrones, judging the twelve tribes of Israel"—Jesus to the twelve disciples (Matt. 19:28).

"I go to prepare a place for you. And if I go and prepare a place for you, I will come again, and receive you unto myself; that where I am, there ye may be also." (John 14:2b–3)

"And I will pray the Father, and he shall give you another Comforter, that he may abide with you for ever . . ." (John 14:16a)

"Thou Lord . . . shew whether of these two thou hast chosen, that he may take part of this ministry and apostleship, from which Judas by transgression fell." (Acts 1:24b–25)

"If any man shall add unto these things, God shall add unto him the plagues that are written in this book: and if any man shall take away from the words of the book of this prophecy, God shall take away his part out of the book of life, and out of the holy city." (Rev. 22:18)

Bible Word Study

The Old and New Testaments are rich in words that describe both time and eternity. Hebrew has more words for eternity than Arabic or Greek, but Greek has many different words for time.

Eternal (Hebrew)

quedma (*kayd-maw*)—The front, of place (absolutely the forepart) or time (antiquity). Translated in the KJV as "eternal," "everlasting," "foreward," "old."[1] (For more information on both *quedma* and the next word, *olam*, turn to the "Bible Study Words" section in Chapter One.

olam (*o-lawm*)—Concealed, i.e., the vanishing point; generally time out of mind (past or future), i.e., eternity; always. Translated in the KJV as "ancient" (time), "any more," "continuance," "eternal," "perpetual." Combined with another Hebrew word to mean "without end."[2]

There is an interesting link between the OT words for time as related to God, and the key word for eternity in the NT.

"The concept of a beginning in time which is dominant in the verb can be seen in an even more specialized sense in the noun *arche*, when it is used to translate *olam*, a distant time (only Josh. 24:2; Isa. 63:16) or *quedem*, antiquity, of old (e.g., Hab. 1:12; Ps. 74; Mic. 5:2). So used, it does not mean only the distant past in time (*quedem* meant originally *the beginning* and so *East*), but the state that once was, the beginning of a nation, or of the world. . . . Used in this sense, the meaning of the word *arche* stretches from the previous condition that can be remembered back over the original condition into the past before time (Isa. 37:26)."[3]

Time (Greek)

arche (*ar-khay*)—Beginning, origin, active cause. "The root *arch*—primarily indicated what was of worth. Hence the verb *archo* meant 'to be first.' "[4]

"*Arche* is used 55 times in the New Testament, and is the most common word for the beginning or start of anything, as in Matt. 19:4 when Jesus speaks of the beginning of creation: "Have ye not read that He which made them at the beginning made them male and female?" (also Mark 10:6). In John 1:1, *beginning* refers to "something before time, i.e., not a

---

[1] *Strong's* 6924.
[2] *Strong's* 5769.
[3] Lothar Coenen, *The New International Dictionary of New Testament Theology*, Colin Brown, ed. (Grand Rapids: Zondervan Publishing House, 1971), vol. 1, pp. 164–165.
[4] W.E. Vine, *The Expanded Vine's Expository Dictionary of New Testament Words*, John R. Kohlenberger III, ed. (Minneapolis, Minn.: Bethany House Publishers, 1984), p. 103.

beginning within time, but an absolute beginning. In the beginning was the Word, and the Word was with God and the Word was God."[5]

Other verses in the New Testament in which *arche* is used are: Matt 19:8; 24:8, 21; Mark 1:1; 13:8; John 6:64; 8:44; Acts 11:15; Phil. 4:15; Col. 1:18; Heb. 1:10; 7:3; 2 Pet. 3:4; 1 John 2:14; 3:8; Jude 6 ("first estate"); Rev. 1:8 ("beginning and the ending"); 3:14; 21:6; 22:13 ("Alpha and Omega, the beginning and the end").

"*Arche* developed a special meaning in Greek philosophy: (a) it denotes the point at which something new begins in time, the end of which can be seen from the first. When one spoke of the beginning (*arche*), the end (*telos*) was also in view. Since the beginning comes out of the infinite, the end will also lose itself in it."[6]

Not always does the word mean a beginning in time. It can also mean a principality, a first. This is especially true of Jesus, who is called "the beginning of the creation" (Rev. 3:14). "In John 8:25 Christ's reply to the question 'Who art thou?', 'Even that which I have spoken to you from the beginning,' does not mean that He has told them before; He declares that He is consistently the unchanging expression of His own teaching and testimony from the first, the immutable embodiment of His doctrine."[7]

The phrase in 2 Thess. 2:13, "God hath from the beginning chosen you," has a well-supported alternative reading: ". . . chosen you as *first-fruits . . .*" (*aparchen*).

Some texts that were translated incorrectly have since been corrected. Those translated in the KJV as "since" or "before the world began" or "from the beginning of the world," are rendered correctly in the R.V. as "before times eternal" (Rom. 16:25; Eph. 3:9; 2 Tim. 1:9; Titus 1:2). However, this change was not made in Luke 1:70; John 9:32; Acts 3:21; or Acts 15:18.[8]

chronos (khron-os)—Quantity of time, duration of a period, amount of time; "the time in which anything is done."[9]

Chronos is the most basic word used for time in the Bible, and it is used a number of different ways in the New Testament. Vine notes it is used as a *space of time* (short or long): "The Devil . . . shewed unto him all the kingdoms of the world in a moment of time" (Luke 4:5; 20:9). Or it can refer to the *date* of an occurrence: "But when the time of the promise drew nigh . . . the people grew and multiplied in Egypt" (Acts. 7:17).

Succession of Time: "From the first day . . . I have been with you at all seasons" (Acts 20:18, NASB). ". . . according to the revelation of the mystery, which was kept secret since the world began [times eternal]" (Rom. 16:25, NASB).

Duration of Time: ". . . while the Bridegroom is with them [as long as

---

[5]Coenen, op. cit. vol. 1, p. 166.
[6]Ibid. vol. 1, p. 164.
[7]Vine, op. cit. p. 103.
[8]Vine, op. cit. p. 103.
[9]Ethelbert W. Bullinger, *A Critical Lexicon and Concordance to the English and Greek New Testament* (Grand Rapids: Zondervan Publishing House, 1975), p. 672.

they have the Bridegroom], the attendents of the bridegroom do not fast, do they?" (Mark 2:19, NASB). "While" here is literally "for whatever time."

Date, Past or Future: "Herod . . . enquired . . . what time the star appeared" (Matt. 2:7). "Until the period of restoration" (Acts 3:21, NASB).[10]

kairos *(kah-heer-os)*—Quality of time. Epochs marked by certain features, events.[11]

Fixed or definite period: "The right measure and relation, especially as regards time and place (generally of time). Hence the right time, suitable or convenient time; the opportune point of time at which a thing *should be* done."[12]

"Due measure, fitness, proportion, is used in the New Testament to signify a season." *Kairos* is distinguished from *chronos*, and Jesus used them both when speaking to His disciples: "It is not for you to know the times [*chronos*—lengths of periods] or the seasons [*kairos*—epochs characterized by certain events], which the Father hath put in his own power" (Acts 1:7).[13] Used like this in Matt. 11:25; 12:1; 14:1; 21:34; Mark 11:13; Acts 3:19; 7:20; 17:26; Rom. 3:26; 5:6; 9:9; 13:11; 1 Cor. 7:5; Gal. 4:10; 1 Thess 2:17; 2 Thess 2:6 (laterally for a season of an hour); Eph. 6:18 (always at all seasons).

"The characteristics of a period are exemplified in the use of the term with regard, e.g., to harvest, Matt. 13:30; reaping, Gal. 6:9; punishment, Matt. 8:29; discharging duties, Luke 12:42; opportunity for doing anything, whether good, e.g., Matt. 26:18; Gal. 6:10 ("opportunity"); Eph. 5:16; or evil, e.g., Rev. 12:12; the fulfillment of prophecy, Luke 1:20; Acts 3:19; 1 Pet. 1:11; a time suitable for a purpose, Luke 4:13, literally, 'until a season'; 2 Cor. 6:2.[14]

pleeroma *(play-ro-mah)*—Fullness, completion, "end of an appointed period."[15]

"But when the fulness of time was come, God sent forth his Son, made of a woman, made under the law, to redeem them that were under the law" (Gal. 4:4–5). "That in the dispensation of the fulness of times he might gather together in one all things in Christ, both which are in heaven . . . and on earth; even in him" (Eph. 1:10).

teleioo *(tel-i-o-o)*—To bring to an end, to fulfill.[16]

"And when they had *fulfilled* the days, as they returned, the child Jesus tarried behind in Jerusalem; and Joseph and his mother knew not of it" (Luke 2:43). "My meat is to do the will of him that sent me, and to *finish* his work" (John 4:34). "After this, Jesus knowing that all things were now

---

[10]Vine, op. cit. pp. 1005, 1149–1150.
[11]Ibid. pp. 1004–1005.
[12]Bullinger, op. cit. p. 672.
[13]Vine, op. cit. pp. 1004–1005.
[14]Ibid. p. 1005.
[15]Ibid. p. 466.
[16]Ibid. p. 466.

accomplished, that the scripture might be *fulfilled*, saith, I thirst" (John 19:28). "That I might *finish* my course with joy" (Acts 20:24).

hora (*ho-rah*)—"A portion of time . . . season, time of blossoming. . . . Originally, the season of the year; then, the time of the day, and when reckoning by hours was practised, the hour; hence, *a* definite limited and determined time (thus differing from [*kairos*], which is *the* definite time)."[17]

For verses using *hora* see: Matt. 14:15; 18:1; Mark 6:35; Luke 1:10; 14:17; John 16:2, 4, 25; 1 John 2:18 (twice).

Eternity As Endless Time

Oscar Cullmann in his epochal work "Christ and Time" was convinced that "eternity is understood in Primitive Christianity only as endlessly extended time. It should be added that the erroneous importation into Primitive Christian thinking of the Platonic contrast between time and timeless eternity has no connection with the few 'marginal passages' that mention the existence of God before the creation and after the end of the world. It connects rather with the biblical distinction between the two ages, the 'present' and 'future' age. . . .

"It is a favorite practice to identify the 'present' age with 'time' and the 'future' one with 'eternity.' To this, however, it must at once be replied that the future age in the New Testament is an actual future, that is a future in time. All talk about the coming age that does not take this time quality in full earnest is philosophical reinterpretation."[18]

There has been, of course, some heated discussion over this. In his article, "Biblical Words for Time," James Barr objects. He thinks Cullman is "attaching theological meaning to semantic units divorced from their syntactical context, and translating key words into fixed theological concepts" and "[he] appeals to biblical vocabulary that depend on selective or tendential appropriation of biblical data." Biblical terms, Barr says, designate a "duration relative to the objects they quantify; a simple appeal to Greek or Hebrew words is not decisive for the nature of divine eternity."[19]

Barr thinks Cullmann "overlooks certain references to God himself and to the eternal world where *aion* is used to contrast the eternal nature or condition with that of the present temporal status . . . that do not readily accomodate the notion that eternity is coterminous with the total span of time."[20]

Barr also thinks interpreters like Kittel "err if they think that simple analysis of the Bible's lexical stock produces theological principles; meaning stems from their combination in meaningful statements. . . . A valid

---

[17]Bullinger, op. cit. pp. 672–673.
[18]Oscar Cullman, *Christ and Time: The Primitive Christian Conception of Time and History*, 3rd ed. (New York: Gordon Press, 1977), pp. 65–66.
[19]James Barr, "Biblical Words for Time," *Studies in Biblical Theology*, March, 1962, SCM.
[20]Carl Henry, *God, Revelation, and Authority* (Waco, Tx.: Word Pub.), p. 250.

biblical theology can be built only upon the statements of the Bible, and not on the words of the Bible." [21]

Cullmann in reply agrees you should not base an idea on a single word, or confuse a word with a concept. But he thinks Barr has both oversimplified Kittel's work, not done justice to the scope of his Lexicon and refuted the main point of his own books. Cullman says the New Testament never speculates about God's eternal being. Since it is "concerned primarily with God's redemptive activity it does not make a philosophical qualitative distinction between time and eternity. It knows linear time only . . . it is a frame within which they spoke of God's deeds. Whenever an author in the NT leads us to a view of God's eternal being—a rare occurrence (Gal. 6:9)—one does so starting always from that which the whole message of the NT is about: God's redemptive activity.

"God's self-revelation in activity, not His eternal being, provides the basis from which all questions about things other than His doings are answered. The frame within which the NT writers worked ought to be the same limits which NT scholars accept for their work. This means we must at least attempt to avoid philosophical categories. My critics have derided this standpoint but have not yet proved wrong my exposition of the concept of time found in the NT." [22]

In addition, Dr. Carl Henry notes that Barr not only doubts that the Bible contains any distinctive view of time, but he also doubts that it contains any distinctive view at all of anything; he does not believe the Bible "contains a unified theology devoid of divergent and at times actually contradictory content." [23]

Dr. Henry, while supporting the idea of a "timeless eternity," admits that neither scriptural or lexical appeals are decisive here for either view. He says "we had better freely acknowledge that the Bible contains no express declaration about God's timeless eternity or about time pervading the nature of God. While the inspired writers may presuppose a distinctive view of time and eternity they do not systematically expound or expressly formulate such a view. Without such specific statements we can only discern the writers' intention and test our inferences by the biblical context as a whole." [24]

There are many passages and phrases in Scripture besides those like Gen. 1:1 that assign some kind of time frame to divine action. Terence Fretheim in his valuable book *The Suffering Of God* points out four types of Hebrew phrases indicating that God acts into history in a "real time" sense.

The Divine "Perhaps" (*Ulay*)

"This term is used in human speech to indicate uncertainty regarding the future, often tinged with a note of hope. . . . There are five instances

---

[21]Barr, op. cit. p. 154.
[22]Cullmann, op. cit. p. xxv.
[23]Henry, op. cit. p. 23.
[24]Ibid. p. 249.

where *ulay* is used in divine speech. [In] . . . two of the more striking (Ezek. 12:1–3 and Jer. 26:2–3; cf. 36:3, 7; 51:8; Isa. 47:12; cf. Luke 20:13) . . . it seems clear from such passages that God is quite uncertain as to how the people will respond to the prophetic word. . . . Every indication in these texts would suggest God knowing the depth of Israel's sin should have been able to declare unequivocally that judgment was inevitable. This God does not do; it is possible that some spontaneous response to the preaching of the prophets will pull them out of the fire at the last moment."[25]

Quoting Jer. 3:7, 19, Fretheim points out the integrity of God's command to the prophets is in view here, as they are predicated on the possibility that Israel might respond positively. . . . God has no reason to pretend to the prophet. "These texts show us Israel's future is genuinely open and not predetermined. The future for Israel does not only not exist; it has not even been finally decided upon."[26]

The Divine "If" (*im*)

These conditional constructions in divine speech use the particle *im* ("if") with the imperfect form of the verb in the prodasis: "If ye thoroughly amend your ways . . . then will I cause you to dwell in this place" (Jer. 7:5; negative formulation in 26:4–6).

Fretheim comments: "The people's opportunity to 'dwell in this place' is a future possibility dependent on their amendment of their ways. In order for God's promise to have integrity God's future action must be a possibility and only a possibility too." Two possible futures are mentioned in Jer. 7:13—8:3, and Jer. 22:4–5.[27]

The Divine Consultation

Here God takes into consideration human thought and action in determining His own future action; human response can "contribute in a genuine way to the shaping of the future of both God and Israel—indeed, the world as well."[28]

Fretheim lists God's dealings with Abraham (Gen. 18:7–22) and Moses (Ex. 32:7–14) as examples and offers a striking insight: "A key phrase for understanding this passage [Ex. 32] is God's unusual charge to Moses: 'Let me alone that my wrath may wax hot against them' (32:10). . . . The devastation of Israel by divine wrath is thus conditional on Moses leaving God alone. While we cannot hear the tone of the remark—it may well relate to the isolation desired to suffer grief—God does thereby leave the door to Israel's future open. Remarkably, Moses does not heed the divine request; his boldness matches that of Abraham. He then proceeds to give God a number of reasons why consuming wrath should not be executed

---

[25]Terence Fretheim, *The Suffering of God* (Fortress, 1984), p. 46.
[26]Ibid. pp. 45–46.
[27]Ibid. p. 48.
[28]Ibid. p. 49.

(11–13) and thereby convinces God to reverse the decision (14)."[29]

Fretheim points out that Moses' argument is (a) that if the people have only just been delivered it would not make sense for God to now destroy them; (b) he is concerned for God's reputation in Egypt; and (c) he reminds God of His promises to the fathers.

"While these ought not to be considered arguments God had not thought of before, to have them articulated in a forceful way by one who has been invited into deliberation regarding Israel's future gives them a new status. That is, God takes Moses' contribution with utmost seriousness. . . . God treats the conversation with Moses with integrity and honors the human insight as an important ingredient for the shaping of the future. If Moses thinks these things, they take on a significance they do not carry when treated in isolation by the divine mind." (See also: Num. 14:11–20; 16:20–27; and 1 Sam. 15.)[30]

Another important insight comes from Amos 3:7: "Surely the Lord God will do nothing, but he revealeth his secret unto his servants the prophets." Fretheim says that rather than God's announcing a "fait accompli" to His servants, He may instead be inviting them into the sphere of decision-making with respect to the future of the people. Fretheim suggests that in the areas of divine judgment and decisions having major implications for humanity, God actually calls into account and treats with genuine integrity and respect the opinions and feelings of His own faithful servants who are themselves involved with the destiny of the people: "God does nothing without consultation!"

Passages such as Jer. 7:16 (cf. 11:14; 14:11; 15:1; 18:20) where God speaks with Jeremiah as the chosen mediator and intercessor between Him and the people show that Jeremiah believed that prayer did change things, that God might revoke His decision. Finally, however, Jeremiah realizes Israel is not going to repent and adapts to "what Mauser calls conformity with the wrath of God" (Jer. 18:20–23 and 20:11–12).[31]

The Divine Question

While these are often assumed rhetorical, some of them also involve divine decisions in respect to the future, like Hos. 6:4 (cf. 11:8a): "What shall I do with you, O Ephraim?"; and Jer. 5:7, 9 (cf. v. 29; 9:7, 9): "How shall I pardon thee?" Fretheim suggests these questions are "reflective of the divine council deliberations between God and the prophet" to "elicit repentance," and they relate to the "perception people would have should such judgment be forthcoming."[32]

Here the decision-making process covers the whole people not just the leader; God has announced a decision (Hos. 5:14–15), but "returns to His place to see if repentance might yet be forthcoming."[33]

---

[29]Ibid. p. 50.
[30]Ibid. p. 51.
[31]Ibid. p. 53.
[32]Ibid. p. 55.
[33]Ibid. p. 55.

As we can see from these and many parallel passages, the simple record of Scripture is that God does act into history in "real time" with human beings, and that all changes called for on His behalf have reality and integrity.

God acts into human time, and we can and must respond. The future is not fully fixed, but in some key places is in flux; and the words for time and interaction between God and His people strongly encourage us to intercede on behalf of peoples and nations. Prayer may not always change "things," but we have a God who hears sincere prayer, and He is not only strong to save, but free to do so.

Questions and Answers

Q: *Are the past, present, and future the same to God?*

A: It does not appear to be. The Bible reveals that God recognizes a true distinction. He does things in sequence and never hints that these acts are consimultaneous, or happening all at once, even as far as He is concerned.

Q: *What is meant by the phrase "Eternal Now"?*

A: It means that God lives in an eternally present state—God's being transcends time. But it has also come to mean that God has no true past or future, only an ever-present *now*. Although the idea is popular, some charge that it is an Eastern or Greek concept rather than a biblical idea.

Q: *Is the future fixed?*

A: No. The Bible clearly describes alternative decisions, actions, judgments, responses that man can or may make. The future is a flux of alternatives within certainties laid down by God.

Q: *Can God live in either the future or past?*

A: Apparently not, except in either an immediate remembering or cognitive sense. God has, of course, perfect recall of all past events and perfect knowledge of all future alternatives, but He lives in neither. God is acting—in computer language—in "real time."

Q: *What does "there should be time no longer" (Rev. 10:6) mean?*

A: The history of this planet and this race will come to an end with the final destruction of the present earth and heavens. This "time" began at its creation and will end with its curtailment. However, the biblical phrase simply means Christ will not delay doing this.

Q: *What is the relationship of Einstein's concept of time to what we find in the Bible?*

A: In Einstein's theory, a body approaching the theoretical speed of light approaches infinite mass and zero time. A body at the speed of light would fill all the universe and "time," for it would theoretically stop. This "time" is related to light velocity, which is not really an absolute.

However, biblical time in God's character pre-existed the creation of light and can be considered as ultimately a *creative sequence.*

Q: *If God lived in time, how could He be omniscient?*

A: By omniscience we mean "God's perfect and eternal knowledge of all things which are objects of knowledge, whether they be actual or possible, past, present, or future." God knows the past as perfectly as He absolutely knows the present, and the possibilitites of the future as well as that which is possible in the present.

Q: *Are things which could be possible (contingent events) objects of knowledge?*

A: Yes. An infinite God must know all finite alternatives; they are knowable without being expressed as realities.

Q: *But does God foresee the future actions of men as realities or only as possibilities?*

A: How does God see His own future actions? If they are already realities, they are not yet expressed realities. When God foresees His own free actions, could it not be assumed that He has the power to change them? The Bible seems to say that He not only can but does control His future actions. Free choice is a reality with man because it is a reality in God.

Q: *How does the doctrine of divine foreknowledge fit into this? God says one of the main reasons He is different from idols is His power to foretell the future (Isa. 41:21–22). Strong says: "If God cannot foreknow free human acts then the 'lamb that has been slain from the foundation of the world' (Rev. 13:8) was only a sacrifice to be offered in case Adam should fall, God not knowing whether he would or not, and in case Judas should betray Christ, God not knowing whether he would or not. Indeed, since the course of nature is changed by man's will when he burns towns and fells forests, God cannot on this theory even predict the course of nature. All prophecy is therefore a protest against this view."*

A: The subject of both prophecy and divine foreknowledge in relation to time and eternity deserves a much fuller treatment than possible in this volume. However, the concept of God living in endless time rather than in timelessness does not impair either His power to see the future and proclaim it or detract from His ability to govern it. What He says will come to pass; what He gives to men as alternatives are real alternatives. What He determines will always and without fail be accomplished.

Q: *But how can God be certain of acts that are free? Some say that knowledge of contingency is not necessarily contingent knowledge, or seeing a thing in the future does not cause it to be any more than seeing a thing in the past causes it to be. Foreknowledge may, and does, presuppose predetermination, but is not itself predetermination.*

A: That, of course, is the basic issue. Can an act that *will*—not might, could, should, or even would—happen still be called "free" without fixity? For us to see a thing does not determine its future or past; but in the *timeless eternity* view, God does not just observe man making these choices; He *created us making them*. We have looked at the problem in some detail under the discussion of eternity and also in the appendices. But the Reformed idea of predestination is based on divine decree and not foreknowledge. God's certainty here comes not from foreseen choices but fixity by purpose. Ultimately, we cannot say in this concept that man ever was free; his choices are ultimately determined by divine decree. If, however, choices are creations, and creations never exist as realities until imaged out into the real world, then all moral beings have a real but limited freedom, and God is a purposer, not just a programmer.

Analysis and Discussion

The theology of God's relationship to His creation and history has become a major issue. A literal interpretation of Scripture yields a case for eternity being extended "time." But before we look at the concept of *Super-time*, we must first look at one important question: If we admit that God has acts in time, does that make Him somehow finite? If God acts and thinks in succession of any sort, some theologians and philosophers charge that He must be learning or growing; and if He is growing, He is not infinite; and if He is not infinite, He is not God. Does time dictate limitation?

Our Limitations

We deal with issues that are important, but we argue on the basis of limited knowledge. From Scripture, we know these things to be true:

- Eternity is a characteristic of God's uncreated existence (state, mode of being).
- His existence cannot be durative; God can have no sequence in His essence, substance, or metaphysical nature.
- He cannot grow older or greater.
- God can and does create finite things. His creations do not in any way impair or subtract from His wisdom, power or energy.
- Every creation of God is finite by definition—having origin, each has limits.
- A created being may learn and grow forever without becoming infinite. Its limits are thus fixed by its finite origin, not by its possible unlimited end.
- The act of divine creation, though not itself originating in the finite, is always expressed in the finite. Those acts of creation, at least with respect to the creation, are successive.
- God's actions in creation, at least with respect to that creation, are successive.

God's Unlimitedness

Our identification and relations with God must all be associated with His personality. His personality is expressed to us both biblically and experientially as a *series* of events, experiences, and revelations. That series of events (a sequence) bears a direct parallel to created time, while apparently transcending it. Therefore, time began with the origin of the creation and seems intrinsic to the nature of personality.

Is a God who can make choices limited? Consider the pool of possible options from which I select choices. Although I may select one choice, the number of potential choices remains the same. This holds true for new or repeated selections: I can wear the same green socks five days in a row without reducing the potential possibilities from which I chose. A million sequential selections does not diminish the size of the original options even in a finite pool.

If the choices or actions selected do not drain the potential of a finite pool, neither will they reduce the choices or actions selected from an infinite pool. If a series of choices were not selected, we cannot conclude that those choices were not options; they are merely unrealized options.

Selecting one of many options does not imply the addition of new options, because choosing a different option does not access any data not previously available. Therefore, making many selections in a row from the same pool of choices does not add any new information to the pool. Sequential choices may open experiences for the chooser without adding to his knowledge.

God interacts in sequence with His creation, but divine creations (people) choosing constantly from unlimited potential cannot reduce either God's abilities or His knowledge. Where there is sequence, there can be a form of time. Sequence is the characteristic that reveals time. Therefore, time of some sort can exist in eternity without implying any limitation of God.

Eternity: Timelessness or Endless Time?

Finite constructs, projections from the known to the unknown to illustrate an indescribable infinite, are perilous! However, for the moment let us allow one analogy. We say in theology that God is omnipotent, omnipresent, and omniscient. We also say He is spiritual and not material, eternal and not created, infinite and not finite. All these areas of wonder cannot really be explained, let alone be illustrated.

Think instead, for a moment, of something around us we do see and at least partially understand: three-dimensional space. We say that a three-dimensional figure includes and transcends any two-dimensional one, which in turn includes and transcends any uni-dimensional figure. The plane is greater than the line that it encompasses; the line is more inclusive and greater than any point on it. Put another way, we can say a plane has both a different and a "higher" kind of space than a line, and a line has "higher" space than a point. It would certainly be false to say that a plane has less space than a mere line or a point.

This is obviously true in the physical realm, but can we legitimately leap from this to the spiritual realm? Omnipotence must surely mean that God has *more* power, not *less* power than His creation. We know this much from the express declaration of Scripture. However, by the mere fact of our finiteness, when we begin to amplify any idea about God we are limited, for any projection of our verbal concept of God must be higher, stronger, more wonderful than revealed by the bare words, for we are dealing with the nature of the living God.

Angels on the Head of a Pin

In medieval times, it is said that scholars debated how many angels could dance on the head of a pin. Believe it or not, it was a serious question—Do spiritual beings occupy physical space? How many demons can fit into a man? How does a person get "filled with the Holy Spirit?"

Whatever they decided, we would be safe to say that the statement "God is omnipresent" must imply that He has more "space" than His finite creation. It does not seem to mean He has no extension at all. We finite humans have space to move. God must at least be able to do the same, just as His creation.

The other possibility, that God has *no* space, that omnipresence really means He does not exist at all in the physical realm, is an odd conclusion. But this seems decisively refuted by the Incarnation. The Incarnation proves that God *likes* matter; He is at home on earth and in His creation.

Any definition of His omniscience has to point to the fact that God has *more* knowledge, more wisdom, and more ability of mind and thought than any of His creatures. His understanding is infinite, His knowledge is unlimited, His awareness of anything and everything is total and immediate. The "foolishness of God" is wiser than the wisdom of man. Omniscience certainly will not mean He knows *less* than any part of His creation, that our limits are His limits, or (taken to a ridiculous extreme) that in some mysterious and inexplicable sense He "knows" or "feels" nothing!

Spiritual Means *More*, Not *Less*

Apply the same projection to the nature of God's uncreated being. God, the living Creator-Spirit who spoke into existence the entire universe, must certainly be more "solidly real" than any of His creation. C. S. Lewis insightfully pointed out that at the resurrection of Christ, His passage through the locked and barred doors or walls of the Upper Room were not a demonstration of His having *less* substance, but rather, *more* substance than the walls. The nature of divinity is not less solidity, less reality, less existence, but more solidity, more reality, and more existence. Jesus did not walk through the wall because the wall was more solid then He, but because He was more solid than the wall. He walked through His own creation of matter like a man walks through mist in the morning—after all, He is called The Rock, not The Gas!

God is in every way more than His creation, more intensely real, more powerful, more wise, more present, more enduring, and more wonderful; He is higher and bigger than anything that corresponds to Him in His creation.

A Different Reality?

Some Christian thinkers hoping to maintain the *otherness* of God believe that His infinity does not mean He has less space than His creation, but that He has no real space at all! When they talk about space concerning God, they are not really talking about the same type of space as we do, but an entirely different reality. They believe that God does not live in space at all.

The idea is attractive and possible, though quite unexplainable. But if it is true, then our time-space-and-matter universe has no actual basis in transcendent reality at all—and what is to stop us from treating the rest of God's attributes in the same fashion? If *infinite* meant *spaceless*, why couldn't *omnipotence* signify *powerlessness*, *omniscience* mean *ignorance*, and *spirituality* speak of actual *non-existence*?

If, on the other hand, we believe that creation is not only real, but that the finite images an ultimate reality on a transcendent scale, we have to think that time, space, and matter have some meaning in relationship to God. Hence we say, infinite means that God has much more space than His creation, although His extension obviously must include and transcend all created space. The limits of space are not His limits, and its boundaries are not His boundaries. The word "spiritual" applied to the nature of the divine being likewise means He is the most intense reality, that while His own uncreated being upholds all physical and created spiritual reality, it nevertheless encompasses, is distinguished from, and transcends it.

"Super-Time"

And now I leave you with the $64,000 question: In light of all this, what can we say is meant by "eternal"? Shall we say it means no time at all, a timeless existence in which God has *less* being than all He himself made? Or shall we attempt, instead, to envision this revelation as a transcendent time, a higher, greater, fuller, more special time, a "Super-Time"? Such a "time" allows Him to "go to prepare a place" for us (John 14:2) and in actuality "remember our sins and iniquities no more" (Heb. 10:17). Miracle-time would allow God to shrink the natural process of healing an ear into seconds or alternately to extend His Kingdom as silently and unnoticeably as leaven.

The final question is, of course, which view of time brings God the greater glory and fits the facts and declarations of the Bible best? (2 Pet. 3:8; Job 10:5; Ps. 90:4)

The Foundation of History

Scripture differs in especially one very important way from some of the other major truth-claims of the religious writings of the world—it claims to be a historical record. It claims to be a history book. It is not only a book of principles, mottos, and maxims; it is a book revealing space-time fact. If Christianity is to be refuted, it must be refuted historically, because its capstone claim is that it is a truth of history. In other words, the Bible is not just spiritually or religiously true; it is geographically and archeologically true.

If we had been there when Moses crossed the Red Sea, we might have seen fish darting about in the thundering sides of the towering walls of water. When Elijah called down fire from heaven, we would have felt the red-white heat flash on our faces as the rocks turned to lava and vaporized. Had you stood beneath the cross of the Son of God when He died, you might have reached out to touch the rough wood and felt a splinter driven into the skin of your own finger. If you had been in the garden when Jesus walked out of the tomb on that first Easter morning, you could have shot a full color video of the risen Lord—if you could have stopped your camera shaking long enough to focus.

The Bible is history. It all happened. Therein lies a profound and fundamental difference between its claims on our lives and that of all others.

Eastern History *vs.* Biblical History

Contrast this with the writings of some of the ancient holy books of India. They too contain many fascinating stories, sometimes beautiful lyrical phrases and practical advice on steps to take to encounter the spiritual world. There too are mentioned miracles. The teachings and philosophy are often set in delightful stories, and God is even given a name. But the *Rig-Veda*, *Bhagavad-Gita*, and the other Vedic scriptures do not claim to be diaries. India kept no history; her vision of the universe was an endlessly recurring wheel. It was the British, with their Judeo-Christian assumptions and a concern for their own roots, who gave India her history. No one was there when India's holy books were collected. No one recorded dates and places or documented names of people in the stories. No one could have. They are not records; they are not history; they are only stories.

But the Bible's picture of God's relationship with man begins and ends with *real history*. God began it in the Garden of Eden and will consummate it in his own city. The world is going somewhere, but only the Christian understands where it came from and what its final destination is.

Communism also gives meaning to history, but little or none to the individual. Existentialism affirms and gives honor to the individual, but little or none to history. But when you encounter Jesus Christ you are gripped by both. God never saves man for the man's sake; we are saved to serve our generation and then to fall asleep in the will of God the King. We were made to discover His active reality in the abandonment of our hypocrisy, to not only reflect His glory but to be as He is in the world. We are saved from our past for the future of the world.

We come from a long line who have stood where we stand. The Bible is a record of people who were actually here on earth. We can turn a shovel of sand in an ancient dig in Egypt or the Sinai and come across some of those names. We can cross-check dates with other authenticated sources and find the unmistakable match of the stated and the dated, the revealed and the recorded. Dig up the past in the Holy Land and you will know why the land is spoken of as holy.

Genealogical Significance

Here too is the saga of those strange lists in Scripture, the seemingly interminable catalog of unpronounceable names, those telephone directories of Genesis, Numbers, Luke, and Matthew which the genealogy-conscious Jews kept with jealous and finicky attention to every jot and tittle in duplicated accuracy. And who are these people with funny names, whose children rarely seemed to do anything more significant than to bear more children with even stranger names? Why the lists? Because the Bible is a history book. These people lived, these people loved, these people brought up children and died in a world alive with the visitations of God. The Bible is the record of this. God acts in history and He acts today.

The World Is Not Locked Into Fate

To grasp the implications of God's acting in history is to fuel the drive of missionary, evangelistic, and revival movements. It births concerts of prayer for the changing of nations and the toppling of kingdoms, for the opening of doors no man can close and the toppling of gates even hell cannot hold. God is alive and well and in charge of the future. We never need to be troubled or afraid; it is the Father's good pleasure to give us the kingdom. God is active in time, and because He is working, so must we. Jesus declared, "My father worketh hitherto and I work" (John 5:17).

Life is not a movie. The future is not canned. The Ruler of history can set His own time. It is our solemn duty and privilege to step into the future with Him, and by His power alter it forever for individuals, for nations, for the world—for the kingdom and for the King.

Historical Discussion

Time is what the clock says.

Albert Einstein

We have seen briefly what the Scripture words say about time; we have discussed some of the philosophical implications of each view. We are now better prepared to amplify and define it, by looking at what others in Christian history have said on this subject.

"What is time?" This deceptively simple question has challenged the greatest minds of all ages. Augustine said, "If no one asks me, I know; If I want to explain it to a questioner, I do not know. . . . I still do not know what time is. . . . Time is certainly extendedness; but I do not know what it is extendedness of."[1]

Whatever conclusions we eventually make, we already have much study and research to draw from in the history of philosophy and theology; the nature of time is one that has been deeply analyzed and discussed by some of the world's best thinkers, both Christian and secular. But exactly what is it?

The Nature of Time

First, human time is not an independent entity; it is obviously related (in some way at least) to the existence of a creation. Einstein, time-thinker and father of both the general and special theory of relativity, showed how time and our space-matter universe are interrelated. He comments on the link between time, space and substance: "If you don't take my words too seriously, I would say this: If we assume that all matter would disappear from the world, then before relativity, one believed that space and time would continue existing in an empty world. But according to the theory of relativity, if matter and its motion disappeared, there would no longer be any space or time."

Our previous biblical word studies have shown how different kinds of sequence have given rise to different words for time, depending on the point of interest being analyzed. Thus we have *chronos*, the *amount* of a sequence; *kairos*, the *features* of a sequence; *pleeroma*, the *completion* of a sequence; *teleioo*, the *concluding* of a sequence; and *arche*, the *origin* of a sequence.

Time in the Early Church

Nelson Pike

Pike comments on the early Christian creeds: "Christ, begotten of the Father 'before the ages—*aeons*' (Nicene Creed, A.D. 381). . . . This phrase occurs in previous personal confessions—Lucian, Cyril, Eusebius, and Epiphanius; the Creed of Chalcedon and the Athanasian Creed. It appears to be a firm part of tradition.

"Why is it said that He was 'begotten before the worlds?' . . . 'That none should think there was ever a time when He was not. In other words, by this is expressed that Jesus is the Son of God from everlasting, even as God the Father is from everlasting' (Larger Catechism of the Eastern

---

[1]Augustine of Hippo, *The City of God* (Washington, D.C.: Catholic University Press, 1950).

Church). . . . The point seems to be that to 'exist before the ages' is to exist at all moments *in time*."[2]

St. John of Damascus

"We also speak of the age of ages, inasmuch as the seven ages of the present world contain many . . . generations of men, whereas there is one age containing all ages and which is called the 'age of ages'—both present and future . . . the expression 'age-enduring life' and 'age-enduring chastisement' show the eternity of the age to come. For after the resurrection, time will not be numbered by days at all; rather there will be one day without evening, with the Sun of Justice shining brightly on the just and deep and endless night reserved for the sinners. How then will the time of Origen's millennium be measured?"[3]

John Locke

"I ask those who say they have a positive idea of eternity whether their idea of eternity includes succession or not. . . . The notion they have of duration forces them to conceive that whatever has duration is of a longer continuance today than it was yesterday. . . . nothing [is] more inconceivable to me than duration without succession. . . . But if our weak apprehensions cannot separate succession from any duration whatsoever, our idea of eternity can be nothing but of infinite succession, of moments of duration wherein anything does exist. . . ."[4]

A. W. Tozer

Tozer's dry wit shows in his description of time as sequence: "Time is the medium in which things change. It isn't time that makes you change; it isn't time that took your 32 honest teeth and got you those hypocrites; it isn't time; it's change that does that. In order to change there must be a sequence of change. That sequence is time, and we call it time."[5]

Charles Hodge

Hodge maintained an Eternal Now perspective of God's own existence and actions, but still acknowledged the fact that God must at least recognize some form of succession in events involving other personalities or happenings: "As God's knowledge is infinite, every event must first be ever equally present to His knowledge, from eternity to eternity. Second, these events must be known to Him as they actually occur in themselves (e.g., in their true nature, relations and successions). This distinction therefore holds true; God's knowledge of all events is without beginning, end or succession; but he knows them as in themselves occurring in the

[2]Nelson Pike, *God and Timelessness* (New York: Schocken Books, 1970), p. 180.
[3]St. John Of Damascus, *An Exact Exposition of the Orthodox Faith*, Bk. II, ch. 1.
[4]John Locke, *An Essay Concerning Human Understanding*, Peter H. Nidditch, ed. (New York: Oxford University Press, 1975), Bk. II, p. 172.
[5]A. W. Tozer, (unpublished sermon) "In The Beginning Was The Word."

successions of time, past, present or future relatively to one another."[6]

Hodge admits that we can only think about God as acting in sequence, but he asserts that this results from our finiteness: "Thought is possible to us however only under the limitation of time and space. We can conceive of God only under the finite fashion of first purposing and then acting, of first promising or threatening, and then fulfilling his word, etc. He that inhabits eternity, infinitely transcends our understanding."[7]

Dr. Nathan Wood

Wood, a Christian philosopher, related his specialized studies of the nature of reality to the triune Creator. In his brilliant book *The Secret of The Universe*, he gives a succinct analysis of time defined as sequence: "Essentially time is consecutiveness of successiveness . . . in the physical universe, time is the successiveness of motion in space everlasting. . . . Potential motion is space. Actual motion is the tangible universe. Successive motion is time."[8]

Francis Schaeffer

In Schaeffer's *Genesis in Space and Time*, he uses the concept of time as sequence in contrast to our own limited and created time frame and concludes that the creation is really a new thing *with God*: "We are faced, therefore, with a very interesting question: When did history begin? If one is thinking with the modern concept of the space-time continuum, then it is quite obvious that time and history did not exist before 'in the beginning.' But if we are thinking of history in contrast to an eternal, philosophic 'other,' or in contrast to a static eternal, then history began before Genesis 1:1.

"We must choose our words carefully here, of course. How shall we talk about the situation before 'in the beginning?' To avoid confusion I have chosen the word *sequence*, in contrast to the word 'time' as used in the concept of a space-time continuum. It will remind us that something was there before the beginning and that it was more than a static eternal. After creation God worked into time and communicated knowledge to man who was in time. And since He did this, it is quite obvious that it is *not the same to God* before creation and after creation. While we cannot exhaust the meaning of what is involved, we can know it truly. It is a reasonable concept; one that we can discuss."

Schaeffer also realized the critical importance of maintaining this view, stressing it in contrast to the Eastern or new theologian's impersonal picture of Him: "This subject is not merely theoretical. What is involved is the reality of the personal God in all eternity in contrast to the philosophic *other* or *impersonal* everything which is frequently the twentieth-century theologian's concept of God. What is involved is the reality of the

---

[6]Charles Hodge, *Systematic Theology* (Grand Rapids: Eerdmans, 1960).
[7]Ibid. p. 142–144.
[8]Dr. Nathan Wood, *The Trinity in the Universe* (Grand Rapids: Kregel, 1984), pp. 146–149.

personal God in contrast to a theoretical unmoved Mover, or man's purely subjective thought projection."[9]

Time as an Essential Element of Personality

Time is surely a *moral concept*, an idea finding its origin in the structure of the personality. The idea of history implies that someone has registered something and that someone has found meaning in it later. We can analyze sequence on a macro or micro level; measuring time in different ways (for instance: sand running through an hourglass, a candle burning at a specific rate, the constant decay of a radioactive element, or use some standard such as an electromagnetic radiation frequency—a wavelength of light). But time itself is a puzzle that in the last analysis points to a unique thing about man made in God's image: it seems that time and pre-existent moral consciousness must go together.

As we have seen in the Bible, God reveals himself as a moral being. Because He is personal and moral, He must be a person with whom time apparently has real meaning.

Dr. Robert Blaikie

Blaikie, a Presbyterian apologist and theologian, emphasizes: "God's eternity, as understood in Hebrew tradition that runs throughout the Bible, is not a 'timeless state' as in Greek thought [which is] without a 'before' and 'now' and 'after' . . . in which 'history' is without real meaning. God's eternity . . . is time with the quality of God's presence and God's action in it; and God is a God who acts in our time and history, which is contained within and permeated by His own eternal time."[10]

Dr. Nathan Wood

We have already seen that God, by His uncreated nature, is *eternal*. If we focus on His personality and look at the record of Scripture as God recorded events, we find that our own idea of time is probably derived from the reality of His own. Dr. Nathan Wood also concludes that personality and time are intrinsically linked: "It is possible to think thoughts which have nothing to do with space or motion. But the mind can do nothing at all without consecutiveness, succession of thoughts."[11]

A. D. Ritchie

We must be careful to keep this moral/metaphysical distinction clear. Our failure to distinguish between the "timeless" being of God and His role as Creator, with His being able to originate actions in some true sequence, has led to much unnecessary speculation and confusion. Focus

---

[9]Francis Schaeffer, *Genesis in Space and Time* (Downers Grove, Ill.: InterVarsity Press, 1972), pp.18–19.
[10]Dr. Robert Blaikie, *Secular Christianity and the God Who Acts* (London: Hodder and Stoughton, 1970), p. 147.
[11]Wood, op. cit. p. 150.

only on what He *is* as an infinite being and you are left with a timeless eternity that seems to ultimately exclude any real human choices. "If men are puppets it makes no difference whether you say the strings are pulled by God, necessity, or chance."[12]

J. R. Lucas

What if we do assume that eternity is some unique form of special time without beginning or end? This would in no way detract from any other biblical attribute of our Creator. Time, even an endless time, is not a limitation except to those who do not enjoy life now: "Those who found time hanging heavy on their hands would not, were it not for the fear of death, welcome extra time. The test of time is a severe test of value. Only something supremely worthwhile can stand having infinite time to do it in. Else—if we were like those who devote their lives to killing time— infinite time would be everlasting hell."[13]

Oscar Cullman

But if we confuse morals and metaphysics, if we make no real distinction in our thinking between the being (substance) and character (personality in action) of God, we will fail to see that God is not of necessity divorced from any sort of time, even though He had no origin in time. The fact that He is a true person and can originate a series of choices that did not exist before means that God's personality does seem to operate in some sort of sequence, the intrinsic element of time.

Oscar Cullmann, in his innovative work on time says: "The New Testament knows nothing of any timeless eternity, or of a God who is beyond or outside time and not within it."[14]

Terence Fretheim

"The difference between God's temporality and that of the human is not simply quantitative; it is qualitative," says Fretheim. "God remains the same. God does not waste or wear away like the grass or a change of clothes (Ps. 90:10). God is immune from the ravages of time; time is no threat to God. God's thoughts, name, faithfulness and kingship remain constant 'to all generations' (Ps. 33:11; cf. 102:12; 119:90; 135:13; 145:13; 146:10). . . . The God of the Old Testament is thus not thought of in terms of timelessness. At least since the Creation, the divine life is temporally ordered. God has chosen to enter the time of the world. God is not above the flow of time and history as if looking down from some supratemporal mountaintop on all the streams of people through the valleys of the ages. God is 'inside time' not outside of it. Yet there never was nor will ever be a time when God is not the living God. . . . God's life within the flow of events is quantitatively supreme; God's salvific will remains unchanged;

---

[12]A.D. Ritchie, *Civilization, Science, and Religion* (Pelican Books, 1945), p. 27.

[13]J.R. Lucas, *Treatise on Space and Time* (London: Methuen and Co., 1973), p. 90.

[14]Oscar Cullmann, *Christ and Time: The Primitive Christian Conception of Time and History* (New York: Gordon Press, 1977, 3rd ed.), pp. 62, 23, 24.

God's faithfulness is never compromised; God's steadfast love endures forever. . . . God has so bound himself in relationship with the world that they move through time and space together."[15]

Attempts at Synthesis

As we have seen in previous studies, many Christian writers and thinkers have attempted some form of absolute synthesis of God's time-transcendent being with His personality. We have also noted that this results in a more or less Eastern picture of God and history, a continuous stream in which God, man, and the universe have *always* existed in their past, present, and future forms; where all events are as fixed as a developed strip of movie film.

This "movie strip" concept which we use to analyze time is something quite different from reality. It represents time as space, opening the door to deterministic arguments.

Henry Bergson

"All the difficulties of the problem and the problem itself arise from the desire to endow duration with the same attributes as extensity, to interpret a succession by a simultaneity, and to express the idea of freedom in a language into which it is obviously untranslatable. . . . All determinism will be refuted by experience; but every attempt to define freedom will open the way to determinism."[16]

Dr. Robert Blaikie

Blaikie said: "If with Kant we assume . . . time remembered and thought about can be properly represented by space as conceptually fixed and frozen in event-bits, then freedom, action, and persons are rational problems or impossibilities precluded by determinism. . . . Real time and action when 'captured' in precise thought and logically analyzed in language become divided and immobilized like the individual pictures in a cine film. . . . Action remains logically impossible for the self. . . .

"If we are to escape this impasse, a new foundation for rational thought must be found, with new presuppositions upon which we may think of man not as subject-self distinguished from the world-as-object, but as agent, acting in the world-as-other; as a psychosomatic unity, united in himself, and in action united also with his world at a level of being more fundamental than that on which the intellect sharply distinguishes mind (or soul) from the body, subject from object, real time from remembered time and so makes possible discursive thought. . . . *The foundation we need for modern thought must start with our knowledge of persons and of agents*, with our knowledge of action and of freedom and on this basis build a systematic account of the different sorts of knowledge we have— intuitive, personal revelation through acts and words (whether of man or

---

[15]Terence Fretheim, *The Suffering of God* (Fortress, 1984), p. 44.
[16]Henri Bergson, *Time and Free Will* (Allen Unwin, 1910), p. 221.

God), objective, scientific knowledge and so on. . . . We need new pre-suppositions for a new age of thinking; we must enter a New World of understanding and 'see' man, action, language, God and the world in a new way or else hand over the academic world to cynical nihilism and unfathomable frustration."[17]

All the elements of fixity, flux, and possibility do exist in time; the idea of the future gives us the idea of true alternatives. Without such a concept of sequence being an ultimate reality even in God, it is difficult to avoid the fatalism and determinism that has killed the East's hope of change, reduced the personality of God to an abstraction, and robbed Him—philosophically at least—of His freedom to alter and originate.

Kenneth Foreman

Foreman, a Presbyterian theologian, shows this difference between a true biblical sovereignty and fatalism: "Let us imagine two horsemen. One sits on a horse every moment of which he controls absolutely. Another man sits on another horse. This horse makes various movements which the rider does not command, does not initiate, cannot even predict in detail. . . . But the rider is in control. . . . Which is the better horseman? Little Willie operating his mechanical horse in the corner drugstore or the prize-winning rider at the horse show? Is it actually more to the credit of God that He shall ride this universe like a hobby-horse or like a real living creature? . . . We Christians will not give up believing in the sovereignty of God. We Presbyterians will need not apologize for keeping that high truth central in our doctrine of God. But we do not have to suppose that God cannot be sovereign without robbing His creatures of all their free-dom."[18]

Another logical but somewhat more ugly result of the "eternal now" premise is that we must take a much more rigid interpretation of biblical doctrines such as predestination. Systematic thinkers like John Calvin derived such beliefs as unconditional election (to salvation), limited or special atonement (Christ dying only for a preselected few), and irresist-ible grace (God using force rather than persuasion to change a man's will in order to save him). Even perseverance of the saints as an amoral eternal security can be derived if man has no real choice in salvation, no real choices of faith to make in his future spiritual relationship. This is not to say those who ascribe to such doctrinal stands may either preach or live them in extreme, but it does explain the historic resistance to such doc-trines by the other evangelical and missionary streams of the Church who considered such ideas nonsense, if not blasphemous, and whose beliefs were likewise considered so by their opponents.

Dr. Robert Blaikie

Blaikie again notes: "Although these concepts from Greek philosophy might appear to have some value in Christian theology for 'explaining' the

---

[17]Blaikie, op. cit. pp. 194–195.
[18]Dr. Kenneth J. Foreman, *God's Will and Ours* (Richmond, Va.: Outlook, 1954), p. 30.

omniscience of God, predestination and so on, yet with reference to a God who acts these . . . raise far more problems than they 'solve.' Action cannot be conceived of apart from movement, and movement requires time—real flowing duration."[19]

Yet we cannot greatly fault the logic leading to these conclusions. The ideas are, after all, the product of centuries of thought, argument, and reasonably adequate biblical documentation. That logic is their great strength, despite the stated claim that the strength of the doctrines is the wealth of Scripture on such subjects. The system *makes sense*; if you start from where Calvin started, you ought to come out where he did.

Many of the attempted refutations of this idea are fatally flawed because they begin where their opponents begin, and by dint of much opposing Scripture and a number of leaps in logic, come out in the opposite place—a more Christ-like understanding explored with the right motives for the wrong reasons!

A plain man with convictions of true justice and goodness might find a theology which takes God outside of time morally indefensible. What we need in theology is an idea of eternity that coherently supports the biblical view that future history can be changed because people are truly, personally responsible for their actions. This view intelligently magnifies our view of God's own greatness and sovereign power.

J. Oliver Buswell

Buswell saw clearly the importance of maintaining this view of eternity, if we are to be fearlessly consistent in our view of God as a person. He points out the inherent weakness of some well-known historic thinkers on this point: "A biblical view of God as a Personal Spirit is contrary to the view of Thomas Aquinas that God is the 'fully Realized,' in 'whom there is no potential.' It is also contrary to the pantheistic view of Spinoza, contrary to the transcendent timeless God of Kant and contrary to the pseudo-Calvinism of some of our contemporaries who teach that God is timeless, and those that hold with Jonathan Edwards that God has no freedom of choice. To say that these eminent writers hold views of God which deny His personality seems radical indeed. Some of them, of course, do believe in a personal God, but inconsistently. My point is that to deny that God performs self-conscious, self-determined specific actions in the process of time and that He is causally related to specific events is to deny something which is essential to the concept of personality."[20]

Arthur C. Custance

Custance, while personally exploring the Eternal Now view, reaches a similar conclusion: "The Lord after His resurrection evidently moved in a world which was constituted differently. It was a real world, but a world with a different kind of reality; a spatial world, but a world with a different

---

[19]Blaikie, op. cit. p. 204.
[20]J. Oliver Buswell, *Systematic Theology of the Christian Religion* (Grand Rapids: Zondervan Publishing House), vol. 1, p. 36.

kind of space. Being a world with a different kind of space it was presumably a world with a different kind of time. . . . It involved a sequence of events, and therefore some kind of time order also that corresponds to what we experience, and yet transcends the time frame of our world because it transcends the spatial order of our world. . . .

"Perhaps we should also agree that any dimensionless position implies the possibility of shifts in position, and this at once introduces the idea of sequence, of previous and subsequent position, of present and future position. So if there is any kind of time, it looks as though it would be the fourth dimension of a frame marked off by the three dimensions of past, present, and future, rather than being the fourth dimension of a three-dimensional space. Perhaps it is somewhere in this direction that there will be time-frame in Heaven."[21]

C. S. Lewis

Lewis toyed with a similar thought (while maintaining the idea of a "timeless eternity" for God) in his *Letters to Malcolm*: "Your own peculiar difficulty—that the dead are not in time—is another matter. How do you know they are not? I certainly believe that to be God is to enjoy an infinite present where nothing has yet passed away and nothing is still to come. Does it follow that we can say the same of saints and angels? Or at any rate, exactly the same? The dead might experience a time which is not so linear as ours—it might, so to speak, have thickness as well as length. Already in this life we get some thickness whenever we learn to attend to more than one thing at once. One can suppose this increased to any extent so that though for them as well as us, the present is always becoming the past, yet each present contains unimaginably more than ours. I feel—can you work it out for me and tell me if it is more than a feeling— that to make the life of the blessed dead strictly timeless is inconsistent with the resurrection of the body. . . . For though we cannot experience in our life as an endless present, we are eternal in God's eyes; that is in our deepest reality. When I say we are 'in time' I don't mean that we are impossibly outside the endless present in which He beholds us as He beholds all else. I mean our creaturely limitation is that our fundamentally timeless reality can be experienced by us only in the mode of succession."[22]

Dorothy Sayers

Sayers, though also holding to an Eternal Now picture of eternity, uses the idea of writing a novel to point out the distinction between the time frame of a creation and a Creator: "Neither do we need more than two kinds of time—real time and created time. This duality of time has the advantage of being empirically known, intelligently manifest. The novelist

---

[21]Arthur C. Custance, "Time and Relativity In Creation," *The Doorway Papers* (Grand Rapids: Zondervan Publishing House, 1977), Vol. VI, pp. 36–37.
[22]C.S. Lewis, *Letters to Malcolm* (Huntington N.Y.: John M. Fontana Publishers, 1975), pp. 111–112.

and reader . . . take it so much for granted that they never give it a second thought. Real time is the rhythm or dimension in which the author himself has his being; created time is the time that takes place inside the story— known to the characters in it as a linear movement in one direction, but to the author as a simultaneity in which all its moments are present at once. The two times have nothing in common except that they are both known to the author; there is no sense in which it can be said that the time inside the story I am writing coincides with my time in which I am living—they are related in the way in which we call 'time' is related to what we call 'eternity.'

"But note that the author, though his is the only ultimately effective will and the only real time or causation concerned, is to some extent bound by the laws he has made for his own creation. He must not reverse or confuse the time sequence within the story; neither must he make his created people behave otherwise than in accordance with the natures he has bestowed upon them. Even in an imagined story, the characters have a certain simulacrum of free will that the author must needs respect; and this encourages us to suppose that in the actual created universe a measure of free will may be compatible in the creature with the author's infinite knowledge of the pattern . . ."

Sayers attempts to synthesize from this parallel a model of freedom within necessity. She feels it is helpful to visualize the possible options of man's and God's choices: "Let us then picture the totality of things as a web spread out in as many dimensions of time and space as we may find it easy and convenient to imagine. We shall observe in it certain fixed points; these are nodes of necessity, through which lines must pass in order to make the pattern. The nodes are determined by the artist, but the lines are self-determined and may take any direction they choose, subject to two limitations: (1) However they bend or turn—even if they start off in the opposite direction—they are bound to eventually go through the fixed points. (2) Every movement they make modifies and is modified by the movements of the neighboring lines. The will of the maker readily submits to all these modifications, since the necessity laid upon these lines to come to the nodes means that all possible modifications can only in the end produce a conditioned necessity of their own."[23]

Regardless of our own conclusion on this matter, the study of time as it relates to God will continue to be a major point of discussion in the Christian church in our century.

---

[23]Dorothy Sayers, *Oedipus Simplex*, pp. 250–256.

CHAPTER EIGHT

COROLLARY THREE:
GOD IS AWESOMELY HOLY

Scriptures

"And they made the plate of the holy crown of pure gold, and wrote upon it a writing, like to the engravings of a signet, *Holiness to the Lord* . . . as the Lord commanded Moses" (Ex. 39:30–31)

"For I am the LORD your God: ye shall therefore sanctify yourselves, and ye shall be holy; for I am holy." (Lev. 11:44)

"For I am the LORD that bringeth you up out of the land of Eygpt, to be your God: ye shall therefore be holy, for I am holy." (Lev. 11:45; cf. 19:2)

"And ye shall be holy unto me: for I the LORD am holy, and have severed you from other people, that ye should be mine." (Lev. 20:26)

"I the LORD, which sanctify you, am holy." (Lev. 21:8; cf. 20:8)

"And one cried unto another, and said, Holy, holy, holy, is the LORD of hosts: the whole earth is full of his glory." (Isa. 6:3)

"Sanctify [*hagiason*] them through thy truth: thy word is truth . . . and for their sakes I sanctify [*hagiazo*] myself, that they also might be sanctified [*hegiasmenoi*] through the truth." (John 17:17, 19)

The Son Is Called Holy

"Found with child of the Holy Ghost." (Matt. 1:18)

"The Holy Ghost shall come upon thee . . . that holy thing which shall be born." (Luke 1:35)

Recognized As Such by Demons

"I know thee who thou art, the Holy One of God." (Mark 1:24; cf. Luke 4:34)

Prophesied That He Would Rise Again

"Thou shalt not allow thine Holy One to see corruption." (Acts 13:35; cf. Ps. 16:10)

The Disciples Declared His Holiness

"Of a truth against thy holy child Jesus." (Acts 4:27)

"By the name of thy holy child Jesus." (Acts 4:30)

The Father Is Called Holy

"Holy Father, keep through thine own name. . . ." (John 17:11)

"But as he which hath called you is holy, so be ye holy in all manner of conversation; because it is written, Be ye holy; for I am holy. And if ye call on the Father, who without respect of persons judgeth according to every man's work, pass the time of your sojourning here in fear." (1 Pet. 1:15–17)

The Spirit Is Called Holy

"He shall baptize you with the Holy Ghost." (Mark 1:8)

"That I should be a minister . . . being sanctified by the Holy Ghost." (Rom. 15:16)

The multiple references to the Holy Spirit comprise the bulk of verses where the word *holy* is ascribed to God in the NT.

God Is Uniquely and Awesomely Holy

"Ye cannot serve the LORD: for he is an holy God." (Josh 24:19)

"There is none holy as the LORD: for there is none beside thee; neither is there any rock like our God. (1 Sam. 2:2)

"Who is able to stand before this holy LORD God?" (1 Sam. 6:20)

"LORD, who shall abide in thy tabernacle? who shall dwell in thy holy hill?" (Ps. 15:1)

"O God, thou art terrible out of thy holy places." (Ps. 68:35)

"To whom then then will ye liken me, or shall I be equal? saith the Holy One." (Isa. 40:25)

"For I am God, and not man; the Holy One in the midst of thee." (Hos 11:9)

"Art not thou from everlasting, O LORD my God, mine Holy One?" (Hab. 1:12)

"No man can say that Jesus is the Lord, but by the Holy Ghost." (1 Cor. 12:3)

"These things saith he that is holy, he that is true." (Rev. 3:7)

"Who shall not fear thee, O Lord, and glorify thy name? for thou only art holy: for all nations shall come and worship before thee; for thy judgments are made manifest." (Rev. 15:4)

God's Name Is Holy

"Thou shalt not take the name of the Lord thy God in vain; for the Lord will not hold him guiltless that taketh his name in vain." (Ex. 20:7)

"Neither shall ye profane my holy name." (Lev. 23:32)

"Pollute ye my holy name no more." (Ezek. 20:39)

"[I] will be jealous for my holy name." (Ezek. 39:25)

"They have even defiled my holy name." (Ezek. 43:8)

"Go in unto the same maid, to profane my holy name." (Amos 2:7)

"When ye pray, say, Our Father which art in heaven, Hallowed be thy name." (Luke 11:2)

We Are to Worship Him in His Holiness

"But thou art holy, O thou that inhabitest the praises of Israel." (Ps. 22:3)

"Give unto the LORD the glory due unto his name; worship the Lord in the beauty of holiness." (Ps. 29:2)

"For the LORD is our defence; and the Holy One of Israel is our king." (Ps. 89:18)

"O sing unto the LORD a new song; for he hath done marvellous things: his right hand, and his holy arm, hath gotten him the victory." (Ps. 98:1)

"He sent redemption unto his people: he hath commanded his covenant for ever: holy and reverend is his name." (Ps. 111:9)

"The LORD is righteous in all his ways, and holy in all his works. . . . My mouth shall speak the praise of the LORD: and let all flesh bless his holy name for ever and ever." (Ps. 145:17, 21)

"Rejoice in the Holy One of Israel." (Isa. 29:19)

"Glory in the Holy One of Israel." (Isa. 41:16)

"For thus saith the high and lofty One that inhabiteth eternity, whose name is Holy; I dwell in the high and holy place, with him also that is of a contrite and humble spirit, to revive the spirit of the humble, and to revive the heart of the contrite ones." (Isa. 57:15)

There Is Wisdom in His Holiness

"The fear of the LORD is the beginning of wisdom: and the knowledge of the Holy is understanding." (Prov. 9:10)

"For thou hast said, My doctrine is pure, and I am clean in thine eyes. But oh that God would speak . . . and that he would shew thee the secrets of wisdom, that they are double to that which is!" (Job 11:4–6)

"But God hath revealed them unto us by his Spirit: for the Spirit searcheth all things, yea, the deep things of God . . . which things also we speak, not in the words which man's wisdom teacheth, but which the Holy Ghost teacheth." (1 Cor. 2:10, 13)

There Is Power in His Holiness

"Let them praise thy great and terrible name; for it is holy. The king's strength also loveth judgment; thou dost establish equity, thou executest judgment and righteousness in Jacob. Exalt ye the LORD our God, and worship at his footstool; for he is holy . . . and worship at his holy hill; for the Lord our God is holy." (Ps. 99:3–5, 9)

"So I will show my greatness and my holiness, and I will make myself known in the sight of many nations." (Ezek. 38:23, NIV)

". . . through the power of the Holy Ghost." (Rom. 15:13)

There Is Joy in His Holiness

"Blessed is the people that know the joyful sound: they shall walk, O LORD, in the light of thy countenance. In thy name shall they rejoice all the day: and in thy righteousness shall they be exalted." (Ps. 89:15–16)

"Bless the LORD, O my soul: and all that is within me, bless his holy name." (Ps. 103:1)

"Glory ye in his holy name: let the heart of them rejoice that seek the LORD." (Ps. 105:3)

"Save us, O LORD our God, and gather us from among the heathen, to give thanks unto thy holy name, and to triumph in thy praise." (Ps. 106:47)

"For the Kingdom of heaven is not meat and drink; but righteousness, and peace, and joy in the Holy Ghost." (Rom. 14:17)

He Creates and Redeems in Holiness:

"Fear not, thou worm Jacob, and ye men of Israel; I will help thee, saith the LORD, and thy redeemer, the Holy One of Israel." (Isa. 41:14)

"That they may see, and know, and consider, and understand together, that the hand of the LORD hath done this, and the Holy One of Israel hath created it." (Isa. 41:20)

"I am the LORD, your Holy One, the creator of Israel, your King." (Isa. 43:15)

"Thus saith the LORD, the Redeemer of Israel, and his Holy One, to him whom man despiseth, to him whom the nation abhoreth, to a servant of rulers, Kings shall see and arise, princes also shall worship, because of the LORD that is faithful, and the Holy One of Israel, and he shall choose thee." (Isa. 49:7)

. . . to bring thy sons from far, their silver and their gold with them, unto the name of the LORD thy God, and to the Holy One of Israel, because he hath glorified thee." (Isa. 60:9)

He Judges in Holiness

"The LORD is in his holy temple, the LORD's throne is in heaven; his eyes behold, his eyelids try, the children of men." (Ps. 11:4)

"They have forsaken the LORD, they have provoked the Holy One of Israel unto anger . . ." (Isa. 1:4)

"But the LORD of hosts shall be exalted in judgment, and God that is holy shall be sanctified in righteousness." (Isa. 5:16)

"And the light of Israel shall be for a fire, and his Holy One for a flame . . ." (Isa. 10:17)

"If any man defile the temple of God, him shall God destroy; for the temple of God is holy, which temple ye are." (1 Cor. 3:17)

"And they cried with a loud voice, saying, How long, O Lord, holy and true, dost thou not judge and avenge our blood on them that dwell on the earth?" (Rev. 6:10)

Bible Word Study

The Bible is filled with descriptions of God in His holiness as well as encouragements and exhortations to us to be holy as He is holy. But what exactly does it mean to be "holy"? Let's look at some of the words the Bible uses, and their meanings.

Holy (Hebrew)

The derivation of the words used for "holy" is uncertain. Three main meanings have been suggested:
1. The idea of separation, to be cut off, withdrawn or set apart.
2. From the Akkadian *qudasu*—"brightness or brilliance," the idea of shining and terrible as God in fire.
3. Also from this root, the idea of purity: "Procksch considers *tahor* [taw-hore; *Strong's* 2889] 'pure' as closely related materially to *qodesh* [*Strong's* 6944] 'holy' as *hagnos* 'chaste,' 'clear,' 'pure' is to *hagios* (holy) in the NT."[1]

---

[1]*The Zondervan Pictorial Encyclopedia of the Bible*, Merrill Tenney, ed. (Grand Rapids: Zondervan Pub. House, 1976), vol. 3, p. 174.

qadowsh or qadosh (*kaw-doshe*)—Sacred (ceremonially or morally); God (when used as a noun); or (by eminence) an angel, saint, sanctuary. Translated in the KJV as "holy One," or "saint."[2]

qadash (*kaw-dash*)—To be (causatively make, pronounce, observe as) clean (ceremonially or morally). Translated in the KJV as "appoint," "bid," "consecrate," "dedicate," "defile," "hallow," "keep," "prepare," "proclaim," "purify."[3]

qodesh (*ko-desh*)—A sacred place or thing; rarely abstract. Sanctity. Translated in the KJV as "consecrated" (thing), "dedicated" (thing), "hallowed" (thing), "saint," "sanctuary."[4]

chaciyd (*khaw-seed*)—Properly means "kind," i.e., (religiously) pious, a saint. Translated in the KJV as "godly" (man), "good," "holy" (one), "merciful," "[un]godly."[5]

Forms of the root *qds* occur some 830 times in the OT, about 350 of them in the Pentateuch. The Aramaic *quadis* (holy) occurs 13 times in Daniel.

Holy (Greek)

Greek uses three different word groups.

hieros (*hee-er-os*)—Sacred. Translated in the KJV as "holy."[6]

"That which is determined, filled or consecrated by divine power." *Hieros* with its derivatives denotes the "essentially holy, the taboo, the divine power, or what was consecrated to it, e.g. sanctuary, sacrifice, priest." It means what is intrinsically holy "in and of itself, quite apart from any ethical judgment."[7]

Other related words: *hierateia* "priest's office" (Luke 1:9; Heb. 7:5); *hierateuma* "priesthood" (1 Pet. 2:5, 9); *hierus* "priest" (used 31 times in the NT); *hieron* "temple" (used 71 times in the NT); *hieroprepes* "as becometh holiness" (Titus 2:3); *hierosulos* "robber of churches" (Acts 19:37); *hierosuleo* "commit sacrilege" (Rom. 2:22); and *hierourgeo* "ministering" (Rom. 15:16).[8]

hagios (*hag-ee-os*)—An awful thing; sacred (physically pure, morally blameless or religious, ceremonially consecrated). [9]

[2]*Strong's* 6918.
[3]*Strong's* 6942.
[4]*Strong's* 6944.
[5]*Strong's* 2623.
[6]*Strong's* 2413.
[7]*The New International Dictionary of New Testament Theology*, Colin Brown, ed. (Grand Rapids: Zondervan Publishing House, 1971), vol. 2, pp. 223, 232.
[8]Ethelbert W. Bullinger, *A Critical Lexicon and Concordance to the English and Greek New Testament* (Grand Rapids: Zondervan Publishing House, 1975), pp. 602, 650, 956.
[9]*Strong's* 40.

"The old Greek word *hagos* signifies the object of awe . . . whether in the sense of reverence . . . or in that of aversion."[10]

In contrast to *hieros*, *hagios* is the "most frequent word group in the NT." It contains an "ethical element. The emphasis falls on duty to worship the holy." But its meaning is hard to determine etymologically.

It carries overtones of that which is marked off from the secular . . . most closely related materially to holiness is the term for purity, yet "there is always an energy in the holy that is lacking in the pure or clean."[11]

hosios (*hos-ee-os*)—Properly "right" (by intrinsic or divine character); hallowed (pious, sacred, sure).[12]

Hosios is a rare word in the NT, being used only eight times, five of which are in quotations (Rev. 15:3–4; cf. Ps. 145:17; Rev. 16:5; cf. Deut. 32:4; Acts 2:27; 13:35; cf. Ps. 16:10; Acts 13:34; cf. Isa. 55:3; Acts 17:31; Heb. 7:26).[13]

"On the one hand, it [*hosios*] indicates divine commandment and providence; on the other, human obligation and morality." In its earliest form (*hosie*), it stood for "what was in accordance with divine direction and providence." The adjective *hosios* has the general sense of "sanctioned or allowed by divine or natural law."[14]

In Heb. 7:26, *hosios* is used "absolutely in the way in which elsewhere it can be used only of God. As high priest . . . Christ is completely *hosios*, utterly without sin and utterly pure, so that his offering is sufficient once for all."[15]

In the Septuagint, God is called *hosios* twice as upright in Deut. 32:4, "God observes the decrees which He himself has made. In Psalms 145:17 *hosios* translates *hasid*—God supports the fallen, satisfies the hungry and is near to them which pray to Him."[16]

"The decisive element in the OT concept of the holy, in contrast to the profane . . . is not so much the awesome divine power. Rather, through certain places, objects or occasions men enter into relatively direct contact with the divine power which can be awesome, if men treat it in a profane way (1 Sam. 6:20). The basic idea is not that of separation . . . but the positive thought of encounter which invariably demands certain modes of response."[17]

"God's holiness . . . becomes an expression for His perfection of being which transcends everything creaturely."[18]

"When we leave the realm of the OT and enter that of the NT, two

---

[10]*Theological Dictionary of the New Testament*, Gerhard Kittel, ed., Geoffrey W. Bromiley, trans. (Grand Rapids: Wm. B. Eerdmans Publishing Company, 1964), vol. 1, p. 88.
[11]*The New International Dictionary of New Testament Theology*, vol. 2, pp. 223–224.
[12]*Strong's* 3741.
[13]*The New International Dictionary of New Testament Theology*, op. cit. vol. 2, pp. 237–238.
[14]Ibid. vol. 2, pp. 223, 236.
[15]Ibid. vol. 2, p. 238.
[16]Ibid. vol. 2, p. 237.
[17]Ibid. vol. 2, p. 224.
[18]*Theological Dictionary of the New Testament*, op. cit. vol. 1, p. 91.

facts stand out. First God [the Father] is only seldom described as holy (John 17:11; 1 Pet. 1:15f.; Rev. 4:8; 6:10), and Christ is only once called holy in the same sense as God (Rev. 3:7; cf. 1 John 2:20). The concept of holiness in the NT is determined rather by the Holy Spirit, the Gift of the new age.

"Secondly and following from this, the proper sphere of the holy in the NT is . . . the prophetic. The sacred no longer belongs to things, places or rites, but to manifestations of life produced by the Spirit. But since prophecy did not readily lend itself to the building up of a corporate consciousness, as time went on use was made of the holy priesthood . . . and the royal priesthood of all the saints."[19]

Jesus was called "the Holy One of God" (Mark 1:24; Luke 4:34; cf. Judg. 13:7; 16:17, where this title occurs in the Septuagint. It means the "bearer has been filled by the holy"). Jesus was holy from His conception, filled by the Holy Spirit and was the "holy servant" (Acts 4:27; cf. 3:14) who was denied and rejected like His prophets of the past. "In all these cases holy means belonging to God and authorized by God."[20]

Hallowed Be Thy Name

"Above all, the name of God is holy. This explains why in later Judaism the proper name . . . of God was never pronounced except in temple worship. After the destruction of the temple it was not even known how to pronounce it. It was replaced in . . . the reading of Scripture . . . but even [the] substitutes eventually became taboo. . . ."[21]

"In the Name of God the holy shows itself to be something personal which thus requires of the one who prays a personal attitude to the divine world. Thus the holiness of God the Father is everywhere presumed in the NT, though seldom stated. It is filled out in Jesus Christ . . ."[22]

In the Synoptic Gospels, the verb *hagiastheto* (hallowed) only occurs in Matt. 6:9, 23:17, 19, and Luke 11:2. "To 'hallow' the Name (i.e., the nature of God as known through His self-revelation in history) means, not only to reverence and honor God, but also to glorify him by obedience to his commands, and thus prepare for the coming of the Kingdom."[23]

"The petitions are a cry from the depth of distress. From a world enslaved by evil, death and Satan, the disciples are to lift their eyes to the Father and cry out for a revelation of His glory, knowing in faith that He will grant it. . . .

"The sanctification prayed for is both positive and negative. 'First it means the abolition of everything in the sensory realm contradictory to God's holiness—for the only one who is holy in his being and actions is the one who, like the angels in the service of God, matches his actions with his being and his being with his actions. . . . Secondly, it means the

---

[19]*The New International Dictionary of New Testament Theology*, op. cit. vol. 2, p. 228.
[20]Ibid. vol. 2, pp. 228–229.
[21]*Theological Dictionary of the New Testament*, op. cit. vol. 1, p. 98.
[22]Ibid. vol. 1, p. 101.
[23]*The New International Dictionary of New Testament Theology*, op. cit. vol. 2, p. 229.

elevation and therefore the consummation of all human and historical being in the holiness of God: "You must be perfect even as your heavenly Father is perfect." ' "[24]

Holiness and Fire

The regular association of holiness and fire is striking. God most characteristically clothes himself in fire from the time of Moses onward (Ex. 3:2–3; 19:18; 24:17; Deut. 4:12, 24; 5:22–27; 9:3; Ps. 18:8–14; Ezek. 1:4–28; Hab. 3:3–4; and many other passages often directly related to holiness).

"God often also judges in fire, especially on the Day of the Lord (Isa. 34:8–10; Zeph.1:18; cf. Isa. 9:18–19; Amos 1:3—2:16). Sacred practices are 'intimately and specifically connected with fire' with noteworthy emphasis on holiness in all these contexts (Lev. 2:3, 9–10; 6:16–18; 7:3–5; 10:1–3; 'unholy fire' 16:27; 21:6–10 etc.).

"Fire imagery is frequently used in passages about holiness with nouns such as 'light,' 'heat,' 'smoke,' 'flame,' 'coals,' 'furnace,' 'cauldron,' 'ashes,' 'brimstone'; and verbs such as 'scorch,' 'blaze,' 'consume,' 'burn,' 'kindle,' 'glow,' 'warm' and 'quench.' It is the seraphim ('the fiery ones') who sing 'Holy, holy, holy' before His throne and take the live coal off the altar (Isa. 6:3–6)."

The NT continues the imagery when it says, "Our God is a consuming fire" (Heb. 12:26–29); also in the language of judgment (Luke 12:49), in reference to the Holy Spirit (Matt. 3:11; Acts 2:1–4), in reference to Moses' meeting with God (Acts 7:30), Isaiah's and Ezekiel's visions (Rev. 4:4–11), and the Day of the Lord (1 Cor. 3:12–15).[25]

Another theme related to these words is of course the *reaction* God's holiness produces in the creation; it is called the "fear of the Lord." We shall look at this in much more detail under analysis and discussion, but here are some of the important words related to this facet of God's holiness:

Fear (Hebrew)

Several Hebrew words are translated "fear" in the OT, the principal of these being the noun *yirah* and the verb *yare*. They also mean "dread," "terror," "timidity," "wonderful," "stupendous," "reverence," and "awe."

Fear (Greek)

The chief Greek words for fear are *phobos* and *phobeo*, which are also translated "terror," "alarm," "reverence" and "respect."

---

[24]Ibid. vol. 2, p. 229.
[25]*Interpreter's Dictionary of the Bible*, George A. Buttrick, ed. (Nashville: Abingdon Press, 1962), vol. 2, pp. 617–618.

phobos *(fob-os)*—Alarm or fright. Translated in the KJV as "be afraid."[26]

Phobos is used 47 times in the NT. Used for "fear of Jews" (John 7:13; 19:38; 20:19), of authority or masters (Rom. 13:3, 7; 1 Pet. 2:18), of husbands (1 Pet. 3:2), persecutors (1 Pet. 3:14), "fear of death" (Heb. 2:15), and "fear of torment" (Rev. 18:10, 15).

Most of the other times it is used to describe the reaction of people to the holy supernatural, such as Christ's miracles (Luke 7:16) and resurrection power (Matt. 28:4, 8), the work of the Holy Spirit in the early Church (Acts 2:43; 5:5, 11), and the attitude of the Christian in ministry (2 Cor. 5:11).

We are to "perfect holiness" in that fear (2 Cor. 7:1), "work out our own salvation" in it (Phil. 2:12), husbands and wives are to submit to each other in the fear of God (Eph. 5:21), public rebuke of sin brings this fear (1 Tim. 5:20), and some even "save with fear" (Jude 23).

Phobos "first had the meaning of flight, that which is caused by being scared; then, that which may cause flight." *Phobos* can mean fear, dread, fright, dismay or terror; as well as a *reverential* fear of God—a "wholesome dread of displeasing Him, a fear which banishes the terror that shrinks from His presence . . . and which influences the disposition and attitude of one whose circumstances are guided by trust in God, through the indwelling Spirit of God."[27]

phobeo *(fob-eh-o)*—This word is used 93 times in the NT and derives from *phobos*. It describes both the reaction of people to the supernatural as well as the fear of God itself, as in Matt. 10:28; Luke 12:5; 23:40; Acts 10:2, 22, 35. It is commanded toward God (1 Pet. 2:17; Rev. 14:7), but prohibited in and toward men (Mark 5:36; Luke 1:13; 12:7, 32).

eulabeia *(yoo-lab-i-ah)*—"Signifies, firstly, caution; then, reverence, godly fear . . . in general, apprehension, but especially, holy fear, 'that mingled fear and love which, combined, constitute the piety of man toward God; the OT places its emphasis on the fear, the NT . . . on the love, though there was love in the fear of God's saints then, as there must be fear in their love now.' "[28]

This word was used in describing Christ's prayers (Heb 5:7—"was heard in that he feared") and of grace received to serve God acceptably (Heb. 12:28—"godly fear"). *Eulabeomai*[29] describes the fear of the chief captain in charge of Paul's protection (Acts 23:10), and of Noah's concern for the future of the world (Heb. 11:7).

deilia *(di-lee-ah)*—Timidity.[30] Used just once in the NT (2 Tim. 1:7).

---

[26]*Strong's* 5401.
[27]W.E. Vine, *The Expanded Vine's Expository Dictionary of New Testament Words*, John R. Kohlenberger III, ed. (Minneapolis, Minn.: Bethany House Publishers, 1984), p. 414.
[28]Ibid. p. 415.
[29]*Strong's* 2125.
[30]*Strong's* 1167.

Questions and Answers

Q: *What does it mean to be* holy?

A: The word "holy" is interpreted in two major ways in our world. In the East to be "holy" means primarily to be "wise"; a holy man is one who is perceptive, one who presumably understands the true nature of reality. Holiness implies the idea of revelation, the understanding of the supernatural that is given to the seeker. The weakness of the Eastern concept of holiness lies in the idea that once it is attained, it is a supreme and static state, an infinite perspective literally possessed by the enlightened (i.e., they become "one with God" in that they think as God). The idea exhibits no necessary moral content. One can be holy and still be immoral.

In contrast, the Western understanding of the word "holy" tends to be "good," often with the suggestion of naivete. Someone who is "nice" is probably so because they have been sheltered and are unaware of the real pressures of life. This concept of holiness finds its strength in its emphasis on human responsibility and ethical accountability; one expects a holy man to be good, even though he need not be intelligent. Its weakness lies in the fact that it does not take supernatural help or revelation into account; there is no required dimension of insight, wisdom, nor perception built into it.

The Bible uses "holy" from both perspectives. A holy man or woman is both wise and good; both perceptive and supernaturally aware of the true nature of reality, and responsibly responding by drawing on the power provided to conform his life to that reality despite the pressures of temptation not to.

Q: *What does God mean when He says "be ye holy for I am holy"?*

A: God calls us to live the same way He is living. This begins when we become His children through His Son by faith; it continues as we trust Him day by day for fresh revelation of His love, grace, and power; and it goes on forever into eternity. It is a state of life that flows from a relaxed, happy trust in Christ.

Q: *What does it mean "Be ye therefore perfect, even as your Father which in heaven is perfect" (Matt. 5:48)?*

A: God is not only perfect in His being, but because He lives perfectly truthfully, His conduct wholly conforms to reality and is the epitome of love. To be morally perfect then is to conform our lives to moral light; to live up to that which God reveals in His Word and by His Spirit as best for all of us (2 Thess. 2:13); in a word, by the grace and power of Christ to live intelligently in a universe ruled by Him.

Q: *But God is infinite. How can we be perfect like God?*

A: Only in the same ways we were created to be like Him: in our character, intentions, and in our moral lives. This perfection cannot be physical. We are never going to be perfect in our physical beings in this life; there are no perfect bodies. We are never going to be immortal in this life; death is still the last enemy to be defeated. This cannot mean an infinite perfection. We will never be infinite, neither now nor at any time, as that belongs only to God. Only in one way can we be like Him: to live as He does, as a true child of the Father. The Bible's call for perfection is a call to finite, moral perfection of intention; a willful choice to do good.

Q: *Doesn't the Bible say "Nobody's perfect"?*

A: No, but the bumper stickers and buttons do! On the contrary, we are commanded to seek God and be like Him; to know Christ (Phil. 3:8–10) and to make Him known; and promised abundant supernatural provision to do this supernatural task. The biblical word "perfect" does not mean "faultless." It has three synonyms in Scripture: "blameless" (Phil. 2:15) or having no selfish intention; "sincere" (Phil. 1:10) or honest and transparent, being all you seem to be; and "complete" (Col. 2:10) or mature, to be all we should be at our stage of growth.

Q: *Is being holy a state or a process?*

A: In God, it is a continuous dynamic state of being, an eternal, active conformity to all that is most wise and good; it is complete, ultimate, and unchanging. In His creation, it is and always will be a process. Conformity to moral light may be real, entire, and sincere, but must by its very nature grow.

Q: *Are you saying that no one will ever be perfectly holy in this life?*

A: To use an electronics analogy, holiness has both a *digital* and a *linear* component. A digital circuit is always in one of two states: a high or low, a yes or a no, an on or an off. On the other hand, a linear circuit, like the volume control on your stereo amplifier, has a steady, proportional (or analog) increase. The linear (analog) component of holiness is *wisdom*—God teaches us step by step, line upon line (Isa. 28:9–10). It is progressive, proportionate, and ever increasing.

In contrast, the digital component of holiness is love, or obedience (John 14:23). It is always a "do" or "do not" situation, a "yes" or "no," never a "partially" or a "perhaps." Part of the tragedy of our time is that we have confused the digital with the linear; we expect instant knowledge of everything and dismiss obedience as impractical, futuristic, or only partially possible. God wants continual learners who do exactly what He says, when He says it.

Q: *God calls some people perfect in the Bible (Job 1:8). Can we think of ourselves or call ourselves perfect?*

A: Only God sees what we really know of true moral light, and what we think we know. In our information-rich world it is very easy to fall into the trap of thinking that religious information is the same as spiritual revelation. Only the Holy Spirit can search out the deep things of the heart and bring to light hidden motives and habit patterns of the past that pose as honest intentions (1 Cor. 2:10–11). Because we do not even know ourselves in intimate depth, we ought not to judge or label the heart-motives of others (Matt. 7:1–2).

Q: *Then how can we know if we are holy like God?*
A: We can't! Only God knows the heart, and only God is ultimately qualified to judge our motives. All we can judge of our own lives is our own intentions and actual conduct in the light of a redeemed, clean conscience. We are to concentrate on loving and trusting God and leave the evaluations to Him. We are, however, commanded to "prove all things; hold fast that which is good. Abstain from all appearance of evil. And the very God of peace sanctify you wholly; and I pray God your whole spirit and soul and body be preserved blameless unto the coming of our Lord Jesus Christ. Faithful is he that called you, who also will do it" (1 Thess. 5:21–24).

Q: *What is the safest way of thinking of yourself as a Christian?*
A: We are "forgiven children of God." *Forgiven* so we remember the pit from which we came, *children of God* so we will never be tempted to dwell there again.

Q: *What does it mean that Jesus was "made perfect"? If He was God, how could He be "made perfect"? (Heb. 5:9).*
A: The perfection spoken of here is the same kind of perfection we are called to: the perfection of obedience in the fear of the Lord. The Lord Jesus did the will of His Father, and in a deliberate committal of trust and love, despite the cost and the suffering, He accomplished His task to provide the way back to God. His death was voluntary and deliberate. A major threat to His mission of atonement was premature death at the hands of His enemies. But He was "heard in that he feared" (Heb. 5:7), He learned obedience by the things He suffered (5:8), and now is the "Author of eternal salvation unto all them that obey Him" (Heb. 5:9).

Analysis and Discussion

"Holiness," says J. Muilenberg, "is the given undergirding and all pervading religion; the distinctive mark and signature of the divine. More than any other, the term 'holiness' gives expression to the essential nature of the sacred. It is therefore to be understood, not as one attribute among other attributes, but as the innermost reality to which all others are related."[1]

What does the term "holy" mean when applied to God? Though we have discussed the definition at length, precise definition is still uncertain. We do know it is "akin to glory, honor, abundance" and is the opposite

---

[1] J. Muilenberg, *Interpreter's Dictionary of the Bible*, George A. Buttrick, ed. (Nashville: Abingdon Press, 1962), vol. 2, p. 616.

of "common or profane."[2] As we have seen in our Bible word studies, the root word for "holy" has been related by many scholars to the idea of *separateness*, in which case something holy is something cut off, withdrawn, or set apart for God. The important thing to note here is that *association with God* makes it holy; things are "separate because they are holy, not holy because they are separate." Like the act of repentance, separation has a necessary *to* and a *from*; separation *from* the world and *to* Christ. Nothing is holy because of mere absence or isolation from wrong, but because of a manifest committal to the presence of the Right and the Good.

Another possible source of the root word comes to us from the Akkadian *qadasu*, which means "clear, bright, or brilliant."[3] From this we get the idea of brightness or freshness with an underlying sense of purity (as of fire) and freedom from defect. This root meaning of "shining" has a double significance in that it not only recalls the many times in which God appears as fire, but it also carries the idea of the terrifying. With this special meaning in the context of separation and shining, we turn our attention to the fear of the Lord.

The Fear of the Lord

What was the very first thing God called Israel to do when He called them to be His people and live the way He intended? Perhaps you might think it was to love Him, to serve Him, to keep His commandments, or to walk in all His ways. You would, of course, be right; but none of these is the *first* thing He asked of them. It was to *"fear Him"* and everything else would follow (Deut. 10:12–13). From Old to New Testament, the Bible is full of the emphasis on the fear of the Lord. It is the essence of His school, His prerequisite for admission to divine truth, the prime qualification for learning from the Lord: reverent fear and worship of the Lord is the beginning of wisdom (Ps. 111:10).

Yet equally emphasized throughout Scripture is the divine command *not* to be afraid: "God hath not given us the spirit of fear; but of power, and of love and of a sound mind" (2 Tim. 1:7) and that "there is no fear in love but perfect love casteth out fear, because fear hath torment. He that feareth is not made perfect in love" (1 John 4:18). If we are not to fear in His love, and God has not given us a spirit of fear, what does it mean to fear the Lord? Whatever else the fear of the Lord is, it can be lived with power, love, and a sound mind!

- Power: "Is not this thy fear, thy confidence, thy hope, and the uprightness of thy ways?" (Job 4:6).
- Love: "Oh how great is thy goodness, which thou hast laid up for them that fear thee!" (Ps. 31:19).
- Sound Mind: "The fear of the Lord is the beginning of wisdom." (Prov. 9:10).

---

[2]*The Zondervan Pictorial Encyclopedia of the Bible*, Merrill Tenney, ed. (Grand Rapids: Zondervan Pub. House, 1976), vol. 3, p. 174.
[3]Ibid. vol. 3, p. 174.

Two Kinds of Fear

Why are we told to fear the Lord and yet not to fear? Perhaps the original languages use different words? No. Scripture says that we are to be "perfecting holiness in the fear [*phobos*] of God" (2 Cor. 7:1), using the same word for that forbidden fear (*phobos*) that Paul spoke against (1 John 4:18).

So it seems there are at least *two* kinds of fear in the Bible: a fear that *harms* our spiritual life and a fear that *helps* it. As to the emotion itself, there is in practice no difference; both are equally frightening, and both have equal power to move us. We can profit by asking what kinds of things really frighten people that are not related to the fear of God. Likewise, we should ask what other equally—if not more—frightening situations are related to that fear.

What the Fear of the Lord Is Not

What is ungodly fear? What is a "spirit of fear" (2 Tim. 1:7), the kind of fear that is wrong in the Bible? The word *'dilia'* translated here as "fear" comes from a root that means "wretched, sorry, miserable" and implies someone who is timid or cowardly, someone who "in a heroic age is good for nothing."[4]

God is certainly not to blame for attitudes of cowardice or timidity. The fear we can expect from God will never cause us to be afraid in that way. What else might be mistaken for the "fear of the Lord"? We can answer that in part by asking this question: What is it about someone or something that can cause damaging fear in another?

- We may fear someone exceptionally ugly or monstrous-looking—the stock-in-trade of horror movies and latex-mask makers. But we are not to have the "fear of the Lord" because God is ugly or monstrous. God made creation beautiful as a finite reflection of His own mind and heart. No one ever ran from Christ during His time on earth over His appearance; in fact, little children flocked to Him. God is an infinitely lovely being.
- We may fear someone known to be evil and liable to do harm—such as a rapist, murderer, or armed maniac on the loose. But, God is "not willing that any should perish but that all should come to repentance" (2 Pet. 3:9). God loves man today as much as He loved him before the Fall.
- Our fear may come from seeing some powerful person who is out of control, such as a drunk or angry soldier. But Paul wrote, "If we believe not, yet He abideth faithful; He cannot deny himself" (2 Tim. 2:13). We need never fear God's power, because it is controlled by His perfect love and wisdom. God has power over His own power.
- Fear may come when someone has shown or declared intention to hurt us. But God says, "I know the thoughts that I think toward you,

---

[4]Liddell and Scott, *Greek-English Lexicon*.

saith the Lord, thoughts of peace, and not of evil, to give you an expected end" (Jer. 29:11).

- We fear if someone is utterly alien, something absolutely unlike us— the quintessential *Alien* of the science fiction screens. Fortunately, "God created man in his image, in the image of God created he him" (Gen. 1:27). Nevertheless, we must point out that God is utterly different from us in His essential being in that He is uncreated and we are creations. In His substance or essential nature, He really is other than us; but as a person, as a moral being, we are related to Him as persons. The Infinite relates to the finite on a level of personal relationship rather than substance. The "fear of the Lord" is not related to these elements of terror, revulsion, or horror.

What Is the Fear of the Lord?

If these are some of the wrong motives for fear, what causes proper godly fear, awe, and reverence? Muilenberg writes, "Even the sum of all the attributes and activities of 'the holy' is insufficient to exhaust its meaning, for to one who has experienced its presence there is always a plus, a something more, which resists formulation or definition. . . . Common to all cultures which seek to describe its mysterious nature is an awareness of an undefined and uncanny energy, a sense of the numinous . . . of the imponderable and incomprehensible, an inarticulate feeling of an inviolable potency outside and beyond, removed and distant, yet at the same time near and 'fascinating' invading the everyday world of normal experience; what Rudolph Otto has described as the '*mysterium tremendum*'. . . . Holiness extends into every area of existence. . . . Whenever God's presence is felt, there men encounter the wonder and mystery of holiness."[5]

Humanly speaking, people can be awed, hushed, even sometimes paralyzed with fear in the presence of something or someone who is not evil. God is holy, yet we are to fear Him. The usual reasons for fear are:

- *Immensity*. Take for instance a space-shuttle view of the earth amidst the stars. How do you feel when you begin to consider the awful distance between the heavenly bodies and our planet? What is your reaction to the first glimpse of the fearful depths of a natural wonder like the Grand Canyon or the dizzying heights of a Mt. Everest?

  God's sheer *size* creates fear. He is omnipresent, eternal, endless, and infinite. He is immense beyond anything imaginable. David wrote, "When I consider thy heavens, the work of thy fingers . . . what is man that Thou art mindful of him?" (Ps. 8:3–4).

- *Power*. Anyone who has ever been caught in a fierce storm at sea or seen the crackle of a shorting, high-voltage power line on an electrical tower knows the proper sense of fear that power can create. A flashlight battery has power, but its 1½ volts is convenient, controllable, and safe; a lightning strike of 100,000 volts is not. A

---

[5]Muilenberg, op. cit. vol. 2, p. 616.

dripping tap or a leaky garden hose is relatively inconsequential, even ignorable. No one comments on a dripping tap and you only notice a washing-machine drain hose when it doesn't work. But people will cross the street to watch a broken high-pressure water hose, cross the country to see a major waterfall, and cross the world to visit a Niagara or Victoria falls. Power creates awe.

God is the essence of sheer and ultimate energy. Even if He were just power with no moral qualities or connotations of holiness at all, He would still scare people speechless. While trapped in a raging storm, the disciples were merely afraid, until they woke up Jesus, who with a single command stilled the storm; then, the record says, "they feared *exceedingly*" (Mark 4:41). The demonstration of His power over nature awakened a deeper fear in them.

Aslan, the lion of C. S. Lewis's *Chronicles of Narnia*, could romp with the children, but when he opened His mouth to roar "his face became so terrible the girls did not dare look at it. All the trees in front of him bent before the blast of his roaring like grass in the wind. 'Then he isn't safe?' said Lucy. 'Safe?' said Mr. Beaver. 'Who said anything about safe? 'Course he isn't safe. But he's good. . . . He's wild you know. Not like a tame lion.' "[6]

"The force of holiness is felt in every sphere of existence. It has been called the source of all other kinds of energy. It is this connection which explains holiness as an agency of judgment, redemption, and grace."[7]

- *Majesty*. We sense dignity, grandeur, or sheer awe when we see a world-famous personality or leader. For instance, how would you feel or react on meeting the Queen of England or the President of the United States? How about bumping into a major rock star or a TV movie personality? If they asked you out to lunch would you know easily what to say or do?

Because of His ultimate majesty, God is the King of all kings. He is the expression of ultimate, absolute, and final authority. Scripture tells us that "at the name of Jesus every knee should bow" (Phil. 2:10). Isaiah recorded that "in the year that King Uzziah died I saw the Lord sitting upon a throne. . . . Then said I, Woe is me!" (Isa. 6:1–5).

When God performs an astonishing miracle, the closest most people get to the fear of the Lord is to concentrate on the awe of the miracle, too soon forgetting the God who produced it. We tend to demand reverence in form, like adults who tell children not to talk in church, while we miss its substance.

The basis of all worship is prostrating ourselves before Him in spirit rather than merely in body. In the book of Revelation, the elders "fell down before Him" five times (Rev. 4:10). If true worship occurs,

---

[6]C.S. Lewis, *The Lion the Witch and the Wardrobe*.
[7]*Interpreter's Dictionary of the Bible*, George A. Buttrick, ed. (Nashville: Abingdon Press, 1962), vol. 2, p. 620.

we are on a far lower plane than God.

Kuhn explains the majesty of the Almighty, "This emphasis on the majesty and transcendence of God does not mean however that God is distant, unapproachable or remote. . . . He reveals Himself to be holy majesty specifically (and indeed exclusively) when one draws near Him. It is constantly said God is present among His people. . . . When there is genuine piety and not unworthy calculation, this believing confidence is always sustained by fear and trembling."[8]

- *Beauty*. Things, scenes, or people of extraordinary beauty or loveliness generate an awe or sense of reverence. Some people are moved to tears of joy by the beauty of a Pacific sunset or spring in the Swiss Alps; others by the bittersweet rhapsody of a song or symphony, of a concert, or the grace and wonder of a classic ballet. Helen of Troy, the Queen of Sheba, and Cleopatra were beautiful women in history who inspired legends. The wealth and splendor of Solomon's or Nebuchadnezzar's courts, or even simple things like a spectacular fireworks display can leave a child-hearted crowd astonished, amazed, and awed. Because of His immortal beauty, God is the most lovely, perfect, and absolutely righteous being in the universe. True love for Him creates a sense of anguish at the very thought of evil, rebellion, or compromise.

  Tozer wrote of those who have sought after His beauty, "Come near to the holy men and women of the past and you will soon feel the heat of their desire after God. They mourned for Him, they prayed and wrestled and sought for Him day and night, in season and out, and when they found Him the finding was all the sweeter for the long seeking."[9]

- *Uprightness*. Someone living a sacrificial or morally lovely life creates an awe or respect. This honorable lifestyle has been popularized by the movies telling the stories of the missionary and runner Eric Liddell, Mother Teresa, Ghandi, Gladys Aylward, the "small woman" of China, and Mark Buntain among the slums of Calcutta.

  Historically, when men and women had the fear of God, *the world has been afraid*. Bloody Mary feared John Knox's prayers, and it is recorded that Evan Robert's eyes were so terrifying during the Welsh revival that a friend sitting behind him began to tremble. Charles Finney, looking in sorrow and grief at the light-heartedness of women mocking him and God in a shoe factory, saw them break down and weep their way to God and revival without his saying a word. Jonathan Edward's sermon "Sinners In the Hands of an Angry God" caused the people in the pews of his church to cry out aloud in fear and grip the backs of the pews as if they were sliding into

---

[8]Kuhn, *Theological Dictionary of the New Testament*, Gerhard Kittel, ed., Geoffrey W. Bromiley, trans. (Grand Rapids: Wm. B. Eerdmans Publishing Company, 1964), vol. 1, p. 98.

[9]A.W. Tozer, *The Pursuit of God* (Camp Hill, Penn.: Christian Publications, Inc., 1982), p. 15.

hell. When Jesus delivered the man with the legion of demons, those who came and saw him sitting clothed and in his right mind were afraid (Mark 5:15). The world has always been afraid of people in their right minds.

Whenever we meet God personally and He unveils some small facet of His character and perfection, our reaction (no matter how devoted or godly we are) will always be like Isaiah: "Woe is me . . . because I am a man of unclean lips, and dwell in the midst of a people of unclean lips" (Isa. 6:5).

C. S. Lewis wrote, "You know at bottom that unless the power behind the world really and unalterably detests bad behavior, then He cannot be good. On the other hand, we know that if there does exist an absolute goodness it must hate most of what we do. . . . We cannot do without it and we cannot do with it. God is the only comfort, He is also the supreme terror; the thing we most need and the thing we most want to hide from. He is our only possible ally, and we have made ourselves His enemies. Some people talk as if meeting the gaze of absolute goodness would be fun. They need to think again. They are still only playing with religion. Goodness is either the great safety or the great danger—according to the way you react to it. And we have reacted the wrong way."[10]

Anyone, but especially the sinner, will feel the terror of standing in the presence of God's holiness, His perfect moral uprightness. He stands far above all our trivial attempts at uprightness.

He is absolute light, while we conceal areas of darkness; absolute righteousness, while we are often wrong. He stands absolutely just, even when we are unjust. His absolute truthfulness shines over our bent to lying, and His absolute goodness pierces our bent to evil. "Who is like unto thee, O Lord, among the gods? who is like thee, glorious in holiness, fearful in praises, doing wonders?" (Ex. 15:11).

Separation, Light, and Purity

When God is called the "Holy One," there is a profound sense of all three meanings of holiness. He is separate from all that would displease Him, from all that is not like God. The Bible calls places where God visited man "holy"; they are sites set aside for sacred use or ritual (Ex. 3:5; Josh. 5:15). Objects put at God's disposal such as temple vessels, silver, or food can be holy (1 Sam. 21:4); likewise, people such as Nazarites or temple priests set apart for God's service were called "holy." The basic idea is not a mere negative separation from something, but a positive encounter and commitment which invariably demands particular modes of response; it is a heartfelt way of life and not just a religious thing to be done.

God is always described in terms of a sense of brightness; His holiness is described in terms of *light*, of awesome and terrifying *power*, a *beauty*

---

[10]C.S. Lewis, *Mere Christianity* (Huntington, N.Y.: J.M. Fontana Publishing, 1955), p. 37.

and *majesty* from another world. "Mercy without righteousness is mushy," said E. Stanley Jones. Even the profane peoples of Canaan called God "holy" when they failed to treat his Ark with respect and faced the prospect of disaster by His judgment (1 Sam. 6:20).

The description of God in terms of light extends to *fire*. Tozer said, "Love and mercy and righteousness are His, and holiness so ineffable that no comparisons or figures will avail to express it. Only fire can give a remote conception of it. In fire He appeared at the burning bush; in the pillar of fire He dwelt through all the long wilderness journey. The fire that glowed between the wings of the cherubim in the holy place was called the '*shekinah*,' the Presence through the years of Israel's glory, and when the Old had given place to the New, He came at Pentecost as a fiery flame and rested upon each disciple."[11]

God is also described in terms of *purity*. We find ourselves convinced that in Christ we are in the presence of someone so utterly wise, so wholly absolute and unflinching in His committal to righteousness, justice, truth, and love, that a person who encounters Him lives for the rest of his life with a heart bowed in awe, adoration, and worship. Here the holiness of God is not a characteristic of His substance, but the quality of His character. It is on this basis that we can enter into the imitation of Christ. He calls us to live like Him in love and wisdom; and on that basis holiness becomes simply loving and trusting God day by day, living moment by moment up to the light He gives us.

Gordon Olson, a life-long student of God's character and nature writes, "Holiness is simply intelligence applied to our various relations in proper proportion and esteem. . . . Because 'God is love' (1 John 4:8, 16) living in a state of goodwill or benevolence and because 'God is light' (1 John 1:5) the embodiment of perfectly intelligent conduct, 'God is holy' or worthy of the veneration and worship of all. Holiness in God is a dynamic state of being rather than a static or fixed something somewhere in the divine nature. It is descriptive of the character of God established by right moral action.

"Holiness is a descriptive term applied to moral beings who are voluntarily fulfilling their moral obligation, conforming to their moral light or perception of truth. Holiness is an evaluation due to virtuous beings. It is a tribute of praise or veneration. . . . The Godhead have chosen to be guided by intelligence in all actions—without the least taint of arbitrariness, partiality or self-assertiveness. . . . God's voluntary conformity is perfect and uninterrupted; His holiness or moral worth is absolute (Rev. 4:8). Holiness is not something one *has*, but something one *is*."[12]

Losing the Fear of the Lord

A culture with materialistic presuppositions and a rationalistic world view has no value higher than man himself. Man has been progressively

[11]Tozer, op. cit. p. 40.
[12]Gordon Olson, *Sharing Your Faith* (Chicago: Bible Research Fellowship).

reduced even though the Bible calls man a "living soul" (Gen. 2:7). Descartes called man a "thinking machine," and the behaviorists say we are merely "reacting things!" Without the fear of God, men turn into competing "black boxes."

Custance says, "Starting with divided personalities and proceeding upward through divided homes to divided communities and divided classes we end up with nation against nation. . . . Living has become an end in itself rather than a means to something higher; as a consequence, competition for the means to survive—whether of the individual or the class or nation—has become the guiding principle. When a sense of respect for God vanishes from the world, so goes its sense of morality, justice, and love."[13]

And why have nations, communities, families, and individuals lost that sense of reverence? "Judgment must begin at the house of God" (1 Pet. 4:17). Because we, the Church, now rarely preach, sing, converse, pray, testify, study, talk, or hardly even read about the greatness, power, majesty, beauty, and the holiness of God, we have lost that fear of the Lord that keeps from evil and brings life, honor, riches, and wisdom to do the tasks of life. This understanding of God grants special power to affect our own lives and then our world for righteousness.

The fear of the Lord continues to be the beginning of wisdom, and the knowledge of the Holy is still understanding (Prov. 9:10). We must have a restoration of testimony to His glorious holiness.

People envision God as a little, human, finite Santa Claus. The great danger to the Church is not *secular* humanism, but *evangelical* humanism. The Church can fall prey to fears of nuclear war, lawsuit, censure, the opinions of rich and famous, and a visionless hold-the-fort mentality. "By humility and the fear of the Lord are riches, and honor, and life" (Prov. 22:4).

God is viewed as powerless, careless, or dead. Society needs authentic examples of His healing, delivering, resurrecting power. Without this practical demonstration of the presence and authority of Christ and His kingdom, people will not only suffer under constant enemy oppression, but be needlessly sick, bound, and dying. When the Church began believing the miraculous impossible, science was called in to fill the gap. But a man should not have to become an atheist before He becomes a Christian; he has a right to a supernatural world view. Biblical Christianity will not disappoint him.

When the Church does not expect miracles, she will eventually not even believe in miracles. The life-blood of her testimony to the living Christ, who is "the same yesterday, to day and for ever" (Heb. 13:8), is the belief that He can change the course of events. "The fear of the Lord tendeth to life; and he that hath it shall abide satisfied, he shall not be visited with evil" (Prov. 19:23).

We have also lost the sense of His majesty. Even church people treat

---

[13]Arthur C. Custance, *The Doorway Papers* (Grand Rapids: Zondervan Publishing House, 1977), Vol. VIII, p. 183.

God as if He were a chummy mortal. They approach Him lightly, familiarly, or with back-slapping irreverence. People think little or nothing of blaspheming His name repeatedly in ordinary conversation, comedians mock Him publicly in profane patter, and the media deals with life or death issues as if judgment and eternity were popular myths and merely light entertainment. There is no proper sense of deference and honor, no reverent sensitivity to God's dignity and glory. "Whoso despiseth the word shall be destroyed: but he that feareth the commandment shall be rewarded" (Prov. 13:13).

People do not give themselves to true worship, devotion, and praise of the beauty of the Divine. They are not in love with Jesus. The world of things is deemed more exciting, attractive, and interesting than devotion to Christ and His kingdom. Rare today is what E. Stanley Jones called "the expulsive power of a new affection," the living, experiential detachment from the values, aims, and goals society deems supremely important. Rarer still is the devotion that burns like that recorded in the diary records of Rutherford, St. Teresa, Guyon, McCheyne, and many others as an unrestrained and abandoned passion for the Lord. "By the fear of the Lord men depart from evil" (Prov. 16:6).

God is holy, but sin is taken lightly. People sin without thought of consequence here or before the awful judgment throne to come. An irreligious actor scarcely thinks twice about participating in a part portraying God as a cigar-smoking, mistake-prone old man. Instead of the reality of ensuing judgment after death, people embrace the deceptive occult fantasy of reincarnation.

But "The fear of the Lord is to hate evil" (Prov. 8:13). Therefore, we need to pay careful heed to the advice: "Be not wise in thine own eyes; fear the Lord and depart from evil; it shall be health to thy navel and marrow to thy bones" (Prov. 3:7–8). "But the path of the just is as the shining light, that shineth more and more unto the perfect day. . . . Keep thy heart with all diligence; for out of it are the issues of life" (Prov. 4:18, 23).

Historical Discussion

The nature of Christianity is centrally determined by the concept of the holy.

Bishop R. S. Foster

The doctrine we contend for is not limited to a bare and questionable place, a doubtful and uncertain existence in the holy records, but is repletely, abundantly, explicitly embodied as a cardinal feature throughout the whole system. It breaths in prophecy, thunders in the law, murmurs in the narrative, whispers in the promises, supplicates in the prayers, resounds in the songs, sparkles in the poetry, shines in the types, glows in the imagery and burns in the spirit of the whole scheme, from its alpha to its omega, beginning to end. Holiness! Holiness needed! Holiness required! Holiness offered! Holiness attainable! Holiness a present duty, present privilege, a present enjoyment, is the progress and completeness of its wondrous theme! It is the truth glowing all over and shouting in all its history and biography, poetry and prophecy, precept, promise, and prayer; the great central truth of the system. . . . If God has spoken at all, it is to aid men to be holy.[1]

The Foundations of Holiness

George MacDonald

"Nothing is inexorable but love. . . . For love loves unto purity. Love has ever in view the absolute loveliness of that which it beholds. Where loveliness is incomplete, and love cannot love its fill of loving, it spends itself to make more lovely, that it may love more; it strives for perfection, even that itself may be perfected—not in itself, but in the object. . . . Therefore all that is not beautiful in the beloved, all that comes between and is not of love's kind, must be destroyed. And our God is a consuming fire.

"He will shake heaven and earth that only the unshakable may remain; He is a consuming fire, that only that which cannot be consumed may stand forth eternal. It is the nature of God, so terribly pure that it destroys all that is not pure as fire, which demands like purity in our worship. He will have purity. It is not that the fire will burn us *if* we do not worship thus; but that the fire will burn us *until* we worship thus; yea, will go on burning within us after all that is foreign to it has yielded to its force, no longer with pain and consuming, but as the highest consciousness of life, the presence of God."[2]

G. Campbell Morgan

"What then is sanctification? The root idea of the word so translated in the N.T. signifies something which is awful, that which fills the soul with awe, not necessarily with dread, for there is a vital difference between dread and awe. Dread is of the nature of slavish fear; awe is of the nature of reverence. There should be no dread in the soul of a man when he draws near to God. No man ought to draw near to God save with a sense of awe. The thought is that of something awful, filling the soul with awe. Its use in the N.T. is always of separation to God and therefore of holiness. The vessels of the house of God were holy and sanctified—they were set apart for sacred purposes and consequently maintained in cleanliness by ceremonial ablutions, and that because they were dedicated and consecrated to the service of God alone."[3]

---

[1]Bishop R.S. Foster, *Christian Purity* (1851), p. 9.
[2]George MacDonald, *Anthology*, C.S. Lewis, ed. (New York: Macmillan, 1986) p. 23.
[3]G. Campbell Morgan, "Sanctification," *Twenty Centuries of Great Preaching*, Clyde E. Fant Jr. and William M. Dinson Jr., eds. (Waco, Texas: Word Books, 1971.), vol. 7, pp. 20–21.

The Life of Holiness: The Incarnation of Christ

Catherine Booth

"He proposes to *restore me*—brain, heart, soul, spirit, body, every fiber of my nature—to restore me perfectly, to conform me wholly to the image of His Son. If He could have saved me without restoring me, then He could have saved me without a Savior at all. How do you read your Bibles? How do you read the history of the miracles—the stories of His opening the eyes, unstopping the ears, cleansing the leper and raising the dead? The Lord showed us how to read it. He will heal you if you let Him. These are the sort of words the world wants—the living words, living embodiments of Christianity, walking embodiments of the Spirit and life and power of Jesus Christ. You may scatter Bibles as you have done all over the world. You may preach and sing and talk and do what you will; but if you don't exhibit to the people *living epistles*, show them the transformation of character and life in yourself which is brought about by the power and grace of God—if you don't go to them and do the works of Jesus Christ you may go on preaching and the world will get worse and worse, and the Church too. We want a living embodiment of Christianity. We want Jesus to come in the flesh again."[4]

Charles Finney

"Faith simply receives Christ as King to live and reign in the soul. It is Christ, in the exercise of His different offices, and appropriated in His different relations to the wants of the soul, by faith, Who secures our sanctification. This He does by divine discoveries to the soul of His divine perfection. . . . One great thing that needs to be done, to confirm and settle the will in an attitude of entire consecration to God is to bring about a counter-development of the sensibility, so it will not draw the will away from God. It needs to be mortified or crucified to the world, to objects of time and sense, by so deep and clear and powerful a revelation of self to self, and of Christ to the soul as to awaken and develop all its susceptibilities in their relations to Him, and to spiritual and divine realities. . . . the Holy Spirit, who takes of the things of Christ and shows them to us . . . so reveals Christ that the soul receives Him to the throne of the heart, and to reign throughout the whole being. When the will, intellect and the sensibility are yielded to Him, He develops the intelligence and the sensibility by clear revelations of himself in all the offices and relations to the soul."[5]

Henry Suso

"But what a glorious life that is my child, to serve God freely and . . . in purity of soul!. . . . I tell you, even if there were no reward beyond this world, it would be worth it for its own sake. We walk in this world, but live already

---

[4]Catherine Booth, *Papers on Godliness* (New York: Salvation Army Publishing, 1986), p. 166.
[5]Charles Finney, *Sanctification*, W.E. Allen, ed. (Fort Washington, Penn.: Christian Literature Crusade, 1963), pp. 19, 22.

in heaven! How beautiful is purity of soul! What freedom that is, to serve God, to live for Him alone! Ah, gentle Lord, adorable Wisdom, to wed Thee, to exchange love of the world for love of the Eternal, how exquisite that is! What a sweet yoke, what a light burden, to serve Thee with one's will!"[6]

Living in Holiness: Imitating Jesus

Francois Fenelon

"We must imitate Jesus. This is to live as He lived, to think as He thought, to conform ourselves to His image, which is the seal of our sanctification. . . . To be Christians is to be imitators of Jesus Christ. In what can we imitate Him except in His humiliations? Nothing else can draw us to Him. As all-powerful, we ought to adore Him; as just we ought to fear Him; as good and merciful we ought to love him with all our strength; as humble, submissive, lowly and faithful unto death, we ought to imitate Him. Let us not pretend to reach this state by our own strength. Everything in us resists it. But let us console ourselves in the Presence of God. Jesus Christ has wanted us to feel all our weaknesses. . . . Let us then find all our strength in Him who became voluntarily weak to strengthen us. Let us enrich ourselves by His poverty, and let us say with confidence, 'I can do all things in Him Who strengthens me.' I want to follow, O Jesus, the road which Thou hast taken!'"[7]

George MacDonald

"The righteousness of him who does the will of his Father in heaven is the righteousness of Jesus Christ, God's own righteousness. The righteousness which is of God by faith is God's own righteousness. The man who has this righteousness thinks about things as God thinks about them, loves the things that God loves, cares for nothing that God does not care about. . . .

"The man with God's righteousness does not love a thing merely because it is right, but loves the very rightness in it. He not only loves a thought, but he loves the thought alive in the man. He does not take his joy from himself. He feels joy in himself, but it comes to him for others, not from himself—from God first, and from somebody, anybody, everybody next. . . . The man who really knows God is, and always will be content with what God, who is the very self of his self, shall choose for him; he is entirely God's and not at all his own."[8]

E. Stanley Jones

"Hunger for righteousness is the thesis, merciful toward others and their failings is the antithesis, the pure in heart is the synthesis. The best definition I know of purity of heart is just here; a passion for righteousness

[6]Henry Suso, *Letters*, p. 18.
[7]Francois Fenelon, *Christian Perfection*, Charles F. Whiston, ed., Mildred W. Stillman, trans. (Minneapolis, Minn.: Bethany House Publishers, 1975), pp. 43–44.
[8]George MacDonald, *Creation in Christ*, Rolland Hein, ed. (Wheaton, Ill.: Harold Shaw Publishers, 1976), p. 185.

and a compassion for men. . . . To be pure in heart is literally 'undivided in heart'—undivided not only between good and evil but between virtue and virtue. That heart is pure which does not divide any portion with any evil, but more, does not divide the virtues righteousness and mercy, giving itself alternately to one or to the other, but blends them into the blend of purity. It is controlled by both at once so that the pure heart is righteously merciful and mercifully righteous. This kind of man sees God. The man who seeks law and shows love sees God."[9]

The Fear of the Lord

Joseph Parker

"Throughout the whole of the Bible the fear of the Lord is declared to be the beginning of wisdom. It is not a servile fear. . . . Fear means reverence, veneration, awe, a sense of the grandeur and majesty of the Lord, not only as that term stands for infinity, brilliance and attributes of an intellectual kind, but it stands for holiness, truth, purity, justice and every expression that indicates moral supremacy. He who fears the Lord in the confidence of ultimate justice; he is confident also in the final exposition of providence, being assured that the way of God to man will be so revealed at last that it will be seen to have been the right way, the only true way notwithstanding . . . that God has not given one stroke too much, taken away one treasure too many, or dug one grave too deep; the righteous will be the first to confess that God has done all things wisely, well and lovingly."[10]

Robert William Dale

"It is said that in the presence of the physical universe the man who has a large knowledge of the revelations of modern science may be filled with a wonder and awe that are too rarely present in popular religion. This may be true. Our sense of the infinite greatness of God has been impaired. Religious thought in recent times has deserted the mountain solitudes in which devout hearts learnt to fear and to reverence the Eternal as well as trust and love Him. And a sense of the awful majesty of God is necessary not only for reverential worship and for some of the deeper experiences of the spiritual life, but for many moral virtues. It is the discipline of humility; it is the inspiration of fortitude; it contributes to the vigilant self-command which is one of the guarantees of fidelity to the highest law. The very virtues of a man who is not conscious of living under a power immeasurably above himself will miss a certain refinement and a gracious dignity which are necessary to perfection. But we must take care that the power we reverence is really above us. The servility of slaves held down by a stern and irrepressible force is something different in quality from the loyal courtesy and the manly reverence with which a

---

[9]E. Stanley Jones, *The Christ on the Mount* (London: Hodder and Stoughton, 1931), p. 63.
[10]Joseph Parker, *Preaching Through the Bible* (Grand Rapids: Baker Books, 1978), Vol. VII, p. 192.

free people regard an august throne. Science may render a service to the religious life of our times by its illustration of the immensity and grandeur of God's works; for the universe is great. But our religious awe must be reserved for God himself."[11]

A. J. Gossip

"And the old habits? They have passed. . . . The old modes of stating truth which often had a reverence about them which seems lost? Francis Thompson admits that he found the shoulder of Christ too high for him to lean against. But the new generation does not appear to feel that. Rather it links arms with Christ in the friendliest way; it talks and thinks of the Great Comrade but the old seemly awe that often filled the minds of those who lived with Christ seems gone. And a fine Indian writer, gazing amazedly at us so jaunty and unabashed, says that is what is wrong with modern Western Christianity, declares with white heat that the works of [one popular preacher] are simply irreligious. Here is a man, he cries, a typical representative of the religion of his day, and face to face with Jesus Christ he talks about 'His charm' and suchlike little vivid surface trifles. Quite evidently he is interested, attracted, fascinated if you will; but he is not upon his knees, not down on his face before him. And that is where we ought to be in His presence! That charge is true of most of us. We are not down on our knees; we are not lying on our faces; we are not in the mood that wades into the real deeps of Christianity."[12]

A. W. Tozer

"No one can know the true grace of God who has not first known the fear of God. . . . The presence of the Divine has always brought fear to the hearts of sinful men. Always there was about any manifestation of God something that dismayed the onlookers, that daunted and overawed them, that struck them with a terror more than natural. . . . This terror had no relation to mere fear of bodily harm. It was a dread consternation experienced far in toward the center and core of the nature. . . . I do not believe any lasting good can come from religious activities that do not root in this quality of creature-fear. . . . Until we have been gripped by that nameless terror which results when an unholy creature is suddenly confronted by that One who is the holiest of all, we are not likely to be much affected by the doctrine of love and grace."[13]

---

[11]Robert William Dale, "Faith and Physical Science," *Twenty Centuries of Great Preaching*, Clyde E. Fant Jr. and William M. Dinson Jr., eds. (Waco, Texas: Word Books, 1971), vol. 5, pp. 180–181.

[12]A.J. Gossip, "The Clash of Age and Youth," *Twenty Centuries of Great Preaching*, Clyde E. Fant Jr. and William M. Dinson Jr., eds. (Waco, Texas: Word Books, 1971), vol. 8, pp. 243–244.

[13]A.W. Tozer, "Terror Of The Lord," *The Root of the Righteous* (Camp Hill, Pa.: Christian Publications, Inc., 1955), pp. 38–39.

C. S. Lewis

"In all developed religion we find *three strands* or elements and in Christianity one more. The first of these is what professor Otto calls the experience of the *numinous*. . . . Suppose you were told that there was a tiger in the next room; you would know you were in danger and would probably feel fear. But if you were told, 'There is a ghost in the next room' and believed it, you would feel indeed what is often called fear but of a different kind. It would not be based on the knowledge of danger, for no one is primarily afraid of what a ghost may do to him, but of the mere fact that it is a ghost. It is 'uncanny' rather than dangerous, and the special kind of fear it excites may be called *dread*. With the uncanny, one has reached the fringes of the numinous.

"Now suppose you were told simply, 'There is a mighty Spirit in the room' and believed it. Your feelings would then be even less like the mere fear of danger; but the disturbance would be profound. You would feel wonder and a certain shrinking; a sense of inadequacy to cope with such a visitant and of prostration before it—an emotion which might be expressed in Shakespeare's words 'Under it my genius is rebuked.' This feeling may be described as Awe and the object which excites it as the numinous.

"A modern example may be found (if we are not too proud to seek it there) in the *The Wind in the Willows* where Rat and Mole approach Pan on the island:

"Rat," he found the breath to whisper, shaking, "Are you afraid?"
"Afraid?" murmured the Rat, his eyes shining with unutterable love.
"Afraid? Of Him? O, never, never. And yet—and yet—O Mole, I am afraid."

"Ezekiel tells us of the 'rings' that 'they were so high that they were dreadful' and Jacob rising from sleep says 'How dreadful is this place!' (Ezek. 1:18; Gen. 28:17). We do not know how far back in human history this feeling goes. The earliest men almost certainly believed in things which would excite the feeling in us if *we* believed in them, and it seems therefore probable that numinous awe is as old as humanity itself. But our main concern is not with its dates. The important thing is that somehow or other it has come into existence and it is widespread, and does not disappear from the mind with the growth of knowledge and civilization. . . .

"When man passes from physical fear to dread and awe, he makes a sheer jump and apprehends something which could never be given, as danger is by the physical facts, and logical deductions from them. . . . There seem to be in fact only two views we can hold about awe. Either it is a mere twist of the human mind corresponding to nothing objective and serving no biological function, yet showing no tendency to disappear from that mind at its fullest development in poet, philosopher, or saint; or else it is a direct experience of the really supernatural, to which the name *revelation* might properly be given. . . .

"The *Numinous* is not the same as the morally good. . . . this brings us to the second strand . . . in religion. All human beings that history has heard of acknowledge some kind of *morality*; that is, they feel towards certain proposed actions the experiences expressed by the words 'I ought' or 'I ought not.' . . . Morality, like numinous awe, is a jump; in it man goes beyond anything that can be 'given' in the facts of experience. And it has one characteristic too remarkable to be ignored. The moralities accepted among men may differ—though not, at bottom so widely as is often claimed—but they all agree in prescribing a behavior which their adherents fail to practice. All men alike stand condemned, not by alien codes of ethics, but their own, and all men therefore are conscious of guilt. The second element in religion is the consciousness not merely of moral law, but of a moral law at once approved and disobeyed. This consciousness is neither a logical nor an illogical inference from the facts of experience; if we did not bring it to our experience we could not find it there. It is either inexplicable illusion or else revelation. . . .

"The third stage in religious development arises when men *identify* them [the gods]—when the Numinous Power to which they feel awe is made the guardian of the morality to which they feel obligation. Once again this may seem to you very 'natural.' . . . But it is not in the least obvious. The actual behavior of the universe which the Numinous haunts bears no resemblance to the behavior which morality demands of us. The one seems wasteful, ruthless and unjust; the other enjoins upon us the opposite qualities. Nor can identification of the two be explained as a wish-fulfillment, for it fulfills no one's wishes. We desire nothing less than to see that Law whose naked authority is already unsupportable armed with the incalculable claims of the Numinous. Of all the jumps that humanity takes in its religious history this is certainly the most surprising. It is not unnatural that many sections of the human race refused it; non-moral religion, and non-religious morality existed and still exist. Perhaps only a single people as a people took the new step with perfect decision—I mean the Jews; but great individuals in all times and places have taken it also, and only those who take it are safe from the obscenities and barbarities of unmoralized worship or the cold, sad self-righteousness of sheer moralism. . . .

"Once more [this step] may be madness—a madness congenital to man and oddly fortunate in its results—or it may be revelation. And if revelation, then it is most really and truly in Abraham that all peoples shall be blessed, for it was the Jews who fully and unambiguously identified the awful Presence haunting black mountain-tops and thunder-clouds with the '*righteous* Lord' who 'loved righteousness' (Ps. 11:7).

"The fourth strand is a historical event. There was a man born among these Jews who claimed to be, or to be the son of, or to be 'one with' the Something which is at once the awful Haunter of nature and the Giver of the moral law. The claim is so shocking—a paradox, and even a horror—which we may easily be lulled into taking too lightly—that only two views of this man are possible. He was either a raving lunatic of an unusually abominable type, or else He was, and is; precisely what He said. There is no middle way. If the records make the first hypothesis unacceptable, you must submit to the second. . . .

"At every stage of religious development man may rebel, if not without violence to his own nature, yet without absurdity. He can close his spiritual eyes against the Numinous, if he is prepared to part company with half the great poets and prophets of his race, with his own childhood, with the richness and depth of uninhibited experience. He can regard the moral law as an illusion and so cut himself off from the common ground of humanity. He can refuse to identify the Numinous with the righteous, and remain a barbarian, worshiping sexuality, or the dead, or the life-force, or the future. But the cost is heavy."[14]

Escaping God's Holiness: Moral Algebra

Tony Morphett

"There's a lot of moral and spiritual talk around these days which is based on the idea that as soon as you can't touch something, then you can say it's anything you like. 'That's right for me and wrong for him.' . . . You get people saying, *'My* God wouldn't do that,' as if He were somehow obedient to *their* beliefs and desires, or, 'As long as people are doing what's right in their own minds' (I tell you at the moment of murder, every murderer is doing what is right in his own mind). . . . No. This idea that good and evil, *my* God and *your* God are all relative terms is nonsense. It can't survive in the physical world. 'Well, in *my* view, wood is made of metal.' 'Well, *your* wood may be made of wood, but *mine* is made of metal.' In the physical world, this sort of thinking just gets laughed out of court; the moment it is stated it disappears. Then why is it so popular in our society when it comes down to what is right and wrong and to what sort of being God is?

"Because it's very convenient. If 'good' and 'bad' are decisions I can make as I go along, then I can justify anything I want to do. . . . Christianity has fouled up large segments of my freedom to destroy myself. No. I'm sorry. The trendy view that 'good' and 'bad' are relative terms and we can assign any values we like to them like a madman's moral algebra simply won't do. There is right. There is wrong. They are real. Rightness flows from the same reality that love flows from—and that wood and metal and water flow from. It flows from the underlying reality which all things flow from. Rightness flows from God. Rightness is being in synchronization with the will of God and wrongness is rebelling against that will."[15]

William Law

"There is nothing wise, or holy or just, except the perfect will of God. This is as strictly true as to say that nothing is infinite and eternal but God. No beings, therefore, whether in heaven or upon earth can be wise, holy or just but so far as they conform to the will of God. It is conformity to God's will that gives virtue and perfection to the highest services of the angels in heaven; and it is conformity to the same will that makes the ordinary actions of men upon the earth acceptable to God. The whole nature of virtue consists in conforming to the will of God; the whole nature of sin in declining from it. . . . The most glorious angelic being or lowliest

---

[14]C.S. Lewis, *The Problem of Pain* (New York: MacMillan, 1978), pp. 4–12.
[15]Tony Morphett, *Moral Algebra* (London: Hodder and Stoughton, 1985), pp. 18–19.

of creeping things, all creation is subject to that self-same will of God that designed and planned it. If therefore you would show yourself not to be a rebel from the order of creation, you must act as do those beings both above and below you; it must be your great desire that God's will be done by you on earth as it is in heaven. It must be the settled purpose and intention of your heart to will nothing, design nothing, do nothing but so far as there is reason to believe that it is the will of God."[16]

Frederick W. Faber

Faber said so well what is so little understood in our shallow world:

> My fear of Thee, O Lord, exults
> Like life within my veins;
> A fear which rightly claims to be
> One of love's sacred pains. . . .
>
> When most I fear Thee Lord!
> Then most familiar I appear;
> And I am in my soul most free
> When I am most in fear.
>
> I feel Thee most a father,
> When I fancy Thee most near;
> And Thou comest not so nigh in love
> As Thou comest Lord! in fear.
>
> They love Thee little, if at all,
> Who do not fear Thee much;
> If love is Thine attraction Lord
> Fear is Thy very touch.
>
> Love could not love Thee half so much
> If it found Thee not so near;
> It is Thy nearness which makes love
> The perfectness of fear. . . .
>
> And Father! when to us in heaven
> Thou shalt Thy face unveil,
> Then more than ever will our souls
> Before Thy goodness quail;
>
> Our blessedness will be to bear
> The sight of Thee so near;
> And thus eternal love will be
> But the ecstasy of fear.[17]

[16]William Law, *The Power of the Spirit*, David Hunt, ed. (Fort Washington, Penn.: Christian Literature Crusade, 1961), pp. 19–20.

[17]F.W. Faber, *The Christian Book Of Mystical Verse* (Camp Hill, Pa.: Christian Publications, 1963).

PART THREE

PROPOSITION THREE:
GOD IS TRIUNE

COROLLARY ONE: THE FATHER, SON, AND HOLY SPIRIT
ARE ONE IN NATURE

DECLARATION ONE: THE FATHER IS THE
UNCREATED GOD
DECLARATION TWO: THE SON IS THE UNCREATED GOD
DECLARATION THREE: THE HOLY SPIRIT IS THE
UNCREATED GOD

Holy, Holy, Holy, Lord God Almighty,
Early in the morning our song shall rise to Thee.
Holy, Holy, Holy, merciful and mighty,
God in three Persons, Blessed Trinity.

—Reginald Heber

Praise God from Whom all blessings flow;
Praise Him all creatures here below;
Praise Him above ye heavenly host;
Praise Father, Son, and Holy Ghost.

—The Doxology

CHAPTER NINE

PROPOSITION THREE: GOD IS TRIUNE

Scriptures

"In the beginning God [plural form] created [singular form] the heaven and the earth." (Gen. 1:1)

In the above verse, *God* takes a plural form but *created* takes a singular form. "Although God did not want to show the truth of His nature to a people surrounded by polytheistic nations, lest the truth be corrupted by those who were to preserve it, He was careful to state it in such a way that those who followed would not corrupt it."[1]

"And God said, Let *us* make man in our image, after our likeness." (Gen. 1:26)

"And the Lord God said, Behold, the man is become as one of us, to know good and evil." (Gen. 3:22)

We can gain a valuable insight into the nature of the Trinity in just these last two verses alone. In Gen. 1:26, "*our* likeness" indicates equality, while God's concern in Gen. 3:22 that man will become like "one of *us*" indicates each person is a distinct entity.

"And the Lord said . . . Go to, let us go down, and there confound their language, that they may not understand." (Gen. 11:6–7)

"Then the Lord rained upon Sodom and upon Gomorrah brimstone and fire from the Lord out of heaven." (Gen. 19:24)

"And in the morning, then ye shall see the glory of the Lord; for that he heareth your murmurings against the Lord." (Ex. 16:7)

"The Lord bless thee and keep thee: the Lord make his face shine upon thee, and be gracious unto thee: the Lord lift up his countenance upon thee, and give thee peace." (Num. 6:24–26)

"I will declare the decree: the Lord hath said unto me, Thou art my

---

[1]Arthur C. Custance, *The Virgin Birth and the Incarnation*, (Grand Raapids: Zondervan, 1985).

Son; this day have I begotten thee" (Ps. 2:7); cf. Acts 13:33: "God hath fulfilled the same unto us their children, in that he hath raised up Jesus again; as it is also written in the second psalm, Thou art my Son, this day have I begotten thee."

"Thy throne, O God, is for ever and ever: the sceptre of thy kingdom is a right sceptre. Thou lovest righteousness, and hatest wickedness: therefore God, thy God, hath anointed thee with the oil of gladness above thy fellows." (Ps. 45:6–7; cf. Heb. 1:8)

"Harden not your heart, as in the provocation, and as in the day of temptation in the wilderness: when your fathers tempted me, proved me, and saw my work." (Ps. 95:8–9; cf. Heb. 3:7–9 where this statement is attributed to the Holy Ghost)

"And one cried unto another, and said, Holy, holy, holy, is the Lord of hosts: the whole earth is full of his glory. Also I heard the voice of the Lord, saying, Whom shall I send, and who will go for us?" (Isa. 6:3, 8)

"I heard the voice of the Lord" (Isa. 6:8–10); cf. John 12:41: "These things said Esaias [Isaiah], when he saw his glory, and spake of him"; also Acts 28:25: "Well spake the Holy Ghost by Esaias [Isaiah] the prophet."

"Seek ye out the book of the Lord, and read . . . for my mouth it hath commanded, and his spirit it hath gathered them." (Isa. 34:16)

"Come ye near unto me, hear ye this; I have not spoken in secret from the beginning; from the time that it was, there am I: and now the Lord God, and his spirit, hath sent me." (Isa. 48:16)

"The Spirit of the Lord God is upon me; because the Lord hath anointed me to preach good tidings unto the meek; he hath sent me to bind up the brokenhearted, to proclaim liberty to the captives, and the opening of the prison to them that are bound; to proclaim the acceptable year of the Lord, and the day of vengeance of our God; to comfort all that mourn" (Isa. 61:1–2); cf. Luke 4:21, where Jesus quotes this verse at the beginning of His ministry: "This day is this Scripture fulfilled in your ears."

"After those days, saith the Lord, I will put my law in their inward parts, and write it in their hearts; and will be their God, and they will be my people." (Jer. 31:33); cf. Heb. 10:15–16 where this statement is attributed to the Holy Ghost.

"For thus saith the Lord of hosts; After the glory hath he sent me unto the nations which spoiled you: for he that toucheth you toucheth the apple of his eye. For, behold, I will shake mine hand upon them, and they shall be a spoil to their servants: and ye shall know that the Lord of hosts hath sent me." (Zech. 2:8–9)

"And I will strengthen them in the Lord; and they shall walk up and down in his name, saith the Lord." (Zech. 10:12)

"They shall look upon me whom they have pierced, and they shall mourn for him, as one mourneth for his only son, and shall be in bitterness for him, as one that is in bitterness for his firstborn." (Zech. 12:10)

"Go ye therefore, and teach all nations, baptizing them in the *name* of the Father, and of the Son, and of the Holy Ghost." (Matt. 28:19)

Name, as used in the above verse, means *nature*; the Father, Son, and Holy Ghost share one divine nature.

"Jesus . . . was baptized of John in Jordan. And straightway coming up out of the water, he saw the heavens opened, and the Spirit like a dove descending upon him: and there came a voice from heaven, saying, Thou art my beloved Son, in whom I am well pleased." (Mark 1:9–11)

"For David himself said by the Holy Ghost, The *Lord* said to *my Lord*, Sit thou on my right hand, till I make thine enemies thy footstool. David therefore himself calleth him Lord; and whence is he then his son? And the common people heard him gladly." (Mark 12:36–37)

"Fear not, Mary: for thou hast found favour with God. And, behold, thou shalt conceive in thy womb, and bring forth a son, and shalt call his name Jesus. He shall be great, and shall be called the Son of the Highest: and the Lord God shall give unto him the throne of his father David. . . . The Holy Ghost shall come upon thee, and the power of the Highest shall overshadow thee: therefore also that holy thing which shall be born of thee shall be called the Son of God." (Luke 1:30–35)

"And it was revealed unto him [Simeon] by the Holy Ghost, that he should not see death, before he had seen the Lord's Christ." (Luke 2:26)

"And, behold, I send the promise of my Father upon you: but tarry ye in the city of Jerusalem, until ye be endued with power from on high." (Luke 24:49)

"But this spake he of the Spirit, which they that believe on him should receive: for the Holy Ghost was not yet given; because that Jesus was not yet glorified." (John 7:39)

"And I will pray the Father, and he shall give you another Comforter, that he may abide with you for ever; even the Spirit of truth." (John 14:16–17)

"But the Comforter, which is the Holy Ghost, whom the Father will send in my name, he shall teach you all things, and bring all things to your remembrance, whatsoever I have said unto you." (John 14:26)

"Nevertheless I tell you the truth; It is expedient for you that I go away: for if I go not away, the Comforter will not come unto you; but if I depart, I will send him unto you." (John 16:7)

"Therefore [Jesus] being by the right hand of God exalted, and having received of the Father the promise of the Holy Ghost, he hath shed forth this, which ye now see and hear." (Acts 2:33)

"The grace of the Lord Jesus Christ, and the love of God, and the communion of the Holy Ghost, be with you all. Amen." (2 Cor. 13:14)

"For through him [Christ] we both have access by one Spirit unto the Father." (Eph. 2:18)

"In whom [Christ] ye also are builded together for an habitation of God through the Spirit." (Eph. 2:22)

"For this cause I bow my knees unto the *Father* of our *Lord Jesus Christ*, of whom the whole family in heaven and earth is named, that he would grant you, according to the riches of his glory, to be strengthened with might by his *Spirit* in the inner man; that Christ may dwell in your hearts by faith." (Eph. 3:14–17)

"There is one body, and one *Spirit*, even as ye are called in one hope of your calling; one *Lord*, one faith, one baptism, one *God and Father* of all, who is above all, and through all, and in you all." (Eph. 4:4–6)

"The kindness and love of *God our Saviour* toward man appeared . . . by the . . . renewing of the *Holy Ghost*; which he shed on us abundantly through *Jesus Christ*, our Saviour." (Titus 3:4–6)

"How much more shall the blood of *Christ*, who through the *eternal Spirit* offered himself without spot to God, purge your conscience from dead works to serve the living God?" (Heb. 9:14)

"Elect according to the foreknowledge of God the *Father*, through sanctification of the *Spirit*, unto obedience and sprinkling of the blood of *Jesus Christ*." (1 Pet. 1:2)

The King James Version indicates with different type the Hebrew differences between the two different Persons referred to in some Old Testament texts. They are: Lord GOD (God the Father) LORD God (God the Son).

Whether this was deliberate or not, Custance notes:

"It seems highly proper that where God the Father was in view, the capitals should have been reserved for the second word in the phrase, i.e., GOD; whereas when the Lord Jesus was in view, capitals should have been reserved for the first word in the phrase, i.e. LORD."[2]

Bible Word Study

The word "Trinity" or "Triunity" is not a biblical term but a theological one, describing the idea of three distinct centers of consciousness in the one God.

God is distinctly called "one Lord" (Deut. 6:4; Mark 12:29), but we must examine closely as to how the word *one* is being used. There are two kinds of unity or "oneness" in both English and Hebrew; an *absolute*

---

[2]Ibid. p. 241.

unity and *compound unity*. Absolute unity is that of singularity; I give you one apple, and you get a single apple. But if you ask for "one" bunch of grapes, you don't simply get one grape! "One" in this case is a word of compound unity, the many in the one.

One (Hebrew)

Yachead is the OT word used for absolute unity; a mathematical or numerical one. It is used about 12 times in the OT, but never to describe the unity of God (Gen. 22:2, 12; Zech. 12:10).

Echad however speaks of a compound or collective unity. In marriage "the two shall be one flesh" (Gen. 2:24); a crowd can gather together "as one" (Ezek. 3:1); or be of one mind or heart: "All the rest of Israel were of one heart to make David king" (1 Chron. 12:38). This is the compound plural always used of God when He is called "one" Lord.

Kevin Conner also points out the significance of some of the divine names:

El is a word used of God describing His relationship with His creation or creatures. It means "to be strong, powerful, mighty." *El* signifies the object of worship rather than the divine name; hence God is called:

El-Elyon—The Most High God (Gen. 14:18).
El-Roi—The God who sees (Gen. 16:13).
El-Shaddai—God Almighty, God all-sufficient (Gen. 17:1).
El-Olam—God the everlasting (Gen. 21:33).
El-Beth-El—God of the house of God (Gen. 31:13; 35:7).
El-Elohe-Israel—God, the God of the Prince of God (Gen. 33:20).
El-oah—The one God (Deut. 32:15; Dan. 2:11).
El-Gibbor—The mighty or great God (Isa. 9:6; Jer. 32:18–19).

The Father is *El* (Gen. 14:18–22); The Son is *El* (Isa. 7:14 [Immanu-El]; Isa. 9:6–9); The Holy Spirit is *El* (Job 33:4; 37:10).

Elohim is the plural of *El* and is used about 2,500 times in the OT. It suggests a plurality of persons in the divine Godhead, and also shows the fullness of the Godhead in the Son (Ps. 45:6).

Elohim-Elyon—God the Most High (Ps. 91:1–2; 78:56).
Elohim-Saboath—God of Hosts (Ps. 80:7, 14).

Adon (singular) or *Adonai* (plural)—Master, Owner, Ruler of All (Ps. 147:5; 86:12).

Immanuel—God with us (Isa. 7:14; Matt. 1:23).[1]

God's Own Personal or Distinct Names

"Jehovah" appears in the KJV about 6,800 times, generally translated as LORD. Jehovah is the "I AM that I AM" (or "I will be what I will be"). The tetragrammaton is JHVH or YHWH, which was considered too sacred to speak. God's compound names (i.e., Jehovah Jireh—The Lord will

---

[1]Kevin J. Conner, *Foundations of Christian Doctrine* (Portland, Ore.: Bible Press, 1979).

provide [Gen. 22:14]) are always linked to some need of man.[2]

Gleason Archer comments on God's words to Moses in Ex. 6:3: "And I appeared unto Abraham, unto Isaac, and unto Jacob, by the name of God Almighty [El Shaddai], but by my name Yahweh was I not known to them.

"There is a very special significance to the phrase 'to know the name of Yahweh' or 'to know that I am Yahweh.' This . . . occurs at least twenty-six times in the Old Testament; and in every instance it signifies to learn by actual experience that God is Yahweh, the covenant-keeping God who chastens, cares for, and delivers His covenant people from their foes" (Ex. 6:7; Ex. 14:4).

"Obviously Pharoah knew that the name of the God of Moses was Yahweh (Ex. 5:2). Therefore we are to understand Exodus 6:3 as meaning 'I showed myself to Abraham, Issac, and Jacob as the All-Powerful ruler of Creation . . . (El Shaddai, God Almighty), but I did not show Myself to them as a covenant-keeping God in the miraculous, redemptive way that I am about to display in the deliverance of the entire nation of Israel from Egyptian bondage.'

" 'Yahweh' connotes God's faithfulness and personal care of His covenant people—though this pertains to His dealings with individual believers as well."[3]

Conner presents the compound names of God as follows:

Jehovah (Yahweh or Lord): The Self-Existent one (Ex. 3:14–15).

Jehovah-Elohim: The Lord God, Creator-Redeemer (Gen. 2:4).

Jehovah-Elohim-Saboath: Master Lord of hosts (Ps. 69:6).

Jah-Elohim: Lord God (Ps. 68:18).

Jah-Jehovah: Lord Jehovah for double emphasis (Isa. 12:2; 26:4).

Jehovah-Jireh: The Lord will provide (Gen. 22:14).

Jehovah-Rapha: The Lord that heals (Ex. 15:26).

Jehovah-Nissi: The Lord my banner (Ex. 17:15).

Jehovah-Kanna: The Lord who is jealous (Ex. 20:5; 34:14; Deut. 5:9).

Jehovah-Mekaddeskum: The Lord who sanctifies (Ex. 31:13; Lev. 20:8).

Jehovah-Shalom: The Lord is our peace (Judg. 6:24).

Jehovah-Shaphat: The Lord is judge (Judg. 11:27).

Jehovah-Saboath: The Lord of hosts (1 Sam. 1:3; Ps. 24:10).

Jehovah-Elyon: The Lord most high (Ps. 7:17).

Jehovah-Raah (or Roi): The Lord my shepherd (Ps. 23:1).

Jehovah-Hosenu: The Lord our maker (Ps. 95:6).

Jehovah-Gibbor: The Lord is mighty (Isa. 42:13).

Jehovah-Tsidkenu: The Lord our righteousness (Jer. 23:6).

Jehovah-Shammah: The Lord is there or everpresent (Ez. 48:35).

"The ultimate revelation of the redemptive names is to be found in the name of the Lord Jesus Christ":

Jehovah-Jehoshua-Christos: Jehovah's Savior Anointed (Matt. 1:21;

---

[2]Ibid.

[3]Gleason Archer, *Encyclopedia of Bible Difficulties* (Grand Rapids: Zondervan Publishing House, 1982), pp. 66–67.

Acts 1:24–26; Eph. 1:20; Luke 2:11, 26–27). It is the name of the God-head bodily, and a triune name for the Triune God (Col. 1:19; 2:9; Matt. 28:19–20).[4]

Questions and Answers

Q: *The Bible does not use the words "Trinity" or "Triunity." How can you call something an absolute when the Bible does not even mention it?*

A: These terms are only convenient labels for a teaching that runs through all of Scripture and even nature. Though "triunity" or "trinity" are not used in the Bible, "three" and "one" are, and the teaching of three persons in one substance is the most accepted understanding of Scriptural teaching.

Q: *This doctrine does not make sense at all. Even a child knows that 1 + 1 + 1 does not equal 1! If this is universally true, why is it so contrary to mathematics, a universal language?*

A: The truth of triunity makes perfect sense and *is* fundamentally demonstrated in mathematics. The unity of the Godhead is not a simple unity but an interdependent unity. Expressed mathematically it would never be $1 + 1 + 1 = 1$, for independent unity never gives true equality; but $1 \times 1 \times 1 = 1$, for interdependent unity gives an exact correspondence of equality, and the omission of one part of such an interdependent unity leads to the loss of the entire product $(1 \times 1 \times 0 = 0)$.

Q: *Aren't these different "persons" of the Trinity just different names for the same God? And if different names are proof of different persons, why not ten or twenty persons?*

A: This is a good argument; nevertheless, it is not the names alone that denote the Church's historical view of the Trinity but the unique characteristics consistent with these names. As for the numbers, when we study the texts that describe interaction in deity, there are never more than three persons involved.

Q: *There are plural words in Hebrew for comprehensive qualities like* shamayim *(heaven) or* mayim *(water or life). Why couldn't the use of a plural word for God merely signify the comprehensiveness of God's power and attributes?*

A: The plural form of Hebrew words such as water point to a *unity in diversity*—water can have the form of either individual raindrops or an entire ocean. The word *Elohim* (gods) is such a word, so certainly the idea of "unity and diversity" may include the idea of His comprehensive power and attributes. But there are also passages where God speaks of himself in the plural: "Let us make man . . ." (Gen. 1:26) and "Whom shall I send, and who shall go for us?" (Isa. 6:8). It is these passages that lead us to believe that there is personal interaction

[4]Conner, op. cit. pp. 68–69.

and communication, not just plurality of power, in God's nature.

Q: *The pope, presidents, kings, and even editors sometimes say "we" when they mean "me and the work I stand for." When the Bible uses plural terms to describe God, why couldn't we consider these as mere editorial plurals of royalty or honor?*

A: Good idea, but too modern to match what we really find in Hebrew Scripture. There *were* no kings, presidents, or editors when God first said "us." Klaas Runia says, "In view of the Old Testament emphasis on the unity of God, the plural form for God 'Elohim' is remarkable. It cannot be explained as a 'plural of majesty'; this was entirely unknown to the Hebrews."[1]

Gleason Archer declares, "This first person plural can hardly be a mere editorial or royal plural that refers to the speaker alone, for no such usage is demonstrable anywhere else in biblical Hebrew."[2]

Q: *Couldn't God have been referring to the angels when He said "Let us make man in our image?"*

A: Nowhere in Scripture is it stated that God either consulted the angels in the creation or made us in angelic image. He needs no help in making anything.

Q: *How many spirits are there? If God's essential nature differs because He is spoken of in the plural, then the essential nature of spirits must differ because they likewise are spoken of in the plural (Rev. 3:1).*

A: The essential distinction (hypostasis) is assumed between the persons of the Trinity not only because it is implied by plural references to it, but because the "most satisfactory solution seems to be that within God himself there is some kind of discussion, some interchange of views."[3] In a finite way, man mirrors this when he adopts points of view considering a question in which each point of view is a consideration from a different point of consciousness.

Q: *What does the Bible mean by the phrase "the seven Spirits of God" (Rev. 3:1)?*

A: The Hebrew significance of *seven* suggests, according to Lockyer, "to become satisfied, satiated or filled. . . . The divine significance of seven carries the similar thought of perfection, whether of good or evil. . . . Seven [thus] speaks of the plenitude of the Holy Spirit's power and diversified activity. Seven was the expression of the highest power, the greatest conceivable fullness of force, and therefore was early pressed into the service of religion."[4]

Q: *Aren't the words "wisdom," "word," and "breath" of God merely poetic*

---

[1]Klaas Runia, *Eerdman's Handbook to Christian Belief*, Robin Keeley, ed. (Grand Rapids: Eerdmans, 1982).
[2]Gleason Archer, *Encyclopedia of Bible Difficulties* (Grand Rapids: Zondervan Publishing House, 1982), p. 359.
[3]Runia, op. cit.
[4]Herbert Lockyer, *The Holy Spirit of God* (Nashville: Abingdon Press, 1983), p. 174.

descriptions of how God acts or moves? If we infer a Trinity from these, what about the other persons implied by God's hands, eyes, or arms?

A: All these expressions, poetic or otherwise, do indicate that God is personal and personally active. He himself is present in His world; they are "extensions of His personality, by which He, the Transcendent One, is personally involved in the history of the world. . . . Nevertheless this idea of the extension of God's personality is very important in itself. It shows there is movement in the living God. His being is not rigid or motionless, but as the living God, constantly reaches out towards others. And it is no wonder that later on in the New Testament this very same idea serves as a starting-point for further development. Both Paul and John take up the idea of the word and wisdom of God and apply it to Jesus Christ, while the idea of the spirit of God develops into a purely personal understanding of spirit: the Holy Spirit."[5]

Q: *I still don't see why the spirit couldn't be considered the creative breath or life of one God. His action would be perceived as God's without the need for a hypothetical third person. Why can't we think of it merely as God's actions in His creation?*

A: When Paul wrote concerning Jesus, "In him dwelleth all the fullness of the godhead bodily" (Col. 2:9), he was introducing an entirely new element into the Jewish doctrine of God, a communion of persons within the Godhead. "For this is not a matter simply of an extension of divine personality, but in this man, who is at the same time God, we are faced with *interaction* within the Godhead. No wonder this was *the* stumbling-block for the Jews. Judaism knew the idea of extension of God's personality. But the idea of interaction within the extended personality is not Hebrew or Hellenistic but definitely Christian."[6]

Q: *So there seem to be different persons. Why not just call it* Tritheism *instead of* Trinity? *What is so important about keeping the idea of one God when it seems so obvious there are more than one?*

A: Because the Bible also states that God is one. The early Christians, and Jesus himself, were orthodox Jews. They would never have considered rejecting or redefining Scripture to arrive at some polytheistic picture of deity.

Q: *Jesus prayed, "that they may be one, even as we are one" (John 17:22). When we say that God is "one," aren't we talking about this singleness of purpose or harmony of personal unity?*

A: The Godhead indeed enjoy perfect unity and harmony of purpose in personal relationship that is to be a model for the Church. But the substantial unity of the Godhead is based on other considerations that are metaphysical, not merely moral—that since each member is uncreated, they are thus essentially one in "substance, nature, and essence."

[5]Runia, op. cit. p. 167.
[6]Ibid. op. cit. p. 168.

Q: *But what if Jesus were only God's creation and the Holy Spirit just God's influence or power?*

A: Then Jesus would have commanded us to baptize people into the "name of the Father, and of an exalted man, and of a certain influence of the Father," and the benediction of 2 Cor. 13:14 would read, "The grace of a creature and the love of the Creator and the communion of creative energy be with you all. Amen."

Q: *Not all those who deny the Trinity deny the deity of God, Christ, or the Holy Spirit. A number of otherwise evangelical groups along with other intelligent Christian men in history (Locke, Newton, Milton, and Isaac Watts) did not seem to support the traditional view of the Trinity. While they retained a full belief in the deity of Christ, of God the Father, and of the Holy Spirit, they held these to be but different names of the one God or various descriptions of His personal relationships with His creation. What is wrong with this?*

A: We must be kind here as well as true. The doctrine of the Trinity has been one of the most discussed and debated of all issues in Church history. Each facet of the various arguments over the centuries has had its own powerful and intellectual defenders. The view adopted here is certainly not the only orthodox viewpoint from Church history, but this seems, on the whole, the view which does the least violence to Scripture, normal language, and early Church thought; it also answers more questions philosophically, theologically, and practically than either the simple monadic or tritheistic views, as well as having the greatest historical support by the evangelical Christian church.

Q: *I'm confused. If I pray, who am I talking to?*

A: Technically your prayer goes *by* the Holy Spirit *through* the Son *to* the Father, and the answer comes *from* the Father via the Son *by* the Holy Spirit to your heart. Specifically you can address requests for power, zeal, communication, and relationships to the Spirit; ask the Son for wisdom, leadership, creativity, and authority; and the Father for comfort, counsel, care, and security. Practically, just pray. It will work out fine.

Analysis and Discussion

Though truly a mystery, God's triunity is the best illustrated of the wonders of His nature. The mark of triunity is stamped on everything around us. "Perhaps," says Dorothy Sayers, "the Trinitarian structure of activity is mysterious to us just because it is universal."[1] It is not always easy to recognize something that in essence fundamentally incorporates everything! Creation is so full of reflections of this three-in-one absolute that initially recognizing it can be something like asking a fish what water

[1]Dorothy Sayers, *The Mind of the Maker* (Westport, Conn.: Greenwood Press, 1970).

is like. Nevertheless, since God designed man in his image (Gen. 1:26), we might expect all creation to share in His likeness—to share His own triune structure.

Augustine, in his *Vestigia Trinitatis* ("Vestiges of the Trinity"), noted this imprint of the Creator and of His triune nature on all created things, "All things which are made by divine skill show in themselves a certain unity and form and order. . . . When therefore we regard the Creator who is understood by the things that are made, we must needs understand the Trinity of whom there appear traces in the creature, as is fitting. For in the Trinity is the supreme source of all things, the most perfect beauty and the most blessed delight."

The Origin of Trinitarian Thought

Francis Schaeffer argued that the Trinity has been a neglected church doctrine too long. In both the worlds of philosophy and theology, it has critical and profound implications: it is the *only* answer to questions of existence, unity and diversity, and the reality of personality (as well as love and communication) as men have defined, debated, and argued over for centuries.

Schaeffer writes, "Every once in a while in my discussions someone asks me how I can believe in the Trinity. My answer is always the same. I would still be an agnostic if there were no Trinity, because there would be no answers. Without the high order of personal unity and diversity as given in the Trinity, *there are no answers.*

"The Persons of the Trinity communicated with each other and loved each other before the creation of the world. This is not only an answer to the acute *philosophical* need of unity in diversity, but of *personal* unity and diversity. . . . We must appreciate that our Christian forefathers understood this very well in A.D. 325 when they stressed the three persons in the Trinity as the Bible had clearly set this forth. Let us notice that it is not that they invented the Trinity in order to give an answer to the philosophical questions which the Greeks had at that time understood. It is quite the contrary. . . . The Christians realized that in the Trinity, as it had been taught in the Bible, they had an answer that no one else had. They did not invent the Trinity to meet the need; the Trinity was already there and it met the needs.

"Let us notice again that this is not the best answer; it is the *only* answer. Nobody else, no philosophy has ever given us an answer to unity and diversity."[2]

What Dr. Schaeffer stressed is that the biblical revelation is true to what actually IS in the world; it answers so many major problems and brings light to so many questions. Nathan Wood, the author of the astonishing twenty-five-year study on the nature of triunity in the universe said concerning the early Christians and Scripture:

---

[2]Francis A. Schaeffer, "He Is There and He Is Not Silent," *The Complete Works of Francis Schaeffer* (Westchester, Ill.: Crossway, 1985), vol. 1, pp. 288–289.

"Did the NT writers get triunity from the universe? Is it a conscious speculation? . . . There is no evidence for such an origin. . . . There is no attempt in any way to compare the triunity of Father, Son, and Holy Spirit with space or matter or time or anything in man. . . . Indeed there is no theoretical triunity in the New Testament. The presentation of the Trinity is simple, natural, matter-of-course, a phrase here, an allusion there, now a characteristic, now a relationship as it happens in connection with other things and topics. Indeed the Trinity there occurs largely in the sayings of Jesus and in His simplest, most personal talk about his Father and Himself and about the Spirit. . . . This triunity of the Bible evidently did not come by human speculation to be so exactly what the universe requires."[3]

Indeed, a good case could be made that the biblical idea of the Trinity is the heart of the unique message of Christianity. "The doctrine of the Trinity is not so much a point among many as the very *essence and compendium of Christianity itself,*" says Dr. George Smeaton. "It not only presents a lofty and sublime subject of contemplation to the intellect, but furnishes repose and peace to the heart and conscience. To explain this mystery is not our province. All true theologians . . . have universally accepted it as their highest function simply to 'conserve the mystery.'. . .

"As this doctrine is believed on the one hand or challenged on the other, Christian life is found to be affected at its roots and over all its extent. Every doctrine is run up to it; every privilege and duty hang on it. . . . However a man may begin his career of error, the general issue is that the doctrine of the Trinity, proving an unexpected check or insurmountable obstacle in the carrying out of his opinions, has to be modified or pushed aside; and he comes to be against the Trinity because he has found that it was against him."[4]

The Master Pattern of Reality

Smeaton, summarizing the divine order of the Trinity, says:

> As to the divine works, the Father is the Source *from which* every operation emanates (*ex ou*); the Son is the Medium *through which* (*di ou*) it is performed; and the Holy Ghost is the Executive *by which* (*en o*) it is carried into effect.[5]

Put in a more general way, we can say: essential being or nature generates embodiment; essence and embodiment generate existent reality. This truth about God is the causal, logical, and progressive order of all reality. Also that divine reality *processes from* the Unseen Source (the Father), revealed *through* a Visible Embodiment (the Son), and proceeds *by* that Executive Reality (the Spirit), which relates both by contact (communication), movement (activity), and power (influence). The man or

---

[3]Dr. Nathan Wood, *The Trinity in the Universe* (Grand Rapids: Kregel, 1984), pp. 97–98.
[4]George Smeaton, *The Doctrine of the Holy Spirit* (Carlisle, Pa.: The Banner of Truth, 1980), p. 5.
[5]Ibid. p. 4.

SUMMARY: God Is the Uncreated Triune Creator

Uncreated	Triune	Creator
(Being)	**(Structure)**	**(Person)**
He is		**He does**
Metaphysics	Epistimology	Morals
Nature of Reality	Truth,	Axiology
	Communication	
Infinite	Father	Personal
Spiritual	Son	Active
Glorious	Spirit	Holy

Trinity

Father	×	Son	×	Holy Spirit
Originator		**Mediator**		**Executor**
(*From* Whom)		**(*Through* Whom)**		**(*By* Whom)**
Source		Medium		Effect
(Unseen,		(Visible		(Relating Agent)
Invisible)		Embodiment)		
(Heart)		(Head)		(Hand)
Love		Wisdom		Power

woman who sees, knows, and understands this about God has a wonderful key for seeing His glory expressed everywhere in the true unity of His universe.

From this we can expect any expression of the Trinity to meet the following criteria: (1) There will be exactly three distinct interdependent, essential elements. (2) No one element can be any of the others. (3) No element can exist without the other two. Put symbolically: $1 \times 1 \times 1 = 1$ and $1 \times 1 \times 0 = 0$.

Again Nathan Wood says, "The Three in One as brought to us in the God of the Bible and of the universe of space, time, matter and men is that kind of absolute unity in which each of the three is the whole. . . . Each is most intensively the whole and every part of the whole. The Trinity is not an inert division of God into three parts. . . . It is life. It is multiplied, infinitely intensified reality. It is a living, active, intensified mode of being in which each of the Three interacts, penetrates, intensifies, lives in the other Two and each is the Whole."[6]

---

[6]Wood, op. cit. pp. 180–181.

Triune Patterns of Reality

From this mirror we can begin to explore not only the outer fringes of God's greatness, but also His wonderful universe. Probe any fundamental reality, and you will see His Triune imprint: each element of that unity in diversity will follow the order of the Designer. Here are just some of the many examples of this pattern that can bring out our worship in every avenue of life and perception:

Man
- Soul—The creative invisible source; the origin of individuality.
- Body—The embodiment of the individual in a tangible expression.
- Spirit—That which relates the individual to God and others.

Personal Existence
- Nature—The essential source of personality, the innermost, primal "I" who realizes or sees. "I myself who see."
- Person—The embodied self whom I or others see or realize. "I who am seen by myself."
- Personality—Myself recognized as myself. "I who am recognized by myself." Myself as I touch, affect, and influence others.

Heavenly Creatures
- Seraphim—Worship, power, guard God's holiness.
- Cherubim—Guard the Tree of Life and the Ark of the Covenant. The tangible sign of God's presence.
- "Angels," Witnesses; executives of ministry to God and man.
- Archangels—Michael (Warrior) Who is like unto God?
  Lucifer (Wisdom, Day-star, Son of the Morning).
  Gabriel (Communication, God Is Mighty).

Space
- Height—Potentiality, space related to its source.
- Breadth—Embodiment, the "thickness" of space.
- Length—Relation of space in reference to other space.

Matter
- Energy—Universal, unseen source, potentiality.
- Motion—Particular embodiment of that energy.
- Phenomena—Particular motion in contact with other existences.

Time
- Future—Universal Source, potentiality of events.
- Present—Particular embodiment, realization of future things we know and touch.
- Past—The present after it has related itself to other things.

Universe
- Space—Source of all God's omnipresent outspreading creative energy.
- Motion—Embodiment of the tangible universe, the omnipotence of God upholds all things.
- Time—Everything known is revealed to us by the time-length of its vibrations.

Marriage (Genesis 2:24)
- "Leave"—*From*; the source of a marriage; legal, public act.
- "Cleave"—*Through*; the embodiment of a marriage, personal, tangible.
- "One flesh"—*By*; the consummation of a marriage, relational, motivational.

Family
- Husband—Source of the family.
- Wife—Embodiment of the family.
- Child—Relation of a husband through his wife.

Growth (1 John 2:12–14)
- Child—Basics, learns foundational abilities and accumulates sources of growth.
- Youth—Building, organization and orientation of knowledge in physical, mental, and spiritual embodiment.
- Adult—Belonging, expansion and experience in harmony with others; relates embodied knowledge and maturity to world in executive ways.

Ministries of Christ
- Prophet—Bearer of universal and absolute truth.
- Priest—Embodiment of God's truth, incarnated truth.
- King—Bringer of people into orderly relationship with God's truth.

Loyalty
- Heart—Love. The source of absolute loyalty, spring, unseen fountain.
- Head—Wisdom. The practical embodiment in which loyalty is seen in judging, speaking.
- Hand—Power. The executive expression of commitment, ministry to needs.

Christian Truth
- Spirit—Universal truth, ultimate source, personal experience with God.
- Word—Particular embodiment of an experience in propositional form.
- Church—Record of relationship, what Christians know and believe on the basis of relationships with each other and God in past history.

Perception
- Concept—The universal idea.
- Perception—The particular embodiment of an idea.
- Relation—An idea as it applies to other ideas.

Biblical Wisdom
- *Sophia*—"Wisdom." Knowledge as it relates to ultimates and universals.
- *Phronesis*—"Prudence." Knowledge relating to particular, practical embodiment.
- *Sunesis*—"Understanding." Relates things to other things, puts things together.

Christian Apologetics
- Mystical—Direct personal contact with the Source of truth.
- Propositional—Intellectual, objective embodiment of truth in written form.
- Historical—Relating the experience of the living and written Word in other's lives.

Deductive Logic
- Major Premise—Universal truth; nature of thing under discussion.
- Minor Premise—Particular embodiment of truth in major premise.
- Conclusion—That which proceeds from the major through the minor premise to bring both in contact with the thing under discussion.

Philosophy
- Universal—Idealist; the concern with the way things ought to be, the perfection.
- Particular—Realist; the concern with the way things actually are, what is seen in actual fact.
- Relational—Pragmatist; what works and actually gets things functioning.

Psychology
- Nature—"Higher" self. Will it bring good? Will it cause happiness?
- Person—Self. Personal interest. Will it bring good for me? Bring me happiness?
- Personality—Family, community, and world. Will it be good for them?

Sociology
- Mankind—Universal humanity, human nature.
- Man—Particular embodiment in a person.
- Mannishness—Personality related to others.

Anthropology
- Shem—Revelation, universal.
- Ham—Technological. The practical solution to life's problems in service. Embodiment in practice.
- Japheth—Illumination, puts together the whole pattern.
  (See A. C. Custance, *Noah's Three Sons*.)

Art
- Source—Idea, conception, ideal, inspiration.
- Embodiment—Picture, poem, song, statue, building.
- Work—The object as it affects others in vision, challenge, and in emotion. (See Dorothy Sayers, *The Mind of The Maker*.)

Law
- Love God—Universal ultimate source and primary command.
- Love yourself—Particular embodiment of law we know and experience.
- Love your neighbor—Law as it relates to others.

Love in the New Testament
- *Agape*—Divine love; motive source; ultimate choice.
- *Phileo*—Embodied love in friendship, companionship.
- *Storge*—Relational love of the comfortable and familiar.

Temptation
- World (Spiritual)—Attacks the relationship God has given us for communion with the Father (1 John 2:15–16).
- Devil (Personal)—Attacks our self-image, the relationship with God we enjoy through and in the Son (Matt. 4:1, John 8:44).
- Flesh (Social)—Attacks our relationships with others given by the Spirit (Gal. 5:17).

Witnesses on Earth (1 John 5:8)
- Blood—Witness of salvation to God.
- Water—Witness of salvation to our humanity.
- Spirit—Witness of salvation to others.

Vocal Gifts (1 Cor. 12:10)
- Prophecy—Forth-telling, revelation of the truth of God.
- Tongues—The embodiment of divine revelation in word.
- Interpretation of Tongues—That which relates the Divine to the human.

Power Gifts (1 Cor. 12:9–10)
- Faith—That which lifts vision to the realm of universal; ultimate vision.
- Gifts of Healing—That which restores the physical body to health.
- Working of Miracles—That which demonstrates and relates the Divine to the human.

Wisdom Gifts (1 Cor. 12:8, 10)
- Word of wisdom—Universal principles, basis of ultimate truth.
- Word of knowledge—Facts that are practically applicable to a personal need.
- Discerning of Spirits—Revelation of the spirit that motivates an action.

Righteous Men (Ezekiel 14:14, 20)
- Noah—The father of redeemed righteous men; source of the new world.
- Daniel—He who embodied righteousness in a pagan kingdom.
- Job—He who witnessed to both heaven and earth of righteousness.

Spiritual Israel
- Abraham—Faithful father; originator of 12 tribes, a type of the Father.
- Isaac—From Abraham; obedient son, willing even to be offered in sacrifice; a type of the Son.
- Jacob—Through Isaac; his fruitfulness peopled the 12 tribes, a type of the Holy Spirit.

(For further study, see *The Trinity In The Universe* by Dr. Nathan Wood, Kregel, 1980).

Types in Scripture

Scripture also contains many types and symbols in this same triune pattern. Noah's Ark had three stories (Gen. 6:14–22), and he sent out a bird three times in search of dry land. Abraham held conversation with one of three heavenly visitors in Gen. 18:1—19:24, and as a sign of the covenant, he was told to offer three animals, each three years old. We see Joseph's dream of future leadership as the sun, moon, and stars bowing down to him. The Israelite spies brought three kinds of fruit back from Canaan (Num. 13:23).

Three appears in the requirements for worship. The priests were to declare cleansing for the leper and anointing for the ministry by using blood, water, and oil on the ear, the thumb, and the toe (Lev. 14:12–29). There were three voluntary offerings to God: the burnt offering, the meal (or meat) offering, and the peace offering. Three measures of meal (Matt. 13:33) formed the great meal offering (Num. 15:9) with the same measure used for whole burnt offerings and special occasion offerings such as the new moon and new year celebrations.

In Old Testament divine architecture, both the Temple and the Tabernacle had three-fold structures: the outer court, Holy Place, and the Holy of Holies. The Tabernacle has three separate compartments and three different entrances and it used covering materials of badger, ram, and goat skins (Ex. 36:18–19). The gold-covered table in the Holy Place measured three solid cubits. Decorative colors were weavings of blue, scarlet, and purple; the high priests wore robes with twelve gems set in four rows of three for each of the twelve tribes of Israel. The laver held three thousand baths, supported by four groups of three oxen looking north, west, south and east (1 Kings 7:24–25, 2 Chron. 4:5). The ark of the covenant held three sacred symbols: the tables of the Law, a golden pot of manna, and Aaron's rod that budded (Heb. 9:4). Israel celebrated three main feasts of the Lord: Passover, Pentecost, and the Feast of Tabernacles (Lev. 23). Three young men dared the wrath of Nebuchadnezzar and God's judgment came to Nebuchadnezzar's co-regent Belteshazzar in an awesome, three-fold prophecy.

From Genesis through the Prophets, there is a three-fold cord illustrating and reinforcing every major aspect of Israel's life. The Old Testament itself consists of three great sections: the Law, the Psalms, and the Prophets. The New Testament likewise has three great divisons: Gospels, Acts, and Epistles. The first three books tell essentially the same story of Jesus as the Synoptic Gospels. Jesus was given three gifts from the Wise Kings as a child, and He faced three temptations in the wilderness with three scriptures. He called His disciples in four groups of three, took three of them with Him (Peter, James, and John) during special times of prayer, and even raised three people from the dead. Jesus was denied by Peter three times before the cock crowed (John 18:17; Matt. 26:70–71). Jesus hung on a cross as one of three men crucified together with a sign in three languages over His head. He was silent during a three-hour darkness, and then died during the third hour. Three women came to His tomb when He rose on the third day.

Nathan Wood summed up this profound reality, "Perhaps this is why the human soul has always so instinctively and easily accepted the mysterious triunity of Scripture, just as it has accepted God's love, or wisdom, or power or goodness. It is because the soul is made in His likeness. It is not because we are thoughtless, but because we are profound. It is because we are like that triunity ourselves. And perhaps that is why the simple intuitive vision of children, and of savages, and of the untutored, and the profound intuitive vision of apostles, and saints and great thinkers and the simple and profound intuitive vision of every human heart which follows its instinct has always so readily grasped the teaching of the Triune God. For the soul was made like Him that it might know Him."[7]

Historical Discussion

Holy, Holy, Holy, Lord God Almighty
Early in the morning our song shall rise to Thee.
Holy, Holy, Holy, merciful and mighty,
God in three Persons, Blessed Trinity

Reginald Heber

Praise God from Whom all blessings flow;
Praise Him all creatures here below;
Praise Him above ye heavenly host;
Praise Father, Son, and Holy Ghost.

The Doxology

The Trinity in the Scriptures

Robert Drummond

"Christians are not the only religious people in the world. Christians are not the only people who believe in God. But Christians are the only people who think of God as they do. And when you try to put in a few words what they think and believe, it is this: They believe in God the Father, the Son, and the Holy Ghost—one God. These words are not found in the Bible. There is no one text that sums up the matter in these terms. And yet that is the distinguishing thought of the Christian about God. That is what distinguishes his view about God from that of everyone else.

"Now that doctrine of the Trinity often seems a very perplexing subject. And no wonder; I for one should be very much surprised if when the truth about God is reached we should not find something which is very perplexing to human minds and something which betrays the poverty of human speech. I expect the truth about the infinite God will always tax the fullest resources of finite minds and tongues and still leave men wondering, pondering and adoring.

"And so it is not some strange concoction of the human brain that speaks when we call God the Father, the Son, and the Holy Ghost—one God, but it is just the description in a few words of what men who, as

---

[7]Ibid. p. 88.

Christians, study the Bible and reflect on their own experience of salvation, find there about God—who He is and what He is. And what gives it value and significance is that it satisfies our highest thoughts, finds its room in God, through all eternity, for the play of the highest faculties man knows or possesses. Here is a God who is not blind energy, dumb force, an impersonal passionless unity. But within himself there is room for fellowship, for love."[1]

"It is plain that both Christ and the apostles ascribe distinct personality to the Father the Son and the Holy Ghost. And these utterances are such as to admit legitimately of no other conception than that of the unity of these three persons in the ontological oneness of the whole divine nature (unity of essential being). . . . The same worship is paid, the same works are ascribed to each of these three persons and in such a way as to indicate that these three are united in the fullness of the one living God. The Monotheism of the Old Testament is maintained while glimpses are nevertheless afforded into the tripersonal mode of the divine existence."[2]

"It is admitted by all who thoughtfully deal with this subject that the Scripture revelation here leads us into the presence of a deep mystery; and that all human attempts at expression are of necessity imperfect. The word 'person' it may be is inadequate and is doubtless often used in a way that is misleading. 'Three persons, if they are to be so called, for the unspeakable exaltedness of the object cannot be set forth by this term' (Augustine). And yet the long-standing and prevailing doctrine of the church expresses more nearly than any other the truth concerning God as it comes to us in the Holy Scriptures. And it is to be further born in mind that this teaching of the church has been called forth for the purpose of combating various forms of error. It has not been held as a complete or perfect expression of truth concerning the unfathomable being of God, but rather as a protest against the denials of the personality and supreme deity of the Son and of the Holy Ghost."[3]

J. I. Packer

"God is Triune; there are within the Godhead three Persons; the Father, the Son and the Holy Ghost; and the work of salvation is one in which all three act together, the Father purposing redemption, the Son securing it, and the Spirit applying it.

"The Son is subject to the Father, for the Son is sent by the Father in the Father's Name. The Spirit is subject to the Father for the Spirit is sent by the Father in the Son's name. The Spirit is subject to the Son as well as to the Father, for the Spirit is sent by the Son as well as by the Father."[4]

---

[1]Robert Drummond, *Faith's Perplexities* (New York: American Tract Society), pp. 283–285.
[2]*The People's Bible Encyclopedia*, "Trinity," Charles Randall Barnes, ed. (London: Charles H. Kelley, 1900), pp. 1124–1125.
[3]Ibid., pp. 1124–1125.
[4]J.I. Packer, *Knowing God* (Downers Grove, Ill.: Inter-Varsity Press, 1973), p. 70.

Klaas Runia

"The biblical roots of this doctrine had nothing to do with philosophical speculation: it was born out of the heart of the Christian faith—what was believed about Jesus Christ. It was the coming of Jesus which set in motion the transformation of Jewish monotheism into the Christian doctrine of the Trinity. The same is true of the way this belief developed in history. The church of the first three centuries did not engage in controversies about the Trinity because it was fond of speculation. . . .

"The basic issue was: Is Jesus Christ God, is He really and fully God? If so, what does this tell us about the being of God? At a later stage the same question was asked about the Holy Spirit. . . . The controversy about the divinity and personality of the Spirit was more in the nature of a consequence. The core of the doctrine of the Trinity was and is the divinity of Christ. . . .

"How then can we describe the New Testament picture of God? On the one hand God is one, truly and absolutely one. On the other hand this one God exists as Father, Son, and Holy Spirit. This threefoldness is present throughout the whole New Testament *not as a formal statement but as a pattern to be seen everywhere.*"[5]

The Trinity in the Creeds

Debates on this doctrine called out the best and most difficult thought of the early Church. Amid controversy and intense discussion, three oversimplified views were (and are still) tried, debated, and found lacking the essential Scriptural understanding of the Trinity—not truly matching the facts, the record, or experience:

1. Sabellian *modalism* is an idea based on God's unity. It says the Father, Son, and Holy Spirit are only different ways God shows himself.
2. *Arianism* is also based on God's unity, saying only the Father is God; Jesus Christ is "a god," a created being; and the Holy Spirit is one of God's attributes, merely His power.
3. *Tri-theism* says there are simply three separate, essentially different Gods.

The Church kept this doctrine in the crucible for three centuries. At last some things became clear: precisely what the Trinity was *not*, if not exactly what it was. One well-known, though still limited and inadequate, formulation, the so-called *Athanasian Creed* of 500 A.D., describes God as: "One divine essence [substance or being] existing in three Persons."

Klaas Runia

Runia comments that in the first centuries the term "person" used in this creed was a rather neutral word pointing to a personal relationship.

---

[5]Klaas Runia, "The Trinity," *Eerdman's Handbook to Christian Belief*, Robin Keeley, ed. (Grand Rapids: Eerdmans, 1982), pp. 165, 169.

Now it has quite a different meaning; as a "self-conscious, autonomous individual." As this modern idea of person seems too much like three Gods, many prefer to speak of "three modes of existence."

The essential Christian idea is: "That we worship one God in Trinity and Trinity in unity; neither confounding the persons, nor dividing the substances. . . . For there is one person of the Father, another of the Son, and another of the Holy Spirit. But the Godhead of the Father, of the Son and of the Holy Spirit is all one, the glory equal, the majesty co-eternal. Such as the Father is, such is the Son, and such is the Holy Spirit.

"The One God exists in three different ways. . . . There are not three individual personalities in God. There is one divine personality which contains a threefold distinction. But at the same time we must make quite clear that the one divine Personality exists in three different personal ways. Father, Son, and Holy Spirit are not simply three different modes of revelation. God not only reveals himself as Father, Son, and Holy Spirit; God *is* Father, Son, and Holy Spirit. These three names indicate three genuine distinctions within the one personal God and these three distinctions themselves are fully personal. . . ."[6]

Irenaeus of Lyons

"Without the Spirit it is not possible to hold the Word of God nor without the Son can any draw near to the Father, for the knowledge of the Father is the Son and the knowledge of the Son of God is through the Holy Spirit."[7]

The Importance of the Trinity

Why do Christians consider the significance of this doctrine the very foundation of our Christian faith?

George Smeaton

"The doctrine of the Trinity is not so much a point among many as the very essence and compendium of Christianity itself. It not only presents a lofty and sublime subject of contemplation to the intellect, but furnishes repose and peace to the heart and conscience. To explain this mystery is not our province. All true theologians . . . have universally accepted it as their highest function simply to conserve the mystery. . . . As this doctrine is believed on the one hand or challenged on the other, Christian life is found to be affected at its roots and over all its extent. Every doctrine is run up to it; every privilege and duty hangs on it."[8]

Klaas Runia

"Precisely in this doctrine it becomes clear that God is truly the living God, the God who has life in himself, literally full of life. Some of the

---

[6]Ibid. pp. 163–174.
[7]Ibid. pp. 163, 171–174.
[8]George Smeaton, *The Doctrine of the Holy Spirit* (Carlisle, Pa.: The Banner of Truth, 1980), p. 5.

early church fathers used a remarkable expression. They said God is 'fertile.' Within the three-in-one God are all the possibilities of person-to-person communication. God in no way needed His creation. . . . The doctrine of the Trinity is the end of all pantheism. If in the depth of His own being God is three-in-one He does not need this world in order to come to his full potential.

This doctrine is the basis of all revelation. "In the revelation of the Father through the Son by the Spirit we not only receive some external information about God but we have the guarantee that God himself is speaking to us and opening his divine heart to us. Revelation is really and fully self-revelation.

"But above all the doctrine of the Trinity is of importance for our salvation. It is the answer to our question whether or not our salvation is really God's work. In the final analysis this is the reason why the church is so vitally interested in the divinity of Jesus Christ and the divinity of the Holy Spirit. The vital question to ask about the nature of Jesus Christ is 'In Jesus, do we really meet with God himself?'. . .

"None of this is bald theory. It is echoed in the Christian personal experience. The believer knows by experience that he is a child of the father, that he is redeemed by the Son and that the Holy Spirit is in his life. And he knows that in all three relationships he has to do with the one and the same God."[9]

Nathan Wood

"The universe is one vast evidence of that triunity of Father, Son, and Holy Spirit in God. The entire universe, the outer universe of space and matter and time and the inner universe of the human soul in all its vast triunity reflects that triunity. It demands that triunity in God. The universe is one vast evidence in such detailed exact, scientific correspondence to the divine triunity which it demands and reflects as can be found in no other witness of the universe to anything else about God.

"The triunity of the Father, Son, and Holy Spirit is the explanation of the universe. It is the answer to those great questions: What is the explanation of the universe? What is the principle of the universe? The answer is: Triunity in the image of the triune God is the principle and explanation of the universe. It is the organizing principle of all things. It is the structure and pattern of the universe.

"The answer to all these questions is evident. The formula, the pattern, the secret, the principle, the structure, the explanation of the universe is self-evidently clear. It explains itself. No 'higher mind' is needed to formulate it. It clearly includes God. It is a universal principle. It is a principle which lies in God's nature. It is triunity in the image of a triune God. It reveals one vast unity—sheer space, moving matter, mysterious time, wondrous man, and supreme God bound in one vast unity.

"Get in your heart a vision of the universe. Do not go about in the midst of it blind to the great structure of the universe and of human life.

---

[9]Runia, op. cit. p. 174–175.

See its immense triunity. See it reflecting from leaf and star and space and time and self the triune God. See it as an orderly universe. See it as a whole. See it as one vast, open and visible witness to the Three-in-One."[10]

Dorothy Sayers

"These three are one, each equally in itself the whole work whereof none can exist without the other. . . . If you were to ask a writer which is the 'real book'—his idea of it, his activity in writing it or its return to himself in power, he would be at loss to tell you. Each of them is the complete book separately; yet in the complete book all of them exist together. He can by an act of intellect 'distinguish the persons' but he cannot by any means 'divide the substance.' How could he? He cannot know the idea except by the power interpreting his own activity to him; he knows the activity only as it reveals the idea in power; he knows the power only as the revelation of the idea in the activity. All he can say is that these three are equally and eternally present in his own act of creation, and at every moment of it, whether or not the act ever becomes manifest in the form of a written or printed book. These things are not confined to a material manifestation; they exist in—they *are*—the creative mind itself."[11]

Early Church Fathers on Christ and the Trinity

One of the most important witnesses to the reality of Christ's deity is that of the Ante-Nicene Fathers, those early Christians who were the spiritual children of the early disciples or their preaching. The testimony of these men from the first three hundred years of the Church is of great value because it shows that they uniformly believed and understood the implications of Triunity.

Irenaeus of Lyons, A.D. 120–202

Irenaeus was one of the early Church fathers who with other early Christian teachers and evangelists across the world had to do verbal and written battle with those who either ignorantly or deliberately twisted Scripture to fit their own ideas or practices.

"God stands in need of nothing, and that He created and made all things by His Word while He neither required angels to assist Him in the production of these things which are made, nor of any power greatly inferior to himself and ignorant of the Father . . . but *He himself in himself* after a fashion which we can neither describe nor conceive, predestinating all things, formed them as He pleased, bestowing harmony on all things and assigning them their own place and the beginning of their crea-

---

[10]Dr. Nathan Wood, *The Trinity in the Universe* (Grand Rapids: Kregel, 1984), pp. 103–104.

[11]Dorothy Sayers, "Idea, Energy, Power," *The Mind of the Maker* (Westport, Conn.: Greenwood Press, 1970), p. 41.

tion. . . . 'His own Word is both suitable and efficient for the formation of all things, even as John, the disciple of the Lord, declares regarding Him: "All things were made by Him and without Him was nothing made." ' "[12]

"He . . . will entertain far more becoming thoughts of Him than do those who transfer the generation of the word to which men give utterance to the eternal word of god assigning a beginning and a course of production to him even as they do to their own word. And in what respect will the word of god—yea rather god himself, since He is the word—differ from the word of men if He follows the same order and process of generation? . . .

"If any one therefore says to us 'How then was the Son produced by the Father?' we reply to him that no man understands that production or generation or calling or revelation or by whatever name one may describe His generation which is in fact altogether indescribable. . . .

"Therefore neither would the Lord nor the Holy Spirit nor the apostles have ever named as God definitely and absolutely him who was not God unless he was truly God; nor would they have named any one in his own person Lord except God the Father ruling over all and His Son who has received dominion from His Father over all creation as this passage has it—'The Lord said unto My Lord, sit thou at my right hand until I make thine enemies my footstool.' . . . And this does declare the same truth— 'Thy throne O God is for ever and ever the scepter of Thy Kingdom is a right scepter' (Ps. XLV.6). For the Spirit designates both of them by the name of God—both Him who is anointed as Son and Him who does anoint, that is the Father. . . .

"For she [the Church] is the synagogue of God, which God—that is, the Son himself—has gathered by himself. Of whom He again speaks— 'The God of gods, the Lord has spoken and has called the earth.' Who is meant by God? He of whom He has said 'God shall come openly, our God and shall not keep silence'; that is the Son, who came manifested unto men. . . . "For He is himself uncreated, both without beginning and end, and lacking nothing. He is himself sufficient for himself and still further He grants to all others this very thing, existence. But the things which have been made by Him have received a beginning. . . . He indeed who made all things can alone, together with His Word, properly be termed God and Lord. . . .

"There is, therefore, one and the same God the Father of our Lord, who also promised through the prophets that He would send His forerunner and His salvation—that is His word—He caused to be made visible to all flesh, the Word himself being made incarnate that in all things their King might be made manifest. . . .

"He was God who also 'was made known in Judea' and 'was declared to those who sought Him not.' "[13]

A hundred pages of scriptural evidence follows, stating that Christ was and is truly God and Lord just as His Father.[14]

---

[12]Irenaeus, *Ante-Nicane Fathers*, Alexander Roberts and James Donaldson, eds. (Eerdmans, 1961), Vol. I, pp. 361–362

[13]Ibid. pp. 418–419, 422–423.

[14]Ibid. pp. 425–525, bks. 3 & 4.

Justin Martyr, A.D. 114–165

Justin Martyr's conversion "marks a new era in Gospel history," says a biographer. "The sub-apostolic age begins with its first Christian author—the founder of theological literature."[15]

Justin, a highly trained and well-traveled professional philosopher, became deeply impressed by the "extraordinary fearlessness" of Christians who faced death. Later he was moved by the grandeur and truth of the Old Testament, finally bowing his knee and heart to Christ, becoming an evangelist. Eventually, he himself faced death as a martyr.

Justin not only believed that Christ was truly the uncreated God, but wrote an entire book on the subject, the record of his famous *Dialogue With Trypho* the Jew. Full of Christ's love and full of the Scriptures, Justin assumed the Trinity.

"Our teacher of these things is Jesus Christ who also was born for this purpose and was crucified under Pontius Pilate, procurator of Judea in the times of Tiberius Caesar; and we will prove that we reasonably worship Him, having learned that He is the *Son of the true God Himself*, and *holding Him in second place* and the *prophetic Spirit in the third.* For they proclaim our madness to consist in this, that we give to a crucified man a place second to the unchangeable and eternal God, the Creator of all; for they do not discern the mystery that is herein, to which as we make it plain to you, we pray you give heed."[16]

"And that this may now become evident to you that whatever we assert in conformity with what has been taught us by Christ and by the prophets who preceded Him are alone true and are older than all the writers who have existed; that we claim to be acknowledged, not because we say the same things as these writers said, but because we say true things; and secondly that Jesus Christ is the only proper Son who has been begotten by God being His Word and first-begotten and power; and becoming man according to His will He taught us these things for the conversion and restoration of the human race."[17]

Commenting on Plato's doctrine of the cross, Justin wrote, "For he gives the second place to the *Logos* which is with God who he said was placed crosswise in the universe; and the third place to the Spirit who was said to be borne upon the water, saying 'And the third around the third.' And that you may learn that it was from our teachers—we mean the account given through the prophets—that Plato borrowed his statement. . . . So that both Plato and they who agree with him and we ourselves have learned, and you also can be convinced that by the Word of God the whole world was made. . . ."[18]

In discussing Gen. 1:26–28, Justin wrote, "And you may not change the [force of the] words just quoted and repeat what your teachers assert

---

[15]Justin Martyr, "First Apology," *Ante-Nicene Fathers*, Alexander Roberts and James Donaldson, eds. (Eerdmans, 1961), Vol. I, p. 159.
[16]Ibid. op. cit. Vol. I, pp. 166–167.
[17]Ibid. pp. 170–171.
[18]Ibid. pp. 182–183.

either that God said to himself 'let *us* make.' . . . or that God spoke to the elements. . . . We can indisputably learn that [God] conversed with someone who was numerically distinct from himself and also a rational being. In saying therefore 'as one of *us*,' [Moses] has declared that [there is a certain] number of persons associated with one another and that they are at least two. . . . This offspring which was truly brought forth from the Father was with the Father before all the creatures and the Father communed with Him; even as Scripture . . . has made clear that He whom Solomon calls Wisdom was begotten as a beginning before all His creatures and as offspring by God. . . ."[19]

On Christ As God

"That these things should come to pass, I say our Teacher foretold He who is both Son and Apostle of God the Father of all, and the Ruler Jesus Christ; from whom also we have the name Christians. Whence we become more assured of all the things He taught us since whatever He beforehand foretold should come to pass is seen in fact coming to pass; and this is a work of God to tell of a thing before it happens. . . .

"And this Word of God is His Son as we have before said. And He is called Angel and Apostle; for He declares whatever we ought to know and is sent forth to declare what is revealed; as our Lord himself says, 'He that Heareth Me, heareth Him that sent Me.' From the writings of Moses this will be manifest; for thus is it written in them, 'And the Angel of God spoke to Moses in a flame of fire out of the bush and said 'I am that I am, the God of Abraham. The God of Isaac, the God of Jacob, the God of thy fathers. . . .' But so much is written for the sake of proving that Jesus the Christ is the Son of God and his Apostle being of old the Word. . . . He endured all the sufferings which the devils instigated the senseless Jews to inflict on Him, who though they have it expressly affirmed in the writings of Moses 'I am that I am, the God of Abraham, and the God of Isaac, and the God of Jacob,' yet maintain that He who said this was the Father and Creator of the universe. Whence also the Spirit of prophecy rebukes them and says, 'Israel doth not know Me, My people have not understood Me.' . . . The Jews accordingly being throughout of the opinion that it was the Father of the universe that spoke to Moses, though He who spoke to Him was indeed the Son of God, are justly charged both by the Spirit of Prophecy and by Christ himself with knowing neither the Father nor the Son. For they who affirm that the Son is the Father are proved neither to have become acquainted with the Father, nor to know that the Father of the universe has a Son who also, being the first-begotten Word of God is even God."[20]

Responding to Trypho's suggestion that Christ was *a god*, Justin wrote, "And Trypho answered, '. . . often the prophets employed this manner of

---

[19]Justin, "Dialogue With Trypho," *Ante-Nicene Fathers*, Alexander Roberts and James Donaldson, eds. (Eerdmans, 1961), Vol. I, p. 228.
[20]Ibid. Vol. I, p. 166, 185.

speech saying that Thy God is a God of gods and a Lord of lords, adding frequently the great and strong and terrible [God]. For such expressions are used not as if they really were gods, but because the Scripture is teaching us that the true God, who made all things, is Lord alone of those who are reputed gods and Lords.'

"And I asked Trypho—'Do you think God appeared to Abraham under the oak in Mamre as Scripture asserts?' He said 'Most assuredly.' 'Was He one of those three,' I said, 'whom Abraham saw and whom the Holy Spirit of prophesy describes as men?' He said, 'No; but God appeared to him before the vision of the three. Then those three that the Scripture calls men were angels; two of them sent to destroy Sodom and one to announce the joyful tidings to Sarah that she would bear a son. . . .' 'How then,' said I, 'does the one of the three who was in the tent and who said "I shall return to thee hereafter and Sarah shall have a son" appear to have returned when Sarah had begotten a son and to be there declared by the prophetic word *God*? (Gen. 21:9–12). Have you perceived then that He who said under the oak that He would return, since He knew it would be necessary to advise Abraham to do what Sarah wished him, came back as it is written; and is God as the words declare when they so speak "God said to Abraham, Let it not be grievous in thy sight because of the son and because of the bond-woman?"

" 'Reverting to the Scriptures I shall endeavor to persuade you that He who is said to have appeared to Abraham and to Jacob and to Moses and who is called God is distinct from Him who made all things—numerically, I mean, not in will. For I affirm that He has never at any time done anything which He who made the world—above whom there is no other God— has not wished Him both to do and to engage himself with. . . .

" 'It must be admitted absolutely that some other one is called Lord by the Holy Spirit besides Him who is considered maker of all things; not solely by Moses, but also by David. For there is written by him, "The Lord says to my Lord sit on my right hand until I make Thine enemies Thy footstool" (Ps. 110:1). And again in other words, "Thy throne O God is for ever and ever. A scepter of equity is the scepter of thy kingdom: thou hast loved righteousness and hated iniquity; therefore God, even thy God has anointed thee with the oil of gladness above thy fellows" (Ps. 45:6– 7). If therefore you assert that the Holy Spirit calls some other one God and Lord besides the Father of all things and His Christ, answer me; for I undertake to prove to you from Scriptures themselves, that He whom the Scripture calls Lord is not one of the two angels that went to Sodom but He who was with them and is called God, that appeared to Abraham.'

"And Trypho said, 'Prove this; for as you see the day advances and we are not prepared for such perilous replies; since never yet have we heard any man investigating or searching into or proving these matters; nor would we have tolerated your conversation had you not referred everything to the Scriptures, for you are very zealous in adducing proofs from them; and you are of opinion that there is no God above the maker of all things.' " Justin quoted from memory Genesis 18:13–16, then finished with these words: " ' "And the Lord rained on Sodom and Gomorrah sulphur and fire from the Lord out of heaven; and He overthrew all these cities. . . ." ' And after another pause, I added, 'And now have you not perceived my friends that one of the three who is both God and Lord and ministers to Him who is in the heavens is Lord of the two angels? . . . And He is the Lord who received commission from the Lord who [remains] in the heavens (i.e., the maker of all things) to inflict upon Sodom and Gomorrah the (judgments) which the Scripture describes in these terms: "The Lord rained down upon Sodom and Gomorrah sulphur and fire from the Lord out of heaven."

" 'I shall give you another testimony, my friends,' said I, 'from the Scriptures that God begat before all creatures a Beginning [who was] a certain rational power [proceeding] from himself who is called by the Holy Spirit now *the Glory of the Lord*, now the *Son*, again *Wisdom*, again an *Angel*, then *God* and then *Lord* and *Logos*. . . . The Word of Wisdom, who is himself this God begotten of the Father of all things and Word and Wisdom and Power and the Glory of the Begetter will bear evidence to me when He speaks by Solomon.' " Justin quoted Proverbs 8:22ff.[21]

Justin Martyr expressly taught the full deity of Christ as the uncreated God, and strongly intimates, if not actually states, a Trinitarian doctrine.

Tertullian, A.D. 145–220

Tertullian faced people in his time who were critics of this absolute of wonder of Jesus' divinity. He too believed in and defended a Trinitarian view, devoting an *entire book* to answering critics.

His book begins by dealing with true unity and diversity as follows:

"In various ways the Devil has rivaled and resisted the truth. Sometimes his aim has been to destroy the truth by defending it. He maintains there is only one Lord the almighty Creator of the world in order that out of this doctrine of the unity he may fabricate a heresy. . . .

"In that all are of one by unity [that is] of substance; while the mystery of the dispensation is still guarded which distributes the unity into a Trinity, placing in their order the three persons—the Father, the Son, and the Holy Ghost; three, however, not in condition, but in degree; not in substance, but in form; not in power, but in aspect; yet of one substance, and of one condition and of one power inasmuch as He is one God from whom these degrees and forms and aspects are reckoned under the name of the Father and of the Son and of the Holy Ghost. . . .

"The simple indeed (I will not call them unwise and unlearned) who always constitute the majority of believers are startled at the dispensation [of the Three in One] on the ground that the very rule of their faith withdraws them from the world's plurality of gods to the one only true God, not understanding that although He is the one only God, He must yet be believed in with his own *oikonomia* [office]. . . . They are constantly throwing out against us that we are preachers of two gods and three gods while they take to themselves preeminently the credit of being worshipers of the one God. . . .

<hr>

[21]Ibid. Vol. I, p. 223–224.

"I may therefore lay this down as a fixed principle that even then before the creation of the universe God was not alone, since He had within himself both Reason, and inherent in Reason His Word, which He made second to himself by agitating it within himself. . . . This Power and disposition of the Divine Intelligence is set forth also in the Scripture under the name wisdom. . . .

"Listen therefore to Wisdom herself constituted in the character of a second person. 'At first the Lord created Me as the beginning of His ways with a view to His own works before He made the earth, before the hills were settled; moreover before all the hills did He beget Me'—that is to say He created and generated Me in His own intelligence.

"This then is the perfect nativity of the Word when He proceeds forth from God—formed (*conditus*) by Him first to devise and think out all things under the name of Wisdom—the 'Lord created or formed (*condidit*) Me as the beginning of His ways' (Prov. 8:22) then afterwards begat Me to carry all into effect—'When He prepared the heaven I was present with Him.' Thus does He make Him equal to Him: for by proceeding from himself He became His first-begotten Son, because He is begotten before all things; and His only begotten also because alone begotten of God in a way peculiar to himself from the womb of His own heart—even as the Father himself testifies (Ps. 45)." Tertullian here does not teach that Christ is not eternal nor that He is simply a created being; but that He was "*condidit*" (Latin) generated from the Father in the beginning of His ways-(not His *works*). This he makes very plain:

"The Word therefore is both always in the Father as He says, 'I am in the Father' and is always with God according to what is written, 'and the Word was with God,' and never separate from the Father or other than the Father 'since I and the Father are One.' This will be the prolation taught by the truth, the guardian of the unity wherein we declare, that the Son is a prolation from the Father without being separated from Him. . . .

"Bear always in mind that this is the rule of faith which I profess; by it I testify that the Father and the Son and the Spirit are inseparable from each other and so you will know in what sense this is said. Now observe my assertion is that the Father is one and the Son one and the Spirit one and that they are distinct from each other. This statement is taken in a wrong sense by every uneducated as well as every perversely disposed person as if it predicated a diversity in such a sense as to imply a separation among the Father and the Son and the Spirit. . . .

"Thus the Father is distinct from the Son, being greater than the Son, inasmuch as He who begets is one and He who is begotten is another; He too who sends is one and He who is sent is another."

Tertullian certainly believed in a Trinity, as well as the fact that Jesus was God, although not the Father; and (as Christians have believed) Christ is distinct from and subordinate in a chain of authority to the father.[22]

---

[22]"Against Praxeas," *Ante-Nicene Fathers*. Vol. VII, pp. 597–599, 601; Vol. III, p. 603–604.

Theophilus, A.D. 115–181

Theophilus not only also used the term *Trinity* as if it was a common one, but makes clear that Christ is both uncreated and truly God. Here are his original assertions:

"He is God alone who made light out of darkness, and brought forth light from His treasures. . . . This is my God, the Lord of all, who alone stretched out the heaven . . . God, by His own Word and Wisdom made all things; for 'By His Word were the heavens made and all the host by the breath of His mouth.' Most excellent is His Wisdom. By His Wisdom God founded the earth . . .

"They [the prophets] taught us with one consent God made all things out of nothing; for nothing was coeval with God: but He being His own place and wanting nothing and existing before the ages, willed to make man. . . . God then, having His own Word internal (*endiatheton*) within His own bowels begat Him, emitting Him along with His own Wisdom before all things. He had this Word as a helper in the things that were created by Him, and by Him He made all things. For the prophets were not when the world came into existence, but the Wisdom of God which was in Him and His holy Word was always present with Him. Wherefore He speaks thus by the prophet Solomon—'When He prepared the heavens I was there and when He appointed the foundations of the earth I was with Him, putting things in order.' [Prov. 8:27 *LXX*] . . .

"Moreover God is found as if needing help, to say 'Let us make man in Our image, after Our likeness.' But to no one else than to his own Word and Wisdom did He say 'Let *Us* make.'. . .

"For the sun is a type of God and the moon of man. And as the sun far surpasses the moon in power and glory, so far does God surpass man. . . . The moon wanes monthly and in manner dies, being a type of man; then it is born again, and is crescent for a pattern of the future resurrection. In like manner also, the three days which were before the luminaries are types of the Trinity (*Triados*), of God, and His Word and His Wisdom." (Theophilus uses *wisdom* here for the Holy Spirit, but in other places for the Son.)

Notice that Theophilus uses the word *trinity* as a word in common use. It seems that he used it in the same way in his lost works. It is certain here that God, His Word and His Wisdom constitute this Trinity and it is a Trinity of persons.

"The God and Father indeed of all cannot be contained, and is not found in a place for there is no place of his rest; but His Word, through whom He made all things, being His power and His Wisdom assuming the person of the Father and Lord of all, went into the garden in the person of God and conversed with Adam. For the divine writing itself teaches us that Adam said that he heard the Voice of God. But what else is this Voice but the Word of God who is also His Son? Not as the poets and writers of myths talk of the sons of gods begotten from intercourse, but as truth expounds, the Word, that always exists, residing within the heart of God. For before anything came into being He had Him as a counselor, being His own mind and thought. But, when God wished to make all that He determined on, He begot this Word, . . . the first-born of all creation, not himself being emptied of the Word, but having begotten Reason and always conversing with His Reason. . . .

"And hence the holy writings teach us, . . . 'In the beginning was the Word and the Word was with God,' showing that at first God was alone and the Word in Him. Then he says, 'The Word was God; all things came into existence through Him and apart from Him not one thing came into existence.' The Word then, being God, and being naturally produced from God, whenever the Father wills He sends Him to any place; and He, coming, is both seen and heard, being sent by Him and is found in a place."[23]

Novation, A.D. 210–280

Novation, like other Church fathers, wrote on the personality of the Holy Spirit. He not only used the term "He" concerning the Holy Spirit (as if assuming common use of the word in reference to the Spirit), but makes clear that the Holy Spirit is both uncreated being and truly God. His treatise *On The Trinity* was written about A.D. 257.

"But when the Lord says that God is a Spirit I think that something still more should be understood than merely that God is a Spirit. . . . For we find it to be written that God is called *love* and yet from this the substance of God is not declared to be love; and that He is called *light*, while in this is not the substance of God. . . .

"Moreover, the order of reason and the authority of the faith in the disposition of the words and in the Scriptures of the Lord, admonish us after these things to believe also on the Holy Spirit once promised to the Church and in the appointed occasions of times given. For He was promised by Joel the prophet but given by Christ.

"And He is not new in the Gospel nor yet even newly given; for it was He himself who accused the people in the prophets and in the apostles gave them the appeal to the Gentiles. Assuredly in the Spirit there are different kinds of offices because in the times there is a different order of occasions; and yet on this account, He who discharges these offices is not different nor is He another in so acting but He is one and the same distributing His offices according to the times and the occasions and impulses of things.

"For, said He [Christ], 'I will pray the Father and He will give you another Advocate that He may be with you for ever, even the Spirit of truth' (John 14:16–17). And 'If I go not away that Advocate shall not come to you; but if I go away I will send Him to you.' . . . This is He who places prophets in the Church, instructs teachers, directs tongues, gives powers and healings, does wonderful works, offers discrimination of spirits, affords powers of government, suggests counsels, and orders and arranges whatever other gifts there are of charismata; and thus make the Lord's Church everywhere and in all perfected and completed. . . .

---

[23]Theophilus, "To Autolycus," *Ante-Nicene Fathers*, Alexander Roberts and James Donaldson, eds. (Eerdmans, 1961), pp. 91, 101, 103.

"Of Him also he tells: 'Now the Spirit speaketh plainly, that in the last times some shall depart from the faith, giving heed to seducing spirits, doctrines of demons, who speak lies in hypocrisy having their conscience cauterized.' (1 Tim. 4:1). 'Whoever shall blaspheme against Him hath not forgiveness not only in this world but also not in the world to come' (Matt. 12:32)."[24]

The Common Testimony

The early Church fathers form an impressive testimony of the common acceptance in their day of this marvelous absolute: God is triune. Because they were so close to those who recorded the New Testament, their writings give added weight to its truth.

---

[24]Novation, *Ante-Nicene Fathers*, op. cit. Vol. V, pp. 640–641.

CHAPTER TEN

COROLLARY ONE: THE FATHER, SON, AND HOLY SPIRIT ARE ONE IN NATURE

Scriptures

"Hear O Israel: The LORD our God is one LORD." (Deut. 6:4; cf. Mark 12:29)

There Are None Beside Him

"Unto thee it was shewed, that thou mightest know that the LORD he is God; there is none else beside him . . . there is none else." (Deut. 4:35, 39)

"Wherefore thou art great, O LORD God: for there is none like thee, neither is there any God beside thee." (2 Sam. 7:22)

"For thou art great . . . thou art God alone." (Ps. 86:10)

"That ye may know and believe me, and understand that I am he; before me there was no God formed, neither shall there be after me." (Isa. 43:10)

"Is there a God beside me? yea, there is no God; I know not any." (Isa. 44:8)

There Are None Like Him

"And he said, LORD God of Israel, there is no God like thee, in heaven above, or on earth beneath." (1 Kings 8:23)

"To whom then will ye liken God? or what likeness will ye compare unto him?" (Isa. 40:18)

"To whom will ye liken me, and make me equal, and compare me, that we may be like?" (Isa. 46:5)

"Remember the former things of old: for I am God, and there is none else; I am God, and there is none like me." (Isa. 46:9)

There Is None With Him

"Know therefore this day, and consider it in thine heart, that the LORD he is God in heaven above and upon the earth beneath; there is none else. Thou shalt keep therefore his statutes." (Deut. 4:39–40)

"See now that I, even I, am he, and there is no god with me." (Deut. 32:39)

"There is no god with me; I kill, and I make alive; I wound, and I heal: neither is there any that can deliver out of my hand. For I lift up my hand to heaven, and say, I live for ever." (Deut. 32:39–40)

"That they may know from the rising of the sun, and from the west, that there is none beside me. I am the LORD, and there is none else." (Isa. 45:6)

"Look unto me, and be ye saved, all the ends of the earth: for I am God, and there is none else." (Isa. 45:22)

"Yet I am the LORD thy God from the land of Egypt, and thou shalt know no god but me: for there is no saviour beside me." (Hos. 13:4)

There Is Only One God

"For there is one God; and there is none other but he." (Mark 12:32)

"I and my Father are one." (John 10:30)

"Jesus saith unto him, Have I been so long time with you, and yet hast thou not known me Philip? *he that hath seen me hath seen the Father*; and how sayest thou then, Shew us the Father? Believest thou not that I *am in the Father* and the Father in me?" (John 14:9–10)

"But when the Comforter is come, whom I will send unto you from the Father, even the Spirit of truth, which proceedeth from the Father, he shall testify of me." (John 15:26)

"That they all may be one; as thou, Father, *art in me, and I in thee*, that they also may be *one in us*: that the world may believe that thou hast sent me. And the glory which thou gavest me I have given them; that they may be one, even as we are one: I in them and thou in me, that they may be made perfect in one." (John 17:21–23)

"We know that an idol is nothing in the world, and that there is none other God but one." (1 Cor. 8:4)

"Now there are diversities of gifts, but the *same Spirit*. And there are differences of administrations, but the *same Lord*. And there are diversities of operations, but it is the *same God* which worketh all in all." (1 Cor. 12:4–6)

"Now a mediator is not a mediator of one, but God is one." (Gal. 3:20)

"There is one body, and *one Spirit*, even as ye are called in one hope of your calling; *one Lord*, one faith, one baptism, *one God* and Father of all, who is above all, and through all, and in you all." (Eph. 4:4–6)

"For there is one God, and one mediator between God and men, the man Christ Jesus." (1 Tim. 2:5)

"Thou believest that there is one God; thou doest well: the devils also believe, and tremble." (James 2:19)

Bible Word Study

The Bible uses many different words to convey the idea of oneness. Hebrew alone has at least five different words that are translated *one*. Two of them in particular are significant.

One (Hebrew)

yachad *(Yakh-ad)*—A Unit. From *yaw-khad*, which means to be or become one. Often translated as "only." Also related to *yachiyd*, which means "sole," or by implication, "beloved," "darling"; also "lonely."[1]

Yachad is used in scriptures such as Gen. 22:12 where Abraham offers his *only* son Isaac to the Lord; of Jephtha's daughter, who was his only child (Judg. 11:34); or when God judges or chastises either a nation or "a man only" (Job 34:29). The writer of Proverbs calls himself "my father's son, tender and only beloved in the sight of my mother" (4:3); the writer of the prophetic Psalm 22:20 cries out that God will deliver His "darling" (only one); and others mourn for an "only son" (Jer. 6:26; Zech. 12:10).

The emphasis of this word is a focus on the special or the solitary. It is used significantly this way twelve times in the Old Testament; but *never once* is it used to denote the unity of God. The clear implication is that whatever kind of unity God is, it is not a simple singularity.

bad *(bad)*—Properly means "separation." As an adverb it means "apart," or "only." From *badad*, which means "to divide," "be solitary."[2]

This word and its derivatives are sometimes used when God stresses that people are to trust in Him and in Him alone (Ex. 22:20). Hezekiah used this word when he spread the letter from Sennacherib before God and said, "Save thou us out of his hand, that all the kingdoms of the earth may know that thou art the Lord God, even thou only" (2 Kings 19:19).

David used it when he spoke of going in the strength of God, making mention "of thy righteousness, even of thine only" (Ps. 71:16), and "who only doeth wondrous things" (Ps. 72:18). Samuel exhorted Israel to "return

---

[1] *Strong's* 3162; also 3161, 3173.
[2] *Strong's* 905; also 909.

unto the Lord with all your hearts . . . prepare your hearts unto the Lord, and serve Him only" (1 Sam. 7:3).

echad (*ekh-awd*)—Properly means "united," (i.e., one), or (as an ordinal) "first."[3]

This is the word God uses to describe combining the waters into "one place" (Gen. 1:9); that man is become as "one of us" (Gen. 3:22); two becoming "one flesh" in marriage (Gen. 2:24); and the earth becoming united in "one language and one speech" (Gen. 11:1).

Echad is the word used for compound plurality, for a unity that is not a simple singularity; the kind of word you use for "a bunch" of grapes. It is a collective unity; the "one" of "one nation under God" or "one body."

Significantly, this is the word that is always used with reference to God being *one*. When Israel declares their national faith, *"Shem 'a yisrael yehovah' eloheynu yehovah echad"* ("The LORD our God is *one* Lord"—Deut. 6:4), they use *echad*, meaning compound unity, for *one*. Even the word used here for God (*Elohim*) is a plural.

Bullinger comments on the word *one* here: "Hebrew *echad*—a compound unity . . . It is one made up of others: Gen. 1:5, one of seven; 2:11, one of four; 2:21, one of 24; 2:24, one made up of two; 3:22, one of the three; 49:16, one of twelve and Num. 13:23, one of a cluster. It is not *yahid* (Latin *unicus*—unique, single) . . . which occurs 12 times: Gen. 22:20; 25:16; 35:17; 68:6; Prov. 4:3; Jer. 6:26; Amos 8:10; Zech 12:10. The Hebrew of all the other words for one is *echad*."[4]

Zechariah writes of the time when "the LORD shall be king over all the earth: in that day shall there be *one* [*echad*] LORD and his name one" (Zech. 14:9).

iysh (*eesh*)—Possibly from an unused root meaning "to be extant"; a man as an individual or a male person. Often used as an adjunct to a more definite term (and in such cases frequently not expressed in translation). Many times used in conjunction with other more definite terms to mean "one" in the sense of some person, some man.[5] Though one of the most frequent words for *one* in the OT, it will not be the focus of our study.

One (Greek)

monos (*mon-os*)—Remaining (i.e., sole or single). Translated in the KJV as "alone," "only," "by themselves."[6]

Monos is used by Jesus in His command to serve "only one God" (Matt. 4:10); that the coming day is known to no man nor angel but "my Father only" (Matt. 24:36); and of Jesus himself as the "only-begotten Son" (John 1:14, 18).

---

[3]*Strong's* 259.
[4]Ethelbert Bullinger, *The Companion Bible*, p. 247.
[5]*Strong's* 376.
[6]*Strong's* 3441.

In Christ's prayer to the Father, He calls Him "the only true God" (John 17:3), and Paul calls Him "God only wise" (Rom. 16:27; 1 Tim. 1:17). He is the "blessed and only Potentate" (1 Tim. 6:15) "who only has immortality" (1 Tim. 6:16), and is the one to whom those who stand on the sea of glass and fire sing and proclaim, "Who shall not fear thee, O Lord, and glorify thy name? for thou only art holy: for all nations shall come and worship before thee" (Rev. 15:4).

heis (*hice*)—A primary numeral; one.[7] *Heis* is the most common word for *one* in the NT, being used 271 times.

It is used in Matthew where Jesus says, "There is none good but one, that is, God" (Matt. 19:17); "one is your master, even Christ" (23:8), and "one is your Father, which is in heaven" (23:9).

Mark uses *heis* for "who can forgive sins but God only?" (Mark 2:7). *Heis* is the NT equivalent of the Hebrew *echad*: "The Lord our God is one [*heis*] Lord" (Mark 12:29); and "there is one [*heis*] God; and there is none other but he" (Mark 12:32).

Mary did the "one thing needful" (Luke 10:42); not one sparrow is forgotten before God (Luke 12:6); and there is joy in heaven over "one sinner that repenteth" (Luke 15:10). In John, Jesus claims that He and His Father are one (10:30); He prays that the disciples will be one as He and the Father are one (17:11, 21), and be "made perfect in one" (17:23).

"*Heis* is the word used of "none other God but one" (1 Cor. 8:4), "one God" (1 Cor. 8:6), one Spirit (1 Cor. 12:11, 13), and one Lord Jesus Christ (1 Cor. 8:6). In Galatians, distinction is made between "seeds" (many) and "as of one seed" [Christ] (3:16); that a mediator is not a mediator of one, but "God is one" (3:20); and that in His body there is neither Jew nor Greek, bond nor free, male nor female for we are "all one" in Christ Jesus (3:28). *Heis* is likewise the word used for one Lord, faith and baptism (Eph. 4:5); "one God, and one mediator between God and men" (1 Tim. 2:5); and the fact that the Spirit, the water and the blood "agree as one" (1 John 5:8).

"Unity in the NT is always seen from the standpoint of Christ . . . (Acts 4:12). In Greek and Roman philosophy, the unity of God and the world is demanded by educated reason. In the OT the unity of God is a confession derived from the experience of God's unique reality. The decisive advance in the NT, caused by God himself, is the basing of the unity and uniqueness of God on the unique revelation through and in the one man Jesus Christ, the Revealer and Lord (Matt. 23:8ff.; 1 Cor. 8:4ff.; Eph. 4:1–16; 1 Tim. 2:5f.). . . .

"The reality of the one God comes from the fact that for us (i.e., for our gain) there is one Lord Jesus Christ (1 Cor. 8:6). . . . Indeed the unity of the Spirit is based on Jesus (1 Cor. 13; Eph. 4), not on a unity of outlook based on human enthusiasm. . . . The foundation and continuity of the church's unity are grounded in Him as the one shepherd of the one flock (John 10:14ff.)."[8]

---

[7]*Strong's* 1520.

[8]K.H. Bartels, *The New International Dictionary of New Testament Theology*, Colin Brown, ed. (Grand Rapids: Zondervan Publishing House, 1971), vol. 2, pp. 722–723.

One Faith for Mankind

The Bible does not command us to believe in God; it commands us to make sure the God we believe in is the true God. The first commandment does not forbid atheism but *idolatry*. It follows then that the most obvious consequence of there being but one true God is that there is really only one true faith, and one true spiritual belief system for all mankind.

William Pope points out that in the quest for religious truth, man has always erred from reality in one of two major ways: polytheism (many gods) and pantheism (everthing is God). Between these two poles of error fall all other false representations of God.

The names of God guard us from stumbling into any of these false religious systems. They both secure our view of Him from error and encompass all the reality of which these systems are but perversions. These "essential and personal names for God pervade Scripture; distinct, related to each other and combined with other names. They convey to the mind a representative idea of the Divine Being which although standing for a reality unsearchable in itself, effectually defends it from every perversion of the notion of God."[9]

Elohim—The first pervading name of the Supreme Being in early revelation. It may be derived from a primitive root signifying power, or the effect of power in fear; in its simplest root probably underived. Though "occurring sometimes poetically in the singular it is generally in the plural, expressing the abundance, fullness and glory of the powers of the Divine nature." Treated sometimes as a plural or intensive of majesty, it is always joined with the singular verb; as such it cannot be "consistent with such an abstract monotheism as to leave no place for the Scriptural doctrine of the Trinity."[10]

Jehovah (*YHWH*)—Denotes essential and absolute being, uniting what to man is present, past, and future in one eternal existence. This name is explained by God himself; *He who is*, or *He who is what He is*; uniting as it were the abstract idea of pure being with the process of continual becoming through revelation to His people. He is eternally steadfast in the perpetual revelation of His nature and relations.

Jehovah "was regarded for the most part as too holy to be communicable. Thus although . . . it will be found written, LORD in the King James Version, yet when it was read aloud other names such as *Adonai* were (at all events by the third century B.C.) vocally substituted. . . . Typographically the name is represented by four Hebrew consonants, the Tetragrammaton. Etymologically it represents a slight modification of the Hebrew verb *to be* which also signifies *to breathe*. . . .

"The Hebrew word for *Jew* is derived from the same verb; so that a

---

[9]William Pope, *Compendium of Christian Theology*, 1881.

[10]Owen Barfield, *Saving the Appearances: A Study in Idolatry* (Harcourt Brace Janovich, 1965).

devout Jew could not name his own race without recalling, nor affirm his own existence without tending to utter the Tetragrammaton. Written as all Hebrew words were without vowels, when any true child of Israel perused the unspoken Name *YHWH* it must have seemed to come whispering up as it were, from the depths of his own being!"[11]

These are the two Supreme Names—given by Himself and not derived from heathenism—of the Divine Being in the Bible. All others are variations on them, or these with additional appelatives that link them with the attributes of the Godhead.

Adonai—This plural name of God denotes His dominion as Lord, which Jehovah does not. The Jews mainly used the vowel points of this word in writing and pronouncing the Name to them above every name which they thus veiled in reverence; hence it coalesced with the latter when it was translated and passed into the New Testament as *Kurios*. The testimony of Thomas to the deity of Christ, "My Lord and my God" (John 20:28), echoes the *"Adonai Elohai"* of the Psalms. Revelation 1:8 records the last revelation of God in the person of Christ, which sums up all the divine names in one remarkable verse: "I am Alpha and Omega, the beginning and the ending, saith the Lord, which is, and which was, and which is to come, the Almighty." Here are all the Greek representatives of the Hebrew names Elohim, Jehovah, Adonai, Shaddai; with their meaning as absolute, personal being."[12]

The two great perversions of thought concerning the divine nature which have been found whenever men have been left to their own devices—polytheism and pantheism in all their forms—are by these names explained at once and condemned.

Polytheism (Many Gods)

"Polytheism is the human corruption of these divine truths: that *Elohim* is the god of unbounded internal fullness of life and external manifestations of creative wealth. In heathenism, *Elohim* becomes a universe of deified and worshiped powers; and *Jehovah* degenerates into the special and local imaginary god of each worshiping nation. In the Eastern systems of dualism, *Elohim* was perverted into the creative forces of darkness and evil, *Jehovah* into the coeternal God of light and goodness. . . .

"From beginning to end the Bible contains no acknowledgement of the reality of other gods. It is true we read 'The Lord [Jehovah] is greater than all gods' [Ex. 18:11] (the testimony of Jethro, a heathen) and 'Who is like unto thee, O Lord [Jehovah], among the gods?' in the song of Moses [Ex. 15:11]. . . . But throughout the scriptures the other gods are 'vanities' or 'nothings.' According to Paul, Gentiles 'sacrifice to devils' [1 Cor. 10:20] . . . evil spirits that rule over the empire of idolatry. But Paul, like all the ancient prophets makes the false gods and their idols identical; both being 'nothing in the world' [1 Cor. 8:4].

---

[11]Ibid. p. 1113.
[12]Pope, op. cit. p. 251

" 'The Lord our God is one Lord and His name One and the only true God.' This is the sublime testimony of the opening of Genesis and is confirmed throughout revelation. The Pantheon of heathenism has its altar; but that altar is erected to 'that which is not god.' "[13]

Pantheism (Everything Is God)

"Pantheism in every age, in the East and West, in ancient and modern times has been the prevalent philosophical error in speculation of this high subject. Unlike Polytheism, it aims to simplify the idea of the supreme; but its simplification reduces Him to *pan kai to en*, the unity of the world, or the universe. As such Pantheism makes God the sum of things in the sense of elevating Him above personality. . . .

"Modern Materialism unconsciously adopts a pantheistic character. Its unknown and unknowable *Force* or *Law* is the irrational expression of the same thought. . . .

"Pantheism perverts the doctrine of divine unity by making God the sum of all personalities and forces, but not Himself a distinct Personality. Psalm 94:9 is the refutation of Pantheism in all its future or possible forms: 'He that planted the ear shall He not hear? he that formed the eye, shall He not see?' Still more expressly however is the true unity of God opposed to this one system of false unity in all those passages that speak of the one Creator of all things: 'Thus saith God the Lord, he that created the heavens, and stretched them out; he that spread forth the earth, and that which cometh out of it' (Isa. 42:5)."[14]

One Absolute Personality: Elohim-Jehovah

The scriptural doctrine that protests against both perversions. God is the one Absolute Personality. This is the teaching of both names, especially in their union. Each denotes the soleness, the necessity, the infinity of the divine being as *Spiritus Independens*; and each is connected with man and the creature in such a way as to not only permit, but demand the most definite personality or self-determining relation to the beings whom He calls into existence.

"This double name expresses clearly all Pantheism labored in vain to express, but forever precludes its error. It avows infinite fullness of life and possibility in the eternal essence; but assigns all to the controlling will of a person.

"Scripture scarcely ever approaches the notion of an abstract entity; it invariably makes both *Elohim* and *Jehovah* the subjects of endless predicates and predicative assumptions. 'In Him we live, and move, and have our being' [Acts 17:28]; in Him, a Person to be sought and found. In fact, the personality of God as a Spirit of self-conscious and independent individuality is as deeply stamped upon His revelation of himself as is His

[13]William Pope, op. cit. pp. 251–254.
[14]Ibid.

existence. We are created in His image; our Archetype has in eternal reality the being which we possess as shadows of Him; He has in eternal truth the personality which we know to be our own characteristic, though we hold it in fealty from Him."[15]

I Am—The Personal, Infinite God

"No subtlety of modern philosophy has ever equalled the definition of the absolute *I Am*; the English words give the right meaning of the original only when it lays the stress upon the *Am* for the essential being, and the *I* for the personality of that being."[16]

Variation in Names

"The long succession of names given the Deity in the OT show the confrontation with error in both forms (but especially the Polytheistic) more fully from age to age. These variations gradually introduced are all connected with appendages that guard the majesty of the one God. When the name Jehovah was made prominent as the covenant-name for His own people, certain peculiarities in its use taught important lessons. Neither the people nor individuals might say, 'My Jehovah'; it was enough to say, 'My *Elohim*', or 'Jehovah my Lord.'. . .

"Nor do we ever read of '*the* Jehovah' as if He were or might be one of many. The Scripture often speaks of 'the living God' as if in opposition to the gods which are dead nothings. But it never speaks of 'the living Jehovah,' though it is very frequent to make the eternal life of Jehovah the highest oath, as 'the Lord liveth!'

"Very much importance has been attached to the laws which regulate the use of *Elohim* and *Jehovah* respectively; and one of those laws will be found by careful observation to be the attestation of the unity of God of the whole earth and His peculiar relation to the entire race of mankind as the God of the covenant of redemption yet to be revealed.

"The plural name *Elohim* lays down the indefinite and mysterious foundation for a plurality of Persons in the Godhead; while the singular Jehovah for ever guards the unity of God."[17]

"Herein lay the mystery of the Divine Name. It was 'that name in which there is no participation between the Creator and any thing else.' So wrote the renowned Jewish Rabbi Maimonides in about the year 1190. And again: 'All the names of the Creator which are found in books are taken from His works, except one Name, the Tetragrammaton, which is proper to Him and is therefore called the Name apart—*Nomen separatum*; because it signifies the substance of the Creator by pure signification, in which there is no participation. His other glorious names do indeed signify by participation, because they are taken from His works.' "[18]

---

[15]Ibid. p. 254.
[16]Ibid. p. 254.
[17]Ibid. p. 254.
[18]Barfield, op. cit. p. 115.

Questions and Answers

Q: *What does the biblical phrase "The Lord our God is one Lord" (Deut. 6:4) mean?*

A: Ignatius wrote, "There is then one God the Father, and not two or three; one who is; and there is no other beside Him, the only true God. 'Hath not one God created us? Have we not all one Father?' And there is also one Son, God the Word, 'The only-begotten Son who is in the bosom of the Father.' And again 'One Lord Jesus Christ.' And there is also one Paraclete. 'For there is one Spirit since we have been called in one hope of our calling." And again 'We have drunk of one Spirit.' . . . And it is manifest that all these gifts possessed by believers worketh one and the self-same Spirit. There are not then either three Fathers or three Sons or three Paracletes but one Father, one Son and one Paraclete. Wherefore also the Lord, when He sent forth the apostles to make disciples of all nations, commanded them to baptize in the 'name of the Father, and of the Son, and of the Holy Ghost' (Matt. 28:19), not unto one person having three names, nor unto three persons who became incarnate, but into three possessed of equal honor."[1]

Q: *Why do Christians insist that there is only one God? What's wrong with the idea of more than one?*

A: The very idea of God includes the idea of absolute fullness and perfection, lacking anything. As Aquinas insisted, "God comprehends in himself the whole perfection of being. If many gods existed, they would necessarily differ from one another. Something would belong to one and not the other." If one were missing something unique and God-like that another possessed, he would not be perfect; and lacking completeness, he would hence not be God. "Hence the ancient philosophers, constrained as it were by truth itself, when they asserted an infinite principle, asserted likewise that there was only one such principle."[2]

Q: *How do you explain Deut. 10:17: "For the Lord your God is God of gods, and Lord of lords" in light of a monotheistic viewpoint?*

A: William Pettingill writes, "Satan is called the god of this age (2 Cor. 4:4). The gods of the heathen world are said to be demons in 1 Cor. 10:20. In addition to this there are doubtless many imaginary gods. But Jehovah is Sovereign over them all, and in the absolute sense there is no God but He."[3]

---

[1]Ignatius, "To the Philippians," *Ante-Nicene Fathers*, Alexander Roberts and James Donaldson, eds. (Grand Rapids: Eerdmans, 1961), vol. 1, p. 116.

[2]Thomas Aquinas, "Summa Theologica," *Great Books of the Western World*, Robert M. Hutchins and Mortimer Adler, eds. (Chicago: Encyclopaedia Britannica, 1952), part 1, article 3, p. 49.

[3]William Pettinghill, *Bible Questions Answered* (Grand Rapids: Zondervan Publishing House, 1932), p. 20.

Q: *How do you explain 1 Cor. 8:5–6? What does "gods many and lords many" mean?*

A: The context of the passage answers that question. "We know that an idol is nothing in the world, and that there is none other God but one. For though there be that are *called* gods . . . to us there is but one God, the Father of whom are all things and we in Him; and one Lord Jesus Christ, by whom are all things, and we by Him. Howbeit there is not in every man that knowledge . . ." (1 Cor. 8:4–7).

Q: *But this verse insists that there is* no *other God but one. Since this obviously refers to the Father, doesn't it mean that Jesus cannot be God?"*

A: No, no more than the phrase "one Lord Jesus Christ" says that the Father cannot also be Lord. The teaching of the unity of the Godhead and the deity of each member is too strong in the rest of Scripture to interpret it any other way.

Q: *Doesn't the Bible say we are gods (Ps. 82:6)? Didn't Jesus call people "gods" in reference to that same verse (John 10:34)?*

A: The word "gods" is not used exclusively of the one true God and the devil or false gods (2 Cor. 4:4; Acts 7:43), but is occasionally used generically as a special title of those given honor by God: the prophets, judges, and kings of Israel. For instance, in Ex. 22:9 when a man is charged with trespass, his judges are called *ha-elohim* or "gods," because they represent God and act in His stead. (See also Ex. 18:15–19; 21:6; Rom. 13:1–6.) Thus Ex. 22:28 declares, "Thou shalt not revile the gods, nor curse the ruler of thy people." This is because leaders are, according to Fletcher, "appointed to be types of [Christ,] the Head of the prophets and Judge of all the earth . . . the Sum and Substance of all types and figures . . . King of kings, the Lord of lords."[4]

However in other cases, God himself brings judgment on those leaders he calls "gods." This is especially true of the passage Jesus quotes: "He judgeth among the gods. . . . I have said ye are gods and all of you are children of the most high; but ye shall die like men and fall like one of the princes" (Ps. 82:1, 6–7).

Q: *Didn't God make us little gods when He made us in His own image— spiritual beings like himself?*

A: We are like God only in the sense that we were created to mirror His purity, truth, and love. But remember that He is the only *unmade* one, and it is what He is in His essential uncreated being that makes Him both distinct and different from all the rest of His beloved creation— including man. That spirit God gives us belongs originally to Him, not us. The spirit of which we are created is finite, not uncreated being.

Q: *Could God do something bad?*

A: No, because His conduct is eternally determined by His character, and

---

[4]John Fletcher, *The Works of John Fletcher* (Schmul Reprints, 1974), vol. 2, p. 413.

that character is eternally referenced to His value, something that is unchanging and unchangeable.

Q: *But doesn't the Bible say that God can hate and love at the same time?*

A: The attributes of God are never in conflict with each other. It is as possible for God to love a sinner and hate his sin as it is possible for us to hate what we are doing wrong precisely because we care about ourselves.

Q: *The Bible says that God is the Judge of the whole earth (Gen. 18:25), which means He must uphold all true law, and yet as Father or Redeemer He is willing to let off a sinner. How can He be both merciful and just?*

A: He can be both because mercy and justice are part of the same ultimate law of love that requires the highest good for God and His creation. Sometimes that law demands justice (love for the whole); sometimes, when certain conditions such as atonement and repentant faith are met, it may allow mercy (love for the part in terms of the satisfaction of the whole).

The Unity of His Attributes

Q: *Isn't what God does the same as what He is? For God to exist is the same as to be kind, wise, or anything else, isn't it? (Obviously this is only true about God. It is certainly not true about anyone else.)*

A: The statement *God does = God is* is not the exact equivalent of *God is = God does*. God does not have to create in order to be Creator. But he does have to *be* Creator in order to create. What He *does* is just an indication of what He is; but what He *is* is not necessarily what He does. His existence precedes His actions.

Q: *If you separate God's essence from His attributes won't you eventually wind up with an impersonal abstraction?*

A: True. If we separate even a man's body from his personality we wind up with a dead man. But we are not talking about separation here; we are discussing *distinction*. To say that the triune God is one God in three distinct (not separate) persons is not only helpful but crucial to a biblical understanding of His nature. In a parallel way, we distinguish between the existence of His essential nature and His eternally consequent moral character for a coherent understanding of His ways and His works.

Q: *Isn't there a danger of exalting one attribute over another, saying that God is essentially this or that?*

A: True. But to emphasize one attribute without comparing it to another is not dangerous. The Bible does this all the time. Scripture reveals much about God's holiness but little about His happiness. Yet we know from revelation that God is both holy and happy. The process of thought requires the establishment of categories of some kind. To distinguish is not to divide. To categorize is not to separate.

Q: *But we cannot say, "God is loving," when we really mean, "God is love." We cannot say that God is love only when He does loving things.*

A: True. But neither can we say, "Love is God." Morality and essence are distinct and must be kept so. People can be kind but not be God; Jesus said, "If ye then, being evil, know how to give good gifts unto your children: how much more shall your heavenly Father . . ." (Luke 11:13). Moral attributes exist without the prerequisite of possessing divine being. Human beings, angels, and demons are moral but not divine.

Being and substance are not moral. This, while applied only to the created realm, was one of the errors of the neo-Platonists. The Manicheans thought substance was evil; and Augustine, who perhaps never fully got over the idea, carried some of the implications of that thought into his Christian writing. It is no divine revelation to move from saying "substance is evil" to saying "substance can be good," even if you tack on the idea that only created material substance is intrinsically evil and uncreated spiritual substance is intrinsically good.

Q: *Nevertheless, I believe there is no ultimate difference between virtue and essence.*

A: If virtue and essence are identical on any level, then any one truly virtuous is also truly God. But while careful to express all true virtue in terms that relate ultimately *to* God, the Bible does not say that all virtue *is* God. While one does not have to always be *doing* good things in order to be good, no one can be recognized as good, kind, or just without some expression of that virtue. God's character is known by His actions.

Q: *If so, how could God have always been good without a creation to express that virtue? Toward whom did He act virtuously before creating angels and man?*

A: Toward himself! The Father, the Son, and the Holy Spirit loved one another. Creation was an extended gift of love, God's purpose for other finite personalities is to share the love and virtue that has always existed.

Other Attempts at Unity

Q: *I met a person who calls himself a Unitarian. What does that mean?*

A: It used to mean "either the Christian or Catholic Unitarians, who maintained the truth of divine unity against all sorts of polytheists including Arians, while at the same time asserting this unity necessarily includes the Father, the Word and the Holy Spirit; or the Jewish or Socinian Unitarians who not only confine the Father to a barren, lonesome unity but as far as their influence reaches, tear Him from His beloved Son and even despoil Him of His paternity . . . we are tempted to call them Disuniters, Dividers of God, and manglers of the divine nature."[5]

---

[5]Fletcher, op. cit. p. 461.

Recently however it has become a creedless movement "stressing the many forms of divine revelation and the inherent goodness of man" so rejecting biblical doctrines like the trinity, the deity of Christ, the falleness of man, the atonement, and eternal damnation. It seeks instead to show that a "genuinely religious community can be created without doctrinal conformity," requiring only "openness to divine inspiration."[6]

Q: *What about Universalism? Is it the same thing?*

A: Although Unitarian and Universalist churches merged to form the Unitarian-Universalist association, universalism began in 1779 as a mix of a number of traditions, including Gnosticism and mysticism. Some American ministers adopted it in reaction to extreme predestinarian Calvinism which stressed both a selective atonement and an inherited moral depravity and damnation. The key platforms of Universalism are the ultimate salvation and perfectibility of *all* men (that Hell and judgment, if real, are not eternal), the "varied character of divine revelation, and the humanness of Christ." By 1942 it accepted "all humane men, Christian or not."[7]

Q: *What is the Unity School Of Christianity?*

A: A non-Christian religious institution begun in 1887 by Charles and Myrtle Fillmore from a synthesis of Christian Science and New Thought. It teaches salvation for all through a series of reincarnations and resurrections of the body, eternal life by purifying the body and overcoming sin, want, and illness through "right thinking" (i.e., "realizing that sin, sickness, old age and death are not real"). God is not considered personal, just a "Spiritual Principle, the total of all good," and Jesus is merely the perfect expression of this in all of us, the "true spiritual higher-self of every individual."[8]

Q: *What about the Unification Church?*

A: Unification is an Eastern religious movement founded by the Korean Sun Myung Moon. It incorporates Taoist ideas into its own concept of God and creation. Man is incarnate God just like Christ, Who was prematurely murdered, before He could accomplish His unsuccessful mission of providing God the Father a physical divine family. He, like Elijah who became John the Baptist, was to be reincarnated as a man in Korea, married to a woman, and together they would become the true parents of all mankind. Accepting this couple as divine parents is the Second Coming of Christ and will lead to the perfection and salvation of all mankind.

Q: *A Bahai man I met said that we all ultimately believe in the same God, we just call Him by different names. He said that all religions ultimately teach the same thing, that we don't all have to go through Jesus and*

[6]"Unitarian," *The New International Dictionary of the Christian Church*, James D. Douglas, ed. (Grand Rapids: Zondervan.), pp. 995–999.

[7]"Universalism," *The New International Dictionary of the Christian Church*, p. 1003.

[8]"Unity," *The New International Dictionary of the Christian Church*.

that we are all going to the same final destination. What does the Bible say?

A: "There is a way which seemeth right unto a man, but the end thereof are the ways of death" (Prov. 14:12). "Jesus saith unto him, I am the way, the truth, and the life: no man cometh unto the Father, but by me" (John 14:6).

Q: *If Christians all claim to love the same God and have "unity," then why are there so many different churches?*

A: Unity is not uniformity. True union, like the triune Godhead, is unity in diversity—essential oneness while preserving true difference and distinction. E. Stanley Jones said: "Christians are united in the deepest thing in life, namely in life itself—they share the same life in Christ. They are united in the center, in life, divided at the margin, in polity and ritual.

"But in this their unity with Christ is real, real christians are to be found in all different denominations, and this inner unity in Christ is manifested in very diverse forms.

We have then, three facts underlying the situation—*Unity, Equality,* and *Diversity.* Any scheme of union which does not take cognizance of these three things and build on them will probably fail—and ought to fail."[9]

Analysis and Discussion

Unity is perhaps the great quest of mankind. Ask any group of people old enough to understand and young in spirit enough not to have become too cynical, "What besides the basic physical necessities of life do you think people seek and need most of all in our world?" You may get many answers, but most of them will boil down to words like these: peace, harmony, happiness—*unity*.

The great need of mankind is to learn *to live together happily and in harmony with God*, with one another, with ourselves, and with our world. The quest for unity is the root of thousands of years of study in every field of human endeavor—in religion, the arts, and the sciences and humanities. From the Buddhist hope of Nirvana to the search for the Unified Field in physics, the world seeks unity. It is in just that search that this truth about God provides so many wonderful answers. Here is the basis of all knowledge, the basis of all truth and reality not only in religion but in every other field. As six-year-old Anna put it, "When you begins with the Answer, you can get a squillion questions right."

Unity of God

The very concept of the number *one* implies importance, unity, and commencement. The *first* use of a word or phrase in Scripture is often

---

[9]E. Stanley Jones, *Along the Indian Road* (Nashville: Abingdon Press, 1939), pp. 151–153.

the key to what it means in the rest of the Bible. Words that occur only *once* in the original languages are often emphatic and important. But when we think about the one-ness of God, we are again limited because of the unique nature of His ultimateness and perfection. We are often better able to say what the unity of God does *not* mean.

William Pope points out, "It is impossible to define the unity of God; the word 'unity' in human language gives no adequate notion, barely serving to defend the doctrine of every opposite error. It is set forth as the basis of all worship, of devotion, and obedience and fear (Deut. 6:4–5). This demands perfect consecration, which by the very terms, only one Object can claim (Deut. 4:39–40). Here, supreme obedience is exacted to one sole Authority which can have no rival (Deut. 32:39–40). There is only one Judge to be reverenced and feared for time and eternity."[1]

Unity *vs.* Dualism: The Tao

Today many people have been influenced by a fundamentally occult picture of God and the universe: the notion of *dualism*, two coeternal elements of being passively coexistent or struggling for mastery. You may have noticed the Tao symbol—black and white opposed tadpole-like figures combined to form a circle. The notion of Tao has been applied for centuries in the East in every part of life, from cooking to medicine, the *ying* and *yang*. It originated in Persia, but passed through later Judaism into the heretical sects of the Gnosticism, and spent itself out in Manichaeism.

From dualism comes the idea that there would be no good without evil; without darkness there would be no light; and that right and wrong are simply two sides of the *same* ultimate and eternal reality. Tao recognizes no real opposites; male-female, good-evil, life-death correctly seen are but as one. Dualistic unity is simply a recognition of the oneness of all things. The problem of division, tensions and evil is solved simply: one *accepts* it.

A Unity of Deception

This is, however, a unity of deception. Its consequences are eventual acceptance of all evils that come from a denial of true distinctions: sodomy and bisexuality in sexual morals, reincarnation instead of the final judgment of God, religious participation in sin instead of separation from it, and worship of the creation as Creator. It conflicts fundamentally with that which the true unity of God proclaims—that all true opposites in the universe are testimonies to the reality of absolutes. He, as the Uncreated, does not *need* a universe in order to exist as the Creator He is. He has always been the self-existent One, making the worlds out of nothing by himself and not needing darkness to make the light.

He is not only different from His creation, but He posits and makes

---

[1]William Pope, *Compendium of Christian Theology* (1881), p. 2550.

differences within that creation; therefore there are real differences in the universe between things we see as unlikes and opposites. Good has always existed, long before evil which is parasitic. Evil is neither eternal nor part of the Divine (the original *good*), and the distinctions in the universe are real and significant.

Perhaps the most natural and widespread of all errors is that opposites are eternal. The plethora of polytheistic and dualistic systems have been built on these very foundations. God protests against this, saying, "I am the Lord, and there is none else" (Isa. 45:18). The final reality is not an eternal conflict/combination of good and evil; the final reality is an uncreated Creator who is absolutely and wholly one, not the sum of conflicting and opposite poles and tensions that image reality.

Implications of Divine Unity

Apart from Scripture, what else can we think or say about the unity of God? Pope notes:

- "We cannot really conceive of more than one absolute being. . . . The Foundation or Source of all being cannot without contradiction be multiplied. Unity is not so much an attribute of Deity or a quality of essence so much as a condition of relation; the Supreme is related to His interior self and to his creatures, but as God is unrelated."
- "The term ['unity'] is used only as analogy. Though there is one Divine Nature, the unity of God is not a unity of *kind* because there are no individuals of the same species. In God there is an absolute soleness, *soleitas*; though what lies hidden in the mystery of this essential *oneness* we know but partially. It is wrong to dogmatize upon the nature of a unity to which we have no parallel and which we cannot define by comparison or illustration."
- "The constitution of nature both physical and moral confirms this. Unity is stamped upon the entire creation. . . . Hence the erring philosophy of the world in the better tendencies of its error has seldom been polytheistic or dualistic; its universal tendency towards pantheism declares its indestructible conviction of the Unity of God. This has been its snare, to carry to the extreme of denying all personality or creaturely existence outside of the One and the All."[2]

Unity in God: Divine Simplicity

A further key area we can consider here concerns the question of God's own "internal unity" of attributes—what theologians call His *simplicity*.

Many theologians follow Augustine's idea of internal unity, who equated all of God's attributes with His divine essence; a "fullness of existence that includes eternity, goodness, wisdom, and other perfections." Holding this same view, Dr. Carl Henry claims that the subjective

---

[2]Ibid. p. 2254.

and relational emphasis of contemporary theology "dilutes the force of cognitive revelation and compromises the fact that God in disclosing His name and attributes reveals in His very nature His innermost character, His essential being."[3]

Augustine opted for a vision of God that admits no essential distinction between substance and character, morals and metaphysics, or between action and being. Henry succinctly sums up this view of divine simplicity: "What we mean by the essence or nature of God is a living, personal unity of properties and activities. Divine essence and attributes are integral to each other. God is not a substance essentially distinguished from His psychic properties or attributes. Such a notion would reduce divine essence to a barren concept, a postulation devoid of content or meaning. God's being is not the bearer of the divine attributes; rather God's essence and attributes are identical. . . . He is the living unity of perfections that coordinately manifests the divine essence. . . . God is, in short, the *living unity* of His attributes. The attributes may be thought of as divine activities. God is not an abstract substance but an active spirit consciousness and will. The activities are God's divine qualities or attributes. . . . He is the one living God, deity *sui generis*, who in His revelation and relationships prominently displays now one and then another of His superlative virtues. . . ."[4]

What do we mean when we say that "God is One"? When Augustine wrote of God's "simple multiplicity" or "multifold simplicity," he meant that "God is not compounded of parts; he is not a collection of perfections, but rather a living center of activity pervasively characterized by all his distinctive perfections. . . . The historic Christian view is that all of God's attributes are identical with his essence, indeed constitute the divine essence."[5]

Augustine declared that "in God, *to be* is the same as *to be strong* or *to be just* or *to be wise*." For this very reason, Dr. Henry says the statement " 'God is'—if we know what we are saying—exhausts all that a course on theology can teach concerning Him. If we give the subject 'God' and the predicate 'is' their true and full sense, we must speak of God's essence, names, attributes, and triunity and do so expressly on the basis of His revelatory self-disclosure addressed to his created and fallen creatures."[6]

When we want to think about God, where do we start? Is there anything about Him more basic, foundational or fundamental? We emphasize one perfection at the expense of another. Henry says, "We are not to exalt preferred attributes in a partisan exposition, but are to exalt God who lives in the unity of all His perfections."[7]

Why Distinguish?

Why then do we make a distinction between who God *is* and what He *does*? Although it is true in practice and expression that we cannot *sep-*

---

[3]Carl Henry, *God, Revelation, and Authority* (Waco: Word Publishers), p. 128.
[4]Ibid. p. 13.
[5]Ibid. p. 134.
[6]Ibid. p. 131.
[7]Ibid. p. 136.

arate the nature from either the person and the personality, in actuality (like the persons of the Trinity), each is quite distinct and none of these distinct realities are exact equivalents of the others. The arrangement of any systematic study of God is based on what we think most important about Him. "The order in which being and attributes are discussed is therefore less important than the underlying reason for a given arrangement of the presentation and its content."[8]

This study is written on the premise that the triune God preserves in His own reality that which is reflected in all of His creation, that the proper treatment of truth will always preserve a fundamental unity in diversity, and that while there are dangers in emphasizing any one attribute at the expense of another, there are also dangers in assuming any one attribute identical in function and form to another.

Confounding the Difference

Why make a distinction between what God *is* (His essence or "stuff" of being) and what He *does* (His character and morality)? Is any such distinction necessary when, like other alternate views, it is a philosophical rather than biblical argument?

However and whenever we make distinctions, they will color our thinking. But we have no other way of talking or thinking about an infinite God other than selectively focusing on one distinct attribute at a time. We all do it, no matter what we may think. To claim God's simplicity as *the* basic truth about God certainly does not exempt us from the emphasis of any one attribute.

The claim that *no* attribute is distinctive is as partisan as any claim that *one* attribute is distinctive. Augustine said God was identical in His essence and attributes; but then so did Plotinus, even though he was not a Christian. (If Augustine had fully followed Plotinus in his analysis of the divine nature, he would never have written *The City of God* nor would he ever have reached it.) To *confound the difference* brings at least as many dangers as to *divide the substance*; neither the unitarian or the polytheist represent the reality of the Trinity. To claim God's metaphysical essence and moral attributes are not only a perfect unity but also a mutual identity is as much an extra-biblical claim as any other theological position. It leads to its own difficulties in coherence and conformity to biblical revelation.

Unity in Philosophy

If God is one, then we should expect deep unity also in the realm of His creation; that things will somehow be interconnected and linked in ways that will demonstrate His wisdom, power, and glory. How then should the Christian study God and His world? Another vital area covered by the Bible truth of unity is in the realm of philosophy.

---

[8]Ibid. p. 134.

While theology is the study of God and His relationship to creation, philosophy analyzes the logic of ideas and arguments in every area of life and thought. We know at least three key things about God:

- He *is* and He is the rewarder of them that diligently seek Him.
- He is *love*, and His conduct and character are the epitome of what is just, good, and right.
- He is *light*, He is the essence of what is true and most wise.

We know also by scriptural revelation that:
- God is *uncreated* (the most basic reality of essence and existence).
- He is *creator* (and as such, is both wise and good—holy).
- He is *triune*, the ultimate reason for both the unity and diversity that exists in our universe.

In Philosophy, *anything* you think about at all can be studied, harmonized, and systematized in one or more of three major categories:
- Metaphysics—The "stuff" of being; the overall and varied nature of what is taken to be real. What is there?
- Axiology—Morals, ethics, the implications of personality; the values involved in morality, art, and politics. What is good, important, fit, and right?
- Epistemology—Truth and knowing; logic, methodology, and the claim to truth. How do we know what we know?

A Christian World View

Arthur Frank Holmes, chairman of the philosophy department at Wheaton College, outlines an approach to the building of a *Christian world view*, a mental map of reality and an approach to both discovering and tying together truth in all realms of thought.

He states that the universal desire for a world view comes from four human needs: "the need to unify thought and life; the need to define the good life and find hope, purpose and meaning in life; to guide thought (determine priorities and guide selectivity); the need to guide action."[9]

"At the turn of this century the Scottish theologian James Orr claimed that pessimism was the logical result of the demise of Christian faith. In *The Christian View of God and the World* he addressed the overall character of a Christian view of things. The main design . . . was to show: That there is a definite Christian view of things, which has a character, coherence and unity of its own, and stands in sharp contrast with counter theories and speculations and that this world view has the stamp of reason and reality upon it, and can amply justify itself at the bar both of history and of experience."[10]

On what basis does Holmes approach the development of a mental

---

[9]Arthur Frank Holmes, *Contours of a World View*, Carl F. Henry, ed. (Grand Rapids: Eerdmans, 1983), p. 5.
[10]Ibid. p. 16.

map on which we base our whole concept of reality? How do we know that what we believe is true? He discusses three major approaches to testing a claim to truth:

1. *Fideism*—The person who accepts this approach expresses the thought, "I believe what I am told." This is an uncritical acceptance of ideas without concern about how they stack up against opposing ideas, how they fit with other known facts, or how they actually work in the world. "Perhaps he accepts them on someone else's authority without assessing the competence of that authority. No further evidence or argument is needed. The Marxist may accept Marxist views uncritically because he is personally convinced of their reliability no matter what."

2. *Foundationalism*—This is the opposite approach. The person with this view says, "I figure out what is true from what I already know." This approach tries to "deduce all one's beliefs from basic premises that are themselves both beyond possible doubt (indubitable) and beyond any need for correction (incorrigible). . . ." While you can best use foundationalism to prove propositions, "a world view is more than a set of propositional beliefs and . . . cannot be established one step at a time as the foundationalist wants. . . . Philosophy is always to some extent 'perspectival.' If it is a deductive system, enough indubitable and incorrigible first premises must be available to imply logically both its unifying perspective and its entire detailed formulation. And that seems to be asking for more explicit and indubitable foundations than we actually have. . . ."

   Although the Christian is called to uncritical commitment to God's Word, he has both the right and responsibility to make sure it *is* God's Word. Although there are many things we can deduce from given absolutes of God, we must also make sure what we start with are indeed absolutes. If we start with a false premise, we can come to a wrong conclusion for all the right reasons. The principle of *coherency*, or unity, is a safeguard against either an unquestioning acceptance of error or an errant deduction from a partial truth. We must always ask how something fits with everything else.

3. *Coherentism*—This approach accepts all truth, but also attempts to resolve the contradictions that arise within the world view. Holmes presents three reasons for proffering this approach, all rooted in the biblical implications of the unity of God:

   1. There is "unity in truth—truth itself is an interrelated and coherent whole. The law of noncontradiction in logic (itself a universal principle) insists on the logical consistency of whatever we claim as true. At least no incompatibility can be allowed." God is inherently, intrinsically, and internally noncontradictory; His attributes are harmonious and symmetrical; His character and actions are without internal division or conflict—what theologians sometimes call His *simplicity*. Thus we can expect His

creation to be likewise noncontradictory."

2. "The quest for understanding itself seeks unity amidst diversity, the one among many; the unity of truth expresses that ideal." As part of the ultimate pattern of things, God's own triune structure of unity and diversity is the common structure of all reality.

3. "The theist believes an omniscient God sees everything in relationship to His own creative power and purposes as an interrelated whole. But this interrelated unity of things implies the unity of truth to which the overall coherence of what we believe will bear witness." This unity extends not only to the realm of metaphysics and epistemology; it encompasses also axiology, the realm of morals, relationships, and ultimate values.[11]

Unity in Relationships

"Neither pray I for these alone, but for them also which shall believe on me through their word; that they all may be one; as thou, Father, art in me, and I in thee, that they also may be one in us: that the world may believe that thou hast sent me" (John 17:20–21).

Perhaps the most important application of the principle of unity is in relationships, first, between man and God and secondly, between man and man. Salvation is ultimately a *restoration of relationship* between man and God. Peace is a restoration of unity, integrity, and wholeness to individuals. Family, societal, national, and international peace depend on our ability to live in harmony and unity with one another. If unity is so important and significant, how can we achieve it? What are the conditions of true unity, and how can unity be promoted?

There are only two basic conditions for experiencing happiness. No true peace or harmony is possible until we meet these conditions.

We must have a *common understanding*. Understanding is basic to agreement. Peace demands that both parties have access to true and relevant knowledge. In an age notorious for manipulating media—distorting facts and creating outright lies for ideological, personal or political advantage—we have become cynical. People find it difficult to believe anything. On top of this, we have added problems of language barriers, communication failures, and conditioned ignorance. But there is no way around it, despite the obstacles. If we cannot agree on basic truths and values in our world, we will have no long-term peace, unity, harmony, or lasting happiness.

We also need a *common unselfishness*. Knowledge is not enough. We must also be willing to follow whatever we honestly regard as the best or wisest choice, or education will only make us more-informed hypocrites and clever criminals. Knowledge is not the same as wisdom. The question is always: will we *do* what we know is right? Technologically advanced nations can do inhuman things. Every major thinker in history, both Eastern and Western, has known that the problem of selfishness must be

---

[11]Ibid. pp. 50–51.

eliminated to bring real harmony, unity, and peace to mankind.

Put these essential conditions in simple words and you get "wisdom" and "love."

Wisdom: How can any finite person agree with another as to what is true or valuable? To be sure, we must be able to see all things. How can we say with absolute certainty that anything is true until we compare it with everything else? How can you be sure of the particular unless we see the universal first? We all need a source of utterly trustworthy, infinitely true, wholly dependable, ever available, and universally accessible wisdom. Such a source *cannot* be human. It demands a level of knowledge and wisdom, of precision and justice, beyond our imagining. It cannot be finite.

Love: Just as important and just as humanly impossible is the need to eliminate selfishness. Everyone from Buddha to Marx had their ideas to eradicate selfishness, from wiping out the individual idea of ego to altering economic conditions by wiping out groups of people. Selfishness remains, with one notable exception; all have lived to please themselves. Dr. Karl Menninger, author of *Whatever Became of Sin*, said, "The willful disregard or sacrifice of the welfare of others for the welfare or satisfaction of the self is an essential quality of the concept sin." Augustine called selfishness "the turning away from the universal whole to the individual part," and pointed out that since there is nothing greater than the whole, devoting ourselves to something we say is greater actually makes us smaller. If we begin with selfish people, we will always end up with selfish societies, no matter what we call ourselves and despite how much we know.

We cannot live without a source of love and absolute wisdom. If we give up the fiction that man is a lucky accident of chance, time, and matter, we come to this conclusion: *we were never meant to live alone*.

We are made to need help and power; made to grow forever, never running out of joy and a sense of awe. There is such a source in the universe. We have not been left to find and forge our own way. There is an infinite Love and an Absolute Wisdom available to all, capable of breaking every language, racial, and educational barrier, strong enough to deliver anyone from the chains of selfishness to a universal compassion. There is One source; but only *One*.

That is why our race needs God. That is why we *must* give our lives to Him. There is no other alternative—we must know Him, have His gifts of love and wisdom, or die. We were never meant to live alone; we cannot survive without Him. He is "no respecter of persons; but in every nation he that feareth him, and worketh righteousness, is accepted with Him" (Acts 10:34–35). Only He has never done wrong, never lied, never sinned, or ever been selfish in any way. Only He has the infinite wisdom capable of revealing "true" truth to anyone with an honest heart; only He can be trusted to reveal reality to anyone without distortion or evasion. He has promised to do this if we will use this knowledge wisely. He has promised to cleanse and forgive and allow us to start anew if we turn to Him with all our hearts.

The foundational necessity of the law of love has been dealt with in another section of this study. We have also seen that revelation is essential to wisdom. But in the practical application of these basic principles, which comes *first*? Do we strive first for unity in truth (or wisdom) or for love? Scripture gives us the divine order:

I therefore, the prisoner of the Lord, beseech you that ye walk worthy of the vocation wherewith ye are called, with all lowliness and meekness, with longsuffering, forbearing one another in love; endeavouring to keep the unity of the Spirit in the bond of peace. There is one body, and one Spirit, even as ye are called in one hope of your calling; one Lord, one faith, one baptism, one God and Father of all, who is above all, and through all, and in you all. But unto every one of us is given grace according to the measure of the gift of Christ. Wherefore he saith, When he ascended up on high, he led captivity captive, and gave gifts unto men . . . for the perfecting of the saints, for the work of the ministry, for the edifying of the body of Christ: till we all come in the unity of the faith, and of the knowledge of the Son of God, unto a perfect man, unto the measure of the stature of the fulness of Christ: that we henceforth be no more children, tossed to and fro, and carried about with every wind of doctrine, by the sleight of men, and cunning craftiness, whereby they lie in wait to deceive; but speaking the truth in love, may grow up into him in all things, which is the head, even Christ. (Eph. 4:1–15)

This passage tells us five key things about unity:

- Unity exists ultimately only *in Christ*. Outside of a vital relationship with Him who is our peace, truth, and love, there is no peace, no absolute truth, and no real love.
- Unity is spiritual, real, and *already exists* if we truly belong to Him. Just as the body and the head are intimately and integrally connected, we are to *keep* unity, not make it. Christians are *already* one with one another by their union with Christ.
- The first step to unity is to maintain a *servant's heart*: a spirit of learning based on dependence and humility. The Christian must maintain genuine love for others despite differences.
- Spiritual gifts include *ministries* in His body that will help us not only become more like our Living Head, but better understand and appreciate the unity of the Body of Christ even in its diversity.
- A day is coming when we will not only agree in spirit and in love, but we will come as finite beings to some common agreement that will protect us from becoming victims of deception and ignorance, and enable us not only to love one another, but to say the same things.

Honor—The Key to True Unity

How can we best promote unity in the Church? Paul, speaking of unity in the diversity of the body of Christ in 1 Cor. 12:11–25, says that God has given "more abundant honor to that part which lacked that there should be no schism in the body." The key to promoting unity, according to Paul's simple and profound writing, is to *honor one another*.

Honor changes the climate in which we approach unity. It is the biblical base out of which true relationships are forged. To honor someone else is to appreciate the dealings of God in their life, to see them through the eyes of Jesus as a loved and valuable creature, to genuinely appreciate their unique gifts and callings, and to be excited about the work of Christ in and through them. This simple thing is rarely done. When we fail to obey God in this, our lives can be a source of disunity, and sometimes in neglecting honor (not by design but by default), we contribute to division in the body of Christ. When we honor God in Christ, we promote a deeper unity with Him and with His purposes; and when we go out of our way to sincerely, practically, and continually honor one another, we actively promote unity in His people, spiritual awakening in the Church, and evangelism in His world.

Historical Discussion

The number one is, in all languages, a symbol, or rather a synonym of unity.[1]

M. Mahan

The *Universe*

A. W. Tozer

"Thought and prayer and a spiritual understanding of the Scriptures will reveal the unity of all things. What appears to be a million separate and unrelated phenomena are actually but different phases of a single whole. Everything is related to everything else. It cannot be otherwise, seeing that God is one. All His words and acts are related to each other by being related to Him. . . . Everything that God is accords with all else that He is. Every thought He entertains is one with every other thought. . . .

"The work of Christ in redemption will achieve ultimately the expulsion of sin, the only divisive agent in the universe and the unification of all things. 'For it pleased the Father that in Him should all fullness dwell; and having made peace through the blood of His cross, by Him to reconcile all things unto himself; by Him, I say, whether they be things in earth or things in heaven' (Col. 1:19–20). The nearer the Christian soul comes to Christ in personal experience the more perfect becomes the internal unity even now."[2]

---

[1]M. Mahan, *The Complete Works of M. Mahan*, p. 94.
[2]A. W. Tozer, "The Unity Of All Things" *Born After Midnight* (Camp Hill, Pa.: Christian Publications, Inc.), pp. 115, 117.

Madame Guyon

"Here all is God to the soul, because it is no longer a question of seeing all in God; for to see things in God is to distinguish them in Him. . . . All creatures, celestial, terrestrial, or pure intelligences disappear and fade away, and there remains only God himself, as He was before the creation. The soul sees only God everywhere . . . by an identity of condition and a consummation of unity. . . . It is not that it does not retain its own nature . . . nor does it lose the nature of the creature. . . . The capacity of which I speak is a capacity to extend and lose itself more and more in God. . . . The more it is lost in Him, the more it develops and becomes immense, participating in His perfections, and being more and more transformed in Him as water in communication with its source continually mingles with it. God, being our original source, has created in us a nature fit to be united, transformed and made one with himself."[3]

The Importance of a Christian World View

Arthur F. Holmes

"To rekindle and disseminate that vision [of integrating the whole of human knowledge under the primacy of the Word of God into an organized Christian view] is of strategic importance today. Christianity has vitally important implications for every area of life and thought, implications that need to be developed, but to live and think Christianly in today's world with meaning and hope does not come easily. It means ferreting out the influence of non-Christian assumptions and bringing distinctively Christian presuppositions to bear in their place. To identify and articulate these distinctives systematically in relation to the world of ideas is to develop a Christian world view. Moreover I am convinced . . . that the most persuasive case for Christianity lies in the overall coherence and human relevance of its world view."[4]

This "quest for a unifying world view that will help us see life whole and find meaning in each part," says Holmes "is as old as humankind. . . . What is it that ties everything together, matter and mind, life and death, art and science, faith and learning and makes this a *uni*-verse? . . . What can unify our vision of life? To see things interrelated as a whole is to get one's bearings on the map of life, to find one's way in the confusing interplay of ideas, to find relatedness in what we do."[5]

R. K. Harrison

"The harmony which is represented in the world and its inhabitants is in fact a divinely-imposed order in which each creature fulfills the will of God. In every instance the creative fiat not merely brings entities into

---

[3]Madame Guyon, *Spiritual Torrents*, A.E. Ford and O. Clapp, trans. (1790, 1853), pp. 134, 137, 147–148.
[4]Arthur Frank Holmes, *Contours of a World View*, Carl F. Henry, ed. (Grand Rapids: Eerdmans, 1983), pp. vii-viii.
[5]Ibid. p. 3.

existence but relates them to some specific function within the larger structure. Because of the personal relationship which exists between God and His creation there can be no room in Scripture for the idea of 'Nature' as an autonomous power set in motion by a First Cause. God is depicted as being at all times in control of the world (cf. Job 38:33; Jer. 5:24) which needs His continual undergirding if it is to continue (cf. Ps. 104:29–30). Where there is an expression of the regularity of natural forces, as in the promise given to Noah (Gen. 8:22) it is based upon the covenant mercies and faithfulness of God."[6]

Henry Drummond

"Probably the most satisfactory way to secure . . . an appreciation of the Principle of Continuity is to try to conceive the universe without it. The opposite of a continuous universe would be a discontinuous universe, an incoherent and irrelevant universe. . . . In effect, to withdraw continuity from the universe would be the same as to withdraw reason from an individual. The universe would run deranged; the world would be a mad world."[7]

A Universal Faith and Answer

Ivan Panin

To see God in nothing—that is atheism.
To see God in everything—that is pantheism.
Only to see God over everything, to look for Him
in anything—that is true godliness.[8]

E. Stanley Jones

" 'If God is one and humanity is one why cannot we be one in religion,' asked a thoughtful Hindu one day. . . . We long for the universal—we cannot rest except in the totality of things. . . . I noted three ways by which men hoped to see it come: first by *command*, that is the Muslim way; second by *comprehension*, the Hindu way; third by *Christ*, the Christian way. . . . We must remember that no universal either in religion or in other realms can be arrived at hastily. It will come through patient sifting of truth from error, of the relevant from the irrelevant, of the universal from the temporary and the local. It will come through putting religions under the facts of life, to see which is spiritually fit to survive, which corresponds to the facts of the universe, which can satisfy universal human need. That process of sifting and testing is now taking place. The universal will emerge—is emerging.

"The issue regarding universality is between a patchwork and a Per-

---

[6]R.K. Harrison, "Creation,"*The Zondervan Pictorial Encyclopedia of the Bible*, Merrill Tenney, ed. (Grand Rapids: Zondervan Pub. House, 1976) Vol. 1, pp. 1023.
[7]Henry Drummond, *Natural Law in the Spiritual World* (London: Hodder and Stoughton, 1884), p. 38.
[8]Ivan Panin, "Aphorisms," *The Writings of Ivan Panin*, p. 28.

sonality—the former trying to combine the good points in each and the latter gathering up in himself all that was fine and noble in the past and fulfilling it in himself. Of the two I choose the latter. . . . synchretisms combine, eclecticisms choose, but only life assimilates.

"As He gathers up all that was fine in the past of all nations, so He gathers up into himself all virtues that seem to be in conflict. . . . He combines them in a living whole. For He is the Aggressive and the Submissive, the Idealist and the Realist, the Mystic and the Master, the Realizer and the Regenerator, the Devotee and the Doer, the Terrible and the Tender, the Pure and the Approachable, the Concentrated and the Catholic, the Progressive and the Patient, the Sweet and the Severe, the Judge and the Justifier, the Balanced and the Blazing, the Immaculate and the Imitable, the Sunshiny and the Sad, the Player with the children and the Purposer of a cross, the Victim and Victor, the Son of Man and the Son of God. Out of the conflict is emerging a Universal—Jesus. Other ways of living and other interpretations of life are gradually being eliminated from the minds of thoughtful men and the Universal is emerging."[9]

The Only Answer

Francis Schaeffer

"To have an adequate answer of a personal beginning, we need two things. We need a personal-infinite God and we need a personal unity and diversity in God. . . . We do not need just an abstract concept of unity and diversity but a personal unity and diversity, because we have to end up with a personal God or we have no answer. . . .

"There is only one philosophy, one religion that fills this need in all the world's thought—the East, the West, the ancient, the modern, the new, the old. There is only one philosophy, one religion that fills the philosophic need of existence, of being, and it is the Judeo-Christian God—not just an abstract concept, but rather that this God is really there. He exists. There is no other answer, and orthodox Christians ought to be ashamed of having been so defensive for so long. It is not a time to be defensive. There is no other answer.

"The truth of Christianity is that *it is true to what is there*. You can go to the end of the world and you never need to be afraid like the ancients that you will fall off the end and the dragons will eat you up. You can carry out your intellectual discussions to the end of the game, because Christianity is not only true to the dogmas, it is not only true to what God said in the Bible, but it is also true to what is there, and you will never fall off the end of the world. It is not just an approximate model, it is really true to what is there. When the evangelical catches that, when evangelicalism catches that, we may have our revolution. We will begin

---

[9]E. Stanley Jones, *Christ at the Round Table* (Philadelphia: Century Bookbindery, 1981), p. 282–283, 300, 301.

to have something beautiful and alive; something that will have force in our poor lost world."[10]

E. Stanley Jones

"There is one thing and only one thing that is unshakeable and that is the Kingdom of God. To be able to say that, to be able to say it in a world of relativisms and to say it without fear of contradiction from any source, scientific, religious, or philosophical is important—all important. A Hindu chairman at the close of one of my addresses said: 'If what the speaker has just said isn't true, it doesn't matter, but if it is true then nothing else matters.' . . . All science, all knowledge, all achievements, all nations, all persons, all things must be related to this Unshakable Kingdom in surrender and obedience and alignment or else end in frustration and failure and decay. I have never penned a wilder or wiser statement . . . nor has anybody else. And I can pen it because it is true!"[11]

Unity: The Law Behind Laws

Henry Drummond

"What is wanted is simply a unity of conception, but not such a unity . . . founded on an absolute identity of phenomena. . . . The perfection of unity is attained where there is infinite variety of phenomena, infinite complexity of relation, but great simplicity of Law. . . .

"The spiritual man, it is true is to be studied in a different department of science from the natural man. But the harmony established by science is not a harmony within specific departments. It is the universe that is in harmony, the universe of which these are but parts. And the harmonies of the parts depend for all their weight and interest on the harmony of the whole. . . . The breaking up of the phenomena of the universe into carefully guarded groups and the allocation of certain prominent Laws to each, it must never be forgotten and however much nature lends herself to it, such divisions are artificial . . . mere departments created by ourselves to facilitate knowledge-reductions of nature to the scale of our own intelligence. And we must beware of breaking up nature except for this purpose.

"Science has so dissected everything that it becomes a mental difficulty to put the puzzle together again; and we must keep ourselves in practice by constantly thinking of nature as a whole, if science is not to be spoiled by its own refinements."[12]

"As the vision of Newton rested on a clearer but richer world than that

---

[10]Francis Schaeffer, *He is There And He Is Not Silent* (London: Hodder and Stoughton, 1972), pp. 24–28.

[11]E. Stanley Jones, *The Unshakeable Kingdom and the Unchanging Person* (Nashville: Abingdon Press, 1971), p. 33.

[12]Henry Drummond, *Natural Law in the Spiritual World* (London: Hodder and Stoughton, 1884), pp. 22, 36–37.

of Plato, so seeing the same things in the spiritual world as our fathers, we may see them clearer and richer."[13]

Dorothy Sayers

"The poet does not work by analysis and measurement of observables, but by a 'consistent imagination.' He creates, we may say, by building up new images, new intellectual concepts, new worlds, if you like to form new consistent wholes, new unities out of diversity. And I should like to submit to you that this is in fact the way the creative mind works—in the sciences as everywhere else—in divine as well as human creation, so far as we can observe and understand divine methods of creation. That is, within our experience, creation proceeds by the discovery of new conceptual relations between things, so as to form them into systems having a consistent wholeness corresponding to an image in the mind, and consequently possessing real existence. . . . The atoms and ourselves are, as it were, created out of an undifferentiated universe by an act of consistent imagination which holds us together as one thing."[14]

Owen Barfield

"The plain fact is, that all unity and coherence of nature depends on participation of one kind or the other. If therefore man succeeds in eliminating all original participation without substituting any other he will have done nothing less than eliminate all meaning and all coherence from the cosmos. . . . His science, with the progressive disappearance of original participation, is losing its grip on any principle of unity pervading nature as a whole and the knowledge of nature. . . . There is no 'science of sciences,' no unity of knowledge. There is only an accelerating increase in that pigeon-holed knowledge by individuals of more and more about less and less, which if persisted in can only lead mankind to a sort of 'idiocy'—(in the original sense of the word)—a state of affairs in which fewer and fewer representations will be collective, and more and more will be private, with the result that there will in the end be no means of communication between one intelligence and another."[15]

Parables as Parallels

Archbishop Trench

"The parable or other analogy to spiritual truth appropriated from the world of nature or man is not merely illustrative but also in some sort proof. It is not merely that these analogies assist to make truth intelligible. . . . Their power lies deeper than this, in the harmony unconsciously felt by all men, and which all deeper minds have delighted to trace be-

---

[13]Ibid. p. 33.

[14]Dorothy Sayers, *Christian Letters to a Post-Christian World* (Grand Rapids, Mich: Eerdmans, 1969), p. 90.

[15]Owen Barfield, *Saving the Appearances: A Study in Idolatry* (Harcourt Brace and World, 1965), pp. 143–145.

tween the natural and spiritual worlds, so that analogies from the first are felt to be something more than illustrations happily but arbitrarily chosen. They are arguments, and may be alleged as witnesses; the world of nature being throughout a witness for the world of the spirit, proceeding from the same Hand, growing out of the same root and being constituted for that very end."[16]

Principal Shairp

"This seeing of Spiritual truths mirrored in the face of Nature rests not on any fancied, but in a real analogy between the natural and spiritual worlds. They are in some sense which science has not ascertained, but which the vital and spiritual imagination can perceive, counterparts one of the other."[17]

Maltbie Babcock

This is My Father's world;
And to my listening ears
All nature sings and round me rings
The music of the spheres.

This is My Father's world;
I rest me in the thought
Of rocks and trees, of skies and seas,
His hand the wonders wrought.

This is my Father's world;
The birds their carols raise,
The morning light, the lily white
Declare their Maker's praise.

This is my Father's world;
He shines in all that's fair;
In the rustling grass I hear Him pass,
He speaks to me everywhere"[18]

Unity in Work and Worship

Henry Sloane Coffin

"We fancy we have outgrown the pagan interpretation of our spiritual home, which saw the unseen world peopled with a discordant company of many gods, as for example in Homer where one divinity favors the Greeks and another the Trojans, where three jealous goddesses contend for a prize, where one deity is the defender of Achilles and another the patron of Ulysses. But do we not trust and follow one spirit in our families and another in our business dealings, one spirit in our patri-

---

[16]Archbishop R.C. Trench, *Notes on the Parables of Our Lord* (Grand Rapids: Baker Book House) pp. 12–13.
[17]Principal Shairp, *Poetic Interpretation of Nature*, p. 115.
[18]Maltbie D. Babcock, 1901.

otism and another in our feelings toward men of other races, one spirit in our scientific observations and another in our acceptance of religious beliefs?

"Unconsciously we slip back into a crude polytheism. We do not feel the same Spirit is to be relied on and obeyed in every sphere of life and in our relations with all men. We do not believe that the same motives and incentives which can be used to make a satisfactory home can be trusted in industry and statesmanship. Instead of holding with the seers of Israel to the unity of God, we are back among the rival divinities who filled the Greek Olympus.

"Christianity starts with the parent faith of Judaism in one God, of whom and through whom and unto whom are all things. If we adore God as love in our families, we cannot worship Him as force in international relations, nor as self-interest in commercial dealings, nor as impersonal energy resident in nature. We cannot revere Him as truth in our universities and as tradition in our churches. If to know Him as love is true religion for ourselves and for our children and not too good to be our religion, then we cannot think that to know Him as less than love and be frightened or fatalistic or unhoping is good enough religion for fellow-mortals in Asia or Africa or among the millions of a cosmopolitan city. Our spiritual home is one God, with whom we dwell with our nearest and dearest and with men of other lands and races, one God in whom we have our friendships, form our opinions on public questions and do our business, one God in whom our life is unified— made all of a piece, and all divinely good.

"Dictionaries are useful volumes in the interest of accurate employment of language. Creeds are useful documents in conserving and clarifying what men have experienced in their life of faith. The statements of the Trinity in unity preserve what Christians through many generations have discovered who have made their home in God; but few men have first read the statement and then gone to make the discovery, nor having made the discovery, do they find the statement containing all they have found. Our souls take to God instinctively, as a mother kisses her child or a man and a maid fall in love. No dictionary can ever tell all that is in a kiss, and no doctrinal statement will ever record what God is to those who love Him. Only those who with Jesus live in Him know."[19]

Francis Schaeffer

"The early Christian church cut across all lines which divided men— Jew and Greek, Greek and Barbarian, male and female; from Herod's foster brother to the slave; from the naturally proud Gentiles in Macedonia who sent material help to the naturally proud Jews who called all Gentiles dogs, and yet could not keep the good news to themselves but had taken

---

[19]Henry Sloane Coffin, "The Home Of The Soul," *Twenty Centuries of Great Preaching*, Clyde E. Fant Jr. and William M. Dinson Jr., eds. (Waco, Texas: Word Books, 1971), Vol. VIII, pp. 303–304.

it to the Gentiles in Antioch. The observable and practical love in our days should certainly without reservation cut across all such lines as language, nationalities, national frontiers, younger or older, colors of skin, education and economic levels, accent, line of birth, the class system of our particular locality, dress, . . . cultural differentiations and the more traditional and less traditional forms of worship. I want to tell you it can work."[20]

All Unity Is Ultimately Founded in Christ

Edward Bickersteth

"The great definition which our Lord gives of His people ('them that shall believe on Me through their word') may show us where the true principle of unity is; not in outside form, not in an external uniformity which may merely mask and cover the most entire and complete opposition and enmity within; but in real living faith in God's own Word, uniting all hearts amidst every diversity of outward form; the truth making all free while it unites in harmony with the will of God and the glory of the Savior and the good of man. . . . The unity of faith, hope, and love . . . surmounts all the hindrances and impediments that human infirmity has occasioned and brings us with one heart and one mind to say, 'Glory to God in the highest on earth, peace, good-will towards men.' "[21]

St. Maximus the Confessor

"Perfect love does not divide human nature which is one, according to men's different characters; but looking always on this nature, it loves all men equally; it loves the good as friends and the wicked as enemies, doing good to them, being long-suffering, enduring things caused by them, never returning evil for evil, but even suffering for them if occasion demands in order, if possible to make friends even of them. But if this proves impossible, it still retains its good disposition towards them, always showing the fruits of love equally to all men. Thus our Lord Jesus Christ showing His love for us, suffered for the whole of mankind and gave equally to all the hope of resurrection. . . .

"The aim of divine providence is to reunite by means of right faith and spiritual love those who were cut asunder and scattered by evil. It is in order to 'gather together in one the children of God that were scattered abroad' (John 11:52)."[22]

---

[20]Francis Schaeffer, *The Church at the End of the Twentieth Century* (London: Norfolk Press, 1971), p. 128.
[21]Edward Bickersteth, *The Trinity* (Grand Rapids: Kregel, 1976).
[22]St. Maximus the Confessor (655 A.D.) *Writings From the Heart: The Philokalia* Kadloubovsky and Palmer, trans. (London: Faber and Faber), pp. 294, 335.

Samuel Wesley

> The Church's one Foundation is Jesus Christ her Lord;
> She is His new creation by water and the word:
> From Heaven He came and sought her to be His holy Bride;
> With His own blood He bought her and for her life He died.
>
> Elect from every nation yet one o'er all the earth,
> Her charter of salvation, one Lord, one faith one birth;
> One holy Name she blesses, partakes one holy food,
> And to one hope she presses, with every grace endued.

CHAPTER ELEVEN

DECLARATION ONE:
THE FATHER IS THE UNCREATED GOD

Scriptures

"Doubtless thou art our father . . . thou O LORD, art our father, our redeemer; thy name is from everlasting." (Isa. 63:16)

"But now, O LORD, thou art our father; we are the clay, and thou our potter; and we all are the work of thy hand." (Isa. 64:8)

"A son honoureth his father, and a servant his master: if then I be a father, where is mine honour? and if I be a master, where is my fear? saith the LORD of hosts unto you." (Mal. 1:6)

"Is this the way you repay the LORD, O foolish and unwise people? Is he not your Father, your Creator, who made you and formed you?" (Deut. 32:6, NIV)

He Is a Caring, Merciful Father

"A father of the fatherless, and a judge of the widows, is God in his holy habitation. God setteth the solitary in families [God gives the desolate a home to dwell in]." (Ps. 68:5, 6)

"For the LORD your God is God of gods, and Lord of Lords, a great God, a mighty, and a terrible, which regardeth not persons, nor taketh reward: he doth execute the judgment of the fatherless and widow, and loveth the stranger, in giving him food and raiment." (Deut. 10:17–18)

"Thou hast seen it: for thou beholdest mischief and spite, to requite it with thy hand: the poor committeth himself unto thee; thou art the helper of the fatherless." (Ps. 10:14)

"As a father pitieth his children, so the LORD pitieth them that fear him." (Ps. 103:13)

"The LORD sets prisoners free, the LORD gives sight to the blind, the LORD lifts up those who are bowed down, the Lord loves the righteous. The LORD watches over the alien and sustains the fatherless and the widow, but he frustrates the ways of the wicked." (Ps. 146:7–9, NIV)

He Is Father Even When His Child Is Wayward

"I will be his father, and he shall be my son. If he commit iniquity, I will chasten him . . . but my mercy shall not depart away from him." (2 Sam. 7:14–15)

"He shall cry unto me, Thou art my father, my God, and the rock of my salvation." (Ps. 89:26, 29)

"Return, ye backsliding children, and I will heal your backslidings. Behold, we come unto thee; for thou art the LORD our God." (Jer. 3:22)

"I have surely heard Ephraim. . . . Turn thou me, and I shall be turned; for thou art the LORD my God. . . . Is Ephraim my dear son? is he a pleasant child? for since I spake against him, I do earnestly remember him still . . . I will surely have mercy upon him, saith the LORD." (Jer. 31:18, 20)

He Is Prayed to and Spoken of As God

"But to us there is but one God, the Father, of whom are all things, and we in him; and one Lord Jesus Christ, by whom are all things, and we by him." (1 Cor. 8:6)

"And call no man your father upon the earth: for one is your Father, which is in heaven." (Matt. 23:9)

"But of that day and that hour knoweth no man, no, not the angels which are in heaven, neither the Son, but the Father." (Mark 13:32; cf. Matt. 24:36)

"He said also that God was His Father, making himself equal with God." (John 5:18)

"I and my Father are one." (John 10:30)

"Jesus saith unto him, Have I been so long time with you, and yet hast thou not known me, Philip? he that hath seen me hath seen the Father; and how sayest thou then, Shew us the Father? Believest thou not that I am in the Father, and the Father in me?" (John 14:9–10)

"But when the Comforter is come, whom I will send unto you from the Father, even the Spirit of truth, which proceedeth from the Father, he shall testify of me." (John 15:26)

"That they all may be one; as thou, Father, art in me, and I in thee, that they also may be one in us: that the world may believe that thou hast sent me. And the glory which thou gavest me I have given them; that they may be one, even as we are one: I in them, and thou in me, that they may be made perfect in one." (John 17:21–23)

"One God and Father of all, who is above all, and through all, and in you all." (Eph. 4:6)

"We give thanks to God and the Father of our Lord Jesus Christ, praying always for you . . . giving thanks unto the Father, which hath made us meet to be partakers of the inheritance of the saints in light." (Col. 1:3, 12)

"Every good gift and every perfect gift is from above, and cometh down from the Father of lights, with whom is no variableness, neither shadow of turning." (James 1:17)

He Is Worshiped

"But the hour cometh, and now is, when the true worshipers shall worship the Father in spirit and in truth: for the Father seeketh such to worship him." (John 4:23)

"Be ye therefore perfect, even as your Father which is in heaven is perfect." (Matt. 5:48)

"Abba, Father, all things are possible unto thee." (Mark 14:36)

"Every tongue should confess that Jesus Christ is Lord, to the glory of God the Father." (Phil. 2:11)

"Therewith bless we God, even the Father." (James 3:9)

He Forgives Sin

"And when ye stand praying, forgive . . . that your Father also which is in heaven may forgive you your trespasses." (Mark 11:25)

"Be ye therefore merciful, as your Father also is merciful." (Luke 6:36)

"Father, forgive them; for they know not what they do." (Luke 23:34)

"Blessed be the God and Father of our Lord Jesus Christ, which according to his abundant mercy hath begotten us again unto a lively hope by the resurrection of Jesus Christ from the dead." (1 Pet. 1:3)

"If any man sin . . . we have an advocate with the Father, Jesus Christ the righteous." (1 John 2:1)

He Is the God of Believers

"Behold what manner of love the Father hath bestowed upon us, that we should be called the sons of God." (1 John 3:1)

"Grace to you and peace from God our Father, and the Lord Jesus Christ." (Rom. 1:7; cf. 1 Cor. 1:3; 2 Cor. 1:2)

"But ye have received the Spirit of adoption, whereby we cry, Abba, Father. The Spirit itself beareth witness with our spirit, that we are the children of God." (Rom. 8:15–16)

"[I] will be a Father unto you, and ye shall be my sons and daughters." (2 Cor. 6:18)

"Who [Jesus] gave himself for our sins, that he might deliver us from this present evil world, according to the will of God and our Father." (Gal. 1:4)

"And because ye are sons, God hath sent forth the Spirit of his Son into your hearts, crying, Abba, Father." (Gal. 4:6)

"Now God himself and our Father, and our Lord Jesus Christ, direct our way unto you . . . to the end that he may stablish your hearts unblameable in holiness before God, even our Father." (1 Thess. 3:11, 13)

"Now our Lord Jesus Christ himself, and God, even our Father, which hath loved us, and hath given us everlasting consolation and good hope through grace." (2 Thess. 2:16)

"I will be to him a Father, and he shall be to me a son." (Heb. 1:5)

"Jude, the servant of Jesus Christ, and brother of James, to them that are sanctified by God the Father." (Jude 1)

Bible Word Study

Early Religious Traditions

"The idea of God as Father is not restricted to Christianity, nor even to the Hebrew-Christian tradition. It is found in many ancient religions; in early India, vegetation is the child of Earth (the mother), and Heaven (*Dyaus*—the father). The Greek Zeus, chief of the gods, was regularly addressed as 'Father'; Homer calls him 'Father of men and gods.'

"The mystery religions taught men to believe in a divine father who could give them rebirth; Mithras was called 'father of the faithful.' Osiris was said to be the father of Horus, and the cult of Cybele called upon Attis as father.

"The doctrine of the fatherhood of God is also found in the Greek philosophers, especially those influenced by Plato. In his *Republic*, Plato gives the title 'Father' to the Idea of the Good believed to be the supreme reality and the necessary condition of the existence of other ideas and of the physical universe. In the *Timaeus* he gives the name 'Father' to the Demiurge who he says is creator of the world. . . . Later, the Stoic Epictetus calls God the Father of men, and the later Platonists Numenius and Porphyry say he is the Father of the cosmos.

"The Christian belief in the Fatherhood of God, however, was not derived from Greek tradition, but indebted rather to Hebrew thought. Although 'father' is not a common title of God in the Old Testament, it occurs in many different writings and is found at many stages of human history. As Father, God is creator of man."[1]

---

[1]Arthur Wainwright, *The Trinity in the New Testament*, p. 43.

Jewish Customary Use of "Father"

In the OT, the title "Father" is used chiefly in connection with the election of the nation. He is Father of Israel (Jer. 31:9; cf. Mal. 2:10), and they are His sons (Isa. 1:2; 30:1; 45:11; Jer. 3:22), as is the nation (Hos. 11:1; Ex 4:22). He is also Father of the anointed king (2 Sam. 7:14; Ps. 2:7; 89:27).

In later Judaism the emphasis is on His Fatherhood of the nation, and protective care for the Jewish race; in one passage the Midrash refers to Him as "Father of the whole world," but this is exceptional. In apocryphal writings God's Fatherhood is often connected with His Lordship, and the two titles "Father" and "Lord" are used in close proximity (Ecclus. 23:1, 4; 51:10; Tob. 13:4).

"The favorite rabbinical phrase "Father in heaven" was not to emphasize His transcendence but distinguish Him from earthly fathers. The phrase was often used in worship and God was regularly addressed as "Father" (Wisd. 14:3).[2]

Father (Hebrew)

ab (*awb*)—Father, forefather. A primitive noun apparently derived from such baby sounds as *abab*.[3]

"It is found with slight variations in all Semitic languages; the Sumerians, for instance, had at least three different expressions for father; *a* (later *a-a*), meaning 'begetter'; *ab-ba*, meaning 'head of the family'; and a rarer word *ad-da* related to the Elamite word for father."[4]

The noun *ab* occurs 1191 times in the Hebrew OT, plus nine times in the Aramaic. The divine name "Father" may have been avoided by Jewish believers due to its abuse in the Canaanitish fertility cults.[5]

Worshipers in ancient Babylon addressed deity with names like "Father of the land," but these implied some actual physical or natural relationship between a god and his people (Jer. 2:27; cf. 3:19). Apart from the idea of election (Ex. 4:22–23; Hos. 11:1–4) or adoption (2 Sam. 7:14–15; Ps. 2:7) father-son imagery may have been avoided because of these pagan associations, coming back into use only after the time of the kings (Isa. 63:16; 64:8; Mal. 1:6).[6]

"Early Semitic writings use a cluster of names like 'father,' 'brother,' 'kinsman' to indicate some kind of kinship with God, e.g., Eliab ('My God is Father' Num. 1:9; 1 Sam. 16:6); Ahiezer ('My [divine] brother is help' Num. 1:2); or Ammishaddai ('The god of my kindred is Shaddai'

---

[2]Ibid. p. 43–44.

[3]*Theological Wordbook of the Old Testament*, Laird R. Harris, ed. Chicago: Moody Press, 1980), vol. 1, p. 5.

[4]*Theological Dictionary of the Old Testament*, G. Johannes Botterweck and Helmer Ringgren, eds. (Grand Rapids: Eerdmans, 1974), vol. 1, p. 3.

[5]*Theological Wordbook of the Old Testament*, op. cit. vol. 1, pp. 5–6.

[6]*Interpreter's Dictionary of the Bible*, George A. Buttrick, ed. (Nashville: Abingdon Press, 1962), vol. 2, p. 415.

Num. 1:12); and of course names containing *ab* like Abraham, Abimelech, Abishua, Absolom and Abijah."[7]

"Among the OT's proper nouns that employ the element *ab*, the most famous is Abraham, though at his call he bore the shorter name, Abram (Gen. 11:26—12:1), literally 'Father [God] (is) lofty.' But when Yahweh established his covenant with Abram (17:1–5), he said, 'Your name will be Abraham . . . for I will make you the father of a multitude . . . of nations.' . . . It thereby shifts the application of *ab* from God to Abraham, who hereafter becomes 'father' of the faithful, both in respect to his subjective attitude (of faith, Gal. 3:7; Rom. 4:16) and his objective inheritance (of righteousness, Gal. 3:29; Rom. 4:11, 13)."[8]

"The word *abh* has other meanings besides earthly father. It can mean a grandfather (Gen. 28:13), a founding father or ancestor, especially of a tribe or people, like David (1 Kings 15:11; 2 Kings 14:3), Abraham (Gen. 17:4ff.; Isa. 51:2), Moab (Gen. 19:37), Esau (Gen. 36:9, 43), and Jacob (Deut. 26:5; Isa. 43:27). It refers to the patriarchs (Deut. 1:8; 6:10; 9:5; 29:12), and of the first or former generations (Ex. 3:15; 20:5; Num. 20:15; 1 Kings 14:15; Jer. 7:22; Ps. 22:5). It can mean the founder of a lifestyle or occupation; Jubal was 'father of musicians' (Gen. 4:21); Jonadab, 'father' (founder) of the Rechabite movement.

"It was a key motivation of 'guilds of priests, singers and prophets . . . [who] traced their origin back to some ancestral father.' It was used of someone worthy of special honor, an elder, teacher, priest or prophetic master (2 Kings 2:12; 6:21; 13:14; Judg. 17:10; 18:19). It can mean a protector, someone partly taking the place of a father (Ps. 68:6; Job 29:16), a counselor (Gen. 45:8), or creator (Job 38:28). Each honored representative of the older investing generation was a 'father,' each of the new inheritance a 'son.' "[9]

Old Testament Usage of Father

The word "father" is often used in the OT to denote a strong bond between the past and the present. The expression "lay down with his fathers" is used of dying kings (Gen. 47:30; Deut. 31:16) and "gathered to his fathers" (Judg. 2:10; 2 Kings 22:20) gives the idea of unity in death with previous ancestors.

The phrase "God of [your] fathers" implies His personal protection and care (Gen. 26:24; 28:13; 31:5) and emphasizes the ongoing continuity between generations (Deut. 1:11; 4:1; 6:3; 26:7; 27:3), the danger of apostasy (1 Chron. 12:17; 2 Chron. 20:33; Ezra 7:27), the beauty of returning to God (2 Chron. 19:4; 30:22; 34:33) and the "intimate connection of the present with ancient history and the faith of the forefathers."[10]

True Israel (both Gentile and Jew) identifies with the great OT spiritual heroes as her "fathers" (1 Cor. 10:1). Abraham received the promise of

[7]Ibid. vol. 2, p. 415.
[8]*Theological Wordbook of the Old Testament*, vol. 1, p. 5.
[9]*Theological Dictionary of the Old Testament*, op. cit. vol. 1, pp. 7–8.
[10]Ibid. p. 11.

faith even before he was circumcised and became "father of the faithful" (Rom. 4:11–12) inasmuch as they are like him in faith (Rom. 4:16–17).[11]

"How long a sense of belonging to a forefather can persist through the generations depends on the amount of love and pride which a figure from the past could attract."[12]

Israel courteously and admiringly ascribed the term "father" to such people as a deeply respected priest, an unconditionally acknowledged prophet, or a high-ranking administrator who commanded with loving concern and was freely and spontaneously accepted. These people represented an ideal underlying all more official titles and functions. "For the Hebrews with their strong sense of family, *father* is a distinctly ethical term which had to prove itself in the sphere of law and justice and which in virtue of its rich content could be used to describe a relation of authority even when the reference was to God."[13]

Limitations of Jewish Understanding

Rabbis prayed and taught as many more formal preachers still do. They commonly used expressions like "The Holy One, blessed be He," "He who causes His name to dwell in His house," as well as substitute terms like "heaven," "the place," "the dwelling," "the speaking" or "the word." These terms stressed God's power, presence, dominion or holiness, but never really His fatherliness. The word was there, but not really understood or perceived. They did not even use "the Lord of the World" or the "almightiness" and "Father in heaven" (the most affectionate term used in the synagogue) in one breath.

Their image of God as Father was still restricted to a more legal context which thought of a father in terms of earned merit, a respected teacher or a privileged elite in a way which actually contradicted real fatherly freedom. Yet inherent in this known name was a glorious truth looking ahead to an incomparably deeper view, wholly transcending "mere formality." They had the term; it simply "lacked vitality because it did not express a radical appreciation of the fatherliness of God."[14]

Unusual as it may have seemed to them to do so, the prophets described God's care in metaphors that were probably closer to the truth than they dared think. The father was "an unconditionally recognized and trustworthy authority," watching over those who reverenced Him, as a father cared for his household (Ps. 103:13), and corrected like a beloved son those who went astray (Prov. 3:12; Deut. 8:5). Even stronger in Isa. 1:2ff., God himself as a Father "complains to the court of dumb nature because He has been rejected by the children whom He raised up with

---

[11]Walter Bauer, *A Greek-English Lexicon of the New Testament*, 2nd ed., William F. Arndt and F. Wilbur Gingrich, trans., F. Wilbur Gingrich and Frederick W. Danker, eds. (Chicago: University of Chicago Press, 1979), p. 635.

[12]*Theological Dictionary of the New Testament*, Gerhard Kittel, ed., Geoffrey W. Bromiley, trans. (Grand Rapids: Wm. B. Eerdmans Publishing Company, 1964), vol. 5, p. 961.

[13]Ibid. vol. 5, pp. 961–981.

[14]Ibid. vol. 5, pp. 981–982.

love. The point of comparison between God and the father is nowhere more tenderly revealed than this outburst of bottled up feelings which seek fellowship but do not find it. The prophet is expressing the fact that, even though the word is not used, love is the basic feeling in God's dealing with Israel."[15]

When His people are headed toward a "harsh destiny," God's father-heart is urgently moved. In such a time of crisis, the Psalmist uses the phrase "the generation of thy children" (Ps. 73:15). The author coined his prayer "for the living and the dead who have proved themselves under the assault of affliction and distress." Although the word "father" is not used in Jer. 3:22 or 31:18–20, we see a foretaste of the parable of the Prodigal Son in these passages.[16]

"The confession of God as Father, which developed from so small a root, serves now to express the supreme insight of biblical faith."[17]

Father (Greek)

"Father" is a favorite word in Matthew's Gospel where it is used of God 44 times. Twenty-two of these are unique to Matthew, and in 8 synoptic passages he also uses the word "Father" absent from the parallels. Mark's Gospel uses Father 4 times (Mark 8:38; 11:25; 13:32; 14:36), all after Peter's confession that Jesus was the Christ. Of the 17 times used in Luke, 7 verses are unique to his Gospel (Luke 2:49; 12:32; 22:29, 42; 23:42, 46; 24:49). It occurs very frequently in all of John's writings, both Gospel and Epistles, but is mentioned only three times in Acts (1:4, 7; 2:33).

Paul often uses phrases like "the God and Father of our Lord Jesus Christ" (Rom. 15:6; 2 Cor. 1:3; 11:31; Eph. 1:3; Col. 1:3), and calls God "our Father" (1 Cor. 1:3; 8:6; 2 Cor. 1:2; Gal. 1:4; Eph. 1:2; Phil. 1:2; 4:20; Col. 1:2; 1 Thess 1:3; 3:11, 13; 2 Thess 1:1; 2:16).

The title "Father" is given twice to God in Hebrews: in 1:5 quoting 2 Sam. 7:14 where God is Father of the Messiah; and 12:9 where God is described as the Father of spirits.

"Father" is rarely found in the Pastoral Epistles (1 Tim. 1:2; 2 Tim. 1:2; Titus 1:4). It is used three times in James (1:17, 27; 3:9) and three times in 1 Peter (1:2–3, 17), once in 2 Peter (1:17), once in Jude (v.1), and five times in Revelation (1:6; 2:27; 3:5, 21; 14:1).[18]

pater (*pat-ayr*)—Apparently a primary word; a father (literally or figuratively, near or more remote). Also translated in the KJV as "parent."[19] *Pater* comes from a root "signifying a nourisher, protector, upholder,"[20] and is "probably derived from the Hebrew word *ab*, which is the simplest labial

[15]Ibid. vol. 5, p. 970.
[16]Ibid. vol. 5, p. 973.
[17]Ibid. vol. 5, p. 974.
[18]Wainwright, op. cit. pp. 48–49.
[19]*Strong's* 3962.
[20]W.E. Vine, *The Expanded Vine's Expository Dictionary of New Testament Words*, John R. Kohlenberger III, ed. (Minneapolis, Minn.: Bethany House Publishers, 1984), p. 411.

sound of an infant. Consequently it recurs in all the cognate tongues"[21]

Pater is used 418 times in the NT. Like *ab* in the OT, it carries multiple meanings:

The immediate male ancestor (Matt. 2:22; 4:21f.; 8:21; 10:21; Mark 5:40; Luke 1:17; John 4:53; Acts 7:14; 1 Cor. 5:1).

Forefather, progenitor, ancestor—of Abraham (Matt. 3:9; Luke 1:73; 16:24; John 8:39, 53, 56; Acts 7:2b), and of ancestors (Matt. 23:30; Luke 1:55; 6:23, 26; 11:47f.; John 4:20; 6:31; Acts 3:13, 25; Heb. 1:1; 8:9).

A form of respectful address (Acts 7:2; cf. Acts 22:1).

The generation(s) of deceased Christians (2 Pet. 3:4).

The spiritual heroes of the past (Rom. 4:12).

A designation of the older spiritual members of a church—a respectful address by younger people to their elders (1 John 2:13–14).

Pater was also used figuratively in early Greek literature to mean a *spiritual father.*[22]

abba *(ab-bah)*—"Approximates to a personal name, in contrast to 'Father,' with which it is always joined in the NT. . . . betokens unreasoning trust." Combined with "Father," it "expresses the love and intelligent confidence of the child."[23]

Abba is used only three times in the NT (Mark 14:36; Rom. 8:15–16; Gal. 4:6), and is the common-language (Aramaic) pronunciation in Jesus' time of this Hebrew or Chaldee word. Jesus probably used *abba* more than just the one time expressly recorded (Mark 14:36), but "in all cases, and particulary in address to God. . . . In so doing He applies to God a term which must have sounded familiar and disrespectful to His contemporaries because it was used in the everyday life of the family. In other words He uses the 'simple speech of the child to its father.' "[24]

"*Abba*," says Dr. Robert Frost, "is an Aramaic term of personal endearment akin to our 'papa' or 'daddy.' It is the affectionate language of a child who looks to his father for faithful provision and protection. It is a term of trust based on a personal love relationship."[25]

"The new thing in the usage is that an everyday infant sound is applied without inhibition to God. To Jewish sensibility this is too familiar. For Jesus it is the simplest and sincerest conceivable term to express God's attitude and it also implies a rejection of all religious pretension."[26]

"The Aramaic word *abba* . . . shows how intimate was the relationship between Jesus and God. Abba was a familiar mode of speech reserved for one's own father. Other peoples' fathers would be addressed as *abi* (my father) or *abinu* (our father). . . . Jews did not use this absolute form to address God because it implied too great a familiarity. When Jesus

---

[21]Ethelbert W. Bullinger, *A Critical Lexicon and Concordance to the English and Greek New Testament* (Grand Rapids: Zondervan Publishing House, 1975), p. 277.

[22]Bauer, op. cit. p. 635.

[23]Vine, op. cit. p. 1.

[24]*Theological Dictionary of the New Testament*, op. cit. vol. 1, p. 6.

[25]Dr. Robert Frost, *Our Heavenly Father* (Plainfield, N.J.: Logos Intl., 1978), p. 57.

[26]*Theological Dictionary of the New Testament*, op. cit. vol. 5, p. 985.

used *abba* He was making a startling innovation. He was claiming a relationship with God closer than that claimed by any of His countrymen. He was claiming a unique kind of sonship."[27]

Worship of the Father

A. N. Gibb says: "To the regenerated believer, God is not some far-off deity, too high and holy to take notice of Him, but He is revealed as a loving Father in whose family he has been born, to whom he has been brought near, and who has blessed him with all spiritual blessings in the heavenlies in Christ Jesus (Eph. 1:3; John 1:12–13).

"The title 'Father' . . . suggests intimacy, dearness, love and care." Worship goes to the Father, says Gibb, because of what He is as:

The *holy* Father (John 17:16). He loves righteousness and hates iniquity (Heb. 1:9).

The *righteous* Father (John 17:35). By the righteousness of God we mean God's perfect consistency with His own character.

"The Father of *glory* (Eph. 1:17). By glory is meant displayed excellence. God has displayed all the many perfections and excellences of His character in His Son, and recorded them for us in the holy Scriptures (2 Cor. 4:6). The Father of *lights* (James 1:17). We are told "God is Light." Light is that "which makes manifest" (1 John 1:5; Eph. 5:13). To Him "all things are open and naked," for "known unto God are all His works from the beginning of the world" (Heb. 4:13). He is the Father who manifested himself, and whose outshining glory is seen "in the face of Jesus Christ."

The Father of *mercies* (2 Cor. 1:3). As such He is also "the God of all comfort." David sang "Like as a father pitieth his children, so the Lord pitieth them that fear him" (Ps. 103:13). As the Father of mercies, He knows all the frailties, fears, failings and faults of His people, and the constant need of His correcting and restoring grace. Truly "His mercy endureth forever" (Ps. 107:1). Every need of His children is not only anticipated, but abundantly supplied "according to His riches in glory by Christ Jesus" (Phil. 4:19).

The Father of *all* (Eph. 4:6). The reference here is to the fact that all regenerated believers have "One God and Father of all". . . . In other words there is no aristocracy in His family. All God's children are equally near and dear to Him.

The Father of our *Lord Jesus Christ* (2 Cor. 1:3; Eph. 1:3; 1 Pet. 1:3). An inexpressibly precious title! He is not only Father of the whole family of the redeemed, but He is also the Father of the One whose precious blood has made such a family relationship possible. Christ is "the only begotton Son of the Father." . . . We have the unspeakable privilege and honor of addressing God by the same name as did His Son while on earth, and we may now call Him "Father." Our Lord in resurrection associated Himself with all who loved Him and said, "Go to My brethren, and say

---

[27]Wainwright, op. cit. p. 45.

unto them, I ascend unto My Father and your Father; and to my God, and your God" (John 20:17).[28]

The Origin and Goal of the Gospel

The gospel, notes Thomas Smail, is not primarily a Jesus movement or a Charismatic movement but a "Father movement." It starts "not with the cross of Jesus or with the gift of the Spirit, but with the Father who so loved the world that He gave His Son in His Spirit. And it achieves its purpose, not when the Body of Christ is gloriously renewed (Eph. 5:27), not even when the enthroned Christ has subdued all His enemies and brought every knee to bow before Him (Phil. 2:11), but rather when that same Christ 'hands over the kingdom to God the Father, after He has destroyed all dominion, authority and power' (1 Cor. 15:24). 'When He has done this, then the Son will himself be made subject to Him who put everything under Him, so that God may be all in all' (1 Cor. 15:28). . . .

"Just as the Father is the source of everything both in creation and redemption, so also He is the goal of everything, and the mission of the Son and of the Spirit is to advance His glory and let Him be all in all. I am convinced that it is within this theological context that any authentic renewal . . . has to be prepared to understand itself, and that such an understanding is full of practical consequences of the most important kind."[29]

Questions and Answers

Q: *Why say that God is a Father? Isn't it true that God is the Divine Principle of life and love, a world-soul, or perhaps just a synonym for "Supreme Power" or "Intelligence"?*

A: God *is* both love and life, supreme power, and intelligence; but the Bible clearly reveals Him to be a loving and life-giving *person*, a Father (Matt. 5:48) who is wise and strong enough to take care of any of His childrens' needs.

Q: *Isn't God the Father just another name for Jesus?*

A: "Jesus" is not the collective name for the Father, Son, and Holy Spirit; it is the name of the Son (Matt. 1:21; Luke 1:31). Jesus clearly distinguished himself from the Father (Luke 2:49).

Q: *I believe in the fatherhood of God, that he is father of all. Why do some Christians call people modernists, liberals, or universalists because they believe this? Isn't God everyone's Father?*

A: God does sustain a fatherly relationship to all men because of His creatorship: "He maketh his sun to rise on the evil and on the good,

---

[28]A. N. Gibb, *Worship*, Walterick Publishers).
[29]Thomas Smail, *The Forgotten Father* (London: Hodder and Stoughton, 1980), pp. 20–21.

and sendeth rain on the just and unjust" (Matt. 5:45). But to sin is to abandon our true Father's house and to lose ourselves in a foreign land. What we lose in relationship with our Creator can only be restored in redemption by the Savior. Jesus said of the Pharisees, "You are of your father the devil" (John 8:44) and that no man could come to the Father but by Him (John 14:6).

Q: *I believe that the Father loves so much that no one will be lost. Won't the final restitution of all things (Acts 3:21) prophesied in Scripture demonstrate God's ultimate victory in reconciliation of all people to himself?*

A: The duration of punishment is as lasting as that of eternal life— unending (Matt. 25:46 uses the same word for "eternal" and "everlasting"). The phrase "the times of restitution of all things" (Acts 3:21) does not refer to Satan, demons, or wicked men who willfully rebelled against God, but to the creation "made subject to vanity, not willingly" (Rom. 8:20). Jesus said "Whosoever speaketh against the Holy Ghost, it shall not be forgiven him, neither in this world, neither in the world to come" (Matt. 12:32). If even one person remains unforgiven, *all* men are not reconciled to God.

Q: *Isn't belief in the fatherhood of God a projection of our own need for a father image—like Freud thought, a "father-complex" of sorts?*

A: Many deities in world religions are, in part, a projection of human fears, lusts, or needs; many people form their idea of God in the image of their own aspirations and longings. True, the idea of God being a heavenly father satisfies a basic and deep human need, but is the hunger of an orphan for a dad's affection and security a demonstration of mere fantasy, evidence of a wish-projection with absolutely no basis in reality? An orphaned boy may make up his own ideas of a father, wish these ideas on men who are not his father, and probably have a completely false picture of his real father. But such sad and misdirected dreams and fancies show only this: he has a legitimate need based on the loss of a real person.

Q: *But on what basis can you say that there really is a father to lose? Why can't belief in a Father-God be simply explained as the projection of a human need for a sense of comfort and goodness?*

A: God's goodness and reality are demonstrated in the objective evidence of the life, teaching, death, and resurrection of Jesus Christ. It is verifiable historically quite apart from and unconnected with human psychology. We believe Jesus on objective grounds and *he* called God "Father." We accept belief in God's father-heart not because it is a totally adequate description of God's goodness, but because it is the *least inadequate* available.

Q: *What do you mean when you call God "Father"?*

A: When we use the word "Father," we don't mean God is exactly like a human father, not even the best father who ever lived. We mean that God has the original qualities which we admire when reflected by the best and wisest of all human fathers. One scholar writes, "God bears the loving relationship of such a father to his children to an infinite degree, though His fatherhood included qualities which no consideration, or extension or multiplication of the attributes of a human father could ever lead us to imagine."[1]

Q: *Why do you call God a father? Isn't it equally true that you could call Deity a mother?*

A: God's creation of men and women "in His image" means all essential elements of both maleness and femaleness come from and are originally inherent in God. God is shown with motherly characteristics in the Bible; however, Scripture uses more images of God as a father than as a mother. There are two main reasons for this.

First, Israel, just as the Church today, must never confuse worship of the only true God with the occultic Mother Goddess (under the names of Astarte, Ashera, Diana, Isis, and Ishtar) worshiped around them. In these pagan religions, the Mother Goddess *was* Nature, characterized by magic, cycles of life, as well as fertility ritual and the identification of sexual immorality with spirituality. Falling prey to this type of worship, which included witchcraft, meant spiritual death.

In another sense, all creation (male, female, and neuter) is treated as female, being sustained, protected and cherished by the Creator, as the Church herself is the "Bride of Christ." These images are not some engineered result of male domination of God-imagery, but God-given metaphors reinforced in the sacrament of marriage as analogies of God's care. As Christ is the Husband, so the Church is the Bride; this marriage brings new (spiritual) children into the world.

Q: *But isn't the idea of "Father" the consequence of the male-dominated Jewish society and Scripture selection committees?*

A: No. We must not lose the power and beauty of the metaphor because of its misuse. Harm has been done by stressing the maleness in God to the exclusion of corresponding female imagery, such as that where God is shown as the mother who birthed Israel (Deut. 32:18), carried the nation in her womb (Is.46:3), comforted her continually (Isa. 66:13) and nursed her on her breast (Ps. 131:2). In Gal. 3:28 we are told that in Christ "there is neither male nor female." When Jesus talked to women, He did not emphasize their femaleness, as many in His society did; He spoke to them as people. Some women were His valued, trusted friends and followers. But the abundance of imagery in Scripture (some male, some female, some nature-based, and some neuter) should protect us from becoming too focused on one aspect of God's nature or personality to the harmful exclusion of others. Don't blame Scripture; blame our biased selection of images from it for the loss of important elements identified with femaleness in our world.

---

[1]Leslie Davidson, *The Christian Replies* (London, 1962), p. 44.

Analysis and Discussion

God himself could either be impersonal or so great a personage as to have no direct concern with puny individuals in such an enormous universe. It is these uncertainties which lend all natural religions their strange admixture of doubt and hope. But once the image has been restored, uncertainty disappears. The relationship of creature to Creator becomes the much more satisfying and directly personal one of son to Father. Indeed, if there is one single question that a man may ask himself who is uncertain as to whether he is a Christian or not—who cannot with assurance recall any specific spiritual experience by which to mark a point of re-creation—it is this: "Do I think of God and address Him as my Father?"

Arthur Custance[1]

Old Testament Role Models

Job

The ideal Father is the personification of security, strength and dependability. Perhaps the oldest recorded story in the Bible is the book about Job. Job is often remembered because of his terrible trials, because of the great spiritual battle fought and won in his life. But he is also something of a model father. Much of his attitude to life reflects the strength of a true Father (Job 29:2, 4–17, 21–25).

Stephen B. Clarke points out that as a village elder, Job was a man of means and power who commanded respect because of the way he lived (5:25). "He fits much of the description in 1 Tim. 3:1–7. He is portrayed . . . as someone who lives righteously and as a man trained in wisdom. People rise to greet him out of respect, wait for him to speak, listen to his words, value his opinion. He is a man who wields authority, formal and informal, and who does it effectively. Equally important: he cares for people, especially those who are in need; for the poor, the crippled, the widow, and the orphan. He sees they are provided for and protected. In fact, he sees that righteousness prevails everywhere he has influence, not just among the disadvantaged. . . . He expresses his authority by caring for people and by seeing that life goes well among those he is responsible for. Job takes a concern for the life of the community that is similar to the concern a father takes for his family."[2]

---

[1]Arthur Custance, *Man and Adam In Christ* (Grand Rapids: Zondervan Publishing House, 1977), pp. 124–125.
[2]Stephen B. Clark, *Man and Women in Christ* (Ann Arbor, Mich.: Servant Books, 1980), pp. 53–54.

Abraham

Another wonderful Old Testament role model for fatherhood is found early in Genesis. We have some idea of God's delight over loving and obedient children; but how does the Father feel about sinners? How does He feel about those He knows who are about to die, to be cut off forever and consumed by fire?

We get a glimpse into God's true father heart from one of the most brave and touching father and son records in Scripture—the account of Abraham and Isaac. This story is more than a record of a man's great faith in God; it is also a type of God's great love for fallen man in the sacrifice of His own Son; a glimpse of the weight on God's own heart over our fallen and estranged race. We can see in this story what it meant for God to have to give up His beloved Son. When we have been touched to the core by its truth, we can think about it again for each prodigal who intends to spend one day too many in the far off country.

Abraham loved his son. Isaac was the special, the promised, child of his old age, a child of miracle and destiny. To say that Abraham loved him is as close to maximum understatement as we can get in all the stories of the Old Testament. But Abraham loved God more and was willing to go to ultimate lengths to prove it.

Barnes notes that the phrases "thy son, thine only one, whom thou hast grown to love" and "Isaac" ("he laughs") are descriptive of how much Abraham had grown to love him. "Take thy son, thine only son Isaac, whom thou lovest . . . and offer him there . . . upon one of the mountains which I will tell thee of" (Gen. 22:1–2). "No mention is made of Abraham's personal reaction to this command from God . . . nothing is said of the pain which tore the father's heart." How does God love a man who is about to die? Like Isaac; like His own Son. And how does the Father love sinners? Like all men; like He loves His Son.

"The details continue; in fact they are multiplied to let us feel how each successive step was an added agony for the much tried father. Isaac may by this time have arrived at the age of some 18–20 years. The aged Abraham, his strength cut by his soul agony could hardly have carried this burden. . . . Isaac cannot but sense that some terrible burden depresses his father past anything the son has ever observed in him before. . . . His very address 'My Father' must almost have been felt like a knife thrust by Abraham. . . . And then his father's love devises an answer which is a marvelous compound of considerate love and anticipative faith. He spares Isaac undue pain and leaves the issues entirely with God where his own heart has left them throughout the journey. It marks the high point of the chapter, the one thing about God's dealings with His own that here receives emphatic statement. 'God will provide a lamb for himself for a burnt offering, my son.' (The verb *ra'ah* usually means 'see'—here 'look out for' or provide or choose as in Gen. 41:33; Deut. 12:13; 33:21; 1 Sam. 16:1, 17.) And then it simply says 'And they two went along together.'

"The tension of the narrative grows. You feel how each successive step grows more difficult for the heavy-hearted father. You observe with wonder the strength of his faith which will not suffer him to waver. . . . Now, O marvel of marvels, he actually binds his own son! Isaac's submission to this act is best explained as an act of confidence in his father, a confidence built upon a complete understanding and a deep love which knew that the father could wish his son no harm. . . . That Isaac suffered himself to be bound is an act of supreme faith in God and of full confidence in his father. Usually too little consideration is given to Isaac's heroism, which if it were not for the more marvelous faith heroism of his father, could justly be classed as among the mightiest acts of faith."[3]

Like Abraham, God gave up His Son, His irreplaceable Son, in the face of what seemed to the world a senseless sacrifice; but He did it in an unflinching implicit commitment to ultimate right and truth.

The Final Revelation of God

John Watson's brilliant message entitled "Fatherhood—The Final Idea of God" (1896) radiantly illustrates the great importance Jesus gave to God's fatherhood in almost every major teaching and ministry. Jesus calls God "Father" over 178 times in the Gospels; it is His constant reference point to all kingdom relationships. Watson makes the following points:

- Jesus reasoned truth on the basis of who the Father was: "If ye then being evil, know how to give good gifts unto your children: how much more shall your Father which is in heaven give the Holy Spirit to them that ask him?" (Luke 11:13).
- He labored in the *fellowship* of the Father: "I seek not mine own will but the will of the Father which hath sent me" (John 5:30).
- He rested in the *wisdom* of the Father: "At that time Jesus answered and said, I thank thee, O Father, Lord of heaven and earth, because thou hast hid these things from the wise and prudent, and hast revealed them unto babes" (Matt. 11:25).
- He suffered in *faith* in the Father: "Therefore doth My Father love me, because I lay down My life that I may take it again. . . . This commandment have I received of my Father" (John 10:17–18).
- When the consciousness of God awoke with power in the soul of the Holy Child, Jesus was filled with a sudden enthusiasm: "Wist ye not that I must be about My Father's business?" (Luke 2:49).
- When He had fulfilled His calling and offered His sacrifice, Jesus' soul returned to His Father: "Father, into Thy hands I commend My spirit" (Luke 23:46).

"From Nazareth to Calvary, the love of the Father was Jesus' dwelling-place . . . no one can ignore this constant and radiant sense of the divine fatherhood in the life of Jesus. . . . It goes without saying that Jesus' sense of the fatherhood [of God] must be supreme. It is a contradiction of the Gospels to say that it was exclusive.

"Jesus toiled for three years to write the truth of fatherhood in the minds of the disciples, with at least one result, that it is interwoven with

---

[3]Albert Barnes, *Barne's Notes on the Old Testament* (Grand Rapids: Baker Book House), Vol. II, pp. 619–620, 627.

the pattern of the Gospels. He pleaded also with His friends that they should receive it into their hearts, till St. John filled his epistles with this word. With minute and affectionate care Jesus described the whole circle of religious thought and stated it in terms of fatherhood."

Likewise, in teaching the disciples, the theme of God's fatherhood was reinforced again and again in many contexts:

- *Prayer* was to be to the Father: "Say: Our Father which art in heaven" (Luke 11:2).
- *Relationship* with Jesus was dependent on obeying the Father: "For whosoever shall do the will of my Father in heaven, the same is my brother, and sister, and mother" (Matt. 12:50).
- He commanded people to conform their character to the Father's: "Be ye therefore perfect even as your Father which is in heaven is perfect" (Matt. 5:48).
- *Providence* is the loving oversight of the Father: "Your heavenly Father knoweth that ye have need of all these things" (Matt. 6:32).
- *Repentance* is a return to the Father: "I will arise and go to my father, and will say unto him, Father, I have sinned . . ." (Luke 15:18).
- Jesus described the *future* as living with the Father: "In My Father's house are many mansions" (John 14:2).

"The effect of such passages is cumulative and irresistible. They are better than the proof texts for a dogma; they are an atmosphere in which faith lives and moves and has its being. They are sunrise." By its very nature, God's father heart is wide as well as deep. More than one evangelical exploring these ocean depths has found himself caught in currents of thought usually assigned to those without a true picture of God's holiness or strong justice. While being careful to avoid universalistic or unscriptural concepts and language, we must admit God is kinder and less doctrinaire than some of His people.

"People with dogmatic ends to serve have striven to believe that Jesus reserved 'Father' for the use of His disciples; but an ingenuous person could hardly make that discovery in the Gospels. One searches in vain to find that Jesus had an esoteric word for His intimates, and an exoteric for the people, saying 'Father' to John and 'Judge' to the publicans. It had been amazing if Jesus were able to employ alternatively two views of God according to His audience, speaking now as an Old Testament prophet, now as the Son of God. 'Then spake Jesus to the multitudes and His disciples saying . . . one is your Father, which is in heaven' (Matt. 23:1, 9).

"This attempt to restrict the intention of Jesus is not of yesterday; it was the invention of the Pharisees. They detected the universal note in Jesus' teaching; they resented His unguarded charity. Their spiritual instincts were not wide but they were very keen within a limited range and the Pharisees judged with much correctness that the teaching of Jesus and the privileges of Judaism were inconsistent. If a publican was a son of God, what advantage had a Pharisee? It was natural that they should murmur; we are now thankful that they criticized the Master.

"Jesus made His defense in His three greatest parables, and in the Parable of the Prodigal son He defined the range of the Divine fatherhood beyond reasonable dispute. His deliverance was given with deliberation—in Jesus, most finished parable; the parable was created for a definite purpose—to vindicate Jesus mixing with sinners. It contains Jesus' most complete description of a sinner—from his departure to his return; with emphasis it declares that sinner a son of God—a son that was lost and is found. Between the son in a far country and the son at home is an immense difference; but if he had not been a son from home there had been no home for his return. The possibility of salvation lies in sonship. It would not be fair to rest any master doctrine on a single parable, were it not that the parable is Jesus' definition of fatherhood, given in answer to the practical challenge of privilege, were it not that it simply crystallizes the whole teaching of Jesus on God from His boyhood to His death. If Jesus did not teach divine fatherhood embracing the race, then He used words to conceal thought and one despairs of ever understanding our Master."[4]

Watson did not, of course, believe that all mankind is really saved but ignorant of their salvation, that the Fall had not really taken place, and men are not lost in the biblical sense. God's love is perfectly consistent with His holiness. The Lord Jesus always posed the question of God's fatherhood in decision and love—*Do we want to be God's sons or not?* "There is no reference to a general sonship by nature or estate.

"The word 'Father' is for those who accept Jesus' teaching about 'your Father.' . . . It is always related to the Kingdom, to the rule of a gracious and commanding God and has as its ultimate implication the Lordship of God."[5]

But, as George MacDonald also pointed out with a lot more passion than theological caution, God really is *by right* the true Father of humanity, and salvation is in a very real sense a return home and not an introduction to an alien way of life. God *is* our true Father. The prodigal may not come home, may call himself by another name and even die outside the Father's home lost forever; but the gracious call of the Gospel finds an echo in the soul of every man and woman because that is where man belongs—in His family.

"When Jesus speaks of fatherhood, it is almost a stupidity to explain He is not thinking of any physical relation—the 'offspring' of the heathen poets and that 'Father' is not a synonym for 'Creator.' Jesus rested His own sonship in community of character. God was love, for He gave His only Son, and Jesus was love, for He gave himself. He realized His sonship in community of service: 'My Father worketh hitherto and I work.' The bond between son and Father in the spiritual world is ethical. It is perfect between the Father and the Son in the Holy Trinity; it is only a suggestion

---

[4]John Watson, "Fatherhood—The Final Idea of God, *Mind of the Master* (New York: Dodd, Mead and Co., 1896).

[5]*Theological Dictionary of the New Testament*, Gerhard Kittel, ed., Geoffrey W. Bromiley, trans. (Grand Rapids: Wm. B. Eerdmans Publishing Company, 1964), vol. 5, pp. 990–991.

between a sinner and God. As one can detect some trace of likeness between a father and his son, although the son may have played the fool and defiled the fashion of his countenance, so the most degraded and degenerate of human outcasts still bears the faint remains of the divine image. The capability of repentance is the remains of righteousness; the occasional aspirations after goodness are the memories of home; the recognition of right and wrong is an affinity to the mind of God. The sonship is hidden in Zacchaeus and Mary Magdalene—a mere possibility; in St. John and St. Paul it is revealed—a beautiful actuality, so that this paradox is only the deeper truth, that one may be, and yet become a son, as the ethical likeness is acknowledged and cleansed. Jesus' message was 'You are a son.' As soon as it was believed, Jesus gave power to become."[6]

Fatherhood and Destiny

The consequences of macro-evolutionary thought have left many of the Western world's young reeling. One of the most significant forces to move and challenge people toward commitment to the purposes of the living God is a sense of divine destiny. This sense of destiny not only comes by understanding the scriptural doctrines of election and providence, but by an essential and usually neglected component: a God-given vision of the Father's heart.

One of the great needs of the Church is a revelation of herself as significant, valuable, and in some way as an effective "affecter" of the world around her. To be gripped by a sense of divine destiny, we need two revelations from the Holy Spirit. First, an understanding that we are true sons and daughters of God; and second that the Lord Jesus himself is our big brother, our true spiritual relative as the firstborn Son of the Father.

Think of what the Lord Jesus must have felt when as a child He first realized His mission and calling in life! To read in Scripture things that *He* was to do, and what *He* was to be! To open the scroll and realize with a thrill, "This is me. This is talking about *me*!" Think of the great sense of purpose it must have burned in His child's heart to learn—perhaps at his mother's knee or out in the hills and fields talking not only to Joseph but to His real Father—how He was born, how He had been spared, and something of what His great purpose and mission was to be. The author of Hebrews writes, "Though he were a Son, yet learned he obedience by the things which he suffered; and being made perfect, he became the author of eternal salvation unto all them that obey Him" (Heb. 5:8–9; cf. 2:9–11, 16–18; 3:1–6).

This was His channel of urgency and devotion, the calm and conscious commitment and time-redeeming priority through which His love and wisdom flowed out to the world. A sense of divine destiny molded the Lord's ministry from before the day He left the wood at His carpenter's

---

[6]Watson, op. cit.

bench until the hour He gave up His lovely life on another beam of wood. We have no detailed Scriptural record of most of His early years; but we can envision what it must have been like even for Him to catch the thrill of the beginning of His life ministry.

Bob Frost recalls one such picture: "An elderly friend who has had a proven ministry over many years once shared with me a vision she had of Jesus prior to His earthly ministry.

"He had just completed construction of a table-like bench and was brushing away the remaining traces of sawdust with the sensitive touch of a master craftsman. He was lean and muscular and she particularly noticed the callouses on his hands. She realized there was something special about this occasion and was impressed in her spirit that this was the last piece of work He would ever accomplish in the carpentry shop. She was aware that He worked very hard during the day but spent many hours in the night communing with His heavenly Father.

"He carefully placed His tools in their designated places, folded His apron and laid it on a bench. He then moved directly to the door, turning only once to survey the familiar surroundings of the workshop He had inherited from Joseph following his death. He had followed in the footsteps of Joseph for many years, but the time had now come to minister the words and works of His heavenly Father and fulfill His divine calling. After a brief pause—so much can be gathered up during such moments— He decisively shut the door. My friend knew deep in her spirit that He was on His way to the Jordan to meet John."[7]

Fatherhood: The Key to a Lost Generation

What happens to a generation that loses all sense of the fatherhood of God? Fathers no longer behave as fathers; mothers in turn lose their concern for their daughters.

Elizabeth Moberly, a research psychologist in Cambridge, specializing in psychoanalytic development, points out a very important consequence of this loss; society becomes a hothouse for homosexuality. She notes that sodomy and lesbianism are the eroticization of unmet and genuine *needs*; the needs of a son to be loved by his father and a daughter to be loved by her mother. She writes, "A homosexual orientation does not depend on a genetic predisposition, hormonal imbalance, or abnormal learning processes, but on difficulties in the parent-child relationship, especially in the earlier years of life. . . . The homosexual, whether man or woman—has suffered from some *deficit in the relationship with the parent of the same sex*; and that there is a corresponding drive to make good this deficit—through the medium of same-sex or 'homosexual' re-lationships."

Any family-related spiritual damage can contribute to this problem. A father may be directly to blame who "makes little effort to find time for his son, belittles him, or ill treats him in some way. But . . . a *divorce* may

---

[7]Dr. Robert Frost, *Our Heavenly Father* (Plainfield, N.J.: Logos Intl., 1978), p. 31.

damage a child's relational capacity in this way without the parents wanting this to happen. . . . Above all, *early separation* or *parental absence* at a crucial point in the child's development may in some instances have long term negative effects even if the separation is unavoidable or for good reasons (illness or hospitalization of either child or the parent). . . . The family relationships of a homosexual may in a number of instances seem good—may be good at a certain level. What we are speaking of is intrapsychic damage at a deep level, much of which may not be overt or conscious."[8]

Hidden Orphans

Moberly uses the term "hidden orphans" to describe "children of two-parent families who are no longer able to relate normally to one or the other parent, and hence are unable to receive parental care even if the parent in question is present and offers care. . . . Homosexuality is not an independent entity or condition caused by difficulties in the parent-child relationship. Rather the homosexual relationship is itself a deficit in the child's ability to relate to parents of the same sex which is carried over to members of the same sex in general. Needs for love from, dependency on and identification with the parent of the same sex are met through the child's attachment to the parent. If the attachment is disrupted, the needs normally met through the medium of such an attachment remain unmet."

She goes on to say that early separation, just like the death of a parent, disrupts a child's attachment. "Even if relatively brief, it may lead to the typical process of mourning, protest at the absence of the loved parent, followed by despair, leading finally to detachment. When the child is reunited with the parent it may take some time for normal attachment to be restored, since the child has experienced the parent as hurtful ('He/she abandoned me') even if the separation was unavoidable and there was no intention of hurt. The child may show indifference for a time, repressing his need for attachment or alternate between hostility (detachment) and clinging behavior (attachment).

"But what if the mourning process is never completely worked through? What if . . . the child continues to express his yearning for the love-source experienced as hurtful and at the same time continues to repress his reproaches against the love-source again on account of its hurtfulness and unwillingness to trust the love-source again? The resultant position would be an unmet love-need, consequent on and maintained by a defensive detachment from the needed love-source. This is precisely the kind of condition we have already spoken of. . . . This condition is essentially an unresolved pathological mourning process."[9]

God's Care for the Orphans

"When deficits occur, substitute relationships for parental care are in God's redemptive plan just as parental relationships are in His creative

---

[8]Elizabeth R. Moberly, *Homosexuality: A New Ethic* (Cambridge, England: James Clarke and Co. Ltd., 1983).
[9]Ibid.

plan. A notable scriptural theme is that of care of orphans. . . . Positive guidelines are provided . . . in the concern for making good deficits in parental care (i.e., in caring for orphans). The duty of care for orphans and denunciation of their oppression is a theme found throughout the OT. Ill-treatment of the orphan is condemned, as in Isa. 1:23; Jer. 5:28; and Ezek. 22:7 'Ye shall not afflict any widow, or fatherless child' (Ex. 22:22); 'Thou shalt not pervert the judgment of the stranger, nor of the fatherless' (Deut. 24:17); 'Cursed be he that perverteth the judgment of the stranger, fatherless, and widow' (Deut. 27:19); 'Do no violence to the stranger, the fatherless, nor the widow' (Jer. 22:3); 'Oppress not the widow, nor the fatherless' (Zech. 7:10). One is enjoined to give the orphan his rights (Isa. 1:17) and in the NT such help is seen as essential to acceptable religion (James 1:27). Above all, this concern is linked with the character of God himself. It is God who protects and helps orphans (Deut. 10:18; Ps. 10:18; 146:9) for He himself is 'father of the fatherless' (Psa. 68:5); 'In Thee the fatherless findeth mercy' (Hosea 14:3).

"Thus a key part of counsel to those bound by homosexuality is a *reparenting* by those in the Body of Christ who can represent that unmet need on behalf of and as an expression of the Father's love. The perfect will of God is checked whenever a child is orphaned. However, although the orphan is 'against the will of God' one does not seek to punish an orphan for being an orphan. . . . Unmet needs are to be met—but without eroticization. It is the sexual expression of pre-adult psychological needs that is unacceptable."[10]

Here then is a significant theme in ministering to a generation marked not only by widespread sodomy and lesbianism, but broken marriages and families: the fatherhood and father heart of God.

True and False Images of God

John Dawson's powerful message entitled "The Father Heart of God" compares true and false pictures people have of God as a father in six areas: parental authority, faithfulness, generosity, affection, attentiveness, and acceptance. It has ministered deeply to street-people as well as many Christians from the Western world who have ugly images of fathers from unpleasant or sin-damaged childhoods.

He asks, "Have you ever wondered what God thinks of you? Is it hard for you to believe that He loves you as much as the Bible says He does? One of the most wonderful revelations in the Bible is that God is our Father. What do you think of when you hear the word 'father'? Do you automatically think of protection, provision, warmth and tenderness? . . . God reveals himself in the Bible as a gentle, forgiving Father, intimately involved with each and every detail of our lives. It is not only a beautiful picture but a true one."

John points out what happens to a society when our picture of God, our image of real fatherhood is damaged by sin: "Our heavenly Father is

---

[10]Ibid. p. 36.

at this very moment being slandered and misrepresented all over the world by man's cruelty and selfishness. Not only in the home, but in all forms of human government. His laws of love have been ignored and our mangled hearts continue on in carrying out injustice to all those smaller and weaker than ourselves. What horror is God seeing at this moment? . . . A small boy is slapped awake by a drunken and angry man in the middle of the night . . . A terrified child is beaten mercilessly by the dark, hulking shape of a man he calls "Daddy." A fifteen-year old prostitute with blank, empty eyes mechanically performs through a night of degradation on Hollywood Boulevard. She doesn't care what happens to her. She hasn't felt clean since the night she was molested by her own father.

"A wounded generation stumbles through their youthful years only to visit the same hurts on their own children. Generation after generation it goes on. Is there no one to comfort us? Who will father the children of men? Whose arms are big enough for all the lonely children of the world? Who weeps over our pains? Who will comfort us in our loneliness? *Only God. A broken-hearted father who is rejected by the little ones He yearns to heal.*"[11]

We often forget that God's very attributes of omniscience and omnipresence must necessarily intimately involve Him with every detail of our lives. The Bible seems to indicate that contrary to the "passionless" (apathy) picture adopted in much of Western theology (following Greek and Latin philosophical and judicial images) God is deeply moved, affected, and touched by the pressures, problems and personal heartbreak people go through.

God was there when you experienced cruel teasing in the school yard and you walked alone, avoiding the eyes of others. When you sat in a math class dejected and confused, He was with you. At the age of four when you got lost at the county fair and wandered terrified through the huge crowd, it was God who turned the heart of that kind lady who helped you find your mother. "I led them with the cords of human kindness, with ties of love" (Hosea 11:4, NIV). . . . It was actually God who heard you speak your first real word. The hours you spent alone exploring new textures with your baby hands were a delight to your heavenly Father. Some of His greatest treasures are the memories of your childhood laughter. . . .

Your Heavenly Father was there when you first walked as a child. He was there through hurts and disappointments. He is present now at this moment. You were briefly loaned to human parents who, for a few years were supposed to have showered you with love like His love. But you are and always will be a child of God made in His image. Your loving Father awaits even now with outstretched arms. What would keep you from Him?

"In my own childhood and boyhood," said George MacDonald, "my father was the refuge from all the ills of life, even sharp pain itself. Therefore I say to son or daughter who has no pleasure in the name 'Father,'

---

[11]John Dawson, *The Father Heart of God* (Tyler, Texas: Last Days Ministries, 1983).

'You must interpret the word by all that you have missed in life. All that human tenderness can give or desire in the nearness and readiness of love, all and infinitely more must be true of the perfect Father—of the maker of fatherhood, the Father of all the fathers of the earth, specially the Father of those who have specially shown a father heart.' "[12]

> To Thy house, O God My Father,
> Thy lost child is come;
> Led by wandering lights no longer,
> I have found my home.

> Over moor and fen I tracked them
> Through the midnight blast
> But to find the Light eternal
> In my heart at last.

Gerhard Tersteegen

Historical Discussion

Father! the sweetest, dearest Name
That men or angels know!
Fountain of life, that had no fount,
From which itself could flow!

Frederick William Faber

The Loving Father

Dr. Robert Frost

"I came to realize in my own experience that I had a very faulty concept concerning the fatherhood of God which was limiting the power of the Holy Spirit in my life. There were hurts that needed to be healed, and a renewed understanding of my position as a son in His family. Consequently, for the last few years I have been in the process of becoming better acquainted with my heavenly Father. I have found the same need and heart-cry wherever we have gone in our travels throughout the world. Truly, our heavenly Father desires that His children find the strength and security which only His love can bring. I am convinced this is one of the great but hidden needs within the Body of Christ. Divine sonship and daughterhood rest full-weight upon a genuine heart-knowledge of the Father's love."[1]

Francis Atterbury

"But if we look up to heaven we may there behold that bow which God has placed about the throne, to remind us of that covenant of mercy

---

[12]George MacDonald, *Creation in Christ*, Rolland Hein, ed. (Wheaton, Ill.: Harold Shaw Publishers, 1976), pp. 130–131.
[1]Dr. Robert Frost, *Our Heavenly Father* (Plainfield, N.J.: Logos Intl., 1978), p. vi.

which God has established with us, and ratified and confirmed it with the blood of His dearly beloved Son, to assure every broken heart and truly penitent sinner that though He is a terrible Judge to obstinate offenders yet He will be a gracious and merciful Savior to all those who are reconciled to Him through Christ and have their sins pardoned by His death and satisfaction. . . . God has laid aside the thunder out of His hand, and is ready to embrace us with the arms of a loving and indulgent Father. . . .

"God's mercy is exalted above His justice; for though all God's attributes are equal . . . the goodness of God is that attribute which in a peculiar manner adorns the divine nature and renders it amiable and lovely as well as venerable and adorable. God's mercy which is only the exercise of His goodness towards offenders is represented in the Holy Scriptures with peculiar privileges above the rest of His attributes. God is styled 'the Father of mercy.' . . . He desires to be known by this attribute to the whole world; He is the Lord God, gracious and merciful, and publicly declares that mercy rejoices over judgment. And therefore the rainbow is placed about the throne, to signify to us that God is always mindful of His gracious covenant made with mankind; and that in the midst of justice, He remembers mercy."[2]

Joseph Parker

"There are unfatherly fathers, men who are lower than natural brute beasts made to be taken and destroyed. Yet as a rule fatherhood among men is synonymous with love, trust, care, sympathy, and defence. God takes up all these ideas and gives them infinite expansion.

"'In the fear of the Lord is strong confidence: and His children shall have a place of refuge' (Prov. 14:26). Here is . . . the sublime doctrine of the fatherhood of God. Here too we find God's children need a place of refuge; they have often to flee from the storm, from the wrath of man, and from an apparently angry nature, for every law seems to fight against them: blessed be God, when all outward things are marked by an excitement of an apparently uncontrollable kind, are heaving and tossing as if shaken by an earthquake, the children of God can go not to law but to the Lawmaker himself, yea to the very heart of God and there rest in hope and confidence, and while the storm howls outside around the rock of the sanctuary that holy place can be filled with sacred and triumphant song."[3]

The Foundation of Theology

Dr. Robert Frost

"So often have we emphasized the Kingdom theme of the Sermon on the Mount that we have failed to see that the government of God rests squarely upon a royal family relationship with the Father. What holy won-

---

[2]Francis Atterbury, *Christian Classics*, vol. 5 (Westminster, Md.: Christian Classics, Inc., 1982), p.154–155.
[3]Joseph Parker, *Preaching Through the Bible* (Grand Rapids: Baker Books, 1978), Vol. VII, pp. 34–35, 193–194.

der must have filled the disciples' hearts as again and again they heard Jesus describe their relationship with God in the same terms with which He described His own. This was their introduction to God as beloved sons, whose life relationship with the Heavenly Father was something to be felt with their hearts."[4]

George MacDonald

"The hardest, gladdest thing in the world is to cry 'Father!' from a full heart. I would help whom I may to call thus upon the Father. There are things in all forms of the systematic teaching of Christianity to check this outgoing of the heart—with some to render it simply impossible. Such a cold wind blowing at the very gate of heaven—thank God, outside the gate!—is the so-called doctrine of adoption. When a heart hears—and believes, or half believes—that it is not a child of God by origin, from the first of its being but may possibly be adopted into His family, its love sinks at once into a cold faint—where is its own father, and who is this that would adopt it?

"By the word translated adoption, [Paul] means the raising of a father's own child from the condition of tutelage and subjection to others—to the position and rights of a son. None but a child could become a son; the idea is a spiritual coming of age; only when the child is a man is he really and fully a son.

"How many children of good parents—good children in the main too—never know those parents, never feel towards them as children might, until grown up, they have left the house—until perhaps they are parents themselves or are parted from them by death! . . . God can no more than an earthly parent be content to have only children: He must have sons and daughters—children of His soul, of His spirit, of His love— not merely in the sense that He loves them, or even that they love Him, but in the sense that they love *like* Him, love *as He* loves. For this He does not adopt them. He dies to give them himself thereby to raise His own to His heart. He gives them a birth from above; they are born again out of himself and into himself—for He is the one and the all. "His children are not His real true sons and daughters until they think like Him, feel with Him, judge as He judges, are at home with him, and without fear before Him, because He and they mean the same thing, love the same things, seek the same ends. Nothing will satisfy Him or do for us, but that we be one with our Father! What else could serve! How else should life ever be a good! Because we are the sons of God, we must become the sons of God.

"I will not believe less of the Father than I can conceive of glory after the lines He has given me, after the radiation of His glory in the face of the Son."[5]

---

[4]Frost op. cit. pp. 34–35.
[5]George MacDonald, *Creation in Christ*, Rolland Hein, ed. (Wheaton, Ill.: Harold Shaw Publishers, 1976), p. 135.

Rolland Hein

Although MacDonald wrote that "theologians have done more to hide the Gospel of Christ than any of its adversaries," his criticisms were motivated by "nothing other than a consuming love for Christ and a magnificently stirring concept of the nature of the Father. The strength and captivating moral beauty of his convictions led him to exercise a righteous scorn of all anemic thinking concerning holy things. In his day as in ours not a few self-styled thinkers would attribute to God under the guise of impressive theological jargon actions and attitudes any good man would justly condemn were he to find it in his fellow man. Such depictions of God create within the devout a secret, mostly subconscious, aversion and fear that stifles what would otherwise be a glad creative relationship with the Father of the universe."[6]

The Theme of Jesus' Ministry

John Watson

"Prophets continually call God the Father of the nation; they never (with one doubtful exception) call Him Father of the individual. Psalmists revel in an overflowing imagery for God, but one word lying to their hand they do not use. He is the 'Shepherd of Israel' and 'our dwelling-place in all generations.' He is the 'rock of my Salvation' and 'a very present help in time of trouble.' He is the 'health of my countenance' and 'the shade on thy right hand,' but He is not Father. 'King' is the Psalmist's chief title for God and his highest note is 'the Lord reigneth.'

"These saints are unapproachable in their familiarity with the Eternal; they will argue and complain; they will demand and reproach; but never at any moment are they so carried beyond themselves as to say 'My Father.' They are bold within a limit; they have restraints in their language. It is not a refusal to say Father because the idea is an offense; it is an unconsciousness—because the idea has not yet dawned. The clouds which had gradually risen from the base and sides of the doctrine of God still veil the summit.

"When one passes from the Gospels to the Psalms he is struck by the absence of Father. When he returns he is struck by its presence. The Psalmist never said the word; Jesus never said anything else. With Jesus, God and Father were identical. Fatherhood was not a side of Deity; it was the center. God might be a King and Judge; He was first of all and last of all and through all Father.

"In Fatherhood, every other relation of God must be harmonized and find its sphere. Short of His fatherhood you cannot stop in the ascent of God. Under Fatherhood is gathered every other revelation. . . .

"What an astounding gaucherie it has been to state the intimate relation between God and the soul in the language of criminal law, with bars, prisoners, and sentences. This terminology has two enormous disadvantages. It is unintelligible to anyone who is not a criminal or a lawyer; it

---

[6]MacDonald, op cit. Preface, pp. 7–8.

is repulsive to anyone who desires to love God. Taken to the highest it was the spirit of Moses. Without disparagement to a former dispensation it has been superseded by the spirit of Jesus.

"One is not astonished that some of Jesus' deepest sayings are still unfathomed, or that some of His widest principles are not yet applied. Jesus is the eternal Son and the ages overtake Him slowly. One is aghast to discover that the doctrine which Jesus put at the forefront of His teaching and labored at with such earnestness did not leave a trace on the dominant theology of the early church, and for long centuries passed out of the Christian consciousness. Had it not been for the Lord's Prayer and, in a sense, the three creeds, no witness had been left for fatherhood in Christian doctrine and worship. The Anglican communion has thirty-one articles, with one on oaths, one on the descent into Hell, one on the marriage of priests, one on how to avoid people that are excommunicate, and not one on fatherhood. The Presbyterian communion has a confession with thirty-three chapters which deal in a trenchant manner with great mysteries, but there is not one expounding the fatherhood of God. It is quite allowable that theology should formulate doctrines on subjects Jesus never mentioned such as original sin; and elaborate theories on facts Jesus left in their simplicity, such as His sacrifice. These speculations are the function of that science; but it is inexcusable that the central theme of Jesus' teaching should have been ignored or minimized. This silence from the date of the Greek Fathers . . . has been more than an omission; it has been a heresy.

"One joyfully anticipates the place this final idea of God will have in the new theology. Criticism has cleared the ground and gathered its building materials. A certain conception of God must be the foundation and give shape to the whole structure. No one can seriously doubt that it will be fatherhood and that Jesus' dearest thought will dominate theology.

"No doctrine of the former theology will be lost; all will be recarved and refaced to suit the new architecture. Sovereignty will remain, not that of a despot, but of a father; the Incarnation will not be an expedient but a consummation; the sacrifice will not be a satisfaction, but reconciliation; the end of grace will not be standing, but character; the object of punishment will not be retribution but regeneration. Mercy and justice will no longer be antinomies; they will be aspects of love, and the principle of human probation will be exchanged for the principle of human education.

"While piety imagined God as the father of a few and the judge of the rest, humanity was belittled and Pharisaism reigned; slavery was defended from the Bible and missions were counted as an impertinence. When He is recognized as the universal Father, and the outcasts of humanity as His prodigal children, every effort of love will be stimulated, and the Kingdom of God will advance by leaps and bounds. As this sublime truth is believed, national animosities, social divisions, religious hatreds and inhuman doctrines will disappear. No class will regard itself as favored, no class will feel itself rejected, for all men everywhere will be embraced in the mission of Jesus and the love of the Father."[7]

The Revealed Relationship

Bilquis Sheikh

It was God's fatherhood that broke through the heart of the Muslim princess Bilquis Sheikh. She wrote: "Suddenly a breakthrough of hope flooded me. Suppose, just suppose God were like a father. If my earthly father would put aside everything to listen to me, wouldn't my heavenly Father? . . . Shaking with excitement, I got out of bed, sank to my knees on the rug, looked up to heaven and in a rich new understanding called God 'My Father.' I was not prepared for what happened.

"Suddenly the room wasn't empty any more. He was there! I could sense His presence. I could feel His hand laid gently on my head. It was as if I could *see* His eyes, filled with love and compassion. He was so close that I found myself laying my head on His knees like a little girl sitting at her father's feet. For a long time I knelt there sobbing quietly floating in His love. I found myself talking with Him, apologizing for not having known Him before. And again came His loving compassion like a warm blanket settling around me. . . . I reached over to the bedside table where I kept the Bible and the Koran side by side. I picked up both books and lifted them, one in each hand. 'Which, Father?' I said. 'Which is your book?'

"Then a remarkable thing happened. Nothing like it had ever occurred in my life in quite this way. For I heard a voice inside my being, a voice that spoke to me as clearly as if I were repeating words in my inner mind. They were fresh, full of kindness, yet at the same time full of authority. It asked, 'In which book do you meet Me as your Father?' "[8]

Sonship

D. T. Niles

"The Church is the Christian family. They are children of the one Father. . . . there is only one religion in the world which says God is your Father and mine, and that is the Christian religion. You do not even find that in the Old Testament. Yes, the Old Testament believes God is the Father of Israel as a people, but that God is *my* Father and *your* Father— that takes a lot of believing. It takes a lot of believing to believe that God, the maker of heaven and earth, God Almighty, immortal, invisible, that God is my Father. And when you say 'My Father' it means He is interested in me and everything about me. . . .

"And the New Testament tells us that the only people who believe that

---

[7]John Watson, D.D., *Mind of the Master* (New York: Dodd, Mead and Company, 1896), pp. 257, 269–270.
[8]Bilquis Sheikh, *I Dared Call Him Father* (Old Tappan, N.J.: Chosen Books, 1979), pp. 41–43.

God is Father are those who know him in Jesus Christ. And only those believe that God is Father who are taught by the Holy Spirit that God is Father. We have made this a banal proposition in our time by talking about the fatherhood of God and the brotherhood of man. The consequence of the fatherhood of God is the family of man."[9]

George Buttrick

" 'Beneath the Cross of Christ, I fain would take my stand' for I need to hear Him say 'Father, forgive *him*.' We still do not understand the blackness, the earthquakes, the evil tyranny, the death-dealing sickness; and we should not ask, for heaven's mysteries are far too vast and deep for mortal minds. But we have a better understanding, namely the knowledge through Christ that God can take the whole convergence of sin and death and turn it into His heartbreak and our daybreak. That is how we know that God is *the* Father and *our* Father."[10]

J. I. Packer

"You sum up the whole of the New Testament teaching in a single phrase if you speak of it as a revelation of the fatherhood of the Holy Creator. . . . If you want to judge how well a person understands Christianity, find out how much he makes of the thought of being God's child and having God as His Father. If this is not the thought that prompts and controls his worship and his prayers and his whole outlook on life, it means he does not understand Christianity very well at all. . . . 'Father' is the Christian name for God."[11]

Thomas Chalmers

"Oh! Be prevailed upon. I know that terror will not subdue you; I know that all the threatenings of the law will not reclaim you. I know that no direct process of pressing home the claims of God upon your obedience will ever compel you to the only obedience that is of any value in His estimation—even the willing obedience of the affections to a father whom you love. But surely when He puts on in your sight the countenance of a Father—when He speaks to you with the tenderness of a Father—when He tries to woo you back to that house of His from which you have wandered, and to persuade you of His goodwill, He descends so far to reason the matter, and to tell you that He is no more seeking any glory from your destruction than He would seek glory from lighting into a blaze the thorns and briars. . . .

"Ah! my brethren, should it not look plain to the eye of faith how

[9]D.T. Niles, "What Is The Church For?" *Twenty Centuries of Great Preaching*, Clyde E. Fant Jr. and William M. Dinson Jr., eds. (Waco, Texas: Word Books, 1971), vol. XII, pp. 209–210.
[10]George Buttrick, "The Wonderment of Jesus" *Twenty Centuries of Great Preaching*, Clyde E. Fant Jr. and William M. Dinson Jr., eds. (Waco, Texas: Word Books, 1971), Vol. X, p. 276.
[11]J. I. Packer, *Knowing God* (Downers Grove, Ill.: Inter-Varsity Press, 1973), p. 182.

honest and sincere the God of your redemption is. . . . Do lay hold of it, and be impressed by it, and cherish no longer any doubt of the goodwill of the Lord God, merciful and gracious; and let your faith work by love to Him who hath done so much and said so much to engage it; and let this love evince all the power of a commanding principle within you, by urging your every footstep to the new obedience of new creatures in Christ Jesus your Lord."[12]

George MacDonald

> Oh Christ, my life, possess me utterly.
> Take me and make a little Christ of me.
> If I am anything but Thy Father's son,
> 'Tis something not yet from the darkness won.
> Oh, give me light to live with open eyes.
> Oh, give me life to hope above all skies.
> Give me Thy Spirit to haunt the Father with my cries.[13]

---

[12]Thomas Chalmers, *Twenty Centuries of Great Preaching* "Fury Not In God," vol. III, pp. 299–300.

[13]George MacDonald, *Diary of an Old Soul.* (Minneapolis, Minn.: Augsburg Publishing House, 1965), p. 67.

CHAPTER TWELVE

DECLARATION TWO:
THE SON IS THE UNCREATED GOD

Scriptures

"In the beginning was the Word, and the Word was with God, and the Word was God. The same was in the beginning with God. All things were made by him; and without him was not any thing made that was made." (John 1:1–3)

"And the Word was made flesh, and dwelt among us, (and we beheld his glory, the glory as of the only begotten of the Father,) full of grace and truth." (John 1:14)

"No man hath seen God at any time, the only begotten Son, which is in the bosom of the Father, he hath declared him [put Him on display]. (The original reads "only begotten *God* [theos].") (John 1:18)

"He [Christ] was clothed with a vesture dipped in blood: and his name is called The Word of God." (Rev. 19:13)

"The Jewish people had a very spiritualized apprehension of God's Person. . . . They believed God dealt indirectly with the universe through an agency which they called 'The Word' (*amar*—A Hebrew word which means 'to speak,' 'say.' Its root form is *memra*—derived from the Aramaic, which means 'word'. . . . In the Targum of Onkelos it is used in Gen. 3:8, 10, and 24 'And they heard the voice of the Word *memra* walking.' Even more striking is . . . Deut. 33:27 in which the words 'underneath are the everlasting arms' are replaced by 'by His word was the world created.' ").[1]

"Therefore the Lord himself shall give you a sign; Behold, a virgin shall conceive, and bear a son, and shall call his name Immanuel [God with us]." (Isa. 7:14)

"For unto us a *child is born* [humanity]; unto us a *son is given* [Deity] . . . and his name shall be called Wonderful, Counsellor, The mighty God

---

[1]Arthur C. Custance, *The Virgin Birth and the Incarnation*, (Grand Rapids: Zondervan, 1985), p. 219.

[Jehovah], The Everlasting Father, The Prince of Peace." (Isa. 9:6)

"But thou, Bethlehem . . . out of thee shall he come forth unto me that is to be ruler in Israel; whose goings forth have been from of old, from everlasting." (Mic. 5:2; cf. Ps. 90:2)

"Whence is this to me, that the mother of my Lord should come to me?" (Elizabeth to Mary—Luke 1:43)

"My Father worketh hitherto, and I work." (Here Christ claims divine activity; His work is the same order and power as the Father's.) (John 5:17–18)

"As the Father hath life in himself; so hath he given to the Son to have life in himself." (Only God has self-existent life.) (John 5:26)

"I and my Father are one [*hen*]." (Not *heis*, which is masculine, but *hen*, which is neuter; not one person, but one substance, one essence.) (John 10:30)

"Who [Christ Jesus], being [*huparcho*] in the form of God, thought it not robbery to be equal with God: but made himself of no reputation, and took upon him the form of a servant, and was made in the likeness of men." (*huparcho* denotes eternal existence; originally, eternally existed in the form of God.) (Phil. 2:6–7)

"He that hath seen me hath seen the Father. . . . Believest thou not that I am in the Father, and the Father in me? the words that I speak unto you I speak not of myself: but the Father that dwelleth in me, he doeth the works. Believe me that I am in the Father, and the Father in me." (John 14:9–11a)

"Thomas answered and said unto him, My Lord and my [the] God." (John 20:28)

"Israelites . . . whose are the fathers, and of whom as concerning the flesh Christ came, who is over all, God blessed for ever. Amen." (Rom. 9:4–5)

"Looking for that blessed hope, and the glorious appearing of the great God and our Saviour Jesus Christ." (Titus 2:13; cf. v. 10) A verse with similar wording is 2 Peter 1:1—"Simon Peter . . . to them that have obtained like precious faith with us through the righteousness of our God and our Saviour Jesus Christ." (If the writers of these two passages wished to speak of two distinct persons, a second definite article would have been used in front of the word "Saviour." There is none.)

"But unto the Son he [the Father] saith, Thy throne, O God, is for ever and ever." (Heb. 1:8; cf. Ps. 93:2)

"Take heed therefore . . . over the which the Holy Ghost hath made you overseers, to feed the church of God, which he hath purchased with his own blood." (Acts 20:28)

"Unto him that loved us, and washed us from our sins in his own blood, and hath made us kings and priests unto God and his Father; to him be glory and dominion for ever and ever. Amen." (Rev. 1:5–6)

The Son Is Called God and Worshiped As the Uncreated God

Jesus Is the Savior, Jehovah

"I, even I, am the LORD; and beside me there is no *saviour*." (Isa. 43:11)

"Thou shalt call his name Jesus: for he shall save his people from their sins." (Matt. 1:21)

"Christ Jesus came into the world to save sinners." (1 Tim. 1:15)

"He became the author of eternal salvation unto all them that obey him." (Heb. 5:9)

"Our Lord and Saviour Jesus Christ." (2 Pet. 3:18)

"Neither is there salvation in any other: for there is none other name under heaven given among men, whereby we must be saved." (Acts 4:12)

He Redeems As God

"All flesh shall know that I the LORD am thy Saviour and thy Redeemer, the mighty One of Jacob. (Isa. 49:26)

"Let Israel hope in the LORD . . . and he shall redeem Israel from all his iniquities." (Ps. 130:7–8)

"The great God and our Saviour Jesus Christ, who gave himself for us, that he might redeem us from all iniquity." (Titus 2:13–14)

"Hereby perceive we the love of God, because he laid down his life for us." (1 John 3:16)

"In whom we have redemption through his blood, the forgiveness of sins, according to the riches of his grace." (Eph. 1:7)

"But of him are ye in Christ Jesus, who of God is made unto us wisdom, and righteousness, and sanctification, and redemption." (1 Cor. 1:30)

He Forgives Sins

(Only God has the authority to forgive sins, a fact testified to by the Jews. See Mark 2:7.) "And he said unto her, Thy sins are forgiven." (Luke 7:48)

"Him hath God exalted . . . to give . . . forgiveness of sins." (Acts 5:31)

"In whom we have . . . forgiveness of sins." (Eph. 1:7)

He Is Called God Our Savior

"According to the commandment of God our Saviour . . . grace, mercy, and peace, from God the Father and the Lord Jesus Christ our Saviour." (Titus 1:3–4)

"The kindness and love of God our Saviour toward man appeared . . . by the . . . renewing of the Holy Ghost . . . which he shed on us abundantly through Jesus Christ our Saviour." (Titus 3:4–6)

He Gives Eternal Life

"My sheep hear my voice, and I know them, and they follow me: and I give unto them eternal life; and they shall never perish, neither shall any man pluck them out of my hand." (John 10:27–28)

"For the life was manifested, and we have seen it, and bear witness, and shew unto you that eternal life which was with the Father, and was manifested unto us." (1 John 1:2)

"And this is the record, that God hath given to us eternal life, and this life is in his Son. He that hath the Son of God hath life; and he that hath not the Son of God hath not the life." (1 John 5:11–12)

"And we know that the Son of God is come, and hath given us an understanding . . . and we are in him that is true, even in his Son Jesus Christ. This is the true God, and eternal life." (1 John 5:20)

"He that hath an ear, let him hear what the Spirit saith unto the churches; To him that overcometh will I give to eat of the tree of life, which is in the midst of the paradise of God." (Rev. 2:7)

Jesus Was Called God on Earth

"How great things the Lord hath done for thee." (Mark 5:19)

"[He] began to publish . . . how great things Jesus had done for him." (Mark 5:20)

"How great things God hath done unto thee." (Luke 8:39)

"And Thomas answered and said unto him [Jesus], My Lord and my [the] God." (John 20:28)

"There is one God, and one mediator between God and men, the man Christ Jesus." (1 Tim. 2:5)

"God was manifest in the flesh." (1 Tim. 3:16)

Stephen Prays to Jesus As God

"And they stoned Stephen, calling upon God, and saying, Lord Jesus, receive my spirit." (Acts 7:59)

"And he kneeled down, and cried with a loud voice, Lord, lay not this sin to their charge. And when he had said this, he fell asleep." (Acts 7:60)

The Early Christians Prayed to Jesus As God

"Then Ananias answered, *Lord*, I have heard by many of this man [Saul], how much evil he hath done to thy saints at Jerusalem: and here he hath authority from the chief priests to bind all that *call on Thy name*." (Acts 9:13–14)

Jesus Was Worshiped As God on Earth

"And when they were come into the house, they saw the young child with Mary his mother, and fell down, and worshipped him." (Matt. 2:11)

"And, behold, there came a leper and worshipped him, saying, Lord, if thou wilt, thou canst make me clean." (Matt. 8:2)

"And when they were come into the ship, the wind ceased. Then they that were in the ship came and worshipped him, saying, Of a truth thou art the Son of God." (Matt. 14:32–33)

"And as they went to tell his disciples, behold, Jesus met them, saying, All hail. And they came and held him by the feet, and worshipped him." (Matt. 28:9)

Jesus Is Worshiped As God in Heaven

"And again, when he [the Father] bringeth in the first-begotten into the world, he saith, And let all the angels of God worship him." (Heb. 1:6)

"Saying with a loud voice, Worthy is the Lamb [Jesus] that was slain to receive power, and riches, and wisdom, and strength, and honour, and glory, and blessing. . . . And the four beasts said, Amen. And the four and twenty elders fell down and worshiped him that liveth for ever and ever." (Rev. 5:12, 14)

Jesus Is the Express Image of God

"In whom the god of this world hath blinded the minds of them which believe not, lest the light of the glorious gospel of Christ, who is the image of God, should shine unto them." (2 Cor. 4:4)

"Who, being in the form of God, thought it not robbery to be equal with God." (Phil. 2:6)

"Who is the image of the invisible God, the firstborn of every creature [the original bringer-forth of the creation]." (Col. 1:15)

"Who being the effulgence of his glory, and the very image of his substance, and upholding all things by the word of his power, when he had by himself purged our sins, sat down on the right hand of the Majesty on high." (Heb. 1:3, ASV)

Jesus Is the "I AM" of the Old Testament

Jesus is the I AM that spoke to Moses out of the burning bush (Ex. 3:13–14). He is also the central truth of salvation; rejecting him means spiritual death."Then said the Jews unto Him, Thou art not yet fifty years old, and hast thou seen Abraham? Jesus said unto them, Verily, verily, I say unto you, Before Abraham was, *I am*." (John 8:57–58; cf. Ex. 3:13–14)

"I said therefore unto you, that ye shall die in your sins: for if ye believe not that *I am* [he], ye shall die in your sins. (John 8:24)

"Now I tell you before it come, that, when it is come to pass, ye may believe that I am he." (John 13:19)

"And he said unto them, Ye are from beneath; I am from above: ye are of this world; I am not of this world. I said therefore unto you, that ye shall die in your sins: for if ye believe not that *I am* [he], ye shall die in your sins." (John 8:23–24)

"As soon then as he had said unto them, *I am* [he], they went backward, and fell to the ground." (John 18:6)

Every Knee Shall Bow at His Name

"That at the name of Jesus every knee should bow, of things in heaven, and things in earth, and things under the earth; and that every tongue should confess that Jesus Christ is Lord, to the glory of God the Father." (Phil. 2:10–11; cf. Isa. 45:18, 21–23)

Dishonor the Son and You Dishonor the Father

"That all men should honour the Son, even as they honour the Father. He that honoureth not the Son honoureth not the Father which hath sent him." (John 5:23–24)

Those Who Love the Father Love the Son

"If God were your Father, ye would love me; for I proceeded forth and came from God; neither came I of myself, but he sent me." (John 8:42)

The Whole Bible Speaks of Jesus

"Search the Scriptures; for in them ye think ye have eternal life: and they are they which testify of me. And ye will not come to me, that ye might have life." (John 5:39–40)

Salvation Comes by Confessing Jesus As Lord

"That if thou shalt confess with thy mouth the Lord Jesus, and shalt believe in thine heart that God hath raised him from the dead, thou shalt be saved. For with the heart man believeth unto righteousness; and with the mouth confession is made unto salvation. . . . For whosoever shall call upon the name of the Lord shall be saved." (Rom. 10:9–10, 13)

He Is the King of Kings

"Thy Kingdom is an everlasting kingdom, and thy dominion endureth throughout all generations." (Ps. 145:13)

"His dominion is an everlasting dominion . . . and his kingdom that which shall not be destroyed." (Dan. 7:14)

"Nathaniel answered and saith unto him, Rabbi, thou art the Son of God; thou art the King of Israel." (John 1:49)

"For he must reign, till he hath put all enemies under his feet." (1 Cor. 15:25)

"Now unto the King eternal, immortal, invisible, the only wise God, be honour and glory for ever and ever. Amen." (1 Tim. 1:17)

"Which in his times he shall shew, who is the blessed and only Potentate, the King of kings and Lord of lords." (1 Tim. 6:15; cf. Rev. 19:16)

He Is the Preserver of Life

"Thou preservest them all." (Neh. 9:6)

"Because I live, ye shall live also." (John 14:19)

"In Him we live." (Acts 17:28)

"By Him all things consist." (Col. 1:17)

He Raises the Dead

"And this is the Father's will which hath sent me, that of all which he hath given me I should lose nothing, but should raise it up again at the last day. And this is the will of him that sent me, that every one which seeth the Son, and believeth on him, may have everlasting life: and I will raise him up at the last day. . . . Whoso eateth my flesh, and drinketh my blood, hath eternal life; and I will raise him up at the last day." (John 6:39–40, 54)

"Marvel not at this: for the hour is coming, in the which all that are in the graves shall hear his voice, and shall come forth; they that have done good, unto the resurrection of life; and they that have done evil, unto the resurrection of damnation." (John 5:28–29)

Jesus Is the Divine Judge

"Thou renderest to every man according to his work." (Ps. 62:12)

"I saw in the night visions, and, behold, one like the Son of Man came with the clouds of heaven and came to the Ancient of days, and they brought him near before him. And there was given him dominion, and glory, and a kingdom that all people, nations, and languages, should serve him: his dominion is an everlasting dominion, which shall not pass away, and his kingdom that which shall not be destroyed." (Dan. 7:13–14)

"When the Son of Man shall come in his glory, and all the holy angels with him, then shall he sit upon the throne of his glory: and before him shall be gathered all nations: and he shall separate them one from another, as a shepherd divideth his sheep from the goats; and he shall set the sheep on his right hand, but the goats on the left." (Matt. 25:31–33)

"For the Father judgeth no man, but hath committed all judgment unto the Son." (John 5:22)

"Whosoever therefore shall be ashamed of me and of my words in this adulterous and sinful generation; of him also shall the Son of man be ashamed, when he cometh in the glory of his Father with the holy angels." (Mark 8:38)

"And he commanded us to preach unto the people, and to testify that it is he which was ordained of God to be the Judge of quick and dead." (Acts 10:42)

"Whosoever shall confess me before men, him shall the Son of man also confess before the angels of God: but he that denieth me before men shall be denied before the angels of God." (Luke 12:8–9)

"Because he hath appointed a day, in the which he will judge the world in righteousness by that man whom he hath ordained; whereof he hath given assurance unto all men, in that he hath raised him from the dead." (Acts 17:31)

"The day of wrath and revelation of the righteous judgment of God." (Rom. 2:5)

"Vengeance is mine, I will repay, saith the Lord." (Rom. 12:19)

"Upon the wicked he shall rain snares, fire and brimstone, and an horrible tempest." (Ps. 11:6)

"The Lord Jesus shall be revealed from heaven with his mighty angels, in flaming fire taking vengeance on them that know not God." (2 Thess. 1:7–8)

"And from the wrath of the Lamb: for the great day of his wrath is come; and who shall be able to stand?" (Rev. 6:16–17)

"To give every man according as his work shall be." (Rev. 22:12)

Jesus Is the Jehovah of the Old Testament

Jehovah and Jesus Command Us To Be His Witnesses

"Ye are my witnesses, saith the LORD, and my servant whom I have chosen: that ye may know and believe me, and understand that I am he: before me there was no God formed, neither shall there be after me." (Isa. 43:10)

We are to witness to Jehovah and be His servants. There is no God before Him, beside Him or after Him

"Fear ye not, neither be afraid: have not I told thee from that time . . . ye are even my witnesses. Is there a God beside me? yea, there is no God; I know not any." (Isa. 44:8)

Jesus commands us to witness to Him and be His witnesses in the New Testament

"But ye shall receive power, after that the Holy Ghost is come upon you: and ye shall be witnesses unto me both in Jerusalem, and in all Judea, and in Samaria, and unto the uttermost part of the earth." (Acts 1:8)

"And I answered, Who art thou, Lord? And he said unto me, I am Jesus of Nazareth, whom thou persecutest. . . . And . . . Ananias . . . said . . . The God of our fathers hath chosen thee, that thou shouldest know his will, and see that Just One, and shouldest hear the voice of his mouth. For thou shalt be his witness unto all men of what thou hast seen and heard." (Acts 22:8, 12, 14–15)

Isaiah Saw Jehovah Jesus

"For mine eyes have seen the King, the LORD [Jehovah] of hosts." (Isa. 6:5)

"But though he [Jesus] had done so many miracles before them, yet they believed not on him: that the saying of Esaias [Isaiah] the prophet might be fulfilled. . . . These things said Esaias [Isaiah] when he saw his glory and spoke of him." (John 12:37–41; cf. Heb. 13:8)

Jehovah Jesus Is the Almighty

"I am the Almighty God." (Gen. 17:1)

"I am . . . the Almighty" (Rev. 1:8, NIV)

Jehovah Jesus Is Changeless

"I am the Lord, I change not." (Mal. 3:6)

"Jesus Christ the same yesterday, and today, and for ever." (Heb. 13:8)

Jehovah Jesus Is the Holy One

"I am the Lord thy God, the Holy One [*hagios*] of Israel." (Isa. 43:3)

"Ye denied the Holy One [*ton hagion*] and the just." (Acts 3:14)

Jehovah Jesus Is the Creator

"By the word of the Lord [Jehovah] were the heavens made; and all the host of them by the breath of his mouth." (Ps. 33:6)

"I am the Lord [Jehovah], your Holy One, the creator of Israel, your King." (Isa. 43:15)

"All things were made by him; and without him was not any thing made that was made." (John 1:3; cf. v. 10)

"For by him [Jesus] were all things created, that are in heaven, and that are in earth, visible and invisible . . . all things were created by him, and for him: and he is before all things, and by him all things consist [hold together]." (Col. 1:16–17)

"Thou art worthy, O Lord, to receive glory and honour and power: for thou hast created all things, and for thy pleasure they are and were created." (Rev. 4:11)

The Psalmist Calls Jehovah Jesus the Creator

"Hear My prayer, O LORD [Jehovah] . . . I said, O my God, take me not away in the midst of my days: thy years are throughout all generations. Of old hast thou laid the foundation of the earth: and the heavens are the work of thy hands. They shall perish, but thou shalt endure." (Ps. 102:1, 24–26)

"But unto the Son he saith, Thy throne, O God, is for ever and ever. . . . And, thou, Lord [Jehovah], in the beginning hast laid the foundation of the earth; and the heavens are the works of thine hands: they shall perish; but thou remainest." (Heb. 1:8, 10–11)

Jehovah Jesus Is the Rock of Offense

"Sanctify the Lord of hosts himself . . . a stone of stumbling and for a rock of offence to both the houses of Israel." (Isa. 8:13–14)

"Unto you therefore which believe he [Jesus] is precious: but unto them . . . a stone of stumbling, and a rock of offence." (1 Pet. 2:7–8)

Tempting Jehovah Is Tempting Christ

"And Moses said unto them, Why chide ye with me? wherefore do ye tempt the LORD [Jehovah]?" (Ex. 17:2)

"And the Lord [Jehovah] sent fiery serpents among the people, and they bit the people. . . . Therefore the people came to Moses, and said, We have sinned, for we have spoken against the LORD [Jehovah], and against thee; pray to the Lord, that he take away the serpents." (Num. 21:6–7)

"Neither let us tempt Christ, as some of them also tempted, and were destroyed of serpents." (1 Cor. 10:9)

Jehovah Jesus Is King and Rules the Kingdom Forever

"Thy throne, O God, is for ever and ever; the sceptre of thy kingdom is a right sceptre." (Ps. 45:6)

"Thy Kingdom is an everlasting kingdom, and thy dominion endureth throughout all generations." (Ps. 145:13)

"I am a man of unclean lips, and I dwell in the midst of a people of unclean lips: for mine eyes have seen the King, the Lord of hosts." (Isa. 6:5)

"His dominion is an everlasting dominion . . . and his kingdom that which shall not be destroyed." (Dan. 7:14)

"Nathaniel answered and saith unto him, Rabbi, thou art the Son of God; thou art the King of Israel." (John 1:49)

"For he must reign, till he hath put all enemies under his feet." (1 Cor. 15:25)

"Now unto the King eternal, immortal, invisible, the only wise God, be honour and glory for ever and ever. Amen." (1 Tim. 1:17)

"Which in his times he shall shew, who is the blessed and only Potentate, the King of kings, and Lord of lords." (1 Tim. 6:15; cf. Rev. 19:16)

Jehovah Jesus Is King of Glory

"The LORD of hosts, he is the King of glory." (Ps. 24:10)

"Crucified the LORD of glory." (1 Cor. 2:8)

"Our Lord Jesus Christ, the Lord of glory." (James 2:1)

Jehovah Jesus Is the One Lord

"The LORD shall be king over all the earth: in that day shall there be one Lord and his name one." (Zech. 14:9)

"To us there is but . . . one Lord Jesus Christ, by whom are all things, and we by him." (1 Cor. 8:6)

Jehovah Jesus Is the First and Last

"I am the first, and I am the last; and beside me there is no God." (Isa. 44:6)

"I am the first and the last: I am he that liveth, and was dead . . . I am Alpha and the Omega . . . the first and the last." (Rev. 1:17–18; 22:13)

Jehovah Jesus Fills Heaven and Earth

"Do not I fill heaven and earth? saith the LORD." (Jer. 23:24)

"He that descended is the same also that ascended up far above all heavens, that he might fill all things." (Eph. 4:10)

Jehovah Jesus' Name Is Above All

"Whose name alone is Jehovah, art the most high over all the earth." (Ps. 83:18)

"God hath . . . given him a name which is above every name." (Phil. 2:9)

"That in all things he might have the preeminence." (Col. 1:18)

"Jesus" Means "Jehovah"

Jesus is the Greek transliteration of the older name of "Joshua." Joshua is an abbreviation of two words which means, "Jehovah is Savior" or, "Jehovah saves."

"Thou shalt call his name Jesus: for he shall save his people from their sins." (Matt. 1:21)

Jehovah Jesus Is the Only Savior

"I, even I, am the LORD [Jehovah]; and beside me there is no saviour." (Isa. 43:11)

"Neither is there salvation in any other: for there is none other name under heaven given among men, whereby we must be saved." (Acts 4:12)

Jehovah Was to Be Pierced

"In that day, saith the LORD [Jehovah] . . . I will pour upon the house of David, and upon the inhabitants of Jerusalem, the spirit of grace . . . and they shall look upon me whom they have pierced." (Zech. 12:4, 10)

"But when they came to Jesus, and saw that he was dead already, they brake not his legs: but one of the soldiers with a spear pierced his side, and forthwith came there out blood and water. . . . For these things were done, that the scripture should be fulfulled, A bone of him shall not be broken. And again another scripture saith, They shall look on him whom they pierced." (John 19:33–34, 36–37)

Jehovah Jesus Is the Redeemer

"Thus saith the Lord [Jehovah], your redeemer, the Holy One of Israel." (Isa. 43:14; cf. 48:17)

"Looking for that blessed hope, and the glorious appearing of the great God and our Saviour Jesus Christ; who gave himself for us, that he might redeem us from all iniquity." (Titus 2:13–14)

"Forasmuch as ye know ye were not redeemed with corruptible things . . . but with the precious blood of Christ, as of a lamb without blemish and without spot." (1 Pet. 1:18–19)

People in the Old Testament Knew About Jesus

"Every time the Old Testament uses the word 'salvation,' especially with the Hebrew suffix for 'my' 'thy' or 'His,' it is identical with the word *Yeshua* or Jesus. As Jesus is simply the Greek transliteration of Joshua (salvation), scriptures like Isa. 12:2–4 read like this: 'Behold, God is my Jesus; I will trust, and not be afraid: for the Lord Jehovah is my strength and my song; he also is become my Jesus. Therefore with joy shall ye draw water out of the wells of Jesus. And in that day shall ye say, Praise the Lord.' "

As the phrase LORD God is used for the Lord Jesus Christ in the Old Testament, it can be seen that Jesus:

Talked with Adam and Eve in Eden (Gen. 3:8–9).

Ate with Abraham before judging Sodom (Gen. 18:1ff.).

Wrestled with Jacob until daybreak (Gen. 32:30).

Had communion with the elders of Israel (Ex. 24:10–11).

Met with Joshua on the eve of battle (Josh. 5:13—6:2).

Spoke to Sampson's father about his boy (Judg. 13:21–22).

Was seen by Micaiah sitting on His throne (1 Kings 22:19).

Appeared to David on the threshing floor (2 Chron. 3:1).

"To repeat then, no man has seen God the Father (John 1:18), but many saw God the Son. Is it any wonder then, that the Lord Jesus should say at the time of His incarnation, 'Lo, I come (in the volume of the book it is written of me)' (Heb. 10:7). Where in the volume of the Book is it *not* written of Him?"[2]

The Father Is Not the Son

"Whosoever therefore shall confess me before men, him will I confess also before my Father which is in heaven. But whosoever shall deny me before men, him will I also deny before my Father which is in heaven." (Matt. 10:32–33)

"And He said unto them, How is it that ye sought me? wist ye not that I must be about my Father's business?" (Luke 2:49)

"And Jesus increased in wisdom and stature, and in favour with God and man." (Luke 2:52)

"And the Holy Ghost descended in a bodily shape like a dove upon him, and a voice came from heaven, which said, Thou art my beloved Son; in thee I am well pleased." (Luke 3:22)

"For whosoever shall be ashamed of me and of my words, of him shall the Son of man be ashamed, when he shall come in his own glory, and in his Father's, and of the holy angels." (Luke 9:26)

"And as he prayed, the fashion of his countenance was altered, and his raiment was white and glistering. . . . But Peter and they that were with him were heavy with sleep: and when they were awake, they saw his glory, and the two men that stood with him. . . . And there came a voice out of the cloud, saying, This is my beloved Son: hear him." (Luke 9:29, 32, 35)

"And when Jesus had cried with a loud voice, he said, Father, into thy hands I commend my spirit: and having said thus, he gave up the ghost." (Luke 23:46)

"In the beginning was the Word, and the Word was with God, and the Word was God. The same was in the beginning with God." (John 1:1–2)

"Labour not for the meat which perisheth, but for that . . . which the

---

[2]Ibid. p. 244.

Son of man shall give unto you: for him hath God the Father sealed. Then said they unto him, What shall we do, that we might work the works of God? Jesus answered and said unto them, This is the work of God, that ye believe on him whom he hath sent." (John 6:27–29)

"All that the Father giveth me shall come to me; and him that cometh to me I will in no wise cast out." (John 6:37)

"It is written in the prophets, And they shall be all taught of God. Every man therefore that hath heard, and hath learned of the Father, cometh unto me. Not that any man hath seen the Father, save he which is of God, he hath seen the Father." (John 6:45–46)

"As the living Father hath sent me, and I live by the Father: so he that eateth me, even he shall live by me." (John 6:57)

"As the Father knoweth me, even so know I the Father: and I lay down my life for the sheep. . . . Therefore doth my Father love me, because I lay down my life, that I might take it again." (John 10:15, 17)

"For I have not spoken of myself; but the Father which sent me, he gave me a commandment, what I should say, and what I should speak. And I know that his commandment is life everlasting: whatsoever I speak therefore, even as the Father said unto me, so I speak." (John 12:49–50)

"Let not your heart be troubled: ye believe in God, believe also in me. In my Father's house are many mansions. . . . I go to prepare a place for you." (John 14:1–2)

"And I will pray the Father, and he shall give you another Comforter, that he may abide with you for ever." (John 14:16)

"He that loveth me not keepeth not my sayings: and the word which ye hear is not mine, but the Father's which sent me." (John 14:24)

"I am the true vine and my Father is the husbandman." (John 15:1)

"Henceforth I call you not servants . . . but I have called you friends; for all things that I have heard of my Father I have made known to you." (John 15:15)

"And these things will they do unto you, because they have not known the Father, nor me." (John 16:3)

"At that day ye shall ask in my name: and I say not unto you, that I will pray the Father for you: for the Father himself loveth you, because ye have loved me, and have believed that I came out from God. I came forth from the Father, and am come into the world: again, I leave the world, and go to the Father." (John 16:26–28)

"Father, the hour is come; glorify thy Son, that thy Son also may glorify thee. . . . And this is life eternal, that they might know thee the only true God, and Jesus Christ, whom thou hast sent. I have glorified thee on the earth: I have finished the work which thou gavest me to do. And now, O

Father, glorify thou me . . . with the glory which I had with thee before the world was." (John 17:1, 3–5)

"Touch me not; for I am not yet ascended to my Father: but go to my brethren, and say unto them, I ascend unto my Father, and your Father; and to my God, and your God." (John 20:17)

"Peace be unto you: as my Father hath sent me, even so send I you." (John 20:21)

"Blessed be the God and Father of our Lord Jesus Christ, who hath blessed us with all spiritual blessings in heavenly places in Christ." (Eph. 1:3)

"That the God of our Lord Jesus Christ, the Father of glory, may give unto you the spirit of wisdom and revelation in the knowledge of him." (Eph. 1:17)

"Which he wrought in Christ, when he raised him from the dead, and set him at his own right hand in the heavenly places . . . and hath put all things under his feet, and gave him to be the head over all things to the church, which is his body, the fulness of him that filleth all in all." (Eph. 1:20–23)

"For the life was manifested, and we have seen it, and bear witness, and shew unto you that eternal life, which was with the Father, and was manifested unto us." (1 John 1:2)

Bible Word Study

All the names and titles used of the Son represent the different relationships sustained by Him. F. E. Marsh comments on the significant phrase "Lord Jesus Christ": "To believe on the Lord Jesus Christ is to believe in Him as such. As Lord He is the Sovereign *over* us (1 Pet. 3:15, RSV); as Jesus He is the Savior *for* us (Matt. 1:21); as Christ He is the Sanctifier *within* us (Gal. 2:20).

"These names are not used in an indiscriminate manner. The Holy Spirit never says 'Jesus' when He means 'Christ,' and He never says 'Lord' when He means 'Jesus.' "[1]

There are seven major names and titles given the Son in the New Testament.

kurios *(ku-ree-os)*—Lord, master, owner.

Used over 9,000 times in the Septuagint; the overwhelming majority of those times (6,156) it is used as a replacement for the proper name of God, the Tetragrammaton *YHWH*. Of the 717 NT passages, it is a title

---

[1] F. E. Marsh, *Fully Furnished*, pp. 157–159.

frequently used of Christ with a great flexibility of meanings.[2]

With the definite article *ho* (the), *kurios* is used four times in quotations from the OT (Matt. 1:22; 2:15; 5:33; 22:44), and 14 other times in the first three Gospels (Matt. 9:38; Mark 5:19; Luke 1:6, 9, 15, 25, 28, 46; 2:15; 22–23, 38; 10:2; 20:42).

Used in direct reference to Christ six times in the Gospels (Matt. 21:3; 24:42; Mark 11:3; Luke 19:31; John 13:13–14); in indirect reference to Him twice (Matt. 22:44; Lk. 20:44). Without the article He is directly called "Lord" 11 times (Matt. 7:21–22; 12:8; 25:37, 44; Mark 2:28; Luke 6:5, 46), and indirectly four more times (Matt. 22:43, 45; Mark 12:37; Luke 20:44).

It is used 59 times by Christ's disciples in reference to Christ. Of the many times it is used by others in reference to Christ, 18 times it is rendered "Lord" (Matt. 8:2, 6, 8; 9:28; 15:22, 25, 27; 17:15; 20:30, 31, 38; 28:6; Mark 7:28; 9:24; Luke 2:11; 5:12; 7:6; 18:41; John 6:34; 8:11); and six times it is rendered "sir" (John 4:11, 15, 19, 49; 5:7; 20:15).[3]

"In The NT the title 'Lord' is given to both God the Father and Jesus Christ. In preaching, prayer, and credal confession, Jesus was invoked as 'Lord,' and from the first century to the present day the title has been used of Christ." It was used:

- As an adjective or noun of *possession* in both classical and Hellenistic Greek in the sense of "having power over," or as a "possessor" (the master of a house or owner of a vineyard [cf. *adon*, Ex. 21:5]).
- *A polite form of address*, like "sir," conveying respect (cf. *adoni*, which is used for a husband [Gen. 18:12] or a prophet [1 Kings 18:7])
- *Royal usage* applied to kings, princes and governors. *Kurios* was a favorite title of Roman Emperors; Hebrew kings were addressed as *adoni*. The English equivalents, "My Lord," or, "Your Majesty," do not have the same religious content.
- *Religious.* Used in this sense throughout the Middle East. "In Judaism the title *Adonai* (Lord) became the substitute for the Divine Name in the reading of the Scriptures, and in the Septuagint, *kurios* was used as the Greek equivalent."[4]

"Lord" was an ideal term for the early Church to use for Christ, as *all* these meanings were simultaneously true in Him. A man might begin with polite respect to Christ, move to the understanding of His courtly royal office and conclude with His deity. Stephen used this term in his prayer as he was martyred (Acts 7:59–60), showing he understood Jesus was God.

"It is of peculiar interest to note that Judas never called Jesus 'Lord.' When Christ told His disciples that one of them would betray Him they all, except the traitor, said, 'Lord, is it I?' But Judas exclaimed 'Master, is it I?' (Matt. 26:22, 25).

"The eleven used a word which means Ruler, or Owner, the One who

---

[2]H. Bietenhard, *The New International Dictionary of New Testament Theology*, Colin Brown, ed. (Grand Rapids: Zondervan Publishing House, 1971), vol. 2, pp. 511–513.
[3]Ethelbert W. Bullinger, *The Companion Bible*, Appendix 98, p. 143.
[4]Arthur W. Wainwright, *The Trinity in the New Testament*, pp. 75–77.

has right to exercise Lordship; while Judas only gave to Christ the title of Master, or Teacher. When the other disciple Judas (Jude, Lebbaeus, Thaddeus) called Christ Lord, the word specifically states he was 'not Iscariot' (John 14:22).

" 'No man can say that Jesus is Lord but by the Holy Ghost' (1 Cor. 12:3). When we are told the Last Supper is 'the Lord's supper' it is such because He told us to remember Him in this way and we have no choice but obey Him in the matter. We are exhorted to 'rejoice in the Lord,' which means that walking in obedience to Him brings joy as a consequence. When the believer is told to marry 'only in the Lord' it means he is not only to marry a believer (marrying in Christ) but to take the one the Lord wishes him to have."[5]

"Maranatha," a transliterated Aramaic phrase used directly of Christ in 1 Cor. 16:22, literally means, "Our Lord, come!" Acts 2:21 and Rom. 10:13 both quote Joel 2:32 ("Whosoever shall call on the name of the Lord shall be delivered") and apply it to Christ.

despotes (*des-pot-ace*)—Means *ownership*, especially in the areas of public and family life, but when used of God it includes the exercise of more absolute, unlimited authority and power in heaven and earth.

It occurs about 60 times in the Septuagint. "Where it is used . . . it particularly emphasizes God's omnipotence (cf. Isa. 1:24; 3:1; 10:33; Jer. 4:10; 15:11; Jon. 4:3; Dan. 9:8)."

Despotes occurs 10 times in the NT; five times it is translated as "Master," one of which refers to Christ (2 Tim. 2:21), and the other five times it is translated "Lord," two of which refer to Christ (2 Pet. 2:1; Jude 4). In these two passages, Christ is shown as the one of true power, command and authority whom false teachers do not practically take as their guide. "God is addressed in prayer three times as *despotes* (Luke 2:29; . . . Acts 4:24; Rev. 6:10)."[6]

Iesous (*Jesus*)—Means "Yahweh is help" or "Yahweh is salvation."

A common name in NT times, and the Greek equivalent of the Hebrew name "Joshua" (*Yeshua*). "It is the oldest name containing the divine name Yahweh." Flavius Josephus, the Jewish historian of the first century "names no fewer than 19 bearers of the name Jesus in his voluminous writings in Greek. These come from both the ancient and the recent history of his people and about half were contemporaries of 'Jesus, the so-called Christ.' . . .

"Col. 4:11 mentions a Jewish Christian Jesus . . . and there are fairly clear indications that even Barabbas . . . had Jesus as his first name."[7]

To distinguish the Son of God's name from others, He is sometimes called "Jesus of Nazareth" (Mark 1:9; 10:47; 16:6; Matt. 21:11; 26:69, 71; Luke 18:37; John 19:19), or "son of David" (Matt. 9:27; Mark 10:47; Luke 2:4).

---

[5]Ibid. p. 91
[6]Bietenhard, op. cit. vol 2, p. 509.
[7]Ibid. vol. 2, p. 331.

Jesus is the name associated with Christ's humiliation and shame. In the Gospel record of His early life it occurs 566 times, while "Christ," or "the Christ," only occurs 36 times. When combined with "Christ" it means the one who humbled himself but is now exalted and glorified. The converse, "Christ Jesus," denotes the now exalted one who once humbled himself.[8]

Marsh says the name is also "associated with exaltation for all things in heaven, earth and hell are to bow before Him as bearing the name Jesus (Phil. 2:10). His exaltation was accomplished in His humiliation. Remembering this, it gives additional interest when we find the name Jesus occurs eight times in the Epistle to the Hebrews in connection with His present service and High Priestly glory."[9]

As Jesus He is seen as:

• The exalted man (Phil. 2:9).
• The appointed high priest (Heb. 3:1).
• The gracious forerunner (Heb. 6:20).
• The sure bondsman (Heb. 7:22).
• The efficient opener (Heb. 10:19).
• The living example (Heb. 12:2).
• The holy mediator (Heb. 12:24).
• The loving sanctifier (Heb. 13:12).

Jesus, the name given supernaturally to Joseph and Mary (Matt. 1:21; Luke 1:31), describes His future destiny to "save his people from their sins." The angel of the Lord announced to the shepherds who the child was and where He was born: "In the city of David a Saviour, which is Christ the Lord" (Luke 2:11); and they found according to the heavenly sign Jesus, the "babe wrapped in swaddling clothes" (Luke 2:12).

"It is clear that . . . the name Jesus already contains, in the form of a promise, what is later fulfilled in the title Lord applied to the risen and glorified Jesus of Nazareth for the salvation of all mankind."[10]

Kristos (*Christ*)—Means "anointed." The Greek equivalent of the Hebrew *mesiha* (Messiah). (A title rather than a proper name, except in Acts 2:36.)[11]

The title, "Christ," combined with the proper name, "Jesus," expressed "the faith of the earliest Christians in Jesus of Nazareth as their Master and Lord, Saviour-King and the universal Redeemer promised by God to His people Israel."[12]

Kristos comes originally from the root *chriein*, which means "to rub lightly," and without further specifics has no religious content. It was used

---

[8]Ethelbert W. Bullinger, *A Critical Lexicon and Concordance to the English and Greek New Testament* (Grand Rapids: Zondervan Publishing House, 1975), p. 422.
[9]Marsh, op. cit.
[10]K.H. Rengstorf, *The International Dictionary of New Testament Theology*, Colin Brown, ed. (Grand Rapids: Zondervan Publishing House, 1971), vol. 2, p. 332.
[11]Bullinger, *Critical Lexicon*, op. cit. p. 151.
[12]Rengstorf, op. cit. vol. 2, p. 330.

of bath oil, paint, cosmetics or anything rubbed or smeared on a person, and it is in itself "anything but an expression of honour. Where it refers to people it even tends toward the disrespectful." Its transliteration, "Messiah," is used twice of Christ (John 1:41; 4:25).[13]

In the OT, two officeholders were described as *masiah* (anointed with oil): the *high priest* and the *king*. In both cases "the anointing . . . [was] a legal act, [was] essential for the conferring of the authority connected with the office as it [was] for the resulting responsibility before God as the God of Israel."[14]

The act ultimately relates to the idea of kingship and the sovereign rule of God. The messianic expectation bound on the king during his reign "a special responsibility for the things of God." God even raises up as a chosen instrument a Persian king like Cyrus (Isa. 45:1) as His "anointed." Cyrus "was one of God's chosen instruments in the pursuit of God's universal aim of the salvation of all people through the people He has made His own possession."[15]

From early times Israel expected a messianic, kingly savior figure from the tribe of Judah (Gen. 49:8ff.). "The anointing of a Judaic king seems to have been . . . essentially with the gift and with the solemn ritual transfer of authority, power and honour (Hebrew *kabod*; Greek *doxa*—glory). The anointing gave the one anointed a position of power and the right to exercise it."[16]

The Christship of Jesus is a most interesting subject for it illustrates progressiveness of revelation. In the Gospels we have Christ *personally*, as the anointed and sent one of God (John 1:41; 4:25) and the builder and foundation of His Church (Matt. 16:16–18; Mark 8:29). In the Acts we have Christ *officially* in His exaltation and power, hence the burden of the Apostles' preaching is "Jesus the Christ" (Acts 5:42; 8:5; 9:22; 17:3; 18:5, 28). In the Epistles we have Christ *mystically* (1 Cor. 12:12) as the head of the Church, hence believers are said to be "in Christ" as to their position (2 Cor. 12:2; Eph. 2:6, 10, 13; 3:6) and Christ is said to be in them as to their power of life (Gal. 2:20).[17]

Master—Eight Greek words are translated "Master":
Kurios and *Despotes* (both of which were discussed earlier in this section).
Oikodespotes—Master of a house. Translated "Master" three times (Matt. 10:25; Luke 13:25; 14:21).
Epistates—Addressed to the Lord five times (Luke 5:5; 8:24, 45; 9:33, 49; 17:13).
Didaskalos—Teacher (John 3:2), or Doctor (Luke 2:46). The Lord was addressed as "Teacher" (rendered "Master") 31 times; and called himself

[13]Ibid. vol. 2, p. 334.
[14]Ibid. vol. 2, p. 335.
[15]Ibid. vol. 2, p. 335.
[16]Ibid. vol. 2, p. 336.
[17]Marsh, op. cit. pp. 157–159.

"Master" eight times (Matt. 10:24–25; 26:18; Mark 14:14; Luke 6:40; 22:11; John 13:14).

Rabboni—Aramaic for "My teacher" (John 20:16).

Rabbi—Jesus was addressed five times as "Rabbi" (John 1:38, 49; 3:2, 26; 6:25).

Kathegetes—Guide or Leader. Used three times by the Lord in reference to himself (Matt. 23:8, 10).

The Son of Man—Christ's favorite term for himself, and usually used in conjunction with *dominion in the earth.*

Used 88 times, always with the definite article. In the first occurrence, Matt. 8:20, He has on earth "no place to lay His head"; in the second, Matt. 9:6, He has "power on earth to forgive sins." Of the 88 occurrences 84 are in the Gospels and are all used by the Lord of himself.

In the first of the remaining four (Acts 7:56), Stephen sees "the Son of man standing on the right hand of God" as though not "yet set down and waiting to be sent according to promise" (Acts 3:20; cf. Heb. 10:13).

The second is in Heb. 2:6 where Ps. 8 is shown as fulfilled in Him; and the third and fourth are two verses in Rev. (1:13; 14:14) "where He comes to eject the usurper and rule in righteousness over a restored earth."

In the last verse He wears a golden crown on the same head that had no place to lay on earth, and in His hands is a sharp sickle with which He "reaps in judgment the harvest of the earth." As "Son of Man" all judgment in the earth is committed to Him (John 5:27).[18] In this term we see the value of humanity and the love of God for matter.

The Son of God—Expresses the relation of the Son to the Father (Matt. 1:20; Luke 1:31, 35) and all those who are begotten of God. As the Son of God, Christ is "heir of all things" invested with "all power," and is "the resurrection and the life" (John 11:25), having power to raise the dead (John 5:25).

The "I Am's" of Christ

The Lord Jesus frequently uses the phrase *ego eimi* (I am), the Greek equivalent of the Hebrew *ani hu* which was so often used by God himself (Ex. 3:14).

Isa. 43:10 and John 8:24 are close parallels. Besides this absolute use of "I am" in John 8:24 and 8:58, there are the seven other "I am's" in John's Gospel: (1) The Bread of Life (6:35 cf. 6:41, 48). (2) The Light of the world (8:12; 9:5). (3) The Door (10:7, 9). (4) The Good Shepherd (10:11, 14). (5) The Resurrection and the Life (11:25). (6) The Way, the Truth, and the Life (14:6). (7) The True Vine (15:1, 5).

---

[18]Bullinger, *The Companion Bible*, Appendix 98, p. 144.

Christ the Husband

This marriage symbol shows yet another link between Jesus in the NT and Yahweh in the Old, where God is the bridegroom and Israel is God's bride (Isa. 54:5; Hos. 2:20). "Rabbinic sayings connect the marriage-time with the Messianic age. In the NT the same marriage metaphor is used to describe the relationship of Christ to the Church (Mark 2:19–20; John 3:29; 2 Cor. 11:2; Eph. 5:25; Rev. 19:7; 21:9; 22:17) and the idea is implicit in the parable of the marriage feast (Matt. 22:1–14) and [the parable of] the wise and foolish virgins (Matt. 25:1–13)."[19]

Questions and Answers

Q: *Exactly who was Jesus, a man or a god? If he was a man, why call him God? If he was a god, how could he have become a man?*

A: Christ is called "the brightness of his glory and the express image of his [God the Father] person" (Heb. 1:3a). The Greek here is *karakteer tes hupostasis*, "the representation of his reality." Paul wrote to the Colossians, "in Him dwells all the fullness of the Godhead bodily" (Col. 2:9). We call Him God simply because Scripture overwhelmingly declares He is. We likewise call Him a true man because Scripture tells us that "the Word was made flesh and dwelt among us" (John 1:14) and that He "was made a little lower than the angels" (Heb. 2:9, 14, 16–18).

How deity became man, "infinity compressed to a span," is beyond our human comprehension; that "God was manifest in the flesh" is called indeed "the mystery of godliness" (1 Tim. 3:16). But the Lord Jesus was not God disguised as a man or merely a man aspiring to be God; He was God who became man, "very God and very man."

Q: *If "no man hath seen God at any time" (John 1:18) and no man can see God and live (Ex. 33:20), how could Jesus be God if people saw Him (1 Cor. 15:6; Acts 9:1–9) and yet lived?*

A: The same Scripture that tells us "no man has ever seen God" goes on to tell us "the only-begotten Son, which is in the bosom of the Father, He hath declared (*exeegeomai*) him [put Him on display]" (John 1:18b). Christ reveals the Father (John 14:7–11) as the express "image of the invisible God" (Col. 1:15). He is the tangible, localized manifestation of the invisible, universal uncreated one. No one can see the Father and live except through the revelation of God in the Son.

Q: *In the New Testament Jesus speaks about His Father God being greater than He (John 5:19; 14:28). Doesn't this imply that He is inferior to the Father?*

A: As wives, children, and employees may know, biblical submission does not imply inferiority. Christ submitted himself to the Father, but

---

[19]Wainwright, op. cit. p. 91.

Scripture clearly states that He did not count equality with God something to pursue, as He already was God. The chain of authority in the Godhead is not inferiority. Also, when Christ completed His ministry He was "highly exalted" and given a name "which is above every name: that at the name of Jesus every knee should bow . . . and that every tongue should confess that Jesus Christ is Lord, to the glory of God the Father" (Phil. 2:9–11).

Q: *Paul said that God was the "head of Christ" (1 Cor. 11:3) and that Christ will be subject to God that God may be "all in all" (1 Cor. 15:28). Doesn't this mean that Christ is inferior to God?*

A: As mentioned, Paul speaks both times about legitimate chains of authority: those found in the human family and in the spiritual family. Christ came to put down all rule, authority, and power not authorized by His Father (1 Cor. 15:23–26), and to demonstrate to the universe His absolute lordship (Phil. 2:8–11). But this lordship in a kingdom of service was not to be gained by the raw expression of divine power any more than rightful human leadership is to be established by violence; it was granted by His moral and spiritual worthiness (Heb. 2:9–18; 3:1–6; Rev. 5). Thus Christ, as a lawful and true representative of the Father, triumphed in the power of the Father, opening the way not only to salvation from sin and death, but to the rights and privileges of the kingdom of heaven for all who follow Him.

Q: *God "knows all things" (Isa. 46:9–11; 1 John 3:20), yet Jesus grew in wisdom and stature (Luke 2:52), said He did not know the hour or day of the world's destruction (Mark 13:32), and had to pray each day (Matt. 26:39) to find out what He was to do. How does the Bible explain this?*

A: When Christ walked the earth, He had all the limitations of a real human being: He ate, got tired, wept, suffered, and was tempted. He was to live daily in dependence and obedience to the Father, just as we are to live (Heb. 2:9–18). Although He was always God and remained truly God (by virtue of His uncreatedness), it appears that as a real man He used none of His Godhead powers directly; for the duration of His earthly ministry He did all that a true and trusting son of the Father would do.

Q: *If God cannot be tempted, was Jesus really tempted by the Devil in the wilderness? (Matt. 4:1)*

A: Life without temptation is only possible to a being who is in a position to see and understand all alternatives. The Scriptures show that Jesus on earth really was tempted. This implies that He did not use His omniscience, but chose to face wrong suggestions as ordinary believers must—in faith (Heb. 1:18; 4:14–16).

Q: *"God is not a man" (Num. 23:19), yet Jesus became a man (1 Cor. 15:45, 47). How is that possible?*

A: An omnipotent God, who was not created, yet upholds the life of His creation, surely has both the ability and power to join himself to it! The creation cannot ascend to the uncreated, the finite to the infinite;

but as a line transcends yet includes a point, why would it be a problem for God to condescend, to incarnate himself among His finite and beloved creation, and by so doing glorify it? (See Matt. 19:26.)

Q: *Revelation calls Jesus the "beginning of the creation of God" (Rev. 3:14) and Colossians the "firstborn" of all creation (Col. 1:15). Isn't the Son a created being?*

A: No. The Greek word for "beginning" in Rev. 3:14 is *arche*, or "origin," perhaps better translated "source" or "first cause." Jesus is simply the one who began or originated the whole creation (see also John 1:1).

The word "firstborn" in Col. 1:15 is of Eastern origin, meaning "lordship, dignity, excellence," and may well be translated "chief of all creation." Nevertheless, even apart from this, the verse does not say "first *created*" but continues on to clearly attribute the entire work of creation to Christ as God. If Christ is part of creation, then He made himself, which is absurd![1] Walter Martin says, "Christ is not only the 'First Born' of the New Creation, the second Adam (1 Cor. 15:45, 47), but the 'First Born of the dead' (Rev. 1:5) or the first one to rise in a glorified body. . . . which type Christians will someday possess as in the words of the Apostle John (1 John 3:2)."[2]

Q: *But if He was "firstborn," wasn't there a time when He did not exist? Proverbs 8:22 reads, "The Lord brought me forth as the first of his works, before his deeds of old" (NIV).*

A: Again, born is not *made*. Even with an ordinary baby, the birth is not the origin of life; a person is alive before he is born. Jesus was likewise alive before He was called "firstborn." How long was He alive? Always. If the Father has always existed, He has always had a Son.

Q: *If Jesus is really God, why could he be tempted (Matt. 4:1)? Doesn't the Bible say God cannot be tempted with evil (James 1:13)?*

A: It is clear that Jesus did not use all of His powers as God during His time of *greatest weakness*—from the incarnation to the resurrection. As a true man, fully representing our race, and as a wholly obedient Son of the Father, Jesus never acted independently during His earthly ministry. Everything He did He drew from His Father's power (John 5:19–20; 14:10–12), wisdom (John 7:16; 8:26–28, 40), and in perfect accord with His Father's will (Mark 14:35–39; John 6:38; 8:29; Heb. 10:5–9). In this voluntary limitation of dependence, He lived (as His followers must live) by faith (Matt. 3:14–15; Heb. 2:9–18; 3:1–2), died in faith (Heb. 5:7–9; Col. 1:18–23; Phil. 2:8–11), and rose again by faith (Matt. 16:21; Eph. 1:17–23). He thus could face real temptation and suffering as well as learn obedience.

Q: *Jesus said, "My Father is greater than I" (John 14:28). Doesn't that mean that Jesus is not God in the same sense the Father is God, or maybe not even God at all?*

---

[1]Edward H. Bickersteth, *The Trinity* (Grand Rapids: Kregel, 1976), p. 105.
[2]Walter Martin, *The Kingdom of the Cults*, 1st ed. (Minneapolis, Minn.: Bethany House Publishers), pp. 81–82.

A: All of Jesus' authority while on earth was delegated by the Father (John 6:38; cf. Isa. 42:1–4; Luke 22:29; Matt. 8:9–10). He came down from heaven to do the will of the Father (John 5:30) and always "did those things that please him" (John 8:29). He was given authority as a man, as each believer must in turn be given authority from heaven. But unlike us, He had life in himself (John 5:26), the authority to lay it down or take it up of himself (John 10:17–18), and the Father has committed all judgment to Him (John 5:22–23, 27).

Q: *What does it mean that Christ was "made in the likeness of men" (Phil. 2:7)?*

A: "Likeness" is translated from the verb *homoiomamati*, which is used in 5 other places in Scripture (Rom. 1:23; 5:14; 6:5; 8:3; Rev. 9:7). The adjective *homios*, derived from the root *homos*, refers to (1) the same kind or condition of persons or things; (2) of the same value, character or rights; (3) what is equally divided to all, or in common; or (4) equality in a geometric sense. The verb form thus means "like-shaped" or "image," with the stress on correspondence and similarity to a concrete individual form. Christ, therefore, became the same kind of person as I am, under the same conditions, with the same character potential, sharing what the Father has made available to all of us, and in the same kind of body. It signifies that the Lord Jesus was "bound to us in history and humanity, in temptation, suffering and dying."[3]

Q: *How much did Jesus empty himself (Phil. 2:7 RSV)? Did He give up almost everything as God to become fully human?*

A: Christ never ceased to be God, but for the duration of His earthly ministry He gave up His rights, privileges, and intrinsic authority as God (cf. the words "likeness" and "servant"). This *kenosis* or "emptying" speaks not of attributes but *rights*; it is a question not of nature, essence, or substance, but of *claim to power*. The passage deals with like-mindedness, accord, and humility; it stresses freedom from self-assertion or grasping after privilege. If the essence of divinity is uncreatedness, Christ could never cease to be God because, although He had been born on earth, He had no beginning. He was and is the universe's only uncreated man.

Q: *A Greek definite article (*ton, "the"*) is used in speaking of the Father as God in John 1:1, but there is no article before "God" in the phrase "the Word was a God." Don't you translate constructions like this, "the Word was with the God" and "the Word was a god"? If Jesus is really God, why is there no article?*

A: The rules of Greek grammar demand the reading. "Was" is an intransitive verb. Intransitives "take no objects but instead predicate nominatives which refer back to the subject" (in this case *logos* or "Word"). The Greek order of the second part of this verse is "kai theos en o logos":

---

[3]*The New International Dictionary of New Testament Theology*, Colin Brown, ed. (Grand Rapids: Zondervan Publishing House, 1971), vol. 2, pp. 500, 505.

"and God"—a definite predicate nominative
"was"—an intransitive verb
"the Word"—Colwell's rule "clearly states that a definite predicate nominative like *theos*, 'God,' *never* takes an article when it precedes the verb [was] as in John 1:1."[4]

Q: *But couldn't this verse be translated "the Word was a God"?*

A: If you did you would also have to so translate John 1:6: "and there was a man sent from *a* God whose name was John." (See also Matt. 5:9; 6:24; Luke 1:35, 78; 2:40; John 1:6, 12–13, 18; 3:2, 21; 9:33; Rom. 1:7, 17–18; 1 Cor. 15:10; Phil. 2:11; Tit. 1:1; and many more.)[5]

Q: *The title or expression "God" in John 1:1 could mean simply "a mighty one." God wasn't speaking of absolute deity.*

A: *Theos*, "God," is used 1,343 times in the New Testament. It can indeed mean "mighty one." It is used twice for men made in God's image (John 10:34–35), twice for false gods (Acts 7:40, 43), three times to describe the imaginative idolatrous worship (1 Cor. 8:5; Gal. 4:8), and once for Satan (2 Cor. 4:4). It is used three times to describe true repentance (2 Cor. 7:9–11). The other 1,333 times it refers to true deity—either the Father or the Son. Certainly it *could* mean a mighty one, but the normal use of the word speaks otherwise and the context screams for a pronouncement of true deity.

John was surely not speaking of *relative* deity. Jesus was obviously not a false god, an idol, or the devil. He had no need of repentance because He had not sinned. This leaves us with only one possible alternative to Jesus being absolutely "God," that He is "a god" in the sense that He was made in God's image. But He was never made.

He is certainly unique as a "mighty one"; no other "mighty one" in Scripture is commanded worship by the Father (Heb. 1:6–7); no other "mighty one" is called "Lord" (1 Thess. 1:1); at the name of no other "mighty one" will every knee one day bow (Phil. 2:10–11). The record is plain; if Scripture means anything, its testimony is that Christ is truly and fully God with all the right to absolute reverence, respect, and adoration due Him.

Analysis and Discussion

Jesus Christ, . . . God of God, Light of Light, very God of very God."

Nicene Creed

His Birth: Immaculate Incarnation

No one was ever *born* like Jesus. His birth is unprecedented and unparalleled in history; the first and only baby born to a woman but

---

[4]Martin, op. cit. p. 75.
[5]Ibid. p. 76.

without a human father. Isaiah wrote, "A virgin shall conceive, and bear a son, and you shall call His name Immanuel [God is with us]" (Isa. 7:14). "For unto us a child is born [humanity], unto us a son is given [divinity]: and the government shall be upon his shoulder: and his name shall be called Wonderful, Counsellor, The mighty God, The everlasting Father, The Prince of Peace" (Isa. 9:6). Jeremiah foretold, "For the Lord hath created a new thing in the earth, a woman shall compass [make] a man" (Jer. 31:22).

The story was foretold in a hundred ancient legends of a God-man who would come to bless the world; the seed of the woman was born in due time (Gen. 3:15). Biology refers to the seed of man, and Matthew's careful account lists thirty-nine "begats" showing the ancestry of Jesus, but stops conspicuously short to note that Joseph was the husband of Mary, *"of whom was born Jesus,* who is called Christ" (Matt. 1:16).

Mary was His mother; but Joseph was certainly not his biological father. An ancient curse on Coniah's descendants (Josias of Matt. 1:11) forbade any one of them to fill David's ancient throne or participate in the covenant (Jer. 22:24–30). Therefore, Coniah's descendant Joseph, godly as he was, could not have fathered the one of whom Gabriel had told Mary, "The Lord God shall give unto Him the throne of his father David; and He shall rule over the house of Jacob for ever" (Luke 1:32–33). Only one ignorant young man and two unbelieving groups ever called Jesus the son of Joseph (John 1:45; Luke 4:22; John 6:42). Mary knew differently. Luke points out that Jesus was assumed to be the son of Joseph (Luke 3:23), the verse referring to custom or legal standing made possible only if a stepson was either *named* by his father (Matt. 1:21) or adopted his stepfather's *trade* (Mark 6:3).

Luke's record details *Mary's* lineage. She was, as Joseph was, in the royal line; and as Jesus' real mother, bore him as rightful ruler of Israel. Joseph's father was Jacob; the Heli in Luke 3:23 is Mary's father, Joseph's father-in-law. Genetic law states that we find all the characteristics of the two progenitors in every individual. Therefore, from Mary, Jesus received true humanity, all the way back to Adam. From God, His Father, Jesus acquired true Deity, all the way back into eternity. How the limitless love and life of the ruler of the universe could have compressed into a span of infant humanity is incomprehensible, but that fact is the central reality of the biblical record: "And the Word was made flesh, and dwelt among us, (and we beheld His glory, the glory as of the only begotten of the Father,) full of grace and truth" (John 1:14).

His Wisdom: Incandescent Intelligence

No one ever *spoke* as Jesus spoke. Peter Abelard said, "I think the purpose and cause of the Incarnation was that God might illuminate the world by His wisdom and excite it to the love of Himself." Pascal commented, "Jesus Christ said great things simply as though He had not thought them great; yet so clearly that we see easily what He thought of them. This clearness, joined to this simplicity, is wonderful."

Phillip Schaff wrote, "This Jesus of Nazareth, without money and arms, conquered more millions than Alexander, Caesar, Mohammed, and Napoleon; without science and learning, He shed more light on things human and divine than all the philosophers and scholars combined; without the eloquence of schools, He spoke such words of life as were never spoken before or since, and produced effects which lie beyond the reach of orator or poet; without writing a single line, He set more pens in motion, and furnished themes for more sermons, orations, discussions, learned volumes, works of art and songs of praise than the whole army of great men of ancient and modern times."

People were astonished at His doctrine, for He taught them as one having authority, and not as the scribes (Matt. 7:28b–29). "When the disciples heard it, they were exceedingly amazed" (Matt. 19:25). "They were astonished at His doctrine; for his word was with power" (Luke 4:32). "The common people heard Him gladly" (Mark 12:37). "Never a man spake like this man" (John 7:46). The Sermon on the Mount, the Lord's Prayer, the Great Commandments, the Parables—the Prodigal Son, the Lost Sheep, the Good Samaritan, the Pharisee and the Publican—any of these would do honor to any writer in the world, a power and simplicity of the highest genius without equal or rival. Did early Christians of taste and education compose these and later ascribe them to Christ? They could not do it.

Then from whence came this wisdom if Christ were merely some peasant carpenter? Listen to His own words: "Heaven and earth shall pass away, but my words shall not pass away" (Luke 21:33). "The words that I speak to you, they are spirit, and they are life" (John 6:63). "He that heareth my word and believeth on him that sent me, hath everlasting life, and shall not come into condemnation; but is passed from death unto life" (John 5:24). "If any man will do his will, he shall know of the doctrine, whether it be of God, or whether I speak of myself" (John 7:17). "If a man keep My saying, he shall never see death" (John 8:51). "For whosoever shall be ashamed of me and of my words, of him shall the Son of man be ashamed, when he shall come in his own glory, and in His Father's, and of the holy angels" (Luke 9:26).

Paley points out, "When He delivered a precept it was seldom He added any proof or argument; still more seldom limitations and distinctions. He produced Himself a messenger from God. He put the truth of what He taught upon authority."[1]

Jesus said, "I say unto you, swear not at all. . . . I say unto you, love your enemies" (Matt. 5:34, 44). "Thou shalt love the Lord thy God . . . [and] love thy neighbor as thyself; on these two commandments hang all the law and the prophets" (Matt. 22:37–42). "I am the way, the truth, and the life; no man cometh unto the Father, but by me" (John 14:6). "I am the light of the world; he that followeth me shall not walk in darkness, but shall have the light of life" (John 8:12).

His claims, His words, and His warnings are *immense*, ringing with

---

[1]William Paley, *Evidences of Christianity* (New York: S. King, 1824), pp. 156–157.

authority and majesty. Never did a man speak as Jesus did; and to all audiences—curious, hostile, or adoring—without apparent deliberation or premeditation, without a moment's hesitation or uncertainty. *He answered them all*—critics, lawyers, professional debaters, religious specialists, scoffers—so masterfully and convincingly that they were mad with impotent rage, dismissing their carefully planned tricks in seconds. Study the incidents of the woman taken in adultery (John 8:1–11), the lawyer with his query on eternal life (Luke 10:25–37), the chief priests on authority (Matt. 21:23–46), and the Pharisees' taxation trap question (Matt. 22:15–22). Are these the answers of a mere man?

Robert Dale writes, "It is apparent that His influence on the thought of the human race has been immense. It had guided and governed the highest forms of intellectual energy. For more than a thousand years after the Council of Nicea early in the fourth century, it is hardly possible to mention the name of a single man of great speculative power in Europe, North Africa, or Western Asia who was not a Christian theologian. . . . The great poets, the great painters, the great orators, and the great architects also did homage to the supremacy of Christ. It was confessed that He stood alone, and in Him man had found God. . . .

"He has made the loftiest and sublimest conceptions of God, of the universe, of the dignity and destiny of mankind the common possession, age after age, of uncounted millions who knew nothing of the learning of scholars and were familiar with only the rudest forms of secular literature."[2]

Nathan Wood declared, "No man with vision can ignore Jesus the Son. For we live in a world which is His vivid likeness, amid a universe of interwoven movement which is His seamless robe, and in a present which is His living reflection in the stream of time."[3]

His Purity: Intolerance for Iniquity

No one ever *lived* like Jesus. "Imagine," said Catherine Booth, "the very holiest and best who ever trod our earth putting forth such assumptions and how they would sound! Suppose Moses, who talked with God in the burning bush, or Isaiah, or Daniel the man greatly beloved, or the apostle to the Gentiles who was admitted to the third heaven, or the beloved apostle John—suppose any of these men saying 'I am from above, you are from beneath,' 'I am not of this world,' 'If you believe not I am He, you shall die in your sins,' 'I came forth from the Father and am come into the world.' . . . 'Have I been with you so long time and yet you have known Me? He that has seen Me has seen the Father.' His character supported His assumptions. For over 1,800 years the best of the human race have accepted these without being shocked by them. If He be not Divine, how comes it to be that the greatest of human intellects, the sincerest of

[2]Robert W. Dale, "Faith and Physical Science," *Twenty Centuries of Great Preaching*, Clyde E. Fant Jr. and William M. Dinson Jr., eds. (Waco, Texas: Word Books, 1971), vol. 5.

[3]Nathan Wood, *The Trinity in the Universe* (Grand Rapids: Kregel, 1984), p. 105.

human souls, the most aroused and quickened of human consciences have ventured their all upon this Divine Word and have seen nothing contradictory between His claims and the actual character which He sustained in the world?"[4]

Schaff writes that Jesus was zealous but not fanatical, faithful but not obstinate, kind but never weak, and tender but not sentimental. He was unworldly without being indifferent, unsociable, or unduly familiar. He "combined child-like innocence with manly strength, absorbing devotion to God with untiring interest in the welfare of man, tender love to the sinner with uncompromising severity against sin, commanding dignity with winning humility, fearless courage with wise caution, unyielding firmness with sweet gentleness."[5]

Harry Rimmer pointed out that Jesus was born a Jew, lived a Jewish life under Jewish laws in a Jewish land. Yet to the end of His days He offered no sacrifice for sin. No other person who lived in the circle of Mosaic Law could ever say he needed offer no sacrifice for sin. He admonished His disciples, "When *you* pray, say 'forgive us our debts, as we forgive our debtors,' " but He never prayed for forgiveness. He owed no debts—moral, spiritual, or physical. And Jesus taught the necessity of regeneration; the twelve, all the loyal band of men and women who followed Him, even His mother Mary needed redemption—except himself. *Perfection*, Rimmer wrote, "There is no other word which would suit a descriptive statement of the humanity of Christ. We use that word 'perfect' with all its common connotations and in accordance with your understanding of that term.

"So conscious was Jesus of His human perfection that when He stood surrounded by His enemies He boldly challenged them to produce proof of any error in belief or conduct of which He had ever been guilty. This is a startling fact when we remember that His teachings went contrary to the accepted trend of rabbinical interpretation. Again and again the tyrannical hierarchy of Israel charged Him with violating the law of Moses. On each such occasion He cited the law and showed himself to be the only one of the group who fully comprehended its intentions and its applications. His life was fully open and nothing He did was in secret. . . .

"Shrewd doctors of the law studied His every word and deed under the keenest legal scrutiny that hate could provide, hoping to find legal accusation against Him. No other life that ever lived could have withstood that microscopic examination, but Jesus Christ emerged from the crucible of that survey with reputation untarnished and character unblemished."[6]

Wilbur Smith said, "Fifteen million minutes of life on this earth, in the midst of a wicked and corrupt generation—every thought, every deed, every purpose, every work privately and publicly, from the time He opened His baby eyes until He expired on the cross, were all approved of God. Never once did our Lord have to confess any sin, for He had no sin."[7]

---

[4]Catherine Booth, *Popular Christianity* (New York: Salvation Army, 1986), p. 27.
[5]Bernard Ramm, *Protestant Christian Evidences* (Chicago: Moody Press, 1953), p. 177.
[6]Harry Rimmer, *The Magnificence of Jesus* (1943), pp. 137–139.
[7]Wilbur Moorhead Smith, *Have You Considered Him?*

Rimmer goes on, "The life of Jesus depicts an ideal that has never since been achieved. There have been holy and godly men who have astonished the world with their unselfish plane of sacrificial living, which they have achieved by following the example of Jesus; but none has yet to come up to the ideal set by His conduct. Nineteen centuries of more or less constant progress has lifted the levels of living among civilized people . . . yet after those long years the life of Christ is still recognized as the perfect moral pattern for all ages and all races."[8]

His Holiness: Impeccable Integrity

His *friends* said He was without sin. "Who committed no sin," Peter said, "neither was guile found in his mouth: who, when he was reviled, reviled not again; when he suffered, he threatened not; but committed himself to him who judgeth righteously" (1 Pet. 2:22–23). John records, "And ye know that He was manifested to take away our sins; and in him is no sin" (1 John 3:5). "For he hath made him to be sin for us, who knew no sin . . ." (2 Cor. 5:21) says Paul. His *enemies* had to admit it—Pilate said, "I find no fault in him. . . . what evil hath He done? . . . I am innocent of the blood of this just person" (Luke 23:4, 22; John 18:38; 19:4, 6; Matt. 27:24). The thief on the cross said, "This man hath done nothing amiss" (Luke 23:41). The centurion that crucified Him said, "Certainly this was a righteous man" (Luke 23:47). "And the chief priests and all the council sought for witness against Jesus to put Him to death; and found none" (Mark 14:55). Jesus himself said of His Father, "I do always the things that please him" (John 8:29), and to His critical foes, "Which of you convinceth me of sin?" (John 8:46). Search, go and look through all the great religions and religious leaders of the world; none of them could say this, none of them would have *dared*. But Jesus did, because He lived an absolutely holy and perfect life. He could forgive sins because He was God in the flesh and He himself had never sinned.

His Power: Impressive Impossibilities

"The miracles of Jesus," wrote George MacDonald, "were His Father's normal works wrought small and swift that we might know them." Forty-nine miracles spring from the life of Jesus from His birth to His ascension: seven showing His power over demons (Mark 1:23–26; 7:24–30; 9:14–26; Matt. 8:28–34; 9:32–35; 12:22–23; 17:14–21); many the healing of sickness or impairment including palsy, fever, deafness, blindness, hemorrhage, and leprosy (Matt. 8:5–13; 9:27–31; Mark 1:29–31, 40–45; 2:3–12; 3:1–5; 5:25–34; 7:32–37; 8:22–26; Luke 13:11–17; 14:1–6; 17:11–19; 18:35–43; John 4:46–54; 5:1–16; 9:1–7). He even raised three people from the dead: a widow's son (Luke 7:11–16), Jairus's daughter (Mark 5:22–24, 35–43), and Lazarus who had been dead four days! (John 11). Then He did it himself (Luke 24:1–7).

---

[8]Rimmer, op. cit. pp. 137–140.

He wrought miracles both of deliverance (Mark 4:37–41; Matt. 14:28–31; John 6:17–21; 18:4–6) and judgment (Matt. 8:30–32; 21:18–21). He supplied food and drink by means of miracle (John 2:1–11; Luke 5:1–11; Matt. 14:15–21; 15:32–39; 17:27—tribute money; John 21:6–14). Miracles surrounded Him throughout His life; at His birth (Matt. 2:1–9), His baptism (Matt. 3:16–17), the transfiguration (Matt. 17:1–14), at prayer (John 12:28–30), His death (Matt. 27:45–53), His resurrection (Matt. 28:2), and His ascension (Luke 24:51; Acts 1:9–11), "And many of the people believed on him, and said, When Christ cometh, will He do more miracles than these which this man hath done?" (John 7:31).

He did these without show, without ostentation, and without fanfare. Many times these are called His "works" in the Gospels. This was an ordinary term that speaks volumes of who He is—the God who created nature. Such actions are the natural, necessary outflow of a life that is creative, constructive, and compassionate, backed by infinite power and ultimate love. All of Jesus' miracles were a mirror of His character, full of love and mercy, upholding His Father's glory and meeting His creation's needs. They are as far removed from the apocryphal tricks of magicians and occult as light is from darkness. "Art thou he that should come," asked John the Baptist, "or do we look for another?" "Go," replied Jesus, "and shew John again those things which ye do hear and see: the blind receive their sight, and the lame walk, the lepers are cleansed, the deaf hear, the dead are raised up and the poor have the gospel preached to them" (Matt. 11:2–5).

The most ancient Christian apologist, Quadratus, (of whose works we have only a small fragment on record) and who lived some seventy years after the ascension, wrote to the Roman Emperor Adrian: "The works of our Savior were always conspicuous, for they were real; both they that were healed and they that were raised from the dead were seen, not only when they were healed or raised, but for a long time afterwards; not only whilst He dwelled on this earth, but also after His departure, and for a good while after it; inasmuch as that some of them have reached to our times."[9]

Justin Martyr followed Quadratus by about thirty years. He recorded that things happened of such import and power that even Christ's enemies were forced to acknowledge His supernatural power: "Christ healed those who were from birth blind and deaf and lame; causing by His word one to leap, another to hear, and a third to see; and having raised the dead and caused them to live, He by His works excited attention and induced the men of that age to know Him, who however seeing these things done, said that it was a magical appearance and dared call Him a magician and deceiver of the people."[10]

Even Jesus' *enemies* could not deny He did miracles. When they examined the man born blind whom Jesus had healed, there was a division

---

[9]Eusebius, "Histories," *Ante-Nicene Fathers*, Alexander Roberts and James Donaldson, eds. (Eerdmans, 1961), vol. 1, 4.50.3.

[10]Justin, "Dialogue With Trypho," *Ante-Nicene Fathers*, Alexander Roberts and James Donaldson, eds. (Eerdmans, 1961), p. 258.

among them. "This man is not of God because He does keepeth not the sabbath day," said some. Others said, "How can a man that is a sinner do such miracles?" (John 9:16). "What sayest thou of Him, that he hath opened thine eyes" (v. 17), they asked the blind man. "Is this your son who ye say was born blind?" (v. 19) they questioned his parents. "How then doth he now see?" (v. 19). "Since the world began was it not heard that any man opened the eyes of one born blind," said their healed son. "If this man were not of God he could do nothing" (vv. 32–33).

When Lazarus was raised from the dead, the despairing comment of the chief priests and Pharisees was "What do we? For this man doeth many miracles. If we let Him thus alone, all men will believe on Him" (John 11:47–48).

The earthly life of Jesus was a life filled with the miraculous. These miracles continue down to the present day, because He is the "same yesterday, and to day, and for ever" (Heb. 13:8).

His Life: Immeasurable Influence

If the New Testament is clear on anything, it is this: Jesus Christ was truly God as well as truly man. He is not "a" god, or related to God in some ethical sense. He is called the:

- Altogether Lovely One (Song of Sol. 5:16)
- Author and Finisher of our faith (Heb. 12:2)
- Bread of Life (John 6:35, 48)
- Bright and Morning Star (Rev. 22:16)
- Chief Cornerstone (Eph. 2:20)
- Desire of all Nations (Hag. 2:7)
- Door (John 10:7, 9)
- Good Shepherd (John 10:11)
- Healer of the sick (Matt. 4:23)
- King of kings and Lord of lords
- King (Luke 23:2; John 1:49; 18:37; 1 Tim. 1:17; 6:15)
- Light of the World (John 8:12; 9:5)
- Matchless Teacher (John 3:2)
- Rock of Ages (1 Cor. 10:4)
- Rose of Sharon (Song of Sol. 2:1)
- Vine (John 15:1)
- Way, the Truth, and the Life (John 14:6)
- Wisdom and Power of God (1 Cor. 1:24)
- Alpha and Omega, the First and the Last, the Beginning and the End (Rev. 1:8)—and above all, the Savior God of humanity (1 Tim. 6:15)

One Solitary Life

"Here is a man who was born in an obscure village, the child of a peasant woman. He grew up in another village. He worked in a carpenter shop until He was thirty and then for three years was an itinerant preacher. He never owned a home. He never wrote a book. He never held an office.

He never had a family. He never went to college. He never put his foot inside a big city. He never traveled two hundred miles from the place where He was born. He never did one of those things that usually accompany greatness. He had no credentials but himself. . . .

"While still a young man, the tide of popular opinion turned against him. His friends ran away. One of them denied him. He was turned over to his enemies. He went through the mockery of a trial. He was nailed on a cross between two thieves. While he was dying his executors gambled for the only piece of property he had on earth—His coat. When he was dead, he was taken down and laid in a borrowed grave through the pity of a friend.

"Nineteen long centuries have come and gone and today he is the centerpiece of the human race and the leader of the column of progress. I am far within the mark when I say that all the armies that ever marched, all the navies that ever were built; all the parliaments that ever sat, and all the kings that ever reigned put together have not affected the life of man upon this earth as powerfully as has that one solitary life."[11]

Joseph Parker said: "There are other men who do not come to worship Christ; who simply come to speculate upon Him. . . . the patronage they offer the Son of God! It makes me sad to hear how they damn Him with faint praise. What I dread among you is not that you will destroy Christ, but that you will patronize Him. Jesus Christ is nothing to me if He is not the Savior of the world. . . . You will know what Jesus Christ is most and best when you are in greatest need of such service as He can render.

"No man can entertain an opinion of indifference regarding Jesus. If he has considered the subject at all, he must worship Christ or crucify Him. Where there is earnestness in the inquiry or the criticism, that earnestness ends in homage or in crucifixion."[12]

His Death and Resurrection: Incontrovertible Implication

No one ever *died* like Jesus. Billions have died and millions have been executed. Scores of thousands had died the terrible death of a Roman crucifixion before Jesus. But none of these things makes Jesus' death unique. No one ever died like Jesus, because He died when He did not deserve to die, and like no one else in history, He did not *have* to die. "I lay down My life," Jesus said, "that I may take it again. No man taketh it from me, but I lay it down of myself. I have power to lay it down, and I have power to take it again" (John 10:17–18).

Jesus would not have had to die from old age, sickness, or weakness like any other human being. He had not known sin. He died like any sufferer of a crucifixion would have died, but His death was utterly unlike any other, for it was a death for the sins of the whole world.

He had told His friends He would die, but they did not believe it then. They had not realized that the silent reel of history recording before their

[11]Author unknown.
[12]Joseph Parker, *The Inner Life of Christ* (London: Hodder and Stoughton, 1950).

eyes was fulfilling prophecy, counting down hour after hour in those last few terrible days. Twenty-nine prophecies which spoke of His trial, death, and burial over a period of five centuries were fulfilled within literally twenty-four hours.

As we read of Christ's final hours, just as the prophets foretold, He is betrayed by a friend (Psa. 41:9; 55:12–14; Matt. 10:4; 26:49–50) and sold for thirty pieces of silver (Zech. 11:12; Matt. 26:15), which were thrown down in God's house (Zech. 11:13; Matt. 27:5), and He is forsaken by His disciples (Zech. 13:7; Mark 14:50; Matt. 26:31). He is accused by false witnesses (Ps. 35:11; Matt. 26:59–61), but remains deliberately silent before His accusers (Isa. 53:7; John 19:9). He is wounded and bruised (Isa. 53:5; Zech. 13:6; John 19:3), hit and spit on (Isa. 50:6; Mic. 5:1; Matt. 26:67; Luke 22:63), and cynically mocked (Ps. 22:7–8; Matt. 27:31). He falls under His cross (Ps. 109:24–25; John 19:17; Luke 23:26). At the Hill of the Skull they pierce His hands and His feet (Ps. 22:16; Luke 24:40). He is crucified with transgressors (Isa. 53:12; Matt. 27:38; Mark. 15:27–28; Luke 23:33), is stared on (Ps. 22:17; Luke 23:35), and His clothes are gambled away (Ps. 22:18; John 19:23–24).

"Dead," they said, and thought to themselves, *Now it is over.* Cut off in His prime, "crossed" out like an embarrassing entry in life's ledger, hung up to die, pulled down and buried.

But that was not the end. Not at all. There had been those disturbing statements all along, but who would believe things like, "Destroy this temple and in three days I will raise it up" (John 2:19)? The Romans post a good guard troop in front of the tomb, and seal a very big rock over it to discourage the casual and some last-minute clean-up operations around town; that ought to take care of the legends.

But three days after the cross—an early morning earthquake, a light like the sun, and terrified rumors that radiated out from an empty grave in the garden. Afraid, none of the disciples dare believe the women's incoherent story. He was dead, really dead! They had *seen* Him die with their own eyes, and buried His body wound in many pounds of spice-laden grave cloth on the slab of a borrowed tomb. But they go—just a few of them—half-afraid, half-hoping for a miracle.

And when they see what they see inside the almost empty tomb, they became such soldiers and heroes that they each choose to die rather than deny it, to go gladly to terrible deaths and vicious executions, to lay down their lives in confidence of a reality that had delivered them from the fear of death.

"The grave-clothes lay like the shriveled, cracked shell of a cocoon, left behind when the moth has emerged and hoisted her bright sails in the sunshine. . . . or more accurately like a glove from which the hand has been removed, the fingers of which still retain the shape of the hand. In that manner, the grave-clothes were lying, collapsed a little—slightly deflated—because there were between the rolls of bandages a considerable weight of spices, but there lay a linen cloth that had been wound round the body of Christ. It was when they saw that, that the disciples believed."[13]

His Soon Return: Imminent Intervention

The prophecies and accounts of His life and death make the Bible absolutely unique among all the world's great holy books. At least a *quarter* of the Bible (an estimated 8,352 verses out of its 31,124) contains detailed predictive material; 27 percent of God's Word is prophetic. Out of approximately 590 major events prophesied in Scripture, all but twenty have been perfectly fulfilled. (Lance Lambert)

Consider, for instance, these fourteen predictions of the Christ's birth precisely fulfilled in the baby Jesus. All of them came true, to the letter. The Messiah would be:

- The seed of a woman (Gen. 3:15; Gal. 4:4).
- Born of a virgin (Isa. 7:14; Matt. 1:18, 24–25).
- The Son of God (2 Sam. 7:12–16; 1 Chron. 17:11–14; Ps. 2:7; Matt. 3:17; 16:16; 26:63; Mark 3:11; 9:7; Luke 9:35; 22:70; John 1:34, 49; Acts 13:30–33).
- The seed of Abraham (Gen. 12:2–3; 22:18; Matt. 1:1; Gal. 3:16).
- The son of Isaac (Gen. 21:12; Luke 3:23–34; Matt. 1:2).
- The son of Jacob (Gen. 35:10–12; Num. 24:17; Luke 1:33; 3:23–34; Matt. 1:2).
- From the tribe of Judah (Gen. 49:10; Mic. 5:2; Luke 3:2; Matt. 1:2; Heb. 7:14).
- From the family line of Jesse and David (2 Sam. 7:12–16; Isa. 11:1, 10; Jer. 23:5; Ps. 132:11; Matt. 1:1, 6; 9:27; 15:22; 22:41–46; Luke 3:23–34; 18:38–39; Mark 10:47).
- Born in Bethlehem (Mic. 5:2; Matt. 2:1; Luke 2:4–7; John 7:42).
- Visited by kings bearing gifts (Ps. 72:10; Isa. 60:6; Matt. 2:1, 11).
- The murder of children in connection with His birth (Jer. 31:15; Matt. 2:16–18).
- He shall be called "Lord" (Ps. 110:1; Jer. 23:6; Luke 2:11; 20:42–44).
- He shall be "Immanuel"; God with us (Isa. 7:14; Matt. 1:23; Luke 7:16).[14]

Consider these prophesies of His life and His death: over *three hundred* evidences that revolve around this one Man whose demands on your life and mine cannot be ignored. All predictions were precisely fulfilled.

Consider this also: for every prophecy of Jesus' *first* coming, there are *seven* of His *second*. He is not just the Christ of ancient history, or even of present experience—He is the Coming King, coming in clouds of power and great glory. He is the Rightful Owner of all creation, at whose advent all people will be called into reckoning, small and great, rich and poor,

[13]Peter Marshall, *Mr. Jones, Meet the Master* (New York: Dell Publishing, 1961), p. 126.

[14]Josh McDowell, *Evidence That Demands a Verdict* (San Bernardino, Calif.: Campus Crusade for Christ, 1979).

religious or not. He is not the Christ of a long-gone past; He is the present Savior, and the world's future Judge, a future that is fast moving into present reality.

Historical Discussion

The soft light from a stable door
Lies on the midnight lands;
The wise men's star burns ever more
Over all desert sands....

No flickering torch, no wavering fire,
But Light the Life of men;
Whatever clouds may veil the sky
Never is night again.

Lillian Cox

The Greatest Life

"The life of Jesus Christ . . . must remain ever the noblest and most fruitful study for all men of every age. . . . Men like Galileo, Kepler, Bacon, Newton, and Milton set the name of Jesus Christ above every other. . . ." Jean Paul Richter goes on to tell us, "The life of Christ concerns Him, who being the holiest among the mighty, the mightiest among the holy, lifted with His pierced hand empires off their hinges and turned the stream of centuries out of its channel, and still governs the ages. Spinoza called Christ the symbol of divine wisdom; Kant and Jacobi hold Him up as the symbol of ideal perfection and Schelling and Hegel as that of the union of the divine and human." "I esteem the Gospels," says Goethe, "to be thoroughly genuine, for there shines forth from them the reflected splendor of a sublimity proceeding from the person of Jesus Christ of so divine a kind as only the divine could ever have manifested on earth."

Jean-Jacques Rousseau

"How petty are the books of the philosophers with all their pomp compared with the Gospels! Can it be that writings at once so sublime and so simple are the work of men? Can He whose life they tell be himself no more than a mere man? . . . Where is the man, where is the sage who knows how to act, to suffer and to die without weakness and without display? My friend, men do not invent like this; and the facts attesting Socrates which no one doubts are not so well attested as those about Jesus Christ. These Jews could have never struck this tone of thought of this morality and the Gospels have characteristics of truthfulness so grand, so striking, so perfectly inimitable, that their inventors would be even more wonderful than He whom they portray. Yes, if the death of Socrates be that of a sage, the life and death of Jesus are those of a God."[1]

An Inexplicable Life

James Stalker

"Most lives are easily explained. They are mere products of circumstances and copies of thousands like them which surround or have preceded them. The habits and customs of the country to which we belong, the fashions and tastes of our generation, the traditions of our education, the prejudices of our class, the opinions of school or sect—these form us. . . . But what circumstances made the man Christ Jesus? There was never an age more dry and barren than that in which He was born. He was like a tall, fresh palm springing out of a desert. What was there in the petty life of Nazareth to produce so gigantic a character? How could the notorious wicked village send forth such breathing purity? . . . How clearly behind all the pretentious and accepted forms of piety He saw the lovely and neglected figure of real godliness! He cannot be explained by anything which was in the world and might have produced Him."[2]

Not Just a Man

Napoleon Bonaparte

"I think I understand something of human nature and I tell you all of these [heroes of antiquity] were men, and I am a man, but not one is like Him; Jesus Christ was more than man. Alexander, Caesar, Charlemagne, and myself founded great empires; but upon what did the creations of our genius depend? Upon force. Jesus alone founded His empire of love, and to this very day millions would die for Him. Men wonder at the conquests of Alexander, but here is a conqueror who draws men to himself for their highest good; who unites to himself, incorporates into himself not a nation, but the whole human race!"[3]

"I know men; and I tell you Jesus is not a man. Everything in Him amazes me. His spirit outreaches mine, and His will confounds me. Comparison is impossible between Him and any other being in the world. He is truly a being by himself. His ideas and sentiments; the truth that He announces; His manner of convincing; are all beyond humanity and the natural order of things. His birth and the story of His life; the profoundness of His doctrine, which overturns all difficulties and is their most complete solution; His Gospel; the singularity of His mysterious being; His appearance; His empire; His progress through all the centuries and kingdoms; all this is to me a prodigy, an unfathomable mystery. I see nothing here of man. Near as I may approach, closely as I may examine, all remains above my comprehension great with a greatness that crushes me. It is in

---

[1]Jean-Jacques Rousseau, "Emile I," iv. 1762.
[2]James Stalker, *The Life of Jesus Christ* (Fleming Revell, 1949), p. 82.
[3]*Bertrand's Memoirs* (Paris, 1844).

vain that I reflect—all remains unaccountable! I defy you to cite another life like that of Christ."[4]

God Visiting This World

G. K. Chesterton

"It is quite unlike anything else. It is a thing final like the trump of doom though it is also a piece of good news; or news that seems too good to be true. It is nothing less than the loud assertion that this mysterious Maker of the world has visited His world in person. It declares that really and even recently, or right in the middle of historic times, there did walk into the world this original invisible being; about whom the thinkers make theories and the mythologists hand down myths; *the Man who made the World*. That such a higher personality exists behind all things had always been implied by the best thinkers as well as by all the most beautiful legends. But nothing of this sort has ever been implied by any of them. . . .

"The most that any religious prophet had said was that he was the true servant of such a being. The most that any visionary had ever said was that men might catch glimpses of the glory of that spiritual being; or much more often of lesser spiritual beings. The most that any primitive myth had ever suggested was that the Creator was present at the Creation. But that the Creator was present at scenes a little subsequent to the supper-parties of Horace, and talked with tax-collectors and government officials in the detailed daily life of the Roman Empire, and that this fact continued to be firmly asserted by the whole of that great civilization for more than a thousand years—that is something utterly unlike anything else in nature. It is the one great startling statement that man has made since he spoke his first articulate word. . . . It makes nothing but dust and nonsense of comparative religion."[5]

Jesus Is God

John Watson

"How can one be certain Jesus is God? There are four lines of proof. The first is to cite reliable evidence that Jesus rose from Joseph's tomb. This is for a lawyer. The second is historical—the existence of the Christian church—this is for a scholar. The third is mystical—the experience of Christians—this is for a saint. The fourth is ethical—the nature of Jesus' life—this is for everyone. The last is the most akin to the mind of Jesus who was accustomed to insist on the self-evidencing power of His life. . . . Even His blind generation was arrested by Jesus. There was note in His words that caught the ear, the echo of divine authority; there was an air about Him, the manner of a larger world. No man could convince Him of sin, no man confound Him. He was ever beyond criticism. He ever com-

---

[4]John Cunningham Geikie, *The Life of Christ*, vol. 1, p. 13.
[5]G.K. Chesterton, *The Everlasting Man* (Dodd and Mead, 1925), pp. 334–335.

pelled admiration in honest men. 'You are the Christ,' said a Jewish peasant with instinctive conviction, 'the Son of the Living God.'

"Centuries have only confirmed this spontaneous tribute to Jesus' life. No one has yet discovered the word Jesus ought to have said; none suggested that better word He might have said. No action of His has shocked our moral sense; none has fallen short of the ideal. He is full of surprises but they are all the surprises of perfection. You are ever amazed, one day by His greatness, the next by His littleness. You are ever amazed that He is incomparably better than you could have expected. He is tender without being weak, strong without being coarse, lowly without being servile. He has conviction without intolerance, enthusiasm without fanaticism, holiness without Pharisaism, passion without prejudice. This man alone never made a false step, never struck a jarring note. His life alone moved on those high levels where local limitations are transcended and the absolute law of moral beauty prevails. It was life at its highest. Jesus was the supreme Artist in Life and had a right to say 'I am the Life.' "[6]

George MacDonald

"The cry of the deepest in man has always been to see God. It was the cry of Moses and the cry of Job, the cry of psalmist and of prophet; and to the cry there has ever been faintly heard a far approach of coming answer. In the fullness of time, the Son appears with a proclamation that a certain class of men shall behold the Father: 'Blessed are the pure in heart,' He cries, 'for they shall see God.' He who saw God, who sees Him now, who will always see Him, says, 'Be pure and you shall also see Him.' . . . All that the creature needs to see or know, all that the creature can see or know, is the face of Him from whom he came. Not seeing and knowing it, He will never be at rest; seeing and knowing it, his existence will yet indeed be a mystery to him and an awe, but no more a dismay."

Reality in the Incarnation

G. K. Chesterton

> There has fallen on earth for a token
> A God too great for the sky,
> He has burst out of all things and broken
> The bounds of eternity.[7]

E. Stanley Jones

"I went to my Bible to see whether as a Christian I was a realist or an idealist and came out at the end of two years of investigation convinced that if I am to be a Christian I have to be a realist, for Christianity in its essential nature is realism. If I were to pick out the most important verse in Scripture to me I would pick out this one. 'And the Word was made

---

[6]John Watson, D.D. , *Mind of the Master* (New York: Dodd, Mead and Company, 1896), pp. 81–82.
[7]G.K. Chesterton, "Gloria In Profundis."

flesh' (John 1:14). In all other religions, it is the word became word, a philosophy or moralism. Once, and only once, the Word became flesh, the ideal became real. Everything Jesus taught He embodied. You cannot tell where His words ended and his deeds began, for His words were deeds and His deeds were words and together with what He was, the Word became flesh."[8]

B. R. Brasnett

"Jesus is a true Jew in His love for the concrete, he is not interested in purity, but in the pure of heart, not in sorrow, but in those that mourn. . . . After all, we do not all need a consciously formulated theory of life, but we all have to live. . . . A theory of virtue is not necessary, but it is necessary to know how to be virtuous."[9]

Alexander Whyte

"He who in the fullness of time became the second Adam had from all eternity been the divine Son, and as such the image of the eternal Father. . . . Such an image as that makes further revelations and manifestations of the Father become possible though Him. In some way quite unfathomable to us the divine nature had come nearer us and nearer all creation in the eternal generation of the divine Son. Creation and providence, revelation and grace had all become possible and indeed prophetic in the eternal Sonship. . . .

"The Unconditioned has become conditioned in the second person of the Godhead. The Father in His monarchy and invisibility secures the majesty and invisibility of the Godhead in its secret place; while the Son . . . manifests its goodness and beneficence: hence the Father is the Son's incomprehensibility and invisibility while the Son is the Father's comprehensibility and visibility. . . .

"My brethren it is not an irreverent play on words but a most profound and fundamental truth to say that as Adam in his creation was made in the image of the Son of God, so the Son of God in His incarnation was made in the image of Adam. A body and soul were prepared for Him; not strictly speaking as a new Creation, but as a sanctified extraction and holy reproduction of the body and soul of Mary, which in this respect were just the body and soul of Adam. The body and the mind, the will, the heart the conscience of the man Christ were all made in the image of Adam. The new creation begun in Christ . . . consisted in filling the Adamic mind found in Christ with divine light and divine truth; in filling the Adamic will with filial humility and obedience; filling the Adamic heart with love to God and man and the Adamic conscience with all the communion and peace of the holy and living temple. . . .

"The image of God as seen in Christ, the second Adam, is simply a human understanding enlarged and enlightened without measure; a hu-

---

[8]E.Stanley Jones, *The Unshakeable Kingdom and the Unchanging Person* (Nashville: Abingdon Press, 1971), p. 46.
[9]B.R. Brasnett, *The Infinity of God* (London: Longmans, Green, and Co., 1933), p. 10.

man will emancipated and carried captive under a sweet and blessed restraint to the will of God; a human heart which is a fountain of love to God and grace to men; and a human conscience which lies in His bosom like a sea of glass before the throne of God."[10]

J. S. Whale

"He is what God means by man. He is what man means by God."

Terence Fretheim

"In the Incarnation, God had acted anthropomorphically in the most supreme way. The N.T. far from being the culmination of a progressive spiritualization in the understanding of God speaks of a God unsurpassably infleshed in the human. . . . The N.T. continues to speak of God in terms of such metaphors. This continuity is consonant with developments within the O.T. itself, where one is struck by the constant use of such language. There are no anti-anthropomorphic tendencies to be discerned; even in dreams or visions or glimpses into heaven God is spoken of in such ways. Such passages as Isa. 42:13–14; 63:1–6; and Dan. 7:9 contain some of the more daring anthropomorphic metaphors in the O.T."[11]

Dietrich Bonhoeffer

"If Jesus Christ is not true God, how could He *help* us? If He is not true man, how could he help *us*?"

Jonathan Edwards

"This then was another thing full of wonders; that He who was man as well as God; He who was a servant and died like a malefactor should be made the sovereign Lord of heaven and earth, angels and men; the absolute disposer of eternal life and death; the supreme judge of all created intelligent beings for eternity; and should have committed to Him all the governing power of God the Father; and that, not only as God, but as God-man not exclusive of the human nature. As it is wonderful that a person who is truly divine should be humbled to become a servant and suffer as a malefactor; so it is in like manner wonderful that He who is God-man not exclusive of the manhood should be exalted to the power and honor of the great God of heaven and earth."[12]

Dorothy Sayers

"For Jesus Christ is unique; unique among the gods and men. There have been incarnate gods aplenty and slain-and-resurrected gods not a few; but He is the only God who has a date in history. And plenty of

[10]Alexander Whyte, *With Mercy and Judgement* (London: Hodder and Stoughton, 1882), pp. 25–28.
[11]Terrence Fretheim, *The Suffering of God* (Fortress, 1984), p. 7.
[12]Jonathan Edwards, "Wisdom Displayed in Salvation," *The Works of Jonathan Edwards* (University Press, 1977), vol. 1, p. 144.

founders of religions have had dates, and some of them have been prophets or avatars of the divine; but only this one of them was personally
divine."[13]

God's Goal for Mankind

John Mbiti

"The uniqueness of Christianity is Jesus Christ. He is the stumbling
block of all ideologies and religious systems. . . . He is the 'Man for Others'
and yet beyond them. It is He therefore, and only He who deserves to be
the goal and standard for individuals and mankind. . . . I consider traditional religions, Islam and other religious systems, to be preparatory and
even essential ground in the search for the Ultimate. But only Christianity
has the terrible responsibility of pointing the way to the ultimate Identity,
Foundation, and Source of Security."[14]

E. Stanley Jones

"Many teachers of the world have tried to explain everything—they
have changed little or nothing. Jesus explained little and changed everything. . . . Jesus changes everything He touches. Call Him a man and you
will have to change your ideas of what a man is; call Him God, and you
will have to change your ideas of what God is. . . . He is the one figure
in history that is not local or national. Moses was a Hebrew, Mohammed
was an Arabian, Buddha was an Indian, Socrates was a Greek, Confucius
was a Chinese, but Jesus is the Son of Man. . . . He is the universal Christ.
All nations feel at home with Him when they really know Him."[15]

Ayn Rand

Rand, the non-Christian objectivist philosopher, makes a trenchant
comment on the relationship of a work of art to ideas like absolutes and
ultimates: "Art is a concretization of metaphysics. Art brings man's concepts to the perceptual level of his consciousness and allows him to grasp
them directly as if they were percepts. . . . Just as language converts abstractions into the psycho-epistemological equivalents of concretes, so art
converts man's metaphysical abstractions into the equivalents of concretes, into specific entities open to man's direct perception. . . . Observe
that in mankind's history, art began as an adjunct (and often a monopoly)
of religion. Religion . . . provided man with a comprehensive view of
existence. . . . Art . . . was a concretization of their religion's metaphysical
and ethical abstractions." Rand goes on to say that we need a model to
live by: "When we come to 'normative' abstractions—to the task of defining moral principles and projecting what man ought to be—the psycho-
epistemological process required is still harder. . . . An exhaustive philo-

[13]Dorothy Sayers, *A Matter of Eternity* (Grand Rapids: Eerdmans, 1973), p. 16.
[14]John Mbiti, *African Religions and Philosophy* (Heinemann, ed., 1969), ch. 20.
[15]E. Stanley Jones, *Christ at the Round Table* (Philadelphia: Century Bookbindery, 1981),
    p. 297.

sophical treatise defining moral values will not do it; it will not convey what an ideal man would be like and how he would act; no mind can deal with so immense a sum of abstractions. When I say 'deal with,' I mean retranslate all the abstractions into the perceptual concretes for which they stand—i.e., reconnect them to reality—and hold all in the focus of one's conscious awareness. *There is no way to integrate such a sum without projecting an actual human figure*—and integrated concretization illuminates the theory and makes it intelligible."[16]

Christ the Pattern

And this is of course precisely what we find in Christ; Jesus is God in the flesh, God focused and incarnate, God to see and follow and model one's whole life after.

Dorothy Sayers

"For whatever reason God chose to make man as he is—limited and suffering and subject to sorrows and death—He had the honesty and the courage to take His own medicine. Whatever game He is playing with His creatures, He has kept His own rules and played fair. He can exact nothing from man that He has not exacted from himself."[17]

A. W. Tozer

"The Gospel not only furnishes transforming power to remold the human heart; it provides also a model after which the new life is to be fashioned and that model is Christ himself. Christ is God acting like God in the lowly raiments of human flesh. Yet He is also man; so He becomes the perfect model after which redeemed human nature is to be fashioned. The beginnings of that transformation . . . are found in conversion when the man is made partaker of the divine nature. By regeneration and sanctification, by faith and prayer, by suffering and discipline, by the Word and the Spirit, the work goes on until the dream of God has been realized in the Christian heart. Everything that God does in His ransomed children has as its long-range purpose the final restoration of the divine image in human nature."[18]

Jesus Christ the Central Theme

James S. Stewart

"If there ever was a man of one subject, that man was Paul. 'I determined,' he told the Corinthians quite frankly, 'not to know anything among you save Jesus Christ.' 'To me,' he wrote to the Philippians, 'to live is Christ'—*life means Christ to me*. That was his one theme, given to him

---

[16]Ayn Rand, *The Romantic Manifesto* (Signet, N.J. 1971), pp. 20–21.
[17]Sayers, op. cit. p. 30
[18]A.W. Tozer, *The Root of the Righteous* (Camp Hill, Pa.: Christian Publications, Inc., 1955), pp. 59–60.

straight from God himself: and if ever a time should come when that is no longer the central theme of the Christian Church then the day of the Church will be finished. The one thing that can justify the church is a great passion for Christ. . . . 'At this moment in ten thousand gatherings of His people, men are still, after nineteen centuries of Jesus, thinking about Him, telling of His all-sufficient grace, exploring His eternal truth—and still not anywhere near the end of it. . . . Any other subject under heaven would have been exhausted long ago; this theme remains bewilderingly rich, everlastingly fresh and fertile. The early church had a strange name for Jesus. They called Him 'the Alpha and Omega.' . . . Jesus is simply everything in life from A to Z. There is nothing worth heralding but Jesus."[19]

David Brainerd

"I have ofttimes remarked with admiration that whatever subject I have been treating . . . I have naturally and easily been led to Christ as the substance of every subject. . . . Never did I find so much freedom and assistance in making all the various lines of my discussion meet together and center in Christ as I have frequently done among these Indians. . . . There has at times unawares appeared such a fountain of gospel-grace shining forth . . . and Christ has seemed in such a manner to be pointed out as the substance of what I was considering or explaining that I have been drawn in a way not only easy and natural, proper and pertinent but almost unavoidable to discourse of Him. . . .

"I have frequently been enabled to represent the divine glory, the infinite preciousness and transcendent loveliness of the great Redeemer; the suitableness of His person and purchase to supply the wants and answer the utmost desires of immortal souls . . . and this in such a manner with such freedom, pertinency, pathos, and application to the conscience, as I am sure I could never have made myself master of by the most assiduous application of mind. . . .

"I do not mention these things as a recommendation of my own performances; for I am sure I found from time to time that I had no skill or wisdom for my great work; and knew not how to choose out acceptable words. . . .

"But God was pleased to help me 'not to know anything among them save Jesus Christ and Him crucified.' . . . And this was the preaching God made for the awakening of sinners and the propagation of this work of grace. . . . It was remarkable . . . that when I was favored with any special freedom in discoursing of the ability and willingness of Christ to save sinners and the need they stood in of such a Savior, there was then the greatest appearance of divine power in awakening numbers of secure souls, promoting convictions begun, and comforting the distressed. I have sometimes wondered to see Peter so quickly introduce the Lord Jesus Christ into his sermon [to Cornelius in Acts 10] and so entirely dwell upon Him through the whole of it, observing him in this point to differ very

---

[19]James S. Stewart, *The Strong Name* (New York: Scribner's, 1941), pp. 92–93.

widely from many of our modern preachers; but latterly this has not seemed strange since Christ has appeared to be the *substance* of the Gospel, and the *center* in which the lines of divine revelation meet."[20]

The Fulfillment of Every Need

Catherine Booth

"Now we contend that this Christ of the Bible, the Christ who appeared in Judea 1,800 years ago is now abroad in the earth just as much as He was then, and that He presents to humanity all it needs; that He is indeed, as He represented himself to be, the Bread of Life come down from heaven, the Light, and the Life, and the Strength of man, meeting this cry of His soul which has been going up to God for generations. Here I stand and make my boast, that the Christ of God, my Christ, the Christ of the Salvation Army, does meet this crying need of the soul, does fill this aching void, and does become to man that which God sets Him forth as being in this book. . . . We make our boast of this Christ and we say He is able to save to the uttermost, and He does this now as much as ever He has done in 1,800 years that are past—that He is a real, living, present Savior to those who really receive and put their trust in Him."[21]

C. H. Spurgeon

"Let not Jesus be a shadow to you, or your religion will be unsubstantial; let Him not be a name to you, or your religion will be nominal; let Him not be a myth of history, or your religion will be a fantasy; let Him be not alone a teacher, or you will lack a Savior; let Him be not alone an exemplar, or you will fail to appreciate the merit of His blood; let Him be the Beginning and the Ending, the First and the Last, the All in all for your spirits."[22]

Frederick Faber

> I love Thee so I know not how
> My transports to control;
> Thy love is like a burning fire
> Within my very soul.[23]

Living as a Son

George MacDonald

"The world was His home because it was His Father's house. He was not a stranger who did not know His way about it. He was no lost child,

---

[20]David Brainerd, *Journal of David Brainerd*, Jonathan Edwards, ed. (Chicago: Moody Press, 1746), Appendix 1, Section I.

[21]Catherine Booth, *Popular Christianity* (New York: Salvation Army, 1986), p. 7.

[22]C.H. Spurgeon, *Flashes of Thought* (1874), p. 102.

[23]A.W. Tozer, *The Pursuit of God* (Camp Hill, Penn.: Christian Publications Inc., 1982), p. 41.

but with His Father all the time. Here we find one main thing wherein the Lord differs from us; we are not at home in this great universe, our Father's house. We ought to be, and one day we shall be, but we are not yet. This reveals Jesus more than man, by revealing Him more man than we. We are not complete men, we are not anything near it, and are therefore out of harmony more or less with everything in the house of our birth and habitation. . . . We are not at home in it, because we are not at home with the Lord of the house, the father of the family, not one with our elder brother who is at his right hand. It is only the son, the daughter that abides forever in the house. When we are true children, if not the world, then the universe will be our home, felt and known as such, the house we are satisfied with and would not change."[24]

Joseph Plinkett

I see His blood upon the rose
And in the stars the glory of His eyes;
His body gleams amid eternal snows
His tears fall from the skies.

I see His face in every flower,
The thunder and the singing of the birds
Are but His voice—and carven by His power,
Rocks are His written words.

All pathways by His feet are worn,
His strong heart stirs the ever-beating sea,
His crown of thorns is twined with every thorn,
His cross is every tree.

George MacDonald

"All His life He was among His Father's things, either in heaven or in the world. . . . He claimed none of them as His own, would not have had one of them His except through His Father. Did He ever say 'This is mine, not yours?' Did He not say 'All things are mine; therefore they are yours?' That the things were His Father's made them precious things to Him. Oh for His liberty among the things of the Father! Only by knowing them the things of our Father can we escape enslaving ourselves to them."[25]

Glorious Beyond Words

Samuel Rutherford

"Alas! My books are all bare, and show me little of God. I would fain go beyond books into His house of love to himself. Dear brother, neither you nor I are parties worthy of His love or knowledge. . . . What am I, to shape conceptions of my highest Lord? How broad and how high and

---

[24]George MacDonald, *Life Essential*, pp. 29–31.
[25]Ibid. p. 31.

how deep He is above and beyond what these conceptions are, I cannot tell. . . . I would fain add to my thoughts and esteem of Him and make Him more high and wish a heart and love ten thousand times wider than the utmost circle and curtain that goes about the heaven of heavens, to entertain Him in that heart, and with that love."[26]

Athanasius of Alexandria

"He became what we are that He might make us what He is."

---

[26]Samuel Rutherford, *Letters*, Frank Gaebelein, ed. (Chicago: Moody Press, 1951), p. 609.

CHAPTER THIRTEEN

DECLARATION THREE:
THE HOLY SPIRIT IS THE
UNCREATED GOD

Scriptures

He Is Eternal

"[Christ] through the eternal Spirit offered himself." (Heb. 9:14)

He Has Attributes of Deity

Omnipresence

"Whither shall I go from thy spirit?" (Ps. 139:7)

Omniscience

"Howbeit when he, the Spirit of truth, is come, he will guide you into all truth. . . . He will shew you things to come." (John 16:13)

"The Holy Ghost by the mouth of David spake before concerning Judas." (Acts 1:16)

"The Spirit searcheth all things." (1 Cor. 2:10; cf. Isa. 40:13–14; Rom. 8:26–27)

"The spirit of wisdom and revelation in the knowledge of him." (Eph. 1:17)

Omnipotence

". . . is the Spirit of the LORD straitened [limited or restricted]?" (Mic. 2:7)

"If I cast out devils by the Spirit of God . . ." (Matt. 12:28)

". . . the power of the Highest." (Luke 1:35)

"If I with the finger of God cast out devils, no doubt the kingdom of

God is come upon you." (Luke 11:20)

"Through mighty signs and wonders, by the power of the Spirit of God." (Rom. 15:19)

He Is Co-Creator of Heaven and Earth

"And the Spirit of God moved upon the face of the waters." (Gen. 1:2)

"By his spirit he hath garnished [beautified] the heavens." (Job 26:13)

"By the word of the Lord were the heavens made; and all the host of them by the breath [Spirit] of his mouth." (Ps. 33:6)

"Who hath measured the waters in the hollow of his hand, and meted out heaven with the span, and comprehended the dust of the earth. . . . Who hath directed the *spirit of the* LORD, or being his counsellor hath taught him? With whom took he counsel, and who instructed him?" (Isa. 40:12–14)

"They lifted up their voice to God with one accord, and said, *Lord, thou art God, which hast made heaven, and earth,* and the sea, and all that in them is: who by the mouth of thy servant David hast said, Why did the heathen rage, and the people imagine vain things? The kings of the earth stood up, and the rulers were gathered together against the Lord, and against his Christ." (Acts 4:24–26)

Compare That Verse With: "Men and brethren, this scripture must needs have been fulfilled, which the Holy Ghost by the mouth of David spake before concerning Judas, which was guide to them that took Jesus." (Acts 1:16)

Co-Creator of Mankind and Living Creatures

"[God] breathed into his [man's] nostrils the breath [spirit] of life." (Gen. 2:7)

"The spirit of God hath made me, and the breath of the Almighty hath given me life." (Job 33:4)

"Thou sendest forth thy spirit, they [the living creatures of our world] are created." (Ps. 104:30)

"Until the spirit be poured upon us from on high, and the wilderness be a fruitful field and the fruitful field be counted for a forest." (Isa. 32:15)

"These all wait upon thee; that thou mayest give them their meat in due season." (Ps. 104:27; cf. 136:25; 145:15–16; 147:9)

He Is Called Lord

"And in the morning, then ye shall see the glory of the Lord; for that he heareth your murmurings against the Lord . . ." (Ex 16:7)

Compare that verse with: "As the Holy Ghost saith, Today if ye will hear his voice, harden not your hearts, as in the provocation . . . when your fathers tempted me." (Heb. 3:7–9)

"After those days, saith the Lord, I will put my law in their inward parts, and write it in their hearts; and will be their God, and they shall be my people." (Jer. 31:33)

Compare that verse with: "Whereof the Holy Ghost also is a witness to us: for after that he had said before, This is the covenant that I will make with them after those days, saith the Lord, I will put my laws into their hearts, and in their minds will I write them." (Heb 10:15–16)

"I heard the voice of the Lord," (Isa. 6:8)

Compare that verse with: "Well spake the Holy Ghost by Esaias [Isaiah]." (Acts 28:25)

"The Holy Ghost said, Separate me Barnabas and Saul for the work whereunto I have called them." (Acts 13:2)

"Now the Lord is that Spirit: and where the Spirit of the Lord is, there is liberty. But we . . . are changed . . . from glory to glory, even as by the Spirit of the Lord." (2 Cor. 3:17–18)

"And *the Lord* make you to increase and abound in love one toward another . . . to the end he may stablish your hearts unblamable in holiness *before God*, even our Father, at the coming of our Lord *Jesus Christ* with all his saints." (1 Thess. 3:12–13)

"And the *Lord* direct your hearts into the love of *God*, and into the patient waiting for *Christ*." (2 Thess. 3:5)

He Is Called Jehovah

"The LORD said unto Moses, How long will this people provoke me?" (Num. 14:11)

Compare that verse with: "They . . . vexed his holy Spirit. . . ." (Isa. 53:10–11)

"Where is he that put his holy spirit within him? . . . That led them through the deep. . . . The spirit of the LORD caused him to rest." (Isa. 13–14)

Compare that verse with: "The LORD alone did lead him." (Deut. 32:12)

"The LORD . . . the God of gods . . . The Lord of lords . . . alone doeth great wonders." (Ps. 136:1–4)

Compare that verse with: "Through mighty signs and wonders, by the power of the Spirit of God." (Rom. 15:19)

He Is Called God

"That which is born of the Spirit." (John 3:6)

Compare that verse with: "Whatsoever is born of God." (1 John 5:4)

"Ananias, why hath Satan filled thine heart to lie to the Holy Ghost? . . . Thou hast not lied unto men, but unto God." (Acts 5:3–4)

"Now God himself and our Father, and our Lord Jesus Christ, direct our way unto you." (1 Thess. 3:11)

"For he is our God; and we are the people of his pasture, and the sheep of his hand. Today if ye will hear his voice, harden not your heart." (Ps. 95:7–8a)

Compare that verse with: "As the Holy Ghost saith, Today if ye will hear his voice, harden not your hearts." (Heb. 3:7–8a)

He Is the Spirit of Christ

"But ye are not in the flesh, but in the Spirit, if so be that the Spirit of God dwell in you. Now if any man have not the Spirit of Christ, he is none of his." (Rom. 8:9)

"Because ye are sons, God hath sent forth the Spirit of his Son into your hearts, crying, Abba, Father." (Gal. 4:6)

"Searching . . . what manner of time the Spirit of Christ which was in them did signify. . . ." (1 Pet. 1:11)

He Is the Author of Inspiration

"David the son of Jesse said . . . The spirit of the LORD spake by me, and his word was in my tongue. The God of Israel said, The Rock of Israel spake to me." (2 Sam. 23:1–3)

"Howbeit when he, the Spirit of truth, is come, he will guide you into all truth." (John 16:13)

"Now the Spirit speaketh expressly, that in the latter times some shall depart from the faith." (1 Tim. 4:1)

"All scripture is given by inspiration of God." (2 Tim. 3:16)

"Of which salvation the prophets have enquired . . . the Spirit of Christ which was in them . . . testified beforehand the sufferings of Christ, and the glory that should follow." (1 Pet. 1:10–11)

"Holy men of God spake as they were moved by the Holy Spirit." (2 Pet. 1:21)

He Is Called God of Israel

"The spirit of the LORD spake by me, and his word was in my tongue." (2 Sam. 23:2)

Compare that verse with: "The God of Israel said, The Rock of Israel spake to me." (2 Sam. 23:3)

He Is the Lord God

"The Lord God of Israel . . . spake by the mouth of his holy prophets . . ." (Luke 1:68, 70)

Compare that verse with: "Well spake the Holy Ghost by Esaias [Isaiah] the prophet . . ." (Acts 28:25)

He Is God the Comforter

"I, even I, am he that comforteth you." (Isa. 51:12)

"As a beast goeth down into the valley, the spirit of the Lord caused him to rest." (Isa. 63:14)

"The Comforter, which is the Holy Ghost." (John 14:26)

"But when the Comforter is come, whom I will send unto you from the Father, even the Spirit of truth, which proceedeth from the Father, he shall testify of me." (John 15:26)

"[Walking] in the comfort of the Holy Ghost." (Acts 9:31)

"The God of all comfort . . . who comforteth us." (2 Cor. 1:3–4)

He Is the Living God

"The Spirit of God dwelleth in you." (1 Cor. 3:16)

"Your body is the temple of the Holy Ghost." (1 Cor. 6:19)

"Ye are the temple of the living God; as God hath said, I will dwell in them." (2 Cor. 6:16)

He Has the Power of Life and Death

"The grass withereth, the flower fadeth: because the spirit of the LORD bloweth upon it: surely the people is grass." (Isa. 40:7)

"Which were born . . . of God." (John 1:13)
Compare that verse with: "That which is born of the Spirit." (John 3:6)

"God which raiseth the dead." (2 Cor. 1:9)
Compare that verse with: "The Spirit of him that raised up Jesus from the dead." (Rom. 8:11)

"Being put to death in the flesh, but quickened by the Spirit." (1 Pet. 3:18)
Compare that verse with: "It is the spirit that quickeneth . . ." (John 6:63)

"For the letter killeth, but the spirit giveth life." (2 Cor. 3:6)

"My spirit shall not always strive with man, for that he also is flesh." (Gen. 6:3; 7:22)

"Not by works of righteousness which we have done, but according to his mercy he saved us, by the washing of regeneration, and renewing of the Holy Ghost." (Tit. 3:5)

He Is a Divine Person

He Works and Acts in a Personal Way

"My Spirit shall not always strive with man." (Gen. 6:3)

"For it seemed good to the Holy Ghost, and to us, to lay upon you no greater burden than these necessary things." (Acts 15:28)

"For as many as are led by the Spirit of God, they are the sons of God." (Rom. 8:14)

"For the Spirit searcheth all things, yea, the deep things of God. . . . The things of God knoweth no man, but the Spirit of God." (1 Cor. 2:10–11)

"But if ye be led of the Spirit, ye are not under the law." (Gal. 5:18)

He Speaks

"When they shall lead you, and deliver you up, take no thought beforehand what ye shall speak . . . but whatsoever shall be given you in that hour, that speak ye: for it is not ye that speak, but the Holy Ghost." (Mark 13:11)

"Howbeit when he, the Spirit of truth, is come, he will guide you into all truth: for he shall not speak of himself; but whatsoever he shall hear, that shall he speak: and he will shew you things to come." (John 16:13)

"While Peter thought on the vision, the Spirit said unto him, Behold, three men seek thee." (Acts 10:19)

"And the spirit bade me go with them, nothing doubting." (Acts 11:12)

"And as they ministered to the Lord, and fasted, the Holy Ghost said, Separate me Barnabas and Saul for the work whereunto I have called them." (Acts 13:2)

"For we know not what we should pray for as we ought: but the Spirit itself maketh intercession for us with groanings which cannot be uttered." (Rom. 8:26)

"Now the Spirit speaketh expressly, that in the latter times some shall depart from the faith . . ." (1 Tim. 4:1)

"Prophecy came not in old time by the will of man: but holy men of God spake as they were moved by the Holy Ghost." (2 Pet. 1:21)

"And I heard a voice from heaven saying unto me, Write, Blessed are the dead which die in the Lord from henceforth: Yea, saith the Spirit, that they rest from their labours; and their works do follow them." (Rev. 14:13)

It Is More Serious to Blaspheme Him Than the Son

"All manner of sin and blasphemy shall be forgiven unto men: but the blasphemy against the Holy Ghost shall not be forgiven unto men. And whoever speaketh a word against the Son of man, it shall be forgiven him: but whosoever speaketh against the Holy Ghost, it shall not be forgiven him." (Matt. 12:31–32)

"He that shall blaspheme against the Holy Ghost hath never forgiveness, but is in danger of eternal damnation." (Mark 3:29)

He Is the Living Executive of God's Holiness

He is called the Holy Spirit 93 times in scripture.

"But they rebelled, and vexed his holy Spirit: therefore he was turned to be their enemy . . ." (Isa. 63:10)

"Whosoever speaketh a word against the Son of Man, it shall be forgiven him: but whosoever speaketh against the Holy Ghost, it shall not be forgiven him, neither in this world, neither in the world to come." (Matt. 12:32)

"Ye stiffnecked and uncircumcised in heart and ears, ye do always resist the Holy Ghost: as your fathers did, so do ye." (Acts 7:51)

"Now if any man have not the Spirit of Christ, he is none of his. . . . The Spirit itself beareth witness with our spirit, that we are the children of God." (Rom. 8:9, 16)

"Wherefore I give you to understand, that no man speaking by the Spirit of God calleth Jesus accursed: and that no man can say that Jesus is the Lord, but by the Holy Ghost." (1 Cor. 12:3)

"As the Holy Ghost saith, Today if you hear his voice, harden not your hearts. . . . So I sware in my wrath, they shall not enter into my rest." (Heb. 3:7, 11)

"And hereby we know that he abideth in us, by the Spirit which he hath given us." (1 John 3:24)

"Hereby know we that we dwell in him, and he in us, because he hath given us of his Spirit." (1 John 4:13)

"If any man see his brother sin a sin which is not unto death, he shall ask, and he shall give him life for them that sin not unto death. There is a sin unto death: I do not say that he shall pray for it." (1 John 5:16)

The Father Is Not the Holy Spirit

"And the Holy Ghost descended in a bodily shape like a dove upon Him; and a voice came from heaven which said 'Thou art My beloved son, in whom I am well pleased.' " (Luke 3:22)

"And I will pray the Father, and He shall give you another Comforter that He may abide with you forever." (John 14:16)

"If ye then being evil know how to give good gifts unto your children how much more shall your heavenly Father give the Holy Spirit to them that ask Him?" (Luke 11:13)

"And behold I send the promise of My Father upon you; but tarry ye in the city of Jerusalem until you be endued with power from on high." (Luke 24:49)

"But this spake He of the Spirit which they that believe on Him should receive; for the Holy Ghost was not yet given because that Jesus was not yet glorified." (John 7:39)

"Baptizing them in the name of the Father, and of the Son, and of the Holy Spirit." (Matt. 26:19)

The Holy Spirit is not the Son

"And Jesus when He was baptized, went up straightway out of the water; and lo, the heavens were opened to Him and He saw the Spirit of God descending like a dove and lighting upon Him." (Matt. 3:16)

"And the Holy Ghost descended in a bodily shape like a dove upon Him; and a voice came from heaven which said 'Thou art My beloved Son, in whom I am well pleased.' " (Luke 3:22)

"And Jesus, being full of the Holy Ghost, returned from Jordan and was led by the Spirit into the wilderness." (Luke 4:1)

"The Spirit of the Lord is upon Me; because He has anointed me to preach the Gospel to the poor . . . to preach the acceptable year of the Lord. . . . This day is this scripture fulfilled in your ears." (Luke 4:18)

"And whosoever shall speak a word against the Son of Man, it shall be forgiven him; but whosoever speaketh against the Holy Ghost, it shall not be forgiven Him, neither in this world neither in the world to come." (Matt. 12:32)

"And whosoever shall speak a word against the Son of Man it shall be forgiven him; but unto him that blasphemeth against the Holy Ghost it shall not be forgiven." (Luke 12:10)

"And I will pray the Father, and He shall give you *another* comforter that He may abide with you forever." (John 14:16)

"Nevertheless I tell you the truth; it is expedient that I go away; for if I go not away, the comforter will not come unto you; but if I depart I will send Him unto you. And when He is come, He will convict the world of sin, and of righteousness and of judgement." (John 16:7–8)

"Howbeit when he, the Spirit of truth is come, he will guide you into all truth; for He shall not speak of himself; but whatsoever he shall hear, that shall He speak; and He will show you things to come. He shall glorify Me; for He shall receive of mine, and show it unto you. All things that the Father hath are mine; therefore said I that He shall take of mine and shall show it unto you." (John 16:13–15)

"Then said Jesus unto them again 'Peace be unto you; as the Father hath sent Me, even so send I you.' And when He had said this he breathed on them and saith unto them 'Receive ye the Holy Ghost.' " (John 20:21–22)

Bible Word Study

The Holy Spirit is specifically mentioned in 22 of the 39 OT books, some 86 passages detailing special aspects of His person or work. Of these, the Pentateuch has 14 (one-sixth of the whole) but with none in Leviticus. Two prophetic books, Isaiah (13) and Ezekiel (15), carry one-third of the verses, together exceeding any other two OT books. Judges and Samuel have 7 each with 6 in the Psalms, and 16 verses in the remaining 11 books.

In the New Testament, the Holy Spirit or His work is directly referred to in 261 scriptures, of which the Gospels have 56, Acts has 57, and Paul's Epistles contains 112. The remaining 36 are found in most of the other books, with the exceptions of Philemon and 2 & 3 John, which do not mention the Holy Spirit.

The Holy Spirit As a Divine Person

Having already examined the individual Bible words for "Holy" and for "Spirit," we shall now look at the ways in which the original words are used together to show us clearly that God the Holy Spirit is a distinct, real person.

Wainwright observes that "the theologians of the early Church felt constrained to include the Spirit as the Third Person of the Godhead. . . . The chief reason was their faithfulness to the biblical tradition. Although the New Testament does not contain a developed doctrine of the Spirit, its account of the Spirit's nature and activity is such that no subsequent theologian could neglect the Spirit in his account of the nature of God."[1]

Difficulties in Study

Many passages seem to speak of the Holy Spirit as a dynamic force, like some heavenly "fluid of power" poured out on men, filling and immersing them. For example, the prophecies about baptism with the Spirit do not refer to *"The* Spirit" but to "Spirit" (no definite article).

At Pentecost Peter quoted God's promise of the Holy Spirit, which he found in the prophet Joel: "In the last days . . . I will pour out of my Spirit upon all flesh" (Acts 2:17). "The partitive genitive 'of My Spirit' would be more appropriate to an impersonal essence," notes Wainwright, "than to a person."

[1]Arthur W. Wainwright, *The Trinity in the New Testament*, pp. 202–203.

In one key episode in John's Gospel (John 20:22), Jesus says to the disciples, "Receive ye the Holy Ghost." But in the Greek, there is no definite article before *pneuma* (Spirit). Paul does the same, with phrases such as "in Spirit" (Rom. 8:9), "The one born according to Spirit" (Gal. 4:29), and "Holy Spirit" (with no definite article—Rom. 9:1; 14:17; 15:16). And the writer to the Hebrews says, "Partakers of Holy Spirit" (Heb. 6:4; cf. Heb. 9:8; 10:15, where there is a definite article), and being "fervent in spirit" (Acts 15:29; 18:25; Rom 9:1; 12:11; 14:17; 15:16; 1 Cor. 6:11; 12:3, 9, 13; 14:16).

In the Epistles the number of definitely personal references to the Spirit are small compared with the large number of references which can be otherwise interpreted. And the same is true of Acts and the synoptic Gospels.[2]

The Holy Spirit Is Dynamic and Animate

Some descriptions—like those of the Old Testament records—speak of the Holy Spirit as an animate, independent, personal power; others as if the Spirit is a dynamic, like a fluid force. Yet the writers assume no conflict in this; sometimes both usages are employed in the same passage, as in Acts 2:4, "They were all filled with Holy Spirit" (no article, impersonal sense) and then the disciples "began to speak with other tongues, as *the* Spirit gave them utterance" (definite article).

In Acts 11:12 Peter says, "And *the* Spirit bade me go," a personal usage; and later, in Acts 11:16, quoting Christ, "Ye shall be baptized in Holy Spirit," more like a dynamic.

Paul, confronting Elymas the sorcerer, is said to be "filled with Holy Spirit" (Acts 13:9); but in the same record *the* Holy Spirit speaks (13:2) and sends him out with Barnabas (13:4). Yet all these dynamic descriptions in Acts, in the letters of Paul and John, and the words of Jesus himself in the Gospels, are wholly consistent with passages where the Holy Spirit is described as a Person.

In Acts alone there are 62 references to the Spirit; in 18 of these the Spirit is described as a person who speaks (1:16; 8:29; 10:19; 11:12; 13:2; 28:25), forbids (16:6), decides (15:28), appoints (20:28), sends (13:4), bears witness (5:32), snatches (8:39), prevents (16:7), is lied to (5:3), tempted (5:9), and resisted (7:51; cf. 6:10).

"Most of the other references describe how men are 'filled with the Spirit' (Acts 2:4; 4:8; 9:17; 13:9), and act 'through' (21:4) or 'in the Spirit' (19:21). Although these references do not of themselves imply that the Spirit is a person, they do not contradict any impression given by other passages."

Further, in 1 Pet. 1:11, the Spirit testifies; in 1 Tim. 4:1 He speaks; Hebrews says He speaks and bears witness to the Old Testament (3:7); and eight times in Revelation we are called to heed "what the Spirit saith to the churches" (Rev. 2:7, 11, 17, 29; 3:6, 13, 22; 14:13).[3] There are far

---

²Ibid.
³Ibid. pp. 201–203.

too many such personal references for them to be, as some have suggested, mere metaphors of a dynamic.

Masculine Pronouns

Still further, NT writers deliberately employ language stressing that the Holy Spirit is a divine person.

"Various pronouns that clearly imply personality are repeatedly used of the Holy Spirit. The use of these pronouns is the more remarkable from the fact that in the Greek language the word for Spirit is a neuter noun ... the pronouns that refer to it should [also] be neuter, and yet in numerous instances a masculine pronoun is used, thus bringing out very strikingly how the Bible idea of the personality of the Holy Spirit dominates grammatical construction.

"There are instances, of course, where the natural grammatical usage is followed and a neuter pronoun is used (Rom. 8:16, 26). But in many instances this construction is set aside and the masculine personal pronoun [is] used to refer to the neuter noun."[4]

The Holy Spirit Is Both Giver and Gift

How can we interpret these different treatments of the Holy Spirit? It is clear that He is a Person, and equally clear that many times His work is spoken of as a dynamic.

In an appendix to his Companion Bible, Bullinger observes a clear distinction in these two usages. One, he says, speaks of the work, influence and gifts of God the Holy Spirit, and the other speaks of the Person himself.

He says when no article is used (*pneuma hagion*—holy spirit), it should always be rendered in the sense of "godly attitude."

This usage occurs 52 times in the NT and is often given the wrong meaning when translated—"*The* Holy Spirit" (with the definite article, and capital letters). Properly however, this phrase is never used of the *Giver* (the Holy Spirit), but only and always of His *gift*. This "power from on high" includes whatever gifts the Holy Spirit may bestow "according to His own will." What particular gift is meant is sometimes stated such as "faith," "power," etc.

The second usage, *with* the definite article, always speaks of the divine Person himself. And Bullinger says, "There is *no stronger rendering* available when there are *two articles* present in the Greek (*to pneuma to hagion*—which means 'the Spirit, the Holy')."

The English reader can never tell which of the two very different Greek expressions he is reading. See Acts 2:4, where we read, "They were all filled" with *pneuma hagion*, and "began to speak with other tongues, as *the* Spirit gave." Here the Giver and His gift are strictly distinguished.[5]

---

[4]R.A. Torrey, *What the Bible Teaches* (Fleming H. Revell Company), p. 226.
[5]Ethelbert W. Bullinger, *The Companion Bible*, Appendix 101, p. 147.

Bullinger suggests that in all 52 cases in which no article occurs, the phrase "holy spirit" can be used simply as God's "power" or "force" or a gift—as we say today "he was in good spirits" or as a synonym for attitude.

Used this way of course, we might say Christians are "baptized in *a* holy Spirit" or "filled with *a* holy Spirit." As in 2 Cor. 6:6, this can be a character quality along with patience, kindness, and love unfeigned. Hence we also say "God is Spirit" (John 4:24, NAS) not "a" spirit, for there is no indefinite article in the Greek.[6]

But though this distinction between gift and Giver is important, we must not infer too much by it. Phrases of power or attitude are still perfectly consistent with personality; there is no grounds to imply there is no person behind this power or attitude. For instance, the scripture "God is light" (1 John 1:5) describes dynamically an attribute of God. However, He is not just a "light" but a holy, infinitely wise *Person*. Even the gifts themselves are given by a Person and almost wholly involve the interface of His power and personality with ours.

The Holy Spirit Is More than the Voice of God

Can these words for personality be explained as perhaps God the Father's voice speaking through a dynamic medium of "spirit"?

As already noted, the term "spirit" is neuter, but a number of times in the NT the Greek assigns the masculine to the root, and often includes *auton* or "himself" specifically in a sentence to show that He is a distinct person.

Numerous passages also show that He is distinct from the Father. Thus His words cannot really be explained by saying they are "like radio transmissions" from the original person (the Father), or that the "media" is the Holy Spirit who (like a radio) could be said to "speak" when all the time it is really the voice of the announcer.

In Scripture, as well as in prayer, when you speak to the Holy Spirit (or He speaks to you) you are dealing directly with the true and personal God, who is distinct from the Father and the Son. You cannot lie to an influence; you cannot grieve an impersonal power.

Personality Is Ascribed to the Holy Spirit

Personal Pronouns Used of Him; Actions Attributed to Him

"Even the Spirit of truth; whom the world cannot receive, because it seeth Him not, neither knoweth him: but you know him; for *he* dwelleth (*menei*) with you and he shall be in you" (John 14:17).

"Howbeit when he, the Spirit of truth, is come, *he will guide you* into all truth: for he shall not speak of himself (*eautou*); but whatsoever he shall hear, that shall he speak. . . . He [that one] (*ekeinos*—masculine pronoun referring to the neuter substantive *pneuma*) shall glorify me: for he shall receive of mine, and shall shew it unto you" (John 16:13–14).

---

[6]Ibid. p. 146.

We see from this passage that the Holy Spirit recognizes His personality. "And I will pray the Father, and he shall give you *another Comforter*, that he may be with you for ever" (John 14:16; cf. John 14:26; 15:26; 16:7). Here Jesus (obviously a person), and the Father (also a person), refer to someone who will take Christ's place: another Comforter. So the Holy Spirit is likewise personal, just like the Son and the Father.

The Holy Spirit Referred to As a Person and As God

"Why hath Satan filled thine heart to lie to the Holy Ghost? . . . Thou hast not lied unto men, but unto God" (Acts 5:3–4).

"Now the Lord is that Spirit: and where the Spirit of the Lord is, there is liberty" (2 Cor. 3:17).

"And as they ministered to the *Lord*, and fasted, the *Holy Ghost* said, Separate me Barnabas and Saul for the work whereunto I have called them. . . . So they, being sent forth by the Holy Ghost, departed unto Seleucia" (Acts 13:2, 4).

We know the Holy Spirit is both a person and God because of the nature of His work: to "reprove the world of sin, and of righteousness, and of judgment" (John 16:8). Only a person has the ability, and only God has the authority to show a man his sin.

Since He is the one who shows us how ugly our selfishness is—even when it's religious—it is deeply unwise to grieve Him or resist Him, for in doing so we pit our tiny wills and minds against the Lord himself.

"Grieve not the holy Spirit of God, whereby ye are sealed unto the day of redemption" (Eph. 4:30). The Old Testament shows the consequences: "They rebelled, and vexed his holy Spirit: therefore he was turned to be their enemy, and he fought against them" (Isa. 63:10).

Will we fight against the one we think we are serving? "All manner of sin and blasphemy shall be forgiven unto men: but the blasphemy against the Holy Ghost shall not be forgiven unto men" (Matt. 12:31).

He Has Always Had a Discernible Ministry

God's *ruah* moves upon the primeval waters from the beginning (Gen. 1:2) like a hypostasis or person. David first designated Him the "holy spirit" (Ps. 51:11; cf. Isa. 63:10–11), and, according to Cummings, "Isaiah, whether thinking of Him as his own inspirer or as a fellow speaker, assumes His distinct personality when he says, quoting the Messiah, 'The Lord God, and his Spirit, hath sent me' " (Isa. 48:16).[7]

Cummings also lists 21 different names for the Holy Spirit, each expressing His relationship, deity, attributes and gifts:

His Relationship to the Father

- The Spirit of God (Matt. 3:16).
- The Spirit of the Lord (Luke 4:18).

---

[7]James E. Cummings, *Through the Eternal Spirit*.

- The Spirit of our God (1 Cor. 6:11) and Spirit of the Living God (2 Cor. 3:3).
- The Spirit of your Father (Matt. 10:20).
- The Spirit of Glory and the Spirit of God (1 Pet. 5:4).
- • The Promise of the Father (Acts 1:4).

His Relationship to the Son

- The Spirit of Christ (Rom. 8:9).
- The Spirit of Jesus Christ (Phil. 1:19) and Spirit of Jesus (Acts 16:7).
- The Spirit of His [God's] Son (Gal. 4:6).
- Another Comforter (John 14:16).

His Own Essential Deity and Attributes

- One Spirit (Eph. 4:4).
- Seven Spirits [meaning the perfect Spirit] (Rev. 1:4; 3:1).
- The Lord, the Spirit (2 Cor. 3:18).
- The Eternal Spirit (Heb. 9:14).
- The Holy Ghost (Matt. 1:18).
- The Holy One (1 John 2:20).

The Gifts He Bestows

- The Spirit of Life (Rev. 11:11).
- The Spirit of Holiness (Rom. 1:4).
- Spirit of Wisdom (Eph. 1:17; cf. Isa. 11:2).
- The Spirit of Faith (2 Cor. 4:13).
- The Spirit of Truth (John 14:17; 14:13).
- The Spirit of Grace (Heb. 10:29) and The Spirit of Grace and Supplications (Zech. 12:10).
- The Spirit of Adoption (Rom. 8:15).
- The Spirit of Power, Love and Discipline [a sound mind, KJV] (2 Tim. 1:7).[8]

"The work of God's Spirit may be cosmic, whether in creation (Job 26:13) or in continuing providence (Job 33:4; Ps. 104:30); redemptive, in regeneration (Ezek. 11:19; 36:26–27); indwelling, to uphold and guide the believer (Neh. 9:20; Ps. 143:10; Hag. 2:5); or infilling, for leadership (Num. 11:25; Judg. 6:34; 1 Sam 16:13), service (Num. 11:17; Mic. 3:8; Zech. 7:12), or future empowering of the Messiah (Isa. 11:2; 42:1; 61:1) and His people (Joel 2:28; . . . Isa. 32:15)."[9]

---

[8]Ibid. pp. 36–37.
[9]*Theological Wordbook of the Old Testament*, Laird R. Harris, ed. (Chicago: Moody Press, 1980).

Questions and Answers

Q: *How do we know that the Holy Spirit is both divine and a person?*
A: There are seven major reasons for concluding this fact.
- He acts as a Person (John 14:26; 1 Cor. 12:11).
- Though distinct from the Father and the Son, He has a mission from both (John 15:26).
- He is given coordinate power and rank with the Father and Son (Matt. 28:19; 2 Cor. 13:14).
- He appears in visible form at Jesus' baptism and on the day of Pentecost (Matt. 3:16; Acts 2:3).
- Sinning against Him cannot be forgiven (Matt. 12:31).
- He is distinguished from His gifts (1 Cor. 12:11).
- He is spoken of and treated as a divine person by Jesus and the Apostles in the New Testament (John 14:26; Eph. 4:30).

Q: *Isn't the Holy Spirit merely the influence or power of God?*
A: As God, He influences; but it is the influence of a distinct *person*. "Absolute speech does not come from what is merely an influence, an energy, a power; it is the function of a person. And it is one of the highest prerogatives of a human being. The disciples had lost a personal presence in the person of Jesus. . . . it was most surely to be replaced by the presence of a person. Would it not be calculated to assist the disciples both to believe correctly and to feel grateful that the ever-visible Spirit was nonetheless a person, a being—not a vague influence or phantom?"[1]

If the Holy Spirit were simply God's attribute of power, then Acts 10:38 would read, "God anointed Jesus of Nazareth with the holy power and with power." Romans 15:13 would read, "Now the God of hope fill you with all joy and peace . . . that ye may abound in hope through the power of the holy power," and Romans 15:19 would say, "by the power of the power of God." We would read, "My speech and my preaching was not with enticing words of man's wisdom, but in demonstration of the power and of power," in 1 Cor. 2:4. Finney says it well in that "to suppose the Holy Spirit to be the attribute of power would make nonsense of the Bible."[2]

Q: *But since the book of Proverbs personifies wisdom and Paul personifies love (1 Cor. 13), couldn't the phrase "the Holy Spirit" be a simple personification of God's power?*
A: Not at all. The Holy Spirit is spoken of in Scripture as a person consistently, not occasionally. Smeaton says that this mode of speaking

---

[1]*Pulpit Commentary*, H.D. Spence and Joseph S. Exell, eds. (Grand Rapids: Eerdmans), vol. 41, p. 75.
[2]Charles G. Finney, *Lectures on Theology* (Minneapolis, Minn.: Bethany House Publishers, 1968), p. 148.

of Him is "general, unvaried, uniform; it is adopted by all the sacred writers with one consent; and it is retained even in the simplest passages where they narrate facts or give plain instruction."[3]

Finney writes, "Personification is admissible in poetic language; but not in prose and the plain language of narrative. The Book of Proverbs is written in poetic language; but these attributes, words, works, feelings, and ways are ascribed to the Holy Spirit in plain prose and in the simple language of narrative."[4]

Q: *Why then does the New Testament use "it" to describe the Spirit, as in "the Spirit itself beareth witness with our spirit" (Rom. 8:16, 26)?*

A: That phrase in the original literally reads, "The Spirit witnesses with the spirit of us that we are children of God." Greek, like English, has masculine, feminine, and neuter forms of pronouns like he, she, or it. But in passages such as John 14:26 and 16:13–15 describing the work of the Spirit, the *masculine* form of the pronoun referring to the Spirit (*ekeinos*, "that one") is used instead of the feminine (*ekeine*) or the neuter (*ekeino*). If the Holy Spirit were only a force or influence, John would have used the neuter gender.

Q: *Doesn't the word "spirit" mean "breath" or "wind" in the Bible?*

A: There are no less than 14 distinct personal usages of the word *pneuma* or "spirit" other than just "breath" in Scripture! It is used to speak of the following:

- The divine nature of the Father (John 4:24).
- The divine nature of Christ (1 Cor. 15:45; 2 Cor. 3:6, 17–18).
- The operations of the Holy Spirit (1 Cor. 14:12—concerning spiritual gifts but spoken of as "spirits" in the Greek).
- The new nature (John 3:6; Rom. 8:4), divine nature (2 Pet. 1:4), and the "spirit of adoption" (Rom. 8:15).
- Man's non-material existence (Gen. 2:7; Eccl. 12:7; Ps. 31:5; 104: 29–30; Luke 23:46; Acts 7:59). All people have *pneuma* psychologically, but not all have the divine *pneuma*.
- Character qualities such as fear (2 Tim. 1:7), meekness (1 Cor. 4:21), and humility—poor in spirit—(Matt. 5:3).
- Desires (Matt. 26:41; Rom. 7:15).
- The person as a whole. "My spirit" myself (Luke 1:47; Mark 2:8).
- As an adverb. Something is done essentially, really, truly in the highest degree, the strongest form, or in the greatest measure; they are "fervent in spirit" (Rom. 12:11; Acts 18:25; 19:21; Rom. 1:9).
- Angels (Heb. 1:7).
- Demons (1 Tim. 4:1; Matt. 8:16; 10:1; Luke 4:33; 9:42; 13:11; Mark 9:17; Acts 16:16).
- The resurrection body as distinct from the earthly human body or angelic creation (Phil. 3:21; Luke 24:39; 1 Cor. 15:45).

---

[3]George Smeaton, *The Doctrine of the Holy Spirit* (Carlisle, Pa.: The Banner of Truth, 1980), p. 99.

[4]Finney, op. cit. p. 148.

- It is used in conjunction with the word *hagion* or "holy" in 50 passages of Scripture as the promise of the Father, the gift of the Giver, the power of God (Luke 24:49; Acts 1:5).
- But whenever it is used with the definite article in Greek—*"the* Spirit," it refers to the third person of the Godhead, the Holy Spirit himself.[5]

Q: *The Father and the Son both received worship. Yet there seems to be no case in which the Holy Spirit is worshiped. Why is this?*

A: Because as the third member of the Godhead, the Spirit comes to exalt the Father through the Son. "He shall not speak of Himself" (John 16:13) is an accurate description of the one who comes to reveal all hearts; as the Spirit of worship, it is inappropriate for Him to draw attention to himself while directing honor and thanks to the Father through the Son. As Lampe observes, "It is befitting that He who speaks by all the prophets and apostles as His scribes . . . should speak less of himself when the work abundantly commends the Author."[6]

Q: *What has made the Church think the Holy Spirit is a person?*

A: In the early days of the Church, men like Arius of Alexandria (313 A.D.) challenged the belief that the Holy Spirit was a real person, arguing that He was nothing more than an influence or power God used to do His will. For several centuries, the matter was deeply studied, debated, and researched. The overwhelming conclusion was that the ideas of Arius and his followers could not be supported from Scripture.

The Bible clearly shows the Spirit's actions and personality as those of God: speaking (Rev. 2:7; Acts 13:2), interceding (Rom. 8:26), as well as overseeing and commanding (Acts 14:2; 16:6–7; 20:28). He does the work of God as a person; attributes, words, works, and feelings are all ascribed to the Holy Spirit. One scholar says, "If Jesus and His apostles uniformly represented the Holy Spirit as a person when He is not a person, it would be the boldest personification ever found in any literature on the subject."[7]

Q: *But in other places in Scripture things are sometimes personified. Charity, for instance "suffers long and is kind . . ." (1 Cor. 13:1–8), and "the blood . . . speaks" (Heb. 12:24). Isn't this just another example?*

A: Not at all. The Holy Spirit is spoken of not occasionally but consistently in Scripture as a person. This mode of speaking of Him is "general, unvaried, uniform; it is adopted by all the sacred writers with one consent; and it is retained even in the simplest passages where they narrate facts or give plain instruction."[8]

Q: *Why is no glory given to the Spirit in Scripture?*

A: No person of the Godhead glorifies himself. Christ "glorified not himself" (Heb. 5:5) but said to the Father that His life's work was "that

---

[5]Ethelbert W. Bullinger, *The Giver and His Gifts*, pp. 15–26.
[6]Smeaton, op. cit. p. 114.
[7]Ibid. p. 98.
[8]Ibid. p. 99.

thy Son also may glorify thee" (John 17:1, 4). So, in turn, the Spirit glorifies Christ (John 16:13–14). The phrase "shall not speak of himself" not only means that He would speak in a chain of divine authority, but that He would concentrate on exalting and uplifting the Son, who in turn exalts the Father. But as Smeaton points out, the glorification of the Holy Spirit in connection with the Church is still future. Christ's coming "ushered in a full historical revelation of the Son in word and deed"; and His humbling himself was followed by an equally conspicuous exaltation. "But the work of the Holy Spirit is still unseen. The personality and deity of the Spirit are, however, one day to be displayed in conspicuous glory in connection with His work on the Church, when He shall have completed the marvelous transformation. . . . There is still another stage of revelation when the Spirit shall be glorified in connection with the work which He shall have finished and brought to its destined completeness."[9]

Q: *What is meant by "the ministration of the spirit" (2 Cor. 3:8)?*

A: Smeaton writes that it refers to two things: "(1) That the Holy Spirit as the Author of ministry constitutes the office, raises up the men and endows them with gifts or (2) the Gospel ministry . . . is exercised with the accompanying power of the Holy Spirit sent down from heaven. . . . Whenever the veil is lifted up the reader [of Acts] gets a glimpse into the movements of the Kingdom of God and into the unseen agency of the Spirit which is everywhere declared. And from this we infer His ever present activity in all centuries and localities alike. The Church has not been left to herself."[10]

Q: *What part does the Holy Spirit play in spiritual awakening?*

A: Jonathan Edwards writes, "From the fall of man to our day, the work of redemption in its effect has mainly been carried on by remarkable communications of the Spirit of God." Though God's Spirit always is influencing and attending His work, "the way in which the greatest things have been done . . . always has been by remarkable effusions at special seasons of divine mercy."[11]

And Smeaton comments, "The Church's ever-living Head knows how to usher in creative epochs, to rally His people to some converging point through the lapse of the centuries and to gather up under this powerful influence isolated opinions into one consistent whole. When a previous awakening has spent its force, when the elements of thought or action previously supplied threaten to become effete, a new impulse is commonly communicated by Him who interposes at various stages to make all things new."[12]

Q: *What is Sabellianism?*

A: The idea that the terms Father, Son, and Holy Spirit are merely different

---

[9]Ibid. p. 104.
[10]Ibid. p. 245.
[11]Jonathan Edwards, *History of Redemption*, Period I, part 1.
[12]Smeaton, op. cit. p. 252.

names of a unipersonal God. This theological tenet is named after Sabellius (218 A.D.) who best defended it. It is sometimes called *modalism*, or *the Trinity of mere manifestation*. It was first propounded by Praxeas of Asia Minor in 200 A.D., but the idea was borrowed in part from the Gnostics who not only denied a Trinity but resolved the facts of the theory into mere "appearance" or "manifestation."

Analysis and Discussion

The doctrine of the Holy Spirit, says Wainwright, "has long been a Cinderella of theology. It has suffered from much neglect and has always been one of the most difficult doctrines to discuss. In the New Testament, though there are many statements about the Spirit's activity, the writers' views are not easy to summarize or express in systematic form." As the wind that "blows where it wishes," the one who imparts motion to His creation is never easy to predict! The work of the Holy Spirit in Scripture is associated with power, zeal, creativity, and action; and His ministry is identified with relationship, revelation, and revival.

The Executive God

The first characteristic of the Holy Spirit is that He is the one who carries things out to completion; He acts as the Divine Executive Director; and sometimes not only as Executive but, as the story of Ananias and Sapphira demonstrate, in judgment as Executor (Acts 5:1–11). Herbert Lockyer observes that in the Spirit's role as God, He has (and can confer) administrative, governmental, and legislative powers, inspiring leadership, military efficiency (the direction of troops and the defense of the kingdom), and all functions of government legislation.[1]

The Bible illustrates the executive function of the Spirit in many ways:

- The Holy Spirit gave Joseph power to administer and govern Egypt (Gen. 41:39).
- He empowered *Moses and the 70 Elders* to lead (Num. 11:17–29).
- He prepared *Joshua* to succeed Moses (Num. 11:17–29; Deut. 34:9).
- The Spirit anointed *David* as both a ruler (1 Sam. 16:13) and a writer and as songwriter and poet (Matt 22:43; Acts 1:16; Heb. 3:7; 4:3–7). David's last message was written in the Spirit (2 Sam. 23:1–3).
- *Amasai* was given physical and moral courage (1 Chron. 12:18).
- The Spirit gave *Daniel* power both to interpret dreams (Dan. 4:8–18; 5:11) and political and administrative wisdom (Dan. 5:14; 6:2–3).
- His executive power influences even pagan rulers. Pharaoh was moved by His power (Gen. 41:38). He helped rulers or judges like Othniel (Judg. 3:10), Gideon (Judg. 6:34), Jephthah (Judg. 11:29), and Samson (Judg. 13:25, 14:6; 14:19; 15:14–15).

---

[1] Herbert Lockyer, *The Holy Spirit of God* (Nashville: Thomas Nelson, 1981).

Images of the Holy Spirit

James Elder Cummings points out four important images that recur in both the Old and New Testaments, representing the Spirit's presence and approach to men.[2] Including a fifth image which we add, his list includes:

1. *Breath*—"The value and importance of the atmosphere is self-evident. We can live for days without food and for a lifetime without sight or hearing, but we cannot live an hour without breath. To breathe is the most essential of all our physical functions and is, in Scriptures, almost synonymous with life."[3]

   Compare Ezekiel 37:14, "[I] shall put my Spirit [*ruach*, wind or breath] in you," with 37:9, "Come from the four winds, O breath"; "Say to the wind, Thus saith the Lord." Psalms says, "By the Word of the Lord were the heavens made and all the hosts of them by the breath of His mouth" (Ps. 33:6). We find the same image in Job 33:4; Isa. 59:19; 40:7. In the NT Jesus "breathed on them and said, Receive ye the Holy Ghost" (John 20:22). In Acts 2:2 the disciples heard a "sound as of a rushing mighty wind," and in Acts 17:25, God is said to give "to all life, and breath [*pneuma*]," the only other place in the NT where the word occurs.

2. *Rushing wind*—The image of breath is carried further, as in Ezek. 3:12, "Then the Spirit took me up and, I heard behind me a voice of a great rushing, saying 'Blessed be the glory of the Lord from His place.' " Acts 2:2 says, "suddenly from heaven a sound as of a rushing mighty wind," and Rev. 1:10, "I was in the Spirit on the Lord's day, and heard behind me a great voice, as of a trumpet." These are images of breath, but in greater power and abundance.

   Prophecy is connected to this image of wind and power. Since the Holy Spirit through the Son looks to the Father, we can expect His work to be one of relating that which is *to come*, in terms of that which is, by showing that which has been. The prophetic ministry of the Holy Spirit shows not only the future in the present, but the future in the past, and the present in the past.

   Lockyer lists instances of the Spirit's ministry to true prophets (Hos 9:7), and them receiving divine messages from Him (Ezek. 2:2; 8:3; 11:1, 24; cf. 13:3; 1 Pet. 1:11; 3:19; 2 Pet. 1:21). He inspired the prophecy of Moses and the elders (Num. 11:17–29); Balaam (Num. 24:2); Saul (1 Sam. 9:19–24); Elijah (1 Kings 18:12; 2 Kings 2:16); Elisha (2 Kings 2:15); Azariah (2 Chron. 15:1); Isaiah (Acts 28:25); Jeremiah (Jer. 1:9; 30:1–2); Ezekiel (Ezek. 2:2; 3:12, 14; 8:3; 36:26–27; 37:1, 14; 39:29); Daniel (Dan. 4:8–9); Joel (Joel 2:28; Acts 2:16–17); Micah (Mic. 3:8; cf. 2:7); and finally, all the prophets (Neh. 9:20; Prov. 1:23; Zech. 7:12; Acts 11:28; 2 Pet. 1:21).[4]

3. *Clothing*—"The Spirit of the Lord came upon [literally—clothed

---

[2]James Elder Cummings, *Through the Eternal Spirit*, pp. 27ff.
[3]A.B. Simpson, *The Holy Spirit* (Camp Hill, Pa.: Christian Publications, Inc.), p. 24.
[4]Lockyer, op. cit. pp. 53–56.

himself with] Gideon" (Judg. 7:34) and "the Spirit came upon Ama-sai" (1 Chron. 12:18). Here the man either becomes the outer cloth-ing of God's Spirit (Gideon), or the Spirit so encompasses and clothes him (as perhaps with Amasai) that He "hides the man him-self from observation and causes him to be lost in the manifestation of God."[5]

Both images are repeated in the New Testament. "The Holy Ghost was upon him" (Luke 2:25) reveals the Spirit covering the man as clothing. John 14:17 illustrates the man covering the Spirit: He "shall be in you." The same image is applied to the Lord Jesus in Rom. 13:14, "but put ye on the Lord Jesus Christ," and in Gal. 3:27, "As many of you as have been baptized into Christ have put on Christ."

4. *Pouring water*—This is probably the most frequently used image in both the Old and New Testaments. Moses struck the rock at Horeb and Kadesh and water came pouring out (Ex. 17:6; Num. 20:11). The people sang to the ground as they dug for water at Beer (Num. 21:17). The water-giving Rock followed Israel (1 Cor. 10:4). A. B. Simpson says, "There is no emblem of the Holy Spirit more fre-quently used in the Scriptures than water. Naturally suggestive of cleansing, refreshing and fullness, it expresses most perfectly the most important offices of the Holy Ghost."[6] It is used three times in both Isaiah and Joel and once in both Zechariah and Ezekiel. Peter quoting Joel uses the same image in Acts 2:33 "He has poured forth this, which you both see and hear." (See also Titus 3:6, Heb. 10:19–22).

To these we must add a fifth major image that involves violent motion:

5. *Fire*—One of the most striking images in the religious customs of any society is fire. "Fire" is molecules in violent motion. In religion it often represents purity, power, warmth, light, and judgment. In ancient Greece and Rome, sacred fire was guarded by consecrated priests and vestal virgins; it was the center of the nation and the home. If this fire went out, people suspended all executive and national affairs until it was rekindled. Foreign ambassadors had to walk by the holy fire before being received in the Council of State. A Slavic or Teutonic bride had to bow before holy fire before en-tering her new home, and the American Indian sachem circled the campfire three times before he gave counsel or conferred with a public visitor. Persians worshiped fire and the sun as sacred, and to spit into fire or commit any impropriety in the presence of these holy elements was unpardonable profanity. Among the ancient Is-raelites, Simpson says, "Fire was recognized as identical with life. . . . God had always recognized it in His Word not as an object of superstitious regard but as the symbol of His own transcendent

---

[5]Cummings, op. cit. pp. 27ff.
[6]Simpson, op. cit. p. 66.

glory and the power of His presence."[7]

Abram's covenant with God was made in light and fire (Gen. 15:17), as was Moses' call (Ex. 3:2) and the national covenant (Ex. 20:18). Aaron was called to make the first offering on the altar, after which a fire from the Lord consumed the sacrifice (Lev. 9:24). In almost all the sacred offerings, fire was an important element. The lamb was roasted in fire before being eaten in remembrance by the nation. The sin offering was carried outside the camp and burned with fire. The burnt offering was consumed by fire on the altar. The innards of the peace offering were burned and the meat offering was fine flour mingled with oil and frankincense baked in fire. The incense offering was composed of sweet spices ground and beaten very fine before the mixture was burned in a gold censer.

The ministries of Gideon (Judg. 6:21), Samson (Judg. 13:19–20), Elijah (1 Kings 18:38–39), and David (1 Chron. 21:26–27) all bore encounters with divine fire.

God's Powerful Holy Spirit

One of the distinct characteristics of the Spirit's work is that of empowering or giving spiritual and moral authority to the believer. Henry Drummond says, "In the New Testament alone, where the Spirit is referred to nearly three hundred times, the one word with which He is constantly associated is 'power.' "[8]

In the Old Testament, one of the names of God is "The Mighty One." The word "MIGHTY" (*gibbor* Hebrew) is used many times of the one true God:

- "A great God a mighty, and a terrible" (Deut. 10:17).
- "Our [true Jewish believers] God, the great, the mighty, and the terrible" (Neh. 9:32).
- "The Lord mighty in battle" (Ps. 24:8).
- "The mighty God" (Isa. 10:21).
- "The Great, the mighty God, the Lord" (Jer. 32:18).
- "The Lord thy God in the midst of thee is mighty; he will save, He will rejoice over thee with joy" (Zeph. 3:17).

The Holy Spirit As Creator

Because He is powerful, "Mighty One" is used as another designation for the third person of the Godhead, as the powerful and life-giving Creator who broods upon the face of the waters in the early chapters of earth's history (Ps. 89:12–15).

Along with other words, the word "mighty" (*gebhurah*) came to be used as a substitute for the proper name of God in the Rabbinic Age when

---

[7] Ibid. pp. 87–88.

[8] Henry Drummond, *Natural Law in the Spiritual World* (London: Hodder and Stoughton, 1884).

the name *Yahweh* was no longer allowed to be uttered. "In this way the name and Person of God who has all great attributes, who is Lord and Sovereign over all men, and by whom everything is created and whose sovereignty has always been and will always be exercised, are best expressed." This extends also to the New Testament where "the best-known example of the use of *gebhurah* [Greek *dynamis*] as a designation for God" is found where Jesus "uses the expression in His trial before Caiaphas (Matt. 26:64). . . ."[9]

The Holy Spirit As Enabler

The mighty Spirit of God in the Old Testament became the enabler of the Christ of the New Testament. Christ's life was dominated by the work of the Spirit:

- He was born of the Holy Spirit (Matt. 1:18).
- The Spirit was His Father's gift to Him (Matt. 12:18).
- He was sealed by the Holy Spirit in baptism (Mark 1:10).
- His normal condition in life was to be "full of the Spirit" (Luke 4:1).
- The Holy Spirit was the sphere of His activity (Luke 4:14).
- Jesus was led by the Holy Spirit (Matt. 4:1).
- The Holy Spirit was the power by which He carried out His ministry (Luke 4:18).
- The Holy Spirit was the energy by which Christ overcame Satan's powers (Matt. 12:28).
- The Holy Spirit was the secret of Christ's joy (Luke 10:21).
- His anointing to do good came from the Spirit (Acts 10:38).
- Through the Spirit's strength He offered himself as a sacrifice to God (Heb. 9:14).
- The Spirit raised Jesus from the dead (Rom. 8:11).
- The Lord Jesus was the bestower of the Holy Spirit to His disciples (John 20:22).
- It was the Spirit's authority by which Christ gave His commands (Acts 1:2).
- The Holy Spirit justified Christ (1 Tim. 3:16).

God's Promise of Power in the New Testament

When we come to the record of the New Testament, not only do we see many more examples of God's power in the life of Christ in the Gospels than with the Old Testament prophets, but the Lord Jesus went so far as to promise His Church this supernatural might. They were to wait until they received this equipping before they could carry out the Great Commission. The book of Acts is a record of this demonstrated power.

In what sense can Christians enjoy this power from God? We can better understand the work of the Spirit in our lives by looking at a list compiled

---

[9]*Theological Dictionary of the New Testament*, Gerhard Kittel, ed., Geoffrey W. Bromiley, trans. (Grand Rapids: Wm. B. Eerdmans Publishing Company, 1964), vol. 2, p. 370.

by F. E. Marsh of five words rendered "power" in the New Testament:[10]

1. *arche*—This word signifies "principal, first, the head, or beginning of anything." It is used of the spies who were watching Christ in order to deliver Him to the "power" (Luke 20:20). It is rendered "principality" and "beginning" in order to call attention to Christ's exalted position (Col. 2:10) and to Him who is the commencement of things (Rev. 21:6). Also used of the wicked angels who "kept not their first estate" (Jude 6), the word is mainly associated with a position of power, hence the believer is exhorted to "hold the beginning" of his confidence fast (Heb. 3:14).

2. *exousia*—The word means the right or liberty to act. Those who have washed their robes have a right to the Tree of Life (Rev. 22:14). Paul says he has the right to require the support of the saints (2 Thess. 3:9), but though he had the right he did not use it. Christ claimed this liberty to lay down His life (John 10:18) on the basis of the authority which His Father had conferred upon Him (John 5:27; 17:2). Christ promises power over the nations to overcomers (Rev. 2:26). We as believers have been given the right to become God's children (John 1:12).

3. *iskus*—This inherently forceful word points to the internal quality of any given thing, indicating the character of a person or the quality of an action. It is translated "mighty" and "might" in speaking of God's power (Eph. 1:19; 6:10), and of the ability which God gives to those who minister in His Name (1 Pet. 4:11).

> For strength to ever do the right,
> For grace to conquer in the fight,
> For power to walk the world in white,
> Send the fire!
>
> William Booth

4. *dynamis*—The word dynamite comes from this word. Its significance is power in action or the transference of power from one body to another. It is translated "violence" (the power of fire in action) in Heb. 11:34, "virtue" (Luke 6:19), "strength" (2 Cor. 12:9), "might" (Eph. 3:16), and "power" (Rom. 15:13; 1 Cor. 2:4). All these carry the thought of a power transfer, as when Christ healed the woman as she touched Him (Luke 6:19), as He strengthens Paul, and graces the believer.

This is the word used for the promise of Pentecost in Acts 1:8. Finney comments: "That which they manifestly received as the supreme, crowning and all-important means of success was the power to prevail with both God and man, the power to fasten saving impressions upon the minds of men. This last was doubtless the thing which they understood Christ to promise. . . . It was God speaking in and through them. It was power from on high; God in them making a saving impression upon those to whom they spoke.

---

[10]F.E. Marsh, *Fully Furnished*, pp. 155–157.

This power to savingly impress abode with and upon them. . . . It has existed to a greater or lesser extent in the church ever since. It is a mysterious fact often manifested in a most surprising manner. Sometimes a single sentence, a word, a gesture, or even a look will convey this power in an overcoming manner."[11]

> Oh that the world might know
> The all-atoning Lamb!
> Spirit of faith descend and show
> The virtue of His Name
> The grace which all may find
> The saving power impart
> And testify to all mankind
> And speak in every heart.
>
> Charles Wesley

5. *kratos*—This word speaks of the manifestation of power, the required strength to perform any given action. Translated by the words "strength," "dominion," and "power" in speaking of God's power in action (Luke 1:51; 1 Pet. 5:11; Jude 25; Eph. 1:19; Col. 1:11). The Spirit caused the Word of God to prevail "mightily" as it was preached (Acts 19:20).

Applied to the believer, the word is used to describe what God does in him (Col. 1:11). In every other case in the New Testament except one, *kratos* is used in an objective sense in calling attention to what God has and does. (Heb. 2:14 is the exception, referring to the power Satan had before Christ, who by His death, nullified Satan's dominion.) God alone is the one who has the strength to perform any given thing in the realm of grace.

Whittier said:

> In God's own might
> We gird us for the coming fight
> And, strong in Him whose cause is ours
> In conflict with unholy power
> We grasp the weapons He has given
> The Light, the Truth, and Love of Heaven.

Historical Discussion

I believe in the Holy Spirit, the Lord and Giver of Life, who proceedeth from the Father and the Son, who with the Father and Son together is worshiped and glorified, who spoke by the prophets.

The Nicene Creed

---

[11]Charles G. Finney, *Power From on High* (Fort Washington, Pa: Christian Literature Crusade, 1962), pp. 8–9.

Thou Christ of burning, cleansing flame,
Send the fire!
Thy blood-bought gift today we claim,
Send the fire!
Look down and see this waiting host,
Give us the promised Holy Ghost
We want another Pentecost,
Send the fire!

William Booth

True Evidence of Christianity

C. H. Spurgeon

"The greatest, strongest, mightiest plea for the Church of God in the world is the existence of the Spirit of God in its midst, and the works of the Spirit of God are the true evidences of Christianity. They say miracles are withdrawn, but the Holy Spirit is the standing miracle of the Church of God today. I will not say a word against societies for Christian evidences, nor against the weighty and learned brethren who have defended the outworks of the Christian church. They have done good service and I wish them every blessing, but as to my own soul, I was never settled in my faith in Christ by Paley's *Evidences*, nor by all the evidence ever brought from history or elsewhere; the Holy Spirit has taken the burden off my shoulders and given me peace and liberty. This to me is evidence, and as to the externals which we can quote to others, it was enough for Peter and John that the people saw the lame man healed, and they needed not to speak for themselves."[1]

William Law

"The Holy Spirit's coming was no less to fulfill the gospel than Christ's coming was the fulfillment of the law and the prophets. As all types and figures in the Law were but empty shadows without the coming of Christ, so the New Testament is but dead letter without the Holy Spirit in redeemed men as the living power of salvation. . . .

"Where the Holy Spirit is not honored as the one through whom the whole life and power of Gospel salvation is to be effected, it is no wonder that Christians have no more of the reality of the Gospel than the Jews had of the purity of the Law. . . . For the New Testament without the coming of the Holy Spirit in power over self, sin, and the devil is no better a help to heaven than the Old Testament without the coming of the Messiah. Need any more be said to demonstrate the truth that the one thing absolutely essential to man's salvation is the Spirit of God living and working in the spirit of man? And while we still cling to a religion that does not acknowledge this, it is a full proof that we are not yet in that redeemed state of union with God which is intended by the Gospel."[2]

---

[1] D.L. Moody, *Secret Power*, Preface, p. 8.
[2] William Law, *The Power of the Spirit*, David Hunt, ed. (Fort Washington, Penn.: Christian Literature Crusade, 1961), pp. 23–24.

A New Reformation

Frederick Denison Maurice

"I cannot but think that the reformation in our day which I expect to be more deep and searching than that of the sixteenth century, will turn upon the Spirit's presence and life as that did upon justification by the Son."

George Smeaton

"The personality and deity of the Spirit are, however, one day to be displayed in conspicuous glory in connection with His work upon the Church. . . . The final issue in the glory reflected from every redeemed and perfected saint and from the entire Body of Christ (now scattered over every country and visited from hour to hour with new communications of wisdom grace and power but then seen to be united to their glorious Head) will be worthy of the divine Workman who is carrying on his transforming work and raising up a temple in which the Godhead will dwell forever. At present the divine personality of the Spirit is less perceptible, because it is not beheld in connection with the accomplished work. The redeemed are not yet perfect; the Church is not yet complete. There is still another stage of revelation when the Spirit shall be glorified in connection with the work which He shall have finished and brought to its destined completeness."[3]

Central Reality of the Church

Henry Van Dusen

"In the faith of the Early Church the Spirit was a central, perhaps *the* central reality. It was not primarily a conviction for thought, certainly not a matter of instructed dogma. It sprang directly from vivid, commanding, indubitable experience."[4]

D. L. Moody

"Let others reject if they will at their own peril this imperishable truth. I believe and am growing more into this belief that divine, miraculous creative power resides in the Holy Ghost. Above and beyond all natural law, yet in harmony with it, creation, providence, the divine Government and the upbuilding of the Church of God are presided over by the Spirit of God."[5]

Leslie Newbigin

"Catholicism has laid its primary stress upon a given structure, Protestantism upon the given message. . . . It is necessary however to recog-

---

[3]George Smeaton, *The Doctrine of the Holy Spirit* (Carlisle, Pa.: The Banner of Truth, 1980), pp. 104–105.
[4]Henry Van Dusen, *Spirit, Son, and Father* (New York: Scribner's, 1958), p. 63.
[5]D. L. Moody, *Secret Power*, p. 12.

nize there is a third stream of Christian tradition. Its central element is the conviction that the Christian life is a matter of the experienced power and presence of the Holy Spirit today. . . . If we would answer the question 'Where is the Church?' we must ask 'Where is the Holy Spirit recognizably present with power?' "[6]

A Word of Power

B. R. Brasnett

"If Christianity had no word of power to speak to men who sought to live like Jesus but knew not how, it would be a dead or dying religion. But Christianity has that word of power and that word is the doctrine of the Holy Spirit. . . .

"The Holy Spirit is the Spirit of Jesus and He is the interpreter of Jesus to those who seek to follow Him." It is He who brings us up to date with Jesus. The person and name of Jesus of Nazareth, says Brasnett, "is not an obsolete anachronism, because the Holy Spirit is a present power. His work is practical, calling men to the practical; it is not the function of the Holy Spirit to portray ideal Utopias divorced from all contact with reality, but rather to inspire each man with a vision of perfection realizable here and now and to aid him to its attaining. It is the Spirit's part not so much to fill men with visions of what might have been, if the world and its inhabitants had been other than they are; instead it is His task to make men face reality and show them how, from the things that are, may arise the things that ought to be."[7]

Heinrich Heine

"Ah my child, while I was yet a little boy, while I yet sat upon my mother's knee, I believed in God the Father, who rules up there in heaven, good and great, who created the beautiful earth, and the beautiful men and women thereon; who ordained the sun, moon and stars in their courses.

"When I got bigger, my child, I comprehended yet a great deal more than this, and grew intelligent, and believed on the Son also, on the beloved Son, who loved us and revealed love to us; and for His reward, as always happens, was crucified by the people.

"Now, when I am grown up, have read much, and have traveled much, my heart swells within me and with my whole heart I believe on the Holy Ghost. The greatest miracles were of His working, and still greater miracles doth he even now work. He burst in sunder the oppressor's stronghold, and he burst in sunder the bondsman's yoke. He heals old death wounds and renews the ancient right. All mankind are one race of noble equals before Him. He chases away the evening clouds and the dark

---

[6]Leslie Newbigin, *The Household of God* (New York: Friendship Press, 1954), pp. 94–95.
[7]B.R. Brasnett, *The Infinity of God* (London: Longmans, Green, and Co., 1933), pp. 57–58.

cobweb of the brain which have spoilt love and joy for us, which day and night have lowered on us."[8]

The Necessity of Power

Joseph Alleine

"A man may as well hew marble without tools, paint without colors or instruments, or build without materials as perform any acceptable service without the graces of the Spirit, which are both the materials and the instruments in the work."[9]

Billy Graham

"When God told us to go and preach the Gospel to every creature and to evangelize the world He provided supernatural power for us. That power is given us by the Holy Spirit. It is available to every one of us. . . . I have asked God that if there were ever a day when I should stand in the pulpit without knowing the fullness and anointing of the Spirit of God and should not preach with compassion and fire, I want God to take me home to heaven. I don't want to live. I don't ever want to stand in the pulpit and preach without the power of the Holy Spirit. It's a dangerous thing."[10]

George Fox

"I was to bring them off from all the world's fellowships, and prayings and singings which stood in forms without power; that their fellowship might be in the Holy Ghost, and in the eternal Spirit of God; that they might pray in the Holy Ghost and sing in the Spirit and with the grace that comes by Jesus; making melody in the hearts to the Lord who has sent His beloved Son to be their Savior. . . . I was to bring people off from . . . all their vain traditions which they had instituted since the Apostles' days against all of which the Lord's power was set; in the dread and authority of which power I was moved. . . ."[11]

John Fletcher

"I wait for the fulfillment of that prayer 'That they all may be one, as Thou Father art in Me and I in Thee, that they also may be one in Us; and that they may be one, even as We are one.' Oh for that pure baptismal flame! O for the fullness of the dispensation of the Holy Ghost! Pray, pray, pray for this! This shall make us all of one heart, and of one soul."[12]

---

[8]Heinrich Heine, *Heinrich Heine's Memoirs* (Ayer Co. Publications).

[9]Moody, op. cit. p. 54.

[10]Billy Graham, *Revival in Our Time* (Wheaton, Ill.: Van Kampen Press, 1950), pp. 109, 119.

[11]George Fox, *The Journal of George Fox*, pp. 104–105.

[12]Gilchrist Lawson, *Deeper Experiences of Famous Christians* (Chicago: Glad Tidings Publishing Co., 1911), p. 194.

God With Us by the Spirit

Samuel Shoemaker

"We may feel the presence of the Creator-Father in some part of creation or all of it. We may feel the presence of the Redeemer-Son in a more personal way still. But I think there is often a *nearness* about the presence of the Holy Spirit as if He were taking the initiative with us himself. At rare times this will be so numinous, so charged with a sense of the supernatural, that it will almost frighten us; we shall know beyond all questioning that this is no subjective imagining, but a living Presence. It is as if He had business with us. He had not just come, He had come for something."[13]

George Smeaton

"The Church's ever-living Head knows how to usher in creative epochs, to rally His people to some converging point through the lapse of the centuries and to gather up under this powerful influence isolated opinions into one consistent whole. When a previous awakening has spent its force, when the elements of thought or action previously supplied threaten to become effete, a new impulse is commonly communicated by Him who interposes at various stages to make all things new.

"The first disciples waited in the youthfulness of simple hope not for a spirit which they had not, but for more of the Spirit which they had; and Christianity has not outlived itself. The attitude of the Church in the first days after the ascension when the disciples waited for the Spirit should be the Church's attitude still."[14]

The Power to Save

Charles Finney

The disciples on the Day of Pentecost "received a powerful baptism of the Holy Ghost, a vast increase in divine illumination. This baptism imparted a great diversity of gifts that were used for the accomplishment of their work. It manifestly included the following things: The power of a holy life. The power of a self-sacrificing life. (The manifestation of these must have had great influence with those to whom they proclaimed the Gospel.) The power of a cross-bearing life. The power of great meekness, which this baptism enabled them everywhere to exhibit. The power of a loving enthusiasm in proclaiming the gospel. The power of teaching. The power of a loving and living faith. The gift of tongues. An increase of the power to work miracles. The gift of inspiration, or the revelation of many truths before unrecognized by them. The power of moral courage to proclaim the Gospel and do the bidding of Christ whatever it cost them. But . . . neither separately nor all together did they constitute that power from

---

[13]Samuel M. Shoemaker, *Twenty Centuries of Great Preaching*, Clyde E. Fant Jr. and William M. Dinson Jr., eds. (Waco, Texas: Word Books, 1971), p. 27.
[14]Smeaton, op. cit. p. 252–255.

on high which Christ promised. That . . . supreme, crowning and all-important means of success was the power to prevail with both God and man, the power to fasten *saving impressions* upon the minds of men.

"This was doubtless the thing which they understood Christ to promise. . . . It was God speaking in and through them. It was power from on high; God in them making a saving impression upon those to whom they spoke. This power to savingly impress abode with and upon them. . . . It has existed to a greater or lesser extent in the church ever since. It is a mysterious fact often manifested in a most surprising manner. Sometimes a single sentence, a word, a gesture or even a look will convey this power in an overcoming manner."[15]

Samuel Shoemaker

"It must be perfectly obvious to anyone that what the whole church needs from top to bottom is a deeper conversion, a profounder experience of the power of the Holy Spirit. . . . Awakening in history has never come from regular ecclesiastics getting together to 'do something.' It has come from inspired nobodies whom the church first ignored, then condemned, then (if they got powerful) took over and finally domesticated. . . . Let us look to see where the Holy Spirit is at work now. Maybe we can learn something."[16]

---

[15]Charles G. Finney, *Power from on High* (Fort Washington, Pa: Christian Literature Crusade, 1962), pp. 8–9.
[16]Shoemaker, op. cit. Vol. II, p. 64.

APPENDICES

THE NAMES OF GOD
THE BASIS OF RIGHT AND WRONG
AUGUSTINE ADOPTS THE ETERNAL NOW
MORE QUESTIONS AND ANSWERS CONCERNING
ETERNITY

THE NAMES OF GOD

Adon —One of three titles (*Adon, Adonai, Adonim*) generally rendered "Lord." They all denote the various aspects of headship, but each one has its own peculiar usage.[1]

The title "Lord" (*Adonis*), meaning "owner," is more a title of honor and respect than a name, like "sir," "my lord," or "your honor." Used by a subject to his king (1 Sam. 24:8; 26:17; Jer. 22:18; cf. Gen. 44:18), a wife to her husband (Gen. 18:12), a slave to his master (Gen. 24:12; Ex. 21:5; cf. Mal. 1:6), or by a follower to his leader (Num. 11:28).

"It refers to one's authority and prestige (Gen. 23:6; 45:8) and in this sense could be used as a title in addressing God to whom, in the highest sense, honor and dominion belong." (See Josh. 3:11, 13; Ps. 97:5; Mic. 4:13; Zech. 4:14; 6:5). Used with Yahweh or as a substitute (Ex. 23:17; 34:23; Isa. 1:24; 3:15; 10:16; Amos 8:1; Ps. 90:1; 114:7; Isa. 6:1; 8:11; Mal. 3:1).[2]

It came to mean God's absolute Lordship in transcendent holiness; "*Adon* is the Lord as ruler *in* the earth."[3]

Adonai —The Lord in His relation *to* the earth, and as carrying out His purposes of blessing *in* the earth. With this limitation it was almost equivalent to Jehovah; 134 passages are recorded in the Massorah where this was deliberately done, associating the vowel points of the word Jehovah with *Adon* and converting it to *Adonai*. Later, to distinguish its use as a divine title for God and safeguard it from human over-familiarity, the title was always spoken slightly differently—the short *a* of the diphthong *ai* in *Adon-ai* was lengthened, and the phrase ended in Hebrew by the word "my"—like "m'lord" in medieval England.

Adonim —The plural of *adon*, carrying with it all that *adon* does but in a greater or higher degree, and more especially as owner and proprietor. Rarely used of men; an *adon* (without the article) may rule others who do not belong to him, but *Adonim* is the Lord who rules His own.[4]

---

[1]Ethelbert Bullinger, *The Companion Bible*, App. 4, p. 6.
[2]B.W. Anderson, *Interpreter's Dictionary of the Bible*, George A. Buttrick, ed., (Nashville: Abingdon Press, 1962). vol. 2, p. 414.
[3]Bullinger, op. cit. App. 4, p. 6.
[4]Ibid, App. 4, p. 6.

Elohim —Occurs 2,700 times. Translated "Lord" (KJV) and "Jehovah" (KJV). A plural word (see Judges 9:13; 1 Sam. 4:8; 2 Sam. 7:23; Ps. 86:8). However, the majority of the time it is used in a singular sense even when the accompanying verb is plural (Gen. 1:26; 20:13; 35:7; Ex. 22:9). The implications of the Trinity are obvious; the word is equivalent to Deity or Godhead, and is indicated in the KJV by ordinary small type "God."

Although sometimes used to describe pagan worship (of Chemosh Judg. 11:24), Ashtoreth or Ishtar (1 Kings 11:5), and Baalzebub (2 Kings 1:2), it is mostly used of the one true and absolute "Lord of history and nature, who demands the exclusive homage of His people."[5]

Elohim —May mean "greatness and glory," with the idea of creative and governing power, omnipotence and sovereignty. "Elohim is God the Creator putting His omnipotence into operation."

In Gen. 1:1—2:4 *Elohim* is used 35 times; it is He who creates by mighty power the vast universe; who says, and it is done, and brings into being what is not. The name's early link with creation gives it a primary meaning as Creator: "It indicates His relation to mankind as His creatures (2 Chron. 18:31) where it stands in contrast with Jehovah indicating covenant relationship."[6]

Elohim is possessor and ruler of heaven and earth, He who brings light out of darkness, cosmos out of chaos, habitation out of desolation and life in His image.

Alah —Another possible word from which Elohim could have been derived. It can mean to "declare or swear," and thus suggests a covenant relationship.[7]

"To make a covenant implies the power and right to do so, and establishes the fact of 'absolute authority in the Creator and Ruler of the Universe.' He can swear by none greater than himself so He makes this covenant with Abraham (Gen. 17:7). "I am the Almighty God [*El-Shaddai*] (17:1) . . . I will establish my covenant . . . to be a God [*Elohim*] unto thee," that is to be with him and his children in covenant relationship.[8]

Elohim's covenant sign with Noah is a rainbow (Gen. 6:18; 9:15, 16). Joseph reminds his sons, "I die: and God [*Elohim*] will surely visit you, and bring you out of this land unto the land which he sware to Abraham" (Gen. 50:24). "*Elohim* keeps covenant and lovingkindness with His servants who walk before Him with all their heart (1 Kings 8:23)."[9]

In Jer. 31:33 and 32:40, *Elohim* is used especially of the new covenant in which He will write His reverence and law in hearts.[10]

El —Uncertain derivative, but the root meaning is apparently "power"—

---

[5]Anderson, op. cit. vol. 2, p. 413.
[6]Bullinger, op. cit. App. 4, p. 6.
[7]Nathan Stone, *The Names of God* (Chicago: Moody Press, 1944), p. 9.
[8]Ibid. pp. 9–10.
[9]Ibid. p. 10.
[10]Ibid. p. 10.

the "numinous divine power that fills men with awe and dread." Translated "mighty," "strong," "prominent." Used 250 times, and frequently appears where God's great power is evident.

El is *Elohim* in all His strength and power; God the omniscient (first usage Gen. 14:18–22), and God the omnipotent (Gen. 16:13). He can perform all things for His people (Ps. 57:2) and in [Him] all the divine attributes are concentrated."[11]

Combinations of El

El Bethel —"God of peace" (Gen. 35:7). May alternately be the God who revealed himself in Bethel.

El Elohe-Israel —"El, The God of Israel" (Gen. 33:19–20). Jacob buys a lot near Shechem and dedicates an altar there to Him.

Elyon —First occurs in Gen. 14:18–20 where Melchizedek blesses Abraham in this name, praising God as the "possessor of heaven and earth." God as the "possessor of heaven and earth" divides the nations "their inheritance" (Ps. 78:55). He is "over all the earth" (Ps. 83:18), a title that occurs 36 times.

El Elyon —"Exalted One" or "MOST HIGH" in the KJV. Used in Balaam's prophecy (Num. 24:16) with *El* and *Shaddai*, in both Moses' and David's songs (Deut. 32:8–9; 2 Sam. 22:14), in David's prayers (Ps. 7:17; 9:2; 21:7; 46:4; 97:9), and in other places where His rulership and ownership or absolute preeminence of deity are the focus of worship ("sons of the Mighty"—Ps. 89:6; "God standeth in the congregation of the mighty" and "judgeth among the gods"—Ps. 82:1).

It appears in its Aramaic form by Nebuchadnezzar in Daniel 3:26 ("servants of the most high God"), and is used in his confession of repentance (Dan. 4:2, 24, 32, 34).

In its Greek form, *hupsistos*, it is used nine times in the NT: by the angel to Mary (Luke 1:32, 35), of John as God's prophet (Luke 1:76), the Gadarene demoniac to Jesus (Mark 5:7; Luke 8:28), of Paul to the philosophers on Mars Hill (Acts 7:48), and in referring to the "highest" places (Matt. 21:9; Mark 11:10; Luke 2:14; 19:38; Acts 16:17; Heb.7:1).

El Olam —"God the Everlasting One" or "God of Eternity." The word means "everlasting time," "time whose boundaries are hidden from view." Applied to God it apparently means "His sovereignty continues through the ages, unaffected by the passing of time."[12]

El Roi —"God Who sees me" or "God of Vision." Used by Hagar in the desert as God watched over her and her son (Gen. 16:13).

---

[11]Bullinger, op. cit. App. 4, p. 6.
[12]Anderson, op. cit. vol. 2, p. 412.

El Shaddai —"God, the One of the mountains" (referring to His visits at Sinai, or His lofty rulership) or "God Almighty"

Excluding Genesis and Exodus 6:2–3, *El Shaddai* occurs 35 times in the OT, 29 of which are in Job, who is entranced with God's majesty and power. It occurs as a quote in 2 Cor. 6:18 and Rev. 1:8; 4:8; 21:22.

In every instance it is translated "Almighty," indicated in some editions of the KJV by small capital letters "ALMIGHTY." "It is God *El* not as source of strength but of grace; not as Creator but as Giver. Shaddai is the all-bountiful. It does not refer to His creative power but to His power to supply all His people's needs.

"The first occurrence of *El Shaddai* (Gen. 17:1) is used to show Abraham that He who called him out to walk alone before Him could supply all His needs. We are to "come out" in separation from the world with the same confidence (2 Cor. 6:18).[13]

First and the Last —Isaiah's term to convey God's "eternal sovereignty over the whole sweep of time from beginning to end" (Isa. 44:6; 48:12).

"The prophet does not speak of eternity in abstract and non-historical terms, but presses temporal language to its utter limits by saying concretely, 'Before me there was no God formed, neither shall there be after me' (Isa. 43:10).

"Yahweh's everlasting sovereignty then is hidden within the shadow of the first and the last. . . . Thus the expression 'the first and the last' is a vivid way of saying the whole sweep of human history from beginning to end is under the sway of God who is Creator and Lord and whose directing presence is known in history (Isa. 46:10; cf. 45:21). This same note is accented in the NT under the conviction that God's sovereign Lordship is manifest in Jesus Christ the Alpha and the Omega" (Rev. 1:8, 17; 2:8; 22:13).[14]

Eloah —"Elohim is to be worshiped. *Eloah* is God in connection with His will rather than His power. The first occurrence associates this name with worship (Deut. 32:15, 17); hence it is the title used whenever the contrast (latent or expressed) is with false gods or idols. *Eloah* is essentially the 'living God' in contrast with idols."[15] Also rendered "God" in KJV.

The Jehovah Titles

Jehovah —God's proper name, denoting His person (Gen. 2:4). Derived from the Hebrew verb *havah*—"to be" or "being," a word almost exactly like the verb *chavah*—"to live or life." With this name "we must think of Jehovah as the being who is absolutely self-existent, the one who in himself possesses essential life, permanent existence."[16]

---

[13]Bullinger, op. cit. p. 7.
[14]Anderson, op. cit. vol. 2, p. 416.
[15]Bullinger, op. cit. p. 6.
[16]Stone, op. cit. p. 15.

Translated "LORD" (in caps) in the KJV, and is the most frequently used name for God in the OT, being used 6,823 times.[17]

While *Elohim* is God as Creator of all things, Jehovah is the same God in covenant relation to those whom He has created (2 Chron. 18:31). Jehovah means the Eternal, the Immutable One, He who was and is and is to come. The divine definition is given in Gen. 21:33. He is especially therefore the God of Israel, and the God of those redeemed in Christ.

We can say "the God" *Elohim* or "my God" *Elohim* to distinguish our true God from idols but not "my Jehovah" or "the Jehovah," for Jehovah is the name of that true, living, personal God as distinct from all false gods or idols. Indicated in the KJV by small capital letters LORD and by "GOD" when it occurs in combination with *Adonai*, in which case LORD GOD = Adonai Jehovah.

Whereas *Elohim* is the name used in the more "universal" books of Scripture like Ecclesiastes, Daniel, and Jonah (a God of loving power to the whole creation), the name used in Israel's theocratic and historical books is Jehovah, thus purposely distinguishing God's unique revelation of himself to His people (power and love conditioned by moral attributes).[18]

"All the names of God which occur in Scripture are derived from His works except one, and that is Jehovah. . . . It teaches plainly and unequivocably of the substance of God."[19]

"Jehovah" is the name God uses when He makes a special revelation of himself as the moral, spiritual Personal-Infinite God of continuous, absolute existence; the "I am that I am" or "I will be that I will be" (Ex. 3:14–15; 6:2–3).[20]

As Jehovah, righteousness and holiness were His two great known attributes. Israel was so afraid to profane that name (Lev. 24:16) that they eventually did not say it. To this day Jehovah is never read in the synagogue; *Adonai* is used instead. "Thus the original pronunciation of that name we call Jehovah, regarded as too sacred to be uttered, has been lost to this day."[21]

A Jewish believer points out that the Hebrew phrase, "I am that I am," put in the third person is pronounced, "Ye-he-yeh," and that the Hebrew letter equivalents to the English "w" and "h" are in Hebrew almost identical; they may have indeed, once been the same letter. To speak of God then as "He is that He is" (substituting "w" for the "h") would be said as "Ya-he-weh," perhaps the original pronunciation.

As a name used with atonement (Lev. 1–7), *Elohim* only occurs twice but Jehovah is used 86 times. In Lev. 16, which concerns the Day of Atonement, only Jehovah is used, and it occurs 12 times. It is also associated with salvation (Gen. 7:5; Ps. 89:15, 16; Isa. 45:22, 24; Zech. 13:9).[22]

---

[17]Ibid. p. 14.
[18]Ibid. pp. 17–18.
[19]Ibid. p. 15.
[20]Ibid. p. 16.
[21]Ibid. p. 19.
[22]Ibid. pp. 21–23.

Jehovah has eleven related titles, usually arising from some historic incident, and appearing in this Hebrew scripture order:

Jehovah-Jireh —"Jehovah will see or provide" (Gen. 22:14). The name related to *ro'eh* (seer, prophet: 2 Sam. 15:27; 1 Chron. 9:22; 26:28; 2 Chron. 16:7; Isa. 30:10). It suggests God's vision of future need; His pre-vision leads to provision ("Before they call, I will answer" Isa. 65:24). We say, "God will take care of it."

Jehovah-Jireh commemorates a great lesson and a mighty deliverance. The deliverance Abraham and Isaac experienced at Moriah purified Abraham's love for his son, allowing him to view Isaac as "the gracious gift and possession of God, as a good entrusted to him by God; which he was to be ready to render back to Him at any moment."[23]

After Abraham offered up the ram, which the Lord provided in place of Isaac, Abraham named the spot "Jehovah-jireh" (Gen. 22:14).

In his naming of the place, Abraham shows he had prophetic understanding of God's future messianic provision and manifestation (Heb. 11:19). Mount Moriah (a kindred word to *jireh*) eventually became the very site of Israel's temple (2 Chron. 3:1) where sacrifices were the center of worship. But Abraham saw the greatest sacrifice (John 8:56), and knew indeed that God would provide the true Lamb one day on the "hill of the Lord" for the entire world (John 1:29; 1 Pet. 1:18–19; Rev. 5:11–13).[24]

Jehovah-Rophe —"Jehovah that healeth thee" (Ex. 15:26). The word *rophe* is used about 70 times and always means "to restore, to heal, to cure, or a physician, not only in the physical sense but in the moral or spiritual sense also."[25]

The sweetening of the waters of Marah is a type of God's healing for the infected stream of our human race. Our thirst can never be quenched (John 4:13–14; 7:37–38) by the waters tainted with bitterness and death (Isa. 30:26; 61:1; Jer. 14:19–20; 30:17) until we come to Him who is the incarnation of the Tree of Life (Rev. 22:1–2) and is himself the wellspring of life and health (Rev. 22:17).

Jehovah-Nissi —"Jehovah my banner" (Ex. 17:15). The Amalekites, descendants of Esau's grandson (Gen. 36:12), had become the unceasing and hereditary enemies of Israel, harassing them with open war (Deut. 25:17–18; Ex. 17:8). Joshua (Num. 13:8, 16—"Jehovah is salvation") led Israel's troops against them, while Moses stayed back with his hands held out on a hill behind him, the rod of *Elohim* in his hand.

The use of *Elohim* is significant. It was the name signifying God's "creative glory, might, and sovereignty, the general name of God, the name especially used in relationship to the nations . . . as distinguished from

---

[23]Ibid. p. 51.
[24]Ibid. pp. 54–55.
[25]Ibid. p. 57.

Jehovah in relationship especially to Israel . . . denoting that whether Amalek acknowledged it or not, He was God."[26]

The rod in Moses' hand was the symbol and pledge of God's presence and power. Isaiah, when prophesying of Christ, said a rod would come from the stem of Jesse who would "stand for an ensign of the people" (Isa. 11:1, 10).

"A banner, in ancient times, was not necessarily a flag such as we use nowadays. Often it was a bare pole with a bright shining ornament which glittered in the sun. The word here for banner means to glisten, among other things. It is translated variously pole, ensign, standard, and among the Jews it is also a word for miracle. As an ensign or standard it was a signal to God's people to rally to Him. It stood for His cause, His battle. It was a sign of deliverance, of salvation . . . the word used by the Psalmist as 'lift up' in the expression: 'Lord lift up the light of thy countenance upon us' (Ps. 4:6)."[27]

Amalek, the "firstfruits of the heathen, the beginning of Gentile power and hostility to the people of God" represents the forces of a world order opposed to Jehovah in all ages (Ex. 17:16; 1 John 2:16; 5:19). Their salvation through the Red Sea had been entirely in God's hands (Ex. 14:13); but now the land is to be taken and war is to be fought (2 Tim. 4:7; Jude 3; 2 Tim. 3–4; Eph. 6:11–17).[28]

Jehovah-Mekaddishkem —"Jehovah that sanctifies you" (Ex. 31:13; Lev. 20:8; 21:8; 22:32; Ezek. 20:12).

Unlike other Jehovah names, this name is not transferred or transliterated but translated in the King James Version. It appears as the word "sanctify" in various forms (dedicate, consecrate, hallow, holy) some 700 times in Scripture. Stone writes, "No other name more truly expresses the character of Jehovah and the requirements of His people."[29]

Days, times and seasons were sanctified, or set apart from the rest (Gen. 2:3; Ex. 20:8, 11; Lev. 23; 25:10), so were places like the temple, and the city of Jerusalem, as well as the people (Ex. 13:2; 28:36; Deut.7:6), some even before birth (Jer. 1:5).[30]

The point involved in these was contact with God. "The Sabbath day was holy because God rested in it. . . . The sanctuary itself was so named because it was the dwelling place of Jehovah among His people. . . . As Himself the Holy One, Jehovah is apart from and above all else in the universe. (1 Sam. 2:2). . . .

"It is this holiness of which an old Scottish divine writes: 'It is the balance . . . of all the attributes of Deity. Power without holiness would degenerate into cruelty; omniscience without holiness would become craft; justice without holiness would degenerate into revenge; and goodness without holiness would be passionate and intemperate fondness

[26]Ibid. p. 70.
[27]Ibid. pp. 70–71.
[28]Ibid. pp. 71–73.
[29]Ibid. p. 78.
[30]Ibid. p. 79.

doing mischief rather than accomplishing good.' It is this holiness which gives to God grandeur and majesty, and more than anything else constitutes His fullness and perfection."[31]

Holiness is more than a position or relationship to Jehovah; it is a participation in Jehovah's nature, character, and works (Lev. 20:26–27). In response to His provided power, man can and must respond to God's call for holiness as long as he lives; it calls for continued choice, in a growth process that goes on forever.

Jehovah-Shalom —"Jehovah send peace" (Judg. 6:24).

This word translated "peace" some 170 times can also mean "whole" (Deut. 27:6), "finished" (Dan. 5:26; 1 Kings 9:25), or to make good a loss inflicted by carelessness (Ex. 21:34; 22:5–6). In a physical and material sense of wholeness and completeness it is translated as "welfare" and "well" (Gen. 43:27), and in the sense of fulfilling or completing obligation, it is frequently used as "pay" or "perform" (Ps. 50:14; 37:21; Deut. 23:21). About 20 times it is translated "perfect" (*shalem*—1 Kings 8:61, where the meaning is harmony and wholeness with God).[32]

"And this is the basic idea underlying all the various translations of this one Hebrew word—a harmony of relationship or a reconciliation based upon the completion of a transaction, the payment of a debt, the giving of satisfaction. . . . It expressed the deepest desire and need of the human heart. It represented the greatest measure of contentment and satisfaction in life." (See 1 Kings 4:25; Jer. 23:6.)

"Peace" was the most common greeting in Bible lands (as it still is today), and was also the word used for the peace offering (Lev. 3; 7:11–21). . . . "This restoration of fellowship between God and man, broken by sin, but now atoned for by the shed blood, was indicated by the fact that both God and man, priest and people partook of the offering. . . . Every blessing, temporal and spiritual, is included in restoring man to that peace with God lost by the fall."[33]

Despite the hurt and grief He feels over His wayward world, not only is Jehovah at peace himself in His perfectly balanced divine nature, but He desires peace for all in it (Lev. 26:3, 6; Num. 6:24–26; Ps. 29:11; Isa. 26:12; 48:18; 66:12; Jer. 29:11). He is the God of peace (Rom. 15:33; 2 Cor. 13:11; Heb. 13:20); and Christ himself is the Prince of Peace (Isa. 9:6; Acts 10:36; Col. 1:20).

Jehovah-Zebaoth —"Jehovah of hosts" (1 Sam. 1:3).

Jehovah-Tsidkenu —"Jehovah our righteousness" (Jer. 23:6; 33:16).

Jehovah-Shammah —"Jehovah is there" (Ezek. 48:35).

Jehovah-Elyon —"Jehovah most high" (Ps. 7:17; 47:2; 97:9).

Jehovah-Rohi —"Jehovah my shepherd" (Ps. 23:1).

---

[31]Ibid. p. 80.
[32]Ibid. pp. 90–91.
[33]Ibid. p. 92.

THE BASIS OF RIGHT AND WRONG

In saying therefore, that things are not good according to any standard of goodness, but simply by the will of God, it seems to me that one destroys, without realizing it, all the love of God and all His glory; for why praise Him for what He has done if He would be equally praiseworthy in doing the contrary? Where will be His justice and His wisdom if He had only a certain despotic power, if arbitrary will takes the place of reasonableness and if, in accord with the definition of tyrants, justice consists in that which is pleasing to the most powerful?[1]

Gottfried Wilhelm Leibniz

Why is "good" good? Is "bad" really bad? Does God just make up what is right and what is wrong? If God wants everyone to be unselfish and says that what He calls *love* is the fulfilling of the law, is He playing by the same rules? Or is it rather that because He gets to make up the rules; whatever He says goes? If love is completely unselfish and God wants everyone to be unselfish as He is, isn't He being selfish in calling us to put Him first?

The Grounds of Moral Obligation

Both Jonathan Edwards and later Charles Finney dealt with this question in detail: Edwards, the Calvinist philosopher, in his grand defense of the "necessity of divine volition," and Finney, the Arminian trained as a lawyer, in his unique studies in law and theology. Despite their other differences, their conclusions in this area are united. Both defined true virtue in *agape* love as *benevolence*, and explored its basis in the nature and character of God.

Finney has been unfairly charged by some with the adoption of utilitarian principles in positing what was called "disinterested benevolence" as man's universal and invariable duty. But the idea of love as "benevolence to being in general" did not originate with him and is certainly not

---

[1]Gottfried Wilhelm Leibniz, *Discourse On Metaphysics II*, trans. Dr. George R. Montgomery (La Salle, Ill.: Open Court Publishing Co., 1962), pp. 4–5.

unique to him. Edwards, in 1754, used the same term to describe the same duty.[2]

Charles Finney

One key distinction Finney later made, and one that significantly applies, in the light of Francis Schaeffer's significant book *A Christian Manifesto*, has to do with the final analysis of the *Rex Lex* vs. *Lex Rex* question—is the king above the law or the law over the king? As most students of theology and law—and Finney was both—are being made aware, one uniqueness of the Christian message is that it is not based on the assumption that the one with the biggest stick has the right to rule; the Bible does not proclaim that might is right but a message close to the idea that right is might. This is patently true in the application of prophetic correction to society; we have an absolute standard by which the actions of all rulers are to be measured, one that is entirely independent from limited human knowledge, from some arbitrary edict or whim of changing cultural mores. To the Church the Law is king. As Christians, we understand that Law to be the Law of God.

Finney specifically enjoined readers to master the first chapters of his systematic theology for the sake of understanding the base of all his writings and ministry. In those pages, his key thought is *distinction* (not separation) of morals and metaphysics, differentiating between the natural and moral attributes of God, the *value of God's essence or His uncreated being*, and the holiness and purity of God's *eternal character.*

He writes, "God's ultimate end in all He does or omits is the highest well-being of himself and of the universe, and in all His acts and dispensations, His ultimate object is the promotion of this end. All moral agents should have this same end, and this comprises their whole duty. This intention or consecration to this infinitely and intrinsically valuable end is virtue or holiness in God and in all moral agents. . . . Consequently, all obligation resolves itself into an obligation to choose the highest good of God and of being in general for its own sake and to choose all the known conditions and means of this end for the sake of the end."

Some assume that Finney found good to be independent of God, some kind of "universal rightness." But on the contrary, this is specifically refuted and denied by him, as is utilitarianism as a ground of moral obligation. It is clear that (a) he did *not* believe in either a utilitarian approach to the Gospel, although he had a strong practical emphasis that admittedly fitted well the tenor of his times; and (b) he did *not* intend, nor espouse (though others may have supposed him to) any kind of "good" or moral obligation that exists *separately and independently of God.*

What he did say (and it seems this particular facet of his theology is not only correct, but important to the whole question of law and its relation to the Christian in society) is that even with God, the Law is King. Though Finney says, "it is our highest duty to will God's highest good

---

[2]Jonathan Edwards, "Dissertation on the Nature of True Benevolence," *The Works of Jonathan Edwards* (University Press, 1977), Vol. I, pp. 122–127.

whether God willed it so or not," this does *not* refer to either a ground of obligation outside of God or an independent source of good outside of God. What he said was that God is not an arbitrary being; that holiness is not simply an expression of ultimate power and might; that the Law of God is not founded in His will, but in His essence, His being.

This is critical to Finney's concept of law and grace, of legal and gospel matters, of old and new covenant dealings. To him, God's declared or expressed will is not an invention but *a declaration of already existing truth;* God is valuable and honorable and praiseworthy whether He ever declares that He is or not. The propositional framework followed the reality, and ultimate moral obligation rests on all moral beings whether or not they have ever been directly commanded by God to worship Him. Put another way, God really *is* the greatest, and whether He says so or not does not *make* His greatness a reality or create a new obligation; His words merely give form to the intrinsic reality which has been and ever will be the ultimate fact of the universe. It enforces by declaration what pre-exists *in His own uncreated nature*, as distinguished, not separated from His declarative will. . . .

Some thought this posited a ground of obligation outside the will of God but blame for that cannot be laid on Finney, who very clearly taught nothing of the kind, and certainly did not in any way seek to build some kind of framework in which man could exalt himself at God's expense on the basis of some autonomous ground of good unrelated to God. He never did teach that the good enjoys an "autonomous *ontos*" or self-existent reality that exists independently of God. Good is *not* what God does but what God *does* is good. This is the basis for our moral obligation to God. We cannot say, "Good is *what* God does," but, "What God *does* is good." This is the basis for our moral obligation to God.

Jonathan Edwards

Edwards, like Finney, wrote that whether we look at what God is in His being or what He does as a person, He still deserves to be put first: "From what has been said, it is evident that true virtue must consist chiefly in love to God; the Being of beings, infinitely the greatest and the best. . . .

"As God is infinitely the greatest being, so He is allowed to be infinitely the most beautiful and excellent; and all the beauty to be found throughout the whole creation is but the reflection of the diffused beams of that being who hath an infinite fullness of brightness and glory. . . .

"He that has true virtue, consisting in benevolence to being in general and in benevolence to virtuous being, must necessarily have a supreme love to God both of benevolence and complacence. And all true virtue must radically and essentially and as it were summarily, consist in this. God is not only infinitely greater and more excellent than all other beings, but He is the head of the universal system of existence; the foundation and fountain of all being and all beauty; from whom all is perfectly derived, and on whom all is most absolutely and perfectly dependent; of whom and through whom and to whom is all being and all perfection; and whose being and beauty are, as it were, the sum and comprehension of all existence and excellence: much more than the sun is the fountain and summary comprehension of all the light and brightness of day."[3]

This is how the Christian relates to the Law and the Gospel: "I love God for who *He is*, not just for what *He does*; I serve Him for himself, not just for what He can do for me."

God is good because God's value and ultimate loveliness—His absolute uncreated nature—directs all of His actions and gives meaning to all His statements of virtue. He keeps all commands He gives to mankind. Even He himself cannot alter that intrinsic value. Good is not just what God is doing, that which He might choose to do differently tomorrow; otherwise He might with equal authority commence to do the devil's work and label it "good," changing vice to virtue. All that does not contribute to the highest happiness of God's own nature and being, and all related, created and upheld realities is by definition unwise or unholy, because it militates against the reality of what God *is*, whether or not God decides to inform us of the details of these violations of divine happiness. Notice in all of this that the nature of God is the basis for holy law; but a clear distinction is kept in God's nature between metaphysics and morals, God as the Uncreated and Creator, the Unmade Maker.

Charles Finney

Finney declared, " 'Whether therefore ye eat or drink, or whatsoever you do, do all to the glory of God.' . . . This precept requires us to will the glory of God for its intrinsic or relative value. . . . The glory and renown of God is of infinite value to Him and to the universe, and for this reason it should be promoted. . . .

"The intrinsic nature and value of the highest well-being of God and His universe is the sole foundation of moral obligation. . . . A single eye to the highest good of God and the universe is the whole of morality, strictly considered; and, upon this theory, moral law, moral government, moral obligation, virtue, vice and the whole subject of morals and religion are the perfection of simplicity. If this theory be true, no honest mind ever mistook the path of duty."[4]

L. D. McCabe

McCabe, a godly revivalist and teacher-philosopher also dealt with this issue at some length: "God is not a lawless being. He exists and acts under laws, some of which are superimposed, and some self-imposed. That is, He acts under laws some of which are not dependent on God for their existence and authority, and some of which are dependent on Him for their origin, authority and efficiency. Right and justice for example, have their origin, not in the will or edict of God, but in the eternal fitness of things. 'Fitness or unfitness in moral action,' says Bishop Butler, 'is prior to all will whatever, and determines the divine conduct.' . . . That two and two are four and not five . . . that certain acts are just and right

---

[3]Ibid. , Vol. I p. 125.
[4]Charles Finney, *Systematic Theology* (Minneapolis, Minn.: Bethany House Publishers, 1976), pp. 42, 93–94.

and that certain other acts are unjust and wrong are equally certain, and would be certain if theism is false and atheism is true. These principles and laws which govern them are not dependent on God for their existence and verity, and He cannot change them. Four units cannot be five and right can never be wrong anywhere in the universe or at any period of duration. Under these laws God exists. They are as eternal as His own essence and He cannot but act in harmony with them. They are super-imposed.

"But it does not follow that God is limited thereby in any sense as would imply imperfection in His nature. It is the crowning excellence and glory of His nature that He never does and never will violate a single principle of right, justice, goodness, and truth. All this would be equally true if there were not a single intelligence in the universe besides God. But when God created . . . human beings, laws adapted to their consti-tution and circumstances became necessary for their government; and the establishment of those laws imposes certain obligations upon himself as well as upon them. They are bound to obey His laws. He is equally bound to act in harmony with them and the modes of administration which they require. Men, being fallible, may violate their obligations; God being in-fallible, never will. Having created mankind under a law of liberty, He cannot himself violate that law in government over them in any single proceeding involving their moral character and destiny. . . . He wishes— He intensely desires—that they may do right. But He cannot force them to obedience, because a forced obedience is no obedience at all.

"This will be said to be a limitation of omnipotence. It is a self-imposed limitation. But this . . . does not imply any imperfection in His attribute . . . It simply affirms God is law-abiding, that He will be true to the law which He had imposed on himself and mankind and which He had an-nounced as the basis of His moral government. It merely affirms He will not constrain those acts of free beings for which He holds them account-able and responsible."[5]

C. S. Lewis

Lewis in turn knew that freedom in God never implied the possibility of His being either sinful or stupid. He wrote: "Whatever human freedom means, Divine freedom cannot mean indeterminacy between alternatives and choice of one of them. Perfect goodness can never debate about the end to be attained and perfect wisdom cannot debate about the means most suited to achieve it. The freedom of God consists in the fact that no other cause other than himself produces His acts and no external obstacle impedes them—that His own goodness is the root from which they all grow and His own omnipotence the air in which they all flower."[6]

A. W. Tozer

The saintly A. W. Tozer presses this idea home: "God being who He is must always be sought for himself, never as a means toward something

[5]L. D. McCabe, *The Foreknowledge of God and Cognate Themes*, pp. 201–202.
[6]C.S. Lewis, *The Problem of Pain* (New York: MacMillan, 1978), p. 23.

else. . . . Whoever seeks God as a means toward desired ends will not find God. The mighty God, maker of heaven and earth, will not be one of many treasures, not even the chief of all treasures. He will be all in all, or He will be nothing. . . .

"Bernard of Clairvaux begins his radiant little treatise on the love of God with a question and an answer. The Question: 'Why should we love God?' The Answer: 'Because He is God.' He develops the idea further, but for the enlightened heart little more need be said. We should love God because He is God. Beyond this the angels cannot think. Being who He is, God is to be loved for His own sake. He is the reason for our loving Him, just as He is the reason for His loving us and for every other act He has performed. . . . God's primary reason for everything is His own good pleasure. The search for secondary reasons is gratuitous and mostly futile. . . . But it is the nature of God to share. His mighty acts of creation and redemption were done for His good pleasure, but His pleasure extends to all created things. One has but to look at a healthy child at play or listen to the song of a bird at sundown and he will know that God meant His universe to be a joyful one."[7]

Dorothy Sayers

Sayers points out what happens when we try to live our lives as if we and our desires, rather than Christ, were the most valuable things in life: "If we refuse to assent to reality: if we rebel against the nature of things and choose to think that what we at the moment want is the center of the universe to which everything else ought to accommodate itself, the first effect on us will be that the whole universe will seem to be filled with an implacable and inexplicable hostility. We shall begin to feel that everything has a down on us, and that being so badly treated, we have a just grievance against things in general."[8]

John Hicks

God's nature and seeking His happiness is, of course, the very nature of agape love. John Hicks of Princeton pointed out: "Unlike *eros*, *agape* is unconditional and universal in its range. It is given to someone, not because he has special characteristics, but simply because he is, because he is there as a person. The nature of *agape* is to value a person in such wise as to actively seek his or her deepest welfare and happiness. . . . The divine commands come with the accent of absolute and unconditional claim, a claim which may not be set in the balance with any other interest whatever, not even life itself. This element of demand can be viewed as an expression of the divine love, seeking the best that is within man. Even between human beings there is nothing so inexorably demanding as a love that seeks our highest good and cannot be content that we be less than our potential best. Because it is infinite, the love of the Creator for

[7]A.W. Tozer, *Man—The Dwelling-Place of God*, pp. 57–59.
[8]Dorothy Sayers, *Introductory Papers On Dante*, p. 64.

the creatures made in His image implies a moral demand of this kind that is absolute and unqualified.[9]

Robert MacIntosh

Thus understood, there is no conflict between justice and mercy, no opposition in attributes, no dichotomy between law and love. As Robert MacIntosh observed: "The true God is law and love in one. What Dale said with fine eloquence, of law being 'alive' in God—it reigns on His throne, sways His scepter, is crowned with His glory"—we must say indeed of law, but still more emphatically of love. Eternal and immutable righteousness is no limitation upon God; it is the self of His self, the heart of His heart, the soul of His soul. It is true that His will is over all things, but assuredly it is not true that right and wrong are constituted by divine fiat. His will affirms righteousness and love—in His decree for us and for other reasonable and moral beings; in His every act; in His purpose that sin shall not go unpunished, but still more that redemption shall triumph. . . . Freedom, in a God of holiness, to create rational beings who shall *not* be under the law of righteousness and love is a meaningless thing or else is a blasphemy. The true freedom of our God is *in* His righteousness and *in* His love. "Justice and judgment are the habitation of His throne; mercy and truth go before His face. In that true freedom He eternally dwells, and we must come to dwell in it as His guests—no! rather as His sons."[10]

Man's Chief End

All men must and ought to bow the knee to this wise and ultimately wonderful God, who himself does what He commands, who lived himself so as to "fulfill all righteousness" (Matt. 3:15); who calls on His people to "walk in the light" even as "He is in the light" (1 John 1:7); the Good Shepherd who goes before the sheep (John 10:4).

That God obeys His own law is a profoundly moving and lovely distinction. It carries great power in presenting the Gospel to an age of not only innate rebellion, but an age which seeks to justify rejection of His righteous rule by charging that God's laws are the whims of a megalomaniac, and ultimately arbitrary. But law, understood as these men presented it, is the very antithesis of the humanism bandied about today. It neither reduces God's awesome sovereignty, nor encourages the elevation of man. Instead, it clarifies and protects the doctrine of God's authority from the false charge of arbitrariness and tyranny, gives a scriptural and sensible base for the declaration of the Gospel from God who has commanded all men everywhere to repent (Acts 17:30) and fixes the chief end of man squarely where the Westminster Confession does—"to glorify God and to enjoy Him forever."

---

[9]John Hicks, *The Judeo-Christian Concept Of God* (Prentice-Hall, 1963), pp. 4–14.

[10]Robert Mackintosh, *Historic Theories of the Atonement* (London: Hodder and Stoughton, 1920), p. 310.

Samuel Rutherford

Rutherford wrote in one of his remarkable letters, woven by Mrs. A. R. Cousin into poetry, that has become a much-loved hymn:

> Oh! Christ He is the fountain
> The deep sweet well of love!
> The streams on earth I've tasted,
> More deep I'll drink above.
>
> There, to an ocean fullness
> His mercy doth expand,
> And glory—glory dwelleth
> In Immanuel's land.

AUGUSTINE ADOPTS THE ETERNAL NOW

Augustine's thoughts on the Eternal Now are generally acknowledged to be the first (and perhaps best) of all detailed early discussions on this view of eternity. Later writers often refer his *The City of God* and *Confessions* as key arguments for this concept. It is certainly to his massive influence that we owe the first popularization of the Eternal Now (and other related ideas) that, as we have seen, later came to deeply influence Western theology. Yet, like all philosophers and theologians, Augustine did not operate in a vacuum, and his theory is primarily a philosophical analysis. Though Scripture is quoted in these devotional meditations, their use is more in the nature of incidental "proof-texts" than detailed and coercive evidence; the heart of the proof is adduced from the logic of the premises. And as we have seen in the lexical and biblical studies, Scripture does not tend to support only the idea of eternity as simple and absolute timelessness. It is also plain that the Eternal Now is not an idea unique to Christianity, but it is also a key concept of much of Eastern thought.

Did Eastern thought mold Augustine's own Christian ideas? Compare Augustine's writing on eternity with the passage by Plotinus, the brilliant Eastern philosopher of 205–270 A.D.:

Augustine	Plotinus
The City Of God	*Enneads*
"It is not as if the knowledge of God were of various kinds, knowing in different ways things which as yet are not, things which are, and things which have been. For not in our fashion does He look forward to what is future, nor what is present, nor back upon what is past; but in a manner quite different and far and profoundly remote from our way of thinking. For	"We know Eternity as a life changelessly motionless . . . not this now and now that other, but always all; not existing now in one mode and now in another, but a consummation without part or interval. All its content is in immediate concentration as at one point; nothing in it ever knows development; all remains identical within itself, knowing nothing of change. . . .

Augustine (cont.)	Plotinus (cont.)
He does not pass from this to that by transition of thought, but beholds all things with absolute unchangeableness; so that of those things which emerge in time—the future—indeed are not yet, and the present are now, and the past no longer are; but all of these are by Him comprehended in his stable and eternal presence. . . . Nor does His present knowledge differ from that which it ever was or shall be, for those variations of time, past, present and future, though they alter our knowledge, do not affect His 'with whom is no variableness neither shadow of turning.' Neither is there any growth from thought to thought in the conceptions of Him in whose spiritual vision all things which He knows are at once embraced."[1]	Forever in a now, since nothing of it has passed away or will come into being but what it is now, that it is ever. What future, in fact could bring to that Being anything which it does not now possess. . . . As it can never come to be anything at present outside it, so necessarily it cannot include any past . . . futurity, similarly is banned; nothing could be yet to come to it. . . . One which never turns to any kind outside itself that has never received any accession that is now receiving none and never will receive any. . . ."[2]

A Christian theologian and an Eastern cultist philosopher—why so much alike? Is it that Eastern thought, though filled with many false and destructive pictures of God, has found a limited picture of His nature? Did Plotinus, the Eastern thinker, happen to hit on the same truth of God's eternity that Augustine, the Christian, later received by divine revelation? Perhaps. Many would say so. And of course, Augustine does not come out with the same conclusions as Plotinus, or the Church through the centuries would not have given his writings half as much credence, regardless of their obvious devotional merit.

But there is a simpler explanation possible for this particular Neo-Platonic idea in Augustine's own later writings on the subject of eternity: Augustine was the originator of this idea in the Church and received it not from the Bible, but from Plotinus.

As any reader of Augustine's classic *Confessions* knows, he (like many young people of the past decade in the West) was deeply involved in various forms of Eastern philosophy before becoming a Christian. For some years he studied the thought of a man called Mani. Mani, a man known for bizarre ideas in many areas, thought he was the Holy Spirit and eventually concocted a blend of Zoroastrianism and Buddhism with Scripture. It was later called, naturally enough, *Manichaeism*.

At length, young Augustine became disenchanted with this philosophy. Ill and wrestling with deep personal and philosophical problems in his

[1]St. Augustine, *The City of God*, XI, ch. 21.
[2]Plotinus, "Third Ennead," *Great Books of the Western World*, Robert M. Hutchins and Mortimer Adler, eds. (Chicago: Encyclopedia Britannica, 1952), VII, sec. 4–5, p. 120–121.

life he was possibly searching for a way out of the system he had built himself into without admitting that all he had studied and done before had been false. It seems that in his reading, this same Plotinus first convinced him that the flawed ideas he held about God might be explained otherwise, and thus related to the Christian faith. Accepting the truth of these Eastern writings helped intellectually to convince him to look into Christianity some time before his actual conversion.

Frederick Copleston, a historian, records Augustine's situation as follows: "At this time, Augustine read certain 'Platonic' treatises in the Latin translation of Victorinus, these treatises being most probably the *Enneads* of Plotinus. . . . The function of Neo-Platonism at this period was to render it possible for Augustine to see the reasonableness of Christianity and he began to read the New Testament again, particularly the writings of St. Paul. If Neo-Platonism suggested to him the idea of the contemplation of spiritual things, of wisdom in the intellectual sense, the New Testament showed him it was also necessary to lead a life in accordance with wisdom. . . . His reading of Neo-Platonic works was an instrument in the intellectual conversion of Augustine, while his moral conversion, from the human standpoint, was prepared by the sermons of Ambrose, the words of Simplicianus and Pontitanus were confirmed and sealed by the New Testament. . . .

"A lung ailment . . . gave Augustine the excuse he wanted to retire from his professorship and at Cassiaciacum, through reading and reflection and discussions with friends, he endeavored to obtain a better understanding of the Christian religion, using as an instrument concepts and themes taken from Neo-Platonic philosophy, his idea of Christianity being still very incomplete, and tinctured more than it was to be later, by Neo-Platonism."[3]

Augustine believed that the Platonists excelled beyond all others in rational philosophy (logic) and moral philosophy. While later denouncing the obviously false and superstitious in what he studied, he still did not hesitate to adopt and use in Christianity what he thought still true.

He declared: "If those who are called philosophers, and especially the Platonists have said aught that is true and in harmony with our faith, we are not only not to shrink from it, but to claim it for our own use from those who have unlawful possession of it. . . . They contain also liberal instruction, which is better adapted to the use of the truth, and some most excellent precepts of morality; and some truths in regard even to the worship of the one God found among them. . . . These, therefore, the Christian, when he separates himself from the miserable fellowship of these men, ought to take away from them and to devote their proper use to preaching the Gospel."[4]

Augustine claimed that he read much truth in these writings "not indeed in the same words but to the self-same effect, enforced by many and diverse reasons."

---

[3]Frederick Copleston, *A History Of Philosophy: Medieval Philosophy, Augustine to Bonaventure* (New York: Image Books, Doubleday, 1962), vol. 2, part 1.

[4]St. Augustine, *On Christian Doctrine*, pp. ii, 60, 61.

He connects that recognition of what he saw as truth with the concept of the Eternal Now: "For that *before all times, and above all times*, Thy only-begotten Son remained unchangeably co-eternal with the Father and that of His fullness souls receive that they may be blessed; and that by participation of the wisdom remaining in them they are renewed. . . ."[5]

He is obviously familiar with the writings of Plotinus and his biographer Porphyry, for he mentions and quotes both in numerous places in *The City of God* and is intimate enough with both to distinguish fine points between them.[6] That Augustine studied Plotinus deeply and quoted some of his writings with approval is certain, although much of these treatments are given to the contrast between Scripture and the deficient Platonist concepts concerning sin as matter or substance, demon worship, etc.

Did Plotinus's thoughts on the Eternal Now happen here to match scriptural truth, or did they corrupt it? Was Augustine wise enough in God to later see, as he did with Manichaeism, *all* the subtle errors of the East so convincingly presented by this brilliant Eastern cultist? Copleston says that later his thought was "less tinctured"; but the question is: *How much less?* One thing is certain; before Augustine, the Eternal Now concept is almost unknown in the church; after him, it becomes a dominant doctrine. Whether it will ultimately prove true or not is a different matter, and will be ruled on by a better Judge than ourselves, before whom we, Augustine, and Plotinus—as with all mankind—shall one day stand.

[5]St. Augustine, *Confessions*, IX, 13, 14, p. 107–108.
[6]St. Augustine, *The City of God*, see: e.g., VII, 12; IX 9, 11, 14, 23–32.

MORE QUESTIONS AND ANSWERS CONCERNING ETERNITY

Assuming that eternity does mean "endless time" of some sort, here are the kinds of objections rightfully fielded by those who hold the Eternal Now point of view, along with some possible replies:

Q: *Even though the Bible seems to teach that God acts and experiences things in sequence, aren't those phrases only adaptations of truth to our human way of thinking?*

A: Possibly. But by what authority do we take the weight of scriptural evidence and pit it against a concept that is not conclusively supported biblically, lexically, philosophically or even logically?

Q: *But that is the root of the problem. Logic leads to the conclusion that if God can have new thoughts, He is growing in knowledge. If He is growing in knowledge, He is not infinite. If He is not infinite, He is no longer the God of the Bible! Scripture, therefore, cannot mean what it seems to say. If God accesses in knowledge, couldn't we retrace that accession to a point where God knew nothing at all? That is why, despite the mass of Scriptures that seem to imply this, such a conclusion must be false. Doesn't logic dictate that we interpret these scriptures differently or wind up with a "God" who stands in contradiction to the rest of biblical revelation?*

A: Logic does not lead to such a conclusion. First, it is not necessarily true that "eternal succession" implies a philosophical reduction to a state where God once knew nothing. To eternally retrace an infinite accession may not bring us to any diminished state at all, but rather to a fresh record of His creativity in eternity. Such accession of knowledge may not bear comparison to our finite learning patterns at all; and perhaps here is the area of true mystery. Perhaps "the foolishness of God is wiser than the wisdom of man" in this case.

Secondly, and more importantly, God's so-called "growth" in knowledge need not include "new" facts at all; it may simply be the actualization of *already known* facts regarding possibility or probability. I, for instance, may extend my fingers in a pattern wholly new to me; I do not have to "grow" or "discover" new fingers in order to do so. I know what to expect from my fingers though I have never placed them in every possible position.

A random digital circuit has two known states, high or low. Though these are pre-known parameters in the engineer's design, they are not *pre-programmed*. The ensuing state of the two alternatives, though already allowed for, was neither predestined nor predetermined.

What is true with just two alternatives can likewise be so with the googols of other alternatives open to a mere man, let alone those of the Infinite God! "New" knowledge does not have to imply *added* facts or a true increase of understanding. Anyone can make something truly new by creatively rearranging existing materials or ideas. Who would say the great God cannot also?

Q: *Nevertheless, when the Bible uses such words and phrases, we are to understand them as anthropomorphisms and anthropopathisms: human figures used to convey an otherwise-inexpressible reality.*

A: Anthropomorphisms are symbols or figures designed to express some personal characteristic of God's nature. They are physical illustrations, biological metaphors of some facet of His character. When we read God "covers us with His wings," we do not understand that God has feathers, but we do know what it means to be under the security and care of God's protection and love. The wing becomes a physical image of a personal and spiritual reality, corresponding to personal concern that actually exists in the moral world. But God's personality is no anthropomorphism.

Can we live as if it is true? What then—is the grief or joy of God over our world an "imaginary adaptation" to our way of thinking? Were the sufferings of Christ at Calvary some mere anthropopathism? And the present anger of God against sin and wickedness some figurative adaptation to human understanding? No.

If we allow this, we might also prove that the text "God so loved the world" in reality means He hated it, cared nothing for it, or possibly felt only a "great undefinable abstraction," since nothing in His nature would need to correspond to the reality of ours. All lines of communication would go down with this and God would become the Great Alien. We would be left with an Eastern picture of divinity.

Q: *Aren't you trying to understand God? You cannot use human reasoning here. Surely this area is one of mystery, one in which there are no real solutions, only paradox or parallel lines meeting in infinity.*

A: Isn't the Eternal Now premise human reasoning? It is the "glory of the king to search out a matter." The Bible encourages our devotional search after Him, entering the place of holy mysteries so as to adore and worship Him more. There are indeed some areas where human minds cannot go; but if we confuse mystery with antinomy or paradox with false premise, we patently fail to glorify God with our hearts and minds.

This area is surely not one that must be wholly relegated to the area of "mystery." Plain statements in Scripture and obvious lexical definitions are its roots. A simple Christian cannot help but think along these lines before he encounters others' theologies. Perhaps its "complexity" is a theological and philosophical inheritance, not the evidence of the Bible.

Q: *Possibly some scripture, lexical definitions, and logic may lie with such a view, but historically it finds little support. Have Christians ever held such a view of God's nature? The Jews never thought like that. Therefore, it cannot be valid. Isn't it too new, too radical to be true?*

A: Isn't it too ordinary, too obvious, too old to be *un*true? It is at least the patent assumption of every person in the Bible that God lives, acts, and feels in time. Many Christians (and Jews) outside of Scripture *did* historically hold such a view, or some modified version of it; perhaps *in practice*, the majority of ordinary Christians, more content with loving and obeying God than attempting to define Him, live by this view. Whatever our theory, we probably live as if it is true in our ordinary daily walk with Him.

No man or woman can talk with or about Him without practically thinking of God in this way. Give up this idea and you lose all basis for communication with Him. Show how you can speak of Him at all, let alone argue this point, without using words speaking of time. The question is, is this only because of the limitation of our nature and understanding or is it because of the way the Creator as well as His creation actually are?

Many of those who have written on the subject are disciples of Augustine's premise, and thus of his conclusions; hence the bulk of Reformed literature and the associated speculations of many sincere Christians along such lines. But of those not persuaded that Augustine's thoughts represent the final summit of Christian thinking on the subject, there are strong evangelical voices raised throughout history in support of this position.

Q: *Isn't there one great unanswered objection to this? While it is permissible to ascend from the human to the Divine, to extrapolate upwards from the known to the unknown in theology, it is not permissible to contradict any of God's attributes and glories clearly expressed in other plain statements of Scripture. If we accept this idea as true, what does that do to God's other attributes? Does this not diminish and demean our picture of God's power and greatness? I would rather have a mystery and maintain my sense of wonder than a logical answer that leaves me with a lesser God than I knew before.*

A: God forbid that any opinion, no matter how seemingly "sensible" to our limited intellects, should ever be held at the expense of His declared glories. A "god" we can wholly explain is no bigger than our little minds. We are reasoning Christians when the Bible and the Spirit of Christ direct and correct our opinions and practices. When we let our views correct Scripture, we are no more than rationalists.

To believe that God acts in time does none of this. It does not diminish His knowledge; for a God who is able to create new things is surely greater than a God who cannot. It does not limit His power; for a God who rules a living and active universe without ultimate failure or loss of control is surely more powerful than a God who supervises some programmed machine. A God who can handle shifting complexities in real time and emerge victor is greatly superior to one merely viewing the processed film of canned history. It does not lessen His eternalness, infinity, omnipotence, omniscience, or omnipresence. Not one of His glories is demeaned, not one attribute impaired; indeed, seen rightly, they are all magnified.

All that is lost in adapting this view is an Eastern premise, a possible fabrication of the thoughts of men, a rationalistic imposition on Scripture and reality. On this premise, an imposing theological and philosophical superstructure, filled with moral and theological paradoxes and complexities, has been erected over the centuries. This superstructure, and thus the premise, is too much to surrender for some. But for others, it is too much unlike Him to accept.

BIBLIOGRAPHY

Anselm. *Proslogium: Faith Seeking Understanding*. M. J. Charlesworth, tr. London: Oxford University Press, 1965.

Aquinas, St. Thomas. "Summa Theologica." *Great Books of the Western World*, Robert M. Hutchins and Mortimer Adler, eds. Chicago: Encyclopedia Britannica, 1952.

Archer, Gleason. *Encyclopedia of Bible Difficulties*. Grand Rapids: Zondervan Publishing House, 1982.

Atterbury, Francis. *Christian Classics*, vol. 5. Westminister, Md.: Christian Classics, Inc., 1982.

Augustine, St. *Summa Contra Gentiles*.

————. *The City of God*. Washington, D.C.: Catholic University Press, 1950.

————. "Confessions." *Great Books of the Western World*. Robert M. Hutchins and Mortimer Adler, eds. Chicago: Encyclopedia Britannica, 1952.

Bacon, Francis. *Meditationes Sacrae*.

Barfield, Owen. *Saving the Appearances: A Study in Idolatry*. Harcourt Brace Janovich, 1965.

Barnes, Albert. *Barne's Notes on the Old Testament*. Grand Rapids: Baker Book House.

Barr, James. "Biblical Words for Time," *Studies in Biblical Theology*. March, 1962, SCM.

Bauer, Walter. *A Greek-English Lexicon of the New Testament*, 2nd ed. William F. Arndt and F. Wilbur Gingrich, trans. F. Wilbur Gingrich and Frederick W. Danker, eds. Chicago: University of Chicago Press, 1979.

Bergson, Henri. *Time and Free Will*. Allen Unwin, 1910.

Bickersteth, Edward H. *The Trinity*. Grand Rapids: Kregel, 1976.

Black, Max. *Models and Metaphors: Studies in Language and Philosophy*. Ithaca, N.Y.: Cornell University Press, 1962.

Blaikie, Dr. Robert J. *Secular Christianity and the God Who Acts*. London: Hodder and Stoughton, 1970.

Bonaventure. *Disputed Questions Concerning Christ's Knowledge*.

————. *The Soul's Journey Into God*. SPCK Trans Ewart Cousins, 1978.

The Book of Common Prayer. London: Oxford University Press.

Booth, Catherine. *Papers on Godliness*. New York: Salvation Army Publishing, 1986.

————. *Popular Christianity*. New York: Salvation Army, 1986.

Brainerd, David. *Journal of David Brainerd*. Jonathan Edwards, ed. Chicago: Moody Press.

Brandall, William S. *The Secret of the Universe: New Discoveries on God, Man and the Eternity of Life*. Albuquerque, N.M.: American Classical Coll. Pr., 1985.

Brasnett, Bertrand. *The Infinity of God*. London: Longmans, Green, and Co., 1933.

Brooks, Thomas. *The Complete Works of Thomas Brooks*. Alexander Groshart, ed. AMS Press, 1866.

Brown, Robert McAfee. *The Spirit of Protestantism*. London: Oxford University Press, 1965.

Bullinger, Ethelbert W. *The Giver and His Gifts*. Grand Rapids: Kregel, 1979.

―――. *The Companion Bible*.

―――. *A Critical Lexicon and Concordance to the English and Greek New Testament*. Grand Rapids: Zondervan Publishing House, 1975.

Buswell, J. Oliver. *Systematic Theology of the Christian Religion*. Grand Rapids: Zondervan Publishing House.

Calloway, Tucker N. *The Logic of Zen: Zen-Way; Jesus-Way*.

Calvin, John. *The Institutes of the Christian Religion*. Westminster Press.

Chapman, Colin. *Christianity on Trial*. Berkhamsted, England: Lion Publishing, 1974.

Charnock, Stephen. *The Existence and Attributes of God*. Grand Rapids: Baker Book House, 1979.

Chesterton, G.K. *The Everlasting Man*. Dodd and Mead, 1925.

Chrysostom. *Twenty Centuries of Great Preaching*, vol. 1. Clyde E. Fant Jr. and William M. Dinson Jr., eds. Waco, Texas: Word Books, 1971.

Clark, Robert E.D. "Creator God or Cosmic Magician?" *Symposium on Creation*.

Clark, Stephen B. *Man And Woman in Christ*. Ann Arbor, Mich.: Servant Pubns., 1980.

Clarke. *Demonstration of Being and Attributes of God*.

Conner, Kevin J. *Foundations of Christian Doctrine*. Portland, Ore.: Bible Press, 1979.

Coomaraswamy, Ananda K. *The Dance of Shiva*. New York: Noonday Press, 1952.

Copleston, Frederick. *A History Of Philosophy: Medieval Philosophy, Augustine to Bonaventure*. New York: Image Books, Doubleday, 1962.

Cullman, Oscar. *Christ and Time: The Primitive Christian Conception of Time and History*, 3rd ed. New York: Gordon Press, 1977.

Cummings, James E. *Through the Eternal Spirit*. Minneapolis: Bethany House Publishers, 1965.

Custance, Arthur C. *Man and Adam in Christ: The Doorway Papers*. Grand Rapids: Zondervan Publishing House, 1977.

―――. *The Virgin Birth and the Incarnation*. Grand Rapids: Zondervan, 1985.

Dale, Robert William. "Faith and Physical Science," *Twenty Centuries of Great Preaching*, vol. 5. Clyde E. Fant Jr. and William M. Dinson Jr., eds. Waco, Texas: Word Books, 1971.

―――. *Fellowship With Christ*. London: Hodder and Stoughton, 1891.

Davidman, Joy. *Smoke on the Mountain*. Philadelphia: Westminister Press.

Davidson, Leslie. *The Christian Replies*. London, 1962.

Dawson, John. *The Father Heart of God*. Tyler, Texas: Last Days Ministries, 1983.

Drummond, Robert J. *Faith's Perplexities*. New York: American Tract Society.

Drummond, Henry. *Natural Law in the Spiritual World*. London: Hodder and Stoughton, 1884.

Edwards, Jonathan. *The Works of Jonathan Edwards*. University Press, 1977.

Eerdman's Handbook to Christian Belief. Keeley, Robin, ed. Grand Rapids: Eerdmans, 1982.

Eusebius. "Histories," *Ante-Nicene Fathers*. Alexander Roberts and James Donaldson, eds. Eerdmans, 1961.

Fenelon, Francois. *Christian Perfection*. Charles F. Whiston, ed., Mildred W. Stillman, trans. Minneapolis, Minn.: Bethany House Publishers, 1975.

Finney, Charles G. *Lectures on Theology*. Minneapolis, Minn.: Bethany House Publishers, 1968.

―――. *Lectures To Professing Christians*. New York: Garland Publishing Inc., 1985.

―――. *Power from on High*. Fort Washington, Pa: Christian Literature Crusade, 1962.

―――. *Sanctification*. W.E. Allen, ed. Fort Washington, Penn.: Christian Literature Crusade, 1963.

―――. *Skeletons of a Course of Theological Lectures*. London: Milner and Company.

―――. *Systematic Theology*. Minneapolis, Minn.: Bethany House Publishers, 1976.

Fletcher, John (of Madeley). *Christ Manifested*. 1800.

Fletcher, John. *The Works of John Fletcher*. Schmul Reprints, 1974.

Foreman, Dr. Kenneth J. *God's Will and Ours*. Richmond, Va.: Outlook, 1954.

Forsythe, Peter Taylor. *The Principle of Authority*. London: Hodder and Stoughton, 1912.

Fosdick, Harry Emerson. *Twenty Centuries of Great Preaching*. Clyde E. Fant Jr. and William M. Dinson Jr., eds. Waco, Texas: Word Books, 1971.

Foster, R.S. *Christian Purity*. 1851.

Fox, George. *The Journal of George Fox*. New York: AMS Press, Inc., 1975.

Fretheim, Terence. *The Suffering of God*. Fortress, 1984.

Frost, Dr. Robert. *Our Heavenly Father*. Plainfield, N.J.: Logos Intl., 1978.

Geisler, Norman. *Christian Apologetics*. Grand Rapids: Baker, 1976.

Gibb, A.N. *Worship*. Waltcrick Publishers.

Gossip, A.J. "The Clash of Age and Youth," *Twenty Centuries of Great Preaching*, vol. 8. Clyde E. Fant Jr. and William M. Dinson Jr., eds. Waco, Texas: Word Books, 1971.

Graham, Billy. *Revival in Our Time*. Wheaton, Ill.: Van Kampen Press, 1950.

Great Ideas. Encyclopaedia Britannica, 1959.

Guyon, Madame. *Spiritual Torrents*. A.E. Ford and O. Clapp, trans. 1853.

Hannum, Wilfred. *In the Things of My Father*. London: Epworth, 1954.

Harper, Michael. *The Love Affair*. Grand Rapids: Wm. B. Eerdmans Publishing House, 1982.

Havner, Vance. *Have You Lost the Wonder?* Old Tappan, N.J.: Fleming H. Revell Co., 1969.

Heine, Heinrich. *Heinrich Heine's Memoirs*. Ayer Co. Publications.

Henry, Carl. *God, Revelation, and Authority*. Waco: Word Publishers, 1982.

Hick, Dr. John. *The Judeo-Christian Concept Of God*. Prentice-Hall, 1963.

Hodge, Charles. *Systematic Theology*. Grand Rapids: Eerdmans, 1960.

Holmes, Arthur Frank. *Contours of a World View*. Carl F. Henry, ed. Grand Rapids: Eerdmans, 1983.

Humphreys, Christmas. *Buddhism*. New York: Penguin Books, Inc., 1967.

Ignatius. "To the Phillipians," *Ante-Nicene Fathers*. Alexander Roberts and James Donaldson, eds. Grand Rapids: Eerdmans, 1961.

Interpreter's Dictionary of the Bible. George A. Buttrick, ed. Nashville: Abingdon Press, 1962.

Jacob, E. *Theology of the Old Testament*. New York: Harper, 1958.

Jeans, Sir James. *The Mysterious Universe*. New York: MacMillan, 1930.

Jenny, Hans. *Cymatics Basel*. Basileus Press, 1966.

John, St. (of Damascus). *An Exact Exposition of the Orthodox Faith*.

Jones, E. Stanley. *Along the Indian Road*. Nashville: Abingdon Press, 1939.

————. *Christ at the Round Table*. Philadelphia: Century Bookbindery, 1981.

————. *The Christ on the Mount*. London: Hodder and Stoughton, 1931.

————. *The Christ of Every Road*. Nashville, Tenn.: Abingdon, 1930.

————. *Selections from E. Stanley Jones: Christ and Human Need*. Eunice and James Matthews, eds. Nashville: Abingdon Press, 1972.

————. *The Unshakeable Kingdom and the Unchanging Person*. Nashville: Abingdon Press, 1971.

Jowett, John Henry. *The Best of John Henry Jowett*. Gerald Kennedy, ed. London: Epworth Press, 1951.

Justin. "Dialogue With Trypho," *Ante-Nicene Fathers*. Alexander Roberts and James Donaldson, eds. Eerdmans, 1961.

Law, William. *The Power of the Spirit*. David Hunt, ed. Fort Washington, Penn.: Christian Literature Crusade, 1961.

Lawson, Gilchrist. *Deeper Experiences of Famous Christians*. Chicago: Glad Tidings Publishing Co., 1911.

Leibniz, Gottfried Wilhelm. *Discourse On Metaphysics II*. Dr. George R. Montgomery, trans. LaSalle, Ill.: Open Court Publishing Co., 1962.

Lewis, C.S. *Letters to Malcolm*. Huntington N.Y.: John M. Fontana Publishers, 1975.

————. *Mere Christianity*. Huntington, N.Y.: J.M. Fontana Publishing, 1955.

————. *Miracles*. New York: MacMillan, 1978.

————. *The Problem of Pain*. New York: MacMillan, 1978.

————. *Reflections on the Psalms*. Huntington, N.Y.: John M. Fontana Publishers, 1961.
————. *The Weight of Glory*. Grand Rapids: Eerdmans, 1973.
Locke, John. *An Essay Concerning Human Understanding*. Peter H. Nidditch, ed. New York: Oxford University Press, 1975.
Lockyer, Herbert. *The Holy Spirit of God*. Nashville: Thomas Nelson, 1981.
Lucas, J.R. *Treatise on Space and Time*. London: Methuen and Co., 1973.
McCabe, L. D. *The Foreknowledge of God and Cognate Themes*. Cincinnati: Cranstant Stowe, 1878.
MacClaren, Alexander. *A Year's Ministry*. London: Hodder & Stoughton, 1903.
MacDonald, George. *Anthology*. C.S. Lewis, ed. New York: MacMillan, 1986.
————. *Creation in Christ*. Rolland Hein, ed. Wheaton, Ill.: Harold Shaw Publishers, 1976.
————. *Diary of an Old Soul*. Minneapolis, Minn.: Augsburg Publishing House, 1965.
————. *The Miracles of Our Lord*. Rolland Hein, ed. Wheaton, Ill.: Harold Shaw Publishers, 1980.
McDowell, Josh. *Evidence That Demands a Verdict*. San Bernardino, Calif.: Campus Crusade for Christ, 1979.
Mackintosh, Robert. *Historic Theories of the Atonement*. London: Hodder and Stoughton, 1920.
MacMurray, John. *The Self as Agent*. Faber and Faber, 1957.
Mahan, M. *The Complete Works of M. Mahan*. J. H. Hopkins, ed. New York: Pott, Young, & Co., 1875.
Marshall, Peter. *Mr. Jones, Meet the Master*. New York: Dell Publishing, 1961.
Martin, Walter. *The Kingdom of the Cults*. Minneapolis, Minn.: Bethany House Publishers, 1985.
Maximus, St. (The Confessor). *Writings From the Heart: The Philokalia*. Kadloubovsky and Palmer, trans. London: Faber and Faber.
Mbiti, John S. *African Religions and Philosophy*. Heinemann Ed., 1969.
Merton, Thomas. *Seeds of Contemplation*. Greenwood, 1949.
Meyer, F.B. *Friendship With God: Moses*. London: Morgan and Scott.
Miller, Basil. *George Washington Carver*. Grand Rapids: Zondervan, 1943.
Miller, Calvin. *The Singer*. Downers Grove, Ill.: InterVarsity Press, 1975.
Moberly, Elizabeth R. *Homosexuality: A New Ethic*. Cambridge, England: James Clarke and Co. Ltd., 1983.
Moltmann, Jurgen. *The Trinity and the Kingdom of God*. SCM, 1981.
Moody, D.L. *Sermons of D.L. Moody*. 1900.
————. *Secret Power*. Chicago: Bible Institute Colportage Assoc., 1908.
Morgan, G. Campbell. "Sanctification," *Twenty Centuries of Great Preaching*, vol. 7. Clyde E. Fant Jr. and William M. Dinson Jr., eds. Waco, Texas: Word Books, 1971.
Morphett, Tony. *Moral Algebra*. London: Hodder and Stoughton, 1985.
Morris, Leon. *Testaments of Love*. Grand Rapids: Wm. B. Eerdmans Publishing Company, 1981.
Nee, Watchman. *Spiritual Reality*. Richmond, Va.: Christian Fellowship Publishers, 1970.
The New International Dictionary of New Testament Theology. Colin Brown, ed. Grand Rapids: Zondervan Publishing House, 1971.
The New International Dictionary of the Christian Church. James D. Douglas, ed. Grand Rapids: Zondervan Publishing House.
Newbigin, Lesslie. *The Household of God*. New York: Friendship Press, 1954.
Olson, Gordon. *Sharing Your Faith*. Chicago: Bible Research Fellowship.
Origen. "Homily VI in Ezekiel."
Owens, Virginia Stem. *And the Trees Clap Their Hands*. Grand Rapids: Eerdmans, 1983.
Packer, J.I. *Knowing God*. Downers Grove, Ill.: Inter-Varsity Press, 1973.
Palmas, Gregory. *Triads*.
Paley, William. *Evidences of Christianity*. New York: S. King, 1824.
Panin, Ivan. *The Writings of Ivan Panin*. The Book Society of Canada, 1918.
Parker, Joseph. *Preaching Through the Bible*. Grand Rapids: Baker Books, 1978.
————. *The Inner Life of Christ*. London: Hodder and Stoughton, 1950.

The People's Bible Encyclopedia. Charles Randall Barnes, ed. London: Charles H. Kelley, 1900.

Pettinghill, William. *Bible Questions Answered*. Grand Rapids: Zondervan Publishing House, 1932.

Pike, Nelson. *God and Timelessness*. New York: Schocken Books, 1970.

Plotinus. "Third Ennead," *Great Books of the Western World*. Robert M. Hutchins and Mortimer Adler, eds. Chicago: Encyclopedia Britannica, 1952.

Pope, William. *Compendium of Christian Theology*. New York: Philip & Hunt, 1881.

Pulpit Commentary. H.D. Spence and Joseph S. Exell, eds. Grand Rapids: Eerdmans.

Ramm, Bernard. *Protestant Christian Evidences*. Chicago: Moody Press, 1953.

Ramsay, Sir William Mitchell. *The Cities of St. Paul*. Grand Rapids: Baker Books, 1949.

Rand, Ayn. *The Romantic Manifesto*. Signet, 1971.

Rimmer, Harry. *The Magnificence of Jesus*. 1943.

Ritchie, A.D. *Civilization, Science, and Religion*. Pelican Books, 1945.

Robertson, F.W. *Sermons on Religion and Life*. London: J.M. Dent and Co., 1906.

Russell, Bertrand. *Why I Am Not a Christian*. New York: Simon and Schuster, 1957.

Rutherford, Samuel. *Letters*. Frank Gaebelein, ed. Chicago: Moody Press, 1951.

Saphir, Adolph. *The Life of Faith*. N.Y.: Gospel Publishing House.

Saunders. *Of God and Freedom*.

Sayers, Dorothy. *Christian Letters to a Post-Christian World*. Grand Rapids, Mich: Eerdmans, 1969.

———. *A Matter of Eternity*. Grand Rapids: Eerdmans, 1973.

———. *The Mind of the Maker*. Westport, Conn.: Greenwood Press, 1970.

Schaeffer, Francis A. *The Church at the End of the Twentieth Century: The Church Before the Watching World*. London: Norfolk Press, 1971.

———. *Genesis in Space and Time*. Downers Grove, Ill.: InterVarsity Press, 1972.

———. *The Complete Works of Francis Schaeffer*. Westchester, Ill.: Crossway, 1985.

———. *He Is There and He Is Not Silent*. London: Hodder and Stoughton, 1972.

Shairp, Principal. *Poetic Interpretation of Nature*.

Sheikh, Bilquis. *I Dared Call Him Father*. Old Tappan, N.J.: Chosen Books, 1979.

Shoemaker, Samuel M. *Twenty Centuries of Great Preaching*. Clyde E. Fant Jr. and William M. Dinson Jr., eds. Waco, Texas: Word Books, 1971.

———. *With the Holy Spirit and with Fire*. New York: Harper, 1960.

Simpson, A.B. *The Holy Spirit*. Camp Hill, Pa.: Christian Publications.

Singh, Sadhu Sundar. *The Gospel of Sadhu Sundar Singh*. Allen Unwin, 1927.

Smail, Thomas. *The Forgotten Father*. London: Hodder and Stoughton, 1980.

Smeaton, George. *The Doctrine of the Holy Spirit*. Carlisle, Pa.: The Banner of Truth, 1980.

Smith, Wilbur Moorhead. *Have You Considered Him?*.

Stalker, James. *The Life of Jesus Christ*. Tappan, N.J.: Fleming Revell, 1949.

Stewart, James Stuart. *The Strong Name*. New York: Scribner's, 1941.

Stone, Nathan. *Names of God*. Chicago: Moody Press, 1944.

Strong, James. *Strong's Exhaustive Concordance of the Bible*.

Suso, Henry. *The Letters to His Spiritual Daughters*. Kathleen Goldman, trans. England: Aquin Press, 1953.

Swinburne, Richard. *The Coherence of Theism*. London: Oxford Press, 1977.

Talmage, T. De Witt. "The A and the Z," *Twenty Centuries of Great Preaching*. Clyde E. Fant Jr. and William M. Dinson Jr., eds. Waco, Texas: Word Books, 1971.

Theological Dictionary of the New Testament. Kittel, Gerhard, ed., Geoffrey W. Bromiley, trans. Grand Rapids: Wm. B. Eerdmans Publishing Company, 1964.

Theological Dictionary of the Old Testament. G. Johannes Botterweck and Helmer Ringgren, eds. Grand Rapids: Eerdmans, 1974.

Theological Wordbook of the Old Testament. Laird R. Harris, ed. Chicago: Moody Press, 1980.

Theophilus. "To Autolycus," *Ante-Nicene Fathers*. Alexander Roberts and James Donaldson, eds. Eerdmans, 1961.

Torrance, Thomas F. *The Ground and Grammar of Theology*. Edinburgh, Scotland: University Press, 1980.

————. *Theological Science*. New York: Oxford University Press, 1969.

Torrey, R.A. *What the Bible Teaches*. Fleming H. Revell Company.

Tozer, A.W. *Born After Midnight*. Camp Hill, Penn.: Christian Publications, Inc.

————., ed. *The Christian Book of Mystical Verse*. Camp Hill, Penn.: Christian Publications, Inc., 1975.

————. "In the Beginning Was the Word." (Unpublished sermon).

————. *How To Be Filled With the Holy Spirit*. Camp Hill, Penn.: Christian Publications, Inc.

————. *Man: The Dwelling-Place of God*. Camp Hill, Penn.: Christian Publications, Inc., 1966

————. *The Pursuit of God*. Camp Hill, Penn.: Christian Publications, Inc., 1982.

————. *The Root of the Righteous*. Camp Hill, Penn.: Christian Publications, Inc., 1955.

————. *That Incredible Christian*. Camp Hill, Penn.: Christian Publications, Inc., 1964.

Trench, R.C. *Notes on the Parables of Our Lord*. Grand Rapids: Baker Book House.

Van Dusen, Henry. *Spirit, Son, and Father*. New York: Scribner's, 1958.

Vaughan, Rev. C.J. *Suggestive Thoughts*.

Vine, W.E. *The Expanded Vine's Expository Dictionary of New Testament Words*. John R. Kohlenberger III, ed. Minneapolis, Minn.: Bethany House Publishers, 1984.

Vivekananda, Swami. *The Complete Works of Swami Vivekananda*, 5th edition. Calcutta: Advaita Ashram, 1951.

Wainwright, Arthur W. *The Trinity in the New Testament*. London: SPCK, 1962.

Watson, G.D. *Our Own God*. Schmul Reprints.

Watson, John (D.D.). *Mind of the Master*. New York: Dodd, Mead and Company, 1896.

Wesley, John. *The Works of John Wesley*. Grand Rapids: Baker Books.

Whyte, Alexander. *Santa Teresa: An Appreciation*. Olipant, Arduson, and Ferrur, 1898.

————. *Father John of the Greek Church: An Appreciation*. Olipant, Arduson, and Ferrur, 1898.

————. *With Mercy and Judgement*. London: Hodder and Stoughton.

Wilder-Smith, A.E. *The Creation of Life: A Cybernetic Aproach to Evolution*. Wheaton, Ill.: Harold Shaw Publishers, 1970.

Wood, Dr. Nathan. *The Trinity in the Universe*. Grand Rapids: Kregel, 1984.

Wuest, Kenneth S. *Word Studies in the Greek New Testament*. Grand Rapids: Eerdmans Publishing Company, 1973.

Yonggi Cho, Dr. Paul. *The Fourth Dimension*. Plainfield, N.J.: Logos Int.

The Zondervan Pictorial Encyclopedia of the Bible. Merrill Tenney, ed. Grand Rapids: Zondervan Pub. House, 1976.